Supervision
Managing for Results

Eighth Edition

John W. Newstrom

Professor of Human Resource Management
Department of Management Studies
University of Minnesota—Duluth

Lester R. Bittel

Professor of Management Emeritus
James Madison University

 Glencoe McGraw-Hill

New York, New York   Columbus, Ohio   Woodland Hills, California   Peoria, Illinois

PHOTO CREDITS:

Bill Aron/PhotoEdit 537; Bruce Ayres/Stone 246, 473, 575; Peter Beck/The Stock Market 145; Ron Chappel/FPG International LLC 8, 414; Paul Conklin/Uniphoto 518; Jim Cummins/FPG International LLC 133; Used by permission of Eveready Battery Company, Inc. Energizer,® Energizer Bunny® and the Energizer Design are trademarks of Eveready Battery Company. Inc. 211, 212; Fisher-Thatcher/Stone 295, 567; Spencer Grant/Stock Boston 329, 445; Charles Gupton/Stock Boston 386; W. Hodges/Corbis-Westlight 508; Walter Hodges/Stone 13, 169, 218, 434; Hulton Getty/Stone 243; Chuck Keeler/Stone 127, 128; Michael Keller/Uniphoto 38, 486; Mike Malyszko/FPG International LLC 219, 292; Chuck Mason/Photo Network 81; Michael Newman/Photo Edit 61, 100; NIST Public & Business Affairs 429, 430; Eric O'Connell/FPG International LLC 1,2; Jose L. Pelaez/The Stock Market 197; Photo Edit 224; Jon Riley/Stone 53, 189, 368; Andy Sacks/Stone 278; Shili Sports/FPG International LLC 361; Ariel Skelley/ The Stock Market 337; Superstock 111, 158, 394, 469, 470; Tecmap/Corbis-Westlight 379, 380; Telegraph Colour Library/FPG International LLC 72, 267; Uniphoto 34; Visual Horizons/FPG International LLC 69, 70, 98

Library of Congress Cataloging-in-Publication Data

Newstrom, John W.
    Supervision: managing for results / John W. Newstrom, Lester R. Bittel.—8th ed.
        p. cm.
    Includes bibliographical references and index.
    ISBN 0-07-822280-X
    1. Personnel management. 2. Supervision of employees. I. Bittel, Lester R. II. Title.

    HF5549 .B52 2000
    658.3'02—dc21

                        00-059615

Glencoe/McGraw-Hill

A Division of The **McGraw·Hill** *Companies*

Send all inquiries to:
Glencoe/McGraw-Hill
21600 Oxnard Street, Suite 500
Woodland Hills, CA 91367

    Study Guide: ISBN 0-07-822281-8
    Instructor's Manual with IPC: ISBN 0-07-822282-6

ISBN 0-07-822280-X

Printed in the United States of America.

2 3 4 5 6 7 8 9 10   027   06 05 04 03 02 01

CONTENTS IN BRIEF

PREFACE xii

PART ONE **Supervisory Management 1**

CHAPTER 1 The Supervisor's Role in Management 2
CHAPTER 2 Creating a Positive Workplace Within
a Dynamic Environment 29
CHAPTER 3 Supervision and the Management Process 49

PART TWO **Planning and Problem Solving 69**

CHAPTER 4 Setting Goals, Making Plans, and Carrying Out Policy 70
CHAPTER 5 Problem Solving and Managing Information 98

PART THREE **Organizing, Staffing, and Training 127**

CHAPTER 6 Organizing an Effective Department 128
CHAPTER 7 Staffing with Human Resources 156
CHAPTER 8 Training and Developing Employees 183

PART FOUR **Energizing the Workforce 211**

CHAPTER 9 Motivating People at Work 212
CHAPTER 10 Leadership Skills, Styles, and Qualities 237
CHAPTER 11 Effective Employee Communication 263

PART FIVE **Working with Individuals and Teams 291**

CHAPTER 12 Appraisal of Employee Performance 292
CHAPTER 13 Counseling and Performance Management 319
CHAPTER 14 Building Cooperative Teams and Resolving Conflicts 351

PART SIX **Controlling 379**

CHAPTER 15 Keeping People, Plans, and Programs on Track 380
CHAPTER 16 Controlling Costs and Budgets 405

PART SEVEN **Improving Productivity and Quality 429**

CHAPTER 17 Stimulating Productivity, Quality, and Innovation 430

PART EIGHT Contemporary Concerns of Supervision   469

CHAPTER 18   Managing a Diverse Workforce 470
CHAPTER 19   The Supervisor's Role in Employee Safety and Health,
              and Labor Relations 502

PART NINE Personal Development Portfolio:
              Toward Mastery of Your Job   537

FILE 1   Taking Charge of Your Career 540
FILE 2   Managing Job-Related Time 547
FILE 3   Coping with Stress 553
FILE 4   Moving Up in Your Organization 557

PART TEN   Appendixes   567

PART ELEVEN Your Career in Supervision and Management
              with Action Planning Checklists   575

GLOSSARY OF TERMS 605
INDEX 617

CONTENTS

PREFACE xii

PART ONE   **Supervisory Management   1**

CHAPTER 1   **The Supervisor's Role in Management** **2**
 ● Members of a Unique Team ● Many Competencies Required
 ● Linking Goals and Efforts ● Converting Resources Into Outputs
 ● Skills to Be Developed ● A Concern for Both Work and People

Superscope Howdy! 20
Cases for Analysis
   Case 1   The Brand-New Supervisor 25
   Case 2   The Rejected Refrigerators 26
   Case 3   Which Comes First—Departmental Performance
        or Employee Development? 26
   Case 4   Too Much to Keep Up With 27

CHAPTER 2   **Creating a Positive Workplace Within
        a Dynamic Environment** **29**
 ● Seven Pressures to Cope With ● The World of Work
 ● Employee Expectations ● Understanding Employee Perceptions
 ● Quality of Work Life

Superscope The New Workplace 33
Cases for Analysis
   Case 5   Mildred and the Mickey Mouse Job 46
   Case 6   Hot Job, High Turnover 47
   Case 7   The Disgruntled Customer Service Clerk 48

CHAPTER 3   **Supervision and the Management Process** **49**
 ● A Body of Knowledge from Which to Draw ● The Management Process
 ● Management Principles ● Management Approaches (or Schools)
 ● Systems and Situations

Superscope The Unpredictable Women in the Relay
        Adjustment Room 59
Cases for Analysis
   Case 8   The Automated Insurance Office 67
   Case 9   The Subordinated Quality Goal 68

PART TWO   Planning and Problem Solving   69

CHAPTER 4   **Setting Goals, Making Plans, and
Carrying Out Policy** **70**
● Road Maps of an Organization ● Goal Setting ● The Planning Process
● Scheduling Guidelines ● Methods and Techniques ● Policies

Superscope   A Smart Way to Set Goals 75
Cases for Analysis
    Case 10   The Disorganized Shipping Dock 94
    Case 11   Cora's Goals 96
    Case 12   The Rush Order's Doubtful Deadline 97

CHAPTER 5   **Problem Solving and Managing Information** **98**
● Problems: Cause and Effect ● Systematic Problem Solving
● Decision Making: Rational and Intuitive ● Information as a Raw Material
● An MIS of Your Own ● Keeping the System Human

Cases for Analysis
    Case 13   The Big Cookie Burnout 123
    Case 14   The Uncertain Reduction in Force 125
    Case 15   The Blue Jeans MIS 126

PART THREE   Organizing, Staffing, and Training   127

CHAPTER 6   **Organizing an Effective Department** **128**
● Organizing for Effectiveness ● Types of Organizational Structures
● Authority, Responsibility, and Accountability ● Delegation for Leverage
● Guidelines for Organizing

Superscope   New Forms of Portraying Organizations
            Are Emerging 137
Cases for Analysis
    Case 16   The Overworked Chorus Director 152
    Case 17   The New Quality Control Department 153
    Case 18   Margaret's Delegation Decisions 154

CHAPTER 7   **Staffing with Human Resources** **156**
● Forecasting Workforce Requirements ● The Staffing Process
● Interviewing Job Candidates ● Making the Selection Decision
● Orientation Training ● Minimizing the Potential for Absences and Turnover

Cases for Analysis
    Case 19   The Biased Interview 179
    Case 20   Who's the Best? 181
    Case 21   The Superior Job Candidate 182

CHAPTER 8   Training and Developing Employees **183**
- Training: Process and Purpose ● A Training Partnership
- Factors in Learning ● Training Methods and Aids
- Obtaining Results from Training

Superscope   Job Instruction Training (JIT) 195
Cases for Analysis
   Case 22 From Theory to Practice 207
   Case 23 The New Telephone Procedure 208
   Case 24 It Sounds Good, But Will They Use It? 209

PART FOUR **Energizing the Workforce** **211**

CHAPTER 9   Motivating People at Work **212**
- The Importance of Individuality ● A Powerful Pattern of Motivation
- Satisfaction and Dissatisfaction ● Achievement, Expectancy, and Equity
- Motivation and Rewards ● Motivation in the Work Itself

Superscope   Performance Motivators 219
Cases for Analysis
   Case 25 The Conflicting Coffee Breaks 234
   Case 26 Putting Maslow Into Practice 235
   Case 27 The "Disposable" Workforce 236

CHAPTER 10   Leadership Skills, Styles, and Qualities **237**
- Leadership Defined ● Leadership and Motivation ● Leadership Styles and Concepts ● Selecting an Appropriate Style ● Leaders and Followers

Superscope   Important Leadership Traits 238
Cases for Analysis
   Case 28 The New Supervisor of Nurses 260
   Case 29 The Experienced Transferees 261
   Case 30 Joe's "Pretty Good" Diner 262

CHAPTER 11   Effective Employee Communication **263**
- The Communication Process ● Methods of Communication
- Nonverbal Communication ● Communication Guidelines
- Orders, Instructions, and Requests

Superscope   Avoiding Trouble When Issuing Orders 280
Cases for Analysis
   Case 31 The Man Who Wouldn't Move 286
   Case 32 Now That I've Got It, What Do I Do With It? 287
   Case 33 Modifying the Medium 288

PART FIVE   **Working with Individuals and Teams**   **291**

CHAPTER 12   **Appraisal of Employee Performance** **292**
- Purposes of Appraisal ● Factors and Format ● The Appraisal Interview
- Special Considerations ● Legal and Financial Aspects

Superscope   Eight Ways to Tarnish the Halo 300
Cases for Analysis

     Case 34   The Downgraded Performance Appraisal 315
     Case 35   Polishing the Halo 316
     Case 36   Betty's Carpet-Cleaning Service 317
     Case 37   The Dissatisfied Mechanic 317

CHAPTER 13   **Counseling and Performance Management** **319**
- Problem Performers ● Employee Counseling ● Reducing Absenteeism
- The Problems of Substance Abuse ● Performance Management
- Administrative Guidelines

Superscope   Behavioral Clues to a Troubled Worker 322
Superscope   Common Pitfalls in Discipline 341
Cases for Analysis

     Case 38   The Irrational Documents Clerk 347
     Case 39   A Difference of Opinion 348
     Case 40   She's a Charmer, But... 349
     Case 41   "That Was the Week That Was" 350

CHAPTER 14   **Building Cooperative Teams and**
                 Resolving Conflicts **351**
- Group Dynamics ● Group Participation ● Developing Cooperative
Teams ● Resolving Conflict in Groups ● Securing Cooperation

Superscope   What Factors Contribute to and Detract
                 from Cohesion? 354
Cases for Analysis

     Case 42   Problems, Problems, Everywhere! 376
     Case 43   Tell Them to Lay Off Me! 377
     Case 44   Inviting Participation 378

PART SIX   **Controlling**   **379**

CHAPTER 15   **Keeping People, Plans, and Programs on Track** . . . **380**
- A Dual Role ● Control Standards ● The Control Process
- Control Targets ● Handling Employee Resistance

Superscope   Confrontation as Control 393
Cases for Analysis

     Case 45   The Overworked Copying Machine 400
     Case 46   Seven Situations Under Control 402
     Case 47   The Wayward Bus Line 403

CHAPTER 16 Controlling Costs and Budgets **405**
  ● Accounting Records ● Budgeted Costs ● Cost Improvement Strategies
  ● Cost Improvement Sources ● Employee Reactions

  Superscope Where Do Cost Data Come From? 407
  Superscope Continuous Improvement 414
  Cases for Analysis
        Case 48 The High-Flying Sales Staff 424
        Case 49 Kindly Make Every Effort... 426
        Case 50 The "Up-Up-and-Away" Computer Supplies 427

PART SEVEN   **Improving Productivity and Quality   429**

CHAPTER 17 Stimulating Productivity, Quality,
            and Innovation **430**
  ● Understanding Productivity ● Methods Improvement
  ● Quality and the Supervisor ● Statistical Quality Control
  ● Toward Total Quality Management ● Innovation and Creativity

  Cases for Analysis
        Case 51 As the Wheels Turn 464
        Case 52 The Hard-to-Meet Quality Standards 465
        Case 53 The Dried-Out Burger 467
        Case 54 The Best and the Worst of It 467

PART EIGHT   **Contemporary Concerns of Supervision   469**

CHAPTER 18 Managing a Diverse Workforce **470**
  ● A Diverse Workforce ● The Legal Basis ● Disadvantaged Minorities
  ● Women in the Workplace ● Younger and Older Workers
  ● Special Problems in a Changing Environment

  Superscope Facts About ADA Complaints Filed with EEOC 477
  Superscope From Veterans to Nexters 489
  Cases for Analysis
        Case 55 Jackrabbit Jokers 499
        Case 56 Upward on Cannery Row 500
        Case 57 Banking Jobs for All Ages 500

CHAPTER 19 The Supervisor's Role in Employee Safety and
            Health, and Labor Relations **502**
  ● Safety at Work ● OSHA's Mandated Safety Standards
  ● Accident Prevention: The Basics ● Labor Unions and Labor Law
  ● Collective Bargaining and Contract Representation
  ● Grievance Procedures

  Superscope The Occupational Hazard of Chicken
                Plucking and Computer Keyboarding 505
  Superscope Overruling the Supervisor 526

Cases for Analysis

    Case 58   Their Aching Backs 534

    Case 59   Mary's Pinched Ring Finger 535

    Case 60   Nine Who Did Wrong 535

PART NINE

Personal Development Portfolio: Toward Mastery of Your Job   537

FILE 1   **Taking Charge of Your Career** 540

FILE 2   **Managing Job-Related Time** 547

FILE 3   **Coping with Stress** 553

FILE 4   **Moving Up in Your Organization** 557

Cases for Analysis

    Case 61   Passed Over Again 564

    Case 62   "Get Your Priorities Straight!" 564

    Case 63   The Unfaceable Day 565

    Case 64   Who Should Get the Pay Raise? 566

PART TEN

Appendixes   567

PART ELEVEN

Your Career in Supervision and Management with Action Planning Checklists   575

GLOSSARY OF TERMS 605

INDEX 617

ABOUT THE AUTHORS

JOHN W. NEWSTROM has taught management courses and supervisory development seminars for over 30 years. He has been a training consultant to numerous federal, state, and local governmental organizations, as well as to firms in various industries. As a Professor of Human Resource Management at the University of Minnesota at Duluth, he was awarded the prestigious Morse-Alumni Award for Outstanding Contributions to Undergraduate Education. He is a member of the University's Academy of Distinguished Teachers. He has served on the national Board of Directors of the American Society for Training and Development. He is co-author of numerous books, including *Organizational Behavior*, *Games Trainers Play*, *The Manager's Bookshelf*, and *Leaders and the Leadership Process*.

LESTER R. BITTEL is a widely recognized authority on management and supervision. His books on supervision have been translated into seven languages and distributed throughout the world. At retirement, he had over 30 years' experience in business as an industrial engineer, plant manager, training director, magazine editor, and corporate executive. He is Professor Emeritus of Management and a Virginia Eminent Scholar at James Madison University.

PREFACE

Today's work environment demands that supervisors do more than know how to supervise. They must manage to bring about results consistent with organizational goals and objectives. The eighth edition of *Supervision: Managing for Results* is written to help them do just that.

Our Approach

The overall approach of this book continues to be guided by seven interlocking objectives:

1. To offer readers practical advice about how to handle real-life, on-the-job situations.
2. To recognize an ever-changing social and work environment.
3. To provide useful insights based upon the job-tested experience of its authors and their associates.
4. To cover all the vital aspects of supervision.
5. To reflect the latest professional concepts of supervisory practice and organizational behavior.
6. To employ the most effective techniques for helping readers enjoy and assimilate the material presented in the text.
7. To maintain a good-humored perspective on what continues to be one of the world's most demanding jobs.

With these objectives as a foundation, *Supervision: Managing for Results* provides a useful aid to a wide and diverse readership, which includes

- **Instructors,** who use it as a basic text in preparing their students for the complex world of supervisory management.
- **Students** of first-level management in commerce, industry, and government, who turn to it as a central source of information about the practice of supervision.
- **Supervisors,** who find it to be a complete reference guide of methods for dealing with people, managing their jobs, and planning their own advancement.
- **Managers,** who may gain from it an insight into the problems—human, technical, and personal—supervisors must face daily.
- **Training directors** and other human resource development professionals, who use this text for guiding the training of supervisors in the interpersonal and administrative skills of their jobs.
- **Members of self-managing teams,** who discover it to be a source for understanding the new roles they must play in the absence of a formal leader.

In This Edition

Supervision: Managing for Results reflects an extensive reexamination of every aspect of coverage. It provides readers with the very latest information and the most current points of view from authoritative sources. Throughout, there has been a rigorous updating—of data, language, legal interpretation, situations, and examples. Coverage includes applications to and examples from clerical, office, service, institutional, and government settings.

Several chapters, such as Chapter 8, Training and Developing Employees, Chapter 9, Motivating People at Work, Chapter 11, Effective Employee Communication, and Chapter 14, Building Cooperative Teams and Resolving Conflicts, contain substantial amounts of new material. Others, such as Chapter 13, Counseling and Performance Management, and Chapter 17, Stimulating Productivity, Quality, and Innovation, have taken on a new thrust and focus. All chapters have been thoroughly updated to reflect the best thinking and most current solid practice in supervisory techniques.

The Personal Development Portfolio has been retained in this edition. It provides practical guidelines for (1) planning a career, (2) managing job-related time, (3) coping with stress, and (4) moving up in an organization.

Of special assistance to potential and practicing supervisors are the three checklists that appear in the appendixes in Part 10:

- Appendix A, "Planning the Day's Work"
- Appendix B, "Supervisory Responsibility Survey"
- Appendix C, "Checklist for Accepting the Assignment of a New Department"

Your Career in Supervision and Management With Action Planning Checklists has also been retained. The checklists provide readers with a practical way to measure and plan for their application of supervision concepts and techniques in the workplace.

Included in this edition is new or expanded coverage of the following topics:

- Organizing, staffing, and training
- Empowerment and servant leadership
- Team building and self-directed teams
- Learning organizations and continuous improvement
- The communication process
- Workforce diversity
- Open-book management
- Trust, loyalty, and commitment

Unique Learning Techniques

This edition retains the two learning methods that differentiate *Supervision: Managing for Results* from most other texts in its field:

1. **A question-and-answer approach with immediate feedback.** This approach helps to reinforce understanding and to develop application proficiency in a manner similar to that of programmed learning. Additionally, the format enables readers to relate concepts to the problems they face daily at work. It also makes the text a convenient desk or workbench reference.

2. **Practical advice in the form of dos and don'ts.** Although the text is unswervingly based upon accepted theory, the authors do not back away from offering straightforward advice about how to handle difficult situations. Especially in the sticky matters of interpersonal relationships, our intention is to provide supervisors with a starting point for their actions and responses, rather than to leave them with what otherwise might be interpreted as a set of equivocating observations.

Building upon this foundation, a number of learning aids are now incorporated in this edition. Collectively, they add greatly to the ease of reading and to the effectiveness of instruction.

Chapter Features

Most chapters contain the following features:

- **A set of learning objectives,** which alerts readers to what they should know or be able to do as a result of reading the chapter. These objectives are numbered, too, to relate them to concepts discussed in the chapter.
- **A concept statement,** which previews each numbered section within the chapter.
- **Superscope,** which highlights the current thinking on a relevant supervision topic.
- **Boxed Features,** including Did You Know?, Quips & Quotes, Internet Connections, and Ethical Perspectives, expand text topics.
- **Job Tip Boxes** provide practical suggestions for readers to implement on the job.
- **Quick Tests** following each topic section help readers assess their understanding of the material covered.
- **Definitions** of terms are shown in the margin when the term is introduced.

A set of Review and Application learning aids appears at the end of the text material in each chapter. The Review aids include:

- **Key Concepts to Remember,** which enlarges upon and summarizes each of the numbered concepts presented in the chapter.
- **Reading Comprehension,** which consists of 10 questions that probe the reader's understanding of the text material.

The Application aids include:

- **Self-Assessment,** with a self-scoring guide, which challenges readers to judge how well they have grasped material presented in the chapter.
- **Skill Development, Role Play,** and **Group Exercises** are included in most chapters to help readers apply what they have learned.
- **Cases for Analysis,** three or more for each chapter, each calling for analysis and solution. These cases are numbered sequentially, beginning with Chapter 1 and concluding in the *Personal Development Portfolio.* Of special note are the cases that appear first in each chapter. These are uniquely structured in the *case-in-point* format—that is, each case presents the reader with five alternate solutions, often called "forced-choice" solutions. The reader is asked to rank the appropriateness of each alternative from first to fifth and to be prepared to defend these choices.

Teaching and Learning Resources

A *Study Guide* and an *Instructor's Manual* containing an *Instructor's Productivity Center (IPC)* CD-ROM supplement this textbook. The *Instructor's Manual* contains a number of useful instructional aids, transparency masters, and additional case studies for class or seminar use. The *IPC* contains the ExamView Test Generator with True/False, Multiple Choice, and Completion questions. The *IPC* also contains PowerPoint presentation slides for each chapter in the text.

Videos

Five videos are included on the *Instructor's Productivity Center.* These videos correlate to the Parts in the text. A correlation guide is provided in the *Instructor's Manual.*

ACKNOWLEDGMENTS

The authors accept full responsibility for the validity of everything that appears in this text. We are, of course, deeply indebted to hundreds of our associates and thousands of practicing supervisors whose thoughts and deeds have contributed directly and indirectly to this work. We could not have built this program without them, and we regret that we cannot name them all. We are especially indebted to Gregory R. Fox, Vice Chancellor for Finance and Operations at the University of Minnesota at Duluth, who prepared the *Study Guide*, the *Instructor's Manual*, and the test items for the ExamView Pro test generator for this edition. Greg's experience as the director of the Duluth Center for Continuing Education adds considerably to the practicality and authority of the ancillary programs.

We are also grateful to the following individuals for their reviews of the seventh edition of the text and the eighth edition manuscript:

■ **James E. Donovan**
Detroit College of Business
Dearborn, Michigan

■ **Victoria Osendorf**
St. Cloud Technical College
St. Cloud, Minnesota

■ **Thomas R. Etling**
St. Louis Community College
St. Louis, Missouri

■ **Kenneth R. A. Rasheed**
Chattahooche Technical Institute
Marietta, Georgia

■ **Deborah M. Jones**
High-Tech Institute
Phoenix, Arizona

■ **Eva Clare Stein**
York Technical Institute
York, Pennsylvania

■ **Thomas W. Lloyd**
Westmoreland County
    Community College
Youngwood, Pennsylvania

■ **Allen B. Young**
Bessemer State Technical College
Bessemer, Alabama

John W. Newstrom
Lester R. Bittel

PART One

Supervisory Management

The Supervisor's Role in Management

Learning Objectives

After studying this chapter, you should be able to

- Identify the level of the supervisor's position on a management team.

- Describe the major competencies that supervisors are expected to bring to their work.

- Explain the linkage that supervisors provide between management goals and employee performance.

- Discuss the resources that supervisors must manage and the results obtained from them.

- Identify the key behaviors that are likely to positively affect employee attitudes and performance.

- Discuss the need for balancing a concern for output and a concern for the people who perform the work.

① MEMBERS OF A UNIQUE TEAM

CONCEPT ▶ Supervisors are an essential part of the management team.

What is management? Why is it important?

Management is the process of obtaining, deploying, and utilizing a variety of essential resources to contribute to an organization's success—both effectively and efficiently. Managers are deemed to be *effective* if they achieve their goals, and they are *efficient* if they do so with a minimal amount of resources for the amount of outputs produced. One of the most important resources of an organization is its employees. *Managers* devote a large portion of their efforts to planning, organizing, staffing, energizing, and controlling the work of human and other resources. One clear distinction between managers and other employees, however, is that managers direct the work of others rather than perform the work themselves.

Are all managers alike?

No. Managers, and the work they do, differ somewhat by the organization they are in (for example, for-profit versus nonprofit organizations), the size of the firm, their industry, their country's cultural norms, their personal values and experiences, and especially by their level in the organization's hierarchy. This latter difference is illustrated in Figure 1-1. At the top of an organization are its executives (often a chief executive officer—the CEO—and some vice-presidents). *Executives* are in charge of, and responsible for, a group of other managers. Executives establish a vision for

Management. The process of obtaining, deploying, and utilizing a variety of essential resources in support of an organization's objectives.

Manager. An individual who plans, organizes, directs, and controls the work of others in an organization.

Executive. A top-level manager in charge of a group of subordinate managers; this person establishes broad plans, objectives, and strategies.

Internet CONNECTION

A.M.A. Access the American Management Association, a nonprofit membership organization providing an education forum for managers.

Executives

Middle managers

Supervisors

Nonmanagerial employees

◆ **FIGURE 1-1**

Managerial levels. Where do first-level supervisors fit into the diagram?

Middle manager. A person who reports to an executive and who directs supervisory personnel toward the attainment of goals and the implementation of plans of an organization.

Supervisor. A manager who is in charge of, and coordinates the activities of, a group of employees engaged in related activities within a unit of an organization.

Nonmanagerial employees. Often referred to as <u>employees</u> or <u>associates</u>, workers who receive direction from supervisors and then perform specific, designated tasks.

the organization, define its mission, develop broad strategies, set objectives and plans, and implement broad policy guidelines. Then they motivate, direct, and monitor the work of managers who report to them.

Middle managers plan, initiate, and implement programs that are intended to carry out the broader objectives set by executives. Middle managers motivate, direct, and oversee the work of the supervisors (and any other managers and employees) who report to them.

Supervisors are managers who normally report to middle managers. Supervisors have the responsibility of getting the "line" employees to carry out the plans and policies set by executives and middle managers. Supervisors plan, direct, motivate, and monitor the work of ***nonmanagerial employees*** at the operational level of the organization. Examples of line employees include production workers, bank tellers, short-order cooks, lab assistants, programmers, nurses, and thousands of other "hands-on" and knowledge (e.g., professional) workers. Some supervisors—about half of the total—are called *first-level supervisors*, as they have only nonmanagerial employees reporting to them. Others are called *second-level supervisors*, because they supervise a combination of other supervisors as well as nonmanagerial employees.

In many organizations, the relative number of middle managers shrunk significantly during the 1990s. This was due mainly to a desire to cut administrative costs, the increasing use of computer-based information systems to fulfill the middle manager's former role, a desire to "flatten" the organizational hierarchy, and the growing capacity and desire of many employees to take on greater responsibilities. As a consequence, supervisors now have greater challenges and expanded roles in the planning and controlling of their employees' work. In turn, supervisors have become increasingly dependent on the information provided by management information systems.

Where did the term *supervisor* come from?

In earlier days, the supervisor was the person in charge of a group of towrope pullers or ditchdiggers. That person was literally the "fore man," since he was up forward of the gang. His authority consisted mainly of chanting the "one, two, three, up" that set the pace for the rest of the workers. In Germany, the supervisor is still called a *vorarbeiter* ("fore worker"); in England, the term *charge hand* is used. Both terms suggest the leadperson origin.

The term *supervisor* has its roots in Latin, where it means "looks over." It was originally applied to the master of a group of artisans. One hundred years ago, it was not uncommon for the master in a New England shop to have almost complete power over the workforce. The master could bid on jobs, hire his own crew, work them as hard as he pleased, and make his living out of the difference between his bid price and the labor costs.

Today, the supervisor's job combines some of the talents of the "foreman" (or leader) and of the "master" (skilled administrative artisan).

Legally, what makes a supervisor a supervisor?

The federal laws of the United States provide two definitions of a supervisor.

1. The Taft-Hartley Act of 1947 (or Labor-Management Relations Act) says that a supervisor is

   …any individual having authority, in the interest of the employer, to hire, transfer, suspend, lay off, recall, promote, discharge, assign, reward, or discipline employees, or responsibility to direct them or to adjust their grievances, or effectively to recommend such action, if in connection with the foregoing the exercise of such authority is not merely of a routine or clerical nature, but requires the use of independent judgment.

   The act specifically prohibits supervisors from joining a union of production and clerical workers, although they may form a union composed exclusively of supervisors.

2. The Fair Labor Standards Act (FLSA) of 1938 (or Minimum Wage Law) as amended set the tone for the above by defining a supervisor as

   …an executive whose primary duty consists of the management of a customarily recognized department or subdivision; who customarily and regularly directs the work of two or more employees; who has the authority to hire or fire other employees or whose suggestions and recommendations as to the hiring or firing and as to the advancement and promotion or any other change in status will be given particular weight; who customarily and regularly exercises discretionary powers; and who does not devote more than 20 percent of his (or her) hours of work to activities which are not closely related to the (managerial) work described above.

   The law also stipulates that supervisors be paid a salary (regardless of how many hours they work). This latter provision makes some supervisors unhappy, since it makes them exempt from the provision of the law that calls for overtime pay after a certain number of hours have been worked. Many employers, however, voluntarily compensate for supervisory overtime in one way or another.

The thrust of these two laws is to make supervisors, once and for all, a bona fide part of management.

SALARY V. OVERTIME

Assume that you have worked in a three-person office for several years. Recently, the supervisor of the unit retired. The manager came to you and explained that a "budget crunch" prevents the company from replacing the supervisor, but that you have been selected to assume some of the supervisory roles while still performing most of your previous duties. Your job will consist of about 70 percent technical tasks (as before) and about 30 percent supervisory tasks (including overseeing the work of the other two employees). You would receive the title of "Supervisor" and switch to a salaried position, but you will no longer qualify for overtime. According to the FLSA, is there a legal or ethical issue involved here? Explain.

Why does frontline supervision get so much attention?

Because it represents just about the most important single force in the American economy. Supervisors, as an occupational classification, form a major segment of the overall labor force. In the United States alone, there is a supervisory management force 2 million strong. It holds the power to turn on—or turn off—the productivity of most organizations. These supervisors are the men and women who maintain the crucial interface between the management hierarchy and the vast body of employees who put their hands on, or apply their minds to, the real work of enterprise.

Recognition—and acceptance—of supervisors by top management has helped them to emerge finally as essential and integrated members of the management group and to assume all the responsibilities of full-fledged managers. The way hasn't been easy. Too often it has been painfully slow. Even today there are companies where the supervisor's status is shaky. But on the whole, no single group of women and men has achieved and deserved such stature and attention in so short a time after so long a wait as has supervisory management.

Are supervisors permitted to do the same work as the people they supervise?

Within the 20 percent stipulation of the Fair Labor Standards Act, there is no law stopping it. Most companies with labor unions, however, often have a contract clause that prohibits the supervisor from performing any work that a union member would ordinarily do (except in clearly defined emergencies, in which the supervisor would do as she or he sees fit).

This is a valid and practical point. Few companies want supervisors to do the work their other employees are hired to do. Supervisors are most valuable when they spend 100 percent of their time supervising. It makes little sense for a $30,000 per year supervisor, for instance, to do the work of a $7.00 per hour operator.

Do employees ever do the work of supervisors?

Yes! An increasingly common trend, discussed in Chapter 14, is for members of so-called self-managed teams to share many of the responsibilities (and perform many of the roles) that supervisors previously performed. This has resulted in a blurring of the supervisor-employee distinction and vastly increased the need for supervisors to become better coaches so as to develop these skills in their employees. Some observers even predict that the title of supervisor will go away, to be replaced by *team leader* and other descriptors.[1] Other commentators assert that "supervisors today play a more important organizational role than ever before."[2] Whichever direction is true, much of the material in this book will be highly relevant to nonmanagerial employees as well as current supervisors.

Quick Test 1

1	T or F	Supervisors are more like managers than they are like nonmanagerial employees.
2	T or F	Supervisors are the type of employee group most likely to be downsized in a cost-reduction effort.

2 MANY COMPETENCIES REQUIRED

CONCEPT ▶ Supervisors must bring to their managerial work a broad range of technical and human relations competencies.

How does a person become a supervisor?

Three out of four supervisors are promoted from the ranks of the organization in which they serve. Typically, they are long-service employees. They have greater experience, have held more different jobs in the organization, and have significantly more education than the employees they supervise. Usually, it is apparent that supervisors are chosen from among the best and most experienced employees in the organization. This isn't necessarily a good thing. Demonstrated knowledge and skill in the technology at hand is very helpful to a supervisor, of course. It says nothing, however, about the skills of management that are needed, too. Just as many superior athletes fail as coaches while lesser athletes succeed, there is similar fate among supervisors who can't handle the human relations aspects of the job.

Other than those supervisors who rise from the ranks, about 10 percent enter the position directly from a college or technical institute or are specially prepared by a company-sponsored training program. Another

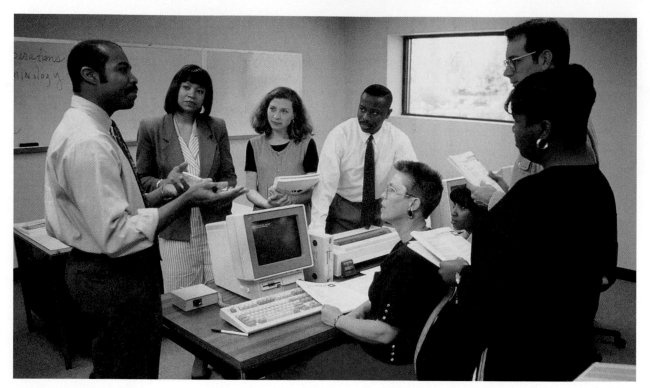

▲ Learning is a lifelong process. **What is your next step in preparing for a career in supervision?**

15 percent are hired into the position from another company or organization.

How long does the transition into supervision usually take?

Just because someone is named to be a supervisor doesn't mean the complete change takes place overnight. The transition from worker to supervisor often moves through five distinct stages:

1. **Taking hold.** This is usually a short phase, where the focus is on learning how to run the department, establishing personal credibility, and beginning to build a power base.
2. **Immersion.** This lasts longer, while a supervisor gets to know the real problems of the department and becomes fully informed about the operations there.
3. **Reshaping.** During this period, a supervisor gradually rebuilds the department to fit his or her style, makes meaningful contributions to operating procedures, and begins to place an "imprint" on the way of doing things.
4. **Consolidation.** In this phase, the supervisor works to remove deeply rooted problems while also perfecting the changes made in previous periods.
5. **Refinement.** This is an opportunity for fine-tuning the operations, consolidating the gains, and searching out new opportunities for making improvements.

YOU NEED TO READ

■ Did you know that supervisors who wish not only to succeed in their current position but achieve future promotions *read widely*? They obtain practical ideas by reading publications such as *Supervision*; they broaden their knowledge about business by scanning publications such as *Business Week* or *Fortune*; and they stay in touch with what's happening in the corporate world by reading the business section of their metropolitan newspaper or even scanning selected portions of the *Wall Street Journal*. Here's some valuable advice: Talk to a couple of managers and ask them what they read, and what they would recommend you read. They'll be impressed, and you'll gain some valuable information!

What personal characteristics does higher management look for in selecting supervisors?

The job of supervision is so demanding that higher management tends to look for *super*people to fill the role. Most firms, however, do establish a set of criteria against which supervisory candidates are judged. The most sought-after qualities in a supervisor are

- Energy and good health.
- The social skills to get along with people.
- Job know-how and technical competence.
- Self-control under pressure.
- Dedication, dependability, and perseverance.
- High self-esteem and a positive outlook toward others.
- Teachability.
- Communications skills.
- Problem-solving skills.
- Leadership potential.
- A positive attitude toward management.[3]

In addition, firms are increasingly seeking supervisory candidates who can build a cohesive team, grasp a wide range of financial data, demonstrate strong integrity and credibility in their dealings with others, and adapt to a variety of changes.[4] Personal characteristics sought include creativity, stress tolerance, initiative, independence, tenacity, flexibility, and risk taking.[5]

How can a newly appointed supervisor make the job of crossing over to the managerial ranks a less turbulent one?

A person who is made a supervisor crosses over from one style of thought to another. As an employee, an individual's concerns are with self-satisfaction in terms of pay and the work itself. As a manager, this same person is expected to place the organization's goals above all other job-related concerns. This means that a supervisor worries first about meeting quotas, quality, and cost standards; second about the employees who do the work; and last about her- or himself.

To make the task more difficult, the newly appointed supervisor usually has already made the long climb to the top of the employee ranks. Now the person must cross over to a new field of achievement—management, as shown in Figure 1-2. It will take a while to get a toehold at the supervisory level. For many, however, it will be the beginning of another long climb—this time to the top of the management heap.

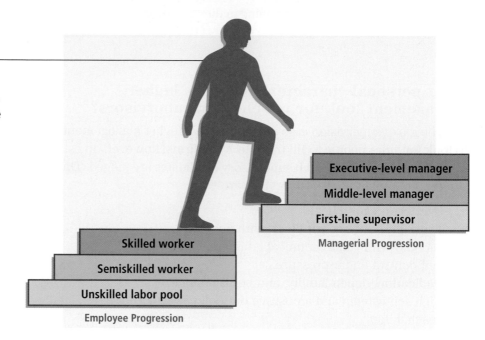

◆ **FIGURE 1-2**

Crossing over from employee ranks to managerial ranks—from "top of the heap" to "bottom of the heap." What differences can the new supervisor expect?

Executive-level manager

Middle-level manager

First-line supervisor

Managerial Progression

Skilled worker

Semiskilled worker

Unskilled labor pool

Employee Progression

The pressures from managers above and from employees below make some new supervisors very uncomfortable. This need not be so, says Professor Keith Davis, one of the most astute observers of organizational relationships. Davis agrees that the supervisor takes pressure from both sides, but he likens the role to a keystone in the organizational arch (Figure 1-3). He suggests that the keystone (the supervisor) takes the pressure from both sides and uses this pressure to build a stronger arch.

Experienced supervisors add this advice for a new person:

Don't throw your weight around. Admit your need for help and seek it from other supervisors and your boss. Make a practice of coming in early and sticking to your job for the full day; employees despise supervisors who push for productivity but who goof off themselves. Keep yourself physically prepared and mentally alert; the job will be more demanding than you expect. Don't indulge in petty pilfering of supplies or use of shop equipment and time to do personal work;

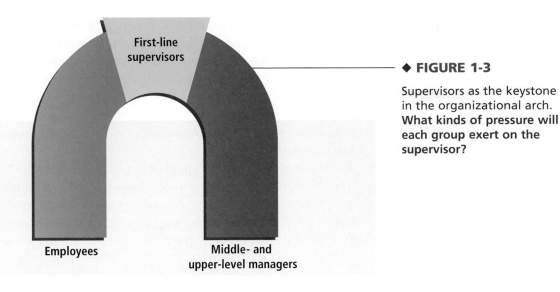

◆ **FIGURE 1-3**

Supervisors as the keystone in the organizational arch. **What kinds of pressure will each group exert on the supervisor?**

employees may try this themselves but they sure don't respect management people who do. Plan to listen a lot, and remember to control your temper even when you are pushed a bit too far.

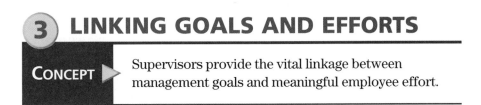

| 3 | T or F | Most new supervisors are drawn directly from college and technical institute programs. |
| 4 | T or F | The transition into supervision is rapid and painless. |

Quick Test 2

3 LINKING GOALS AND EFFORTS

CONCEPT ▷ Supervisors provide the vital linkage between management goals and meaningful employee effort.

When it comes to job responsibilities, what is expected of supervisors?

Responsibilities encompass four—occasionally five—broad areas within an organization:

- **Responsibility to management.** Supervisors must, above all, dedicate themselves to the goals, plans, and policies of the organization. These are typically provided by higher management. It is the primary task of supervisors to serve as a "linking pin" for management to make sure that these are carried out by the employees they supervise.

- **Responsibility to employees.** Employees expect their supervisors to provide direction and training; to protect them from unfair treatment such as sexual harassment; respect their privacy; and to see that the workplace is clean, safe, uncluttered, properly equipped, well lit, and adequately ventilated. They also expect to be treated as intelligent and mature adults. As a result, the term subordinate has often been replaced by *employee, team member, partner,* or *associate.*

- **Responsibility to staff specialists.** The relationship between supervision and staff departments is one of mutual support. Staff people are charged with providing supervisors with guidance and help as well as with prescribing procedures to be followed and forms to be completed. Supervisors, in turn, aid the work of the staff departments by making good use of their advice and service and by conforming to their requests.

- **Responsibility to other supervisors.** Teamwork is essential in the supervisory ranks. There is a great deal of departmental interdependence. The goals and activities of one department must harmonize with those of others. This often requires the sacrifice of an immediate target for the greater good of the organization.

- **Relationships with the union.** Labor union and management views are sometimes in conflict, and the supervisor and shop steward will often see things differently. It is the supervisor's responsibility, however, to keep these relationships objective, to neither "give away the shop" nor yield responsibility for the welfare of the organization and its employees.

Quick Test 3 ▶	**5**	T or F	Of all the expectations placed upon them, supervisors are primarily concerned with their responsibilities to management.
	6	T or F	Supervisors may be called upon to sacrifice their own immediate targets for the greater good of the organization.

CONVERTING RESOURCES INTO OUTPUTS

(4)

| CONCEPT ▷ | Supervisory performance is judged by how well supervisors manage their resources and by the results they get from them. |

Of all that is expected of supervisors, which tasks loom largest?

Four types of problems demand priority:

1. **Meeting operating or production schedules.** Take all the fancy talk away, and the supervisors' basic job is still one of "getting the job done." You must see that services are rendered on time, goods are finished on schedule, deadlines are met, and projects completed when promised.

2. **Living up to prescribed standards of quality.** In many organizations, quality has become the primary objective. This means that you must maintain a delicate balancing act to get out the production while seeing that goods and services meet the quality standards.

3. **Keeping operating costs in line.** It may seem unfair, but supervisors must do even more than meet deadlines and maintain quality standards. You must also attain these operating goals efficently. Simply stated, you must keep your departmental expenses within the allowed or budgeted limits.

4. **Maintaining cooperative attitudes with employees.** Even with computers and automation, employees remain the true "engines" of an organization. Keeping those engines tuned so they function when, how, and as fast as they should is your ultimate challenge as a supervisor.

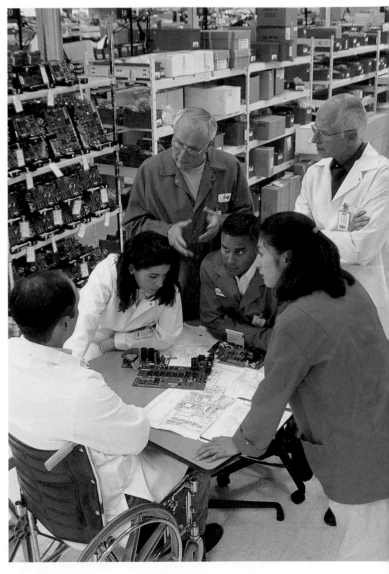

▲ Meeting schedules is an important aspect of the supervisor's job. **What might be the effects of a missed schedule?**

How will supervisory performance be judged by higher management?

It will be judged by two general measures: (1) how well you manage the various resources made available to you to accomplish your assignments and (2) how good the results are in terms of several criteria (see Figure 1-4).

◆ **FIGURE 1-4**

Measurement of supervisory performance. Will more resources (e.g., more people, more money) necessarily assure better results?

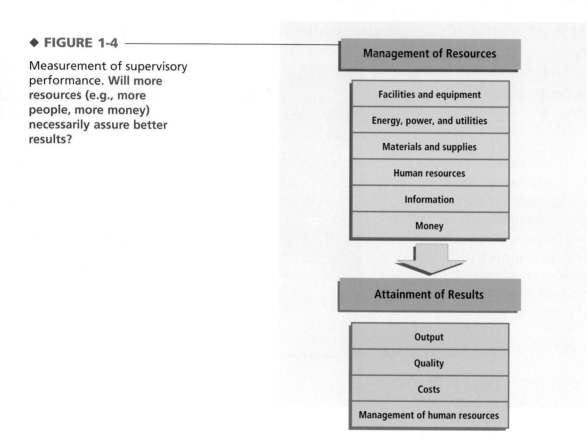

Management of Resources

Facilities and equipment

Energy, power, and utilities

Materials and supplies

Human resources

Information

Money

Attainment of Results

Output

Quality

Costs

Management of human resources

Management of Resources. Resources are the things that, in effect, set you up in business as a supervisor. They include the following:

- **Facilities and equipment.** Examples are a certain amount of floor space, desks, benches, tools, production machinery, and computer terminals. Your job is to keep these operating productively and to prevent their misuse.
- **Energy, power, and utilities.** Among these resources are heat, light, air-conditioning, electricity, steam, water, and compressed air. Conservation is the principal measure of effectiveness here.
- **Materials and supplies.** Included are raw materials, parts, and assemblies used to make a product and operating supplies such as lubricants, stationery, computer disks, paper clips, and masking tape. Getting the most from all of your materials and holding waste to the minimum are prime measures here.

- **Human resources.** This refers to the workforce in general and your employees in particular. Your biggest job is to see that these people are productively engaged at all times.

- **Information.** Examples are the information made available by staff departments and found in operating manuals, specifications sheets, and on computer screens. Your success often depends on how well you can utilize the data and know-how made available to you through these sources.

- **Money.** All the above can be measured by how much they cost, although the actual cash will rarely flow through your hands. Nevertheless, supervisors are expected to be prudent in decisions that affect expenditures and may have to justify these in terms of savings or other benefits.

Attainment of Results. It follows that if you manage each of your resources well, you should get the desired results. Whatever your particular area of responsibility and whatever your organization, you can be sure that you will be judged in the long run by how well you meet these four objectives:

- **Output, or production.** Specifically, your department will be expected to turn out a certain amount of work per day, per week, and per month. It will be expected that this will be done on time, to specification, and within budget.

- **Quality and workmanship.** Output volume alone is not enough. You will also be judged by the quality of the work your employees perform, whether it be measured in terms of the number of product defects, service errors, or customer complaints.

- **Costs and budget control.** Your output and quality efforts will always be restricted by the amount of money you can spend to carry them out. Universally, supervisors attest to the difficulty of living up to cost or expense and budget constraints.

- **Management of human resources.** You will face many potential problems in the areas of employee turnover, theft, tardiness, absenteeism, discipline, and morale. Managing these dimensions of employee satisfaction and behavior will be a key element of your overall success.

| 7 | T or F | The most important task of a supervisor is to maintain cooperative employee attitudes. |
| 8 | T or F | Output, quality, and costs are all considered key resources to be managed by a supervisor. |

◀ *Quick Test 4*

CONCEPT ▶ Supervisors strengthen their contribution to the management process by developing their technical, administrative, and human relations skills.

Where do supervisors fit in the management process?

Management process. Covers the five key functions of planning, organizing, staffing, energizing, and controlling organizational resources for the attainment of results.

They are an essential part of it. Supervisors perform exactly the same functions as all other managers in their organization—up to and including the chief executive. Each specific task, every responsibility, all the various roles that supervisors are called on to perform are carried out by the ***management process*** (Figure 1-5). This process, which is repeated over and over, daily, weekly, and yearly, consists of five broad functions:

- **Planning.** Setting goals and establishing plans and procedures to attain them.
- **Organizing.** Arranging jobs to be done in such a way as to make them more effective.
- **Staffing.** Selecting and placing just the right number of people in the most appropriate jobs.
- **Energizing.** Motivating, communicating, and leading.
- **Controlling.** Monitoring the process, its output and quality, its costs, and the people who carry it out.

The management process is explained in detail in Chapter 3.

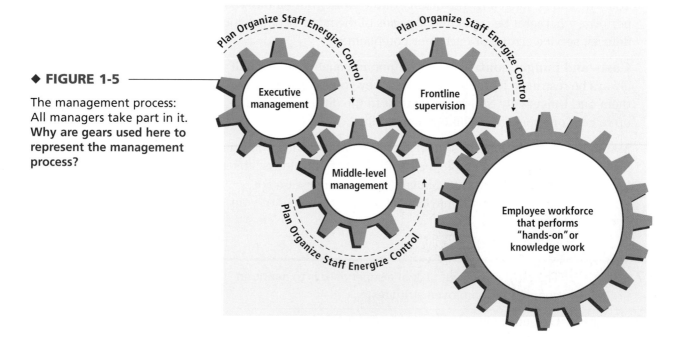

◆ **FIGURE 1-5**

The management process: All managers take part in it. **Why are gears used here to represent the management process?**

How do supervisory job roles differ from those of other levels of management?

They differ only in degree. Higher level managers spend more time planning and less time directing, for example. The people who studied this matter came up with several useful conclusions. They first divided all the tasks and responsibilities we have listed so far in this text into three kinds of roles. *Roles* are the parts played by actors on a stage; they are also the real-life parts played by managers and supervisors in an organization. These three roles can be classified as those requiring the following:

- **Technical skills.** Job know-how; knowledge of the industry and its particular processes, equipment, and problems.

- **Administrative skills.** Knowledge of the entire organization and how it is coordinated, knowledge of its information and records system, and an ability to plan and control work.

- **Human relations skills.** Knowledge of human behavior and an ability to work effectively with individuals and groups—peers and superiors as well as subordinates.

The observers then concluded that the role of the supervisor emphasizes technical and human relations skills most and administrative skills least. This emphasis tends to reverse itself with higher level managers, as illustrated in Figure 1-6. Note the importance of human relations at all levels!

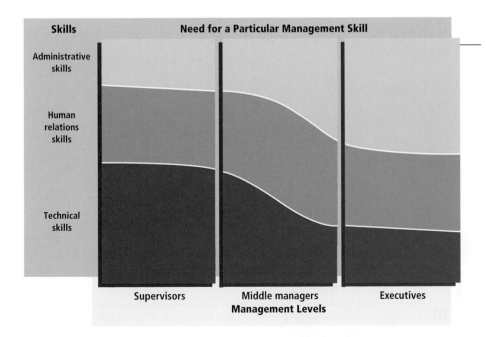

◆ FIGURE 1-6

How the need for managerial skills varies at different levels of management. **Why are human relations skills so important to a supervisor?**

What are the main supervisory behaviors associated with results?

Though they vary somewhat from job to job and firm to firm, there are a number of regularly performed duties of the supervisory job that require attention. The broadest category could simply be called *performance management*. This is an ongoing process of clarifying and communicating performance expectations to employees, and then providing coaching and feedback to reinforce the desired actions by them.[6] In addition, supervisors need to engage in personal time management, attend meetings and conferences, solve problems, provide training to employees, and handle a wide range of communications.

A comprehensive review of relevant research studies on supervisory effectiveness produced a profile of behaviors associated with improved subordinate attitudes and performance. The highlights are illustrated in Table 1-1. The list may seem formidable, but most of the listed skills can be acquired by supervisors who are willing to learn from their experiences, accept the coaching offered by their managers, and take advantage of developmental opportunities provided by their employers.

TABLE 1-1

Key Behaviors of a First-Level Supervisor

- Accepts criticism and suggestions
- Lets subordinates know what s/he thinks of their work
- Goes to bat for subordinates (supports them where appropriate)
- Emphasizes production, gives directions, and plans operations
- Follows the chain of command (linkages between levels of management)
- Keeps one's boss informed

- Gives praise verbally to subordinates
- Develops and trains subordinates for better jobs
- Uses rewards and punishments wisely
- Displays competence in human relations
- Creates an open climate for discussion of problems
- Displays consideration, tact, and diplomacy
- Identifies with higher management (supports organizational goals)

Source: Adapted from Steven Kerr, Kenneth D. Hill, and Laurie Broedling, "The First-Line Supervisor: Phasing Out or Here to Stay?" *Academy of Management Review*, 1986, vol. 11; no. 1, pp. 103–117.

Quick Test 5 ►

9	T or F	Supervisors, managers, and executives all engage in planning, organizing, staffing, energizing, and controlling.
10	T or F	Administrative skills are the most important ones for supervisors to develop and exhibit.

A CONCERN FOR BOTH WORK AND PEOPLE

(6)

CONCEPT ▶ Effective supervisors balance the application of their skills between the work to be done and a concern for the people who perform this work.

Supervisory balance: What does it mean?

Simply this: Pay as much attention to human relations as to technical and administrative matters combined.

In other words, be as ***employee centered*** as you are ***job*** or ***task centered*** in your interests. Or, said still another way, spend as much time maintaining group cohesiveness, direction, and morale as you do pushing for productivity or task accomplishment.

It would be misleading to conclude that being nice is the answer to employee productivity. It isn't. As in sports, nice players often finish last. The important conclusion from research is that supervisors who focus on job demands to the exclusion of their interest in the welfare and the development of their people don't get the results they are looking for. Conversely, supervisors who bend over backward to make work easy for their employees don't get good results either. It takes a balance between the two approaches, as shown in Figure 1-7.

> **Employee-centered supervision.** A method of supervision that places an emphasis on a genuine concern and respect for employees, and on the maintenance of effective relationships within a work group.

> **Task-centered supervision.** A method of supervision that places an emphasis on the job or task that employees are expected to perform to produce results.

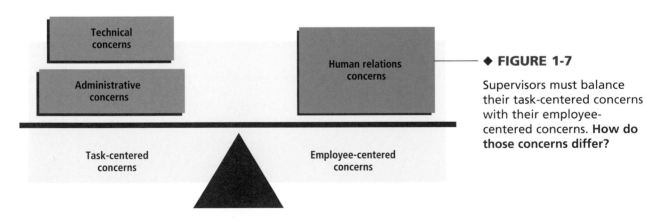

◆ **FIGURE 1-7**

Supervisors must balance their task-centered concerns with their employee-centered concerns. **How do those concerns differ?**

What's a normal day in the life of a supervisor?

Many supervisors say that there is no such thing as a normal day. One thing is certain, however: A supervisor's day is full of interruptions. Estimates are that a typical supervisor handles from 50 to 80 problems a day. Thankfully, many of these are simple or short-lived. Nevertheless, solving problems quickly and systematically is the name of the game. Accordingly, anything supervisors can do to put order and system into their days is strongly encouraged. Appendix A outlines a daily work sequence that can guide supervisors in establishing an orderly structure for their day.

Quips & Quotes

The best way to change behavior is to change your point of view.

—Sigmund Freud

"Getting to know you" is an important aspect of balancing a supervisor's human relations concerns with technical and administrative ones. Here's how this was accomplished by two notable managers when they took over responsibilities in a new organization:

When the new president, Mickey Drexler, took over The Gap, the now-famous but then-slumping vendor of designer blue jeans, he walked up to every sales clerk in the organization and asked, "What's up?" Then he stopped talking and listened. His next question was: "What should we do?" Employees' replies covered just about everything from new products to store design, lighting, and displays.

Based in part by suggestions from employees, The Gap made a spectacular turnaround to gain a major share of the jeans market.

When Lynn V. Cheney assumed the chair of the National Endowment for the Humanities, her credentials were sound, but she was an unknown commodity to the staff. So, after receiving her confirmation from the U.S. Senate, the first thing Cheney did was to walk through the agency and shake hands and introduce herself to all 250 members of the staff. "It took two days," she said, "but many of these staff members had been there five to ten years. They had talent and knowledge I needed to depend upon."

Quick Test 6 ▷	**11**	T or F	Supervisors should focus on their employees more than on their tasks to be accomplished.
	12	T or F	Most days in the life of a supervisor are highly predictable and relatively interruption-free.

CHAPTER 1 REVIEW

KEY CONCEPTS TO REMEMBER

1. **Members of a Unique Team.** Supervisors occupy the vital first level of management that interacts directly with the workforce. They are essential to an organization's success, and by law they are members of the management team of an organization.

2. **Many Competencies Required.** To be able to learn and perform well in their roles, supervisors must bring to the position a wide range of personal qualities and competencies. Competencies most frequently expected of supervisors include energy and good health, an ability to get along with people, job know-how, self-control under pressure, dedication and dependability, problem-solving skills, leadership potential, and a genuine belief in the contribution that good management can make to the attainment of an organization's goals.

3. **Linking Goals and Efforts.** Supervisors must respond to the interests of the many groups present in an organization: the management team, their own employees, staff specialists, other supervisors, and—where present—the labor union. The most critical function that supervisors perform for these constituents is to act as the linkage, or interface, between higher management's goals, plans, and policies and the employees who actually perform the work of an organization.

4. **Converting Resources into Outputs.** Supervisory effectiveness is judged by two major measures: (a) how well supervisors manage the resources made available to them and (b) the quantity and quality of the results they derive from the use of these resources. Resources include facilities and equipment; energy, power, and utilities; materials and supplies; human resources; information; and money. Results are focused on output attained from resources, its quality, and the containment of costs.

5. **Skills to Be Developed.** As managers, supervisors regularly engage in the management process of planning, organizing, staffing, energizing, and controlling. Supervisors improve their effectiveness in this process by developing their technical (or know-how) skills, their administrative (planning, implementing, and innovating) skills, and their human relations (interpersonal) skills. Compared with executives, supervisors rely much more on their technical skills and far less on their administrative skills. While human relations skills are important at all levels of management, they often become a make-or-break factor for supervisors.

6. **A Concern for Both Work and People.** In carrying out their responsibilities, supervisors must be careful not to be overzealous in either (a) pushing employees too hard for production or (b) being overly protective of these employees. The most effective supervisors strike a balance between a concern for the work to be done and a concern for those people who must do the work.

READING COMPREHENSION

1. There is one clear distinction between managers and their employees. What is it?
2. How many levels of management are there in a typical organization? At which level are supervisors found?
3. What characteristics of a supervisory management job are stressed by the two laws that define this position?
4. Why might a company object to the supervisor of an order processing department spending most of his or her time operating the keyboard of a computer?
5. Energy, good health, and self-control are among the characteristics looked for in a supervisor. Why are these qualities important?
6. Name the four main groups of constituents within an organization with which a supervisor must interact. Describe the nature of a supervisor's responsibilities to each.
7. Which two broad categories of performance are typically used to judge the effectiveness of supervisors at their work?
8. Research studies have identified a variety of tasks that supervisors must perform (Table 1-1). Sort these out according to the three categories of supervisory skills: (a) technical, (b) administrative, and (c) human relations.
9. How is supervisory management similar to higher level management? How is it different?
10. What is meant by the fact that supervisors are advised to achieve "balance" in the application of their skills?

APPLICATION

Self-Assessment

▶ *Are you ready to be a supervisor?*

Read the following statements carefully. Circle the number on the response scale that most closely reflects the degree to which each statement accurately describes you. Add up your total points and prepare a brief action plan for self-improvement. Be ready to report your score for tabulation across the entire group.

	Good Description									Poor Description
1. I like to work under deadlines.	10	9	8	7	6	5	4	3	2	1
2. I am keenly sensitive to the needs of other people.	10	9	8	7	6	5	4	3	2	1
3. Most employees work for social and esteem reasons, as well as the money they can earn.	10	9	8	7	6	5	4	3	2	1
4. I don't mind being held accountable for other people's work.	10	9	8	7	6	5	4	3	2	1
5. I have a lot to learn about supervision and management.	10	9	8	7	6	5	4	3	2	1

	Good Description									Poor Description
6. The work of employees should be criticized when it is not acceptable.	10	9	8	7	6	5	4	3	2	1
7. I believe that people who break the rules should be disciplined.	10	9	8	7	6	5	4	3	2	1
8. Given a fair chance, most people want to do a high-quality job.	10	9	8	7	6	5	4	3	2	1
9. Most employees are willing to give a fair day's work for a fair day's wage.	10	9	8	7	6	5	4	3	2	1
10. Most managers are quite good at helping me and others do their work.	10	9	8	7	6	5	4	3	2	1

Scoring and Interpretation

SCORING

Add up your total points for the 10 questions. Record that number here, and report it when it is requested. _____

INTERPRETATION

81 to 100 points. Your attitudes and beliefs are appropriate for supervisory positions.

61 to 80 points. Examine your attitudes and beliefs and discuss them with current supervisors and managers to determine need for revision.

Below 60 points. Your attitudes and beliefs may be substantially inconsistent with current organizational practices. They could be detrimental to your career.

Identify your three lowest scores and record the question numbers here:

_____, _____, _____.

ACTION

Write a brief paragraph detailing an action plan for how you might change your beliefs. For example, if you scored low on item 6, you may wish to obtain additional training in the skill of performance feedback. Include a target date for mastering the skill.

Skill Development

Interview ◀

Assume that you want to become one of the best supervisors that you know—one who is truly outstanding. According to an earlier discussion in this chapter, this might require strong capabilities in several of the following qualities. Identify three key people whose opinions you value and who have had an opportunity to observe you closely (e.g., your supervisor, your spouse, a co-worker). Ask each of them for specific suggestions for how you could improve in some of these areas:

1. Physical health— _____
2. Personal energy— _____
3. Ability to get along with people— _____
4. Technical competence— _____
5. Self-control under pressure— _____
6. Dependability— _____
7. Teachability— _____
8. Communications— _____
9. Problem-solving— _____
10. Leadership— _____

ACTION

Commit yourself to a one-month, three-month, and twelve-month plan of improvement by following these suggestions. At the end of each time period, return to the three people and ask them if they've seen any change in you on any of the ten criteria.

Group Exercise

▶ *Considering Your Future*

STEP 1: Form into two teams (A and B) for a mini-debate on the topic, "The position of the first-line supervisor will be phased out of most organizations."

STEP 2: The "A" team should take the affirmative position (arguing in favor). The "B" team should take the negative position (arguing against).

STEP 3: Complete an exploratory investigation (projecting historical trends, conducting interviews, etc.) to support your position.

STEP 4: Conduct the debate. After all arguments have been heard, search, through informal discussion, for a likely "middle ground" about the issue.

Case 1

The Brand-New Supervisor

Sheryl had just the kind of personality you'd like in a supervisor. She was focused, energetic, and friendly. She was brand new on the job, however. She had just received an associate degree in data processing from a nearby community college, where she had worked her way through as a night tabulator at a local branch bank. Based on her good work there and grades in college, the bank selected her to replace the retiring day supervisor of its eight-person data processing department.

From the start on her new job, things had not gone quite right for Sheryl. For instance, almost immediately Sheryl spotted several inequities in the existing distribution of assignments. Accordingly, she prepared a more efficient—and more equitable—assignment schedule. She was disappointed, however, that her employees did not recognize how fair the new assignments were. Instead, they found all sorts of ways to make the schedule inoperable. Similarly, when Sheryl tried to show the keyboard operators some of the new techniques she had learned in college, they watched politely but continued to function as before. Then, after a few weeks, Sheryl discovered that the employees had arranged their own system of coffee and lunch breaks, without regard to the rules set forth in the bank's human resource manual. When Sheryl insisted that the employees conform to the rules in the manual, there was almost a rebellion.

Try as she might, things did not improve for Sheryl. The cruelest blow, however, fell at the end of Sheryl's first month on the job when the bank manager called her into the office to review her progress. The manager said, "What's going on out there? I'm hearing all sorts of vague complaints from your employees. Furthermore, our records show that the output and quality from your department has fallen off sharply since you took over. What do you intend to do about it?"

◀ Analysis

If you were Sheryl, which of the following actions would you consider to be most effective for you to take? Rank the alternatives on a scale of 1 (most preferable) to 5 (least preferable). You may add another alternative if you wish. Be prepared to justify your ranking.

Ranking

_____ **a.** Ask for the bank manager's help and support in enforcing rules and changing the assignments in your department.

_____ **b.** Rethink your approach, by placing an emphasis on establishing cooperative relations equal to what you now place on the technical and administrative matters.

_____ c. Back off on the changes you have tried to initiate, and learn to "go with the flow."

_____ d. Make a concerted effort to build a better relationship with your staff, based on a mutual understanding of the department's goals.

_____ e. Crack down now on enforcing rules and assignments before you completely lose control.

Case 2

The Rejected Refrigerators

"You've got to get your department in order!" That's the word Dave received from his boss yesterday. Dave supervises a spot-welding department in an appliance manufacturing plant. His boss's complaint was twofold: Not only was Dave's department producing too many refrigerator bodies that were later rejected at inspection, but the cost of raw materials consumed by the department was also far more than expected. Dave couldn't understand the connection. He did know, however, that in order to speed up their production rates, his welders did damage a lot of raw materials. He also knew that often in their haste, the welders jammed the spot-welding equipment.

Analysis

a. How might there be a connection between the rejects and overconsumption of raw materials and jamming of the welding equipment?

b. What should Dave do to "straighten out his department"?

Case 3

Which Comes First—Departmental Performance or Employee Development?

Fred supervises the tabulation section in the accounting division of a public utility in the Northeast. He is a stickler for performance, and places a major emphasis on his staff's ability to meet monthly output quotas. Accordingly, he was disturbed when one of his more effective employees asked whether Fred could arrange her assignments so that she could learn something about billing operations in the division. "What do you want to do that for?" he asked. "I want to improve my chances for advancement," the employee said. "I'll have to think about it," said Fred. "I don't want to do anything that interferes with your meeting your production quotas."

a. What do you think of the employee's request? Will it interfere with her output or productivity?

b. What answer do you think Fred should give?

Too Much to Keep Up With

Tami, supervisor of the word processing section of a federal agency, was having one of those days. She had been pressing her staff of keyboard specialists to complete a major report in time for distribution to the press by the next morning. She was interrupted, however, by a call from the human resources department. "Would you come up here, please," said the personnel officer. When Tami arrived, she was irritated to find that one of her employees had registered a grievance related to Tami's continuing pressure for performance.

"Your handling of people leaves much to be desired," said the personnel officer.

"What am I supposed to do," responded Tami, "hold every employee by the hand all day? We've got work to do out there, and I expect each person to pitch in."

"Few people will complain about that," said the personnel officer, "It's the way you go about it that causes the trouble. You're getting a reputation of being too heavy-handed."

"I've got all I can do to keep up with the details of this job," said Tami. "Every day, I'm handling problems involving letter, memo, and report writing; telephone techniques; resource and reference materials; calculating, transcribing, and copying machines; and now this new baby—electronic filing. I was put into this job because of my know-how, wasn't I? Without it, the department would be in a hopeless mess. I can't help it if one or two employees are unhappy."

"It's more than one or two employees who are unhappy," said the personnel officer, "and it's up to you now to do something about it."

a. What do you think of Tami's view of her responsibilities as a supervisor?

b. Where will her strengths and weaknesses as a supervisor likely be?

c. What might Tami do to improve her overall effectiveness?

Chapter References

1. "Future Directions for Management Development," *Issues and Trends Report*, Fall 1996, Alexandria, VA: ASTD, pp. 1–4.
2. David K. Lindo, "Are You an Obstacle Course or a Key Resource?" *Supervision*, October 1996, pp. 3–5.
3. Lester R. Bittel, "Dimensions of Supervisory Competencies," in *The Complete Guide to Supervisory Training and Development* (Reading, MA: Addison-Wesley, 1987).
4. James M. Kouzes and Barry Z. Posner, *Credibility* (San Francisco: Jossey-Bass, 1993).
5. William C. Byham, "Assessment Center Method," in Lester R. Bittel and Jackson E. Ramsey (eds.), *Handbook for Professional Managers* (New York: McGraw-Hill, 1985), p. 41.
6. Maureen Driscoll, "Performance Assessment: An Opportunity, Not a Chore," *Corporate Report Ventures*, August 1996, pp. 28–9.

Answers to Quick Tests ▶

Quick Test 1	Quick Test 2	Quick Test 3
1. T	3. F	5. T
2. F	4. F	6. T
Quick Test 4	Quick Test 5	Quick Test 6
7. F	9. T	11. F
8. F	10. F	12. F

CHAPTER 2

Creating a Positive Workplace Within a Dynamic Environment

Learning Objectives

After studying this chapter, you should be able to

- Distinguish between a supervisor's work environment and that of higher level managers.

- Identify the four characterizing features of work.

- Discuss the general expectations that employees have for their jobs.

- Explain how and why different people have different perceptions of the nature of their work.

- List a number of ways by which supervisors can improve the quality of work life for their employees.

1 SEVEN PRESSURES TO COPE WITH

CONCEPT ▶ The unique environment in which supervisors work shapes their horizons, tends to restrict their options, and yet provides opportunities for flexible and creative responses.

In what ways does the supervisors' world differ from that of their superiors?

Higher level managers tend to be outward-oriented. They are likely to be more influenced by forces and events outside the company or institution than by those within. Supervisors, on the other hand, are more inside-oriented.

A company president or agency executive has concerns for such things as how to increase shareholder value, what the competition is doing, whether or not the company's creditors can pay their bills, how dependable suppliers are likely to be, sources of funding, or how to keep stockholders and the public satisfied. Higher level executives are also concerned with general economic conditions, proposed government regulations, and public opinion.

Supervisors are concerned with, and restrained by, a number of more immediate factors. As shown in Figure 2-1, a supervisor's environment is characterized by seven important factors. Some factors were mentioned in Chapter 1 as "responsibilities." Regardless of terminology, these factors also establish the supervisor's environment. They include the following:

Etiquette. Check the Internet for guidelines for using e-mail, including etiquette tips.

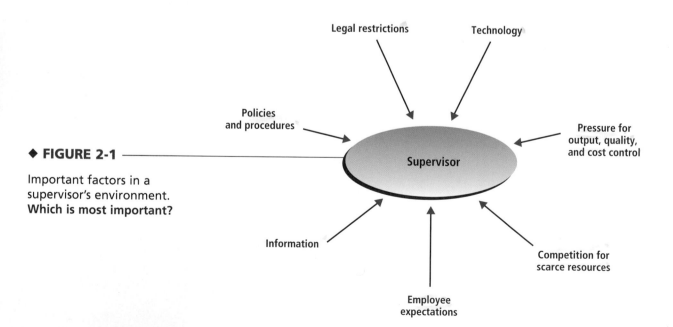

◆ **FIGURE 2-1**

Important factors in a supervisor's environment. **Which is most important?**

1. Technology, existing and changing, such as the processes and equipment, the know-how, and the way things are done in a particular company, department, or organization.
2. Legal restrictions, such as those affecting employee safety, health, and rights to equal opportunity, fair pay, privacy, freedom from harassment and discrimination, accommodation of diverse backgrounds and values, and representation by a union.
3. Organizational policies and procedures, to which supervisors, as well as their employees, must conform.
4. Pressures from above to meet the organization's goals for output, quality, and cost control.
5. Competition with other supervisors for scarce resources, such as employees, equipment, space, skills, and budgets.
6. A wide array of information that must be generated, processed, maintained, and utilized.
7. Rising expectations of employees for considerate treatment, meaningful work, and an opportunity to participate in decisions that affect them.

How do time horizons differ?

Higher level executives are, rightfully, more concerned with the long-term future than are supervisors. Executives, and most middle managers, are paid to plan for and create results that will happen next month or next year. Supervisors, who are on the firing line, have a shorter time horizon. A delay of 15 minutes in the arrival of operating supplies can loom large in importance when 15 employees are idled by it. Consequently, supervisors keep their eyes on hour-by-hour and day-to-day problems. For most supervisors, a "month from now" is a long look ahead.

Does this mean that supervisors don't need to look ahead?

Not at all. Supervisors should also keep a sharp eye out for changes—both external and internal—that may affect their future operations. For example, there is hardly an organization whose operational practices won't change in the next 10 years due to one of the following changes predicted for the external environment:

- Increasing pace of change in technology, affecting low-tech, as well as high-tech, industries.
- Globalization of business operations, requiring that a supervisor's operations be competitive with those that are thousands of miles—and maybe even an ocean—away.
- Changes in the composition of the workforce, including more women and immigrants, an increasing number of older workers, and a shortage of applicants with the necessary technical skills.

- Greater emphasis on the ***quality of work life* (QWL)** for employees, including flexible work hours and variety in assignments.
- Increasing concern for legal rights of employees as guaranteed by federal and state legislation.
- Economic uncertainty, requiring organizations to expand or contract their operations, or change structure quickly and efficiently.

As you can see, supervisors are caught in a web of uncontrollable circumstances, and they will be even more so in the future.

Quick Test 1 ▶

1	T or F	Most supervisors need not be concerned with environmental issues such as technology, scarce resources, or legal restrictions.
2	T or F	Supervisors and higher level managers both share the same emphasis on long-term issues and problems.

2 THE WORLD OF WORK

CONCEPT ▶ The traditional world of work is characterized by various degrees of employee conformity, the exercise of authority by managers, the blending of personal interests with organizational goals, and the need for record keeping.

What is meant by *work*?

Webster helps here. The dictionary identifies several relevant aspects in these five definitions of ***work***:

- Activity in which one exerts strength or faculties to do or perform.
- Sustained physical or mental effort valued to the extent that it overcomes obstacles and achieves an objective or result.
- Labor, task, or duty that affords one the accustomed means of livelihood.
- Strenuous activity marked by the presence of difficulty and exertion and the absence of pleasure.
- Specific task, duty, function, or assignment, often a part or phase of some larger activity.

Note the key words: physical, mental, effort, exertion, obstacles, difficulty, result, and means of livelihood. Note, too, the implication of work as a part of a larger activity and its age-old association with the absence of pleasure! An emerging definition of *work*, then, is an activity involving physical or mental effort to perform tasks and overcome difficulties so as to attain valued organizational results and a means of personal livelihood. Twenty-first century supervisors need to try to combine work with pleasure for their employees, as measured by the degree of personal satisfaction they can derive from their jobs or work environment.

Why do most people work?

For two relatively universal reasons: first, for the money it brings and for what necessities and pleasures that money will buy; second, for the satisfaction work can bring—either from being with other people or from a sense of personal accomplishment.

Which reward is more important to most workers, money or job satisfaction?

That depends. Most of us want both, of course. But until each of us has a paycheck that is big enough for our own highly personal situation, job satisfaction may take a backseat. However, it almost never disappears—at least for long.

In what ways does a bureaucracy affect the things people do?

Especially within organizations, four factors make work unique:

1. Rules, regulations, and procedures sometimes demand a degree of conformity in each employee's action and thus limit free choice. Many people find it hard to channel their efforts into paths that are set by others. Modern supervision tries to keep rules to a minimum and to stress the opportunity for self-control especially when employees have previously demonstrated their capacity to act responsibly.

▲ Most people work for money and what it buys. **What other rewards motivate people to work?**

Bureaucracy. An organized system of work characterized by policies and rules, a chain of command, an emphasis on organizational goals, and many written records.

2. A chain of authority makes each person receive direction from and report to a boss, and the boss in turn reports to another boss, and so on. In practice, this means that most companies are run by relatively few top-level managers. In organizations with many layers in the hierarchy, lower level managers and employees at the bottom of the organizational pyramid often feel that they have little say in what happens. Employees may not have been asked to make constructive suggestions about how to run the business. Supervisors who invite help from employees tend to make the work more appealing to them.

3. Those who hold managerial responsibility are expected to place their own personal interests behind those of the organization. It is no secret that a great many managers do not do so. Instead, they take care of themselves first and the company's resources, especially employees, later. Employees who work for this kind of manager may find very little job satisfaction and may expend their effort in complaints.

4. Much of what happens or is expected to happen is put into written records. Outside of work, most of our activities are loosely defined and rarely put into writing. Written documents—those that record the past and those that set goals for the future—are threatening to many people. They fear that no mistake will be forgotten and that every promise will be remembered. Because of so much formal communication, employees often feel more comfortable with supervisors who pass on the word in easy, give-and-take conversation.

These four factors were first identified in the 1890s by German sociologist Max Weber, who prescribed them for an "organized system of work directed by hired managers." He called this system *bureaucracy*.

Quick Test 2 ▶	**3**	T or F	Most employees work for one thing and one thing alone—the money it provides them.
	4	T or F	Most bureaucracies no longer have policies, rules, or a chain of command.

③ EMPLOYEE EXPECTATIONS

CONCEPT ▷ Despite the constraints of a bureaucracy, the great majority of employees are reasonably satisfied with their work.

How many people are truly happy at their work?

According to a number of authoritative studies, from 80 to 90 percent of all employees are reasonably satisfied with their jobs. This doesn't necessarily mean that they are ecstatic about them; it just means that on balance the positives outweigh the negatives. The figures also show that African Americans and those in other cultural groups are not as satisfied as are whites, and females are less satisfied than males. Furthermore, factory workers tend to be less satisfied than white-collar workers. And one of the clearest conclusions is that job satisfaction tends to improve with age. Younger people are by far the most dissatisfied with their work. Why is this? Perhaps because their expectations are much higher regarding the rewards of working. They have been raised in an era of abundance.

Despite some recent declines, the general level of job satisfaction is still surprisingly high. High enough, it seems, to give supervisors an even break in attempting to move employees toward organizational and departmental goals.

What is it today's workers expect from their jobs that is often lacking?

Something that challenges their skills and offers fair pay in return for this extra effort. According to Daniel Yankelovich, a noted surveyor of public opinion and director of the nonprofit Public Agenda Foundation, most people can choose either to work hard or to just get by. Only 1 person in 5, reports Yankelovich, says he or she does his or her very best. For one thing, workers assume that an increase in output may not benefit them, but only the consumer, stockholders, or management. Down deep, however, most employees will work harder and better, says Yankelovich and other observers, if the work they do makes sense to them and is truly appreciated by their bosses. In fact, 8 out of 10 Americans say that their jobs are too easy. Instead, they'd prefer a challenging job to an easy one where they merely "put in their time."

Supervisors can minimize both kinds of employee complaints. First, they can make sure that employees have enough to do, especially of the kind of work that capitalizes on their talents and skills. Second, supervisors can live up to their promises about promotions or relief from boring assignments for those who do go all out to do a good job.

Employees, workers, colleagues, cast members, crew members, team members, associates? What should supervisors call subordinates, and why does it matter?

That depends. The dictionary term for an employed person, at any level, is "employee." It has also been a common practice to think of employees at lower levels of an organization as "workers," even though an economist would say that *all* employed persons are workers. These two terms (employee and worker) have traditionally been used to differentiate lower level, nonexempt employees from managerial (or exempt) employees. In recent years, however, a trend has emerged for designating employees—at whatever level—as "colleagues" or "team members" or "associates." This reflects a recognition of the wisdom in considering the status of nonmanagement employees as *collegial* (to be in partnership) with management. Wal-Mart stores, in particular, have popularized the use of the term "associates." Not every organization, of course, subscribes to this terminology. Progressive employers do, however, recognize that each employee—regardless of rank or designation—(1) shares a responsibility for helping an organization to attain its goals, and furthermore, (2) has the potential to contribute, not only the prescribed physical and mental effort, but also ideas of value. Consequently, the term used should be selected with care, used consistently, and backed up by daily actions consistent with it.

| **Quick Test 3** ▶ | **5** | T or F | The general level of job satisfaction remains relatively high among the workforce today. |
| | **6** | T or F | The vast majority of employees report that they do their very best on their jobs. |

(4) UNDERSTANDING EMPLOYEE PERCEPTIONS

| CONCEPT ▶ | Individuals have differing perceptions of their work and differ in their responses to it. |

What are the chances of developing a 100 percent enthusiastic workforce?

Very slim. This is because of two important factors—individual differences and the role of perceptions. Extensive research on employee characteristics shows that they vary substantially—despite obvious similarities—in many ways. People differ in physical dimensions and appearance as well as in emotional and intellectual capacities, and this produces predictable differences in their desires for jobs and rewards. Each employee further develops a unique set of perceptions about the work itself (and their supervisor), affected by past experiences, mental models, and even trivial events. Therefore, it is likely that there will always be some dissatisfied employees (perhaps 1 or 2 out of 10), an equal proportion who are readily satisfied, and a broad group in between.

What are some key examples of employee perceptions at work?

Taken as a whole, today's employees are better educated than any workforce in history, and this leads to higher expectations. Applicants and subordinates are fully aware of their civil—and employment—rights. This leads to a widespread feeling that "I'm entitled." In fact, public law has legalized a great many **entitlements**, such as those related to equal employment opportunity, representation by a labor union, workplace adjustment for disabilities, family leave, due process, and privacy. One entitlement often leads to a demand for another, and seeing someone else receive an entitlement leads to a request for their own ("Me, too!").

At the extreme, a mentality of entitlement leads some people to believe that society owes them a living, and a pleasant one at that. And any employee can become discouraged by the **downsizing** of organizations or closing of plants that were once thought to guarantee secure employment for a lifetime. As a consequence, many employees have lost faith that hard work, dedication, and perseverance will assure job success or even job security. Towers Perrin, a respected consulting company, reports that less than half of all employees believe that they'll retire from their current employer. One explanation for this, however, is the diminishing level of *employee loyalty* (strong employee commitment to the employer), replaced by an increasing level of employee self-interest. Both employers and employees are asking "What have you done for me lately?" and if the answer is shaky, either side is more willing than ever to cut the proverbial umbilical cord.

It's no wonder, then, that so many employees place the burden of their need for job satisfaction on the supervisor. In turn, the supervisor needs all the skills and patience that he or she can muster to motivate today's workers to perform at the levels that society—to say nothing of their employers—expects of them.

What causes employees to perceive similar kinds of work in such different lights?

The way people perceive things, including their jobs or the work they are asked to do, is influenced by five factors:

1. **Past experience with similar work.** If the work has been unpleasant with another company or boss, an employee may anticipate that the experience will repeat itself everywhere. The opposite

Entitlement. The perception by employees that they ought to receive certain benefits, protections, and privileges from their employer.

Downsizing. A reduction in the number of people employed by an organization, usually in order to respond to unfavorable economic conditions or in an attempt to improve efficiency.

Did You Know ?

Fewer Do the Work

■ According to the American Management Association (AMA) 1999 survey on downsizing the workforce: 36 percent of work became automated, 17 percent of positions open were filled by temporary workers, and 80 percent of the individuals responding to the survey stated the work was delegated to remaining workers.

Source: American Management Association.

Many employees like the concept of telecommuting. **What are its advantages? Its disadvantages?** ▶

Ethical
PERSPECTIVES

Is Telecommuting Productive?

Your company is starting a new telecommuting initiative. You attended the companywide question-and-answer session today. Now you are questioning telecommuting—the presenters focused on the positive side for the employee. As a supervisor, you know there will be issues or situations that will be difficult to monitor—you will still be responsible for your department's productivity. Next week, there will be a meeting to discuss the management of the telecommuters. What will be on your list to discuss?

will be true for a person whose experience with this work has been favorable.

2. **Assumptions about the motivation of others.** An unhappy person may blame her or his problems on the actions of aggressive co-workers or an unfair boss. For some unfortunate people, this becomes a guideline in dealing with *all* interpersonal relations. On the other hand, a person who views others as supportive and friendly may perceive every work situation in that light.

3. **Expectations about what will happen.** "It's a foregone conclusion," we hear people say. This is based somewhat upon past experience and somewhat upon our beliefs about the motivation of others. Unfortunately, it reflects a rigidity of mind and the unwillingness of some employees to give a new job or a different assignment a fair try.

4. **The reliability of information.** Some employees make judgments about their work on the basis of what others tell them. This knowledge may be correct, or it may be unreliable hearsay or bitter prejudice. Supervisors can contend with this problem by providing accurate information upon which employees can then make valid decisions.

5. **The present state of mind.** All of us are subject to mood swings. If the boss proposes a new task, for instance, on a day when an employee feels good, the reaction is likely to be more positive than it would be if the idea were proposed on one of those inevitable "bad days."

Are there any programs or systems that can improve employee perceptions of their work environment?

Yes. *Flexible work schedules* (sometimes called *compressed work-weeks*) can do this. As pressures rise for better use of the organization's facilities (space in particular), as workers wish to explore new lifestyles and pursue recreational interests, as the numbers of single-parent and dual-career households increase, and the cost and time associated with commuting rises, flexible work schedules can help. Many forms of these compressed schedules exist, with the more common ones being four 10-hour days or even the use of 12-hour shifts (three days one week and four days the next.) Under *flextime* systems, employees have the chance to tailor their work schedules to their personal needs and reduce the number of commutes per week; employers benefit from fewer daily start-up and shut-down cycles and the broader band of hours available for customer service. Another flexible approach is *job sharing*, in which two people divide the duties in one job and split the total time at work according to mutually negotiated agreements with their supervisor.

Telecommuting has also become increasingly popular in recent years, with the availability of computers, voice mail, fax machines, and e-mail. Telecommuters work in their homes and usually have electronic connections with their place of work. They avoid the hassles of commuting, they experience less interruptions, and they can spend more time with family members. Employers like the results, too, as productivity often rises by 10 to 20 percent, space needs are reduced, and new applicants become interested in the jobs available. Of course, not all jobs, and not all employees, are well-suited for telecommuting. Supervisors need to make a special effort to provide resources, give clear instructions, keep telecommuters in the information "loop," be available for questions, and provide frequent feedback.

Flexible work schedule. A system by which employees can choose—and periodically change—the blocks of time in which they will work.

Job sharing. The process of taking one job and splitting its duties into two such that the combined time and efforts of two persons will satisfy all the work demands.

Telecommuting. Working at one's home, while being connected electronically to the employer's office.

◀ *Quick Test 4*

| 7 | T or F | Most employees are basically very similar in their thoughts, feelings, and perceptions. |
| 8 | T or F | Telecommuting provides substantial benefits for both the employee and the organization. |

Facilitating. An approach
to management in which a
supervisor assists and guides
employees in their efforts
to perform their jobs rather
than emphasizing orders,
instructions, and control.

5 QUALITY OF WORK LIFE

CONCEPT ▶ Supervisors can improve the quality of work life when they *facilitate*, rather than direct, the work of their employees and encourage feedback from them.

To what extent can supervisors be held responsible for dissatisfied employees?

Only to the extent that employees who ordinarily ought to be satisfied with their work begin to project a general dissatisfaction with it. One observer advises that when a state of "poor satisfaction" occurs, it may also be evidence of "poor management." Some organizations even make managerial bonuses dependent on the level of employee satisfaction in their unit.

What can supervisors do to improve the quality of working life?

There are two views. The first is that improved productivity—greater output from the inputs of labor, materials, money, and machines—continues to be the foundation for a better work life. Higher productivity buys the tools that make work easier and the time for each employee to find the best way of adapting to the task. The second is the conviction on the part of many qualified observers that a greater involvement in decision making at the job level is essential. The early generation of managers believed just the opposite. They divided jobs into the smallest and easiest pieces. Their goal was to create foolproof jobs. The trouble with this view is that the majority of human beings *want* to "work smarter," although not necessarily harder. As a consequence, they will respond to job conditions that make the fullest use of their manual and mental skills and see how their efforts contribute to the overall objective. They enjoy working in situations that enable each woman and man to make a demonstrably valued contribution to the finished product or service.

To most people, an improved quality of work life simply means that their hours spent at work will not be wasteful ones. They want to feel that, somehow, their lives will be more worthwhile as a result of working than they would be with no job at all.

What can supervisors do to make work more enjoyable?

Some basic (and easy-to-implement) approaches will make for greater satisfaction among employees in general.

Offer employees an opportunity for "bottom-upward" feedback. This is one good way to find out what each person expects from work, even if it cannot always be provided.

View many supervisory functions as facilitating rather than directing. Few people want to be told how and when to do every little thing. Not every worker who is given an inch will take a mile. So try to provide the kinds of information and tools an employee needs to get the job done—the right blueprint or specification, a key bit of know-how. A physical or mental assist, when needed or asked for, encourages employees to enforce their own discipline.

Stay flexible when and where you can. The supervisor whose department rules can't be bent to accommodate a worker's individuality on occasion makes employees feel hopelessly locked in. Keep to a minimum all directives that begin with the words *always* or *never*. Think in terms of *most of the time*, or *on the average*, when you will not permit this or insist on that. Be adaptable, not rigid.

Try to be a part of the total organization. Know your own superior as well as you can. Find out the company's basic objectives about costs, production, and quality. Understand the real intent of company policy toward employees. If you have this information, you will be in a better position to intercede for your employees. The supervisor who goes to bat for the team members is often the supervisor an employee can face on a rainy Monday morning when there is a temptation to remain in bed.

◄ Quick Test 5

9	T or F	Supervisors have an impact on the satisfaction of their employees.
10	T or F	Most employees want to receive clear directions and be told exactly how to do each task in their jobs.

KEY CONCEPTS TO REMEMBER

1. **Seven Pressures to Cope With.** Supervisors face a different set of restraining factors in their immediate work environment than do higher level managers. Specifically, a supervisor's horizons and options are greatly influenced by (a) technology, (b) legal restrictions, (c) organizational policies and procedures, (d) pressures for improved output, quality, and cost control, (e) competition with other supervisors for the organization's scarce resources, (f) the need to manage an enormous amount of information (or paperwork), and (g) the rising expectations of employees. Additionally, supervisors need to be more concerned with day-to-day, short-term events than do higher level managers, who are expected to be prepared much farther in advance for important changes in the external environment.

2. **The World of Work.** Work is a unique activity that is characterized, according to Max Weber, by (a) the necessity of employee conformity to rules, regulations, policies, and procedures, (b) the exercise of authority over others by managers, (c) the subordination of personal interests to the goals of the organization, and (d) the presence of written records for planning and control.

3. **Employee Expectations.** The great majority of employees (from 80 to 90 percent) are reasonably satisfied with their jobs. Many good employees, however, would be better satisfied if their work required more of them and—as a result—was more challenging.

4. **Understanding Employee Perceptions.** Individuals perceive their work differently for different reasons. An employee's perception of the job is affected by past experience, assumptions about the intentions of others that will affect the situation, expectations about what will happen, the reliability of information about the job and its prospects, and the employee's present state of mind.

5. **Quality of Work Life.** Supervisors can help to improve the quality of work life by maintaining a flexibility that accepts individual differences. Such supervisors also encourage "bottom-upward" feedback. Most importantly, these supervisors facilitate, rather than direct, the work of their employees.

READING COMPREHENSION

1. Who might be more concerned with general economic conditions: a supervisor or a company president? With an employee's request for a less boring assignment? Why?

2. What factors distinguish a supervisor's work environment from that of a higher level manager? Also, explain the difference in their time horizons.

3. List the four characteristics of a bureaucracy identified by Weber. Which is presumed to be the most threatening to most employees and why?

4. Contrast the work or job you have done for pay with a task you have done on a voluntary basis. Into which did you put more physical or mental effort? Why?

5. Think of persons you consider to be happy in their work. Describe one such person, the kind of work performed, and the kind of supervision provided.

6. Yankelovich says that only one person out of five does his or her very best on a job. Why don't others do their best, too?

7. What's the difference between an employee's expectation of certain job

conditions and a legal entitlement to them? Give some examples of the latter.

8. Ralph has been asked to perform a particularly nasty job. Surprisingly, he accepts it without hesitation, and he does it well. Ted, when given the same assignment, tries to duck it. When forced to accept it, Ted botches the job.

What factors might explain the differing responses to this assignment?

9. Have you ever had a job that was easy but dull? What could you have done to make it more interesting?

10. Explain the difference between a supervisor who facilitates the work and one who directs it.

APPLICATION

Self-Assessment

What is your level of satisfaction with your present (or previous) job?

Consider the job that you hold right now (or one you have held recently). Read each statement below. Circle the number on the response scale that most closely reflects the degree to which each statement accurately describes your feelings. Add up your total points and be ready to report your score for tabulation across the entire group.

	Strongly Agree									Strongly Disagree
1. I have many opportunities to learn new things on this job.	10	9	8	7	6	5	4	3	2	1
2. My contributions are respected and appreciated by others.	10	9	8	7	6	5	4	3	2	1
3. My job requires that I use many of my skills.	10	9	8	7	6	5	4	3	2	1
4. If my work merits criticism, it is done in a fair and tactful manner.	10	9	8	7	6	5	4	3	2	1
5. In general, I feel like I am kept pretty well-informed.	10	9	8	7	6	5	4	3	2	1
6. I believe that the job I do is very worthwhile to the organization.	10	9	8	7	6	5	4	3	2	1
7. The expectations of quantity and quality of output are challenging, but fair and reasonable.	10	9	8	7	6	5	4	3	2	1
8. When I express ideas or make suggestions, they are listened to.	10	9	8	7	6	5	4	3	2	1
9. My pay is reasonably fair for the work that I do.	10	9	8	7	6	5	4	3	2	1
10. I put a lot of myself into my work.	10	9	8	7	6	5	4	3	2	1

Scoring and Interpretation

SCORING

Add up your total points for the 10 questions. Record that number here, and report it when it is requested. _____

INTERPRETATION

81 to 100 points. Congratulations! You seem to be reasonably well satisfied with your job.

61 to 80 points. There is clearly room for improvement. Set up a meeting with your boss to explore what might be done to provide more satisfaction at work.

Below 60 points. Your job lacks substantial opportunities for satisfaction and this could cause other problems for you and the organization.

Identify your three lowest scores and record the question numbers here: _____, _____, _____.

ACTION

Begin thinking about the possibilities of changing jobs, changing employers, or taking a serious look at your overall attitude toward work and its rewards.

Skill Development

▶ Building Loyalty

Loyalty is one's commitment toward someone or something. Conduct a mini-study on loyalty by talking to five employees. Ask them how committed they are to their employer today. Then talk to five managers, and ask them how committed their employees are to the organization today. Are the responses consistent? If not, why?

Employees' Comments	Managers' Comments
1. _____	1. _____
2. _____	2. _____
3. _____	3. _____
4. _____	4. _____
5. _____	5. _____

ACTION

Develop a basic plan for increasing loyalty among members of an organization's workforce. What are the five most important actions your employer could take to substantially raise the level of loyalty among its employees? List those below.

1. _____
2. _____
3. _____
4. _____
5. _____

Role Play

Group Exercise ◄

Form into groups of three persons each. Two of you per group should assume one of the roles identified below, with the third person acting as an observer. Then engage in a brief discussion between Krista and Carlos, in which you each try to put forth the most persuasive arguments for your position.

KRISTA. As a new supervisor looking for ideas, you have recently read material similar to that in this chapter regarding an organization's responsibility for creating a high quality of work life for its employees. You feel very comfortable with that approach and hope you can convince some of your colleagues to join together in proposing it to higher management. You are about to meet with a colleague now for a preliminary exchange of ideas.

CARLOS. As a new supervisor, you have been bombarded with ideas for improvement. Many of these seem overly simplistic or soft-hearted, and fail to consider the organization's need for good, old-fashioned hard work from employees. Krista has asked that you get together for a discussion to increase the quality of work life among employees, and you are going to try hard to convince her to back down on that proposal. You are about to meet with her now.

OBSERVER. You are about to overhear a conversation between two supervisors—Krista and Carlos—on the topic of quality of work life. Do not participate in the discussion, but take notes on the effectiveness of each person's argument, their use of facts versus unfounded opinions, their persuasiveness, their listening skills, and their overall communication skills. When they are finished, do not judge who "won" the argument, but simply give them both feedback for improvement in future conversations of this type.

CASES FOR ANALYSIS

Case 5

Mildred and the Mickey Mouse Job

Two employees of the Zebra Hosiery Mills were waiting outside the plant for transportation home on a cold, wet afternoon. Mildred, a 30-year-old loom operator, said, "One more day like this and it's bye-bye Zebra for me."

"What's the problem?" asked Leon, her co-worker.

"This job is boring me to death," said Mildred. "It's Mickey Mouse all day long. I work my fingers raw racking up those yarn spools. Two hours straight before the break. Then lunch. Then the afternoon break. That's the same routine four times a day. I handle over 800 spools. Toward the end of each period I can hardly wait until I count the two-hundredth spool."

"Wow," said Leon. "I never thought of it that way. It just strikes me that it's an easy way to make $75 a day."

"Easy, nothing," said Mildred. "I could show them how to make it easier. All we'd need is some gizmo to let me rack up two spools at a time. But that pumpkin head I work for hasn't listened to a new idea in thirty years."

"That could be," said Leon. "But I'm satisfied as long as the supervisor stays off my back. I just don't like to be hassled."

"If she were to hassle you, you'd know you were something besides a machine," said Mildred. "If there were some place closer to home, I'd walk out on Zebra tomorrow."

"I could get a job nearer to my home," said Leon, "but I'd only make $65 a day. The extra $10 is worth fifteen minutes longer on the bus."

"Not for me," said Mildred. "I've got kids to feed when I get home. I don't want them out on the streets longer than they have to be. I'd take a cut if my job was next door to where I lived."

At this point Leon's bus arrived. "See you tomorrow—if you don't decide to quit," he said as he climbed aboard.

"Fat chance," said Mildred to herself. "What other choices do I really have?"

If you were Mildred's supervisor, which of the following actions would you consider to be the most effective in handling Mildred's dissatisfaction with her job? Rank the alternatives on a scale from 1 (most preferable) to 5 (least preferable). You may add another alternative if you wish. Be prepared to justify your ranking.

_____ **a.** Demonstrate to Mildred that she is well paid for the work she does compared with the rates for other work in the mill.

_____ **b.** Ask what Mildred would do to make her job more interesting. Then try to incorporate her suggestions.

_____ **c.** Change the job so that Mildred would rotate assignments with co-workers doing related work in the same department.

_____ **d.** Ignore Mildred's complaints, since your attention may lead her to expect more than you can deliver.

_____ **e.** Suggest that, if Mildred is so unhappy, she look for another job elsewhere.

Case 6

Hot Job, High Turnover

After Eileen H. graduated from high school in June, she spent most of the summer hanging around the public swimming pool during the day and with the gang in the shopping mall parking lot at night. By fall, however, her parents insisted that she find a job. The best she could get was a second-shift job as a lay-up operator at the local fiberglass boat factory. The work was difficult and disagreeable. The plant was hot, and the fumes from the plastic solvents were irritating. The pay was just above the minimum wage standard. The only thing really good about the job was her supervisor, Ray J. He was regarded by the boat plant workers as a "good guy." Ray was troubled, however, by the number of young people like Eileen who stayed on the job only a month or two before quitting.

To reduce the chance of Eileen's leaving, Ray should
a. Make the work easier for Eileen.
b. Ask her for ideas about how to make the work more pleasant.
c. Emphasize the value her job adds to the final product.
d. Try to get her a 50-cent-an-hour raise.

Circle the course of action you think would be most suitable, and be prepared to explain the reasons for your choice.

Case 7

The Disgruntled Customer Service Clerk

"I expected to be moved to the day shift when I took this job," complained Aldo, a night telephone customer service clerk for a credit card company. Aldo is married and, because his wife works nights, too, he had hoped that he could change shifts so that he could stay home with their two young children during the evenings. When Aldo's supervisor replied that there was little or no chance for his changing shifts, Aldo was greatly irritated. "I'm doing a first-rate job and have done so for six months. You told me when I was hired that I might make the change to days after I'd shown that I could do the job."

"I said that there was a possibility," said the supervisor, "but there are no openings available now."

"That's not true," said Aldo, "You've hired at least one day-shift clerk since I've started here. I think I'm entitled to be switched right now."

Analysis

In order to handle this request with the most appropriate results, Aldo's supervisor should say:

a. "You're not entitled to anything. I'll give you a chance to change shifts only when and if it is convenient."

b. "No one is automatically entitled to fill a day-shift opening, but I'll try to fit you in the next time."

c. "Sorry, I forgot about you. I'll switch you to days right away, even if it means overstaffing that shift for the time being."

d. "Many factors affect how day-shift jobs are filled. I'll try to comply with your request, but only after giving consideration to all the factors involved."

Circle the course of action you think would be most suitable, and be prepared to explain the reasons for your choice.

Answers to Quick Tests

Quick Test 1	Quick Test 2	Quick Test 3
1. F	3. F	5. T
2. F	4. F	6. F

Quick Test 4	Quick Test 5	
7. F	9. T	
8. T	10. F	

CHAPTER 3

Supervision and the Management Process

Learning Objectives

After studying this chapter, you should be able to

- Identify the four most useful sources of generally accepted managerial expertise.

- List the five functions of the management process and discuss how they involve a supervisor.

- Given any of Fayol's management principles, explain its application.

- Name the four most widely used approaches to management practice and discuss the particular suitability of each.

- Explain the value of contingency management in handling situations that occur in an organizational system.

A BODY OF KNOWLEDGE
(1) FROM WHICH TO DRAW

CONCEPT ▷ Supervisors become active in the management process by applying established management principles and practices to operating problems.

What does it really take for a supervisor to become a manager?

Thinking and acting like one. Management is characterized by a professional—or disciplined—approach to the work environment. Individuals who move into supervision must begin to think in a systematic way. They need to approach their work positively, rather than passively. They should accept the responsibility of making things happen for the better in an organization. They shift their roles from those that entail just following orders, to roles that require making task assignments, helping others to solve problems, and making decisions. They become increasingly aware of their involvement in a complex system of organizational activities, and they act accordingly.

Where can knowledge about management be learned?

Newly appointed supervisors are not left alone without guidance. Fortunately, they have a vast background of management experiences to draw upon. First of all, supervisors can begin their new assignments by immersing themselves in the five responsibilities outlined for them in the management process. They can look next for guidance to a set of 10 basic management principles. Then they can select an approach from any of three "schools" (or theories) of management practice. And they can learn many "tricks of the trade" about effective supervision by interacting with a managerial *mentor*—an experienced person willing to engage in frequent dialogue to provide development guidance and support. Over a period of time, supervisors finally acquire a sense of the many factors at play in their spheres of influence. And from this sensitivity, they develop an invaluable flexibility. This enables them to do the right things at the right times, on the basis of the peculiarities of each situation they face.

Quick Test 1 ▷

1	T or F	Despite their new responsibilities, supervisors are still pretty much just order-followers.
2	T or F	One of the most valuable skills for a supervisor to have is flexibility.

2 THE MANAGEMENT PROCESS

CONCEPT ▶ The management process differentiates the work of managers from that of all others in an organization.

Why is there so much emphasis placed upon the management process?

There are two reasons. First, the process serves to differentiate the work of managers from the work of nonmanagers. Second, the management process provides a valuable underpinning that guides the practice of management and its various approaches.

The five functions of the management process were shown in Figure 1-5 of Chapter 1 to illustrate the interdependence of all levels of managers within an organization. The five functions are shown again here in Figure 3-1. This time the figure illustrates the typical sequence in which the functions are performed in an orderly manner.

Why is it called a process?

It is called a *management process* because it moves progressively from one stage to another in a fairly consistent sequence. In a production shop, for example, a supervisor first plans the daily schedule, then organizes the tasks and resources, then assigns people to their workstations, then directs the process by giving orders and instructions, and, finally, controls, or checks up on, results. In a typical office, a similar management process takes place as supervisors plan the workday, organize the work and the clerical force, direct others by communicating and motivating, and control by seeing that work procedures are followed properly.

This process is carried on repeatedly, day by day, month by month, and year by year. For this reason many people refer to it as the *management cycle*.

Management process. The major managerial functions of planning, organizing, staffing, energizing, and controlling carried out by all managers in a repetitive sequence or cycle.

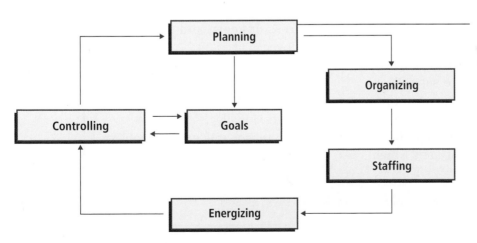

◆ **FIGURE 3-1**

Functions in the management process. **Which function demands the most of a supervisor's time?**

Peter Drucker's
comment regarding the
planning process:
Trying to predict the
future is like trying to
drive down a country
road at night with no
lights while looking out
the back window.

How do the five management functions involve a supervisor?

These five functions are carried out, to a greater or lesser degree, by supervisors, by middle managers, and by top executives. From a supervisor's standpoint, each function has a particular significance:

Planning. This is the function of setting goals and objectives and converting them into specific plans. For a supervisor, the outcomes of planning will include operating schedules, quality specifications, expense budgets, timetables, and deadlines. The planning process also establishes policies, standard operating procedures, regulations, and rules.

Organizing. In performing this function, a supervisor lines up all available resources. These include departmental tools, equipment, materials, and—especially—the workforce. It is at this stage that the organizational structure of a department is designed and its work divided up into jobs.

Staffing. This is the function whereby supervisors figuratively put flesh on the organizational structure. Supervisors first figure out exactly how many and what kind of employees a department will need to carry out its work. They then interview, select, and train those people who appear to be most suitable to fill the open jobs.

Energizing. This function gets the blood flowing in an organization. Supervisors energize the vital human resources of their department by providing motivation, communication, and leadership.

JOB tip!

BE SUPPORTIVE

■ To attract qualified applicants, to retain productive employees, and to unleash worker energies and creativity, supervisors need to create more supportive work environments. Employees are looking for, and expecting, a more nurturing workplace, a more compassionate supervisor, and diminished stress on the job. Supervisors in the twenty-first century need to demonstrate caring, respect, trust, flexibility, appreciation of diversity, and a high degree of integrity.

Specifically, supervisors can
- Clarify their own ethical values, and display them consistently at work.
- Express concern and support for employees.
- Exhibit faith in the capabilities of employees to make sound decisions.
- Show their adaptability by "bending" a bit occasionally.
- Placing reasonable expectations on employees.

Source: Pamela Leigh, "The New Spirit at Work," *Training and Development*, March 1997, pp. 26–33.

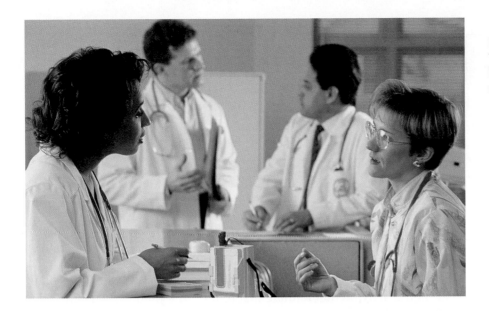

Controlling. Once departmental plans are set in motion, supervisors must periodically keep score on how well the plans are working out. To do so, supervisors measure results, compare them with what was expected, judge how important the differences may be, and then take whatever action is needed to bring results into line. Controlling is closely linked to planning (as Figure 3-1 shows), because control actions are guided by the goals established during the planning process.

In theory, supervisors perform the five functions of the management process in the order listed above. In practice, however, supervisors perform all the management functions in one way or another each time action is in order. They may find themselves shortcutting the management process sequence or turning back on it, inasmuch as each problem situation is unique and calls for its own solution.

This process must have an objective, mustn't it?

Yes, of course. The purpose of the management process is to convert the resources available to a supervisor's department into a useful end result. Said another way, a supervisor is in charge of seeing that inputs are transformed into outputs in his or her department, as illustrated in Figure 3-2. This end result, or output, is either a product or a service.

A *product* might be a pair of shoes, a loaf of bread, a bicycle, or steel strings for a guitar. Your product may be partially complete, so that it becomes the material resource for the next department in your factory. It may become the raw material for use in another manufacturing plant. Or, it may be ready, like a pair of shoes, to be sold directly to a consumer without further work performed on it.

Supervisors and other managers are responsible for converting an organization's resources into useful results. **What role(s) does the supervisor play in the conversion process?**

Input resources	Conversion process	Output results
Workforce Equipment Materials Information Money		Products Services Profits

A *service* may be providing accounting information for a production department, inspecting a product as it is being made, or creating a schedule for others to follow. A service may be provided directly for a consumer, as in supplying an insurance policy or handling cash and checks for a bank customer. It may be maintaining machinery in a plant or washing windows in a shopping center.

Whether the endpoint is a product or a service, the management process is designed to make sure that the result is at least as valuable as the combined cost of the initial resources and the expense of operating the process. In a business enterprise a *profit* is made when the result can be sold at a price that is higher than the total cost of providing it. If the reverse is true, the business assumes a *loss*.

Quick Test 2 ▶

3	T or F	In the management process, supervisors usually staff before they can organize.
4	T or F	Equipment and materials are typical measures of output results.

③ MANAGEMENT PRINCIPLES

CONCEPT ▶ Management principles provide basic guidelines for supervisory decisions and actions.

Management principles.
A set of guidelines established by Henri Fayol and others for carrying out the management process.

How do management principles relate to the management process?

They stem from the same source according to Henri Fayol, an especially effective chief executive of a French mining company. Fayol was the first person to conceive of management as a separate "process of administration," consisting of several distinct functions and based on certain "principles." Fayol's writings (1916) led to the current generally accepted notion of the management process. His **management princi-ples** as stated in those writings are acknowledged as universally appli-cable guidelines for carrying out the management process.

Exactly what are the principles of management?

They consist of a number of practical guide-lines, held by many authorities to contain the "essence of management." Here, arbitrarily num-bered, are those principles that appear to have the greatest value for today's supervisors:

Office-Related Information. Access links to business management, communications, business news, and business research information.

1. Work should be divided so that each person will perform a special-ized portion. In making a sailboat, for instance, one person will lay up the hull, another caulk, and another make sails. Fayol called these ideas **division of work** and specialization. Division of work provides clarity in job assignments, while specialization helps workers increase their skill levels.

2. Managers must have the right (*authority*) to give orders and instructions, but they must also accept *responsibility* for whether the work is done correctly. A supervisor needs the right to ask a work crew to load a freight car, for example, but if the car is loaded improperly, the supervisor must accept the blame.

3. Managers are responsible for extracting *discipline* and building morale among members of their workforce, but they must also reciprocate by offering something of value. Said another way, if you want loyalty and cooperation from employees, you must be loyal and cooperative in return.

4. An individual should have only one boss. Fayol called this **unity of command**. Experience bears this out: if an employee reports to more than one superior, confusion and conflict are likely to result.

5. Every organization should have only one master plan, one set of overriding goals. Such **unity of direction** is lost if the purchasing department, for example, slows down the production department's output by buying materials from a less costly but undependable supplier when the company's overall commitment is to ship orders on time.

6. Similar to the principle of unity of direction is Fayol's insistence that all individuals, especially managers, must place their personal interests second to those of the total organization. If persons in authority went their own way, Fayol reasoned, all others in the organization would suffer as a result.

7. Pay and rewards (remuneration) should reflect each person's efforts and, more importantly, each person's contribution to the organiza-tion's goal. It was a novel idea in Fayol's time that each employee should be paid according to individual worth rather than at the whim of a manager who might be inclined to play favorites.

Division of work. The principle that performance is more efficient when a large job is broken down into smaller, specialized jobs.

Unity of command. The principle that each individual should report to only one boss.

Unity of direction. The principle that there should be a single set of goals and objectives that unifies the activities of everyone in an organization.

8. Orders and instructions should flow down a ***chain of command*** from the higher manager to the lower one. Fayol also said that formal communications and complaints should move upward in the same channel. In practice, however, it has proved to be a good idea to permit and encourage the exchange of work information sideways between departments (or commands) as well. The real trouble seems to occur when a manager bypasses a supervisor with instructions to an employee or when an employee goes over a supervisor's head to register a complaint. This is known as *blindsiding*.

9. Employees should be treated equally and fairly. Fayol called this *equity*. It invites dissatisfaction and conflict among employees, for example, when a supervisor gives one employee a break while picking on another.

10. Managers should encourage initiative among employees. Fayol advised, "It is essential to encourage this capacity to the full. . . . The manager must be able to sacrifice some personal vanity in order to grant this sort of satisfaction to subordinates. Other things being equal, a manager able to permit the exercise of *initiative* on the part of subordinates is infinitely superior to one who cannot do so." This classic principle forms the basis for the modern practice of empowerment (to be discussed in Chapter 9).

Quick Test 3 ▶

5	T or F	Unity of direction and unity of command mean pretty much the same thing.
6	T or F	The chain of command principle should always be rigidly adhered to.

MANAGEMENT APPROACHES (OR SCHOOLS)

CONCEPT ▶ Four widely accepted approaches to management practice have evolved, each with its particular suitability.

To what extent can supervisors develop their own approaches to handling their operational situations?

They have a great deal of leeway. Four managerial approaches, however, have evolved into popular usage over the past century and proven helpful to supervisors. These approaches to management practice are sometimes called "schools" or theories. Each has its special usefulness.

1. ***Systematic management* approach.** This is known by other names, too, such as scientific, classic, traditional, process, functional, or rational. All names imply a systematic approach that relies on measurement and analysis of the various tasks and activities that take place at work.

2. **Behavioral approach.** This was previously known as the human relations school. It is based on the thought that a manager who understands human behavior well enough is able to get employees to willingly cooperate with, and work productively toward, company goals.

3. **Quantitative approach.** This approach emphasizes the use of data, models, and decision aids. It relies on the sciences of mathematics and statistics. It is also known as the *management sciences approach* to management.

4. **Contingency approach.** The ***contingency management*** approach challenges a supervisor to study each (significant) organizational situation carefully to identify its major elements. Then it calls upon a vast body of prior research studies and managerial experiences to identify what have proven to be the most effective practices in similar situations. The supervisor then will have reasonable confidence that actions taken will produce the most desirable results.

Some authorities add still another concept: the *systems approach*. This is an outgrowth of the quantitative approach, and it makes much of the fact that all the elements and resources of an organization are parts of an interlocking system. Thus, a manager cannot take action regarding one element without that action's having an effect upon one or more other elements in the organization.

A summary of the management approaches is presented in Table 3-1.

When does the systematic management approach work best?

A systematic approach is almost always a good way to attack any problem. It requires that you gather facts first. What has really happened to the data bank? When did it happen? Who was inputting? Were reasonable controls set for its operation? How close has actual output been to what was expected?

It emphasizes the value of accurate measurements. How much? How big? How long? How many?

It presumes that most activities are best performed according to a set path. Are the procedures carefully spelled out? Were they followed?

The problem with the systematic approach is that it too often expects that organizations will operate perfectly or that people will function like machines. Its founder, Frederick W. Taylor, was an engineer who hoped that human beings could be motivated by wage incentives to imitate machines. Later advocates of scientific management were also engineers—Henry L. Gantt, who conceived the production control chart, and

Systematic management. The traditional approach to management that emphasizes the functions performed in the management process as well as systematic measurement and analysis of the various tasks and activities of the workplace.

Contingency management. The selection and use of a management practice that is most appropriate for a particular problem or situation, based on prior research.

Ethical PERSPECTIVES

Shift Work

Eight percent of the 90 million full-time U.S. workers clock in for evening or night shifts according to the Bureau of Labor Statistics. An additional 7 percent sometimes work shifts that include evenings or nights.

What is management's and/or a supervisor's responsibility to support shift workers?

	TABLE 3-1	
Different Approaches to Management Practices		
Approach	**Emphasizing Productivity as a Result of the Following**	**Impact on Supervision**
Systematic Management Related to scientific, classic, traditional, rational, process, or functional management	Systematic process, management principles, measurement and standards, and firm direction and control	Greater reliance on established company policies and procedures and on prescribed relationships in formal work groups
Behavioral Management Related to human relations or organizational behavior management	Individual or group motivation stimulated by management's concern for people and their relationships	Greater reliance on participatory techniques and upon individuals and groups to solve operational problems
Quantitative Management Related to management sciences	Use of advanced mathematical and statistical methods as well as theories about how information and other resources interact in an organization system	Greater reliance on staff-directed and/or automatic programs to prescribe operating procedures and to signal for control actions
Contingency Management Related to situational management	Belief that supervisors and other managers must analyze the conditions that prevail in a particular situation and apply relevant research findings	Greater need for careful analysis of different situations along with the skills and flexibility to apply different management methods selectively

Frank B. Gilbreth, who perfected the art of the motion study of workers. Other proponents were mainly business executives.

When should behavioral management be used?

Behavioral management. A management approach that seeks to stimulate cooperation on the basis of an understanding of, and genuine concern for, employees as individuals and as members of a work group.

There is rarely a time when ***behavioral management*** shouldn't be considered. The stickiest problems in business or elsewhere involve human beings. Supervisors need to know all they can about why people act the way they do. Exaggerated human conflict can be very wasteful. Use of what we know about the psychology and the sociology of human behavior can prevent or at least minimize this conflict. Many authorities on management, beginning with Elton Mayo, have demonstrated the controlling influence that human relations can have in any organization. Mayo, in his famous experiment at the Hawthorne Works of the Western Electric Company in the 1930s, drew attention to the possibility that the performance of workers is more nearly related to psychological and social factors than to the physical makeup of the workplace (see SuperScope, p. 59). Optimism for the human relations approach was highest in the 1950s, when it was thought that a cookbook of methods could be given to supervisors. The idea was that if you follow the right directions and prescriptions, people will act the way you want. Alas, this simpleminded approach never fulfilled this promise.

The Unpredictable Women in the Relay Adjustment Room

It happened at the Hawthorne Works of the Western Electric Company near Chicago during the depths of the Great Depression. Management was then, as now, complaining that employees weren't as productive as they ought to be. The Hawthorne Works was following Taylor's wage-incentive program to the letter, but the results weren't what they hoped for. The company thought it was time to find another approach to improving productivity. It brought in two psychologists from Harvard to study the problem. The professors set out to find a relationship between physical working conditions and productivity. They chose to conduct their experiments with the group of women workers who adjusted the mechanical relays that were later to be mounted on telephone switchboards.

First, the professors raised the lighting levels in the work area, and worker productivity increased. Then they lowered the lighting levels. Incredibly, worker productivity increased again. Next, the researchers altered other environmental factors such as rest periods, the length of the workday, and noise levels. To the professors' astonishment, it made little difference to these women whether conditions were improved or made worse. Productivity always increased!

"What is happening?" the researchers asked. They observed that other, less obvious things than working conditions were of vital importance to these employees. The professors discovered that the workers involved in the project took their participation as a sign of status and recognition of their value by management. As a consequence, they worked harder to do better, whatever the conditions.

The Harvard professors, Elton Mayo and Fritz Roethlisberger, concluded that all workers (regardless of gender) are deeply affected by psychological and social conditions. Employees can and do react to such things as individual recognition, group pressures, and an opportunity to become involved in decisions that affect their work.

Most authorities now strongly suggest that supervisors should develop skills in applying behavioral knowledge. The watchwords would appear to be *go slowly*. Clear up technical problems first. Let people try to solve their own problems. Don't oversimplify management tasks. They are all complex because so many factors—materials, machinery, instructions, time pressures, conflicting objectives, hidden relationships—can influence the outcome of a supervisor's actions.

What's unique about the *Japanese management* approach?

In Japan, managers seek a consensus of agreement from the employees and other managers in their organization before moving ahead in a new direction. This leads to mutual goal setting at lower, as well as higher, levels. Once a consensus is reached, employees feel committed to goals and plans. As a consequence, they tend to work together with greater unity and initiative and to require fewer controls and less supervision. The underlying concept, of course, is similar to the participation (sharing of responsibilities and goal setting) urged by advocates of the behavioral approach to management.

Japanese management. The participative practice of seeking consensus of agreement from employees and other managers before choosing or implementing a course of action.

Where will the quantitative approach be most effective?

Quantitative management.
A management sciences approach to management that emphasizes the use of advanced mathematics and statistics and the application of information theory.

Where people problems are fewest and process factors are greatest. The *quantitative management* method is a numbers approach. It helps in setting up production and maintenance schedules, in controlling quality statistically, in mapping out shipping routes, and in setting workloads for bank tellers and airline reservationists. Quantitative methods have been applied successfully to just about every operational problem where employees' interests and motivations are not controlling factors. Without any doubt, management sciences techniques should be in every supervisor's tool kit. More often than not, of course, supervisors will need the help of industrial engineers, statisticians, or systems analysts to put these techniques to work. On the other hand, these specialists will need a supervisor's keen eye to spot potential applications.

Quick Test 4 ▶			
7	T or F	The quantitative approach relies on measurement and analysis of various tasks and activities.
8	T or F	The contingency approach to management relies heavily on a supervisor's intuition to make the right choice.

⑤ SYSTEMS AND SITUATIONS

CONCEPT ▶ Supervisors need to view their operations from a systems perspective.

The systems approach has been mentioned as important. What should I know about this?

System. An interrelated set of elements functioning as a whole.

A *system* is an interrelated set of elements functioning as a whole. Each element (or part) is dependent on some of the others in the system: A change in one part will affect the functioning of other parts. The human body is an example of a system; so is a clock or an automobile engine.

An organization (a private company, nonprofit institution, or public agency) functions as a system. Within a system, there may be many smaller (nested) systems that interact among themselves and with the larger system. In a company that makes women's sportswear, for example, the design, fabricating, shipping, and sales departments may function as individual systems, although they influence—and are influenced by—each

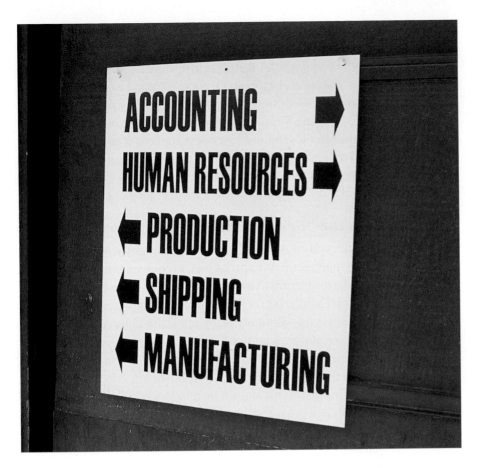

◄ What system is being shown in this photo? How many components of the system can you identify?

other. A supervisor, therefore, not only must manage her or his departmental system to keep things flowing smoothly but also must ensure that the department interacts productively with the other departments within the overall company system.

What's important to remember about systems? They require *inputs* (air, food, and water for the body; raw materials for a manufacturing facility), they take *action* on those inputs (the body digests food; the mill refines raw ore), and they produce *outputs* (humans create energy, just as a coal-fired electrical generating plant does).

It may be tempting for some supervisors to focus exclusively on the actions necessary in their unit for building an efficient operation. However, they must also maintain the system, and this requires viewing themselves as *boundary managers* who pay attention to internal and external suppliers and customers as well. It also means that they dare not take a narrow view, blindly accenting success of their unit while other units and the organization suffer. Supervisors need to take a holistic (systems) view of their responsibilities within a larger system.

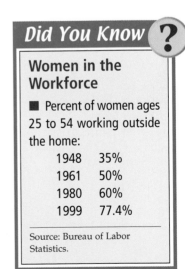

Did You Know ?

Women in the Workforce

■ Percent of women ages 25 to 54 working outside the home:

1948	35%
1961	50%
1980	60%
1999	77.4%

Source: Bureau of Labor Statistics.

How does the systems perspective relate to the contingency approach mentioned earlier?

They are highly compatible. Both require that a supervisor become aware of causal connections between factors. A causal connection exists when you have reason to believe that one action (A) produces a predictable result (B). At the simplest level, systems are series of clearly related causes and effects; the contingency approach seeks to identify proper choices to make based on known causal connections. In effect, a supervisor is continually asking causal questions such as, "If I do this, will I get a valued result?" or "If I do something else, can I get a better result?"

What, then, is the "best" management approach to use?

As a supervisor, you must be ready to employ any one or combination of the various management approaches; no one of them is necessarily the "best." If you are starting a new project, you may wish to accent the systematic approach at first. If you are involved in implementing a major organizational change, you will likely draw upon the behavioral approach to understand employee fears and soften their resistance. And there is almost never a time in which you would want to neglect the causality connections implicit in the systems view. Rarely, however, can you rely upon a single approach. Instead, there should be a balance in the application of management approaches or you will be "typecast" as a narrow person and will overlook some important factors.

Quick Test 5 ▶			
9	T or F	An organization can be viewed as a system of interrelated elements.
10	T or F	When thinking about the various approaches to management, it is best to pick one and rely on it entirely.

KEY CONCEPTS TO REMEMBER

1. **A Body of Knowledge From Which to Draw.** Supervisors are expected to act in a disciplined, or professional, way. They act rationally and think positively. Their manner is characterized by problem solving rather than fault finding. They draw from a vast body of accumulated knowledge concerning the management process, Fayol's management principles, and several basic approaches to management practice.

2. **The Management Process.** Managerial work is different from nonmanagerial work in that managers, including supervisors, devote most of their time and energy to planning, organizing, staffing, energizing, and controlling. These functions require that supervisors become problem solvers and decision makers.

3. **Management Principles.** Fayol's management principles provide guidelines for handling many management situations. They are general in nature, however, and are subject to interpretation and judgment in their application. Among the most important principles are division of work, managerial right to authority, unity of command, unity of direction, subordination of interest to the organization, chain of command, and equity.

4. **Management Approaches (or Schools).** Effective managers apply any or all of the several approaches to management practice that have evolved over the last century. These are systematic (traditional, scientific, or classic) management, behavioral (human relations) management, quantitative (management sciences) management, and contingency management.

5. **Systems and Situations.** Most problems that face supervisors are complex and are influenced by many factors that are present in an organizational system or outside of it. Thus, the management approach emphasized should depend on an analysis of each particular situation. Both the analysis and choice are aided by viewing organizations as systems of interconnected parts.

READING COMPREHENSION

1. Supervisors are advised to have a disciplined approach to their managerial responsibilities. What does this mean?
2. Name three basic sources that help to guide supervisors in their roles as managers.
3. Give a specific example of an activity that might be included in each of the five functions of the management process.
4. What is the purpose, or objective, of the management process?
5. Why did Henri Fayol advise that an organization should have unity of direction?
6. In light of modern experience, should communications be rigidly confined to an up-and-down direction of the chain of command? Explain.
7. Why can't a supervisor rely exclusively on the systematic management approach?
8. Name three applications for which the quantitative approach has been found successful. What do these applications have in common?
9. Explain how the human body, an auto engine, and a football team can be described as systems.
10. What is the basic message of the contingency view of management?

APPLICATION

Self-Assessment

▶ *Which of your supervisory skills need additional development?*

Read the following statements carefully. Circle the number on the response scale that most closely reflects the degree to which each statement accurately describes you. Add up your total points and prepare a brief action plan for self-improvement. Be ready to report your score for tabulation across the entire group.

	Good Description									Poor Description
1. I am good at setting goals and working to achieve them on time.	10	9	8	7	6	5	4	3	2	1
2. I can successfully define a problem and work it through to completion.	10	9	8	7	6	5	4	3	2	1
3. I enjoy assigning tasks to others and holding them responsible for results.	10	9	8	7	6	5	4	3	2	1
4. I am an attentive listener; I don't interrupt others.	10	9	8	7	6	5	4	3	2	1
5. I am able to stimulate others toward task achievements without offending them.	10	9	8	7	6	5	4	3	2	1
6. I am willing to criticize the work of others when their work is not acceptable.	10	9	8	7	6	5	4	3	2	1
7. I have consciously chosen a style of leadership that I will use.	10	9	8	7	6	5	4	3	2	1
8. I enjoy training people how to do things and coaching them to success.	10	9	8	7	6	5	4	3	2	1
9. I am good at explaining things to others in a clear fashion.	10	9	8	7	6	5	4	3	2	1
10. Once a goal is set, I strive hard to meet it on schedule.	10	9	8	7	6	5	4	3	2	1

Scoring and Interpretation

SCORING

Add up your total points for the 10 questions. Record that number here, and report it when it is requested. _____

INTERPRETATION

81 to 100 points. You seem to have a basic set of skills that are appropriate for supervisory positions.

61 to 80 points. Take a close look at some of your skills and discuss them with current supervisors and managers to see if they need improvement.

Below 60 points. Some of your supervisory skills may be substantially inconsistent with current organizational practices and could be detrimental to a career in supervision.

Identify your three lowest scores and record the question numbers here:

_____, _____, _____ .

ACTION

Write a brief paragraph detailing an action plan for how you might sharpen each of these skills. Then pay particularly close attention to the chapters that follow that provide key information about those topics.

Skill Development

Identifying Causal Implications ◄

Assume that a high-level manager asked you to conduct an analysis and make a recommendation regarding this question: *"Should this organization implement a casual-dress policy for all employees on all workdays?"* To prepare your report, you will need to do some exploratory investigation (e.g., searching the Internet for relevant articles; interviewing managers and employees for their views) to uncover supporting materials and demonstrated effects. In particular, you should point out the likely positive consequences of casual dress as well as the likely negative consequences of casual dress on the worksheet below.

Positive Effects	Negative Effects
1. _____	1. _____
2. _____	2. _____
3. _____	3. _____
4. _____	4. _____
5. _____	5. _____
6. _____	6. _____
7. _____	7. _____

ACTION

Following your analysis of the effects of this change, state a conclusion that you would feel comfortable supporting. (Note that this is an exercise demonstrating the system implications of a single policy change inside an organization.)

Group Exercise

▶ *Reaching a Consensus*

STEP 1: Form small groups of about five persons each. Jointly consider Fayol's 10 principles of management as presented in the text.

STEP 2: Arrive at a group consensus on which of Fayol's principles you would place as the highest (and the lowest) priority.

STEP 3: On the list below, rank the 10 principles from 1 (highest priority) to 10 (lowest priority). Use each number from 1 to 10 only once.

STEP 4: Present your results to the class, and discuss the reasons for any substantial differences among groups.

Principle (or Concept)	Group Rank
Specialization of jobs	_____
Authority of managers	_____
Need for discipline	_____
Unity of command	_____
Unity of direction	_____
Subordination of personal interest to that of the organization	_____
Pay according to individual worth	_____
Chain of command	_____
Equitable treatment of employees	_____
Encouragement of initiative	_____

Case 8

The Automated Insurance Office

George's trouble began when the work of his recording clerks was switched from a paperwork system to a computerized one. George was supervisor of the fire-damage claims department of the Alpha Insurance Company. For years, his recording clerks had been judged as very efficient in "moving paper" through the department. Nevertheless, a companywide change in data processing had radically altered the clerks' jobs. Instead of typing and collating multileafed forms in several operations, the clerks now accomplished the same thing by making one simple entry at computer terminals. Or at least that was the way it was supposed to happen.

In fact, the recording clerks seemed to have developed an uncanny knack for uncovering every flaw in the system. As a consequence, records would be unaccountably "lost" in the computer network. Or they would be "unintentionally" merged with others. Or the printers would inexplicably malfunction.

Of course, all this put George on the spot with his superiors. "Why is it," asked George's boss, "that the computerized records system is working well in every other department of the company, but not in yours?" George did not have a ready answer, but he vowed to find out—and to correct the situation as soon as possible.

◀ *Analysis*

If you were George, which of the following actions would you consider to be the most effective in correcting this situation? Rank the alternatives on a scale from 1 (most preferable) to 5 (least preferable). You may add another alternative if you wish. Be prepared to justify your ranking.

_____ **a.** Meet with the records clerks to find out from them the specific nature of their difficulty with the new system and to elicit their suggestions on what can be done to resolve the problems.

_____ **b.** Ask the company's computer programmer to redesign the data processing system for the claims office so that it is foolproof.

_____ **c.** Monitor the recording operation yourself to demonstrate to the records clerks that their output is falling far short of what is possible under the new system.

_____ **d.** Meet with the records clerks to emphasize that the computerized system is working very well elsewhere and that the fault must lie with their work rather than the programming.

_____ **e.** Ask the company's computer programmer to meet with the records clerks to demonstrate the proper operation of the automated system.

Case 9

▶ *The Subordinated Quality Goal*

At a recent speech to its customers at an industrial conference, the company president said, "The All-Purpose Gear Corporation is committed to producing the best gears in the business. You can be sure that our quality can measure up to any of those of our competitors and can top most of them." To back up this message, the president plastered the company bulletin boards with posters that read: "Quality Comes First at All-Purpose Gear."

Employees in Matilda M.'s gear-grinding department, however, were hearing a slightly different story. On more than one occasion, Matilda was heard to say to an employee that she supervised, "If you don't meet your production quota, don't give me any of this 'I had to slow down because I was concentrating on quality' stuff. As far as I'm concerned, that is an unacceptable excuse. Meet your production quota first, and then start worrying about quality."

Analysis ▷

a. What do you think of Matilda's statement?
b. How might her employees react to it?
c. If production quotas really do interfere with employees meeting quality standards, what do you think Matilda should do about it?

Answers to Quick Tests ▶

Quick Test 1	Quick Test 2	Quick Test 3
1. F	3. F	5. F
2. T	4. F	6. F

Quick Test 4	Quick Test 5	
7. F	9. T	
8. F	10. F	

PART Two

Planning and Problem Solving

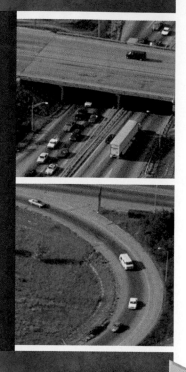

Setting Goals, Making Plans, and Carrying Out Policy

▶ Learning Objectives

After studying this chapter, you should be able to

- Differentiate among the various terms associated with the planning process.

- Create a relevant set of goals for a department supervisor.

- Explain the planning process and the differences between long- and short-range plans and between standing and single-use plans.

- Discuss various guidelines for developing efficient departmental schedules.

- Identify and explain the applications of the Gantt chart, the PERT chart, and the work-distribution chart.

- Discuss a supervisor's responsibilities for interpreting and implementing a company's policies.

ROAD MAPS OF AN ORGANIZATION

1

CONCEPT ▶ Planning establishes the goals and provides the road map for almost all of a supervisor's actions.

Aren't managers and executives paid to do the organizational planning? Why should this chore be part of a supervisor's workload?

It's true that top managers bear the primary responsibility for setting an organization's direction. In particular, they provide the framework for a supervisor's efforts through creation of a vision, values, mission statement, and strategic plans. Further, managers are often aided in this process by planning and scheduling specialists. Let's take a quick look at the major elements of an organization's master planning process.

A corporate *vision* provides a dramatic look at what the entire organization might be like at a distant point in the future—perhaps 5 to 10 years out. It is a broad image of the possibilities that lie ahead. A statement of corporate *values* lays out the beliefs and standards that are very important for an organization to adhere to. Examples might be adherence to cutting-edge technology, attaining superior quality, or providing outstanding customer service. A *mission statement* typically specifies what business the firm is in and what its primary areas of emphasis are. It answers the questions, "Who are we, and what do we do?" From this, top managers develop a corporate *strategy* that sets the overall pattern for how the vision will be achieved and the mission fulfilled. Examples of corporate strategies include acquisitions of related companies, expanding existing products into new markets, diversification, or even downsizing. The key lesson is that *supervisors must custom fit their own units into these master planning pieces.* Supervisors, not executives, make the day-to-day assignments and adjustments needed to make a master plan effective. Without conscious awareness of what is going on above you, your own planning efforts will be wasted.

Unless supervisors accept their share of this managerial responsibility, they will waste (a) time—because of avoidable delays; (b) materials and supplies—because of unwarranted haste, spoilage, or unnecessary accumulation of inventories; (c) machinery—because of operation below its optimum capacity; (d) space—because of overcrowding and poor coordination of incoming supplies and outgoing production; and (e) human resources—because of underutilization or improper assignments.

Vision. A statement of an organization's ideal future.

Values. What an organization believes in and guides its practices by.

Mission statement. A statement that clarifies the nature and purpose of a business.

Strategies. The major methods for achieving an organization's vision and mission.

Internet CONNECTION

Personal Growth. Access the **Education and Research Center** providing an online library for personal growth.

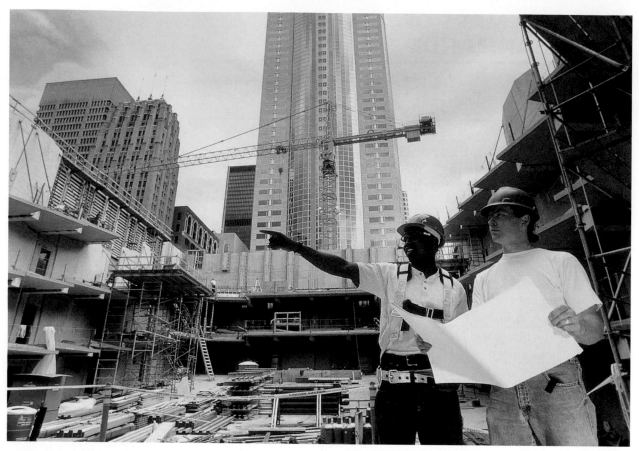

▲ Top management does the long-range planning. Supervisors are more concerned with today, tomorrow, and next week. **How do supervisors fit into the long-range plans of top management?**

How far ahead should supervisors plan their work?

Long-range plans should be handled largely by those in higher levels of management. As a supervisor, your target is necessarily much closer at hand. American Management Association studies show that supervisors spend 38 percent of their thinking time on problems that come up the same day, 40 percent on those one week ahead, 15 percent on those one month ahead, 5 percent on those three to six months ahead, and 2 percent on those one year ahead.

Check your own habits. If you feel you're too busy to worry about anything but today, chances are you spend most of your time fighting fires that can be avoided by planning a week to a month ahead of time.

Typically, a supervisor is responsible for short-range (or tactical) plans and higher executives for long-range (or strategic) plans. In military language, tactical plans are those concerned with a particular engagement or skirmish or battle; strategic plans are those on which the major battle or entire war is based.

Plans, planning, policies, goals: What is the difference?

There are some subtle, but useful, differences among the terms. *Plans* are what come out of the *planning* process. Plans, or programs, are what you intend to do in the future. Before you can develop plans, however, you must set targets. These targets are called **goals** or **objectives**. After you have set these goals (that is the simplest term to use), you establish general guidelines for reaching them. These guidelines are called **policies**. Policies are, in effect, master plans that have been derived from organizational objectives. Only after policies have been set should the specific, operational plans be formulated. Operational plans will include (a) **schedules**, which dictate what must be done as well as establish starting and finishing times, (b) **procedures**, which prescribe the exact methods to be used and sequence to be followed in carrying out a plan, and (c) **standards**, which prescribe the level (quantity or quality) of performance expected.

Finally, you may choose to lay down some *rules* and **regulations**. These will establish the limits (or controls) within which employees are free to do the job their own way.

Take this example. You are thinking ahead (planning) about what your department will do during the annual spring cleaning. You make a list of things that you want to accomplish: filing cabinets cleared of all obsolete material, shelving cleaned and rearranged, tools repaired and put in tip-top shape. These are your goals. Next, you establish some sort of policy. For example, cleaning will be done during normal working hours without overtime; discarding obsolete papers will conform to legal requirements; repairing tools may be done by your own maintenance department or by an outside machine shop. Then you lay out your own optional plan (schedule and/or procedures) of how the housekeeping will be done, when, and by whom. Then you clarify how everyone will know when they have done a satisfactory job. Finally, you set down some firm rules or regulations for your work crew: Only file clerks will make judgments about what paperwork will be discarded; before tools are sent outside for repair, employees must check with you; employees who clean shelving must wear protective gloves. Figure 4-1 illustrates common relationships among these terms.

Goals. Short-term and long-range targets (objectives) toward which an organization strives.

Policies. Broad guidelines that must be followed in pursuit of goals.

Schedules. Detailed date-and-time indications of how facilities, equipment, and employees are to be used to accomplish organizational goals.

Quips & Quotes

The tragedy of life doesn't lie in not reaching your goals. The tragedy lies in having no goals to reach.

—Benjamin E. Mays

◄ **Quick Test 1**

1	T or F	Supervisors are responsible for creating vision, values, mission statements, and strategies.
2	T or F	Operational plans such as schedules, procedures, and standards should be prepared after goals and objectives are created.

Relationship among the various outputs of the planning process. **What is the intended outcome(s) of this process?**

Organization-wide Planning process
• vision • values • mission • strategies

↓

Goals and objectives

General policies	→	Specific plans and programs	→	Budgets and standards

Standing procedures		Operating procedures and schedules	←	Control procedures

Standing rules and regulations		Operating rules and regulations

Feedback from control may modify results of standing procedures and operating procedures.

② GOAL SETTING

CONCEPT ▷ A supervisor's goals shape the targets toward which all of her or his plans and actions should be directed.

Why must goals come before plans?

Because plans are the means to an end; goals are ends. Logically, then, you must first decide where it is you want to go and what it is that you want your unit to accomplish. These are, of course, your goals or objectives. You should set them carefully and systematically. This can be done by following these seven steps:

1. **Consider the goals of the entire organization, not just those of your department.** Think about the needs and wishes of customers—those the company serves as well as those "customers" your department serves internally.

To add practicality to your goal-setting process, keep these bits of advice in mind:

- Look backward before you define tomorrow's goals. The future can often be foretold simply by projecting last year's history forward. If you were able to complete 1,500 units a week last year, it figures that you ought to be able to complete 1,500 units a week next year.

- When you do sense that changes may make history obsolete, define your new goals within ranges. That is, instead of an absolute goal of, say, 8 percent reduction in expenses, aim for a range of from 5 to 10 percent.

- Always set the routinely attainable goals first. Then, you can consider goals that require problem solving and innovation. Don't commit to more than you can deliver. Set only those goals that you believe you can attain with the resources at hand.

- Allow for environmental and organizational influences that can affect your plans for better or worse. Give special attention to human factors—especially the extent to which your employees will support or obstruct your plans.

- Follow up by creating a feedback loop. Monitor your goal-achievement success to see what lessons you can learn for future improvement.

Finally, be assured that the more often you set goals, the more accurate you will be. It's one activity that improves with experience.

2. **Assess the strengths and weaknesses of your department.** Ask how they will help or hinder you in trying to meet company goals and in trying to serve external and internal customers.

3. **Look for areas of improvement.** Keep your mind alert to new opportunities, such as ways to improve quality or reduce costs. Don't restrict your thinking to what your goals were last year or how you met them. If you can forecast what may happen to change conditions next year, this will help focus your attention on goals that will be more meaningful in the months to come.

4. **Consult with those who will have to help you carry out your plans and with those who can offer you their support along the way.** Employees who are involved in setting goals are more likely to be committed to success in reaching the goals. Staff departments that are consulted in advance may direct your attention to potential pitfalls or to goals that will get the full measure of their support.

5. **Pick a relevant and reasonable set of goals.** These should meet two standards. They should (a) contribute to the organization's goals and (b) be attainable by your department, given its resources.

6. **Arrange your department's goals in a hierarchy of objectives.** That is, *prioritize them* by placing the most important ones at the top of your list and the least important at the bottom.

7. **Watch out for limitations.** Think about restrictions that may be imposed on you by your company or by the need to coordinate with or serve other departments. Your department cannot operate in a vacuum. It must base its plans on realistic planning premises.

With what kinds of goals are supervisors usually concerned?

Typically, the goals you set for yourself—or that are set for you, at least partially, as part of a company's overall objectives—are targets to be aimed at in the near future. They pin down your department's output, quality of workmanship, and allowable expenditures. Often, they also include goals in such employee-related areas as departmental attendance, labor turnover, and safety, as shown in Table 4-1. These goals may be stated in terms of tomorrow, next week, or next month, or as far ahead as a year. More often than not, the goals are quantitative (expressed as numbers, percentages, or dollars) rather than merely qualitative (described with such words as *improve, maintain, good,* or *better*). In short, results will be *measurable.*

TABLE 4-1

Typical Performance Goals for a First-Line Supervisor

Area of Measurement	Last Year's Record	Next Year's Goals
1. Ratio of jobs completed on schedule to total jobs worked	85% average, 92% highest, 65% lowest in June	90% average, minimum acceptable 75%
2. Percentage of job costs held to within 3% of standard costs	91% average, 95% highest, 75% lowest in June	90% average, bring up low figure to 87% or better
3. Rejects and rework	Less than 1% rejects; rework averages 7%	Keep rejects to less than 1% but cut rework to 3%
4. Labor stability	Two quits, one discharge	No quits of employees with over three years service
5. Absences, latenesses	5% absences, 7% latenesses	5% absences, 2% latenesses
6. Overtime	Only on jobs okayed by sales department	Only on jobs okayed by sales department
7. Accidents	No lost-time accidents; 37 calls to dispensary for minor ailments	No lost-time accidents; reduce number of dispensary visits to 30 or less
8. Customer satisfaction	Average of 15 complaints per month	33% reduction in complaints per month received

In many companies and organizations, the degree to which you and your department attain your goals becomes the determining factor in what kind of raise you'll get or how good a job for which you can be groomed. This is one big reason why it is so important to lay out a detailed set of plans for meeting your goals.

How can goals be made more compelling?

By making sure that they aren't confused with activity for activity's sake. Professor Ed Locke has identified several criteria for the setting of objectives, and he concluded that goals should be something to strive for, not just something to do. A few meaningful goals are better than a long "laundry list" of activities to make sure that you look good when performance appraisal time comes around. Accordingly, Locke and others suggest the following key guidelines for making your objectives more effective. A goal should be

Clearly focused on output. For example, when you are stating a goal, it's all right to say "100 orders will be handled each day," but it is not all right to say, "We will improve productivity." The former is an output; the latter is a vague statement of aspirations.

Explicit. That is, goals should be clearly stated in terms, or numbers, that make the output measurable. It should be clear to any observer whether or not the goal was achieved.

Time-oriented. The targeted output must always be related to a specific time period, such as "10 tons per day," "50 shipments by the end of the month," or "5 percent reduction of absenteeism for the year."

Achievable. Don't set impossible goals; they must be attainable or they will haunt you later on!

◄ Quick Test 2

3	T or F	After setting several goals, it is probably not important to prioritize them according to their relative importance.
4	T or F	Good goal statements should be output-oriented, explicit, time-oriented, and achievable.

③ THE PLANNING PROCESS

CONCEPT ▶ The planning process should be systematic, yet it should allow for flexibility.

Once goals have been set, how does the planning process proceed?

In six steps (see Figure 4-2). Effective plans flow from clearly stated goals, such as those appearing in Table 4-1. Plans detail *how* goals will be achieved. These plans, however, depend upon your following a systematic planning process, just as you did when setting goals.

1. **Develop a master plan.** This should focus on your main objective. If, for example, the company's goal is to have higher quality products or services, the master plan for your department should give this top priority.
2. **Draw up supporting plans.** This requires that you think about how each activity in your department can contribute to your master plan. Machinists may need more explicit blueprints. Assemblers may need brighter workplace lighting. Clerks may need a different order-entry procedure.

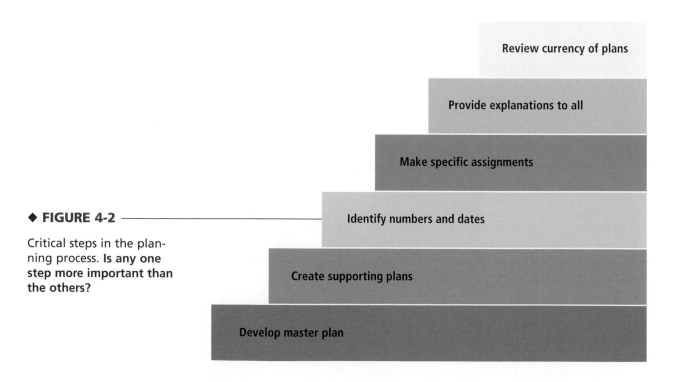

◆ FIGURE 4-2

Critical steps in the planning process. **Is any one step more important than the others?**

Review currency of plans

Provide explanations to all

Make specific assignments

Identify numbers and dates

Create supporting plans

Develop master plan

3. **Put numbers and dates on everything you can.** Plans work best when employees know how much or how many are required of them. Since plans are for the future—tomorrow, next week, or next month—times and dates are essential, too.
4. **Pin down assignments.** Plans are for people. Responsibility for carrying out each part of a plan or procedure should be assigned to a particular individual.
5. **Explain the plan to all concerned.** Plans should be shared. Their rationales should be explained and their goals justified. Employees who know *why* are more likely to cooperate.
6. **Review your plans regularly.** Circumstances and restrictions change. Your plans should be examined periodically to see whether they should be changed, too.

Should a supervisor's plans be flexible or rigid?

They should be stated firmly and clearly so that everyone concerned can understand them and recognize their importance. They should not be so rigid, however, that they prevent your making changes to accommodate unexpected circumstances. A good plan should be flexible enough to anticipate and allow for an alternate course of action. Suppose, for example, you planned to start a new order or project on Monday, but the necessary materials are not on hand. Your plans should permit postponement of that project and insertion of a productive alternative without delay.

In what way are plans or programs usually classified?

They are usually classified according to their duration (long or short) and usage (standing or single-use).

Long-range plans are typically set by higher management and are expected to be in operation from one to five years.

Short-range plans are those with which supervisors are most concerned. These are usually based on operations of one year or less. At the department level, sort-range plans may be in effect for a day, a week, a month, or a quarter.

Standing plans include just about any activity that goes on without much change from year to year. Standing plans cover general employment practices, health and safety matters, purchasing procedures, routine discipline, and the like.

Single-use plans are used only once before they must be revised. A plan for the assembly of a new machine is an example. It will be used only once.

Generally speaking, then, supervisors will follow short-range, single-use plans for day-to-day operations. But supervisors will also be guided by many standing plans that implement routine, relatively unchanging goals and policies.

What is a good way to double check your plans and projects?

Try using this six-point planning checklist (adapted from Rudyard Kipling's poem "Six Honest Serving Men"—what, why, where, when, how and who):

1. **What** is to be done? Spell out the objectives in terms of output, quality, and costs.
2. **Why** should this activity be done? Will it save money? Generate revenue? Add to customer satisfaction?
3. **Where** is this activity to be performed? At the workplace? In the field? Where is the finished product or service to be delivered? To the adjoining department, the shipping dock, the home office?
4. **When** must this activity or project be completed? Just as important, when must it begin? A starting date is often as vital to a plan's success as its deadline. And this date cannot be determined without first having a reliable time estimate to do the job. That way, if you know, for example, that it will take three days to complete a project that's due on Friday morning, you must start working on the project the first thing Tuesday morning.
5. **How** is this activity to be performed? Answers to this question should verify the job methods and equipment to be used and the procedures and sequences to be followed.
6. **Who** is to perform this work? This not only means that you must assign responsibility for this task; you must also specify the nature of the authority that goes with the job. That is, you must specify the extent to which that individual can control the resources needed to complete the task, such as tools, machinery, materials, and additional labor.

How do controls relate to plans?

Controls keep results in line with plans. When a plan is moving directly toward its goal, the track is kept clear. The supervisor need apply no control. But when actions stray from their planned targets, the supervisor must take corrective action to bring them back in line. When planning a department's goals, a supervisor must also plan its control limits, which provide the feedback needed to trigger corrective actions.

Quick Test 3 ▶			
5	T or F	Supervisors are usually more concerned with short-range plans than with long-range ones.
6	T or F	If a good job of planning has been done, supervisors usually don't need to concern themselves with controls.

▲ Schedules are more obvious for some organizations, but critical to all. **How can supervisors avoid missing deadlines?**

 SCHEDULING GUIDELINES

CONCEPT ▶ Scheduling brings the planning process right to the employee level.

Should you schedule your department to operate at 100 percent capacity?

No. This is a poor practice because it leaves no cushion for emergencies. It's best to call on your past experience and plan only for short periods at 100 percent. No department can run for very long without some unforeseen emergency arising. These emergencies may be only unexpected absences or special rush orders, but you must leave room to cope.

What happens if you underschedule your staff?

Exactly what you would expect: Employees often find a way to stretch the job to fill the time. One way to minimize this is to have a backlog of second-priority jobs on tap for assignment. If regular orders are slow coming in, you can catch up with some of the work that often needs to be done but is not allowed for in the master schedule. These assignments might include cleaning out files in an office, sorting and discarding obsolete inventory in the stockroom, or undertaking any kind of general cleanup. However, if this condition persists, some employees must be transferred or laid off.

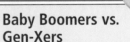

Baby Boomers vs. Gen-Xers

■ Seventy-three million-plus baby boomers are in the labor market. They tend to work a 50-hour work week. The Gen-Xers (born between 1964 and 1980) get the job done and go home at 5 P.M., choosing to focus on life outside of their job.

Source: Bureau of Labor Statistics.

Can you expect as much from employees when they work overtime, or should you make an allowance for it in the schedule?

You should probably expect a 5 to 10 percent drop in productivity. Authorities differ on this one, probably because there has been very little definitive research on the subject. Stress and fatigue inevitably take their toll. The more extended the overtime, the greater the drop in output—and probably in the quality of work produced. Our own impression is that a 10 percent drop is predictable for scheduling purposes.

What should supervisors do when they are pressured for faster deliveries or tighter deadlines?

Resist your first instinctive response to say you can't deliver. Hopes and expectations have no place in planning. Your schedules and promises must be based on fact. Only facts—available equipment and its condition, people and their reliability, material supply and its delivery—can be used as a successful base for planning.

A firm, dependable promise will satisfy most superiors. But don't yield to the temptation to be overcautious. Don't allow for more time than you think the situation actually warrants.

Don't say, for instance, "We can't possibly deliver these parts before the 16th," and then finish the job on the 11th. Others in your plant depend on the accuracy of your forecasts. If everyone allowed too much leeway, that would eat up time and money just as overscheduling might.

Give the best sure date you can figure on. Otherwise, you'll lose both friends and respect among your associates and your superiors.

Quick Test 4 ▶			
7	T or F	Employees often increase their productivity rate during overtime hours, as they are anxious to get done early and go home.
8	T or F	It is better to make realistic and dependable promises for output than to be overly optimistic or pessimistic.

⑤ METHODS AND TECHNIQUES

CONCEPT ▶	Supervisors may draw from a range of established planning and scheduling techniques.

What is a Gantt chart? How does a supervisor use it?

Henry Laurence Gantt, an industrial engineer, developed the first production control chart. Its form seems obvious today, since most organizations now use one or another version of it to plan and chart output performance. Its essentials are displayed in Figure 4-3.

To understand the unique value of the **Gantt chart**, put yourself in the place of a supervisor who has just been handed five production orders, stamped serially from 101 to 105. These orders indicate what machines the work must be processed on, the sequence that must be followed, and the estimated number of hours it will take each machine to complete its work.

These orders contain essentially the same kind of information found on a route sheet. The route sheet, however, often includes operations performed in different departments. Thus, it is not unusual for the supervisor to collect this information from several route sheets, or the production-control department may issue a number of separate orders to each departmental supervisor.

If the supervisor were to load the machines (they could be benches, workstations, desks, and so on) with the assumption that each order must be finished before another one is begun (straight-line or point-to-point scheduling), the schedule would look something like Chart A in Figure

Gantt chart. A visual device for scheduling jobs in the most productive sequence and then controlling work progress.

Log of orders for Charts A and B

Order number	101			102			103			104			105		
Operation sequence	1	2	3	1	2	3	1	2	3	1	2	3	1	2	3
Machine number	A	B	C	C	A	B	B	A	C	A	C	B	B	C	A
Machine time (hrs.)	4	8	2	10	4	6	6	4	8	4	10	12	4	2	6

Chart A

	Monday	Tuesday	Wednesday	Thursday	Friday	Monday	Tuesday
Machine A	101			102		103	
Machine B		101			102	103	
Machine C			101	102			103

Chart B

	Monday	Tuesday	Wednesday	Thursday	Friday	Monday	Tuesday
Machine A	101	104	102	105	103		
Machine B	105	101		102	103	104	
Machine C	102		105 101	104		103	

◆ FIGURE 4-3

Development of a Gantt chart from a series of production orders. Log of orders shows prescribed operation sequence for each job. Chart A shows orders lined up in sequence as they were received. Chart B shows orders rearranged (overlapped) for maximum loading at each machine, with the prescribed sequence of operations for each job maintained. Note the increased utilization of available machine times afforded by the Gantt-chart scheduling. **Is that the only benefit of using a Gantt chart?**

4-3. The flow of work would be orderly, but the equipment would be extremely underutilized. Worse still, many orders would be delayed. To correct these deficiencies, Gantt overlapped orders and disregarded the sequence in which they were accepted, while still rigidly adhering to the operation sequence each order specifies. Chart B in Figure 4-3 shows how the supervisor can juggle orders, starting order 105 on machine B and order 102 on machine C and at the same time beginning order 101 on machine A. By rearranging and overlapping the jobs, the supervisor can have all five orders finished by Friday afternoon. Furthermore, the supervisor has greatly increased the overall machine utilization. Machine A is now scheduled to be in operation 18 of the first 24 hours of the week (through Wednesday). It works 4 hours on 101 and 4 hours on 104, is idle for 2 hours, then works 4 hours on 102 and 6 hours on 105, and is idle again until the close of the shift on Wednesday. Machine B utilizes 22 hours during the same period: 4 hours on 105, 8 hours on 101, idle for 2 hours, 6 hours on 102, and 4 hours on 103. Machine C utilizes all 24 hours: 10 hours on 102, 2 hours on 105, 2 hours on 101, and 10 hours on 104. This predicts utilization rates of 75 percent, 92 percent, and 100 percent, respectively. Although in reality, a supervisor might not be able to juggle the work so efficiently all week long, such a chart indicates what judicious overlapping of jobs can accomplish.

How does the PERT Chart relate to the Gantt chart?

It borrows the ideas of juggling a number of different but related tasks of varying time requirements from the Gantt chart. PERT ties these to the critical events as they should occur and demonstrates graphically how these are all tied together. Finally, PERT enables the planners to identify the bottlenecks in a complex schedule, plan, or program.

What do the initials P-E-R-T stand for? Where is PERT used?

PERT chart. A graphic project-planning device that shows relationships among many tasks and the critical bottlenecks that could delay progress toward completion.

They stand for *program evaluation and review technique*. In plainer English, **PERT** is a technique for planning any project that involves a number of different tasks that must be coordinated. It is a graphic technique that enables the planner to see the progressive relationships among many jobs; PERT is also known as the critical-path method (CPM), because it alerts the supervisor to the sequence of tasks that take the longest time to complete the critical path. Any delay on the critical path will delay the entire project.

The technique dramatizes the value of conceiving of doing two or more things simultaneously. It may take 12 minutes to get a haircut, 5 minutes for a shoeshine, and 10 minutes to browse through the newspaper. You could take 27 minutes to do all three, in sequence, one after the other—or you could do all three in 12 minutes by doing them simultaneously, or (as planners say) in parallel.

The PERT method is most useful for scheduling one-of-a-kind projects. It is used to plan and schedule construction projects such as roads, bridges, and dams. It is used to plan the building of very large engines, airplanes, and ships; PERT is helpful, too, in scheduling a number of jobs that must be done in a short period of time. For example, a plant closes for two weeks in the summer and tries to get everything cleaned and repaired during that period. It is also useful for starting a new program in a government agency or for introducing a new product to the market.

◆ **FIGURE 4-4**

PERT chart for planning the installation of a large machine. **Why is a PERT chart so useful to supervisors?**

A is the starting point, and M is the finishing point—the time when the machine is completely installed and ready to run. B, C, D, etc. indicate the completion points for a variety of intermediate tasks such as digging the pit, constructing the forms, pouring the foundation, assembling the supporting iron work, pipework, installing electrical connections, mounting the machine in place, training the operators, debugging, etc. All arrows prescribe the paths that must be followed between one task and another. Numerals beside the arrows indicate the estimated time (in hours) needed to complete each task. The critical (longest, or bottleneck) path is indicated by the solid arrows. Its estimated time from A to M is 47.5 hours (40+5+2+0+0.5). All other paths from A to M (indicated by the dotted arrows) are shorter. On the other hand, if the project were pursued in alphabetical (point-to-point) sequence, the total time needed would be 107.5 hours.

Work distribution chart. A visual device for allocating tasks equitably among the members of a department, according to time required and skill levels available.

What makes PERT so different from ordinary scheduling methods?

The program evaluation and review technique helps a scheduler to plan ahead, to look for critical jobs that will tie up a whole program unless they are begun and completed before they create bottlenecks. For example, it may be logical to wait until a machine foundation pit has been dug and the concrete has been poured before constructing the supporting ironwork for the machine (see Figure 4-4). But if steel is in short supply and the ironwork job will take four weeks to fabricate, then perhaps it's wiser to begin this part of the job before digging the pit. And if there are several other jobs that can't be begun until the ironwork is in place, you can see how critical it is to anticipate the ironwork job and ensure its completion on time; PERT charting helps you to identify these critical jobs ahead of time.

What is the basis for scheduling and assigning office and clerical work?

Office scheduling should be based on the same considerations given to production scheduling: (a) the number of tasks to be done, (b) the time it will take to do each task, (c) the number and qualifications of employees available to do the work, and (d) the capacity and availability of proper machines and equipment, when they play a part. A good way to put this all together is to use a *work distribution chart*, which provides a rule-of-thumb guide to indicate how much work the department can handle with its present staff.

Table 4-2 shows how repetitive, routine work in an office (or in most service-related operations) might be balanced among employees by means of a work distribution chart. (Machine capability and availability are not considered to be factors in this example.) Note that the supervisor has tried to group together activities of roughly the same skill levels into job assignments for each person. For example, Agee handles mail sorting and dispatching and part of the copying—fairly simple work. Bonds and Case handle the balance of the copying plus the filing chores, which are slightly more difficult. Diego, Epes, and Foxx are assigned to basic keyboarding, which requires a modest level of skills. Gray does the more difficult keyboarding (using complex software) and check writing, both considered to need the highest level of skills in the department. Hiti is the receptionist.

A work distribution chart is also useful for planning the work of maintenance and construction crews and for retail employees.

Quick Test 5 ▶	**9**	T or F	Gantt charts and PERT charts are different names for the same performance planning methods.
	10	T or F	Work distribution charts help to assign activities of similar skill levels to each person.

TABLE 4-2

Work Distribution Chart
A Technique for Planning and Scheduling Office Work and Similar Servicelike Operations

Weekly Tasks or Activities	Total Hours per Week	Weekly Time Distribution in Hours per Employee							
		Agee	Bonds	Case	Diego	Epes	Foxx	Gray	Hiti
Reception/switchboard	40								40
Mail in	20	20							
Mail out	10	10							
Keyboarding:									
Tabulating	80			10	20	20	30		
Forms	20				10	10			
Letters	30				10	10	10		
Reports	30							30	
Copy machine	40	10	15	15					
Check writing	10							10	
Filing in	25		15	10					
Filing out	15		10	5					
Total hours	320	40	40	40	40	40	40	40	40

---

6 POLICIES

CONCEPT ▶ Policies provide the guidelines that help keep an entire organization working toward the same goals in the same way.

What is meant by *company policy*?

Company—or organization—policies are broad guidelines for action. At their best, these guides are a reflection of a company's objectives and a statement of its basic principles for doing business. In a major way, they represent a public commitment to employees, suppliers, customers, and the community. In a very practical way, however, they are intended as a guide for supervisors and managers for getting their jobs done. Many policies at the operational level give supervisors the opportunity to use their own best judgment in implementing them. Other policies are reinforced by firm rules and procedures that greatly restrict supervisory discretion.

ASK QUESTIONS

■ Policy implementation often involves supervisory judgment, which can prove to be good or flawed. To avoid getting burned later about policy matters, ask yourself these questions: Would my boss want to talk this over with me first? Is a union contract relevant to this? Is there a precedent for handling this issue? Who can I consult for advice on this? Have I gathered all the facts?

Does policy apply only at high levels?

Policy is generally set by managers high up in the company organization. But policy can be no more than a collection of high-sounding words unless the supervisor translates them into action on the firing line.

Consider the following example of a disciplinary policy. Note how its formality decreases, and its action-orientation increases, as it works its way down from the executive suite to the first-line action by the supervisors:

Company president: "Our policy is to exercise fair and reasonable controls to regulate the conduct of our employees."

Division executive: "The policy on attendance in this division is that habitual absenteeism will be penalized."

Area manager: "Here are the rules governing absences in this region. It's up to you supervisors to keep an eye on unexcused absences and to suspend any employee absent or late more than three times in three months."

Local supervisor: "Sorry, I'm going to have to lay you off for three days. You know the rules. You took time off on your own without warning or getting approval."

Note that no real action takes place until the supervisor puts the words of the policy into effect.

Is policy always in writing?

Far from it. Many rigid policies have never been put down in black and white. And many firm policies have never been heard from an executive's lips. But employees and supervisors alike recognize that matters affected by such policies must be handled in a certain manner and usually do so.

The existence of so much unwritten policy has led many authorities to the conclusion that all policy is better put into writing so that it may be explained, discussed, and understood. Nevertheless, there are many companies that don't subscribe to this way of thinking, and their policies remain implied rather than spelled out. This can lead to genuine misunderstandings and more "exceptions" to the policy.

Should a supervisor deviate from organizational policy?

No. That's a very dangerous thing to do. Policies exist for a good reason; they are set to guide action. It's a supervisor's responsibility to act within policy limits.

Supervisors can influence a policy change, however, by making their thoughts and observations known to the boss, the human resources department, and the top management. After all, supervisors are in the best position to feel out employees' reactions to policy, both favorable and unfavorable. You do your boss and your company a service when you accurately report employees' reactions. And that's the time to offer your suggestions for improving or modifying the policy. In a nutshell, provide your best input, and then agree to abide by the decision.

How responsible will employees hold you for company policy?

If you have done a good job of convincing employees that you fully represent the management of their company, your actions and company policy will be one and the same thing in their eyes. Naturally, you will sometimes have to carry out policy that you don't fully agree with—policy that may be unpopular with you or with your employees. Resist the temptation to apologize for your actions or to criticize the policy to employees. When you do, you weaken your position.

If you have to reprimand an employee, don't say, "I'd like to give you a break, but that's company policy." Or when sparking a cleanup campaign, don't say, "The manager wants you to get your area in order." Handle such matters positively. Give the policy your own personal touch, but don't sell the company down the river or you're likely to be caught in the current yourself.

11	T or F	Policies generally apply only to high-level executives; supervisors need not be concerned with them.
12	T or F	Policies usually ought to be put into writing so that they will be more clearly understood and administered more consistently.

◀ Quick Test 6

CHAPTER 4 REVIEW

KEY CONCEPTS TO REMEMBER

1. **Road Maps of an Organization.** Planning is the process of systematically working out ahead of time what you and your work unit will do in the future. Good planning reduces needless waste of a department's resources. It is planning that establishes an organization's goals and standards and the policies that guide their attainment. From these goals and policies, plans emerge in the form of procedures and schedules. Organizational policies, which are general in nature, are made increasingly specific as they move down the line as rules and regulations. Supervisory planning is mainly concerned with short-term objectives spanning a few days, a week, a month, or—at most—a year.

2. **Goal Setting.** Goals are usually arranged in a hierarchy. The goals of a supervisor's work unit should support those of the overall organization. The unit's goals should be clearly stated, output and time-oriented, and should be attainable within the limitations of the unit's resources.

3. **The Planning Process.** The planning process flows from the goals into the development of plans for implementing them. Plans must be supported by details, such as times and dates as well as the anticipated assignment of equipment, facilities, and people. Plans may be long range (more than one year) or short range (anything less than one year). There are standing plans, which cover procedures that remain in effect over a long period of time, and there are single-use plans, which cover operating schedules and budgets.

4. **Scheduling Guidelines.** When developing schedules for their own units, supervisors should not press their resources too far; nor should they underschedule them. The use of overtime to complete schedules is usually a costly practice, not only in labor premiums but also in reduced productivity.

5. **Methods and Techniques.** Supervisors should master a variety of planning and scheduling techniques for handling different scheduling problems: (a) the Gantt chart for mixed production runs; (b) PERT, or CPM, for one-of-a-kind projects; and (c) the work distribution chart for standing assignments, especially those in office, service, and retail situations.

6. **Policies.** Decisions and actions in every enterprise are guided by a body of operating principles, called policies, that either have been set down in writing or have evolved informally (like common law) as a result of decisions and actions that management has taken under similar circumstances in the past. Supervisors are expected to act within the limits of these guidelines. In the eyes of employees, then, supervisors are inseparably identified with the policies of the employing organization, since it is at that level that these principles are translated into specific actions.

READING COMPREHENSION

1. How do vision, values, mission statement, and strategy concern a supervisor?
2. How are plans, goals, and policies related?
3. Why must establishing goals precede developing plans?
4. Identify each of the following as either a standing plan or a single-use plan: a department's monthly budget, a fire-drill procedure, this week's production schedule, the methods prescribed for filling out a purchase order.
5. How are plans and controls related?
6. Why is it not considered good practice to schedule operations at 100 percent of capacity?
7. In what ways is a Gantt chart like a calendar? In what ways is it different?
8. In what ways is a PERT chart similar to a Gantt chart? What is the principal difference between the two?
9. When would it be wise for a supervisor to check with the boss before carrying out a particular policy?
10. A company's policy manual states, "It is our intention to listen with an open mind to employee complaints." What supplementary information might a supervisor need to better interpret that policy?

APPLICATION

Self-Assessment

How good are your planning skills?

Read the following statements carefully. Circle the number on the response scale that most closely reflects the degree to which each statement accurately describes you. Add up your total points and prepare a brief action plan for self-improvement. Be ready to report your score for tabulation across the entire group.

	Good Description									Poor Description
1. I can read the organization's vision, values, mission, and strategy and see how my department fits into that picture.	10	9	8	7	6	5	4	3	2	1
2. I know, and could explain to an employee, the difference between a policy, a procedure, and a regulation.	10	9	8	7	6	5	4	3	2	1
3. Once my plans are in place, I recognize the need for an associated set of controls.	10	9	8	7	6	5	4	3	2	1
4. I feel comfortable that I could create and use a Gantt chart in my department.	10	9	8	7	6	5	4	3	2	1
5. If I were to see a PERT chart for a major project, I could identify the critical path.	10	9	8	7	6	5	4	3	2	1

		Good Description										Poor Description

6. I understand the basis upon which a work distribution chart is constructed.   10 9 8 7 6 5 4 3 2 1

7. I am familiar with the nature of policies and know when I could change them.   10 9 8 7 6 5 4 3 2 1

8. I could construct goals for my department that incorporate the suggested guidelines.   10 9 8 7 6 5 4 3 2 1

9. I can differentiate between standing and single-use plans.   10 9 8 7 6 5 4 3 2 1

10. I am effective at answering the six questions in planning (what, why, where, when, how, and who).   10 9 8 7 6 5 4 3 2 1

Scoring and Interpretation

SCORING

Add up your total points for the 10 questions. Record that number here, and report it when it is requested. _____

INTERPRETATION

81 to 100 points. You seem to have a basic set of planning skills.

61 to 80 points. Take a close look at some of your planning skills (those with lower self-assessments) and discuss them with a manager to see if they need improvement.

Below 60 points. Some of your planning skills may be substantially inconsistent with effective planning practices and could be detrimental to your success as a supervisor.

Identify your three lowest scores and record the question numbers here: _____, _____, _____.

ACTION

Write a brief paragraph detailing an action plan for how you might sharpen each of these skills. Pay particularly close attention to the related material in the chapter as you review the relevant sections there.

Skill Development

Goal Setting ◄

STEP 1: Pair up with another person. Working independently, each of you should develop (write out) a set of personal goals and associated action plans for the next year. Then exchange them with your partner.

STEP 2: Assess the degree (grade their product on A to F scales) to which your partner incorporated the following guidelines from the chapter regarding effective goals and plans.

STEP 3: Share your evaluation of your partner's goals with him or her, and offer your feedback.

STEP 4: Encourage your partner to revise his or her goals. Revise your goals based on feedback from your partner. Discuss what you have learned from this exercise.

Grade	Incorporation of Chapter Principle
_____	Goals are based on an assessment of strengths and weaknesses.
_____	Goals fit into some larger system (e.g., one's family).
_____	Consultation with others who are affected or can help.
_____	Goals are relevant and reasonable.
_____	Goals are arrayed in a hierarchy of importance.
_____	Goals clearly focus on output.
_____	Goals are explicit (the outcome is measurable).
_____	Goals are targeted toward a specific time for completion.
_____	Goals appear to be achievable.

Group Exercise

Identifying the Critical Path ◄

STEP 1: Working in small groups, brainstorm the various steps involved in a relatively simple task (such as building a birdhouse to give to an elderly person). Be sure to consider all the probable steps (such as identifying the recipient, drawing up the plans, obtaining the materials, etc.) as well as the major completion points.

STEP 2: Provide time estimates for each of the activities, and then consider which of the activities can be done simultaneously with other activities (complete the worksheet on the next page).

STEP 3: Draw up a PERT chart for the entire process, and identify the critical path (longest possible time line).

STEP 4: Report to the class what major principles this exercise has demonstrated for you.

Major Activity	Time Estimate	Completion Point
_____	_____	_____
_____	_____	_____
_____	_____	_____
_____	_____	_____
_____	_____	_____
_____	_____	_____
_____	_____	_____

CASES FOR ANALYSIS

Case 10

The Disorganized Shipping Dock

Jackie J. is in charge of the shipping dock at the Black & White Dairy Products plant. Every day, she oversees the shipment of hundreds of pallet loads of milk-filled cartons, thousands of cases of ice cream and cottage cheese, and hundreds upon hundreds of boxes of butter packages. The daily routines in the shipping department run like this: The night before, Jackie is notified by a computerized dispatch order of the products to be shipped the next day. At that time, she is also given a tentative loading schedule for the 25 company-owned trucks and another for the 10 or more trucks that are expected from distributors and the large grocery chains.

The following morning, Jackie directs her crews to begin removing the products scheduled to be shipped from where they have been stored in chilled "holding rooms." Using specially designed fork-trucks, her crews bring these products by pallet loads to a chilled and sheltered shipping apron. Such deliveries must follow a carefully planned sequence so that these perishable products will be exposed to blasts of outdoor temperatures for the least possible amount of time. If all goes right, the products arrive at the apron at the same time that a truck backs in for that particular load. If the timing is wrong, considerable spoilage of goods can take place as they wait for the proper truck or are shunted aside to give priority to the next truck arriving.

To handle this complex schedule, Jackie supervises a crew of 15 employees: 10 fork-truck drivers; 3 "rovers," who perform a variety of labor-grade duties such as handling small or split loads by hand truck and cleaning up spills from broken cartons and leakage from milk containers; and 2 dispatchers who coordinate the arrival of empty trucks and direct and verify their loading.

Lately, however, Jackie's department has not been running smoothly. For instance, there has been an unusual amount of breakage and spoilage on the dock. Jackie's boss made critical mention of this when the monthly spoilage report was issued. Then, too, hardly a day has gone by when there haven't been three or more trucks backed up waiting for loads that have not as yet been brought up from the holding rooms. Repeatedly, the traffic manager has been on Jackie's back for this. There has also been an occasional misloading of a distributor's truck, which necessitated either refunds or returns. The sales manager has made unpleasant remarks to Jackie about that.

When things didn't improve, Jackie decided that she had had enough. So, one Friday afternoon she called her crew together to find out what was going wrong. Here's what she heard:

"You never let us know until the last minute what is to be pulled from the holding rooms," said one fork-truck driver.

"When you issue the requests to bring stuff forward, you don't make it clear who should do it," said another.

"You have never made the load sequences clear to me," said one of the dispatchers.

"As to the trucks backing up," said the other dispatcher, "I thought you were coordinating truck arrivals."

"We could do a lot more to speed up loading if we knew beforehand what the small and split-load orders were," said the rovers.

◀ *Analysis*

If you were Jackie, which of the following alternatives would you pursue to get things running more smoothly? Rank the alternatives from 1 (most preferable) to 5 (least preferable). You may add another alternative if you wish. Be prepared to justify your rankings.

_____ **a.** Consider that the majority of the crew's comments are more likely excuses for poor performance rather than valid suggestions for improvement.

_____ **b.** Bring the crew's comments to the attention of the traffic manager and the sales manager so they can improve scheduling of the over-the-road truck drivers and clarity of orders with distributors.

_____ c. Ask the crew's help in preparing a master plan of operation that, over the long haul, will best fit the reality of shipping conditions.

_____ d. Clarify your daily plans so that crews will know the removal schedule in advance and what their particular assignments will be.

_____ e. Draw up and post a detailed shipping schedule each day; then advise the crew that it must be followed to the letter.

Case 11

Cora's Goals

The order-entry department of a large wholesale distributor owes part of its success to the careful planning done by its supervisors. The department's new computer system has caused some problems, but things generally have been running smoothly. Cora, the supervisor, is now establishing objectives for the coming year, and she wants to set reasonable, but measurable, goals for some important indicators of her department's operations.

The order-entry process consists of (a) accepting mailed or telephoned orders; (b) looking up or verifying the stock number, price, and current availability of each item ordered; (c) looking up the customer number; (d) adding the customer number and requesting a credit check if the customer is new; and (e) entering the customer number, items ordered, and quantities (as well as out-of-stock indicators, if applicable) on a keyboard computer terminal. The computer then automatically prepares packing lists, shipping labels, and invoices and makes appropriate entries in accounting records.

Analysis

Your assignment is to prepare a list of objectives for Cora and her department. Use Table 4-1 in the text as a model. Supply whatever numbers you think are reasonable and appropriate for the order-entry department. Among the items you should consider are processing time, costs, accuracy, overtime, lateness and absenteeism, employee turnover, and damage to equipment through misuse.

The Rush Order's Doubtful Deadline

"Can you handle this rush order for 1,500 cases of hairspray for one of our nonbrand customers?" asked the sales manager of a toiletries company one Friday afternoon. "It's got to be shipped by the end of the third week in March." The sales manager was speaking to Chico Juarez, supervisor of the packaging department.

"I don't know for sure," said Chico. "Monday will be March 1, and the very best we can do while working a five-day week is 100 cases a day."

"That's great," said the sales manager. "Three weeks at 500 cases a week should allow you to make the deadline."

"Not so fast," said Chico, "I've got to check out all the possibilities before I can agree to that deadline."

◀ *Analysis*

When Chico took a look at his records, this is what he discovered:

a. The packaging machine is due for an overhaul on the second weekend of March.

b. Absenteeism runs very high in his department when employees have to work Friday nights during the high school basketball play-offs in March.

c. The plant superintendent has recently issued an edict that prevents the department from working overtime.

d. Past records show that unscheduled downtime for repairs on the packaging machine have been running about 10 percent. This has cut down proportionately on scheduled production.

Should Chico commit himself to shipping this order at the end of the third week in March? If not, when would be a reasonably sure date? Be prepared to explain your reasoning and to show your calculations.

◀ **Answers to Quick Tests**

Quick Test 1	Quick Test 2	Quick Test 3
1. F	3. F	5. T
2. T	4. T	6. F

Quick Test 4	Quick Test 5	Quick Test 6
7. F	9. F	11. F
8. T	10. T	12. T

Problem Solving and Managing Information

Learning Objectives

After studying this chapter, you should be able to

- Recognize and define a problem or a potential problem.

- List the nine steps in problem solving and decision making that lead to the removal of a problem's cause.

- Discuss the rational and intuitive approaches to decision making and explain cost-benefit analysis, decision trees, and ABC analysis.

- Describe a management information system and differentiate between data and information.

- Understand how supervisors can use information systems to implement open-book management.

- Discuss the impact on employees of computerized information handling systems and suggest ways to alleviate the stress associated with systematization.

① PROBLEMS: CAUSE AND EFFECT

CONCEPT ▶ Problems in organizations occur because of change, and they are revealed by gaps between expected and actual outcomes.

What, exactly, is a problem?

A problem has several defining characteristics. At its most complex, a problem is (a) an unsettled matter or disturbing condition (b) that raises puzzling questions as to its specific nature and (c) demands resolution by decisive action; however, (d) its proper settlement is often clouded by difficulty, uncertainty, and doubt, and—as a consequence—(e) it may require considerable thought and skill to find an effective solution. A simpler and more useful definition, however, is this: A *problem* exists when there is a substantial difference between an expected condition (such as that spelled out by a performance standard or departmental goal) and the actual condition that has occurred or is now occurring. Further, *supervisory problems* usually require making a choice from among multiple options to be considered. Given this simpler characterization, studies show that supervisors may solve as many as 80 problems a day. If this figure were only half true, supervisors are called upon to find answers to, or render decisions on, 10,000 problems a year. Thankfully, the great majority of these problems are minor. Nevertheless, the figures are staggering and are of major concern to every supervisor.

As a practical matter, it is helpful to think of problems as falling into two classifications:

Current problems. These are ones that have already been observed or are occurring right now. Examples include merchandise that has spoiled, a valued employee who has quit, costs that are running out of line, and shipments that are not meeting delivery dates. These need immediate solutions to correct what has already happened or what is now taking place.

Potential problems. These lie in the near future. Nevertheless, you must be alert to their eventual presence. You will recognize these in such forms as how to finish a certain project on time, when to assign overtime, where to place the new copy machine, and when to tell employees about an impending change in their work schedules. It is important that you identify such potential problems in advance. Then you can apply "preventive" problem solving to them.

Problems, and their solutions, are, of course, inseparably related to the management process. Problems arise all along the way. Supervisors must solve them when they plan, organize, staff, energize, and control. Otherwise, problems will interfere with the attainment of the department's goals.

Problems are often brought about by change. **How should supervisors deal with problems?** ▶

Problem solving. A process of systematically analyzing gaps between expected and actual conditions to find and remedy their causes.

What causes a problem?

Change does. If everything operated exactly as it should, and the situation remains as it has been, very few problems would occur. Unfortunately, change, especially unwanted change, is always with us—and increasingly so in the 21st century. Changes occur in materials, tools and equipment, employee attitudes, specifications received from customers, the work space itself, and just about anything else you can imagine. The trick to *problem solving* is often the ability to spot the unwanted and unexpected change that has slipped into an otherwise normal situation.

How can you recognize a problem or a potential problem?

A problem exists when there is a gap (or variance) between what you expect to happen and what actually happens (see Figure 5-1). Your budget, for example, calls for 2,200 insurance policies to be processed this week; the count at 5 P.M. on Friday shows that you completed only 1,975, a gap of 225 policies. Or you expected to hold the total number of employee absences in your department to 300 days this year; the total is 410, a gap of 110 days.

It is almost the same with potential problems. You know what you would like to have occur in the future: a project completed, a perfect safety record, fewer than 10 customer complaints. These are your plans. But when you look ahead at your procedures and the potential for mishaps, you think that your department will fall short of its targets—that there will be gaps. In a nutshell, you find problems by spotting a gap (deviation or variance) between actual and expected performance.

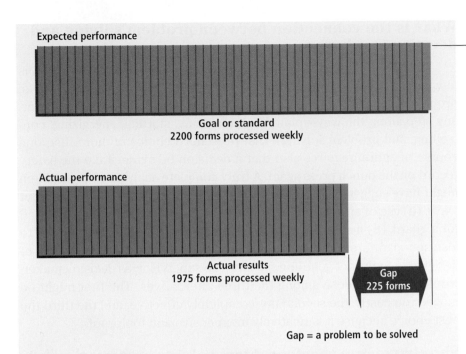

◆ **FIGURE 5-1**

How gaps between actual performance and goals, or standards, help to identify, or "find," problems. **What causes gaps to occur?**

Expected performance

Goal or standard
2200 forms processed weekly

Actual performance

Actual results
1975 forms processed weekly

Gap
225 forms

Gap = a problem to be solved

1	T or F	A problem exists when there is a gap between what you expect to happen and what is predicted to happen.
2	T or F	Current problems require corrective action; potential problems require preventive action.

◀ *Quick Test 1*

② SYSTEMATIC PROBLEM SOLVING

CONCEPT ▶ Problems should be approached systematically, with the goal of removing their causes.

How are problems solved?

By removing whatever it is that has caused, or will cause, a gap between the expected (or desired) condition and the actual condition. That's the main idea, at least. Suppose, for example, that your hoped-for safety record of zero accidents is spoiled by three accidents on the punch press machine. You will want to (a) find their cause (bypassing of the safety guard by the operators) and (b) remove it (by designing a foolproof guard).

Finding and removing the cause or causes, however, is usually difficult and requires considerable examination and thought. There will be more discussion about the problem-solving process later.

Quips & Quotes

You're either part of the solution or part of the problem.

—Eldridge Cleaver

What is the connection between problem solving and decision making?

The two processes are closely related (see Figure 5-2). A decision is always needed in the choice of the problem's solution. In many ways, problem solving involves **decision making.** As you will see in a moment, any step along the way—planning, organizing, staffing, energizing, controlling, and problem solving—that presents a choice of more than one course of action requires also that a decision be made. Take the safety record on the punch press again. A truly complete analysis of the problem might have suggested that the cause could be removed in three different ways: (a) use of an automatic feeding device that would remove the need for a guard, (b) institution of an educational and disciplinary program to instruct operators about the proper operation of the present guard, or (c) design of a foolproof guarding system. The supervisor, as decision maker, would have to choose among the three alternatives. The first might be judged too costly, the second not completely effective, and the third the best choice because it is relatively inexpensive and foolproof.

Should you approach problem solving systematically?

Yes. There are few exceptions to the rule that the best results come from a systematic approach. By moving from step to step progressively, you avoid the cardinal mistake in problem solving: jumping to a conclusion before you have fully explored all aspects of the problem. Here, as illustrated in Figure 5-2, is the fundamental approach to problem solving and decision making.

Step 1: State the problem clearly and specifically. Stay away from a general statement, such as "We have a problem with quality." Instead, narrow it down and put figures on it if you can, as in, "Between the first of the month and today, the number of rejects found at final inspection totaled 32, compared with our standard of 15 rejects."

Step 2: Collect all information relevant to the problem. Don't go too far afield, but do find data that may shed light on process changes, materials used, equipment function, design specifications, employee performance, and assignments. Much of the data will not tell you anything except where the source of the problem is not. If your information shows, for example, that there has been no change in the way materials have arrived or machinery has been used, good! You can look elsewhere.

Step 3: List as many possible causes for the problem as you can think of. Remember that a problem is a gap between expected and actual conditions. Something must have occurred to cause that gap. Most particularly, something must have been changed. Is the present operator different from the former one? Was a power source less regular than before? Has there been a change, however slight, in the specifications?

| 1. State the problem clearly. | 2. Collect relevant information. | 3. List possible causes. | 4. Select the most likely cause. | 5. Suggest alternative solutions. | 6. Evaluate alternatives. | 7. Choose one solution. | 8. Plan for imple-mentation. | 9. Implement and follow up |

Problem finding

Decision making

Problem solving

◆ **FIGURE 5-2** ————————

The problem-solving process. How problem solving and decision making overlap. **Why is using a systematic approach so important?**

Step 4: Select the cause or causes that seem most likely. Do this through a process of elimination. To test a cause to see if it is a probable one, try seeing (or thinking through) what difference it would make if that factor were returned to its original state. For example, suppose a possible cause of rejects is that compressed air power is now only 75 pounds instead of 90 pounds. Try making the product with the pressure restored to 90 pounds. If it makes no difference, then power irregularity is not a likely cause. Or perhaps you think that the new operator has misunderstood your instructions. Check this out with the operator. See if your instructions are, in fact, being followed exactly. If not, what happens when your instructions are followed? If the rejects stop, then this is a likely cause. If the rejects persist, this is not a likely cause.

Step 5: Suggest as many solutions as you can to remove causes or overcome obstacles. There is rarely only one way to solve a problem. If the cause of an employee's absenteeism, for instance, is difficulty in getting up in the morning, this cause can be removed in a number of ways. You might change the shift, insist that the employee buy an alarm clock, make a wake-up telephone call yourself, or show how failure to get to work is job threatening. The point is to list as many "cause removal" suggestions as possible.

Some causes, of course, cannot be removed, as when the problem arises from an edict for change (such as to "cut costs by 5 percent") received from above. If so, it is helpful at steps 3 and 4 to identify "obstacles to be removed" if the problem is to be solved. Then, at this step, look for ways to overcome the most difficult obstacles.

Step 6: Evaluate the pros and cons of each proposed solution. Some solutions will be better than others. But what does better mean? Cheaper? Faster? Surer? More participative? More in line with company policy? To judge which solution is best, you'll have to have a set of criteria like the ones just listed. Evaluation requires that you make judgments based on facts. Consult the information gathered in step 2. Also, consult anyone who can offer informed opinions about the criteria you have chosen.

Step 7: Choose the solution (or combination of solutions) you think is best. Yes, this—like what you did in step 6—is the decision phase of problem solving. In effect, you will have weighed all the chances of success against the risks of failure. The strengths of your solution should exceed its weaknesses.

Step 8: Spell out a plan of action to carry out your solution. Decisions require action, so you should indicate how to implement the solution. Pin down exactly what will be done and how, who will do it, where, and when. How much money can be spent? What resources can be used? What is the deadline?

TABLE 5-1

Guide for Seeking Help in Problem Solving and Decision Making

Factors	1. You Decide Alone	2. You Consult with One of Your Employees	3. You Consult with a Group of Your Employees
Whose problem is it?	Yours alone	His or hers	The group's (ours)
Amount of time	None available	Have some time available	Plenty of time available
Expertise	You are fully expert	Expert advice is needed to fill gaps in your own knowledge	Yes, as for no. 2
Technical know-how	You have full know-how	Need to fill in gaps in your technical know-how	Yes, as for no. 2
Can others add anything to the decision?	No	Yes	Yes
Will you accept suggestions?	No, not likely	Yes, from someone you respect	Yes, from an effective unit
Will it help others to carry out the project if they are involved in the decision?	No significance; you will carry out the project yourself	Yes, helpful and essential	Yes, necessary and essential
Coordination of effort	Not needed; you will handle it all	Necessary either with your superior or your employee	Needed and necessary among your employees
Learning value	No value to anyone else	Potential value to the employee	Potential value to your whole group

Step 9: Implement the solution, and follow up. Decisions, by themselves, are quite passive unless they are put into action. Follow the steps specified in the solution, and then monitor the results to see if the problem initially identified has been eased to your satisfaction. Without taking this critical step, you will never be able to improve your problem-solving skills!

When should you solve problems on your own, and when should you go to others for help?

This depends upon a number of factors. Table 5-1 shows how to look at the whole picture before deciding to handle a problem on your own or to ask another person or a group of employees for assistance.

3	T or F	Problem solving is one part of the larger decision-making process.	◄ *Quick Test 2*
4	T or F	The first step in problem solving is to collect all relevant information.	

③ DECISION MAKING: RATIONAL AND INTUITIVE

CONCEPT ▶ Decisions are the logical outcome of problem solving.

How can you recognize the need for a decision?

Whenever there is more than one way of doing things, a decision is needed. Any kind of choice, alternative, or option calls for a decision. You might ask, "If this is so, why are so many decision opportunities overlooked?" The answer is that managers and supervisors alike get overly comfortable with the status quo, and even fixated on it. In effect, they say, "If it ain't broke, don't fix it." Such supervisors miss the point that there are always alternatives. There is always the choice to do something or not to do it, to speak or to remain silent, to correct or to let well enough alone. All too often a supervisor's decision is made by default. The supervisor does nothing. The tide of events carries the department until a crisis occurs. In reality, however, doing nothing represents a choice. It is a decision not to change, not to plan for improvement, not to anticipate a potential problem.

How systematic must the decision-making process be?

Most decisions should be systematically approached, but only up to a point, unlike the purely problem-solving steps. A systematic approach to decision making (often called the rational or logical approach) should be followed through step 6 (evaluating the pros and cons of each proposed solution) and well into step 7 (choosing the solution you think best). At that point, it may help to give some weight to your intuition before making the final choice. Decisions that affect the future, even if the future is only tomorrow, always contain a degree of uncertainty that logic cannot fully remove. In view of the limits of logic, many authorities believe that at this point you can often draw valuable insights from that part of your brain from which hunches, premonitions, unconscious thoughts, and creative ideas emerge. Intuition can also be useful at step 5, where you are trying to generate the maximum number of possible solutions.

Are decisions based on intuition as good as those based on logic?

If a decision works out well, it won't make any difference how it was reached. Many decisions based on hunches have proved to be correct. They are harder to explain and defend, however, when they go wrong. More important, any decision is likely to be better if its goals are clearly understood. The logical approach helps to strip away distractions and irrelevancies. Intuition often adds a valuable dimension by calling on some inner sense we don't clearly understand. Many authorities believe the best decisions come from the dual approach—a combination of logic and hunch.

What is meant by mathematical decision making?

Mathematical decision making refers to the use of certain mathematical, statistical, or quantitative techniques to aid the decision maker. These aids are very valuable in many instances, but they are only aids. The techniques do not make decisions. They arrange numerical information in such a way that it can be analyzed mathematically, but the executive, manager, or supervisor must make the final decision on the basis of an interpretation of the results. Further, the benefits of mathematical analyses are very dependent on the quality and relevance of inputs received ("garbage in; garbage out").

How can supervisors make use of decision trees?

Decision tree. A graphic portrait of the possible outcomes of alternative solutions.

A ***decision tree*** is essentially a graphic portrait of steps 5 and 6 in the problem-solving process. It shows how each alternative solution forks into various possibilities. Suppose, for example, that a supervisor is faced with a decision about how to treat Edgar, an employee whose attendance has been very poor. One alternative (A_1) is to enforce strict discipline by laying Edgar off for three days. A second alternative (A_2) is to provide constructive encouragement. A third alternative (A_3) is to try a little of both. Figure 5-3 shows how these alternatives work on a decision tree.

The supervisor can presume that there are only three ways Edgar can react. He may respond only to strict discipline, he may respond only to encouragement, or he may respond favorably to both. The probable changes in performance from each kind of response are diagrammed, with outcomes ranging from very little improvement to great improvement. Thus, the improvement in Edgar's performance differs according to each decision strategy and to each possibility of how Edgar might respond to it.

Edgar may react three different ways to the A_1 alternative. If he responds to discipline, there may be great improvement; if he responds only to encouragement, then there will be very little improvement. Or, if he responds favorably to both discipline and encouragement, there may be moderate improvement. Similarly, Edgar may react three different ways to alternatives A_2 and A_3. The decision tree helps the supervisor to visualize the various outcomes or possible changes in Edgar's performance. On the basis of such an analysis, you may be better able to choose the alternative that has the best chance of being effective.

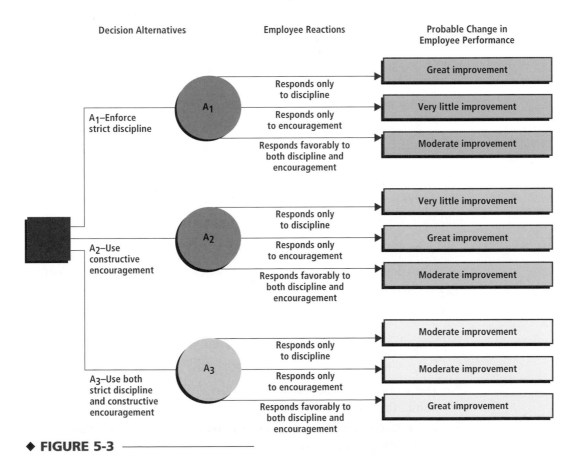

◆ **FIGURE 5-3**

Example of a decision tree. Alternative outcomes of various applications of discipline versus constructive encouragement in trying to improve an employee's performance. **Does a decision tree replace the problem-solving process?**

Even if you never construct a decision tree on your own, keep the concept in mind. It will add another dimension to how you think about alternative paths to choose from and their consequences.

What is meant by cost-benefit analysis?

Cost-benefit analysis. A technique for weighing the pros and cons of alternative courses of action.

It is not unlike the closing steps in problem solving and decision making. This is the phase in which you examine the pros and cons of each proposed solution. ***Cost-benefit analysis*** adds all the costs (both quantitative and qualitative) of implementation and compares them with the projected value of the resulting product or services. This type of analysis has become a popular technique for evaluating proposals in the public sector. Take, for example, a proposal for a local government to offer a child care service to its residents. Typically, the benefits of such nonprofit services are hard to quantify; that is, it is hard to place a dollar value on them. Accordingly, many cost-benefit analyses include qualitative judgments of benefits as well as dollar estimates. These analyses also need to identify any *unintended* consequences of proposed solutions.

Cost-benefit analysis is similar to *input-output analysis*, which is an attempt to make sure that the cost and effort expended in carrying out a decision will at least be balanced by its outputs, or results. In business, when outputs exceed inputs, the result is a profit. If there is an excess of benefits over costs in nonprofit organizations, the excess is called a *surplus*.

What is a *programmed decision*?

Programmed decision. A solution to a recurring problem that can be established for continual use every time the problem reappears.

Decisions that are spelled out in advance by a standard procedure or policy are said to be "programmed." That is, a supervisor has only to identify the problem correctly as one that has arisen before. There's no point in solving it a second time. As a consequence, the supervisor simply applies the previous solution or the decision that is dictated by standard procedures and policies. By avoiding the necessity of having to "reinvent the wheel" each time the same problem comes up, a supervisor saves time and energy.

Some problems occur so frequently that you can set up a routine decision for them. You must remember, however, that what worked before may not work again. It can be risky to follow past experience blindly without considering other possible solutions.

When should you engage in group decision making?

Only whenever *all* these factors are in play:

- The work group can contribute information, know-how, and viewpoints that you need but don't have.
- You are truly ready to respect their opinions and are prepared to act on their suggestions.
- You sense that such participation is needed to induce a commitment from the group to implement the decision.
- You've got adequate time.

Seeking help from a work team in making a decision involves the same considerations as were charted in Table 5-1 for problem solving. In any event, be forewarned that such a consultative approach should not be taken lightly. Employees who participate will be resentful if they sense that they are being manipulated. Their involvement in the process, while not necessarily at an equal level of authority with yours, must be absolutely genuine. Otherwise, the process will backfire and you will be worse off than if you hadn't gotten them involved.

What can be done to make your decisions more effective?

Besides starting with a specific goal in mind and laying a foundation of facts and systematic analysis, there are two other kinds of insurance to which you can turn.

Pick your spots. Try to make decisions only where the potential for payoff is great. You can identify this kind of opportunity by using ABC analysis (see Figure 5-4). The ABC analysis concept is based on an established economic fact: A vital few problems or opportunities for action account for the greatest loss or greatest gain. Most problems and opportunities are basically of little consequence. Statisticians call this the *80/20 principle*. It means that 80 percent of your problems will account for only 20 percent of your losses or profits. Conversely, 20 percent of your problems (the vital few) will account for 80 percent of your losses or profits. In ABC analysis, the vital few are called A items; the inconsequential many, C items; and those that fall somewhere in between, B items. If you were to take an inventory of items in your stockroom, for example, it is a sure bet that a relatively few items would account for most of its value. A great many items, however, such as paper clips and

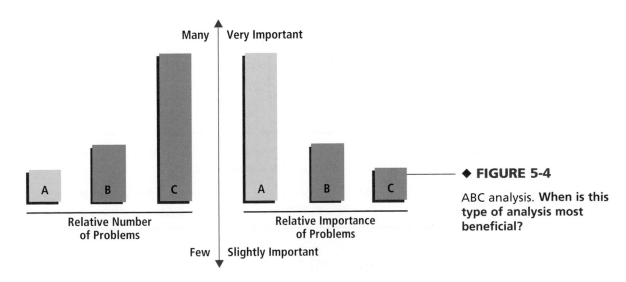

◆ FIGURE 5-4

ABC analysis. **When is this type of analysis most beneficial?**

PLAYING THE ROLE

■ The next time you are participating in a group problem-solving meeting, make an explicit effort to play each of the following roles (as they seem appropriate). There are two keys to success: (1) being aware of *when* they are needed, and (2) having the *flexibility and willingness* to apply them. The six roles are

1. Data-gatherer—Solicit information, ideas, and opinions from others
2. Rational person—Provide key facts and relevant information

3. Emotion-injector—Express the depth and breadth of feelings on an issue
4. Uplifter—Offer your assessment of the benefits and advantages
5. Devil's advocate—Identify the costs, drawbacks, and disadvantages
6. Evaluator—Place everything in perspective, considering all inputs

   The likely result will be wider respect for your contributions as well as better decisions from the group, and that is a win-win product!

---

erasers, would account for only a small portion of the inventory's total worth. Astute purchasing managers concentrate on the vital few items, not the trivial many. You should apply the same principles to your selection of problems and decisions to address.

Maintain your perspective. Statistically, problems fall in what is called a *normal distribution*, and so do the results of most decisions. We say, "You win some and you lose some." That's really what a normal distribution tells us. If you make 10 decisions, one or two will work out fine. One or two are likely to be "bombs." The rest will fall somewhere in between. Knowing this, you should keep the following guidelines in mind when you make decisions. These will help you to improve your "batting average."

1. Don't reach too high. Don't set your objectives at the very top; allow some room for mistakes.
2. Don't overcommit or overextend your resources on one problem; you may need them later for an unanticipated problem.
3. Always prepare a backup approach (often called plan B), a way to alter your course and attain at least part of the objective.

| *Quick Test 3* ▶ | **5** | T or F | A decision tree is a graphic portrait of the nine steps in the problem-solving process. |
| | **6** | T or F | Unless the costs (inputs) exceed the benefits (outputs), there is little reason to proceed with a proposed solution. |

INFORMATION AS
④ A RAW MATERIAL

CONCEPT ▶ Information is the substance with which problems are solved and decisions are made.

In seeking information to solve a problem or make a decision, what should be the cutoff point?

Stop looking when the trouble and cost of obtaining the extra information exceeds its value. The rule is: The more critical and lasting the effect of the decision, the more you can afford to look for the last scrap of vital information. Don't spend two days hunting for background data on a purchasing decision, for example, if the item plays an insignificant part in your process and will be used only once or twice. On the other hand, it might pay to defer a decision to hire a full-time employee until you have made a reference check.

Do guard against using the absence of information as an excuse for procrastination. Some decisions are especially hard to arrive at and unpleasant to carry out. When you are faced with these situations, there is a temptation to put off an answer (yes, answers are decisions—or should be) by asking for more information. Rarely is the questioner fooled by this tactic, and rarely does the additional information add much to the quality of the decision. Therefore, *practice being decisive.*

Computers make it possible for organizations to develop enormous data banks. **How do managers at all levels use data banks?** ▼

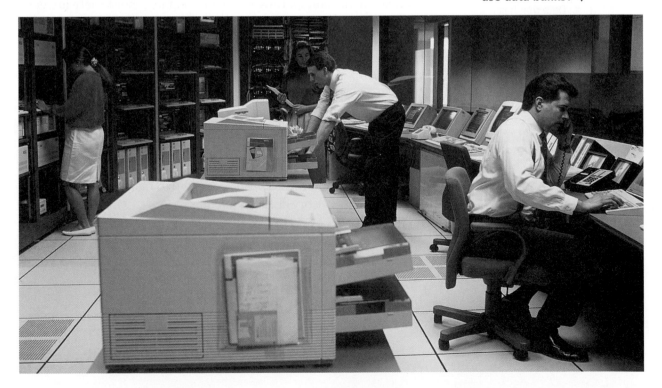

The burden of information collection and analysis has now become so enormous, however, that most organizations provide support with some form of management information system.

What, really, is a management information system? Why has it become so important?

You may better understand a *management information system (MIS)* if you compare it to an accounting system. Like the traditional accounting system, it collects data from an organization's operations, sorts it out, analyzes it, and delivers consolidated reports to a manager for use in planning and control, problem solving, and decision making. The two systems, however, differ enormously in terms of the amount of data accumulated and the speed and complexity of the sorting-out and analytical process. It's no surprise that the ultra-high speed "facilitator" is the computer. This makes an MIS a network of computer-based, as well as manual, data processing procedures that provide timely and useful information for managers in carrying out their work.

The ultimate objective of an MIS is to tie together all of an organization's past and present data into a very large library with instant electronic recall. Managers at all levels draw from this library (called a *data bank*) any kind of information that aids short-range or long-term decisions. The goal is to create a fully integrated MIS system.

Should a distinction be made between data and information?

It may seem like hairsplitting, but MIS designers insist there are good reasons to distinguish between them.

Data can be described as merely facts and figures that, until processed, contribute little to decision making.

Information is data that has been processed for specific use by managers and supervisors in problem solving and decision making related to planning, organizing, staffing, energizing, and controlling.

Quick Test 4 ▶			
7	T or F	Data are like raw materials (facts and figures); information has been processed to make it useful for supervisory decision making.
8	T or F	Supervisory decisions can be made easily despite the absence of vital information.

⑤ AN MIS OF YOUR OWN

CONCEPT ▶ Supervisors are vital participants in an organization's management information system.

Where do supervisors fit in the MIS computer picture?

Supervisors become involved in computer operations in two basic ways:

1. You may simply be an *end user* of the MIS. If so, make the most of these outputs. Understand what they mean, what you are supposed to derive from them, and what kind of actions you are supposed to take on the basis of them. Is the computer printout you get a yard long but only six items apply directly to you? Should you make a correction today? Or can you wait until the next report before you get moving?

2. You may be a *prime source* of inputs. If so, find out specifically what information your department is sending to the computer. Which records are selected for keyboarding? Exactly what form should they be in when they leave your department? Are the measures your employees are collecting exactly the same as those required for the computer? For example, are you tallying in inches when the computer needs metric figures? Or are you transmitting daily figures when the computer wants hourly data?

Can supervisors design their own management information systems?

Yes. Even if their parent organizations have an MIS, supervisors can and should develop their own concept of how information needed for decisions is gathered and routed to them. Figure 5-5(a) shows a basic management information system. Figure 5-5(b) shows how a supervisor can adopt the same principle to explain departmental information needs, sources, and uses. *Primary data* is new information that is collected and analyzed for the specific purpose of running a particular operation. *Secondary data* is any useful information previously collected for another purpose and published by trade associations, business magazines, the U.S. government, or any other source outside the department.

Secondary data for your department may simply be the data you can gather from other departments in your own company, agency, or institution.

In Figure 5-5(b), the supervisor set performance standards at 500 units a day, labor costs at $4,000 a week, and the average weekly reject rate at 1.5 percent. The supervisor based the decisions for these standards on past records for the department and on what could be learned about industry standards for similar operations.

To make the MIS work, the supervisor requested the following: daily output figures from the shop clerk; weekly labor costs gathered from the time cards, processed by the payroll section, and recorded by the accounting department; and the weekly defects rate from the quality control department.

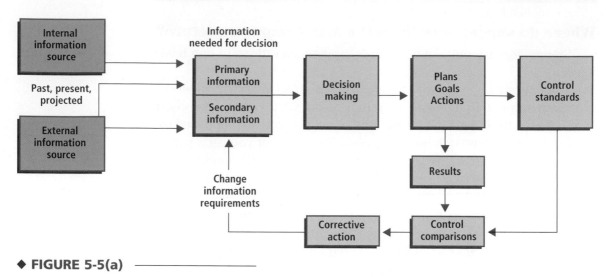

◆ **FIGURE 5-5(a)** ─────────────

Basic components of a management information system. **What is the difference between primary and secondary data?**

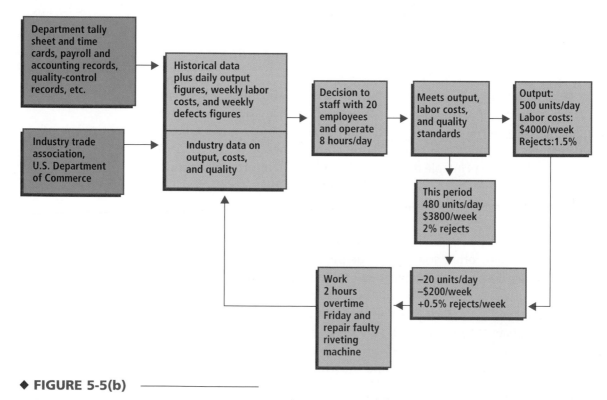

◆ **FIGURE 5-5(b)** ─────────────

Assembly supervisor's departmental information system. **What solutions resulted?**

For this week, the supervisor's daily output has been only 480, or 20 below standard. Labor costs were $3,800, or $200 less than budgeted. The weekly reject rate was up to 2 percent, or 0.5 percent over standard. On the basis of these control comparisons, the supervisor has decided to take corrective action. The entire staff will work overtime for two hours on Friday to raise output. The supervisor will also place a maintenance request to fix a faulty riveting machine, to which the higher reject rate is attributed.

Should employees have access to information from MIS?

Yes! According to author John Case and others, the best way to do this is through a program called **open-book management**. Many companies are now sharing a wide range of financial (e.g., sales, expenses) and operating (e.g., productivity data, absenteeism rates) information with employees. Along with "opening the books," they also train their workers to understand and use the data, emphasize how each employee's work can influence the financial results, empower employees to make decisions leading to improvements, post the key results conspicuously, and hold celebrations when milestones are achieved. Many organizations then provide bonus rewards to those employees whose actions led to success and allow others to participate in the gain via stock ownership programs. Clearly, MIS systems have made open-book management possible.

Open-book management. The practice of sharing extensive information with employees, training and empowering them to use it, and rewarding them for the results.

9	T or F	Supervisors have a role to play in MIS systems as both sources and end users of inputs.	◀ *Quick Test 5*
10	T or F	For open-book management to work well, employees need to be trained in how to use the information wisely.	

6 KEEPING THE SYSTEM HUMAN

CONCEPT ▶ Computerized handling of information introduces problems of stress and adjustment to a supervisor's workforce.

How does computer-based information handling affect people at work?

Computer-generated information has its good aspects and its unfavorable ones. Even these draw conflicting responses. For example, consider these views:

1. **Systematic information and reports reduce job tensions and conflicts by making things more orderly.** There will always be conflict among people, jobs, and operations. The computer should

lessen the intensity of conflict, however, because the interfaces will be fixed and predictable. Once an information issue is resolved between the production and the maintenance supervisors, it should be less bothersome, because it will arise in the same manner each time and can be anticipated.

2. **Systematization creates job dissatisfaction because it requires that individuals fit their work into a rigidly prescribed format.** Those employees who dislike close supervision and control will feel the same way about any system that makes similar demands. Supervisors must do a better job than in the past of placing people in work that best suits their concept of job satisfaction.

3. **Systematization tends to make work monotonous because it reduces the opportunity to be creative.** If the job is one that is fully dominated by the system, this will be true. People who prefer routine to initiative may like it, however. For many jobs, the computer has just the opposite effect. It removes the routine and calls out for creative solutions to the problems it identifies.

4. **Systematization depersonalizes work; people serve the machine more than the machine serves people.** This is unfortunately true at lower levels of employment. At skilled and managerial levels, however, the system takes over much of the tiresome work and allows people to devote a greater portion of their efforts to work that matches their education, experience, and capabilities.

What can be done to make employees more receptive to MIS and to computers in general?

Management information systems and other applications of computer technology are with all of us to stay. Happily, employees coming out of high schools and colleges today are much more familiar with it than are those of previous generations. Nevertheless, there are several positive approaches that you as a supervisor should take.

Internet CONNECTION

Check out timely topics in **Human Resource Management** on the Internet.

1. **Try to reduce tension by allowing employees to bring their irritations into the open.** Tempers are likely to flare highest when a new system is being debugged. Suppose Helen says, "Nothing matters anymore except getting the data to the electronic monster on time." Try responding like this: "I agree that the computer now seems to be dominating our work in the department. Perhaps it won't be that way once we get used to it. After all, look how we adjust ourselves to the exact time for a TV show or a sports event. Let's stick with it and see if we can get the better of this situation."

2. **Acknowledge that it is only normal to be fearful of what the computer may do to jobs and job security.** Suppose that Trang says, "When they redesigned the last computer setup, six people in the payroll section were transferred to the sales order department,

and not one of them likes it over there. What's going to happen when these MIS analysts finish up with us next month?" Don't dismiss Trang's fear as something silly. Instead, agree that computers and information systems have made changes in the company. And, yes, some of these changes have been hard to accept. But assure Trang that you will do whatever you can do to make certain that higher management is aware of her present contributions. You will also look around to see where and how her talents can best be used if there is a change in her job.

3. **Focus your attention on trying to make sure that people are assigned to the work they do best and like best.** Abe, Hillary, and Malcolm like routine work so that they can socialize to the maximum; assign them to repetitive work that is undemanding mentally. Ella, Donna, and Vortek have strong creative qualities; assign them to work that requires initiative. All six persons may have to work in a computer-oriented world, but usually enough different kinds of work are available to satisfy individual preferences. People and job matches won't be perfect, of course. But when supervisors show they are willing to make the effort, this act in itself helps to counteract anxieties about computers depersonalizing the work.

4. **Help your employees see the benefits of MIS.** One of the greatest potential advantages is the creation of a *learning organization.* Here, organizations use their computer systems to catalog, systematically sort, and make available a wide range of evolving expertise and knowledge to other employees. As one person learns or creates something, the new knowledge is entered into an MIS where it is instantly available to help others in the company. Cooperative learning takes place, and co-workers across the country are able to gain and apply new techniques almost instantly. Learning organizations have spawned the need for systematic *knowledge management* programs, where companies seek to gain a competitive edge by identifying what they don't know, need to know, and already know. In this way, employees with a question can benefit by using the MIS to search out others with valuable expertise. Additionally, as employees upgrade their own skills, they receive the psychic benefit of being consulted (and praised!) by others throughout the organization. Supervisors need to train their employees to use the knowledge management system for the benefit of themselves and others.

Learning organization. A company in which new ways of thinking are nurtured, people are continually learning how to learn, and the results are widely shared and used at all levels.

Knowledge management. The process of creating and using human and technological networks to capitalize on a company's expertise, experience, and learning.

| 11 | T or F | The effects of systematization of information handling are almost always clearly negative. |
| 12 | T or F | Everyone plays a role in creating a learning organization, not just the corporate training department. |

◀ *Quick Test 6*

KEY CONCEPTS TO REMEMBER

1. **Problems: Cause and Effect.** Effective supervisors are able to (a) recognize the existence of a problem or the need for a decision, (b) anticipate potential trouble spots, and (c) identify opportunities for improvement. Problems are caused by changes or other factors that disturb normal procedures or conditions. Problems can be recognized by a gap between what is expected (or planned) to happen and what actually occurs.

2. **Systematic Problem Solving.** Problems are solved by removing or correcting the cause of the disturbance, which, in turn, closes the gap in performance. Problem solving should always be approached systematically. The process can often be improved by seeking help from those individuals or groups of employees who are best informed and/or more closely involved in the problem and in implementing its solution.

3. **Decision Making: Rational and Intuitive.** Decision making is an inseparable part of the problem-solving process. It is the phase in which solutions, ideas, and new courses of action are examined critically and then chosen on the basis of their chances for success or failure in meeting related objectives. Decision making may be approached mathematically—using a variety of techniques, such as the decision tree—or intuitively. It is always more effective, however, when based on firm objectives and sound information. Work groups can make useful contributions to problem solving and decision making, but their involvement must be genuine.

4. **Information as a Raw Material.** Effective problem solving depends on the quantity and quality of information upon which analysis and judgments are made. Increasingly, formal management information systems (MISs) provide operational information for decision-making purposes in a convenient form for managers and supervisors.

5. **An MIS of Your Own.** Supervisors stand at both ends of the MIS and computer systems. As end users, they receive computer outputs that provide them with operational and cost data. As prime sources of input, supervisors collect and transmit all sorts of sales, production, quality, and cost data to the system. MIS principles also allow the use of open-book management that puts important information in the hands of all employees.

6. **Keeping the System Human.** Computerized information gathering and monitoring pose a real or imagined threat to many employees. Supervisors should face these problems openly and try to reduce tensions and dissatisfactions by making job assignments as attractive as possible and by accenting the benefits that employees will receive.

READING COMPREHENSION

1. How would you recognize the existence of a problem?
2. What is the primary cause of most problems? Why do they occur?
3. Differentiate between problem solving and decision making.
4. Under what circumstances might it be better for supervisors to seek help in solving a problem rather than handling it all by themselves?
5. If you were asked to decide which of five projects might be chosen for a public health care program under your supervision, what technique might you use? Why?
6. Supply some examples of how a company's policies, rules, or standard procedures help to "program" a decision for a supervisor.
7. What four requirements must be met if participation of a work group in the decision-making process is to be successful?
8. Distinguish between data and information.
9. Which of the following are considered primary data for a supervisor's departmental MIS? Production tallies collected at the end of the day, inventory-status records retrieved from a company's central data file, a count of errors that have occurred in the department during the week, comparative cost data from the U.S. Department of Commerce.
10. The development of a learning organization may create both favorable and unfavorable working conditions. Describe these and explain what a supervisor might do to improve an employee's ability to adapt to these conditions.

APPLICATION

Self-Assessment

How good are your problem-solving skills?

Read the following statements carefully. Circle the number on the response scale that most closely reflects the degree to which each statement accurately describes you. Add up your total points and prepare a brief action plan for self-improvement. Be ready to report your score for tabulation across the entire group.

	Good Description									Poor Description
1. I regularly monitor the actual performance in my department and compare it to expected levels to uncover variances.	10	9	8	7	6	5	4	3	2	1
2. When problems appear in my area, I can usually see them coming in advance.	10	9	8	7	6	5	4	3	2	1
3. I am aware that more problems than normal can be expected under conditions of rapid or frequent change.	10	9	8	7	6	5	4	3	2	1

	Good Description									Poor Description

4. As soon as a major problem appears, I try to create a clear statement of it that highlights the gap clearly and specifically.

10 9 8 7 6 5 4 3 2 1

5. When solving a problem, I generally try to brainstorm as many solutions as I can before selecting one.

10 9 8 7 6 5 4 3 2 1

6. I recognize the importance of differentiating between problem finding, problem solving, and decision making.

10 9 8 7 6 5 4 3 2 1

7. I usually follow a systematic process of choosing whether to decide alone, consult an employee, or involve a group of employees.

10 9 8 7 6 5 4 3 2 1

8. I consciously try to focus my attention on the 20 percent of problems that account for about 80 percent of my results.

10 9 8 7 6 5 4 3 2 1

9. I feel very comfortable following the key steps in implementing an open-book management process.

10 9 8 7 6 5 4 3 2 1

10. I take systematic actions to ensure that my employees feel like they are part of a learning organization.

10 9 8 7 6 5 4 3 2 1

Scoring and Interpretation

SCORING

Add up your total points for the 10 questions. Record that number here, and report it when it is requested. _____

INTERPRETATION

81 to 100 points. You seem to have a basic set of problem-solving and information management skills.

61 to 80 points. Take a close look at some of your problem-solving and information management skills (those with lower self-assessments) and discuss them with a manager to see if they need improvement.

Below 60 points. Some of your skills may be substantially inconsistent with effective problem-solving and information management practices and could be detrimental to your success as a supervisor.

Identify your three lowest scores and record the question numbers here: _____, _____, _____.

ACTION

Write a brief paragraph detailing an action plan for how you might sharpen each of these skills. Then pay particularly close attention to the related material in the chapter as you review the relevant sections there.

Analyzing the Potential for Open-Book Management

Assume that your manager asked you to study the practice of open-book management, and make a recommendation regarding this question: "Should this organization implement open-book management at this time?" To prepare your report, you will likely wish to scan both of John Case's books on the subject (*Open-Book Management* and *The Open-Book Experience*), ask some employees for their reactions, scan the Internet for relevant information, and interview some managers for their reactions. In particular, you should identify the likely positive consequences of open-book management as well as the probable negative consequences on the worksheet below.

Positive Effects

1. _____
2. _____
3. _____
4. _____
5. _____
6. _____
7. _____

Negative Effects

1. _____
2. _____
3. _____
4. _____
5. _____
6. _____
7. _____

ACTION

Following your analysis of the effects of this change, state a conclusion that you would be comfortable supporting. (Note that this is an exercise that builds on the availability of timely financial and operating information, as well as the willingness of the organization to provide the MIS-generated data freely to all employees. The exercise also gives you an opportunity to demonstrate your cost-benefit analytical skills.)

Chapter 5 ▲ Problem Solving and Managing Information   **121**

Group Exercise

▶ *Problem Solving*

STEP 1: Form into groups of six. Select a problem to address, such as "How to make this course more exciting." Agree to follow the problem-solving steps outlined in the chapter.

STEP 2: Be sure to generate an explicit analysis of both the costs and benefits of your final recommendation.

STEP 3: During the discussion, each person should note who plays each of the six roles, and how often they do so, by placing a check mark in the appropriate box below each time you note a contribution from that person.

STEP 4: When the group is finished with its task, answer the following questions:

1. What role does each person think exemplified his or her primary contributions?

   Provide feedback to each person about your observational data on their roles.

2. What role(s) seemed to be over/underemphasized in the group? Why?

3. Are there other types of roles that would be useful in a group such as this?

Group Members

Member Roles	A	B	C	D	E	F
Data-gatherer						
Rational person						
Emotion-injector						
Uplifter						
Devil's advocate						
Evaluator						

Case 13

The Big Cookie Burnout

What seemed like a simple problem with an obvious solution turned out to be anything but that. It happened in the baking department of one of the nation's largest cookie makers. Too many batches of cookies, more than 10,000 dozen of them, were spoiled due to overheating. And when the finger-pointing was over, it was Arsenio, the department supervisor, who ended up as the fall guy.

Arsenio hadn't intended it that way. In fact, he was so sure that Joanna, the chief baker on the oven line, was at fault that he suspended her on the spot. It had seemed like an open-and-shut case. Chief bakers were supposed to monitor oven temperatures continuously, even though temperatures were automatically controlled by a sophisticated series of thermostats. The chief baker could override the automatic controls, however, if at any time she felt that the oven was getting hotter or colder than the optimum temperature. This was accomplished by switching the control to "Manual" and then manipulating a lever to increase or decrease the flame levels in the oven.

Monitoring was easily accomplished by observing a number of temperature-indicating devices. The main temperature indicator was an automatic recorder mounted at the chief baker's workstation at the front end of a 200-foot-long oven. It was there that the raw cookies entered the oven. The cookies had previously been formed by an extruding machine that squeezed the dough mixture through a battery of nozzles onto a stainless-steel conveyor belt. After entering the oven, the belt automatically carried the cookies through the oven at a predetermined speed. According to the kind of cookies being baked, it took from 12 to 18 minutes for them to move from one end of the oven to the other.

Besides the main temperature recorder, temperature indicators were mounted every 50 feet or so along the oven's side. The automatic temperature controls could also be switched to manual control at each of these points.

On the day of what came to be known as the Big Burnout, the cookies were not just "overdone," they were burnt to a crisp. So, after first blowing his stack and shunting the spoiled cookies to the garbage truck, Arsenio demanded of Joanna, "How could you ever have let this happen?"

"I can't understand it," said Joanna. "I never left my workstation. I must have looked at the recorder a dozen times during that period. And while oven temperatures were nudging the high side occasionally, they always seemed within the control limits."

"So," said Arsenio, "you were too lazy to get off your duff and check the oven-side thermometers."

"That's not true. I can't remember whether or not I checked them because I was talking with the extruder-machine operator at that time about a problem he was having with his equipment. That distracted me."

"That's no excuse," said Arsenio, "and I don't believe for a moment you were talking about machine problems. You were probably arguing about last night's ball game. Anyway, your job is to watch the ovens, not to chat with every person in the shop. And no matter what the main recorder indicated, you're supposed to be monitoring the oven-side thermometers. It's obvious that somewhere along the line, temperatures got too high, and you should have been there to take over. By not doing your job right, you made a big mistake that cost the company a lot of money. So, I'm going to suspend you for a couple of days to give you a chance to get your head straight about this job."

To Arsenio's dismay, Joanna's suspension did not stick. The reason? After listening to Joanna's story, the bakery manager asked the plant engineer to examine the oven equipment. The plant engineer found that temperatures indicated by the main recorder were accurate, as were all the oven-side thermometers. He also checked the automatic temperature controls and found them to be functioning properly. He then asked the extruder-machine operator about the problems Joanna had spoken of. "The nozzles have been jamming lately," said the operator, "and I've had to shut the belts down from time to time to clean them."

"Don't you realize," said the plant engineer, "that when you shut the belt down, the belt in the oven stops, too? It's no wonder the cookies burned up. Next time you want to stop the belt, be sure to let the chief baker know in advance. Meanwhile, we'll see if we can't adjust the automatic temperature control system so as to avoid this problem."

Analysis ▶

What do you think of Arsenio's approach to handling this problem? Of the five alternative opinions provided below, which do you think is most appropriate? Rank the alternatives on a scale from 1 (most appropriate) to 5 (least appropriate). You may add another alternative, if you wish. Be prepared to justify your ranking.

_____ **a.** Arsenio was justified in suspending Joanna because he had no way of knowing the whole story at the time.

_____ **b.** The suspension was justified because no matter what the extruder-machine operator had done, the chief baker should have discovered the belt stoppage before damage was done.

_____ **c.** Arsenio's only mistake was that he did not clearly identify and specify the problem to begin with.

_____ **d.** Arsenio's biggest mistake was to jump to a conclusion without having all the facts.

_____ **e.** Arsenio solved the problem as best he could under the circumstances.

Case 14

The Uncertain Reduction in Force

The commissioner of a federal agency sent this directive to its regional offices: "Due to an unanticipated reduction in funding, all offices will be expected to reduce their staffs by 10 percent by the quarter's end. We regret this decision, but we have been advised that due to improvements in our procedures, there should be a similar decrease in employee workloads. Please make your plans accordingly."

When this notice arrived on the desk of Kathy M., supervisor of a 10-person clerical unit of a regional office, she said to herself, "No problem." Kathy believed that the reduction could easily be reached by the transfer or separation of Joey, her least productive employee. She notified him of her decision immediately.

Unfortunately for Kathy, several things soon occurred to make the reduction in force (RIF) directive become a major problem: (1) Joey objected to the method used for selecting him to be RIFed, and he filed a grievance; (2) when queried, the agency issued a policy memo that pointed to the selection of an individual other than Joey for separation; (3) one clerk got sick and another quit before the quarter ended; (4) the workload did not diminish as promised; (5) the staff mounted a slowdown as their response to the threatened cuts; (6) at the last minute, the agency found additional funding and modified its directive to advise that the effective date of the RIF would be postponed until the end of the next quarter.

◀ *Analysis*

a. Should Kathy have waited before telling Joey of her decision? Why or why not?

b. What should Kathy do now? In other words, how should she go about solving the potential problem, which will need a solution by the end of the next quarter?

Case 15

The Blue Jeans MIS

"What's that pile of papers on your desk?" asked Dora's friend, who supervised the department next door to Dora's.

"Oh, that!" answered Dora, who supervised the customer service section. "They're the latest batch of reports from data processing . . . and also last week's reports and the reports from the week before that."

"How can you get by without studying them?" asked her friend.

"A better question is how would I ever get time to look at them," said Dora. "They are more a nuisance than a help. Half the stuff in them doesn't even apply to my department. And most of the rest arrives too late to do me any good or doesn't tell me what I really want to know. Besides, I'd rather fly this department by the seat of my blue jeans than get cross-eyed looking at an endless batch of figures."

"You're sure laid back," said Dora's friend, "but if I were you, I'd ask the MIS people if they couldn't do something to make your reports more useful to you."

Analysis ▶

---

a. What is wrong with Dora's attitude toward the MIS reports she now receives?

b. What might the MIS people do to make the reports more useful to her?

Answers to Quick Tests ▶

Quick Test 1	Quick Test 2	Quick Test 3
1. F	3. F	5. F
2. T	4. F	6. F

Quick Test 4	Quick Test 5	Quick Test 6
7. T	9. T	11. F
8. F	10. T	12. T

Three

Organizing, Staffing, and Training

CHAPTER 6

Organizing an Effective Department

Learning Objectives

After studying this chapter, you should be able to

- Describe the organizing process and its outcome, and differentiate between formal and informal organizations.

- Identify and differentiate among various organizational structures and formats including functional, line-and-staff, divisional or product, matrix, and centralized and decentralized organizations.

- Define *authority*, *responsibility*, and *accountability* and explain their relationships.

- Understand the benefits to be derived from delegation and explain several effective approaches to it.

- Discuss the relationship of the organizing process to the chain of command and explain the concept of organizational culture.

① ORGANIZING FOR EFFECTIVENESS

CONCEPT ▶ Organizing arranges jobs and groups of jobs in a department so that employees can perform their work in the most effective way.

What is an organization?

An **organization** is the structure derived from grouping people together so that they can work effectively toward a goal that members of the group want to achieve.

The goals of a business organization are primarily profits for stockholders, and salaries and wages for managers, supervisors, and employees. There are other important goals, of course, such as supplying goods and services valued by the general population. While the goals of non-profit and public organizations do not include profit, members of such organizations expect them to provide compensation in addition to delivering valued services to others.

Members of an organization also look to it as a source of personal satisfactions, such as companionship, accomplishment, and status.

At a broader level, society expects organizations to act in ethically and socially responsible ways.

What is the distinction between organizing and an organization?

Organizing is the process of arranging the pattern of work relationships. An *organization* is the structure, or framework, that comes out of the organizing process.

Why organize in the first place?

Without an organization, we would have nothing but chaos in the workplace. We take organizations for granted because we have lived so long with them at home, in places of worship, and in the educational system. Little that we do together—anywhere—would be effective, however, if we didn't agree among ourselves on who should do what. We need look no further than team sports to see the extent of organizational structure that prevails. What would professional football be, for instance, without its highly organized structure of tasks for offense, defense, special teams, and special situations (that is, first-down run, third-down pass, goal-line defense, etc.)?

The overriding value of an organization, then, is its ability to make more effective use of human resources. Employees working alone, and potentially at cross purposes, require the coordination and direction that

Organization. The structure derived from systematically grouping the tasks to be performed and from prescribing formal relationships that strengthen the ability of people to work more effectively together in pursuing common objectives.

an organization can provide. People working together within a sensible organizational structure have a greater sense of purpose and teamwork, and they accomplish vastly more than people whose efforts are allowed to run off in any direction they choose.

Are all organizations formal?

No. In a good many of our activities, even in complex manufacturing plants, some people just naturally take over responsibilities and exercise authority without anyone's ever spelling them out. Chances are that in a group of 15 employees who you might imagine are all at the same level, you'll discover some sort of *informal organization*. It may be that the person who sweeps the floors actually has the greatest influence in that group. This person is an informal leader. Acting as staff assistant may be the lift truck driver, who is the informant. The rest of the group may either work hard or stage a slowdown at a nod from a third member of the group, who has authority as surely as if the company president had given it.

So be alert to informal organization—among the employees you supervise, in the supervisory group itself, and in the entire management structure.

How does the organizing process proceed?

Organizing follows planning. The organizational structure must provide the framework for carrying out the plan. Suppose, for example, a supervisor plans to load a trailer by 5 P.M. The goal will be met if one employee is assigned to remove cartons from the stockroom, another to operate a fork truck, another to stack cartons in the trailer, and another employee to verify and prepare the inventory and shipping documents.

Essentially, the organizing process moves from the knowledge of a goal or plan into a systematic *division of labor*, or *division of work*. Typically, the process follows these steps:

1. Making a list of all the important tasks that must be performed by the organization to accomplish its objectives.

2. Dividing up these tasks into activities that can be performed by one person. Each person will then have a group of activities to perform, called a *job*. This specialization allows each person to become more proficient at his or her special job.

3. Grouping together related jobs (such as production jobs or accounting jobs) or sequenced jobs in a logical and efficient manner. This creates specialized departments or connected sections of the organization.

4. Establishing relationships between the various jobs and groupings of jobs so that all members of an organization will have a clear idea of their responsibilities and of either their dependence on, or their control over, people in other jobs or groups of jobs.

Which comes first, the organization or the work to be done?

If there were no job to do, there would be no reason for having an organization. So there is little reason to set up an elaborate organization just for the sake of having one. The best organization is a simple one that puts people together so that the job at hand gets done better, more quickly, and more cheaply than any other way. Good organizations are also flexible, so that they can adapt to changing conditions.

1	T or F	An organization is the process of arranging the pattern of work relationships.
2	T or F	Planning comes first; then organizing helps carry out the plans.

◀ *Quick Test 1*

2 TYPES OF ORGANIZATIONAL STRUCTURES

CONCEPT ▶ Organizational structures follow several traditional patterns.

Which is the most basic of all organizational structures?

The *functional organization*. In it, each group of related activities is collected under one functional head. Thus, in Figure 6-1, the meats supervisor may have under her all the meat cutters, trimmers, and packers; the stockroom supervisor all the receivers, inspectors, and pricing clerks; and so forth. The functional approach to organizing yields the simplest structure. It also provides the basic framework from which other types of structures are built. *It is, essentially, a line organization.*

Functional organization. An organizational structure in which tasks are grouped according to a particular operating function, such as production, sales, information handling, and so on.

◆ **FIGURE 6-1**

Example of a functional organization structure for a supermarket. **What are the advantages of this structure?**

Store manager

Grocery supervisor | Dairy and frozen foods supervisor | Vegetables and produce supervisor | Meats supervisor | Stockroom supervisor | Checkout supervisor

How is a line-and-staff organization formed?

A ***line-and-staff organization*** adds to the basic features of functional (or line) organization *staff groups* that either give advice to, or perform services for, the line functions. A line-and-staff organization is illustrated in Figure 6-2.

What is the difference between line and staff groups?

An organization works best when it gets many related jobs done effectively with the minimum of friction. This requires coordination and determination of what to do and who is to do it. Those managers and supervisors whose main job is to see that products and services are produced and delivered are usually considered members of the *line* organization. Other management people who help them to decide what to do and how to do it, assist in coordinating the efforts of all, or provide service or special expertise are usually called *staff people*.

In manufacturing plants, line activities are most commonly performed by production departments, sales departments, and, occasionally, purchasing departments. The production supervisor is likely to be a member of the line organization.

Line-and-staff organization. The most common form of organizational structure, in which line managers hold accountability for results that most directly affect profits or institutional goals, and staff managers hold accountability for results that most directly affect the processes by which line managers accomplish their goals.

◆ **FIGURE 6-2**

Example of a line-and-staff organization for a manufacturing company. **When does this structure work best?**

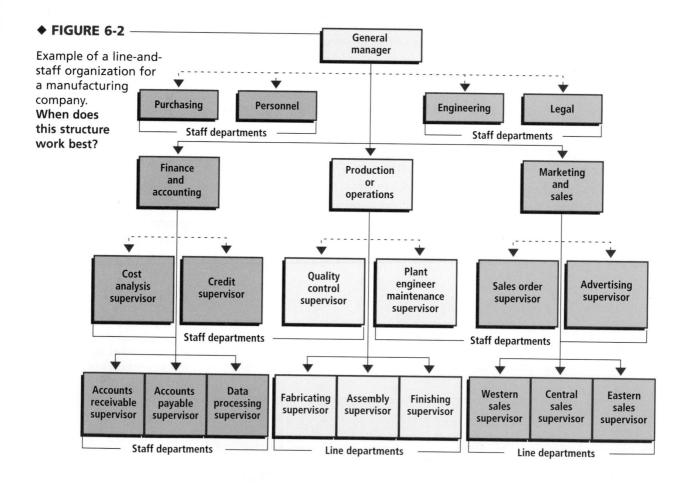

Departments that help the line departments control quality and maintain adequate records are typically staff departments. Industrial engineering, maintenance, legal, research, MIS, and the human resource (personnel) department, are some examples of typical staff activities.

In service organizations such as banks and insurance firms, the line organization may represent the primary "action" operations (such as deposits, withdrawals, and record keeping, or premium collections and claim settlements), and the staff organization may represent such support groups as computer departments and actuarial.

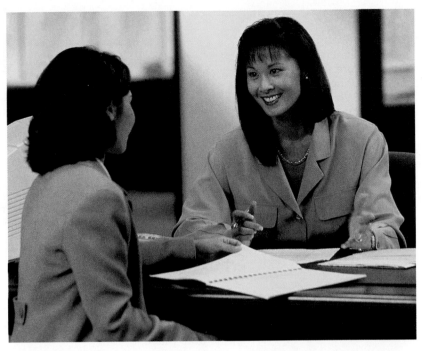

▲ HR departments are staff departments. **What functions do they perform?**

In hotel and motel chains, the line may be everything connected with the operation of a geographic unit, and the staff may be such home-office activities as advertising, accounting, and legal.

At the risk of oversimplifying, it may help you to think of line people as the doers, and staffpeople as the advisers. Each function—line and staff—is important in its own way, and collectively they help the organization achieve its goals. However, conflicts sometimes emerge between the two functions for a variety of reasons. The groups may compete for influence, be jealous of each other's status, question the limits of the other group's authority, want to claim credit for accomplishments, or be unclear about areas of responsibility. These problems are often predictable and need to be addressed before they become detrimental to the desired working relationship.

In what other ways may organizations be structured?

The great majority of organizations combine some form of functional segmentation along with a line-and-staff format. This allows for a great many variations. Among the most common are these:

Divisional or product. All functions needed to make a particular product, for example, are gathered under one highly placed manager. If a firm manufactures tractors for farmers, road graders for construction contractors, and lawn mowers for home use, it might "divisionalize" to make and sell each major product in its product line, as shown in Figure 6-3. Note that under each vice president each division is essentially a functional one; as a consequence, labels such as "functional" and "divisional" can be misleading.

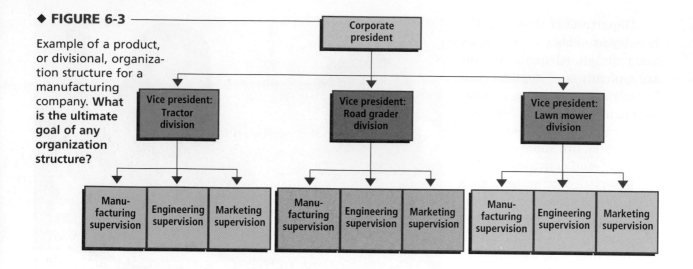

Example of a product, or divisional, organization structure for a manufacturing company. **What is the ultimate goal of any organization structure?**

Geographic. A firm may divide all of its activities, or only some, such as sales, according to the geographic region where these take place.

Customer. A company may also choose to organize some or all of its activities according to the types of customers it serves, such as farmers, contractors, and homeowners. This kind of organization is closely related to the product organization.

Regardless of organization type, always remember that the purpose of the organizational structure is to make your department's work fit together more closely with the work of other departments, while satisfying customer needs.

The matrix organization: What's that all about?

This is a nontraditional format, especially suited for projects, task force work, or other one-of-a-kind enterprises. It is commonly used in research and development organizations and engineering firms for major projects or contracts. It allows a project manager to call upon—for a limited period—the time and skills of personnel with various functional specialties. When the project is completed, the specialized personnel return to their home units to be assigned to another project. Because project managers can exercise their authority horizontally across the basic organization while the specialists receive permanent authority from their functional bosses above them vertically on the chart (Figure 6-4), this form is called a *matrix* organization. The matrix organization has the drawback of requiring employees to report to more than one superior—a functional supervisor and one or more project supervisors. There is also some loss of control by both supervisors and the potential for communication breakdowns. Nevertheless, the format has proved to be effective in its chosen applications.

How do you distinguish between a centralized organization and a decentralized one?

A *centralized* organization focuses decision-making authority among a few people at the top of an organization. It tends to have many levels of management, to concentrate its facilities in one location, to perform certain functions (such as engineering, labor negotiations, computer operations, and purchasing) from a single source, and to gather together its power and authority at headquarters. A *decentralized* organization tends to have the opposite characteristics, especially when a company is divided into distinctly separate units with varying degrees of independence. These units may be set up along product lines, according to geography or according to methods of marketing and distribution.

Centralized organizations tend to have more levels of management, have tighter controls, and allow employees less freedom to make their own decisions. Decentralized organizations have fewer levels of management, have looser controls, and allow employees greater freedom in their actions.

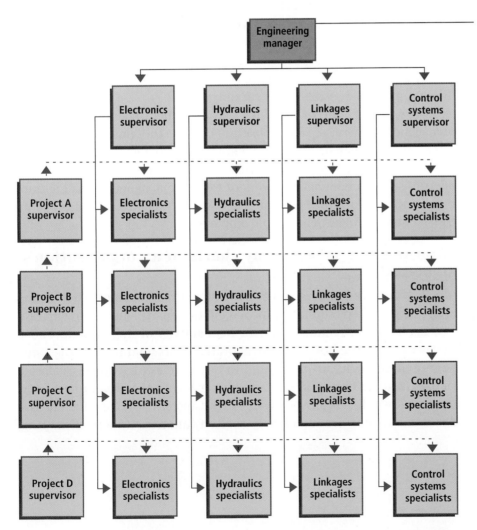

◆ **FIGURE 6-4**

Example of a matrix organization structure. **What is the primary disadvantage of a matrix structure?**

A decentralized approach pushes decision-making authority toward lower levels of an organization. As a result, it is more likely to release employee ingenuity in solving problems and pleasing their customers. Decentralization also provides opportunities for those workers who enjoy contributing their knowledge and ideas, thus creating satisfied employees.

How wide should a supervisor's span of control be?

Authorities disagree on this point, depending on several key factors. A traditional rule of thumb suggests that no supervisor should have the responsibility for more than five to eight separate activities. The span should be shorter when employees are geographically dispersed, the firm is centralized, the activities are specialized and complex, new problems are encountered frequently by employees, or when the workforce is new and not well trained. Wider spans are more appropriate when several employees all perform similar activities in a single area, when they have experienced workers close by to demonstrate proper methods, when the organization is decentralized and when the supervisor can easily be contacted on short notice to respond to problems. More and more, organizations are finding that twenty-first century employees can learn to work independently, can discover when to ask for advice or assistance, and will enjoy figuring out how to solve problems on their own. Under these conditions, spans of controls will invariably widen.

The *span of control* is defined as the number of people that a single manager can supervise. When this is the case, it is not unusual for a supervisor to have a span of 30 or more employees, provided they are engaged in only a few simple, related activities. However, corporate cost-cutting decisions (often eliminating layers of middle management) and a more highly trained workforce have increased some supervisors' spans of control, sometimes to as many as 100 employees.

What purpose is served by charts of an organization's structure?

They help you understand organizational relationships. Such charts are really simple pictures of how one job or department fits in with others. Each box, or rectangle, portrays an activity or department. Those boxes on the same horizontal level on the chart tend to have the same degree of authority or power and to have their work closely related. Departments in boxes on the next higher level have greater authority; those at lower levels have less authority. Clusters of boxes that enclose departments performing closely related functions (such as shaping, fabricating, assembly, and finishing in a manufacturing plant) are typically shown at the same level and report vertically above to the head manager of that particular function (such as the production manager).

Boxes containing line departments tend to descend from the top of the chart to the bottom (where supervisors' departments typically are) in vertical chains. Boxes that enclose staff departments tend to branch out to either side of the main flow of authority.

Organization charts can be drawn in any way that shows relationships best, even in concentric circles. For practical purposes, however, most charting is done in the manner just described and illustrated in the figures for this chapter. Two notes of caution: First, organizational structures and staffing change constantly. Accordingly, organization charts go out of date very quickly. Second, informal relationships and actual communication patterns don't show up on organization charts. Therefore, they have limited capacity to show "how things really get done."

3	T or F	Staff groups give counsel and advice; line groups see that products and services are produced and delivered.	◀ *Quick Test 2*
4	T or F	Centralized organizations tend to have fewer levels in their hierarchy; decentralized ones have more.	

AUTHORITY, RESPONSIBILITY, AND ACCOUNTABILITY

3

CONCEPT ▷ The organizational structure provides the framework for the formal assignment of responsibility and delegation of authority.

Responsibility. The duty or obligation to perform a prescribed task or service or to attain a specified objective.

Authority. The legitimate power to issue orders to other people in an organization and to obtain resources from it.

Delegation. The assignment, or entrustment, to subordinates of organizational responsibilities or obligations along with appropriate organizational authority, power, and rights.

Are authority and responsibility the same thing?

No. Authority should go hand in hand with responsibility, but the two are no more alike than the two sides of a coin. Your ***responsibilities*** are those things you are held accountable for—such as costs, on-time deliveries, and accuracy. Responsibilities are also spoken of as your assigned *duties*—such as checking time cards, investigating accidents, scheduling employees, and keeping production records. ***Authority*** is the power you have been given to carry out your responsibilities. A supervisor's authority includes the right to make decisions, to take action to control costs and quality, and to exercise necessary discipline over the employees assigned to help carry out the responsibilities.

It's an axiom that you shouldn't be assigned a responsibility without enough authority to carry it out. If a supervisor is charged with responsibility for seeing that quality is up to specifications, that supervisor must also be given authority to stop the production line when the quality falls off or to take any reasonable steps necessary to correct the condition.

Where does your organizational authority come from?

Authority, like responsibility, is usually handed down to supervisors from their immediate bosses. The bosses, in turn, receive their authority and responsibilities from their immediate superiors. And so it goes, on up to the company president or CEO, who receives assignments from the board of directors. This process of handing down authority is known as ***delegation.***

The biggest chunk of authority rests with the company president, who may split this chunk into as few as three pieces (to vice presidents of production, sales, and financing) or as many as 20 (to vice presidents in charge of 20 different products). As the authority comes down the line to you, the pieces get smaller. But they also get much more specific.

Your plant superintendent may have the responsibility of producing goods in sufficient quantities to meet sales requirements, whereas your responsibility may be to see that 10 milling machines are operated at optimum capacity so that 200,000 product units are produced each month. Similarly, the plant superintendent's authority may permit the exercise of broad disciplinary measures, whereas yours may be limited to recommending disciplinary action for employees who break rules or whose output is not up to production and quality standards.

Most companies try to make the responsibilities and authorities at each level of management fairly consistent. For instance, a supervisor in Department A should have the same general responsibilities as a supervisor in Department Z. And their authorities would be generally the same even though the specific duties of each might differ widely.

Appendix B in the back of the book provides a checklist that might help you and your boss decide on those duties, policies, and actions for which you should be held responsible.

What other sources can you draw on for getting things done?

In addition to your organizational "right" to act, you may often need to draw on other, more personal sources. Your employer tries to establish your organizational rights by granting you a title or a rank, by depicting you on an organization chart, and by providing some visible demonstration of status, such as a desk or an office or some special privilege. Ordinarily, you must supplement this institutional authority with some of the following bases of power:

- Your job knowledge (expertise).
- Your personal influence in the organization (capacity to convince others to help you or your team).
- Your interpersonal skills (caring, trustworthiness, or charisma).
- Your ability to get results (even doing some of the work, if necessary).
- Your empathetic and persuasive ability (communication skills).

All these sources are important because employees tend to discount your formal organizational authority over them. They expect you to earn your power and their respect. When employees voluntarily come to accept your authority as deserved or earned (referred to as the *acceptance* theory of authority rather than the *institutional*), you will find that your relationships with employees improve greatly.

Should a distinction be drawn among authority, responsibility, and accountability?

Yes. Although the distinction may appear to you to be only a technical one, it is not. As your boss, for example, I might be held accountable to higher management for the way in which operating supplies are conserved in my department. But I have the prerogative to assign this responsibility to you—if I also grant you the authority to take any steps needed to protect these supplies. If you were to misuse these supplies or to lose track of them, I might discipline you for failing to discharge your responsibility in this matter. But I'd still be held accountable to my boss (and would be subject to discipline) for what happened—no matter which one of us was at fault. My **accountability** is my nonassignable liability for the way my

Accountability. A non-assignable liability for the way in which an organizational obligation held by a supervisor is discharged, either personally or by subordinates.

responsibilities are carried out. Therefore, when you assign a minor responsibility to one of your employees (together with necessary authority to carry it out), you will still be held accountable to your boss for the way in which this responsibility is fulfilled by your subordinate. In other words, you can assign responsibility to others and delegate authority to them, but you will always remain accountable.

How much leeway do supervisors have in taking authoritative action?

There is no hard-and-fast rule to follow. Generally speaking, a company may establish three rough classifications of authority within which supervisors can make decisions:

- **Class 1.** Complete authority. Supervisors can take action without consulting their superiors.
- **Class 2.** Limited authority. Supervisors can take action they deem appropriate as long as it fits within company policy, and the superior is told about the action soon afterward.
- **Class 3.** No authority. Supervisors can take no action until they check with their superiors and receive their approval.

If many decisions fall into class 3, supervisors will become little more than messengers. To improve this situation, first learn more about your company's policy and then spend time finding out how your bosses would act. If you can convince them that you would handle matters as they might, your bosses are more likely to transfer class 3 decisions into class 2 and, as you prove yourself, class 2 decisions to class 1.

Note that the existing company policy would still prevail. The big change would be in permitting supervisory discretion. And this would be because you have demonstrated that you are qualified to translate front-office policy into front-line action.

How do staff people exert their influence?

More often than not, staff departments suggest, advise, or provide information. They may suggest a different, and improved, way of doing something, advise that your department is off target (on quality, for instance), or provide information for your use and guidance.

If supervisors are smart, they will make every use they can of the staff department's knowledge. If you were building a house yourself for the first time and someone offered to give you free the advice of a first-rate carpenter, a top-notch mason, a heating specialist, and an experienced painter, you'd jump at the chance. The same holds true in accepting the advice and guidance available from staff departments and other specialists when you are tackling a management problem.

You should be alert, however, to the fact that in many organizations, staff units are granted functional authority. ***Functional authority*** entitles

Functional authority. The legitimate authority granted to a staff department to make overriding organizational decisions involving its particular functional specialty.

a staff department to specify the policies and procedures to be followed in matters within their specialties. For example, supervisors might be told they cannot hire a new employee unless he or she has been screened by the employment department; nothing can be ordered from outside the company without a completed purchasing requisition; maintenance repairs cannot be made without an approved work order; the production-control department will have final say on the scheduling of customer orders; and so on.

In still other variations, organizational policy may specify that while supervisors have final authority over a functional matter, they may be required either to consult with the functional specialist before taking action or to reach an agreement beforehand on the intended action.

| 5 | T or F | Authority means the duties that you have been assigned. |
| 6 | T or F | Only line people have authority; staff personnel do not. |

Quick Test 3

4 DELEGATION FOR LEVERAGE

CONCEPT ▶ Delegation of selected tasks by supervisors can greatly add to their personal effectiveness.

When should you delegate some of your work?

Delegate when you find you can't personally keep up with everything you feel you should do. Giving minor time-consuming tasks to others will save your time for more critical tasks. Let one employee double-check the production report, for example, and send another employee down the line to see who wants to work overtime.

Arrange to have certain jobs taken over when you're absent from your department in an emergency or during vacation. Keep it to routine matters, if you will, and to those requiring a minimum of authority. But do try to get rid of the tasks of filling out routine requisitions and reports, making calculations and entries, checking supplies, and running errands.

How can you do a better job of delegating?

Start by thinking of yourself as primarily a manager. Recognize that no matter how good a person you might be, you'll always have more responsibilities than you can carry out yourself.

The trick of delegating is to concentrate on the most important matters yourself. Keep a close eye, for instance, on the trend of production

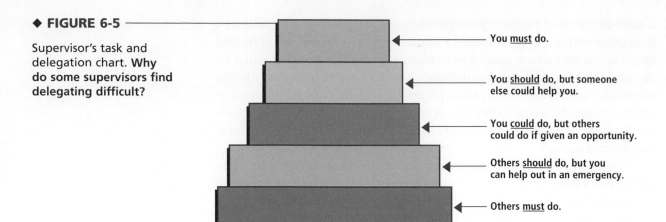

◆ FIGURE 6-5

Supervisor's task and delegation chart. **Why do some supervisors find delegating difficult?**

You <u>must</u> do.

You <u>should</u> do, but someone else could help you.

You <u>could</u> do, but others could do if given an opportunity.

Others <u>should</u> do, but you can help out in an emergency.

Others <u>must</u> do.

costs—that's a big item. But let someone else check the temperature of the quenching oil in the heat treater—assuming that's less important.

Trouble begins when you can't distinguish between the big and the little matters. You may feel you can put off checking the production record: It can wait until the day of reckoning at the end of the month. You may think that unless the quenching oil temperature is just right, the heat treater will spoil a $500 die today. But in the long run, you'll be overwhelmed if you don't see that the small jobs must get done by someone else.

Be ready, too, to give up certain work that you enjoy. A supervisor must learn to let go of those tasks that rightfully belong to a subordinate. Otherwise, larger and more demanding assignments may not get done. And don't worry too much about getting blamed by your boss for delegating to an employee work the boss has given to you. Generally speaking, supervisors should be interested only in seeing that the job is done the right way, not in who carries it out. See Figure 6-5 for an idea of how to decide which jobs should be targeted for delegation.

What tasks should not be delegated?

As important as delegation is, don't go too far. Some things are yours alone. When a task involves technical knowledge or advanced skills that only you possess, it would be unwise to let someone less able take over. Of course, it's wrong to trust confidential information to others. And you wouldn't want to overload employees by delegating too much to them. Finally, you wouldn't normally allow one employee to appraise another. That's a task for you to control.

What should you tell employees about jobs delegated to them?

Give them a clear statement of what they are to do, how far they can go, and how much checking you intend to do. Let employees know the relative importance of the job so that they can judge how much attention it should receive. There's no point in letting an employee think that making a tally will lead to a promotion if you consider it just a routine task.

Tell employees why you delegated the job. If it shows you have confidence in them, they will try that much harder. But if they think you're pushing off all the dirty jobs onto them, they may deliberately make mistakes.

Don't mislead employees about their authority. You don't want them going far beyond your intentions. But do define the scope of the task and see that others in your department know that this new task isn't something an employee assumed without authorization. Let it be known that you gave the assignment and that you're seeking cooperation from the other workers.

Why should employees accept a delegated job?

Employees who accept a delegated job outside their own job responsibilities are really taking the job on speculation. They have a right to know what's in it for them:

- **Employees who take on an extra duty get a chance to learn.** If they have never seen how the individual records in the department are tabulated, here's a chance for them to get a better perception of what's going on.

- **Delegated jobs provide more job satisfaction.** Employees thrive on varied assignments. This is a chance to build interest by letting employees do something out of the ordinary.

- **Delegation is sometimes a signal of your confidence in others.** If you can truthfully say that you wouldn't trust anyone else with a certain delegated task, this will help build employee pride and a feeling of status.

- **Delegation provides direct preparation for a promotion.** An employee who performs well on a variety of delegated tasks demonstrates the competence needed when a supervisory position opens up.

You may also want to try the concept of "completed staff work." You assign a problem requiring judgment and common sense to a subordinate, and he or she is to provide you with a complete solution according to these specifications:

1. Consult other personnel who are affected by, or who can contribute to, the problem's analysis.
2. Provide concrete recommendations about how to proceed.
3. Work out all the details.
4. Avoid overly long and complex explanations.
5. Present a single, coordinated plan of action in written form.

When can delegating go wrong?

Delegation of personal tasks will invite trouble if you are tempted to engage in any of the following practices:

- Delegating only dirty work, trivial work, or boring work that cannot be justified as representing a genuine opportunity for self-development.
- Overloading a subordinate beyond the limits of his or her time or ability.
- Failing to match responsibility with the appropriate authority to obtain the resources needed to complete the job successfully.
- Undercontrolling or overcontrolling the subordinate. You should keep an eye on progress at all times. Otherwise, try to stand aside and let the subordinate handle the assignment independently. Of course, if someone asks for advice or help, be ready to provide it.

Quick Test 4 ▶

7	T or F	Supervisors should concentrate on delegating the most important matters to others.
8	T or F	The sole purpose of delegating to others is to relieve yourself of unwanted tasks.

(5) GUIDELINES FOR ORGANIZING

CONCEPT ▶ Organizing respects the principles of management while providing an important clue to the organization's culture.

What is the relationship of the chain of command to the structure of an organization?

The term *chain of command* is a traditional military phrase used to imply that delegation of responsibility and authority and of orders and information in an organization should originate at the top and then proceed toward the bottom from each management level to the next lower level. In a rigid chain of command, you would neither skip any levels nor cross over to another chain of command. The same procedure would be followed regarding information and requests going up the line. Your boss is entitled to firsthand information about your work and its progress.

Is it a bad practice to go out of channels?

It's best to conform to the practice in your company. *Channel* is a word used to indicate the normal path that information, orders, or requests

▲ The military perfected the concept of chain of command. **Is it ever acceptable to go outside the chain?**

should travel when following the chain of command. The channel that customer orders travel in going from the sales manager to the production supervisor might be from the sales manager to the production manager, from the production manager to the department superintendent, and from the department superintendent to the supervisor. It would be going out of channels if the sales manager gave the order directly to the supervisor.

Since responsibility is assigned and authority is delegated through the channels of a chain of command, for the most part it's better to handle your affairs (especially decisions) through them, too. It avoids your making changes without letting your boss know what's going on. And it prevents others from feeling that another manager is going over the boss's head.

On the other hand, there are occasions when chain-of-command channels *should* be circumvented. In emergencies, or when time is essential, it makes sense to get a decision or advice from a higher authority other than your boss if your boss is not readily available.

For purposes of keeping people informed and exchanging information, channels sometimes get in the way. It is often common practice to discuss matters with people in other departments or on other levels of the company, but take care that you don't betray confidences. If you do cross channels, it's a good practice to tell your boss you are doing so, and why. That way, you won't seem to be doing something behind your boss's back. And that is something you should never do.

Organizational culture. The underlying (often implicit) set of assumptions, beliefs, attitudes, and expectations shared by members of an organization.

Are there any organizational practices to avoid?

Yes, but not very many. Once an organization is set up, practicality ought to prevail. In fact, some odd—and informal—arrangements occasionally work out very well. For example, one leading manufacturing company has operated for years without a visual organization chart. Its maverick president believes that the staff will develop the most effective relationships without one, and apparently it has. Nevertheless, in the design stages, at least, there are a few hazards of organization that ought to be guarded against:

1. **Don't let the chain of command get too long.** Keep the number of responsibility levels at a minimum; otherwise, some information will never trickle all the way to the bottom.
2. **Don't ask one person to report to two bosses without previously clarifying priorities.** Anyone caught in this nutcracker knows the dilemma: Which boss's work comes first?
3. **Don't make fuzzy job assignments.** When there is a gray area between two positions, overlap, conflict, and duplication of effort are invited. Clarify each person's job.
4. **Don't be too rigid.** Try to retain flexibility for contingent situations—those problems that inevitably crop up and need handling by nonstandard assignments.

How does structure relate to organizational culture?

The formal organizing process creates the broad framework within which you operate. It arranges work into jobs and serves as a vehicle for defining authority relationships. But it also provides a clue to employees about the kind of work environment, or culture, they will encounter. An *organizational culture* is the underlying set of assumptions, beliefs, attitudes, and expectations shared by members of an organization. It tells members "the way things really are around here," providing important signals regarding acceptable behavior. An organization with many layers of management, rigid policies, and centralized decision making sets one tone for its employees. Another firm that embraces humor, creativity, and informality will be totally different.

How do you learn about the organization's culture?

Although all firms have a culture, they are usually very different. Even within an organization, different cultures can emerge in different divisions or departments. But you can still identify the overall culture through close examination. Read about the company's history and its heroes and heroines, pay attention to popular slogans and myths, watch the common rites and ceremonies, and examine the early actions of newly hired executives.

Most of all, ask for advice from a variety of peers about accepted practices and valued behaviors. In addition to learning about your own culture, you will also discover that most cultures are

- Implicit and fuzzy, not explicit.
- Relatively stable, although they do change slowly over time.
- A product of top management beliefs and visions for the future.
- A powerful factor affecting employee behavior.

Your role as a supervisor is to help your employees understand the organization's culture and learn the norms governing their expected behavior and how to "fit in." You are a key link in shaping their attitudes and behavior (their socialization into the culture). If you communicate the culture clearly, they are more likely to avoid mistakes, while still being able to retain their individuality. Then both the company and the employee will be satisfied.

Internet CONNECTION

The Manager Journal. Access some of the ideas that are shaping business thinking in this journal.

9	T or F	There are legitimate times when the chain of command doesn't need to be followed.	◀ *Quick Test 5*
10	T or F	It is possible to discover an organization's culture through reading, observation, and inquiry.	

CHAPTER 6 REVIEW

KEY CONCEPTS TO REMEMBER

1. **Organizing for Effectiveness.** The organizing process creates the organizational structure. This structure prescribes the way that different individuals with different skills, and performing different tasks, can combine their efforts effectively into logical groupings (or departments) for the pursuit of common goals. Such structures also encourage order and harmony in the workplace.

2. **Types of Organizational Structures.** A variety of organizational structures can be built. The basic structure is the functional organization, which is often modified to incorporate staff, as well as line, departments. Other traditional forms are the divisional (or product), geographic, and customer organizations. The matrix organization is a newer form that is especially suitable to projects and task forces. When a great deal of authority is retained at the top, an organization is said to be centralized; when authority is pushed downward, an organization is said to be decentralized.

3. **Authority, Responsibility, and Accountability.** The formal organizational structure provides the framework—or chain of command—for determining accountability, and for the formal distribution of responsibilities and the authority needed to discharge them. Accountability is nonassignable liability for the way responsibilities are carried out; a responsibility is a duty or an obligation; authority is the power to carry out that obligation. When delegating a task to someone, it is imperative that a proper amount of authority be transferred, too. It is imperative that responsibility and authority be balanced. A supervisor's authority is affected by the authority often granted to staff specialists. While their main responsibility is to advise or provide service, staff departments may also have functional authority in matters involving their specialties.

4. **Delegation for Leverage.** In addition to the formal allocation of job duties that occurs during the organizing process, there is also an opportunity for supervisors to engage in the delegation of tasks to their subordinates. Such delegation, fairly and prudently practiced, adds greatly to the amount of work a supervisor can accomplish.

5. **Guidelines for Organizing.** Certain principles prevail in the establishment of effective organizations. Among them are (a) an awareness of the chain of command and a respect for the channels it creates and (b) an adherence to the principle of an employee having only one boss. Organizations are more than just their structures, however. Their cultures (beliefs and expectations) can have a powerful impact on employee behavior.

READING COMPREHENSION

1. What features distinguish a formal organization from an informal one?
2. Explain the part that the division of work plays in the organizing process.
3. Jill is an assembly supervisor in a plastics novelty company. Her department receives maintenance services on its presses from a plant engineering department. A quality control department

inspects the output of Jill's department and advises her when it is not meeting standards. What common form of organizational structure do these relationships imply? Identify the kinds of departments represented here.

4. Name three traditional kinds of organizational structures besides the functional and line-and-staff organizations. Why might they be used?

5. What is a major drawback of the matrix organization?

6. Distinguish between responsibility and authority, and explain how the two are related.

7. Give an example of functional authority.

8. In what way does the concept of accountability place restrictions on the delegation process?

9. What are some of the benefits a subordinate may gain from accepting a delegated task?

10. How can a supervisor learn about an organization's culture?

APPLICATION

Self-Assessment

How good are your organizational skills? ◀

Read the following statements carefully. Circle the number on the response scale that most closely reflects the degree to which each statement accurately describes you. Add up your total points and prepare a brief action plan for self-improvement. Be ready to report your score for tabulation across the entire group.

	Good Description									Poor Description
1. I understand the differences between the formal and the informal organization.	10	9	8	7	6	5	4	3	2	1
2. I know when to use the chain of command, and when it is appropriate to use other channels.	10	9	8	7	6	5	4	3	2	1
3. I recognize the different implications of having a centralized or a decentralized organization.	10	9	8	7	6	5	4	3	2	1
4. I understand the need to balance responsibility with appropriate delegation of authority.	10	9	8	7	6	5	4	3	2	1
5. When delegating, I am careful not to either overcontrol or undercontrol.	10	9	8	7	6	5	4	3	2	1

	Good Description									Poor Description
6. I feel comfortable working with staff personnel who have substantial functional authority.	10	9	8	7	6	5	4	3	2	1
7. When I delegate, I am careful to explain not only what is to be done and how, but why.	10	9	8	7	6	5	4	3	2	1
8. I am aware of what organizational charts can and cannot portray.	10	9	8	7	6	5	4	3	2	1
9. I could make an effective case for either a wide or narrow span of control.	10	9	8	7	6	5	4	3	2	1
10. I often pay attention to the visual, as well as the less visible, clues about my organization's culture.	10	9	8	7	6	5	4	3	2	1

Scoring and Interpretation

SCORING

Add up your total points for the 10 questions. Record that number here, and report it when it is requested. _____

INTERPRETATION

81 to 100 points. You seem to have a basic set of organizational skills.

61 to 80 points. Take a close look at some of your organizational skills (those with lower self-assessments) and discuss them with a manager to see if they need improvement.

Below 60 points. Some of your skills may be substantially inconsistent with effective organizational practices and could be detrimental to your success as a supervisor.

Identify your three lowest scores and record the question numbers here:

_____, _____, _____.

ACTION

Write a brief paragraph detailing an action plan for how you might sharpen each of these skills. Then pay particularly close attention to the related material in the chapter as you review the relevant sections there.

Determining the Appropriate Span of Control ◀

Assume that your manager asked you to review the factors affecting a span of control decision, apply them to your work unit, and make a recommendation regarding this question: *What is the best span of control for this unit?* To prepare your report, you will likely wish to review the text's discussion on span of control, scan the Internet for relevant information, and collect relevant information from within your department. In particular, you should recognize that even if you have an equal number of factors pushing in both directions, it is the *strength* and *relevance* of some forces that will determine your final conclusion. Record your findings on the worksheet below.

Forces for a Wider Span	**Forces for a Narrower Span**
1. _____	1. _____
2. _____	2. _____
3. _____	3. _____
4. _____	4. _____
5. _____	5. _____
6. _____	6. _____
7. _____	7. _____

ACTION

Following your analysis of the forces driving toward both wide and narrow spans in your unit, state a conclusion that you feel comfortable supporting. (Note that this exercise has no single precise numeric answer but should result in a strong directional conclusion. The exercise also gives you an opportunity to demonstrate your analytical skills.)

Role Play

Delegation ◀

Pair up with two other persons. Designate one person as Pat, the second as Lee, and the third as an observer. Read your respective roles (do not read each other's until the role play is over) and engage in a conversation until you resolve any difference of opinion (or determine that you are unable to do so). Then discuss these questions:

1. What did Pat do well?
2. What could Pat have improved upon?
3. Were Lee's reservations/objections legitimate? Why or why not?
4. What lessons did you learn from this exercise?

PAT. You are first-line supervisor for a staff of mortgage lenders. Although several members of your team are capable, one in particular (Lee) seems destined to advance to managerial ranks. Your own workload has grown substantially in recent months, and the only way to stay ahead of deadlines is to delegate some assignments to your employees. In addition, you want to provide developmental opportunities for workers like Lee and keep them intellectually challenged. Therefore, you have decided to assign Lee the task of preparing a comprehensive statistical and analytical report on mortgage trends (within the bank, the local area, and nationally) over the past five years. You anticipate that the preparation of this report will require about 20 to 40 hours of effort (in addition to Lee's normal responsibilities). You are about to talk with Lee now to announce this opportunity.

LEE. You are one of eight mortgage lenders on the staff of a local financial institution. You all report to Pat, who is generally a first-rate supervisor. Work has been extremely busy for the past several months, and you hope that things slow down pretty soon. Unfortunately, it always seems like you get additional projects dumped on you under the pretense of "developmental delegation," while the other lenders plod along at their normal pace. In addition, a major golf tournament is drawing celebrity pro golfers into the city in the near future, and you intend to ask Pat for several days off to attend this event. Pat has called you into the office, and you are about to speak to Pat now.

CASES FOR ANALYSIS

Case 16

The Overworked Chorus Director

Dick was exhausted. A few months ago, he was asked by the company president to coordinate the firm's annual employee party. The event had grown from a simple summer picnic in the "good old days," to a complex musical extravaganza. He was put in charge of selecting a theme, renting an auditorium, choosing the music, choreographing the numbers, designing the sets, conducting auditions for the singers, and leading the rehearsals. All the work usually had to be done in the evenings, even though he had been promised release time from his job.

It seemed as if there were people running everywhere, and there was a question, idea, comment, or complaint every minute. Dick had tried to get organized a few weeks ago, and had appointed four section leaders—one each for the sopranos, altos, tenors, and basses. Each section had 15 singers in it, including the section leader. Then he had recruited three aides—a choreographer, a stage manager, and a publicity person. Finally, in desperation, he talked his friend Larry into being the assistant director, hoping that Larry could relieve him of some pressure by leading the chorus in rehearsals.

◀ *Analysis*

a. What are Dick's organizational problems?
b. What is his span of control?
c. Draw his organizational chart.

◀ **Case 17**

The New Quality Control Department

The Boonetown Forging Company has never had a full-fledged inspection or quality control department. Up until this year, the various functions have been carried out, irregularly, by the manufacturing and engineering departments. Recently, the company secured a large government contract and was told that it must set up a quality control department that can ensure proper product quality. Dan Crown, formerly a supervisor in the engineering department, was told that he could head the new department if he could come up with an acceptable organization. Dan got right to work, and after a few days this is what he had written in his notebook:

The Need. Make sure that no forged products are shipped that do not meet government standards for size, weight, strength, and so forth.

Cost. Keep number of staff and cost of operating this department to a minimum, commensurate with the need for quality assurance.

Tasks to Perform

1. Implement design and engineering of product to conform to specifications.
2. Implement design and engineering of processes and equipment that can manufacture to specifications.
3. Specify, acquire, and maintain proper measuring instruments.
4. Inspect incoming raw materials and parts.
5. Inspect parts in process and assembly.
6. Inspect final products.
7. Inspect tools.
8. Establish and administer statistical control procedures for sampling of materials and for inspection.

Analysis ▶

Dan has been told that, as the department's manager, he can appoint as many as three supervisors to assist him if he needs them.

Put yourself in Dan Crown's position, and draw up what you think would be an effective organization chart.

a. Divide up the tasks into three logical groupings, or functions.
b. Decide which functions are most likely to be considered "line" for the quality control department's objectives and which should be "staff."
c. Construct a line-and-staff structure somewhat like that shown in Figure 6-2.
d. Decide which of the functions really requires a supervisor.

Case 18 ▶ *Margaret's Delegation Decisions*

The Metropolitan Planning Agency was set up to help the governments in a medium-size metropolitan area make plans for guiding future development in their area. The process carried out by the agency includes talking to local officials and members of the public to find out local goals; gathering and analyzing statistical information on population, economic growth, and so forth; as well as writing plans suggesting concrete steps the governments and citizens may take to reach their public goals. The plans may then be adopted by the governments and achieve legal status.

Margaret Walsh is a supervisor for the agency, overseeing nine employees who actually do the planning. Margaret used to be a planner herself, but now her work is entirely supervisory. The following list shows 10 activities, or duties, for which Margaret's department is responsible:

_____ 1. Assign sections of overall plan to individual planners.
_____ 2. Gather data on which the plans will be based.
_____ 3. Judge whether plan reports are of acceptable overall quality.
_____ 4. Decide what objectives will be included in plans.
_____ 5. Establish the number of planner-hours to be allocated to each project.
_____ 6. Meet with local officials to get their opinions for inclusion in plans.
_____ 7. Write community plans.
_____ 8. Work with governing bodies in their legal adoption of plans.
_____ 9. Present information about plans to the public.
_____ 10. Keep track of whether activities are being carried out within budget.

Mark each activity on the list to show whether Margaret should or should not delegate it. Use one of the following lettered actions to indicate your decision.

a. She must do it.
b. She should do it, but someone else could help her.
c. She could do it, but others could do it if given an opportunity.
d. Others should do it, but she can help out in an emergency.
e. Others must do it.

Quick Test 1	Quick Test 2	Quick Test 3	◀ *Answers to Quick Tests*
1. F	3. T	5. F	
2. T	4. F	6. F	
Quick Test 4	**Quick Test 5**		
7. F	9. T		
8. F	10. T		

CHAPTER 7

Staffing with Human Resources

▶ **Learning Objectives** _____

After studying this chapter, you should be able to

- Know the factors that affect workforce requirements and understand the implications of overstaffing and understaffing.

- Identify the six steps of the staffing process and explain the extent of a supervisor's participation in each.

- Discuss the critical aspects of the selection process and the role of application blanks, tests, and reference checks.

- Explain the main features of an employment interview and identify the types of questions that are most suitable and those areas that are restricted by equal employment opportunity legislation.

- Explain the importance of, and topics to cover in, employee orientation programs.

- Explain how careful selection and orientation can reduce employee turnover and absences, and show how to calculate specified turnover and absenteeism measures.

FORECASTING WORKFORCE REQUIREMENTS

1

CONCEPT ▶ Effective staffing helps meet performance goals, but it depends on careful analysis of work requirements and needs for employees.

Why should supervisors be concerned about the staffing process?

People are an organization's most vital resource. They will make or break your department's performance. People are costly resources, however. They should be selected very carefully, just as you would do a thorough investigation before choosing an expensive piece of capital equipment. You must also take equally good care of employees after their hiring, similar to the preventive maintenance schedule followed for new machinery.

A supervisor's primary goal is to achieve departmental performance results. This is a challenging task that extends across staffing and retention into training and motivation (the subjects of future chapters). It begins with estimating the number of workers needed to staff the department, playing an active and educated role in selecting the employees the organization hires, and maintaining the working conditions that attract and hold the best employees.

How do you engage in human resource planning for your department?

It's a matter of looking ahead, obtaining inputs, making assumptions based on past experience, working cooperatively with the human resource department, and remaining flexible. Here's a sketch of how it works.

1. Find out what your department is expected to produce—numbers of products or level of service—for the next week, month, quarter, or as far ahead as you can obtain input. Seek information on new products, redesign efforts, new service expectations, and other factors. Study the firm's sales and service projections.

2. Calculate how much the work schedule means in terms of total worker-hours for each type of job. Check your records for historical times for similar jobs, or carefully estimate the time required for each job. Be as specific as possible, and allow adequate time for setups, changeovers, breakdowns, preventive maintenance, and other activities.

3. Convert your total hours to worker-days by dividing by the number of hours in the standard work day for your organization. Then divide the total by the number of working days during the period to find the number of employees you'll need. But don't stop here.

4. Check how many indirect persons—maintenance, material handlers, setup persons—you'll need to service the required number of employees during this period (if they weren't included in step 2). Add the number of indirect employees to the number of direct to get the total needed.
5. Make allowances for absences, training, and leaves. How many days of absences do employees in your department average per month? How many worker-days per month do all your employees combined lose due to workshops, parental leaves, etc.?
6. Search for other ways to meet your schedule. Many organizations today are concerned with "right-sizing"—rigorously examining their level of employment to identify the minimum number of employees they require. This places pressure on supervisors to search for creative alternatives to permanent employment. Options include the use of overtime, transfers, or borrowed employees from other departments, stretching the initial time lines for job completion, and using temporary or part-time employees to meet peak demands.

What are the implications of overstaffing or understaffing?

Neither overstaffing nor understaffing are desirable. **What are the problems associated with under-staffing?** ▼

If you plan for too many employees, department costs will go up and your efficiency will suffer. Idle employees may become bored unless you can channel their free time into meaningful activities. The advantage of slight overstaffing, however, is that it does allow you to cover varying

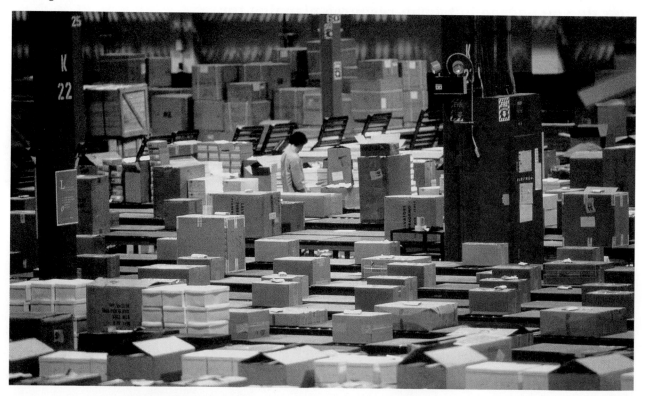

demand (peak loads) and to handle production emergencies with greater flexibility. In addition, spare time can be a great opportunity for on-the-job coaching, informal training, and team-building activities.

Understaffing also has negative consequences. It can get you behind schedule and undermine an organization's effort to engage in time-based competition. Late deliveries may infuriate a customer and result in lost business. It can also give employees the feeling of being overworked and stressed out. And it doesn't give you much flexibility. But understaffing—at least short-term—can stimulate your creativity to find and use alternative staffing techniques and also challenge employees to rise to the occasion. And a key advantage resulting from using either overtime for present employees or temporary-help agencies on a short-term basis to solve an understaffing problem is that you don't have to incur—at least directly—the additional benefits costs that would be associated with new hires.

Your goal, then, is to balance the workforce. This means making sure that the number of employees on hand closely matches the workload, despite brief periods of staff shortages and excesses.

Quick Test 1

| 1 | T or F | Proper staffing and retention can help a supervisor achieve departmental performance goals. |
| 2 | T or F | It is far better to be understaffed than to be overstaffed. |

2 THE STAFFING PROCESS

CONCEPT ▶ Effective staffing places the right numbers—and kinds—of workers on the right jobs at the right times through a systematic process.

How is organization staffing accomplished?

It is done through a six-step procedure (see Figure 7-1). The first step is to specify the kinds of jobs and the characteristics of workers that will meet the production and service requirements. These jobs must fit within the organization structures described in Chapter 6. Then it is important to forecast the total number of different employees needed to complete a given work schedule. Supervisors often play a key role in providing these estimates. Recruitment comes next; applicants are sought from inside and/or outside the company for unfilled job openings. Preliminary screening then takes place, usually by human resource department staff. They accept applications, administer employment tests, conduct reference checks, and keep legal files on the search process. Then the most appropriate individuals from among the candidates are selected. In many

The staffing process. **Should members of the work group be involved in the selection of new workers?**

organizations, supervisors play a key role in the actual selection decisions. In addition, a contemporary trend is for work group members to be involved in the selection process. After one or more persons are hired, it is essential that proper orientation takes place.

How can hiring decisions be improved?

Haphazard and discriminatory hiring practices have been exposed, condemned, and hopefully are becoming a thing of the past. They have increasingly been replaced with more formalized employment procedures, systematic data gathering, and well-trained personnel conducting the process. Modern organizations begin the hiring process with a careful *job analysis* that defines the knowledge, skills, and abilities needed by an employee to succeed. Hiring personnel then ask prospective employees to fill out an ***application blank*** that seeks relevant information about the nature and relevance of their work experience and education. This is usually followed by a preliminary screening interview conducted by the human resources department.

Personal *references* (relating to one's character) and **employment references** (relating to work history) may then be checked. A variety of *tests*—psychological, knowledge, honesty, performance, and medical—may be administered. Since many organizations are sharply reducing their corporate staff and decentralizing hiring authority to operating units, each of these procedures will be discussed briefly.

Application blank. A form used by an organization to legally and systematically gather and record information from a job applicant about his or her qualifications, education, and work experience.

References. People who give information on those seeking employment.

What information can be gained from the application blank?

Before ever examining any application blanks, you should develop a clear image of the kind of employee you want. Vague descriptions, like "a good worker," are not very useful. Instead, specify the qualities you are looking for to suit the job that is open. Reflect on the better employees you've had in the past and their characteristics. Try making a checklist of qualifications, and indicate whether each one is necessary or just desirable. Consider factors like the following:

- **Experience.** What type is best? How long should they have worked on similar jobs? Is related experience acceptable?
- **Specific skills.** Is it imperative that they be able to interpret blueprints? Or is it sufficient that they be literate?
- **Speed and accuracy.** Does the job require dexterity? Is the pace likely to overwhelm some people? Can quality work be expected on a consistent basis?
- **Initiative.** Will employees be working without close supervision? Will they need to make decisions on their own?
- **Teamwork.** Will new employees work alone, or with others? Is close interaction required? Will there be a good "fit" with present employees? After these factors are identified, then examine the application blank for relevant information. What skills do they list? How stable is their employment history? Have they worked in a team-oriented workplace before?

What kinds of tests can help to select better employees?

Properly chosen, administered, and interpreted, employment tests can be a big help in picking better workers *if* they are legally defensible. For example, *aptitude* tests may attempt to find out whether a person has the ability to learn a particular kind of job. *Personality, intelligence,* and job or career *interest* tests are widely used for applicants seeking higher level management positions, but these tests are somewhat more difficult to justify as being job related. *Honesty* tests, which purport to measure applicant attitudes toward ethical behavior, have grown in popularity as employers try to hold down the costs of internal theft.

Tests may be simple and direct, such as those that show whether an applicant can read and write or perform the simple arithmetic that record-keeping on the job may demand. Of particular interest to supervisors are ***performance*** (or work sampling) ***tests***, which measure the ability of applicants to do the major parts of the job for which they may be hired. Although it is only possible to sample work requirements and obtain limited data, at least these tests provide an opportunity to observe the candidate in action. For instance, an applicant may claim competence at using the computer program Lotus 1-2-3. A 15-minute tryout on a specific task

Performance test. An employment test that enables job applicants to demonstrate that they can actually perform the kind of work required by the job in question.

will provide powerful evidence whether that claim is valid. But remember: the test used must be relevant to the particular job you are seeking to fill.

What criteria do tests have to meet before being used?

All tests used should be fully validated and their reliability established before they are used to screen applicants for jobs. This is done for two reasons—(a) to meet legal requirements, and (b) to increase the likelihood of desirable selection decisions. *Validity* simply means that the test really measures what it is supposed to measure. *Reliability* means that it can do that consistently. For example, if an applicant were to take a test repeatedly over several weeks, the scores would be nearly the same (unless the applicant learned the answers in the interim).

Underlying the challenges of validity and reliability is the requirement that any test given to applicants (a) should be directly related to the job's content, (b) should not discriminate unfairly against the persons taking it, and (c) should not unduly invade their privacy. In other words, it would not be right to require that an applicant for a data-entry job pass a test designed for an administrative assistant. Nor should the test explore issues of lifestyle that are the employee's own business.

What about the use of medical evaluations?

Many employers no longer require physical examinations by a company nurse or doctor, at least not until *after* an employment decision has been made. At that point, applicants may be required to provide urine, hair, or blood samples to be tested for evidence of drug usage. Since the Americans with Disabilities Act provides protection for the qualified disabled, the employer risks a charge of discrimination if it appears that a non-job-related disability affected a hiring decision. Supervisors should ask only whether there is a physical or mental impairment that would make it impossible for the person to perform the job, or if there are specific positions for which the applicant should not be considered. Beyond that, supervisors should look for ways in which they can make reasonable accommodations that would allow differently abled persons to succeed on the job.

Should you check employee references?

Absolutely yes! It's foolhardy to hire anyone without checking with the last employer or two. You can at least find out the actual job the applicant held and verify the dates of employment. Most former employers will not tell you much more for fear of illegally prejudicing the applicant's chances. For this reason, it is wise to ask the job candidate to sign a *release*, which authorizes you to contact personal and employment references, as well as obtain verification of education and employment backgrounds. One good way to discover the applicant's own views about his or her employment record is to ask, "What do you think your last employer would say about your performance, work habits, and attendance?"

Validity. The proven ability of a test to measure what it purports to measure.

Reliability. The demonstrated ability of a test to yield similar scores for a candidate if the test were repeated (after a sufficient period of time to allow forgetting).

Personal references, on the other hand, are usually not of much value. Few applicants will supply you with names of others who will say something bad about them. Since personal references are often friends, relatives, or clergy, it is difficult for them to provide candid and objective assessments of someone they know to be seeking a job.

◀ **Quick Test 2**

| 3 | T or F | The first step in the staffing process is to forecast future needs. |
| 4 | T or F | Employment tests can still be helpful even if they lack validity and reliability. |

③ INTERVIEWING JOB CANDIDATES

CONCEPT ▶ Interview questions should be strictly job related and must be free from any implication of bias.

What are the objectives of job interviews?

Simply stated, an ***employment interview*** has three broad purposes—to give information, to get information, and to "make a friend." In short, the interview is a face-to-face exchange during which you need to provide a candid overview of the job and work environment, obtain key data that allow you to decide which candidate is the best, and build a positive relationship with the applicants so that the persons who are rejected this time will apply again for future positions, and the person who is accepted will be "sold" on the job and the employer (and will accept employment).

Employment interview.
A face-to-face exchange of information between a job applicant and an employer's representative designed to develop qualitative information about the applicant's suitability for employment.

What information should you give to job candidates?

An important task is to provide applicants with a ***realistic job preview***. If you tell about only the good features, or (worse yet) if you oversell the job, the individual hired will likely be disappointed and soon quit. Your goal is to provide a realistic portrait—a healthy balance of both favorable and unfavorable job tasks. Specify the fixed requirements that are inescapable. Mention the job title, major tasks, relationships to other jobs, and degree of discretion allowed. Describe the job environment, equipment used, safety factors, physical demands, and working conditions. Better yet, show them the work site and job location.

It's especially wise to forewarn an applicant about any conditions that might be considered undesirable, such as fumes, dampness, and shift work. Don't scare the applicant, but be sure the key facts are known ahead

Realistic job preview.
A balanced presentation of positive and negative features about a job that allows a candidate to reach an informed judgment.

of time. Better that the applicant turn down the job than to walk off it after two weeks of costly training.

You should also describe the positive aspects of the job—opportunities for advancement, the organization's benefit programs, and so forth. This is the time to do some sound, factual selling, but don't make promises about raises, job security, or promotions. These can come back to haunt you later on. And don't neglect to inform applicants that you are taking a few notes during the interview so as to better help you remember their positive attributes. When presented in this way, most applicants will be pleased to see you stop to jot down a few things they have said.

How do you build a positive relationship with the candidates?

Your first task is to build rapport with them. Welcome them, extend a warm handshake, put them at ease, and possibly offer refreshments. Explain that your goal is to obtain enough information about them to make a sound judgment about their prospects of job success. Never turn the interview into a "grilling" by asking point-blank questions, or firing a series of questions at the candidates, or challenging their answers. Since job seekers are already on guard, this will only create greater caution and defensiveness. And when you are finished, thank them for their time and indicate clearly how and when they will hear a decision from you.

What kinds of interview questions are most useful to ask?

You won't learn much from questions that can be answered with a simple "yes" or "no." For example, will you really gain much by asking a question like "Did you get along well with your co-workers in the last place you worked?" Instead, ask a structured series of *open-ended questions* that begin with *what, where, why, when,* or *who*. These questions give applicants a chance to talk and, while talking, to show you a lot about themselves. If the applicant does most of the talking and you do most of the listening, you'll have lots of time to gather data and form a reasoned opinion. And that's the purpose of the interview.

Ask open-ended questions such as the following:

- Tell me about your education. How do you feel that it would help you do the kind of work you are applying for?
- Where did you get your most valuable work experience? How did it prepare you for this job?
- When did you first decide to do this sort of work? What have you found most difficult about it? Most pleasant?

- Why did you leave your last job? Would you like to go back there if you could?
- How would you describe the nature of your relationship with your last supervisor?

Then follow up with a carefully prepared set of behavioral-based questions that elicit responses from the applicant in terms of what he or she would do (or has done) in specific work-related situations. For example, ask the applicant, "Tell me about a recent situation at your current job when you had to deal with a conflict and how you went about it." The answers to these behavioral questions are a rich source of information that helps you better predict the applicant's future behavior based on past performance.

CAUTIONS WHEN CONDUCTING A JOB INTERVIEW

■ James Menzies Black, former director of human resources for a major railroad, offers this advice during interviews:

- **Don't be too formal.** When you are relaxed, the applicant will be, too.
- **Don't concentrate heavily on note taking.** While it's acceptable to jot down a few notes, a trained memory will allow you to wait until the interview is over to capture your final thoughts.
- **Don't high-pressure applicants.** Glowing pictures fade quickly once employees are on the payroll. And misled employees won't trust your word.
- **Don't hire overqualified applicants.** Unless there are valid reasons to do otherwise, you want a close match between job requirements and employee qualifications.
- **Don't tell applicants why you rejected them.** It's not your job to do this, and you may say something that becomes the basis for a subsequent lawsuit.
- **Don't make moral judgments or give advice.** An applicant's personal life is no concern of yours. And the areas of advice probably don't relate to valid job requirements, anyway.
- **Don't ask trick questions that may embarrass them.** Be direct. Your job is to discover what you can about the individual's capacity to perform the job.
- **Don't give feedback on your reactions through facial expression, tone of voice, or gestures.** If an applicant sees a reaction, he or she may simply alter their answers to meet your preferences.
- **Don't be too impatient.** The best information often comes after you pause and invite further explanations.
- **Don't be misled by your prejudices.** Keep an open mind.

What kinds of interview questions should you avoid asking?

Be extremely careful. An ounce of prevention can save you from a ton of trouble. Prepare your questions in advance, and follow them consistently with all candidates. Before using the questions, consult someone from the human resources department to obtain their reaction. The following is just a partial list of areas to avoid or in which to use great caution:

Race or color. Don't ask.

Religion. Don't ask.

National origin. Don't ask.

Sexual preference. Don't ask.

Age. Don't ask, unless you need to know whether the applicant is legally old enough to work for you.

Marital status, family intentions, or employment of spouse. Don't ask.

Disability or past illnesses. Don't ask about past or present disability, though you may seek to determine if the applicant can perform the primary tasks required for the job.

Citizenship. You may not ask if the applicant is an American citizen, though you may ask whether the person has the legal right to work. But don't press for details beyond that.

Arrests. Don't ask about arrest records. However, it is acceptable to inquire about convictions for major crimes—especially if they are relevant to the job.

In addition, if an applicant *volunteers* any of the above information, be sure to avoid taking notes about it, and also inform the candidate that topics such as that will not be used in the selection decision.

Quick Test 3 ▶

5	T or F	A realistic job preview provides a portrait of all the reasons why a candidate should accept the job.
6	T or F	Open-ended questions are preferable to those answerable by a "yes" or "no" for getting candidates to talk.

④ MAKING THE SELECTION DECISION

CONCEPT ▷ Use the available information carefully to screen out the less-qualified candidates and find the ones with the greatest chance of success.

How do you use the information gained to make a sound decision?

First, recognize that there are no guarantees in hiring, only probabilities. No one has a perfect record of predicting success, but you do want continual improvement of your batting average. Second, remember that selection is more a process of screening out the poorer candidates than identifying the best one. You are looking for information that will disqualify some, while moving others higher on your list. Third, you are seeking corroborative evidence—information from two or more sources that confirms a tentative conclusion. That's why you don't rely on a single selection tool, but use multiple items such as the application blank, references, tests, and interviews.

Review the information gathered. Be especially alert to the following:

Desirable characteristics. Are the applicant's achievements well documented? Has the individual received some recognition in a previous job?

Problematic attitudes. Does the person engage in unnecessary boasting? Unnecessary criticism of a former employer or work colleagues? Failure to listen? Will those behaviors continue and affect work performance in the new job?

Work motivation. How willing is this person to work? To volunteer for extra assignments? To help out other workers? To seek creative solutions to technical problems?

Remember, most people looking for work are trying to put their best foot forward. And they may have been well trained to present a smooth appearance. But if an interviewee can't show you something positive during the interview, there's a good chance that you won't see anything better on the job.

◀ **Quick Test 4**

7	T or F	Selection is basically a process of screening out the less-qualified candidates.
8	T or F	It is reasonable to expect that supervisors will have a perfect record in hiring successful employees.

Orientation. The process in which new employees are introduced to their jobs, co-workers, and work environment through tours, personal introductions, and explanations.

5 ORIENTATION TRAINING

CONCEPT ▶ New employees need an orientation to their job, co-workers, and work environment.

Why do new employees need an orientation?

Providing an *orientation* for recently hired workers is a little like introducing friends at a club meeting where they are strangers. You'd want to introduce them to others and try to make them feel at home. You'd show them where to hang their hats and coats and where the rest rooms are. If you wanted to have them think well of your club, you might tell them something about its history and the good people who belong to it. If you had to leave them for a time to attend to some duty or other, you would come back occasionally to see how they were getting along. It's the same way with new employees who report to you. You want them to think well of you and to feel at home in your department from the beginning, so treat them accordingly.

Internet CONNECTION

Access the **Society for Human Resource Management** for information on workplace trends and developments in human resource management.

What should be included in orientation programs for new employees?

Orientation sessions should cover the major topics of probable interest to employees, as well as the items that you think are important to their success. These include the following:

- Pay rates, pay periods, when pay is first received, deductions from pay, and how pay increases may be earned.
- Hours of work, such as reporting and quitting time, lunch periods, breaks, and cleanup time.
- Information about the organization's vision, values, mission, and goals.
- Work-related policies, such as disciplinary procedures, harassment, and so forth.
- Opportunities to use an alternative work schedule, such as four 10-hour days.
- Availability of overtime and overtime pay, and premium pay for working shift schedules.
- Time reporting systems.
- Employee options under the company's benefit plans, such as group life, health, and dental insurance.
- Procedure to follow when sick.
- Procedure to follow when late.

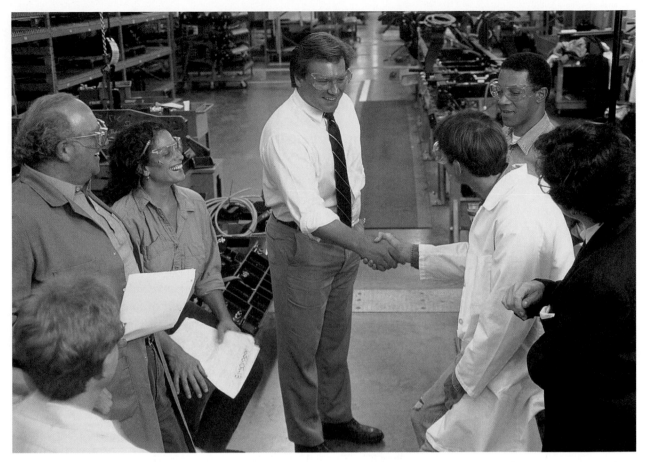

▲ The first day on a new job can be difficult. **How can current employees help a new person "fit in"?**

- Basic safety rules, the procedure for reporting accidents, and the joint employee-company responsibility for identifying hazards under the Occupational Safety and Health Administration (OSHA) law.

Orientation should also include the following activities:

- Tour of the department and other areas of the company.
- Introduction to co-workers.
- Discussion of the organizational culture.
- Assignment to a work area and identification of necessary resources.
- Location of cafeteria and rest rooms.
- Location of first-aid facilities.

This basic information is a lot for new employees to swallow at once. So don't be afraid to ask questions to gauge their understanding or to repeat what you tell them several times. Better still, give them some of the more detailed information in small doses. Give them some today, a little tomorrow, and as much as they can take a week from now.

Note that in many companies, new employees receive an orientation talk from the human resources department. As valuable as this talk may be, it won't help new employees half as much as an informal, one-on-one chat with their supervisor. You are an important person in their eyes, and you also want to begin developing a healthy work relationship with them. Grab the opportunity to do so!

How can you increase the chances that a chosen employee will succeed?

One powerful device is the *self-fulfilling prophecy*. This is the process of believing something to be true, and then acting so as to make it more likely to happen. You can use this in three ways. First, tell the chosen candidate that you were pleased to offer the job to your first choice—someone who really stood out over the others. Your statement of high expectations will set a challenging goal at which the new hire can aim. Second, tell your existing employees that you have selected a new worker with a strong track record and high likelihood of success. Ask them to help the new employee "learn the ropes" and fit in. Third, remind yourself that your reputation is on the line with every new hire. Ask yourself what you can do to help the new employee become productive.

Quick Test 5 ▶

9	T or F	Once an employee is selected, a supervisor's work in staffing is basically over.
10	T or F	The self-fulfilling prophecy can draw together expectations of success from co-workers, the employee, and the supervisor.

(6) MINIMIZING THE POTENTIAL FOR ABSENCES AND TURNOVER

CONCEPT ▶ The selection process should seek to minimize the employment of people whose unsuitability will result in excessive absences and/or turnover.

What's the connection between the staffing process and high turnover and absenteeism among employees?

A high incidence of turnover and absenteeism among employees is a major indicator of an ineffective staffing and selection process. Other signs of ineffective staffing include excessive tardiness, poor quality of work, low productivity, poor customer relations, and missed deadlines. Experts also identify low creativity and poor teamwork as other symptoms.

It is difficult, costly, and time-consuming to recruit, select, relocate, and train new employees. For example, it may cost $50,000 to add an engineer or a systems analyst to the payroll. Even a conservative estimate of the cost of keeping a semiskilled worker on the payroll for a year is well over $30,000, when you consider salary, fringe benefits, training, overhead, and other costs. Consequently, each employee who works for you must return about $30,000 or more in productive effort before his or her cost of employment can break even. When the cost of hiring employees to replace those who quit or are discharged (turnover) is added to the losses of their costly services due to absenteeism, you can readily see why it is so important to hire people most suitable for the work in the first place and to orient them well.

How do you measure employee turnover?

Employee turnover is the relationship between how many people come to work for you and don't stay (for any reason). Turnover includes employees who are hired or rehired, and employees who are laid off, quit, retire, die, or are discharged.

For consistency, the U.S. Department of Labor suggests that the rate of turnover compare only the *total* number of separations with the *average* number of employees on your payroll during a particular period. The *rate of turnover* is calculated as follows:

$$\frac{\text{Number of separations} \times 100}{\text{Average size of workforce}} = \text{Turnover percentage}$$

For instance, if you had an average of 50 employees during the month, but 1 quit and you laid off 2, the turnover would be 3. Your turnover rate would be $(3 \times 100) / 50 = 6$ percent a month. While that doesn't sound so bad, you should realize that if that happened consistently, your turnover rate for the year would be a substantial 72 percent (6×12).

Turnover rates vary widely from department to department, from organization to organization, and from industry to industry. Therefore, it is important to find out what your employer's past turnover experience is, and what is considered "acceptable" in your situation.

Decisions as to what *kind* of separations and hires to include in turnover computations vary from organization to organization, too. For example, some firms distinguish between voluntary and involuntary separations, while others try to identify "functional" and "dysfunctional" separations (the loss of unproductive and productive employees, respectively). And some firms have aggressively sought to downsize their workforce through stimulating *attrition*—the use of natural events and causes such as resignations and early retirements. Obviously, if certain kinds of separations or hires are excluded, the turnover rates will be lower. So it's good to know exactly what the specifications are when comparing turnover rates, or when trying to control yours.

Employee turnover. A measure of how many people come to work for an organization and do not remain employed there, for whatever reason.

Attrition. The gradual reduction of a workforce by means of natural events and causes, such as retirements, deaths, and resignations, as opposed to reductions planned by management, such as discharges, layoffs, and early retirement programs.

Absenteeism rate. The average number of days absent per employee, or the percentage of scheduled worker-days lost.

What causes high turnover?

In general, employee turnover is considered to be the single best long-term measure of employee morale. High morale should contribute to lower turnover; and lower morale will be followed by higher turnover. Many other factors—such as an unusually high or low unemployment rate—may confound this relationship, of course. But one thing stands out: a highly dissatisfied employee has a higher *propensity* to think about quitting and is more likely to search for a new job. Then, when an opportunity arises, the dissatisfied worker will jump at the chance.

There are many causes of voluntary turnover decisions. Dissatisfaction with a poor supervisor, unhappiness with pay or benefits, transfer of a spouse to another city, desire to seek a less stressful job, or a belief that greater job security lies elsewhere may all lead to employee resignations. Many times the problem leading to involuntary turnover, though, is simply having the wrong person in the job—the result of a poor staffing procedure. Something broke down, especially during the interviewing and selection stages. Even a potentially good employee may have been assigned to the wrong job during the placement process. Accordingly, high turnover rates can be greatly reduced by careful hiring and placement. And it is far easier to provide effective supervision for employees who are well matched to their jobs.

What are the negative effects of absenteeism?

Absences (like turnover) are costly, to the organization as well as to the employee. If it costs about $30,000 a year to keep a person on the payroll, then each day that a person is absent and receives pay can cost your department something like $125 (based on 240 working days a year) in lost effort. But there are other negative effects as well. Absences frequently create a need for permanent overstaffing, or for hiring temporary employees, or for overtime caused by delays in getting an operation started or a machine running. And absent employees cause aggravation to both the supervisor and the co-workers who have to pick up an extra workload. In many cases, your **absenteeism rate** is one of the biggest obstacles you have in your workforce planning—from day to day or from month to month.

There are two popular ways to compute absenteeism rates:

1. Absenteeism rate =
$$\frac{\text{total days absent}}{\text{average size of workforce}} = \text{average days absent per employee}$$

2. Absenteeism rate =
$$\frac{\text{total days absent} \times 100}{\text{worker-days worked} + \text{worker-days lost}} = \frac{\text{percentage of scheduled}}{\text{worker-days lost}}$$

Computation of these averages, when compared to norms for your industry, your geographical area, or comparable departments, can give you a good idea of whether you have a problem on your hands. Absences (and *tardiness*, which is simply short-term absenteeism) can usually be controlled by good supervision. Often all it takes is to monitor the data and share it with your workers, asking their cooperation. Preferably, though, you can avoid many problems by screening out applicants who have displayed these undesirable characteristics in the past or are likely to develop them on the job in your organization—simply because they are unsuited for the work they were hired to do or were not given a realistic job preview.

How can better hiring reduce turnover and absences?

Selecting the proper person to fit first the company and then the available job opening hits the turnover and absenteeism problem at its source. With millions of people keeping an eye out for a better job, this creates a substantial opportunity for upgrading the quality of your workforce as new hires are made. But knowledge of the causes and consequences of turnover and absenteeism should also drive supervisors to reexamine their own behavior, departmental working conditions, and other job factors for possible improvements.

Keep in mind that employees, too, are continually assessing the suitability of their employment after being hired. They ask themselves: "Is this still the right job for me? Is this an organization I want to continue working for?" An effective staffing procedure—coupled with effective supervision—is more likely to find these employees answering "yes!" to these questions.

11	T or F	Employee turnover is best measured by the length of time a specific employee stays on the job after being hired.	◀ *Quick Test 6*
12	T or F	Supervisors should be mostly concerned with overall departmental absenteeism rates and generally not with individual absenteeism problems.	

KEY CONCEPTS TO REMEMBER

1. **Forecasting Workforce Requirements.** Supervisors know they need to get results through people—good people. And supervisors, better than anyone else, should know the kind of requirements the work in a department demands of employees—that is, what skills, aptitudes, and interests are required—and the number of such individuals needed to get the work done economically, on time, and well. Forecasts of the numbers of employees needed to staff a department are determined by workload projections, work schedules, vacations, and anticipated absenteeism rates. A proper balance should be struck in the size of the workforce so that a department is neither overstaffed nor understaffed.

2. **The Staffing Process.** Staffing of an organization is accomplished through a six-step procedure—(a) specifying the kinds of jobs and the characteristics of employees needed to attain work requirements, (b) forecasting the number of different employees needed, (c) recruiting those candidates for unfilled job openings, (d) preliminary screening of job candidates, (e) selecting the most appropriate individuals from among the candidates, and (f) orientation. Supervisors have their greatest responsibility in steps *a*, *b*, and *e* of this process, but they also need to be aware of the role of other selection tools. They should be prepared to exert a major influence in the selection of the right kind of people by participating fully in describing jobs, specifying criteria for applicants, and interviewing candidates. A strong understanding of the legal requirements for fair treatment, and of the need for valid and reliable selection tools, is essential.

3. **Interviewing Job Candidates.** Supervisors should remember the three objectives of job interviews, and be sure to provide applicants with a realistic job preview covering both favorable and unfavorable features. After establishing rapport, ask open-ended questions that focus on education, experience, skills, and job-related attitudes. Extreme care should be taken during the interview to avoid bias or any implication of it. All questions used should relate to a performance requirement of the job. Avoid questions that might generate information regarding race, color, religion, national origin, sexual preference, age, marital status, disability, or citizenship.

4. **Making the Selection Decision.** Effective selection is based upon matching an individual's knowledge, skills, and abilities (or aptitudes for learning) with those required by the job. Selection judgment is improved when a number of candidates are interviewed so comparison is possible. In addition to checking demonstrable skills, look also for evidence of past achievements, negative attitudes, and work motivation.

5. **Orientation Training.** New employees require special attention and they are often receptive to any help received. Orientation is a valuable tool for sharing important information regarding pay, benefits, and safe work practices with workers and for developing a relationship with them. They should also be introduced to their co-workers and shown relevant areas of the department and company.

6. **Minimizing the Potential for Absences and Turnover.** Careful selection of employees helps to prevent a high incidence of absences and turnover later on. Employees whose capabilities and interests match those of the job tend to be better satisfied with their work and reflect this in better attendance and staying power. It is costly to replace experienced employees with new ones all the time. Absences are costly, too, both in lost productive efforts and in disruptions to efficient work scheduling.

READING COMPREHENSION

1. What factors affect the determination of the optimal size of a department's workforce?
2. In which aspect(s) of the staffing process are supervisors *not* likely to play a major part? Which unit usually handles those aspects?
3. Gerry expects that his sales order department will have to handle peak loads during the spring and fall seasons. Should he plan to staff a year-round workforce large enough to handle these peak loads when they occur? Why or why not? What are his alternatives?
4. What is meant by the validity and reliability of selection tools?
5. What is meant by an "open-ended" question, as used during an employment interview? Provide some examples.
6. What kinds of information can generally be obtained from a job candidate without infringing upon rights guaranteed by equal employment opportunity legislation? What kinds cannot?
7. What are the risks of hiring a college graduate for a job that requires only a high school education, as long as the applicant was willing to take the job at the prevailing wage rate?
8. How can a supervisor use realistic job previews, orientation, and the self-fulfilling prophecy to increase the success of new employees?
9. Which factors are generally considered to be the main causes of excessive employee turnover?
10. What are the differences between the two ways of computing absence rates?

APPLICATION

Self-Assessment

How good are your selection skills? ◀

Read the following statements carefully. Circle the number on the response scale that most closely reflects the degree to which each statement accurately describes you. Add up your total points and prepare a brief action plan for self-improvement. Be ready to report your score for tabulation across the entire group.

		Good Description										Poor Description

1. Before submitting a hiring request, I carefully specify the type of job to be filled and the kind of personal characteristics I am seeking.   10 9 8 7 6 5 4 3 2 1

2. I recognize that recruiting and selecting applicants should be a joint effort with the human resources department.   10 · 9 8 7 6 5 4 3 2 1

3. When I'm planning for an increase in the size of my workforce, I am careful to include estimates of indirect, as well as direct, labor.   10 9 8 7 6 5 4 3 2 1

4. When interviewing applicants, I try to avoid asking questions that can be answered with "yes" or "no."   10 9 8 7 6 5 4 3 2 1

5. I can readily report my department's annual turnover rate and provide and explanation for it.   10 9 8 7 6 5 4 3 2 1

6. When deciding on the proper staffing level, I am careful to avoid either substantial understaffing or overstaffing.   10 9 8 7 6 5 4 3 2 1

7. In a difficult job market with few applicants, I still feel the obligation to talk about the less pleasant aspects of an open job.   10 9 8 7 6 5 4 3 2 1

8. Although it might be tempting to leave employee orientation up to the human resources department, I still take those responsibilities very seriously.   10 9 8 7 6 5 4 3 2 1

9. I am extremely careful not to ask questions about, nor make note of (or use) information about, factors such as an applicant's age, race, and gender.   10 9 8 7 6 5 4 3 2 1

10. I am fully aware of the meaning of, and need for all selection methods to have, validity and reliability.   10 9 8 7 6 5 4 3 2 1

Scoring and Interpretation

SCORING

Add up your total points for the 10 questions. Record that number here, and report it when it is requested. _____

INTERPRETATION

81 to 100 points. You seem to have a basic set of selection skills.

61 to 80 points. Take a close look at some of your selection skills (those with lower self-assessments) and discuss them with a manager to see if they need improvement.

Below 60 points. Some of your skills may be substantially inconsistent with effective selection practices and could be detrimental to your success as a supervisor.

Identify your three lowest scores and record the question numbers here:

_____, _____, _____.

ACTION

Write a brief paragraph detailing an action plan for how you might sharpen each of these skills. Then pay particularly close attention to the related material in the chapter as you review the relevant sections there.

Skill Development

Interviewing Prospective Employees ◄

Assume that you have an opportunity to interview several prescreened candidates for an important position in your department. Your overall goal is to answer the question, *Who is the best applicant for this job?* To prepare your questions, you will likely wish to review the text's discussion on effective interviewing, search the Internet for relevant guidelines, remind yourself to stay away from issues and topics that are illegal or inappropriate, and consult with staffpersons in the human resources department for their advice. In particular, you recognize that it will be desirable to ask the identical (or very similar) questions of all applicants, so that you can directly compare their responses.

Compile a list of applicant questions below. See **Action** on next page for detailed instructions.

1. _____

   _____

2. _____

   _____

3. _____

   _____

4. _____

   _____

5. _____

   _____

7. _____

_____

8. _____

_____

9. _____

_____

10. _____

_____

ACTION

Prepare a list of the 10 most useful questions you can, stated in the proper format. Include both open-ended and behavioral questions. Ask someone in the human resources department to review your questions.

Group Exercise

▶ *Evaluating Orientation Programs*

STEP 1: Form into teams of three persons. Each team should select a local company to explore. Contact that organization and request permission to interview someone there regarding his or her process for orienting new employees to the organization and their jobs.

STEP 2: During the interview, obtain a specific list of topics covered and the approximate time allocated to each topic. See if you can determine how much time is spent on providing factual information versus how much is spent on making the new employee feel comfortable and helping him or her "fit in."

STEP 3: Combine your results with other groups by completing the matrix on the next page, showing time estimates for the various topics by each organization.

STEP 4: Determine if there are differences across the organizations. If so, why? Which pattern seems to be the best from your perspective? What recommendation(s) could you make?

Organization

Topic	A	B	C	D	E	F	G	H
Pay								
Hours of work								
Alternative work schedules								
Time reporting system								
Benefit plans								
Sick leave								
Tardiness procedures								
Safety								
Physical facility tour								
Co-worker introductions								
Organizational culture								
Other								

CASES FOR ANALYSIS

The Biased Interview

Case 19

"Nancy, the carpenter's position you're applying for is very demanding physically. We work outdoors in some of the coldest, wettest, windiest weather. And building forms with heavy, rough-cut lumber is a totally different ball game from trimming a few windows with clean, dried pine." That's Jake Barnes talking, site supervisor for the Jarvis Construction Company.

Nancy sat straight up in her chair and answered with pursed lips: "I'm strong, healthy, and an experienced backpacker. I haven't had a serious illness for years."

"I'm glad to hear that," said Jake. "Your application says that you have worked only indoors doing remodeling and trim work. I don't know whether you can stand this hard work."

"Mr. Barnes, I wouldn't have answered your ad if I were not sure of my physical capabilities," replied Nancy.

"We've had a lot of turnover here; I only want to hire carpenters who will stick with us. I see that you are married; do you plan to have children soon?"

Nancy crossed her arms. "I don't plan to, but I don't see how that would make a difference. During my last pregnancy, I never missed a day of work until right before the baby was born. I was back to work six weeks later."

Jake went on: "Another thing, Nancy. You would be the only woman in the crew. Can you handle hearing 'man talk'?"

"Mr. Barnes, I'm interested only in doing good work and getting more experience. I've often worked with men; it's never been a problem. Wouldn't you like to know something about my work experience, about my training?"

"Oh, I already know you're a good carpenter. I called your last boss. It's just that this job is really demanding, and I don't know whether you can handle it."

That did it for Nancy. She said, "You're not giving me a fair chance at this job, Mr. Barnes, and I'd like to speak to the owner." Jake agreed to call in Mr. Jarvis. Nancy spoke to him with considerable heat. "This isn't fair. Mr. Barnes has assumed from the start that I can't handle this job. He implies that I'm not strong enough, that I might be unreliable if I had another baby, and that I am unqualified because I'm a woman and the other carpenters are men. Won't someone listen to my qualifications? I'm a good carpenter, and I can do a good job for you."

Analysis ▶

If you were Mr. Jarvis, how would you proceed? Of the following five alternatives, which do you think might be most effective? Rank the alternatives on a scale from 1 (most preferable) to 5 (least preferable). You may add another alternative if you wish. Be prepared to justify your ranking.

_____ **a.** Finish the interview with Nancy, but choose not to hire her. The issues Jake was raising, although delicate matters, are legitimate concerns for this position.

_____ **b.** Finish the interview and hire Nancy. It has been established that she has the carpentry and work skills that qualify her for the job. Plan a number of coaching sessions for Jake to improve his job-interviewing skills.

_____ **c.** Finish the interview and hire Nancy. Fire Jake Barnes because of the serious possibility of his involving the company in crippling legal action because of his illegal job interview questions.

_____ **d.** Tell Nancy that it was improper for her to insist on seeing you. Jake is an authorized management representative of the company. It is not always possible to bypass the organization's chain of command just because one fails to succeed at a lower level. Send the hiring decision back to Jake, with whom it legitimately rests.

_____ **e.** Finish the interview and hire Nancy. Sit down with Jake and Nancy in an effort to improve their personal attitudes toward each other.

Case 20

Who's the Best?

Patrick and Maria each run a separate shipping department, but they work for different divisions of the same company. In an attempt to improve communications between them and learn from each other's mistakes and successes, Patrick and Maria agreed to meet once a month over a cup of coffee. They both had been told to monitor their absenteeism and turnover rates in an attempt to control costs. "Mine are the lower," said Maria. "No, they aren't," replied Patrick, "mine are." So they agreed to pull out their actual data for the past six months. Here's what they found:

	Maria	Patrick
Crew size	25	30
Working days	120	120
No. of separations/month	1	1
Attendance records of employees:		
working all 120 days	10	10
working 116 days	10	0
working 115 days	0	10
working 112 days	0	9
working 110 days	3	0
working 100 days	2	0
working 92 days	0	1

Analysis

Calculate their respective annual turnover percentages, the average days absent per employee, and the percentage of scheduled worker-days lost. Who has the better record, Maria or Patrick?

Case 21

The Superior Job Candidate

"At last," said Eduardo, "I've found the perfect stock clerk. Marcia has a wealth of experience. She has taken advanced courses in inventory planning and computerized controls. Compared to our other clerks, Marcia is far superior."

That was how Eduardo felt when he hired Marcia. Within a month, he felt less enthusiastic about her. Marcia could handle just about any assignment—perfectly. Trouble began, however, when it became apparent that the work of a stock clerk at Eduardo's company was mostly routine. In fact, Marcia found most of her work boring, and she let the other clerks know about it. In many ways, Marcia's superior attitude was disruptive, especially when she was asked to work along with others on group projects. Matters came to a head when Marcia confronted Eduardo on the Friday afternoon of her fourth week. "I'm extremely dissatisfied with my job," she said. "I've been here a month and there hasn't been a challenge in anything I've done. Can't you find more important assignments for me? Otherwise, I don't see much of a future in working here."

Analysis

a. What is the basic problem here?
b. How might it have been avoided?
c. Should Eduardo accommodate Marcia's request? Why?

Answers to Quick Tests

Quick Test 1	Quick Test 2	Quick Test 3
1. T	3. F	5. F
2. F	4. F	6. T

Quick Test 4	Quick Test 5	Quick Test 6
7. T	9. F	11. F
8. F	10. T	12. F

CHAPTER 8

Training and Developing Employees

Learning Objectives

After studying this chapter, you should be able to

- Explain why employees need to be trained and what should be emphasized.

- Discuss the training roles of supervisors and their relationships with the training department.

- Understand how employees learn best and how these learning principles can be used in the four-step method of training.

- Choose appropriate training methods and aids to assist the learning process.

- Define transfer of training and explain the actions a supervisor can take to ensure that a payoff is received from training.

1 TRAINING: PROCESS AND PURPOSE

CONCEPT ▶ Employees need systematic, guided training that aims toward improving job performance.

How important is education and training today?

It is extremely important. An extra year of high school adds about $100,000 to a typical worker's lifetime earnings. And, despite rising costs, a college education provides about a 10-percent rate of return to the individual. Within an organization, training can hold the key to productivity gains and improved customer service. Some companies, such as Motorola, have even required all managers to spend at least 1.5 percent of their payroll on training, and the overall average at that company is 2.4 percent. Employees in many firms are taking classes on quality, design-for-assembly, just-in-time inventory, process reengineering, and statistical process control. Trained employees who learn to use their heads as well as their hands hold the key to a company's future.

Will employees learn without being trained?

Yes. That's the danger. Whether employees are trained systematically or not, they will learn. What they learn may be good, or, more likely, it will be only partially correct. In some instances, what is learned may be downright wrong. A good illustration is the case of an assembler of tiny parts in an electronics plant. Her work was regularly judged to be of poor quality. Her supervisor wanted to get her off the job. The assembler insisted that she was doing her work exactly like the others on the production line. On close investigation it was found that the assembler, who did her work with the aid of a binocular microscope, was looking through the microscope with only one eye at a time. No one had ever told her that to get the right depth of vision she had to use both eyes. As soon as she was instructed in this technique, which took only about three minutes, her work was as good as that of her colleagues.

The point is that there are four ways to provide training: hit-or-miss, sink-or-swim, trial-and-error, and structured and systematic. The only dependable way is the last one: structured and systematic. It is based on a careful study of what the job requires in terms of knowledge and skills. Then it involves an orderly period of instruction provided by an individual who is familiar with the job, well versed in training techniques, and aware of the learning process. Even then, supervisory follow-up is essential.

What are the key steps in a systematic approach to training?

There are six steps (see Figure 8-1). At a minimum, supervisors need to determine whether training is needed at all (other solutions include improved equipment, clearer performance expectations, or better supervisory support). Then they should specify exactly what the purpose (objectives) of the training will be. After this, they will need to decide what the substance will be and what training method(s) should be used to produce the knowledge, skills, and attitudes necessary for improved performance. After the actual training experience occurs, two more steps remain: evaluating the effectiveness of the training, and implementing an ongoing program for facilitating and encouraging trainees to use their new skills (transfer the training to the workplace) and perform well. Several of these topics will be discussed further in this chapter.

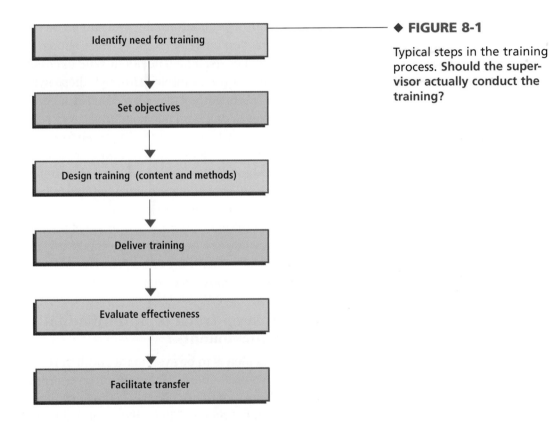

◆ **FIGURE 8-1**

Typical steps in the training process. **Should the supervisor actually conduct the training?**

What is the primary purpose of training?

Historically, training programs have been presented for a variety of reasons, and not all of them stand up to close inspection. Employees have been sent to training as a reward for good performance, as an attempt to correct their bad habits, as a way to fill "down time" during slack periods, as an attempt to change their attitudes, and for a host of other reasons. However, *most good training is conducted to improve employees' present or potential job performance*. It is driven by a focus on customer wants and desires, and how to meet those needs. It keeps a close eye on measurable performance outcomes and is often highly solution-oriented. As a consequence, good training is practical, efficiently presented, and directly relevant to the trainees' jobs. And trainees learn best when the employer's expectations are clearly defined, relevant models are demonstrated, constructive feedback is given, and useful materials are provided for a later reference when needed.

How will you know that training is needed?

There are two major ways to identify **training needs**, which are gaps between expected and actual performance. Both ways—informal and formal—are potentially useful. Informally, you should be on the alert for any of these conditions: too much scrap or rework, subpar production rates, out-of-line operating costs, a high accident rate, excessive overtime, and even a general state of poor morale. Although these symptoms may indicate the need for training, they may also result from employee selection, motivational problems, or job-related conditions. As a result, interpretation of these symptoms is best supplemented by some formal analysis of needs.

Formal approaches to assessing training needs are more structured. They attempt to identify the people who need training and the type of training they need and even to determine whether training is a viable solution to performance problems. Common methods of assessing needs include the use of surveys, interviews, and skills tests, and the observation of employees while at work. If these methods are employed regularly, they can be especially useful for identifying trends or for making comparisons with other employees or departments.

How can you keep track of an individual's training needs and achievements?

The overriding idea is to be systematic, both in recording prior skills that have been acquired and in planning future training on the basis of needs that have been identified. The record-keeping process can be a very simple one, like that shown in Figure 8-2, or it can be as detailed as you like. The important thing is to use it to (a) record what each worker can already do, (b) indicate what each worker doesn't need to be able to do, (c) plan ahead for what each worker has to learn and how that will be achieved, and (d) set definite dates for completing training in each part of the job.

An analysis such as that illustrated in Figure 8-2 is sometimes called a *skills inventory*. It tells you what skills each worker has acquired as well as the total skills capability and training needs of your department.

Quips & Quotes

Investing in employees' future is more important than immediate compensation. Programs that improve work skills and future career development are seen as particularly effective.

—Eric Rolfe Greenberg, AMA Director of Management Studies

	Answer telephone calls	File correspond-ence	File reports	Make logbook entries	File sales order forms	Prepare day-end report	Etc.
White	V	V	V	V	V	V	
Cruz	V	V	V	11-10	—	—	
Smith	11-1	11-20	—	V	V	12-1	
Klein	—	—	V	11-15	12-1	12-8	
Etc.							

V means the worker can already do the job.

— means the worker doesn't need to know the job.

11-1, 11-15, etc., indicate the dates the supervisor has set to have the workers trained to do the jobs required.

◆ **FIGURE 8-2**

Sample job instruction timetable or skills inventory. **How will this supervisor use this information?**

◀ *Quick Test 1*

1	T or F	The first step in the training process is to define one's objectives.
2	T or F	The primary purpose of training is to improve the job performance of employees.

② A TRAINING PARTNERSHIP

CONCEPT ▶ Supervisors are the primary source of employee training, but the training department, skilled co-workers, and the employee are also key partners.

Why is a supervisor responsible for training employees?

Traditionally, supervisors have concentrated on planning, organizing, motivating, and controlling activities in their departments. But an emerging role in organizations calls for the supervisor also to be a teacher and coach. Employees want to grow and take on new responsibilities, and supervisors must be there to show them how. And this goes beyond teaching basic skills for task performance; it includes helping employees become lifelong learners who know how to analyze situations, solve problems, and integrate new ideas.

Coaching is an effective way to help employees learn. A supervisory coach alertly watches for improvement opportunities, demonstrates supportive behaviors (empathy and concern for worker needs), asks

Coaching. Helping employees learn through supervisory observation, demonstration, questioning, and timely feedback.

BECOME A BETTER COACH

■ You can become a better coach if you follow some of these practical suggestions. When you engage in one-on-one coaching, make sure your comments are

- Personalized (tailored to the employee's unique needs).
- Specific (clear and detailed, with useful examples).

- Discreet (done in a private setting, so as to avoid embarrassing people).
- Timely (offered when the employee is ready to use the information).
- Performance-oriented (focused on how to attain identifiable results).
- Regular (ongoing and continued across several occasions).

open-ended questions that stimulate employee thought, and gives timely feedback in a constructive manner. And the payoff will come. Just like collegiate athletes and their relationship to their coaches, workers are also intensely loyal to their "coaches."

Make up your mind that coaching is one of your most important concerns. It is, or should be, part of the job description. Coaching needs to be done every day, for training is the only surefire way to build a workforce that returns full value for every dollar invested. As a supervisor, you are judged by your ability to get the people who work for you to create a product or perform a service accurately and at low costs. Employee training is your most powerful tool in accomplishing that end.

When does a good supervisor begin training an employee?

Teachable moments. The specific times when employees are most likely to learn.

When a new employee is hired. There are two reasons for this. First, new workers who get off on the right foot by knowing what to do and how to do it are like a baseball team that builds a 10-run lead in the first inning. With a head start like that, there's a good chance of eventual success. The second reason revolves around the idea of the **teachable moment**. This is the time when new employees are most receptive to instruction because they want to learn and succeed. Good supervisors respond to this need and begin training almost immediately.

Must supervisors do all the training themselves?

No. Two other parties can share in this responsibility. First, the organization's training department can prove extremely helpful in preparing individuals to conduct training. This department may offer *train-the-trainer* courses, in which they take highly knowledgeable or highly skilled persons (often called subject-matter experts) and turn them into capable trainers. The courses focus primarily on presentational skills, thus helping a qualified person communicate the key points and develop trainee skills without either boring or overwhelming the trainees. In a nutshell, the training department provides information to the subject-matter expert on

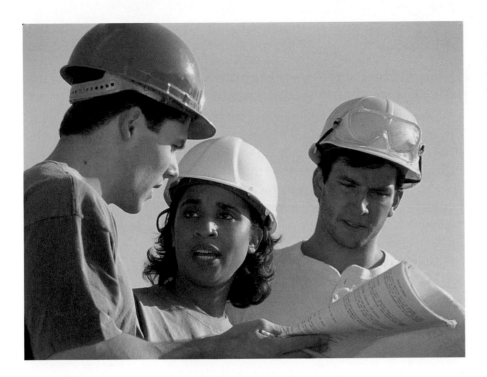

◀ Many supervisors are now involved in training their employees. **Should supervisors delegate the training to others?**

how to train. Train-the-trainer courses help a new trainer identify objectives, prepare appropriate course materials, determine the best pace at which to proceed, anticipate problems that may arise and how to address them, and choose the best mix of information presentation and skill practice. Don't overlook the value of these courses for yourself or others; the training skills gained can be invaluable.

The second party who can play a role is the trainee. Many employees can take some responsibility for *self-directed learning*. They learn at their own pace, asking for assistance only when needed. They refer to manuals (or ask co-workers) for explanations, and periodically submit the results of their initial efforts for supervisory evaluation. And the feelings of accomplishment can be enormous when they realize, "I did it myself!"

Employees who are capable of self-directed learning may also wish to capitalize on the wealth of information that is becoming available on the Internet (Web-based training). They can do this independently through focused searches for relevant information, or they can take advantage of online courses (called *distance learning*), available at their fingertips. The existence of a wide array of electronic tools such as e-mail, whiteboards, and chat groups have created the possibility of a *virtual classroom*, capable of providing just-in-time training to workers.

Caution: Even if you have qualified job instructors in your department, you can never completely delegate your training responsibilities. It's also important to be aware of, and show a personal interest in, every employee's progress. This will stimulate employees to want to learn and become equal partners in the training process. In other words, even with the help of designated trainers and self-directed learners, you must

Self-directed learning. The process by which trainees learn at their own pace by consulting resources and asking for guidance when they think it is needed.

Virtual classroom. The use of Web-based electronic programs to provide just-in-time training to employees.

continue to supervise the training and the trainees to be sure that they are meeting your expectations.

If supervisors are responsible for training, what's the role of a company's training department?

The function of a company training (or human resources development) department is to identify training needs, specify and/or provide training programs and methods, conduct evaluations of training, and assist or supplement supervisors and other managers in meeting their training responsibilities. They may also centrally conduct certain training that needs to be standardized across departments, such as orientations on company history and new products, literacy training, team development, or statistical quality control.

Generally, the training department people are experts in teaching methods. For example, training specialists can be of real help in determining specific training needs. They can help you recognize and interpret the training symptoms mentioned previously. You'll want their help, too, in learning how to be a good instructor and in training some of your key employees to be trainers.

Quick Test 2 ▶

3	T or F	Effective supervisors should wait for a problem to occur before training a new employee.
4	T or F	Self-directed learners should be encouraged to make use of Web-based training resources.

---

③ FACTORS IN LEARNING

CONCEPT ▶ Much is known about how employees learn best, and these ideas should be built into any training program.

What's the difference between acquiring knowledge and learning a skill?

Knowledge. Job-relevant information.

Skill. The ability to perform a job-related action.

Knowledge is information that can be learned from reading, from listening to an expert, or from keen observation. *Skill*, the ability to perform a job-related action, is a combination of relevant knowledge and physical or perceptual abilities. It is acquired through guided practice. For example, in operating a four-speed (manually shifted) sports car, you may be told that it is vitally important to reach certain minimum speeds before shifting from one gear to another. To apply this information, you will need to acquire a very special skill, a "motor" skill. Smooth shifting of gears will take place only after hours of practice learning the "feel" of pushing in the clutch and coordinating that with a sense of how fast the auto is moving. And all of this must tie in with a special movement of the gear shift by hand.

Almost all jobs in which an individual must place his or her hands, feet, or eyes on the material or equipment at the workplace require a unique combination of information and motor skills. In simple terms, then, the trainee on a job must not only acquire knowledge (knowing what to do and understanding why) but also learn a skill (being able to perform properly).

What can you do to make the job easier to learn and to teach?

Jobs that seem simple to you because you're familiar with them may appear almost impossible to a person who has never performed them before. You may have heard the advice given to the diner faced with the overwhelming task of eating an elephant: "Just take one bite at a time!" Similarly, experience has shown that the trick to making jobs easier to learn is to break them down into simple (bite-size) steps. That way, employees need to learn only one step at a time, adding steps systematically, rather than trying to grasp the whole job in a single piece. At an early stage, however, it is useful to portray the entire task to the trainees so that they can see how each step fits into the larger picture.

Breaking down a job for training purposes (a *job breakdown analysis*) involves two elements:

Job breakdown analysis. The segmentation of a particular job into important steps that advance the work toward its completion.

1. You must observe the job as it is done correctly and divide it into its logical steps. (See Figure 8-3 for an example.)

2. For each step in a job breakdown, you must now consider the second element, called the key point. A *key point* is anything at a particular step that might make or break a job or injure the worker. Essentially, it's the knack or special know-how of experienced workers that makes the job go easier or faster for them. The key point for one step in the customer relations representative's job would be to have the knack of sorting out the real complaint from a variety of frustrations expressed by the customer. For another step, it would be the capacity to personalize a standard solution to fit the unique problem and individual.

Key point. The essential element that makes or breaks the job.

Figure 8-3 shows how this customer relations job might be broken down into several steps with their appropriate key points for training purposes. Table 8-1 lists a number of factors, and sample questions for each, that will help you identify key points in product- and machine-oriented jobs for training purposes. In professional and service-related jobs, key points often will revolve around factors such as logic, courtesy, timeliness, and accuracy.

JOB BREAKDOWN SHEET FOR TRAINING	
Task: Responding to customer complaints	**Operation:** Preparing written letter using word processor
Important Steps in the Operation	**Key Points**

Step: A logical segment of the operation during which something happens to advance the work	Key point: Anything in a step that might:
	  Make or break the job
	  Injure the worker
	  Make the work easier to do (i.e., knack, trick, special timing, bit of special information)

1. Read the customer's letter.	Knack–avoid defensive reactions.
2. Identify all issues raised.	Take notes using only key words.
3. Select a specific problem to be solved.	Identify the real complaint from a variety of frustrations expressed.
4. Consult the company policy manual.	Use the table of contents or index to find relevant material.
5. Determine acceptable response.	Knack–ask yourself how you would feel if you received that reply.
6. Pick appropriate standard paragraphs from computer files.	Refer to list of key words, and match with those in file paragraphs.
7. Tailor the letter to fit the individual.	Personalize letter by frequent use of customer's name and specific problem.
8. Proofread the product for errors.	Review letter once now; set it aside for a while; return to it when you are "fresh."

◆ **FIGURE 8-3**

Sample job instruction breakdown. **Can you give an example of a key point?**

Where will the key points for a job be found?

They may be found in a number of places: in an operating or maintenance manual prepared by the manufacturer of equipment; in a record of "bugs" or peculiarities that has been gathered on a particular operation, procedure, or piece of equipment; or in the mind and/or know-how of an experienced operator. One of the reasons that training results are often poor when an experienced employee has been asked to break in a new one is that the older employee may "conveniently" forget or, more likely, not be aware of key points that she or he has come to take for granted through years of experience. Since experienced employees have "internalized" these key points, they may no longer be conscious of what they are doing. Their descriptions of the job may be either incomplete (missing key points such as "Speed up the engine if you feel that the auto is about to stall while shifting gears") or altogether wrong (such as "Depress the clutch pedal after you have moved the gearshift"). As you (or a trained observer) break down a job for training purposes, you'll want to check all three sources of

TABLE 8-1

Key Points Are Those Things That Should Happen, or Could Happen, at Each Step of a Job That Make It Either Go Right or Go Wrong. Key Points Include Any of the Following:

1. **Feel.** Is there a special smoothness or roughness? Absence of vibration?

2. **Alignment.** Should the part be up or down? Which face forward? Label in which position?

3. **Fit.** Should it be loose or tight? How loose? How tight? Can you show the trainee? When can you tell that a part is jammed?

4. **Safety.** What can happen to injure a worker? How are the safety guards operated? What special glasses, gloves, switches, shoes are needed?

5. **Speed.** How fast must the operation proceed? Is speed critical? How can you tell if it's going too fast or too slow?

6. **Timing.** What must be synchronized with something else? How long must an operation remain idle—as with waiting for an adhesive to set?

7. **Smell.** Is there a right or wrong smell about anything—the material, the cooking or curing during the process, the overheating of a machine?

8. **Temperature.** Is temperature critical? How can you tell whether it is too hot or too cold? What can you do to change the temperature, if necessary?

9. **Sequence.** Is the specified order critical? Must one operation be performed before another, or doesn't it make any difference? How can the worker tell if he or she has gotten something out of order?

10. **Appearance.** Should surfaces be glossy or dull? Should the part be straight or bent? How can you correct an unsatisfactory condition?

11. **Heft.** Is weight important? Can you demonstrate how heavy or light a part or package should be?

12. **Noise.** Are certain noises expected (purring of a motor)? Unacceptable (grinding of gears)?

13. **Materials.** What is critical about their condition? How can the worker recognize that? When should the material be rejected? What should be done with rejected material?

14. **Tools.** What is critical about their condition? Sharpness? Absence of nicks or burrs? Positioning? Handling?

15. **Machinery.** What is critical about its operation? How is it shut down in emergencies? What will damage it? How can this be avoided?

16. **Trouble.** What should be done in the case of injury to persons or damage to materials, parts, products, tools, or machinery? How can damage be recognized?

key points—manuals, records, and current employees. Table 8-1 also lists a number of questions that help to identify key points for training purposes.

In what sequence must the parts of a job be taught?

The best way to teach a job is to present its elements in a logical order. Alternatively, you might start with the easiest part and proceed to the most difficult. This isn't always possible, of course. But if you can arrange your employee training in a systematic sequence, learning will go more smoothly and teaching will also be easier.

How skillful should you expect a trainee to become?

At one time, a supervisor expected employees to learn every facet of a narrowly defined job, and learn to do it well. Specialization was popular, and workers were expected to perform a few tasks skillfully for a particular job. Workers might receive additional pay as they progressed from minimum levels of competency to intermediate capabilities to mastery level. But this approach had potential weaknesses—worker boredom, inflexibility across employees, and limited opportunities for advancement and wage increases.

Now a new trend has emerged—the idea of **multi-skilled employees** and *skill-based pay*. As employees acquire skills and demonstrate competency within a certain domain, they are certified as capable in that job and deserving of its pay. They are encouraged to learn new skills in another job or skill block, and by doing so qualify for a higher rate of pay. They are more valuable to the company because they can shift back and forth across multiple jobs, depending on production demands. They get better within a job and better at performing multiple jobs. The variety and challenge keep them interested. Employees are always learning something new, so the need for training never ends.

How do you get employees to want to learn?

The answer lies in three directions—personal payoff, challenge, and engaging their minds. Employees must see how training will pay off for them before they dive into training with all their hearts. So show the younger employees, through examples, how training can help them to get ahead, build job security for them, and increase their incomes. Then show employees how learning new jobs or better methods makes the work more interesting. And be sure to explain why a job is done a certain way. Employees need to know not only *what* to do and *how* to do it but *why* it needs to be done.

How much should you teach at one time?

This depends on how quickly a trainee can learn and how difficult the job is. Each learner is different. Some catch on quickly; others are slow. It's better, therefore, to gauge your training speed to each situation. If an employee has trouble learning, try to find out why. With new employees, for example, it may simply be that they are nervous and trying so hard that they don't concentrate. So be patient. Help them relax. Make it easy for them to succeed. And when they complete even a small part of the new task successfully, be sure to praise them. Many companies use **job instruction training (JIT)**, a systematic, four-step method of teaching employees a specific job skill (see the following Superscope).

Multi-skilling. The development of capacities to perform two or more key tasks by a single employee.

Job instruction training (JIT). A systematic four-step approach to training employees in a basic job skill.

SuperSCOPE ▷ Job Instruction Training (JIT)

There are four cornerstones to systematic job instruction training:

Step 1: Get the workers ready to learn. People who want to learn and are relaxed are the easiest to teach. Help them feel at ease. Explore their present knowledge, their experience, and their attitude toward learning. Let trainees know why the task is important and must be done right.

Step 2: Demonstrate how the job should be done. Begin by telling the employees how to perform the first step (and why). Then, demonstrate the procedure by doing it yourself. Next, check for their comprehension, and, finally, have them demonstrate it to you. This is a double process—tell and show (by you), followed by another tell and show (by the trainee).

Step 3: Try the workers out by letting them do the job. Let the employees try the job under your guidance. Observe for a while so that you will know how they are doing. Praise their success, and provide constructive feedback when they are wrong. Make sure they learn from their mistakes.

Step 4: Put the trainees on their own gradually. Every pilot must "solo" eventually, and employees aren't much different. Once you see that trainees can do the work reasonably well, turn them loose for a while. But check on their progress and workmanship regularly. And never assume they are completely trained. Not only might they forget, but there is always something an employee can learn to do—or learn to do better.

How smoothly should the training process proceed?

The learning process doesn't go smoothly for most people. We all have our ups and downs, depending on the material to be learned and even on the time of day. Expect progress to be slow at first as the trainees struggle to set aside old ways of doing things. They may learn quickly for a while and then taper off to a plateau temporarily. They may even backslide a little. If this happens, reassure the trainees that their halt in progress is normal. Don't let them become discouraged. If necessary, go through the demonstration again so that they can get a fresh start. And pile on the encouragement.

How quickly do people forget what they have learned?

Rapidly. Research indicates that our learning disappears quickly unless we keep working at it. So for employees to become expert at the job you're teaching, you must keep repeating the important things you want them to retain. And they must practice new skills regularly under your supervision. It's not enough for them to qualify at a minimum level; they must overlearn a skill so that it becomes almost automatic. This is one reason why follow-up (step 4 in the JIT approach) is so vital.

Can you teach old dogs new tricks?

Yes. Older workers can and do learn new methods and new jobs. And although they may learn at a slower rate than younger workers, this is mainly because older workers frequently have to unlearn what was taught to them in the past. Older workers often don't have the same incentive to learn that younger ones do. They tend to feel more secure in their jobs and have less interest in advancement. For these reasons, step 1—getting the worker ready to learn—is of prime importance when you are teaching older workers.

Quick Test 3 ▶

5	T or F	Good training provides a balanced emphasis on both knowledge and skill.
6	T or F	Most employees are extremely practical; they only want to know what to do and how to do it.

4 TRAINING METHODS AND AIDS

CONCEPT ▶ Effective training uses a variety of training methods and aids to facilitate employee learning.

What training methods should be used for instructing employees?

The key is to be aware of the many options available, recognize their unique strengths and weaknesses, and use the most appropriate one or ones. Training methods can be divided into those that primarily occur on the job (such as coaching or job rotation) and those that take an employee off the job (classroom lectures, for example). Other methods, such as apprentice training, combine elements of both settings. The key questions to ask in making a good decision about methods to use are these: What is my objective (knowledge acquisition or skill development)? How much time, space, materials, or special preparation is required? Will the method make trainees be active or passive? How many employees must be trained at one time? If new job skills are the desired product, supervisors will often use one-on-one methods, since they provide personalized attention and have high impact on the trainees.

World News. Check out world news links at **Knowledge Management**.

What's the purpose of visual aids?

A classic Chinese proverb states, "I hear and I forget; I see and I remember; I do and I understand." Training that only tells a worker how to do something may soon be forgotten. Visual aids, when used to supplement job instruction, demonstrate clearly that "one picture is worth a thousand words." Any device that helps trainees visualize what you're telling them speeds up the learning process and helps them retain it. Training that appeals to the visual senses will always be more effective.

◀ Many trainers now use multimedia in their presentations. **What is the primary advantage in doing so?**

Visual aids may include a variety of devices, such as transparencies, slides, films, posters, or flip charts. Visual aids may also be simple and inexpensive, such as writing key points on a chalkboard or distributing a diagram of the steps in a process. The best visual aid, of course, is actual demonstration right on the equipment a worker will use.

Audiovisual instruction continues to upgrade the training field. Audio cassettes can present information to workers during their free time. Videos can provide both information and realistic demonstrations right at the job site. And many forms of *computer-assisted instruction* (also called computer-based training) use interactive videodisks and CDs, which involve exciting graphic displays, realistic experiences, and even touch-screen responses.

A special form of visual aid, one that is both inexpensive and useful, is the *job aid*. These can be checklists, flow charts, worksheets, or listings of step-by-step instructions that remind a worker how to perform a task. They minimize the fear of forgetting something and are especially useful when a procedure is performed infrequently, a mistake would be costly, or a supervisor is not close by.

Job aids. Materials placed on or near the work area that help employees to remember key points and to perform effectively.

How good are off-the-job training methods?

Although individualized training is effective for developing job skills, it can still be expensive and time consuming for the supervisor. Some training can be conducted in small groups off the job at less cost per person with equal success. This is particularly true when new policies or procedures need to be explained to all workers or when employees need to know the theory and background behind an operation. But remember that most line employees are active individuals, and their attention span during a lecture is brief. The best training methods still draw on that Chinese proverb mentioned previously and *involve the participants actively in their learning.* As a result, many training programs use some form of experiential method where workers are performing a task and drawing their own learning from it. They hear, see, and do, and they understand and remember.

Another alternative that relieves the supervisor of direct training responsibility is the use of self-paced instructional methods. *Programmed learning*, for example, exposes a trainee to a small block of information and then tests the trainee immediately to see if the material has been grasped. If the trainee answers the questions correctly, another block is provided. If the trainee cannot respond correctly, the block is repeated or rephrased and then the trainee is questioned again. This is a "small-bite" approach that allows trainees to move ahead at their own pace as they master the material. It also uses regular feedback to reinforce learning.

Quick Test 4			
7	T or F	Training methods are used to deliver instruction; visual aids are used to supplement that instruction.
8	T or F	Most trainees enjoy being passive during instruction; they are content to listen to the experts.

⑤ OBTAINING RESULTS FROM TRAINING

CONCEPT ▶ Training is effective only if it has a demonstrable payoff and is transferred to the job.

What are the direct and indirect costs of training?

All training, structured or catch-as-catch-can, is costly. There are direct costs of training materials, visual aids, and outside instructors. Indirect costs include the time of both supervisor and trainees, the effects of errors made, and the lost productivity during training. But the alternative—not training—may be the most expensive of all. The key is to plan carefully for systematic training to avoid the need to repeat it later. And there are many ways to hold down costs, like having a new employee learn while working alongside an experienced one.

What benefits can a supervisor expect from training?

In addition to making a better showing for your department in terms of improved quality and quantity of output or service, training puts you in a favorable light in other ways. Effective employee instruction

- Smoothes the way for intradepartmental transfers.

- Allows you more time for other supervisory tasks, such as scheduling work.
- Provides a reserve of trained personnel in your department for emergencies.
- Wins the confidence and the cooperation of your workers.

Perhaps most important of all, training your employees makes you a prime candidate for promotion. To achieve this result, you should try to assess, and improve, the payoffs from training. Measure the productivity of an employee before training and again after it is over. Compare the performance of trained workers to that of untrained ones, and project the improvements for the whole year. This analysis will convince you to continue your training efforts, and it will justify the time and costs of training.

How will you know if training has been successful?

The only sure way is to measure some aspect of it; never *assume* that it was successful. All training—whether formal or informal, short or extensive—is expensive in some ways. Therefore, alert supervisors are always concerned about the benefit/cost ratio of the training that they support. There are four classic indicators of the success of training:

1. **Trainee reactions.** Did they stick it out until the end? Did they feel something useful was being shared? Were they satisfied with the time spent and the materials received? If not, they will be less inclined to attend future sessions or to urge others to participate.

2. **Trainee learning.** Did they acquire new information? Can they pass knowledge-based tests following the training? Can they now explain a process or procedure that they were not aware of before training?

3. **Trainee behavior.** Did they acquire new skills? Can they demonstrate specific skills at a higher level than previously possible? Can they now pass behavioral certification tests?

4. **Results.** Based on a combination of knowledge, skills, and attitudes, do the trainees now perform their jobs in ways that produce demonstrably better products or service than before the training? Has their speed increased? Quality improved? Mistakes declined?

All of these indicators are important, but the biggest payoff lies in demonstrated results. Results "speak" best to upper management when you are requesting additional support of future training efforts, so be sure that you focus your primary attention on results.

How can a supervisor increase the probability that training will transfer to the job?

Many supervisors are effective trainers. Many employees want to learn new skills. Yet evidence suggests that much training (especially in the classroom) doesn't result in improved job performance. Training has failed if it has not been transferred to the job. The reasons are diverse—lack of supervisory reinforcement, impractical training, or even peer-group norms that create barriers to its use.

Training is successful only to the degree that ***transfer of training*** takes place. This is the degree to which employees are able to transfer to their jobs the knowledge and skills they gain in learning sessions.

What can you do to aid the transfer of training? Discuss the objectives of training in advance with your new employees so that they will know what to expect. Point out effective workers to them so that they can have successful role models. Have these skilled co-workers ***model***, or demonstrate, the performance of key job skills. Visibly monitor trainee performance; this lets the trainees know what you think is important. Praise successful behaviors regularly so that your new workers will feel good about their developing skills. Above all, consider training an important supervisory function and give it the attention it deserves.

How should you modify training for new entrants to the workforce?

Millions of people will enter the U.S. labor force in the next decade; a majority of these will be drawn from various ethnic, immigrant, or economically disadvantaged groups. How can they be trained to make them fully contributing workers? Training fundamentals do not vary much from situation to situation or person to person. It is more a matter of intensifying the fundamental techniques. Companies such as Daimler/Chrysler, Western Electric, Lockheed Martin, and the Equitable Life Assurance Society have found that the following guidelines need special emphasis:

1. **Make the training specific.** Avoid generalizations and abstractions. Talk about concrete things such as pounds, inches, steel, and paper. Show how each new subject relates to a job or to a product.
2. **Rely on demonstrations.** Actions and illustrations, plus live demonstrations, communicate far more effectively than do words alone with an audience for whom speaking, reading, and other verbal skills are underdeveloped. Repeat and repeat the demonstration until you are sure the trainee has understood what you are doing.
3. **Overtrain rather than undertrain.** Err on the side of providing more information and more skills than are needed for the work to be done. That way, trainees will be less likely to underperform on the job, and they'll have more confidence in their ability to do it well.
4. **Offer personal aid.** It may not seem germane to a training effort for a supervisor to help a trainee get a ride to work, have a garnishment reduced, or even provide jail bail, but it helps to keep the trainee's mind on what is being learned and, of course, it builds confidence in the boss.

Transfer of training. The process in which trainees effectively apply to their jobs knowledge and skills gained in off-the-job training.

Modeling. The process in which a skilled co-worker or supervisor explains and demonstrates the performance of a key job skill.

5. **Provide lots of follow-up.** In some cases, the most meaningful training takes place when a supervisor shows a trainee again on the job what may have already been shown in training. That's because it is on the job that learning becomes most relevant and least academic.

6. **Reassure and recognize frequently.** It may seem like pampering to assure a person repeatedly that progress is good or to tell that person (and others) constantly how well the work is going; but people who are from culturally or linguistically diverse backgrounds, who have been economically disadvantaged, or who have disabilities may benefit from an abundance of encouragement to reinforce their confidence in themselves.

7. **Use the buddy system.** Appoint a co-worker, preferably a person from a similar or sympathetic background, from whom the trainee can get private counseling. The first days on a new job are often full of hazing and mistakes. At one St. Louis plant, for instance, a trainee inadvertently was doused with oil on his first day in the shop. He would not have returned to the job after lunch, he said, if his buddy hadn't shown him that it was an accident and assured him that it wouldn't happen again.

9	T or F	Once an employee has been trained, the supervisor's responsibility pretty much ends.
10	T or F	Training is training; supervisors should standardize their training efforts regardless of the backgrounds of their employees.

KEY CONCEPTS TO REMEMBER

1. **Training: Process and Purpose.** In the absence of sound training, employees learn their jobs haphazardly, inaccurately, or not at all. Only through careful assessment of needs, systematic instruction, and responsible follow-up can a supervisor be confident that employees will learn how to perform their work in the most effective manner. Record keeping is easier when a skills inventory is prepared for each employee.

2. **A Training Partnership.** Training is an important supervisory role, as well as a powerful tool for achieving bottom-line results. Although supervisors are ultimately responsible for the success of training, they can delegate some assignments to skilled employees. They should also call upon the training department for assistance in planning and designing good training programs.

3. **Factors in Learning.** Learning—the acquisition of knowledge and development of skills—can be accelerated in many ways. Identifying the key points through a job breakdown analysis, sequencing them logically, showing as well as telling, repeating major ideas, and adapting to individual needs will all help the trainee. The four-step method of job instruction training (JIT) will also ensure that the process is systematic.

4. **Training Methods and Aids.** The process of instruction should use a variety of methods and aids, all carefully chosen to support the objectives of training. Programmed learning and computer-assisted instruction relieve the supervisor from direct instructional tasks while providing instant feedback to trainees on their performances.

5. **Obtaining Results From Training.** Training can be costly, both directly and indirectly. Fortunately, it can also produce tremendous benefits if it is planned and conducted well. To facilitate the transfer of training from classroom to work site, supervisors can use a number of methods, such as discussing objectives, providing role models, monitoring performance, and praising successful behavior.

READING COMPREHENSION

1. Why is training an important supervisory function?
2. Mark's department is finally receiving the new computer terminals that other departments have had for several months. Would it be a good idea for Mark to let his employees learn all about the operation of the new terminals by reading the manufacturer's instruction manual? Why or why not?
3. What information can you gain from a skills inventory?
4. What is the difference between training that focuses on knowledge versus job skills? Why might both be important for a supervisor to accent?
5. Betty Jo, a checkout clerk in a discount store, has been told by her supervisor that she apparently understands how the cash register works but is too slow in operating it. Why does Betty Jo's acquisition of knowledge about her work differ from her skill development? How are these two factors related?
6. In a job breakdown, how do key points differ from important steps?
7. Why wouldn't a supervisor want to teach a job's sequence of steps rigidly in the same order as they are performed?
8. Derek, a new supervisor, is worried that his employees will not be excited about

the training he plans to conduct for them. What can he do to stimulate them to want to learn?

9. What guidelines can a supervisor follow to make training more successful?

10. Danielle, a recent immigrant to the United States, has just been hired for her first full-time job after several months of temporary jobs while she worked on her English language skills. What advice do you have for her supervisor as she begins training Danielle?

APPLICATION

Self-Assessment

How good are your training skills?

Read the following statements carefully. Circle the number on the response scale that most closely reflects the degree to which each statement accurately describes you. Add up your total points and prepare a brief action plan for self-improvement. Be ready to report your score for tabulation across the entire group.

	Good Description									Poor Description
1. I am familiar with, and generally follow, the steps in the systematic approach to training.	10	9	8	7	6	5	4	3	2	1
2. I view training primarily as one approach to improving an employee's work performance.	10	9	8	7	6	5	4	3	2	1
3. I recognize the importance of carefully keeping a skills inventory for each employee.	10	9	8	7	6	5	4	3	2	1
4. I understand the tremendous importance of my role as a coach in helping employees succeed.	10	9	8	7	6	5	4	3	2	1
5. I am familiar with the ways in which an employee could engage in self-directed learning, especially by using the Internet.	10	9	8	7	6	5	4	3	2	1
6. I am capable of identifying and explaining the key points of a job to an employee.	10	9	8	7	6	5	4	3	2	1
7. I am fully aware that employees are as much interested in the "why" of training as they are the "what."	10	9	8	7	6	5	4	3	2	1
8. I understand the unique value of providing job aids to employees.	10	9	8	7	6	5	4	3	2	1

	Good Description									Poor Description

9. When training a new employee, I would first concentrate on ways to produce a quality product or service, and then turn to speed.

10 9 8 7 6 5 4 3 2 1

10. I accept the need for, and importance of, actively supporting newly-learned behaviors back on the job.

10 9 8 7 6 5 4 3 2 1

Scoring and Interpretation

SCORING

Add up your total points for the 10 questions. Record that number here, and report it when it is requested. _____

INTERPRETATION

81 to 100 points. You seem to have a basic set of training attitudes and skills.

61 to 80 points. Take a close look at some of your training attitudes and skills (those with lower self-assessments) and discuss them with a manager to see if they need improvement.

Below 60 points. Some of your skills may be substantially inconsistent with effective training practices and could be detrimental to your success as a supervisor.

Identify your three lowest scores and record the question numbers here: _____, _____, _____.

ACTION

Write a brief paragraph detailing an action plan for how you might sharpen each of these skills. Then pay particularly close attention to the related material in the chapter as you review the relevant sections there.

Skill Development

▶ *Identifying Barriers to Transfer of Training*

Assume that the employees in your department will soon participate in a major training program to provide them with twenty-first century job skills. However, you are concerned that some barriers might stand in the way of their learning and application. Review the list of possible barriers on the next page, and select the three most relevant and powerful ones, marking them with an X.

Possible Transfer-of-Training Barriers	Most Critical (3)
1. Participants may lack knowledge of what the training is all about.	_____
2. Participants weren't involved in the design of the training.	_____
3. Participants don't want to take the training.	_____
4. Supervisor is reluctant to release employees for the training.	_____
5. Performance expectations haven't been shared with the trainees.	_____
6. The program as proposed overlaps heavily with information available from other sources.	_____
7. Top-level managers are unlikely to show their support for the training.	_____
8. The organization's culture doesn't support the results of training.	_____
9. Supervisors haven't been adequately briefed on the nature of the training.	_____
10. Participants are unlikely to see the benefits of being trained.	_____

ACTION

Prepare a report that suggests how you intend to prevent those problems or overcome them. To prepare your report, you will likely wish to review the text's discussion on transfer of training, scan the Internet for relevant guidelines, and consult with colleagues and staff persons in the human resources department for their advice.

Role Play

Determining the Costs and Benefits of Training ◀

Pair up into sets of two persons. One of you will take the role of a supervisor (A), and the other will be the supervisor's manager (B). Read only your role, and when you are ready, engage in a discussion with the other party that reaches some balanced agreement.

A. Assume that you are a new supervisor. After an analysis of the current performance of employees in your department, you believe that they need a variety of training programs in order to meet future expectations. You intend to propose these programs to your manager but first need to prepare the strongest rationale possible in support of such efforts. Brainstorm all possible benefits (both direct and indirect, short-term and long-term) that might accrue from training your employees. List those in the spaces below and be prepared to talk about these in a discussion with your manager.

1. _____ 5. _____

2. _____ 6. _____

3. _____ 7. _____

4. _____ 8. _____

B. Assume that you are the manager of a new supervisor. This person has requested a meeting, indicating that the purpose is to propose a considerable funding increase for new training programs for the supervisor's department. You are a strong believer in a balanced approach, looking at both the benefits and costs of training. Since you expect the supervisor to focus on the probable benefits of training (while likely ignoring the considerable costs), you decide to prepare a set of counterarguments that identify all the likely costs (both direct and indirect, short-term and long-term) that might accrue from training these employees. List those in the space below and be prepared to share them in a discussion with this supervisor.

1. _____ 5. _____

2. _____ 6. _____

3. _____ 7. _____

4. _____ 8. _____

After the initial presentation of each person's perspectives, combine your joint information into creating a *general model for benefit/cost analysis of training* that can prove beneficial in looking more objectively at future training proposals.

From Theory to Practice

Case 22

Kelly McWhinny is the new manager of staffing and development for a large mining operation employing nearly 2,000 people. As she began her new job, she reflected on some of the ideas a university professor had presented in a course on human resource development. As she recalled, he suggested that trainee learning was directly proportional to the number of human senses involved in the learning experience and the degree to which the trainee is active, not passive. This sounded similar to the Chinese proverb, "I hear and I forget; I see and I remember; I do and I understand."

This simple theory made intuitive sense to Kelly, but she was still not sure how to use this information in the selection of training methods. Although she realized that each method currently under consideration varied in cost, she was equally concerned with the human side of each: Would the trainee be likely to learn as much from each method?

Analysis

Assist Kelly in her assessment of the following training methods by ranking them from 1 to 5 (1 = highest; 5 = lowest) according to the degree to which each method is likely to engage the trainee's multiple senses and involve them actively in the learning process.

Method	Rank
Listening to a lecture	_____
Apprenticeship	_____
Outside reading	_____
Demonstration	_____
Coaching	_____

Case 23

The New Telephone Procedure

The supervisor of a rural office of a large electrical utility received a terse memo. It indicated that executives at headquarters were unhappy with the way some employees in the company were greeting customers when answering the phone. To avoid the possibility of problems in the rural office, the supervisor made a list of unacceptable practices and distributed the list to all employees during the next staff meeting. He explained that "pressure from the home office" was the major reason for his preparation of the list. During the next several days, the supervisor made a point of listening in on at least two phone conversations of each employee to make sure that the workers were not violating the preferred practices.

Analysis ▷

In the table that follows, put a check mark in the first column for each guideline for effective training that the supervisor apparently ignored or even violated; put a check mark in the second column for each guideline that the supervisor appears to have practiced or respected.

Guidelines for Effective Training	Ignored Guideline	Respected Guideline
1. Demonstrate how the job should be done.	_____	_____
2. Let the workers perform the job while being guided.	_____	_____
3. Periodically check on employee progress.	_____	_____
4. Explain why the procedure is to be used.	_____	_____
5. Break the job down into important steps and key points.	_____	_____
6. Present the parts of a job in a systematic sequence.	_____	_____
7. Provide a familiarization period for learning about the employee.	_____	_____
8. Assess whether the employee had a need for the training.	_____	_____

It Sounds Good, But Will They Use It?

Your company's director of training and development recently contracted with a firm to present a workshop for all employees entitled "Effective Time Management." As a member of the training committee, you have examined some of the materials and attended the pilot session. You are convinced the daylong program contains some good ideas and is skillfully presented but are concerned as to what extent the employees will use these ideas on the job. If they don't use them, valuable production time will have been lost.

◀ *Analysis*

Before suggesting ideas for improvement, you decide to assess those barriers that inhibit transfer of training. Of the following, which do you think is most likely to impede transfer? Rank the items on a scale from 1 (most likely) to 6 (least likely).

_____ **a.** Trainees usually dislike change and naturally resist it.

_____ **b.** Trainees want to change, but a lack of resources on the job prevents it.

_____ **c.** Trainees resist change because of negative peer pressure.

_____ **d.** Supervisors don't provide positive reinforcement for the new behaviors acquired in the workshop.

_____ **e.** Trainees are excited about change while attending a well-run workshop, but lose enthusiasm once separated from the trainer.

_____ **f.** The overall organizational climate doesn't support change.

Quick Test 1	Quick Test 2	Quick Test 3
1. F	3. F	5. T
2. T	4. T	6. F
Quick Test 4	**Quick Test 5**	
7. T	9. F	
8. F	10. F	

◀ *Answers to Quick Tests*

PART Four

Energizing the Workforce

CHAPTER 9

Motivating People at Work

Learning Objectives

After studying this chapter, you should be able to

- Recognize some of the factors that influence the development of each person's unique personality.

- Describe the major needs that employees typically have, and explain how they influence motivation and behavior.

- Explain the differences between satisfaction and dissatisfaction, and discuss how a supervisor can affect the contributing factors.

- Understand the concepts of expectancy theory, drives for achievement, power, and affiliation, and the impact of equity and inequity as they affect employee motivation and morale.

- Discuss the ways in which money and recognition can be used to reinforce desirable employee behaviors.

- Identify the elements found in a people-centered approach to job design and explain how, when they are used to empower employees, they provide motivation and improve the quality of work life.

THE IMPORTANCE OF INDIVIDUALITY

1

> **CONCEPT** ▶ People behave differently because of their uniquely different personalities and backgrounds.

Why do people act the way they do?

If you mean, "Why don't employees act the way I wish they would?" the answer would be lengthy and still probably not very useful to you. But if you are really asking, "Why do people sometimes act in such unpredictable ways?" the answer is simple: *People—their personalities and their behavior—are a product of their backgrounds.* Their actions at work, which may look irrational to someone who doesn't try to understand them, are in reality very logical—at least internally. If you could peer into people's backgrounds and into their psychological makeup, you'd be able to predict with surprising accuracy how one person would react to criticism or to a new task assignment. And this is a key part of the supervisor's job—seeking to understand employees before deciding how to motivate and lead them.

An example: The dog that's been scratched by a cat learns to steer clear of all cats. *It generalizes its past behavior*, perhaps even more than it needs to. Workers who have learned from one boss that the only time they are treated with respect is when the workload is going to be increased will quickly become suspicious when a new boss tries to be friendly. To the new boss such employee actions look absurd. But to the workers it's a logical thing to do.

What determines an individual's personality?

Just about everything. An individual's personality cannot be neatly pigeonholed (as we so often try to do) into simple categories. It is unfair and unwise to label people as pleasant or outgoing or friendly or ill tempered or unpleasant or suspicious or defensive. An individual's **personality** is the sum total of everything the person is today. It is exhibited in many ways—the clothing worn, the hairstyle chosen, the food preferred, the conversation enjoyed or avoided, the manners and gestures used, the methods of thought practiced, and the way situations are handled. All of these are important cues, if you are alert enough to detect and interpret them.

Each person is the product of parents, home life, education, social life, peer pressures, and prior work experiences. And each person's personality is uniquely different from everyone else's. It results from heredity and upbringing, schooling or lack of it, neighborhoods, work and play experiences, parents' influence, religion—all the social forces around them. From all these influences, people develop their individuality in a

Personality. An individual's unique way of behaving and of seeing and interpreting the actions of other people and events.

way that enables them to cope with life's encounters, with work, with living together, with aging, with success and failure. As a result, personality is the total expression of the unique way in which each individual deals with life. Consequently, when supervisors deal with employees, they are dealing with persons who have brought all their previous experiences with them to the job. The supervisor's task, then, is captured in an old saying, "Seek first to understand others before you can expect to be understood by them."

Are all people different from each other?

Each person is, and has the right to be, a distinct individual. As a matter of fact, the differences inherent in any work group collectively bring a rich variety of assets to the job. But to predict and adapt to human behavior, you first have to understand the major work-related ways in which people are different—and there are many. The most significant personality traits (deeply ingrained ways that people are inclined to think, feel, and act) include

- **Positiveness.** The degree to which an employee is sociable, friendly, and upbeat. These people enjoy work that brings them into frequent contact with others.
- **Criticalness.** The degree to which employees are typically negative, pessimistic, feel distressed, or get down on themselves. These employees, however, may play a key role in adding critical thinking and objective assessment to a group's deliberations.
- **Agreeableness.** The degree to which a person is likable, cares for others, is cooperative, and builds good relationships with co-workers. These employees are often good customer-contact persons because they are courteous and desire to please others.
- **Conscientiousness.** The degree to which a person has self-discipline, perseveres at tasks, and carefully follows directions. These employees are valuable because they require less attention and supervision.
- **Openness to experience.** The degree to which employees are receptive to new challenges, enjoy learning, and are willing to take risks. These employees are often adventuresome and innovative.
- **Self-monitoring and self-controlling.** The degree to which employees are sufficiently aware of their actions to engage in an acceptable manner; they regularly assess how they are doing and are willing (and able) to make adjustments in their own behavior.
- **Self-esteem.** The degree to which employees feel good about their skills, believe they are capable, and can handle a variety of challenges. These employees respond well to challenges and do not let minor setbacks disrupt their work lives.

The important conclusion in dealing with a diverse pool of employees is the recognition that although individuals will demonstrate more or less of these personality traits, each employee can be capable and productive if you are willing to adapt to their nature. Once you understand this, the next step is to grasp the underlying reasons for doing anything at work. These reasons are called *needs* or *drives*.

1	T or F	To understand an employee's current behavior, it would be helpful to know about his/her personal background.
2	T or F	A supervisor's first priority is to try to predict the behavior of employees.

A POWERFUL PATTERN OF MOTIVATION

2

CONCEPT ▶ Individuals strive to satisfy a hierarchy of five basic needs.

Motivation. The process that impels a person to behave in a certain manner in order to satisfy highly individual needs.

What do employees want from life—and their work?

Most of us, including employees, seek satisfaction from life in relation to what the psychologist A. H. Maslow called the "five basic needs." (See Figure 9-1.) And we seek a good part of this satisfaction from our work. Dr. Maslow outlined the basic needs as explained here and conceived of them as a sort of hierarchy, with the most initially compelling ones coming first and the more sophisticated ones last.

We Need to Be Alive and to Stay Alive. We need to breathe, eat, sleep, reproduce, see, hear, and feel. But in today's world these needs rarely dominate us. Real hunger among workers, for example, is rare. All in all, our first-level needs are satisfied. Only an occasional experience— a couple of days without sleep, a day on a diet without food, a frantic 30 seconds underwater—reminds us that these basic needs are still with us.

We Need to Feel Safe. We like to feel that we are safe from accidents or pain, from competitors or criminals, from an uncertain future or a changing present. Not one of us ever feels completely safe. Yet most of us feel reasonably safe. After all, we have laws, police, insurance, social security, union contracts, and the like, to protect us.

We Need to Be Social. From the beginning of time we have lived together in tribes and family groups. Today, these group ties are stronger than ever. We marry, join clubs, and participate on recreational teams. Social need varies widely from person to person, just as other needs do. Few of us want to be hermits. Not everyone, of course, is capable of frank and deep relationships—even with a wife or husband and close friends. But, to a greater or lesser degree, this social need operates in all of us.

We Need to Feel Worthy and Respected. When we talk about our self-respect or our dignity, this is the need we are expressing. When a person isn't completely adjusted to life, this need may show itself as undue pride in achievements, self-importance, boastfulness—a bloated ego.

But so many of our other needs are so easily satisfied in the modern world that this need often becomes one of the most demanding. Look what we go through to satisfy the need to think well of ourselves, and have others do likewise. When a wife insists her husband wear a jacket to a party, she's expressing this need. When we buy a new sports car even though the old sedan is in good shape, we're giving way to our desire to show ourselves off.

We even modify our personalities to get the esteem of others. No doubt you've put on your company manners when out visiting. It's natural, we say, to act more refined in public than at home—or to cover up our less acceptable traits.

We Need to Do the Work We Like—and Do It Well. This is why many people who don't like their jobs turn to hobbies for expression, and why so many people get wrapped up in their work. We all know men and women who enjoy the hard burden of laboring work, or machinists who hurry home from work to run their own lathes, or bored terminal operators who stay up late in their own homes playing with their own computers. These behaviors are largely an expression of the desire to fulfill oneself—what Maslow called *self-actualization*. This need rarely is the be-all and end-all of our lives. But there are very few of us who aren't influenced by it.

Which employee needs are the most powerful?

The one or ones that have not yet been satisfied. Maslow's greatest insight was the realization that once a need is satisfied, it will no longer motivate a person to greater effort. If a person has what is required in the way of job security, for example, offering more of it, such as guaranteeing

◆ **FIGURE 9-1**

Maslow's hierarchy of needs. **Which needs are met first?**

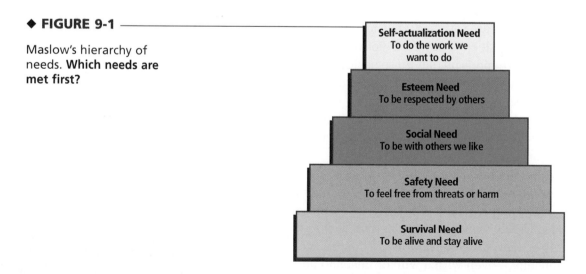

Self-actualization Need
To do the work we
want to do

Esteem Need
To be respected by others

Social Need
To be with others we like

Safety Need
To feel free from threats or harm

Survival Need
To be alive and stay alive

employment for the next five years, will normally not cause a person to work any harder. The supervisor who wishes to see greater effort generated will have to move to an unsatisfied need, such as the desire to be with other people on the job, if this employee is to be expected to work harder as a result.

It should also be noted that people tend to move up and down the hierarchy as one of their needs is threatened. For example, rumors of downsizing and layoff can shift attention quickly back to "safety and security."

| 3 | T or F | According to psychologist A. H. Maslow, employees all have five basic needs of equal strength. |
| 4 | T or F | The most powerful motivational need may vary from person to person. |

Quick Test 2

3 SATISFACTION AND DISSATISFACTION

CONCEPT ▶ Supervisors are key forces in providing employees with need satisfaction.

In what way can a job satisfy a person's needs?

It's a fact: Many people are happier at work than at home! Why? Because a challenging job with cooperative peers and a supportive supervisor goes such a long way toward meeting one's needs. Even though all of us may complain about some parts of our jobs (or our bosses) from time to time, most of us appreciate having a good job in a solid organization. At home, the problems may pile up and seem insurmountable—a nagging spouse, sick children, aging parents, a barking dog next door, and a stack of bills to pay. But if one can find an appreciative supervisor at work, a stimulating job that is viewed as important, and the predictability of a decent paycheck and the possibility of future promotions, the average worker will enjoy coming to work.

Or look at it this way. Even an entry-level job with a thriving organization often provides satisfaction of the first two basic needs: (a) a livelihood that provides for food, shelter, and clothing and (b) a sense of safety from the fears of job loss or accidents. Satisfaction of the other three basic needs—to have social contacts, to be respected by others, and to use one's talents—is often more a function of a person's supervisor than of the job itself.

▲ The supervisor can help employees find satisfaction at work. **What need can be met in a work situation?**

A good supervisor can satisfy the *social need* by showing direct care and concern for employees, greeting them warmly, demonstrating empathy, and inquiring about their current activities. The supervisor can also help a worker break into a work group and acquire friends. For instance: "This is Paula Brown, our new records clerk. We're really glad to have her join the agency. I've told her what a great bunch of people you all are, and she's looking forward to meeting each of you. Since it's almost break time, how about taking Paula along to the vending area and showing her where she can get a cup of coffee?"

To satisfy the *esteem need*, a good supervisor will make sure workers know when their work is appreciated. For example: "Paula, I've looked over your report for August, and I couldn't find a single error in it. Not only did you point out some fruitful suggestions, but the report reads very well. I'm pleased with your effort."

To satisfy the *desire to do worthwhile work*, a good supervisor gives thought to assigning tasks that will stretch employees' minds and skills, while drawing on their aptitude and training. The supervisor might say to Paula, "We'll start you on this task until you get the hang of things. Then, in a couple of weeks, we'll give you a chance to broaden your experience by taking on some of Tom's responsibilities. And the more tasks you master, the more promotable you'll be."

How are the causes of satisfaction and dissatisfaction different?

Behavioral scientist Frederick Herzberg made these distinctions between them:

Satisfaction for an employee comes from the presence of truly motivating factors (satisfiers) such as interesting and challenging work, utilization of one's capabilities, opportunity to do something meaningful, recognition of achievement, and responsibility for one's own work.

Dissatisfaction occurs when the following factors are *not* sufficiently present on the job: good pay, adequate holidays, long enough vacations, paid insurance and pensions, good working conditions, and congenial people to work with. These are called maintenance (hygiene) factors.

Whose responsibility is it for job satisfaction— the organization's or the supervisor's?

The employer has a huge stake in creating a productive work environment that helps attract, retain, and motivate good employees. The organization can do much to establish an overall climate, policies, and working conditions to make the supervisor's job easier. But a supervisor's day-to-day relationships with his or her employees is, ultimately, a very

Satisfaction. The positive state that exists when truly motivating factors (satisfiers)—such as interesting and challenging work, full use of one's capabilities, and recognition for achievement—are provided.

Dissatisfaction. The state that exists when "maintenance" or "hygiene" factors such as good pay, job security, fringe benefits, and desirable working conditions are lacking.

---

*Super*SCOPE ▷ Performance Motivators

What *really* produces high performance motivation among employees? Clay Carr, chief of the Civilian Personnel Office for the Defense Logistics Agency in Columbus, Ohio, suggests seven key factors:

- **Goals.** Targets that are clear to employees, worthy of devoting effort to, and challenging enough to make them stretch before achieving them.
- **Standards.** Preferably explicit and pre-established criteria that tell an employee how successful performance will be measured.
- **Feedback.** Information provided on progress toward accomplishing a goal, or data indicating where a shortfall occurs.

- **Opportunity.** Ensuring the employee has the time to devote to the task and is allowed to participate.
- **Means.** Providing adequate resources (technology, procedures, scheduling, and information) to allow for high performance.
- **Competence.** The unique knowledge and skills that an employee can apply to a job.
- **Motive.** Providing reasons such as autonomy, support, recognition, time, and money to encourage employees to want to do something.

A key issue for all supervisors is to determine which of these factors are under their control (even in a classic hierarchical organization) and then actively apply them to each employee.

Source: Adapted from Clay Carr, "The Ingredients of Good Performance," *Training*, August 1993, pp. 51–54.

personal one. No amount of policies and procedures, cafeterias, generous fringe benefits, or clean rest rooms can take the place of a concerned supervisor who treats each employee with respect, and helps he or she feel needed and appreciated. Clearly, responsibility for the dual tasks of removing dissatisfaction and increasing satisfaction is one that is shared by you and the parent organization (see Figure 9-2).

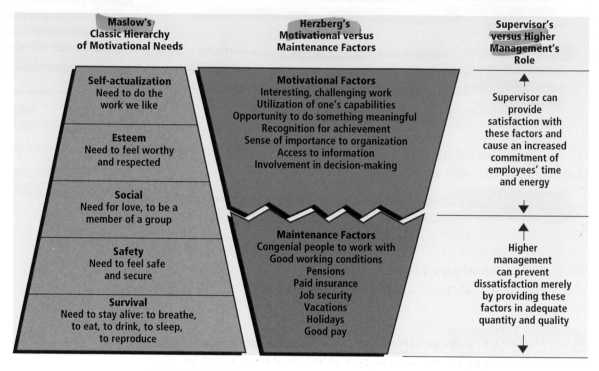

◆ **FIGURE 9-2**

Employee needs that supervisors can satisfy. **Which is the more challenging— removing dissatisfaction or increasing satisfaction?**

Quick Test 3 ▶	**5**	T or F	Satisfaction and dissatisfaction are basically two different feelings (positive and negative) about the same set of factors.
	6	T or F	Supervisors are most directly responsible for affecting motivational, not maintenance, factors at work.

ACHIEVEMENT, EXPECTANCY, AND EQUITY

4

CONCEPT ▶ Employee performance is greatly influenced by the workers' opportunities for personal achievement, their expectancy of what the job will provide, and their desire for equity in the workplace.

What important drives do employees typically have?

Researcher David McClelland discovered that people have varying degrees of drive toward achievement, power, and affiliation. Some people—those with *achievement* motivation—thrive on pursuing and attaining goals. Often they are the ones who aspire to supervisory and management careers. But many other people feel its strong pull, too. You can recognize achievement-driven persons, according to McClelland, if they

1. Like to be able to control the situations in which they are involved in.
2. Take moderate risks but not great chances.
3. Like to get immediate feedback on how they have done.
4. Tend to be preoccupied with a task orientation toward the job to be done.

Achievement-oriented persons rise to challenges well, seek new horizons to conquer, and thrive on freedom of choice. But if left unchecked, they may be inclined to take off in an independent direction and balk at working closely with other employees.

Individuals who are *power* driven may see almost every situation at work as one in which they must seize control or dominate others. They love to influence others around them and change situations whether or not it is needed. The extreme power seekers tend to be abrasive and insensitive to others' feelings. They insist on doing a job their own way rather than admitting that your instructions may be more effective. But they are also willing to assert themselves when a decision needs to be made.

Employees who are strongly motivated by *affiliation* are usually friendly and like to socialize with others. They enjoy being with friends and value others whom they find compatible. This drive may even distract them from their performance requirements, but they will usually respond to an appeal for cooperation.

In contrast to basic needs that are felt instinctively, these three drives are usually acquired from life's experiences. The supervisor's task is to identify the strength of each drive in an employee, and then tap into its positive features by attempting to satisfy that dimension.

In addition to having their needs and drives satisfied, what other factors are important to employees?

Using their capabilities fully and being rewarded commensurately are other major concerns. An employee's **expectancy**, her or his judgment about the attractiveness and probability of a prospective reward, strongly influences that person's willingness to take on a new task. It is tempting, but too simple, to suggest that every employee is concerned with only one question—"What's in it for me?" Many employees *do* want to perform well and satisfy their supervisor's requests. They recognize that the organization's success and their need for satisfaction go hand in hand. To achieve these goals, however, they require answers to several questions, such as the following:

Expectancy. An individual's judgment about the attractiveness and probability of a reward.

1. Can I do what management is asking me to do? (Do I have the skills, resources, and time?)
2. If I do the job, will I be rewarded? (Will management recognize my work, be satisfied with it, and reward me?)
3. Will the reward I receive be satisfactory to me? (Will it be something I value, large enough to meet my needs, and received soon enough to be useful?)

As you can see, a person's effort will be greatly influenced by the answers received. But two factors stand out. First, the questions may be *implicit* only in the employee's mind, suggesting that the supervisor has to stay one step ahead of the employee. You should anticipate such questions and be ready to raise them and offer solid answers. Second, the answers to *all* of these questions must be positive, for employees will see no reason to exert their effort if any of the factors are missing or unsatisfactory. As a baker knows when mixing a cake, all the ingredients are important to the overall product.

How important is it to treat different employees in a similar manner?

Equity. An employee's perception of the fairness in the application of rewards to oneself and others for their efforts.

Extremely important. This is because many employees are highly concerned about **equity**—the perception of fairness involved in rewards given by their supervisor to different employees. They are interested not only in their own efforts and rewards balance, but also in how that balance compares with the rewards received by others for their efforts. Here's how it works. Maria looks at the range of rewards (both satisfiers and hygiene factors) that she receives, and compares this with the effort (talent, skills, and time) that she contributes to her employer. Even if this ratio is initially satisfactory to her, she may still be unhappy if she senses that Nelson is contributing less or receiving more than she. When inequity exists, Maria is likely to withhold some of her contributions (consciously or unconsciously) to bring her ratio into a better balance. This has an important lesson for supervisors: They must manage not just objective reality (actual rewards given), but also the *perception* of fairness that exists in the mind of each employee. As we shall see in Chapter 11, the task of communicating is never-ending!

A few other points about the distribution of rewards also deserve mention, however. It's a fact of life that the package of rewards given to one employee will differ from that given to another employee. This suggests that one role of a supervisor is to explain this fact—both in advance and at the time that rewards are given—to help employees understand the differential reward phenomenon. One reason for this practice is that people are motivated by different needs (as discussed earlier in this chapter). The main principle to follow is this: Be consistent in what you reward so that employees will see the pattern and the rationale for it. Supervisors walk a shaky tightrope as they try to balance two objectives: consistency *within* rewards for an employee, and equity *across* employees.

7	T or F	One good thing about the drives for achievement, power, and affiliation is that there is almost no negative side to them.
8	T or F	Perceptions of equity involve not only a judgment of the balance of effort and rewards but also the comparison to similar employees' rewards.

◀ *Quick Test 4*

⑤ MOTIVATION AND REWARDS

CONCEPT ▷ Supervisors need to use money and other means to encourage and reward effective employee behaviors.

How does money relate to the motivational concepts discussed earlier?

Quite obviously, money is important to employees for several reasons. They use it to buy groceries, pay the rent or mortgage, contribute to charitable causes, and fund their children's education. It also serves as a status symbol, for it provides a clue about the value that organizations place on them and their jobs. Further, it demonstrates one's achievement in life, provides access to social organizations, and is a source of power and influence over others. Pay also satisfies lower order needs (physiological and security) and helps remove the dissatisfaction associated with the absence of several maintenance factors in Herzberg's motivational model. Finally, pay serves as a clear measure of equity when employees wonder if they are receiving rewards equivalent to their contributions and the rewards that their peers are receiving. Therefore, pay—and its careful administration—cannot be ignored as a means of motivation.

Quips & Quotes

Motivation is what gets you started. Habit is what keeps you going.

—Jim Ryun

Meeting a goal can be very satisfying. **How can a supervisor reinforce that satisfaction for the employee?** ▶

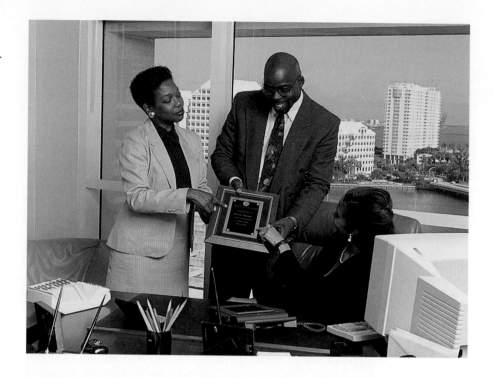

Should supervisors supplement pay with personal recognition?

Absolutely! Employees are constantly asking themselves (and their employers), "What's in it for me?" So supervisors had better be ready with the answers. When money is tight, creative supervisors still have many options for recognizing employees. The process is straightforward:

1. **Specify the desired outcomes.** Is it better customer service? Is it more deliveries per day? Be sure to communicate your goals in terms of what behaviors you are expecting and the results that should appear from their efforts.

2. **Involve the employee in choosing the form of recognition.** Some people prefer public praise; some do not. Some will smile for

a week after receiving a humorous T-shirt or coffee mug; some will not. Demonstrate that you care enough to ask, and the results will have greater impact.

3. **Monitor the employee's performance.** Be observant, and gather evidence indicating how things are going. Then share the data with the employee.

4. **Immediately provide recognition for early evidence of results achieved.** Don't wait for "just the right moment," for that day may never come. Commend the employee now, and celebrate the results. Find creative ways to do this, and don't hesitate to rely on the element of surprise.

◀ **Quick Test 5**

9	T or F	One of the keys to motivation is the proper use of money and other economic rewards.
10	T or F	Personal recognition of employees should be reserved for extraordinary performance.

6 MOTIVATION IN THE WORK ITSELF

CONCEPT ▶ Employees can be greatly motivated by the design of their jobs and their involvement in work decisions.

How can work be tailored to provide the greatest motivation for the persons who perform it?

By redesigning jobs according to *people-centered* considerations. Most work is first designed according to process-centered constraints revolving around technology and natural work flows. That is, emphasis is given to the dictates of (a) product or service specifications, (b) tool, machine, and equipment requirements, (c) process-flow sequences, (d) computer-assisted controls, and (e) work space layout. Only by a subsequent redesign (sociotechnical) that considers social as well as technological factors will most work be made more satisfying and convenient to human beings.

Many present-day efforts are being directed at process *reengineering*. This approach challenges old ways of doing things and encourages the removal of unnecessary steps. Jobs are combined into one, information technology is put to work, and work is performed where it makes the most sense. At the same time, present-day *job redesign* efforts stress a better accommodation of the psychological, as well as the physiological, needs of workers. And that is where supervisors enter the picture most actively.

Job redesign. The process of carefully restructuring a job to foster productivity and to appeal to the interests of the employees who carry it out.

What are the basic dimensions that job design focuses on?

Fast Company is a magazine with informative features regarding all aspects of a "company." The online version contains an archive of articles.

AT&T was a pioneer in experiments with work design. Authorities there and elsewhere identified five core dimensions of jobs. When all five dimensions are designed into a job, it is fully enriched and most likely to be motivational. As a result, high performance is expected, employees will be satisfied, and absenteeism and turnover lowered. The five dimensions are the following:

1. **Task identity** (whole job from beginning to end). This functional completeness enables an employee to start a task from scratch and see a definable product or service once the job has been completed.

2. **Task significance** (important work). This refers to the perceived impact that the job has on other people, on a finished product, or on the customer.

3. **Skill variety** (different skills and abilities used). The need to employ more than one skill and accomplish more than one task in getting the job done helps to relieve the sense of confinement and monotony.

4. **Autonomy** (freedom for self-direction). This is the reality as well as the feeling that the employee can make meaningful choices about how the work gets done, without direct interference or close supervision from others.

5. **Feedback** (direct information from the work itself). This is the possibility that an employee can tell immediately by looking at the finished product or service whether it has been done rightly or wrongly. The worker does not have to wait for hours, days, or weeks for a supervisor or inspector or accounting report to provide this information.

Can employees be motivated through being involved in work-related decisions?

Empowerment. Providing lower level employees with the authority to examine problem situations and resolve them as they arise.

Absolutely. Most workers have the intellectual capability, and the desire, to be more involved in decisions about their jobs. What they have lacked in the past has been the opportunity and sometimes the specific information and skills to make a meaningful contribution. *Empowerment*—the authority of lower level employees to examine problem situations and help resolve them as they arise—has become both a demand for a greater role by workers and a management practice responding to that demand. Sometimes supervisors drag their feet because they fear a loss of control. And sometimes employees try to exercise their new freedom too fast. But the potential motivational impact of empowerment is enormous, and the practice should not be overlooked by any supervisor.

How are empowerment and job redesign related?

Maximum employee involvement is allowed in the design of each individual's job. Process considerations are not ignored. Instead, employees are trained to view technical demands and requirements as problems they are invited to help solve with the help of their supervisor. The major feature of the people-centered approach lies in its stress on genuine participation by employees, singly or in groups, in making their work more effective and their jobs more attractive.

One increasingly common example of empowerment is for organizations to provide employees with decision-making opportunities with vendors, customers, or clients. Not only can employees use and demonstrate their expertise, but they gain valuable knowledge about product and service problems while gaining stature for being an important person who can solve problems.

How are jobs changed through redesign programs?

Two approaches—job enlargement and job enrichment—can each result in substantially changed jobs. Each has its merits, especially when it is tailored to the type of employees holding the job and their needs.

Job enlargement extends the boundaries of a job *horizontally* by adding differing tasks at the same level of expertise. The concept is to let manufacturing employees be responsible for the production step just before and just after the one they currently are doing. Thus, punch press operators might fill their own tote boxes and carry the punched parts to the next operation. It provides an opportunity to get away from a fixed place all day and a chance to converse for a minute or two with adjoining operators and to feel that the job isn't limited to the second or two it takes to load the press and wait for the die to stamp out a part.

Job enrichment is very different than the job-enlargement concept. It expands a job *vertically* by adding higher skill activities and by delegating greater authority. For example, the punch press operators might set up their presses with the die required for each new job, inspect their own work with gauges typically used by roving inspectors, and maintain their own output tallies.

Where does the biggest payoff come from in job redesign?

For the company or organization, it comes in greater output per employee; improved quality of product or service; and—often most important—fewer absences, lower turnover rates, and greater cooperation from employees.

Job enlargement. Extends the boundaries of a job by adding differing tasks at the same level of expertise.

Job enrichment. Expanding a job vertically by adding higher skill activities and delegating greater authority.

Quality of work life (QWL). The extent to which the work itself provides motivation, satisfaction, and the chance for personal growth.

For employees, there can be little doubt that job redesign adds a number of attractive ingredients to their work. Experts say that it improves the *quality of work life* (QWL) itself. It offers greater freedom and flexibility and at the same time makes the work more challenging. Job redesign utilizes more of an employee's skills and does this more effectively than traditionally chosen methods.

Quick Test 6 ▶

11	T or F	Fully enriched jobs will likely result in higher performance, satisfaction, absenteeism, and turnover.
12	T or F	Job enlargement is likely to increase an employee's sense of skill variety; job enrichment is likely to increase an employee's task significance and autonomy.

KEY CONCEPTS TO REMEMBER

1. **The Importance of Individuality.** Individual behavior is dependent on a vast heritage of background characteristics. One's personality is shaped by the forces of home environment, education, and work experience. This individuality causes people to behave as they do, even though such behavior often appears illogical to others who haven't taken the time to understand that person.

2. **A Powerful Pattern of Motivation.** Most people are motivated to satisfy five basic needs, arranged in a hierarchy. The physiological needs of survival and safety are at the bottom. The psychological needs of being social, winning the respect of others, and performing well the work they want to do are at the top. Each individual places different priorities on these needs, and these priorities vary from time to time. Once a need has been satisfied, it no longer serves to motivate behavior, and a supervisor must appeal to the next level of unsatisfied needs.

3. **Satisfaction and Dissatisfaction.** The two-factor theory says that the three lower level needs—survival, safety, and social—do not provide motivation; they are "hygiene" or "maintenance" factors that create dissatisfaction if they are not satisfied. Only the two higher level needs—for esteem and for self-actualization—are genuine satisfiers. Since supervisors often have little control over many of the dissatisfiers, their main motivational routes are through application of the satisfiers.

4. **Achievement, Expectancy, and Equity.** Employee motivation is also influenced by (a) the degree to which an individual seeks achievement, affiliation, or power, (b) the expectancy of rewards and the value placed upon them, and (c) the desire to receive equitable treatment at work. In all of these factors, supervisors must be sensitive to the employee's perception of working conditions and rewards.

5. **Motivation and Rewards.** Employees need, want, and value money for a wide range of reasons, and that is a big part of the reason why they work. They also desire recognition for their efforts and results, and that is an area where supervisors can have a powerful impact—if they are observant and systematic in rewarding employees.

6. **Motivation in the Work Itself.** When jobs are redesigned through a people-centered approach that blends individual needs and technology, the work becomes more nearly the kind of work employees want to do. Job enlargement and especially job enrichment fulfill needs for variety, whole tasks, significance, autonomy, and feedback, thus providing their own motivational force. Work redesign is most successful when employees are empowered to make meaningful decisions about products and services.

READING COMPREHENSION

1. What sorts of things affect the development of an individual's personality?
2. Why is it possible for two employees to have entirely different reactions to the same boss?
3. If an employee's survival, safety, and social needs were satisfied, which of Maslow's five needs should a supervisor appeal to next?
4. How might an individual's priorities of needs change with his or her growing maturity?

5. When worker motivation is still low despite good pay, fringe benefits, and desirable working conditions, what can a supervisor do to increase motivation?

6. How does Herzberg distinguish between satisfiers and dissatisfiers (hygiene factors)?

7. Explain the three estimates an employee makes about a work assignment in deciding whether he or she will try harder.

8. An employee told her supervisor, "I'm being paid fairly for the work I do; it's just that others are getting more for doing the same thing!" Explain the source of her dissatisfaction, and then indicate how the supervisor should respond to her.

9. Name at least five factors that, if built into jobs, add to the potential of the work itself to motivate employees.

10. After some changes had been made in the job, an employee complained to the supervisor, "This is job enlargement, all right, but it sure isn't job enrichment." What did the employee mean?

APPLICATION

Self-Assessment

▶ *How good are your motivational skills?*

Read the following statements carefully. Circle the number on the response scale that most closely reflects the degree to which each statement accurately describes you. Add up your total points and prepare a brief action plan for self-improvement. Be ready to report your score for tabulation across the entire group.

	Good Description									Poor Description
1. I believe it is wise to understand an employee's personality before trying to motivate that individual.	10	9	8	7	6	5	4	3	2	1
2. I understand the importance of removing dissatisfaction before trying to motivate an employee.	10	9	8	7	6	5	4	3	2	1
3. I believe that an employee's psychological needs are potentially as important as the individual's physiological needs.	10	9	8	7	6	5	4	3	2	1
4. I fully understand the difference in motivational impact between job enlargement and job enrichment.	10	9	8	7	6	5	4	3	2	1

	Good Description									Poor Description
5. I can see how I would have to motivate individuals differently if they have strong achievement, affiliation, or power drives.	10	9	8	7	6	5	4	3	2	1
6. I accept the role of the supervisor in making sure that employees perceive that their rewards are equitable.	10	9	8	7	6	5	4	3	2	1
7. I believe in empowering people to the greatest extent possible, based on their abilities and interest.	10	9	8	7	6	5	4	3	2	1
8. I understand the importance of building factors such as opportunities for variety, significance, and autonomy into employee jobs.	10	9	8	7	6	5	4	3	2	1
9. I am the kind of supervisor who is quick to share a word of "thanks" or praise with employees.	10	9	8	7	6	5	4	3	2	1
10. When I give feedback to employees, I usually focus on what they did well and the results that they achieved.	10	9	8	7	6	5	4	3	2	1

Scoring and Interpretation

SCORING

Add up your total points for the 10 questions. Record that number here, and report it when it is requested. _____

INTERPRETATION

81 to 100 points. You seem to have a basic set of motivational attitudes and skills.

61 to 80 points. Take a close look at some of your motivational attitudes and skills (those with lower self-assessments) and discuss them with a manager to see if they need improvement.

Below 60 points. Some of your skills may be substantially inconsistent with effective motivational practices and could be detrimental to your success as a supervisor.

Identify your three lowest scores and record the question numbers here: _____, _____, _____.

ACTION

Write a brief paragraph detailing an action plan for how you might sharpen each of these skills. Then pay particularly close attention to the related material in the chapter as you review the relevant sections there.

Skill Development

Using Motivational Concepts

Assume that you have been promoted to be the supervisor of a dozen employees in your department. You are eager to develop a high-performing unit, and recognize the importance of motivating each employee to the highest level. You have decided to use what you know about motivational concepts. Indicate below how you would plan to obtain relevant information about each of the ideas listed for each employee. Then prepare a report that suggests how you intend to use that information to motivate your employees. To prepare your report, you will likely wish to review the text's discussion on various motivational concepts, scan the Internet for relevant guidelines, and consult with colleagues and staff persons in the human resources department for their advice.

Motivational Concept	Information Needed	Application
1. Maslow's need hierarchy	_____	_____
	_____	_____
2. Herzberg's satisfaction and dissatisfaction model	_____	_____
	_____	_____
3. McClelland's achievement, affiliation, and power drives	_____	_____
4. Employee expectancies	_____	_____
	_____	_____
5. Perceptions of equity	_____	_____
	_____	_____
6. Need for money	_____	_____
	_____	_____
7. Need for personal recognition	_____	_____
8. Job design dimensions	_____	_____
	_____	_____
9. Empowerment	_____	_____
	_____	_____
10. Job redesign	_____	_____
	_____	_____

Group Exercise

Motivational Debate ◀

Careful reading and review of the chapter will suggest that many of the motivational tools available to supervisors can be classified into either extrinsic or intrinsic factors. *Extrinsic factors* are those that provide motivation from outside the employee (and are often more easily manipulated by supervisors); they include the lower order needs (Maslow), dissatisfiers (Herzberg), and many others. *Intrinsic factors* are those that provide motivation from inside the employee; they include the higher order needs (Maslow), satisfiers (Herzberg), and many job design dimensions.

STEP 1: Form into two groups, and prepare yourselves for a debate.

STEP 2: Team A will take the position that extrinsic factors are most important for a supervisor to use for motivation, while Team B will take the position that intrinsic factors are most important for a supervisor to use for motivation.

STEP 3: Conduct the debate. Be prepared not only to present your side but to look for flaws in the other side's arguments. Make notes in the spaces below.

Arguments for Extrinsic Motivation	Arguments for Intrinsic Motivation
1.	1.
2.	2.
3.	3.
4.	4.
5.	5.
6.	6.
7.	7.
8.	8.
9.	9.
10.	10.

CASES FOR ANALYSIS

Case 25

The Conflicting Coffee Breaks

Two employees, Janet and Martha, work side by side as bank tellers. For several months, they relieved one another for their coffee breaks. Janet took the first break from 9:45 to 10 A.M., and Martha took the second one, from 10 to 10:15 A.M. However, a new supermarket opened in the shopping center, and there was suddenly a large influx of shoppers coming in to cash checks right after 10 A.M. Accordingly, Jack Smith, their boss, asked Martha to postpone her coffee break until after 10:30 A.M. but told Janet she could continue on the same break as before. Martha thought this request over, and when she came in the next day, she told Mr. Smith that the new arrangement was unfair. If anyone should postpone her break, it should be Janet, because she had had the early one for a long time. When Mr. Smith asked Janet her opinion, Janet said that she had been handling the peak load alone from 10 to 10:15 A.M. for a long while. Now she ought to get the choice because she is still going to be on duty during the extended peak period.

Analysis ▶

If you were Mr. Smith, what would you do? Rank the following five alternatives on a scale from 1 to 5 in the order in which they appeal to you (1, most preferable; 5, least preferable). You may add another alternative if you wish. Be prepared to justify your ranking.

_____ **a.** Tell Martha that she is selfish for not going along with a simple adjustment, and insist that she comply with your request.

_____ **b.** Agree to Martha's suggestion instead, and tell Janet you expect her to cooperate.

_____ **c.** Point out that the morning hours are busy for only a very short time, so this shouldn't be a factor.

_____ **d.** Ask Martha and Janet to resolve this problem between themselves, as long as there is double coverage from 10 to 10:30 A.M.

_____ **e.** Set up a rotating schedule.

Putting Maslow Into Practice

Hollie, who supervises the cassette reproduction room for a large audio manufacturer, made the following statements when talking to employees. Hollie is very aware of the five basic motivational needs described by A. H. Maslow: survival, safety or security, social, esteem or respect, and self-actualization.

◀ *Analysis*

You can help Hollie by identifying the need she is appealing to and suggesting a way in which that need can be satisfied at work. On a separate sheet of paper, write the letters *a* to *e* to correspond to each of the following statements. After each letter on your list, write the number 1, followed by the need Hollie is appealing to, and then write the number 2, followed by your suggestion for satisfying this particular need at work. Use this example as a guide.

"Al, I know you're struggling on your present wages to meet expenses, but your work is good and you can expect regular pay increments."

1. Survival needs
2. Introduce merit pay programs

a. "If the boss approves, Marcie, I'm going to see that you get some free time to develop those product specification changes you suggested."

b. "I know that some of the organization changes around here have bothered you, Bob, but you can be sure of having a good job here for as long as you want."

c. "Debbie, the boss asked me why the stripping bottleneck suddenly disappeared, and I told him it was mainly the result of your good work."

d. "Felix, you don't have to stop talking with the others whenever I come into the room. I don't mind if you talk, as long as it doesn't interfere with your work."

e. "You can relax about that rent payment now, Harry. Your job has been reevaluated, and you'll be getting a nice increase in salary."

Case 27

The "Disposable" Workforce

Ramon was in shock. Just two weeks ago, he had been promoted to the position of Supervisor of Security for a large electronics plant on the West Coast. After 13 years in the profession, he was proud of his work record and looked forward to building a committed group of security officers. Then the bombshell hit. Corporate executives announced that the company was in severe financial difficulty, and "belt-tightening" measures would be implemented immediately. Ramon's boss directed him to lay off all 17 security personnel, and contract for plant security through hiring temporary and part-time workers as needed. Ramon had read something about the "new workforce"—millions of people working by the hour, day, or project and often receiving limited benefits. Now he would be supervising a loose-knit group of part-timers, leased employees, or "peripherals," as his boss was already calling them.

Analysis ▷

a. How will this "new workforce" differ from the old?
b. What can Ramon do to motivate the part-time workers?

Answers to Quick Tests ▷

Quick Test 1	Quick Test 2	Quick Test 3
1. T	3. F	5. F
2. F	4. T	6. T
Quick Test 4	**Quick Test 5**	**Quick Test 6**
7. F	9. T	11. F
8. T	10. F	12. T

CHAPTER 10

Leadership Skills, Styles, and Qualities

Learning Objectives

After studying this chapter, you should be able to

- Describe the essential skills of leadership.

- Explain the relationship between leadership and motivation, and differentiate between the assumptions of Theory X and Theory Y.

- Recognize the various leadership styles, explain the benefits and prerequisites of a participative approach and the potential reasons for its failure.

- Discuss the factors a leader should consider when selecting a leadership style, and explain two models for choosing a style on a situational basis.

- Discuss the leader's responsibility for being an effective follower, actions for helping employees become self-leaders, the impact of substitutes for leadership, and the role of servant-leader (steward).

① LEADERSHIP DEFINED

CONCEPT ▶ Given certain characteristics, a supervisor may acquire and develop the skills required for effective leadership.

What is leadership?

Leadership. The process of influencing and supporting others to follow you and to do willingly the things that need to be done.

Everyone will give you a different answer to this one—a set of traits (see Superscope), a certain behavior, a standard style. Our definition is this: *Leadership is the process of influencing and supporting others to follow you and to do willingly the things that need to be done.* Obviously, the actions you request from others should be reasonable, relevant, and ethical. They should represent appropriate actions that will advance your department toward its goals of higher productivity, improved quality or service, and conservation of its resources. Two other factors stand out in our definition of leadership. First, employee responses need to be more than passive acceptance; you need willing and enthusiastic commitment. Second, as employees develop their skills and experience, they should begin to accept some of the responsibility themselves for seeing what needs to be done.

Super SCOPE ▶ ## Important Leadership Traits

Shelley Kirkpatrick and Edwin Locke have reviewed a half-century of research on leadership traits. Although the research contains some mixed results, they found that several factors consistently seem to differentiate between effective leaders and ineffective leaders. The most important traits of good leaders are the following:

- **Energy.** Good leaders have a high level of personal drive and enthusiasm. They demonstrate a strong work ethic before they ask others to dedicate themselves.
- **Desire.** Effective leaders have personal aspirations to rise to leadership positions, and the desire to guide others to greater achievements. They choose to be leaders.
- **Integrity.** Fidelity, strength of character, and credibility are their hallmarks. Good

leaders set high ethical and moral standards for themselves, and live up to them conspicuously. Their words, supported by their actions, send clear messages to others about the type of behavior they expect.

- **Self-confidence.** Leaders feel good about their past performance and future capabilities. They have appropriate levels of self-esteem, projected through self-assurance in their actions and decisions.
- **Judgment.** Careful analysis and thoughtful consideration precede most actions by effective leaders. However, they can still be decisive when the situation calls for it.

In addition, effective leaders have a firm knowledge of the company's technology, and demonstrate charisma, creativity, and flexibility when needed.

Source: "Leadership: Do Traits Matter?" by Shelley A. Kirkpatrick and Edwin A. Locke, *Academy of Management Executive*, May 1991, pp. 48–60.

BUILDING TRUST

■ The best ways to develop and demonstrate your integrity and honesty with employees, while building a trusting relationship with them, include the following:

• Maintain confidentiality when they confide personal information to you.

• Always tell them the truth, for employees can detect (or eventually discover) lies.

• Strive for fairness, equity, and objectivity in all your interactions.

• Be candid, disclosing, and open, keeping employees well-informed at all times.

• Promise a lot; deliver even more." Fulfill your pledges to them, and then some.

Are good leaders born or made?

Most leaders must learn their skills. They do so by working at self-improvement, observing and studying effective leaders, and carefully analyzing their employees and the situations in which they do their jobs.

How much does a supervisor's personality have to do with leadership?

A good personality helps. Most employees react more positively to a supervisor who has a ready smile, exhibits a sense of caring, and demonstrates personal warmth. But even an outgoing extrovert must be more than skin deep to be effective. Much more important is your real desire to understand and support the people who work for you. Fair play, interest in others, good decisions, and honest character will help make you a stronger leader than you would be if you relied solely on personality.

Much has been written about charisma. Is that important to be a leader?

Charisma is a leadership characteristic that can help motivate workers into early and sustained action. Supervisors with charisma tend to have expertise, be assertive and self-confident, take moderate risks, and express high performance expectations for others. Their language, behavior, spontaneity, and personal energy seem to inspire others around them. Employees trust and respect leaders with charisma, accept their vision of needed departmental actions, and commit themselves to working hard to achieve results. Clearly, it is a trait that supervisors should work hard to achieve, for it is invaluable when changes must be introduced.

What personal skills does leadership require?

The list is almost endless. As specific keys to success, some would focus on time management or on how to run an effective meeting. Others would point toward problem solving or being a good teacher and communicator. Most people would agree, however, that good leaders have mastered the following three skills:

Persuasion. This is the ability to assemble and present to others a good case for what you think should be done. It works equally well with your boss and your employees. Persuasion relies both on a rational development of arguments and on a convincing presentation of them.

Influence. This is the ability to exert power over others. Many people possess or are given power, but few learn how to use it. Supervisors, for example, have the power and authority of their *position*, and the prestige that accompanies it. They have the power of *expertise*, in their greater knowledge of departmental and company operations than is normally possessed by their employees. They also have the power that comes from their capacity to administer or withhold *rewards* from others. But power is like the electrical energy that comes to a light socket—it is useful only when the switch comes on. Similarly, your supervisory power will not make you a leader until you learn to use this power to move others.

Social skills. One of a supervisor's biggest tasks is creating among others a willingness to cooperate with each other. This requires a range of interpersonal skills, beginning with tact, diplomacy, a deep understanding of motivation, and the ability to perceive the needs of others. Leaders must first establish a firm foundation of rapport with their employees; then they can use their powers of influence and persuasion to activate individuals and groups in the pursuit of worthwhile goals.

Quick Test 1 ▶			
1	T or **F**	Leadership is essentially a set of traits that one is (or is not) born with.
2	**T** or F	Supervisory influence can be derived from either position, expertise, or reward power.

② LEADERSHIP AND MOTIVATION

CONCEPT ▷ Leadership relies upon providing direction that satisfies the motivational needs of others, and the direction chosen reflects a supervisor's assumptions about these needs.

How are motivation and leadership related?

Motivation is a power that arises within an individual to satisfy a need. As you've seen earlier in discussions about Maslow's and McClelland's views of motivation (see Chapter 9), needs cover a broad span, from the need for survival and safety to the need for self-esteem and fulfillment, and from the need for achievement to the need for affiliation and power. Leaders, as shown in Figure 10-1, act to provide satisfaction, or to offer a means of satisfaction, for the needs of others. Leaders don't really motivate. A leader succeeds by first understanding the needs of others and then applying persuasion and influence to show others that they will get the most satisfaction from following the leader's views.

A person can have motivation without another person's leadership. Leadership, however, cannot succeed without motivation on the follower's part. Take Mary, for example. She has a powerful need to show that she can perform a higher level job. This may be a strong enough motivation for her to attend night courses to acquire the necessary knowledge and skills. She will do this with or without the encouragement of her supervisor. On the other hand, there is Peter. He has the same aptitudes as Mary. With additional training, he, too, could perform a higher level job. Peter's supervisor sees this aptitude and offers Peter all sorts of encouragement and assistance in acquiring the necessary skills. Peter, however, is content to stay where he is. His social needs are very strong. He wants to continue to enjoy working with the people with whom he's become friendly. Enrolled in a night course at the supervisor's suggestion, he soon drops out. The leadership failed, despite the supervisor's influence and persuasion, because the supervisor was not properly tuned to Peter's motivational needs.

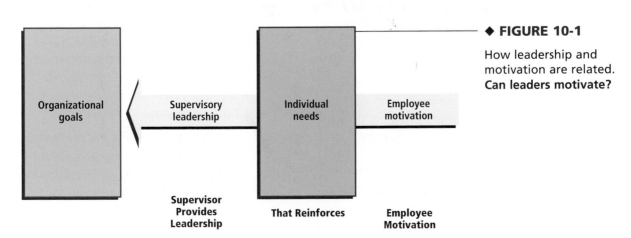

◆ FIGURE 10-1

How leadership and motivation are related. **Can leaders motivate?**

Turn Peter's situation around a little bit and look at it again. Suppose Peter is such a fun lover that his work suffers. His boss tells him that if his performance doesn't improve, he'll lose his job. Peter's reaction is: "So what! I can get another job." At this point, the supervisor uses the knowledge of Peter's social needs to persuade him that he'll enjoy working with his friends at his current job more than he might enjoy working with strangers at some other job. Peter accepts this advice and gets his act together so that he can hold his present job. The leadership provided by Peter's supervisor has succeeded. The supervisor established rapport and was tuned to Peter's motivational needs. She used the power of her position to influence Peter's judgment about the consequences of his performance. And then she persuaded Peter that it was in his best interest to improve the quality of his work.

Theory X, Theory Y. What's this all about?

To get along with people effectively, you must make a couple of fundamental decisions. First, you must recognize your responsibility for managing human affairs at work. Second, you must always weigh this concern of yours against the practical urgencies of technical and administrative matters.

Theory X. A set of assumptions in which a supervisor acts as if she or he believes that most people don't like to work and that they wish to avoid responsibility and prefer job security above all.

Douglas McGregor, late professor of industrial management at the Massachusetts Institute of Technology, had much to offer supervisors in his thoughtful work, *The Human Side of Enterprise*. Most of today's management thinking was forged long ago to meet the needs of a feudal society, reasoned McGregor. The world has changed, and new thinking is needed for top efficiency today. That's the core of this unique philosophy of contrasting Theory X against Theory Y.

Theory X, the traditional framework for management thinking, is based on the following set of implicit assumptions about human nature and human behavior:

1. The average human being has an inherent dislike of work and will avoid it if possible.

2. Because of this human characteristic of dislike of work, most people must be coerced, controlled, directed, or threatened with punishment to get them to put forth adequate effort toward the achievement of organizational objectives.

3. The average human being prefers to be directed, wishes to avoid responsibility, has relatively little ambition, and wants security above all.

Did You Know **?**

How Management and Leadership Differ

Management	Leadership
Get things done	Get right things done
Direct	Inspire
Cope with complexity	Initiate change
Organize and staff for task achievement	Communicate vision
Task achievement	Goal accomplishment

▲ Theory X dictated that personnel be watched constantly. **How do assumptions in Theory Y differ in this regard?**

Do these assumptions make up a straw person for purposes of scientific demolition? Unfortunately, they do not. Although they are rarely stated so directly, the principles that constitute the bulk of traditional management action could have been derived only from assumptions such as those of Theory X.

Theory Y finds its roots in recently accumulated and emerging knowledge about human behavior. It is based on the following set of assumptions:

Theory Y. A set of assumptions in which a supervisor acts as if she or he believes that most people can set challenging goals and provide their own initiative and exert self-control to attain their goals.

1. The expenditure of physical and mental effort in work is as natural as play or rest.

2. External control and the threat of punishment are not the only means for bringing about effort toward organizational objectives. Individuals will exercise self-control in the service of objectives to which they are committed.

3. Commitment to objectives depends on the rewards associated with their achievement. The most important rewards are those that satisfy needs for self-respect and personal improvement.

4. The average human being learns, under proper conditions, not only to accept but also to seek responsibility.

5. The capacity to exercise a relatively high degree of imagination, ingenuity, and creativity in the solution of organizational problems is widely, not narrowly, distributed in the population among both men and women.

6. Under the conditions of modern industrial life, the intellectual potentialities of the average human being are only partially realized.

What makes Theory Y still applicable today?

Under the assumptions of Theory Y, the work of the supervisor is to integrate the needs of employees with the needs of the department. Hard-nosed control rarely succeeds today. In McGregor's words,

> [Supervisors] are dealing with adults who are only partially dependent. They can—and will—exercise remarkable ingenuity in defeating the purpose of external controls that they resent. However, they can—and do—learn to exercise self-direction and self-control under appropriate conditions. [The supervisor's] task is to help them discover objectives consistent both with organizational requirements and with their own personal goals.

In McGregor's mind, *the ability to help employees to discover goals consistent with those of the organization is the essence of leadership*. When a genuine commitment to these objectives is secured, said McGregor, "supervision consists of helping employees achieve these objectives: to act as teacher, consultant, colleague, and only rarely as authoritative boss."

You can see that Theory Y, along with the leadership roles that it implies, is far more in tune with today's employees than is Theory X and the autocratic style of leadership it implies. Good supervisors are willing and able to step back and examine periodically their assumptions about the nature and motivation of the people they supervise. Some will find that they have been using styles of leadership based on inappropriate and outdated assumptions, and they will need to change their own behavior. The important thing is to identify and test your assumptions—would they hold up to close scrutiny by your peers? Your manager? Your own employees? Once you have revised your assumptions, then you need to ask yourself what new style of leadership they imply.

Quick Test 2 ▶

3	T or F	It takes a combination of employee motivation and supervisory leadership to accomplish organizational goals.
4	T or F	Effective supervisors examine their assumptions about people and examine their implications for behavior.

LEADERSHIP STYLES AND CONCEPTS

3

CONCEPT ▶ Leadership styles range widely from a job- or task-centered orientation, to a people- or relationship-centered one, with many other combinations. A participative style has special merit for consideration.

What is meant by "styles" of leadership, and which are the most basic?

A **style of leadership** refers to the total approach a supervisor uses in trying to direct, activate, or otherwise provide a motivational atmosphere for employees. It is a combination of the leadership traits, skills, attitudes, and behaviors that employees *perceive* their supervisor to have and con-sistently use. Leadership is in the mind of the beholder. A traditional way to distinguish among leadership styles was to divide them into three types:

Management Science. Check the Internet for valuable management magazines and journals.

> **Autocratic**, or **directive**, **leadership.** Here, the leader independently sets goals, makes decisions, gives orders, and demands obedience from the people supervised. In some cases, this can produce short-run results, and it may even be appro-priate when time is tight or a crisis is present. However, regular use of a directive style reflects assumptions consistent with Theory X. Most employees dislike—even fear—working for a rigid leader, feeling that they have more to contribute and deserve some respect. As a result, employee commitment may suffer, and absen-teeism and turnover problems may arise (see Figure 10-2).

◆ **FIGURE 10-2**

Clues that employees may fear you. **What happens when employees fear their leader?**

Democratic, or **consultative**, **leadership.** This style continues to be a popular approach. The leader presents problems to a group, consults with relevant individuals, or solicits ideas from those with expertise and interest in the issue before making a decision. This promotes involvement and strong teamwork. The consultative style is similar to what the Japanese call "consensus" management. Some critics argue, however, that it delays decision making, weakens a leader's image, and results in compromises with less than optimum features.

Participative leadership. This style is the most difficult for a supervisor to learn and practice. It relies on the employee's sense of responsibility, training, experience, and good judgment, and the supervisor's capacity to "let go" of some authority. However, it is highly consistent with the need to empower employees (as discussed in Chapter 9) and the assumptions of Theory Y. True participation gives one or more employees the right to explore a problem, gather relevant information, make a decision, and implement it. The positive result is that they are mentally and emotionally committed to its success. But there are risks, too—not all employees are immediately ready for it, and it can be threatening to a supervisor's desire to be in control.

Participative leadership. The act of fully involving employees in decision-making processes such that their ideas are used and they are fully committed to the solution's success.

Participative leadership is challenging for many supervisors. **What are its advantages?** ▼

What are the prerequisites to using a participative style?

Several conditions would ideally be in place before a participative approach could have the greatest chance of succeeding. There must be adequate time to consult with employees, the benefits of allowing participation must exceed the costs, and the issue must be sufficiently interesting to engage the workers' minds and imaginations. It almost goes without saying that the problem must be within the supervisor's area of job freedom (latitude to make decisions). Consequently, not all problems lend themselves to a participative approach, and both the supervisor and the employees must understand this.

What formal programs exist to encourage employee participation?

Clearly, many supervisors can initiate a participative approach on their own. They need to recognize, however, that such an experiment may be nearly irreversible. Once they allow employee involvement in meaningful issues, it won't be relinquished easily. And it also changes their own role dramatically as they become facilitators of the work group—coaching, encouraging, and even "cheering" their success.

On a more formal level, organizations have implemented a wide variety of participative programs, including the following:

- **Suggestion systems.** These programs invite individual employees to submit recommendations for work improvements. After careful evaluation of their practicality and probable cost savings, monetary awards may be made, sometimes amounting to thousands of dollars.

- **Quality circles and total quality management programs.** Some organizations set up voluntary groups of employees that receive training in problem solving, group decision making, and statistical techniques. Employees become involved in the idea of continuously searching for improvements in their operations and striving for quality and service improvements.

- **Employee ownership plans.** Sometimes called employee stock ownership plans (ESOPs), these systems allow employees to purchase shares of common stock in the company, thereby becoming part owners. Employees thus are given a chance to share in profits (through dividend distributions), if there are any, or in losses (if the stock's market price declines). The more substantive ESOPs actually give employees genuine opportunities to share in the management of their companies through formal involvement of representatives at a variety of organizational levels, possibly including a seat on the board of directors.

Did You Know ?

Emotional Intelligence

■ In addition to the need for a reasonable level of IQ (mental capacity), leaders also need a solid level of EQ (emotional intelligence), according to author Dan Goleman. EQ is the ability of supervisors to manage their emotions for the greatest level of interpersonal success. It involves (1) recognizing one's emotions and reflecting on them, (2) actively managing them by deciding to remain in control of them, and (3) engaging in productive self-talk to avoid inappropriate expressions of undesirable emotions (e.g., fear, anger) when crises occur. The good news is this: Emotional intelligence can be developed throughout most of your work life if you are willing to try. Despite past setbacks, you can improve!

If participative management is so good, why does it sometimes fail?

Clearly, it's not for everyone, although most supervisors should thoroughly explore its potential gains. When it breaks down, it is most often due to one—or more—of these factors:

- It may be uncomfortable for supervisors (or employees) to change old habits.
- It may be attempted in an insincere fashion, causing employees to see right through the transparent attempt to manipulate them.
- Supervisors may fail to follow through on the implementation of employee inputs and decisions. When this happens, employees quickly decide it's not worth the effort when the next occasion arises.
- Intense performance pressure, coupled with a decade of downsizings, may produce so much fear and insecurity in employees that they are literally "frozen" in their ability to think clearly and address critical problems, even when given the opportunity to do so.
- Perhaps most significantly, some supervisors fear that allowing their employees to participate results in a loss of power for themselves. Consequently, they cling to their "right" to make decisions in the face of demands from the contemporary workforce to be involved.

Quick Test 3 ▶		
5	T or **F**	It doesn't matter much what supervisory style employees perceive. What matters most is what the supervisor intended to convey.
6	T or **F**	Participative leadership works so well because all problems lend themselves to its use at work.

④ SELECTING AN APPROPRIATE STYLE

CONCEPT ▶ Leadership styles should be selected with a keen sensitivity to the individuals and circumstances involved.

Contingency model of leadership. The belief that the leadership style that will be most effective in a given situation can be predicted by examining the intensity of three interacting factors.

What factors might affect the choice of a leadership style?

Situational leadership models maintain that leaders need to assess several key factors before making a decision on which style to adopt. This is in contrast to older models, which implied that the need for leadership should always be fully balanced between all-out concerns for both people and production. One situational approach, the **contingency model of** *leadership*, advanced by Professor Fred Fiedler and documented in many studies, identifies three critical factors. It asks the leader to examine (a) the quality of leader-member relations, or rapport and good feelings between the supervisor and those supervised, (b) the level of structure in the job, in terms of how carefully procedures and specifications must be followed, and (c) the amount of real power invested in the supervisor by his or her superiors. The model then relates this assessment to research results showing whether a task-centered (authoritative) or people-centered (democratic or participative) style is called for.

What is the particular significance of the contingency approach?

It adds an important consideration when a supervisor is choosing a leadership style. As the term *contingency* implies, the style chosen depends upon the conditions of the three factors in any given situation (see Figure 10-3). Surprisingly, the task-centered, or authoritative, approach, which uses forceful directing and controlling, is most effective in either very favorable or very unfavorable circumstances. That is, it works best when relationships are either very good or very poor, job methods are either precisely defined or not defined at all, and the leader's true authority is either very strong or very weak. In the less clearly defined, or middle, situations, the participative approach is more likely to be successful.

Situational Conditions

Most Effective Leadership Approach

Very favorable conditions → **Task-centered** Production-oriented, directive, authoritative.

Mixed or ambiguous conditions → **People-centered** Relations-oriented, participative.

Very unfavorable conditions → **Task-centered** Production-oriented, directive, authoritative.

1. Rapport   2. Job precision   3. Position power

◆ **FIGURE 10-3**

Choosing a leadership style according to the situation. **Which style is best?**

In other words, an *authoritative style* works out best (a) in situations where the supervisor has lots of real power, the process requires strong control, and rapport with employees is good, and (b) in situations where exactly the opposite conditions prevail.

A *participative style* is best where the supervisor's authority hasn't been clearly spelled out by top management or acknowledged by the employees, where the process and procedures are somewhat flexible, and where the rapport between supervisor and employees is only moderately good.

The contingency approach tends to explain why directive supervisors can be effective in some situations and not in others. Similarly, it helps to show where participative leadership may work best and to suggest where it might fail. An authoritative approach may work for assembly-line workers or for labor crews cleaning up the area. A participative approach seems favorable on jobs for which exact procedures are hard to set or for jobs that require creativity or initiative. These conclusions are contingent on the authoritative leader's having either high or low position power and high or low rapport, and on the participative leader's having moderate rapport and only so-so authority.

Which style of leadership, on average, will get the best results?

Surely the most difficult aspect of leadership involves the decision of when to lead and when to stand back. That is the value in employing the concept of situational leadership. Regardless of whether or not you accept the rather narrow prescriptions of Dr. Fiedler, the situational concept opens your mind to the wisdom of selecting a style that is most suitable for the individuals and circumstances involved.

Many successful managers will tell you that democratic leadership is the best method to use. The fact is, however, that whereas the democratic way may involve the least risk, you'll hamper your leadership role if you stick only to that method. You can play a round of golf with only a driver, but you'll get a much better score if you use a wedge in a sand trap and a putter on the greens.

A good way to consider such choices is to think of leadership as ranging along a ***continuum of leadership*** styles, as shown in Figure 10-4. At one extreme, a supervisor relies upon complete authority; at the other, subordinates are allowed a great deal of freedom. Between the extremes are an infinite number of shadings of leadership styles to choose from.

Should your leadership approach be varied according to an employee's maturity level?

One school of thought believes that it should—provided that you are talking about a person's task-related maturity, and not about chronological age or emotional development. Paul Hersey's and Ken Blanchard's *situational (or life-cycle) model of leadership* suggests that employees vary in two important ways—their task-specific *competence (ability)* and

Continuum of leadership. A range of leadership approaches that progresses from the extremes of autocratic control by the supervisor to complete freedom for subordinates.

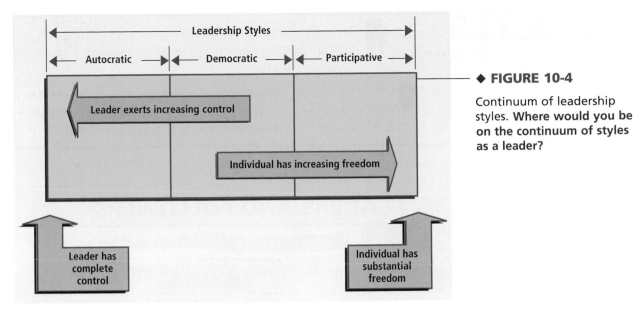

Source: Adapted from "How to Choose a Leadership Pattern," by Robert Tannenbaum and Warren H. Schmidt, *Harvard Business Review*, March/April 1958, pp. 95–101.

their motivation to *perform (willingness,* or *commitment).* Supervisors can help employees develop along both dimensions of task-related maturity by providing appropriate guidance and feedback, offering a variety of job experiences, and clarifying the rewards for cooperative behavior.

Not surprisingly, any work group may have a mixture of members who are at a low developmental stage (low ability and low commitment), intermediate stages (low ability and high willingness, or high ability but low willingness), or high levels of development (high ability and high commitment). The Hersey-Blanchard model suggests that supervisors adapt their approach to *fit the development stage of each employee,* using a directive style for those at low levels, more supportive styles (or mixed directive and supportive) for those at intermediate levels, and a "delegating" style (low direction and low support) for employees who have demonstrated their competence and commitment. The keys to success with this model lie in taking the time to analyze each employee's stage of development, working with them to move them upward, and matching your style to fit their current needs.

Should you ever deviate from the prescriptions of the situational models?

Absolutely. In a crisis, autocratic leadership is called for because it is fast. When an emergency arises—say, a live steam hose breaks loose and whips about, endangering lives—you can't afford the time to consult employees as to what to do. Instead (and with the probable complete support of your crew), you'd probably shout, "Hey, Smitty, cut the steam valve! Sandy, hit the electrical power switch!"

7	T or F	According to the contingency model of leadership, a task-centered approach works well no matter what the situation calls for.
8	T or F	The Hersey-Blanchard model suggests that a supervisor might have to use different leadership styles with employees who are at different levels of task-related maturity.

5 LEADERS AND FOLLOWERS

CONCEPT ▶ Supervisors must consider both themselves and their employees as followers, and also acknowledge that there are substitutes for effective leadership.

Can supervisors afford to focus exclusively on their leadership role?

No. Supervisors are leaders, but they are also followers. To be promoted in your organization, you may need to develop a reputation not only as an effective leader of your current work unit, but also as a loyal supporter of your boss. This requires a completely different orientation, in effect looking upward as well as looking downward. Effective followers avoid competing with their managers for the spotlight, act as team players, and feel comfortable disagreeing occasionally. They also take the initiative to raise penetrating (but useful) questions, constructively confront their manager's ideas and actions, and work hard to anticipate and prevent potential problems. Effective followership is an important role and needs to be balanced with the leadership job.

What responsibility do supervisors have toward helping their employees develop as leaders?

Some supervisors have been dismayed to learn that their own career advancement was put on hold because higher managers felt that there was no one adequately prepared to take the supervisor's place. Don't let that happen to you! In addition to providing job-related training (which we discussed in Chapter 8), good supervisors will also consider the opportunity to be a superleader for their employees. The **superleader**, according to authors Charles Manz and Henry Sims, Jr., is a person who places high priority on unleashing and expanding the capabilities of subordinates. A special focus is on encouraging them to practice self-leadership skills, including self-observation, independent goal setting, rehearsal of desirable activities, self-administration of rewards, and self-criticism. Superleaders, then, create a win–win situation. Employees learn useful leadership skills that may qualify them for promotions, and the supervisor

Superleader. A supervisor who places a high priority on developing the skills of employees to manage themselves and engage in self-leadership.

acquires a self-motivated group of employees who can be trusted to work toward organizational goals under their own volition. Theory Y assumptions again play a large role in affecting one's decision to be a superleader.

I can't be present all the time. What happens to my leadership while I'm gone?

We have already provided one answer—create self-leading employees. Another simple response is that close and constant supervision can actually *inhibit* some productive employee behaviors. And believing that you are indispensable, or that employees will always fool around just because your back is turned, may be an indication that you hold Theory X assumptions. But another fascinating set of alternatives lies in the idea of **substitutes for leadership**.

Have you ever considered the possibility that you can be replaced with factors already or clearly present in the task, organization, or other employees? It's possible. Researchers have found that a supervisor's need to accent a production orientation may be diminished by the presence of strong subordinate experience, clear policies and rules, or a cohesive work group with a positive attitude. Similarly, there are potential substitutes for a supervisor's need to show a high concern for people and be supportive toward them. Intrinsically satisfying tasks, employees with a professional orientation, and individuals with a high need for independence can help relieve the supervisory pressure. The real lesson is, don't cling to a rigid definition of your leadership role. The job has changed and will likely go right on changing!

> **Substitutes for leadership.** Factors in the task, organization, or employees that diminish the need for various kinds of supervisory leadership behaviors.

How do new attitudes in the contemporary workforce affect leadership behavior?

Much has been written about Generation X and the generation of employees already following it. The combination of a "new age" workforce, coupled with a dramatic influx of women, immigrants, and minorities into the labor force, have created some unique challenges for supervisors. Some new workers are less committed to their employers; they will readily quit for a better job—or no job at all. Some new workers don't want to work during "traditional" hours, or wear "traditional" clothing at work. Others sharply protest the need to be placed in a subordinate position to someone who may lack their level of technical expertise. Even simple and nonthreatening behaviors such as wearing decorative jewelry, displaying tattoos, or wearing extreme hairstyles can create challenges for supervisors, if they allow the behaviors to do so.

The key to adapting to these new forces lies in viewing one's job as a **steward**, according to noted author and consultant, Peter Block. He suggests that good supervisory stewards retain their level of accountability for resources and results, while giving up their need to dominate, be right, or (always) be in control. Stewardship implies empowering others, building partnerships with others, and (most of all) having the humility to define

> **Stewardship.** The view that supervisors are stewards of resources and must play the role of servant-leader to help others achieve their goals.

one's role as being in service to others while building employee capabilities and enhancing their performance. The supervisor-as-servant sets aside the idea of status and power differences while searching for ways to help others meet their goals and satisfy their needs through productive work. This type of leadership approach usually proves far more palatable to newer workers, who are less inclined to accept traditional, task-oriented supervision.

Can leaders always be popular with the people they supervise?

Probably not. The very best leaders seem to combine the knack of leading with the knack of winning friends. But most supervisors are not that successful. Instead, they must be satisfied with earning the respect of their followers. Why? Because many of the decisions that you must make as a supervisor will not favor everybody. Sometimes you will please nobody. The result is that you must often be satisfied with the knowledge that your leadership has been responsible, considerate, and equitable—regardless of how unfairly others may judge you.

Quick Test 5 ▶			
9	T or F	A superleader is one who can step in and perform all of his or her employees' jobs if the need arises.
10	T or F	When substitutes for leadership exist, it removes the need even to have a supervisor in that position.

KEY CONCEPTS TO REMEMBER

1. **Leadership Defined.** Leadership requires the ability to develop rapport with others and to apply appropriate persuasion and influence to obtain their willing cooperation in pursuing legitimate organizational goals. Given sound character in the supervisor, the skills of leadership can be acquired and developed.

2. **Leadership and Motivation.** Leadership is not a form of manipulation. Instead, it relies upon gaining a firm understanding of another's motives and providing conditions in the workplace that enable that person to satisfy his or her needs while also helping the organization to attain its goals. It is important that the assumptions concerning an employee's needs are, in fact, correct. The two opposing sets of assumptions about employee motivation are characterized by Theory X (the desire to avoid work) and Theory Y (the desire to perform work that is challenging and worthwhile).

3. **Leadership Styles and Concepts.** Styles of leadership range from the autocratic approach (which is forceful and demanding) to the democratic, or consultative, approach to the participative approach (which encourages employee responsibility and initiative). A participative approach that empowers employees is highly recommended for obtaining high levels of commitment, although the conditions for its success must be evaluated first.

4. **Selecting an Appropriate Style.** The contingency model depends on an analysis of the state of three factors present in a situation: (a) leader–member relations, (b) task structure, and (c) position power of the leader. When the states of all three factors are either very favorable or unfavorable, an authoritative approach is recommended. When the states of the three factors are somewhere between favorable and unfavorable, a participative approach is recommended. A leadership approach can be selected from a continuum of styles that range from strictly autocratic to purely participative. The best choice of style is one that is based on an analysis of a subordinate's task competence and motivation to perform. The more capable and committed the employee, the more likely that a participative style will be appropriate.

5. **Leaders and Followers.** Good leaders recognize their role as followers, and engage in a variety of behaviors that provide support to their own manager. These supervisors also attempt to fulfill their superleader role by helping their employees learn and practice self-leadership skills. Supervisors also learn that other factors can act as substitutes for their leadership behaviors, and that an emerging workforce demands that they act as servant-leaders.

READING COMPREHENSION

1. Which are the three skills most likely to be required of leaders? Can they be learned, or must a leader be born with them?

2. Give an example of how an individual's motivational needs offer an opportunity for effective action on the part of a supervisor.

3. As supervisor of the catalog section of a direct-mail house, Mary has come to believe that without her close supervision, employees in her department would never get their work done. Which of McGregor's assumptions about employees at work does Mary's view represent?

4. Describe what McGregor believed to be the essence of leadership.

5. Compare democratic leadership with participative leadership.

6. According to Fiedler's contingency model of leadership, what is likely to be the best approach in a situation where the supervisor has been newly appointed, relationships with the new group are standoffish, and the task to be performed requires great accuracy? Why?

7. In what ways are various leadership styles related to Theory X and to Theory Y?

8. Provide examples of the use of leadership styles at three different points along the continuum of leadership styles.

9. Which kind of leadership style—autocratic or participative—is least likely to be effective with a relatively incompetent and uncommitted individual? Why?

10. Explain why it is important for a supervisor to manage upward (followership skills) as well as downward (leadership skills).

APPLICATION

Self-Assessment

▶ *How good are your leadership skills?*

Read the following statements carefully. Circle the number on the response scale that most closely reflects the degree to which each statement accurately describes you. Add up your total points and prepare a brief action plan for self-improvement. Be ready to report your score for tabulation across the entire group.

	Good Description									Poor Description
1. I exhibit a high degree of energy, desire to help others succeed, integrity, self-confidence, and judgment.	10 9 8 7 6 5 4 3 2 1									
2. I am aware of the need to demonstrate a substantial level of charisma in order in induce others to make needed changes.	10 9 8 7 6 5 4 3 2 1									

	Good Description									Poor Description

3. I have a high level of persuasiveness, capacity to influence others, and social skills.
10 9 8 7 6 5 4 3 2 1

4. I completely embrace the assumptions about people at work stated in Theory Y.
10 9 8 7 6 5 4 3 2 1

5. I am comfortable playing the roles of teacher, coach, consultant, and colleague to my staff.
10 9 8 7 6 5 4 3 2 1

6. I firmly believe in the value of participative leadership for involving employees.
10 9 8 7 6 5 4 3 2 1

7. I understand why a task-centered leadership style might be effective in some situations, and a people-centered style might work better in others.
10 9 8 7 6 5 4 3 2 1

8. It makes good sense to me to vary the style of leadership to fit the competence and level of commitment of each employee.
10 9 8 7 6 5 4 3 2 1

9. In addition to getting my employees to be productive, I accept the need to help them develop critical self-leadership skills.
10 9 8 7 6 5 4 3 2 1

10. I feel very comfortable viewing my role as a steward and servant to my employees.
10 9 8 7 6 5 4 3 2 1

Scoring and Interpretation

SCORING

Add up your total points for the 10 questions. Record that number here, and report it when it is requested. _____

INTERPRETATION

81 to 100 points. You seem to have a basic set of leadership attitudes and skills.

61 to 80 points. Take a close look at some of your leadership attitudes and skills (those with lower self-assessments) and discuss them with a manager to see if they need improvement.

Below 60 points. Some of your skills may be substantially inconsistent with effective leadership practices and could be detrimental to your success as a supervisor.

Identify your three lowest scores and record the question numbers here:

_____, _____, _____.

ACTION

Write a brief paragraph detailing an action plan for how you might sharpen each of these skills. Then pay particularly close attention to the related material in the chapter as you review the relevant sections there.

Skill Development

▶ *Leadership Skills and Qualities*

Assume that several high-level executives in your organization have indicated that they believe you have great potential for rapid advancement. However, you are concerned that the absence of (or weakness in) some of your leadership skills and qualities might prevent such advancement. Review the list of leadership characteristics below with a close colleague or friend, and select the three on which you need the greatest development, marking them with an X. Then prepare a report that suggests how you intend to improve them. (For example, if you lack in self-confidence and spontaneity, you might consider joining a Toastmaster's Club.) To prepare your report, you will likely wish to review the text's discussion on leadership, search the Internet for relevant guidelines, and consult with colleagues and staff persons in the human resources department for their advice.

Leadership Skills and Qualities	Most Deficient (3)	Action Plans
1. Personal warmth	_____	_____ _____
2. Assertiveness	_____	_____ _____
3. Self-confidence	_____	_____ _____
4. Spontaneity	_____	_____ _____
5. Persuasiveness	_____	_____ _____
6. Risk-taking propensity	_____	_____ _____

Leadership Skills and Qualities	Most Deficient (3)	Action Plans
7. Sense of caring	_____	_____ _____
8. Ability to influence	_____	_____ _____
9. Diplomacy and tact	_____	_____ _____
10. Interest in others	_____	_____ _____

Role Play

Leadership Skills ◄

Five individuals should be identified (through volunteering) for a leadership-development task. Ask each volunteer to select any work-related topic of his or her choice and propose a major change of some sort to the audience (their employees). It could be a new compensation system, a new work schedule, the introduction of new technology, a new office layout, among other ideas. Have them step out of the room to prepare for a few minutes, and then return singly to give a brief, one minute talk to the class, in which they propose acceptance of the change. The other class members should rate each speaker (10 = very high; 1 = very low) on the dimensions shown. Collect and tabulate the information, and feed it back to each speaker privately for the purpose of individual development. Then engage the class in a discussion of leadership.

Leadership Dimension	Speaker				
	1	2	3	4	5
1. Charisma (expertise, self-confidence, assertiveness, spontaneity, high expectations for others)	——	——	——	——	——
2. Persuasion (rational arguments and convincing presentation)	——	——	——	——	——
3. Influence (use of position power, expertise, and rewards)	——	——	——	——	——
4. Social skills (tact, diplomacy, and perception/understanding of others' needs)	——	——	——	——	——

CASES FOR ANALYSIS

Case 28

The New Supervisor of Nurses

This action took place on the general surgery floor of a small hospital in western New York State. For several months, the hospital trustees had debated the feasibility of building an addition that would have moved all critical-care facilities into a modern, fully equipped building. However, just last month, the decision was made not to expand but to modernize the present facilities. During this period of decision making, the administrative organization of the hospital changed markedly. A new administrator from a large city hospital took over and brought in a new nursing head and several new nursing supervisors.

The general surgery floor on this particular shift (3 to 11 P.M.) was staffed by eight longtime registered nurses, three licensed practical nurses, and two nurses' aides. Molly P., the new nursing supervisor for this shift, reported for the first time on Saturday night. She observed during the shift that there were several infractions of sterile procedures, that on two occasions practical nurses administered injections (which, by law, must be handled by the registered nurses), and that the nurses tended to congregate at the nursing station for long periods of time. The first thing that Molly did when she went on shift Tuesday night was to call the entire staff together. She said that they should know that she expected all of them to adhere strictly to sterile procedures, that there must be no abrogation of R.N. responsibilities, and that "coffee klatching" at the nursing station must be kept to a minimum. It appeared that things improved on Wednesday and Thursday nights, but by the middle of the following week, Molly sensed a return to the general laxness that was evident when she first took over.

Molly waited until the next Monday. That night, she met with staff members individually in a quiet room. With each one, she reiterated her determination to "run a tight ship, medically," and then asked for cooperation. From most of the staff members, she got no meaningful replies. However, one of the older R.N.s looked her in the eye and said, "We've handled this floor in our own way for a number of years, and we've had no problems. Our record is as good as any in the hospital. We don't need your big-city ways here. And since the new addition won't be built, the chances are that you won't be here for long, anyway."

If you were Molly, what would you do? Five approaches are listed below. Rank them on a scale from 1 to 5 in the order in which they appeal to you (1, most attractive; 5, least attractive). You may add another alternative if you wish. Be prepared to justify your ranking.

_____ **a.** Continue to insist on a high level of performance while taking steps to weed out those staff members who don't or won't measure up.

_____ **b.** Make changes after the staff is better unified under your leadership.

_____ **c.** Relax the rule about "coffee klatching," but stick to the letter of the procedures for sterile practices and R.N. responsibilities.

_____ **d.** Hold fast to your demands for a medically tight ship, but work along with each person to find a way to convince him or her of the value of operating this way.

_____ **e.** Get together with the other nursing supervisors to make certain that the procedures set down are uniform from floor to floor.

Case 29

The Experienced Transferees

Due to the closing of several company plants, a number of employees have been transferred from other locations to your department. These are men and women reputed to have had good records elsewhere. Most of them have had extensive experience in other departments in the company. An examination of their employment records, however, shows that they have had little or no experience with the line of work performed in your department. However, they appear willing and cooperative.

◀ *Analysis*

Which of the following approaches would you choose to make this group of transferees productive as quickly as possible? Why? Can you identify the leadership style of each alternative?

a. Hold a meeting with them to find out how they think the work should be handled; then proceed to make assignments.

b. Provide explicit directions for now, and accept no suggestions until the transferees have shown you they can do the work properly.

c. Allow the transferees to find out through experience on the job the best way to handle the work.

d. Interview each transferee so that you can better understand his or her preferences, and then make assignments accordingly.

Case 30

Joe's "Pretty Good" Diner

Everything was, as the saying goes, "coming up roses." Joe had bought a small diner several years ago and worked hard to make it successful. Business had grown steadily through careful attention to costs and customer service. Joe had been able to stay on top of things for a long time, handling the ordering of supplies, payroll, hiring and firing, and filling in for the cooks on their days off.

Suddenly, everything changed. A major electronics plant opened up a block away, providing hundreds of new customers daily at Joe's "Pretty Good" Diner.

Analysis ▶

After expanding his seating area, upgrading his menu, changing his decor, and hiring three assistant managers to help out, Joe thought he could sit back and relax. However, on their first day, each new supervisor came to see Joe, asking which leadership style to use. What do you recommend for each of them?

- Mary had been promoted from her job as senior food server. She had received a warm recommendation from the other servers, and Joe put her in charge of the morning shift and told her that he would support almost anything she did. Trusting her completely allowed Joe an occasional morning off to go golfing, too.

- Danny was new to the diner and had received mixed reviews from the employee team who assisted in the selection process. Nevertheless, he seemed to be the best available candidate, so Joe put Danny on probation for six months and sharply limited his decision-making authority.

- Tom was another story. He, like Mary, had been a food server, but his grating personality rubbed his co-workers the wrong way. Joe put him in charge of maintenance and supplies, and in addition gave him all the marketing responsibilities. But he put sharp financial controls on Tom, requiring him to clear in advance all expenditures over $25.

Answers to Quick Tests ▶

Quick Test 1	Quick Test 2	Quick Test 3
1. F	3. T	5. F
2. T	4. T	6. F

Quick Test 4	Quick Test 5
7. F	9. F
8. T	10. F

CHAPTER 11

Effective Employee Communication

Learning Objectives

After studying this chapter, you should be able to

- Explain the process of communication, including the major steps essential for its success.

- Choose appropriate spoken and written methods for communicating with individuals and groups of employees.

- Assess the quality of your nonverbal communication skills and identify needed changes.

- List the major communication guidelines that help create positive working relationships.

- Use your knowledge of the communication process to make orders, instructions, and requests more acceptable to employees.

THE COMMUNICATION PROCESS

CONCEPT ▶ Employee communication is a continuous process involving skillful sending and receiving of messages.

What is the meaning and significance of the term communication in supervision?

Communication is defined as the process of passing information and understanding from one person to another. As a supervisory responsibility, the process is frequently called employee communication, although the communicating process is equally important between supervisors and between supervisor and manager.

The term *communications* is more narrowly used to describe the mechanical and electronic means of transmitting and receiving information, such as newspapers, bulletin-board announcements, computer printouts, radios, telephones, e-mail, voice mail, and video screens. Employee communication has many of the qualities—and limitations—of these means, but it is infinitely more subtle and complex. So employee communication needs to be managed carefully.

How does communication activate the organization?

By providing the linking pin between plans and action. You may have a great set of plans and a fine staff, but until something begins to happen, you will have accomplished nothing. Neither motivation nor leadership can bring about action without communication. This is what starts and keeps the whole plan in motion.

Good supervisors keep learning about employee communication. They recognize that employee perceptions of their leadership are affected by how they pass information on to others through the process of communication. Unless employees know how you feel and what you want, the best management ideas in the world go to waste. Good communication is especially important when a supervisor is trying to build team spirit or when employees are insecure because of rapid organizational changes or threatened cutbacks.

What is meant by the communication process?

In a broad sense, the *communication process* is the series of steps that enables an idea in one person's mind to be transmitted, understood, and acted on by another person. This process is illustrated in greater detail in Figure 11-1. Clearly, it is an essential ingredient in all human relationships. To be effective, it requires that supervisors establish rapport with employees, be sensitive to how others perceive ideas and *information* (knowledge and feelings about tasks and people), and minimize the *noise* (physical or emotional obstructions to understanding) that can detract

---

Communication. The process of passing information and understanding from one person to another.

Did You Know ❓

The Importance of Body Language

■ Some experts suggest that communication between humans is 90 percent body language, 8 percent tone of voice, and 2 percent what you say.

Information. The knowledge, skills, and feelings that are exchanged in the communication process.

Noise. Any kind of distraction, physical or emotional, within an individual or the environment that distorts or obstructs the transmission of a message.

from the process. It also requires that supervisors have better-than-average skill in using the spoken word, the written word, and the nonverbal signals that the face and body send out to others. Last, but far from least, it demands of supervisors that they be good at receiving communications from others. That is, they must be good listeners who are receptive to feedback and questions.

Some people talk about three-dimensional communication. What are they referring to?

Communication should not be a one-way street. For a complex, modern organization to function smoothly, communication must occur in three ways. First, not only must you furnish information downward to employees and upward to your manager, but employees must communicate their ideas and feelings upward to you. Second, since interdepartmental cooperation among supervisors is extremely important, there also must be a horizontal flow of information. Finally, there may also be a need to exchange information with "outside" sources, such as staff groups or external vendors, customers, and government agencies. In effect, this creates a challenging three-dimensional communication process—up/down, left/right, and in/out. All involve transmitting, understanding and receiving *feedback*, information from the recipients that tells the sender how well the message was understood and received.

Feedback. Information provided by those engaged in the communication process that serves to clarify and/or verify understanding and to indicate either agreement or dissent.

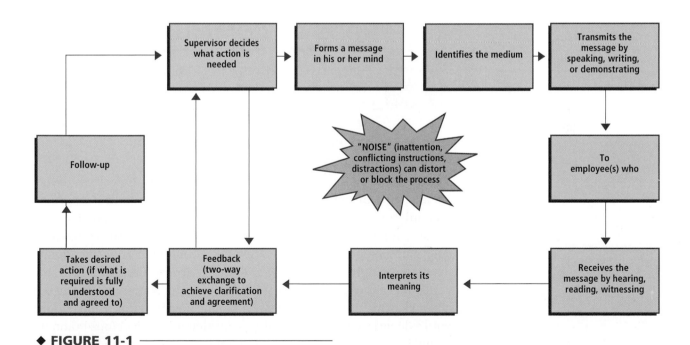

◆ **FIGURE 11-1**

The communication process. **What are some distractions that can block the communication process?**

Some supervisors report receiving 360-degree feedback. What is that?

Valid knowledge of your strengths and weaknesses is essential if you wish to continue improving your skills and preparing yourself for promotion. However, you may not have the capacity to assess your own behavior accurately. As a result, you should consider using some form of *360-degree feedback*. This procedure involves gathering data on your skills, abilities, and style from your manager, peers, subordinates, and even customers. Then you compare the results with organizational norms for a good supervisor, or with your own perceptions, or with data from an earlier survey (to see if you have changed). Finally (often with the help of a "coach"), the supervisor prepares an action plan for personal change. The system works best when it is voluntary and based on anonymous responses from the participants. The product is a rich set of feedback (both positive and negative) that, if used, can aid in your supervisory development.

Quick Test 1

1	T or F	Communication is the process of passing information and understanding from one person to another.
2	T or F	Communication is incomplete unless feedback is received.

② METHODS OF COMMUNICATION

CONCEPT ▶ Effective supervisors select a communication medium on the basis of careful analysis of situational factors.

How can you choose which communication medium to use?

This depends on the specific task as well as on your objectives. If the task is a lengthy or highly technical message or one requiring a permanent record, you'll want to use a written form. On the other hand, if speed, informality, or personal impact is important, the spoken word is often preferred. Another supervisory choice revolves around whether to communicate with a single employee or the entire group. Person-to-person conversations allow you to control the flow of information, have greater impact, and protect privacy. However, opening up communication among the entire department invites employee participation, develops commitment, and helps build team spirit. It demands that you become more of a facilitator, helping the group explore problems and make progress toward goals. All in all, wise supervisors employ a rich variety of methods.

How can person-to-person communication be conducted effectively?

A maximum of "custom tailoring" to an individual employee is not only feasible but definitely in order. This becomes increasingly important as you develop a sound working relationship with each person. That's because an individual who is addressed singly but in the same way as everyone else usually resents such treatment in proportion to the degree of previously assumed familiarity. *People are unique, and they like to be recognized for their differences.* Supervisors can choose among a variety of spoken or written communication methods.

▲ Person-to-person communication permits custom tailoring of the message. **Does this mean there is no chance of a misunderstanding of the message?**

Spoken Communication. In spoken communication, the person addressed is immediately aware of the conditions under which the message is shared. Therefore, speed, tone, mood, gestures, and facial expressions may seriously affect the way the individual reacts.

1. **Informal talks.** These are still the most fundamental form of communication. They are suitable for day-to-day liaisons, directions, exchanges of information, progress reviews, and some disciplinary sessions, and especially for maintaining effective personal relations. Even if the talks are brief, be sure they provide the opportunity for a two-way exchange. And if either party is likely to be emotionally involved in the subject, face-to-face communication should always be used (in preference to writing or using the telephone).

2. **Planned appointments.** These are appropriate for regular appraisal reviews, recurring joint work sessions, and so forth. The parties should be adequately prepared to make such meetings complete and effective by being up to date, by providing adequate data and information, and by limiting interruptions as much as possible. For extended projects or for some employees (especially new ones, those with problems, or those who travel extensively), many supervisors have regular daily (brief), weekly (longer), or monthly (extensive) appointments.

3. **Telephone calls.** These are useful for quick checkups or for imparting or receiving information, instructions, or data. However, your telephone personality sometimes contradicts your real (face-to-face) self, so you should examine how you sound when

talking on the telephone. Also, since the impersonality of routine calls is sometimes resented, you should occasionally follow up with personal notes to confirm the message.

A special concern with telephone calls arises when recipients are not present to receive the calls you make. *Voice mail* systems allow you to leave the desired messages anyway, and the other persons can listen to them at their convenience. These systems help alleviate the frustration of playing "phone tag" (repeated unsuccessful attempts to reach each other), and also give the recipients some control over when to listen to a set of messages. But don't forget some basic rules of phone etiquette for greatest success when using voice mail: Speak slowly and clearly, identify yourself along with the time and date of your call, and clarify whether it is important to respond to your message (and when you plan to be available).

Written Communication. All messages that are intended to be formal, official, or long term, or that affect several persons in a related way should be written. Be sure that you use only a written communication to amend any previous written communication. Oral changes risk being forgotten, may be recalled inaccurately, or are not passed along to co-workers.

1. **Interoffice memos.** Used for recording informal inquiries or replies, interoffice memos can also be of value if several people are to receive a message that is extensive, or if data is numerous or complex. A memo can be a simple way of keeping your boss informed, and it can be read at his or her convenience. Memos should not be overused, or they will lose their impact and be ignored.
2. **Letters.** Usually addressed to individuals, letters are more formal in tone than memos. They are useful for official notices, formally recorded statements, and lengthy communications, even when the addressee is physically accessible. Letters are often valuable as a means of communicating involved thoughts and ideas for future discussion and development, or as part of a continuing consideration of problems.
3. **Reports.** These are more impersonal than letters and often more formal. Reports are used to convey information, analyses, and recommendations to superiors and colleagues. They are most effective when based on the results of conferences, inspections, research, and careful thought. Reports should carefully distinguish objectively determined facts from more subjective guesses, opinions, impressions, and generalizations.

What can you do to communicate most effectively with groups of employees?

Plant or office groups that are uniform in status, age, sex, compensation level, occupation, and length of service provide a valid basis for highly pointed messages. This approach helps avoid the gradually numbing stream of form letters, memos, and announcements that are interesting to only a few. Establishment of such groups on a continuing basis helps to build a sense of unity and group identity that fosters favorable group morale and group response. The appropriateness of different communication forms is summarized in the following paragraphs.

Spoken Communication. Effective spoken communication with groups calls for special skills. However, the skills that are useful in a committee of equals may be inadequate in a mass meeting. Nor does your ability to conduct a conference attended by your own staff mean that you will have equal ability to contribute effectively as a staff member of a conference called by your superior. You may be skillful at resolving conflicts of interest among participants in a meeting, but it is much more difficult to remain objective when, as a member, you are emotionally involved in the discussion of the topic.

1. **Informal staff meetings.** These provide an opportunity for sharing useful information of common interest and for developing strong group cohesiveness. Properly supplemented with individual face-to-face contacts, they are an outstanding means of coordinating activities and building mutual understanding. Hold brief, informal staff meetings regularly or as the need arises—at the beginning or end of the day or even during lunch or coffee breaks.

2. **Planned conferences.** These are relatively formal affairs. A common error is to create an agenda without consulting those who will attend. Most participants appreciate being asked for their input and having sufficient time to prepare any needed data, information, reports, and recommendations. Properly conducted, a planned conference can be extremely useful. If improperly managed, it can waste time, antagonize people, and discourage future participation.

3. **Mass meetings.** Meetings of large numbers of employees or managers can be valuable for celebrating occasions like the introduction of a new product, for making emergency plans when a crisis occurs, for sharing operational results in an "open-book" management context, or for introducing new policies or key personnel. But because of the opportunity for emotions to flare and hostile questions to be asked, such meetings require that the presiding individual have great patience, skill, and a forceful personality.

Written Communication. The effect of a single, isolated written communication to a group of employees is generally unpredictable. But a carefully planned program of written communications can develop a desirable cumulative effect.

1. **Bulletin-board notices.** For lengthy or formal announcements of new policies or promotions, bulletin-board notices are appropriate. They are most effective when they are accompanied by illustrations, when readers are constantly attracted to the area and interested in the topics, and when out-of-date material is promptly removed. Most bulletin-board announcements should be supplemented with other

forms of written communications because there is no certainty that they will be seen or read by all employees.

2. **Posters, exhibits, and displays.** These can serve a useful purpose by visually catching the attention of workers. They are typically expensive, require considerable space, and must be properly prepared. The most common subjects are introducing new company products, promoting quality production or service, increasing safety, cutting waste, and stimulating suggestions.

3. **Audio and visual aids.** Slides, flip charts, videocassettes, videodiscs, audiocassettes, and other visual materials such as PowerPoint (computer-assisted) presentations have great potential value, but only if they are used effectively. Many, such as videos, require a thorough introduction and careful follow-up. Competent preparation and planning coupled with appropriate presentation skills should be applied to the use of all audio and visual materials.

E-mail. Use of the Internet or an Intranet (local area network) to send and receive messages electronically.

4. Electronic communications, or ***e-mail***, has added a whole new dimension to written messages in recent years. By drawing upon high-speed networks of interconnected computers, individuals can now transmit near-instantaneous messages to almost anywhere in the world. While most rules for written communications apply to e-mail, too, the following set of special guidelines is appropriate to consider:

   - Check your e-mail at least once per day, and respond promptly whenever possible; this builds respect and shows that you care about messages received.
   - Send short messages; use capital letters for special emphasis; pay as much attention to grammar, punctuation, spelling, and sentence structure as you would for any other written message. Every communication you send is constantly being evaluated, and it tells the receiver much about you.
   - Limit the use of "emoticons" (e.g., combinations of colons and parentheses for smiles [:)] and frowns [:(]) and acronyms (e.g., BTW for "by the way"); they may irritate or confuse recipients who aren't familiar with them, especially in a multicultural workforce.
   - Do not send emotional messages you'll later regret or anything that violates the privacy of others. And remember: The delete function does not necessarily wipe a message from the computer's storage system!
   - Most importantly, be sure to familiarize yourself with your employer's policies on e-mail and pass these along to your staff. Find out what is inappropriate or an unauthorized use of the Internet and avoid it!

Is any one method of communication better than another?

Each situation has its own best method or combination of methods. Some problems are urgent and demand an immediate response (an informal talk, telephone call, or handwritten memo). Some employees believe only what you put down on paper, so time spent communicating face-to-face with them is virtually wasted. If the same message must be conveyed to a large number of people, a memo or a mass meeting is best. So it seems that the most successful communicating is done by supervisors who (a) quickly analyze the situation they are encountering and (b) know and use many ways of getting their ideas, instructions, and feelings across to others.

Should a supervisor use the company grapevine as a means of communication?

Listen to it, for it's one way of getting clues about what's going on. But don't depend on the **grapevine**, or informal communication network, to provide totally accurate information. And don't make a deliberate practice of leaking information to the work group through the grapevine, for employees will then rely even less on your formal communication methods.

The grapevine becomes most active in the absence of good communication about company rules, employee benefits, opportunities for advancement, and performance feedback. If you don't tell employees—promptly—about the things that interest or affect them, the grapevine will quickly emerge. However, much of the grapevine information will be based on incomplete data, partial truths, and outright lies. And surveys show that even though employees receive a lot of information from the rumor mill and enjoy participating in it, they'd much rather get the real story from a responsible party—their supervisor. You can prevent a lot of emotional upsets among your employees, and build a lot of goodwill, by spiking rumors as soon as they appear. So show employees you welcome the chance to tell the truth. They'll appreciate your candor and integrity.

Grapevine. The informal communication network that employees use to convey information of interest to them.

3	T or F	Supervisors should identify their favorite form of communication and rely on it heavily.	
4	T or F	Studies show that the grapevine is usually 100 percent accurate.	

◄ *Quick Test 2*

3 NONVERBAL COMMUNICATION

CONCEPT Nonverbal behaviors—actions, body language, and active listening—are vitally important communication skills.

What kinds of communications are likely to speak louder than words?

The messages transmitted by your actions. Talking and writing are the communication methods most frequently used, of course. But regardless of what you say, employees will be most affected by what you communicate to them by your actions. What you do—how you treat them—is the proof of your real intentions. Going to bat for an employee who needs help provides concrete evidence of how highly you value that person's contributions on your team.

Even on simple matters, such as training an employee to do a new job, the act of showing how to do it (demonstration) is eloquent even when no words are spoken. Similarly, going to an employee's work site to chat rather than always requesting that the employee come to your office helps project a supportive image. The best communications are generally those that combine spoken or written words with compatible actions.

What other forms of nonverbal behavior should I pay attention to?

You send messages every minute of the day in one form or another. Start to monitor—and work at improving—the clarity of your use of these forms:

1. **Time.** Do you arrive early for meetings or come late? Do you stick to your appointment schedule or keep people waiting? Do you make promises to return phone calls and then "forget"?

2. **Space.** Do you vary the physical distance between you and others, depending on whether the appropriate context is private or public, or whether you are close friends or spirited competitors? Do you consciously seek to eliminate physical barriers between you and your partner?

3. **Symbols and artifacts.** Is your work space devoid of personal mementos, or do you signal your "humanity" through inclusion of photos and other objects? Is your desk cluttered or clean? Is there consistency in the symbolic messages you're sending, or a stark contrast (such as telling employees that there is "no money for raises this year" while flashing a new ring and driving a new car)?

What is the lesson here? Nonverbal cues are vitally important in the overall communication process, and you need to use them to your advantage. Don't just use words to communicate; think about your appearance, facial expression, posture, and your use of time, space, and symbols, too.

Body language. What's that?

Nonverbal body movements or facial expressions that may convey to others what is really on your mind are referred to as *body language.* These signals may be no more than a frown, a shrug of the shoulders, or a gesture with your hands. Unfortunately, they can be misinterpreted both within—and across—cultures. For example,

- Nodding the head up and down can imply agreement with the speaker; shaking the head from side to side can be perceived as disagreement.

- Drumming the fingers or tapping the foot can mean "Hurry up. I'm impatient for you to get to the point."

- Raising the eyebrows can signal doubt, surprise, or skepticism.

- Rolling the eyes often expresses disbelief.

- Tight-lipped frowning can indicate displeasure or even disgust.

Many body movements such as these are unconscious and deeply ingrained, and they would be difficult for you to change. But try to assess whether people are reacting primarily to your words or to your body language. Observe the nonverbal signals from others; these can often provide you with solid clues to what is on another person's mind—but test your interpretations for accuracy. If in doubt, ask for clarification!

How important is listening?

Listening should make up at least a third of your communications. *Active listening* requires good eye contact, alert body posture, and the use of frequent verbal encouragement. It is a skill that must be continually practiced to be maintained. But it can provide great satisfaction both to you and to the speaker. Here are four basic suggestions regarding actions you should avoid:

1. **Don't assume anything.** Don't anticipate what someone will say. And don't let an employee think that you know what is going to be said, even if you do.

2. **Don't interrupt.** Let the individual have a full say. If you are busy, either set a time limit or schedule an appointment for a time when you can get the whole story.

3. **Don't guess about intentions.** Look for the real reason the employee wants your attention. Often this may be quite different from what first appears to be the purpose.

4. **Don't react too quickly.** Try not to jump to conclusions. Avoid becoming upset simply because a situation is explained poorly or an inappropriate word is used. Patience will produce a big payoff in understanding the other person's viewpoint.

Body language. Nonverbal body movements, facial expressions, or gestures that may project and reveal underlying attitudes and sentiments.

Active listening. The conscious process of securing information of all kinds (including feelings and emotions) through attention and observation.

Did You Know

Are You Listening?
■ Employees know when their supervisors aren't listening to them. They report being interrupted, see frequent glances at a wristwatch or other objects, note an absence of reactions, find the supervisor changing the subject or even walking away! When these things occur, they report feeling ignored, insignificant, worthless, unintelligent, and anxious.

Employees use these adjectives to describe a supervisor who is a good listener: courteous, attentive, concerned, respectful, and empathetic. When good listening is experienced, they report feeling liked, valued, respected, important, and intelligent. Clearly, the self-image of employees is readily shaped by the listening skills of their supervisors; what power lies in their hands!

HOW TO BE A BETTER LISTENER

■ Effective listeners know that silence can be golden; they follow the ancient Asian prescription admonishing, "Seek first to understand, *then* be understood." Some suggestions for effective listening include the following:

- Select an appropriate time and place to hear a person out, based on the need for privacy and comfort.
- Avoid, if possible, placing nonverbal barriers—such as a desk—between you and your employee when conversing.

- Be patient; use the "golden pause" to encourage further thought and sharing.
- Provide supportive cues: nod your head, offer a confirming remark, maintain eye contact, echo a few key words, or paraphrase a key thought.
- Listen for feelings expressed "between the lines"; probe non-aggressively for additional thoughts; offer a tentative summary of what you've heard.

However, active listening shouldn't take the place of definite actions and answers on your part. When you sense that an employee is rambling too far afield, return to the point with astute questioning. If an employee is wrong on a point of fact or company policy, make that clear. When group discussions turn into purposeless rap sessions, you have an obligation to set talk aside and take action. And when an employee comes to you with a problem and truly wants you to solve it with your knowledge and experience, give a straightforward reply. Only if you—and the employee—are more interested in helping the individual develop problem-solving skills than in immediately solving the problem should you shift your emphasis to helping the person arrive at his or her own solution. But this can be very time-consuming.

Quick Test 3 ▶

5	T or F	Many body language cues are expressed unconsciously.
6	T or F	Good listeners can usually guess what someone is about to say; they can save time by offering suggested words and phrases.

④ COMMUNICATION GUIDELINES

CONCEPT ▶ Effective communication helps to develop positive working relationships with both a supervisor's boss and employees.

What kinds of things should I tell my boss?

Your success as a leader depends on how freely employees will talk to you and tell you what's bothering them. Your superior, too, needs similar information from you. Make a point of voluntarily keeping your boss informed of the following:

1. **Progress toward performance goals and standards.** This covers items such as deliveries, output, and quality. If possible, warn your boss in advance about foreseeable performance problems, while there is still time to obtain help. Rarely do managers like negative "surprises."
2. **Matters that may cause controversy.** Arguments with other supervisors, a controversial interpretation of company policy, a discipline problem within your department—all are issues that should be brought to the attention of your superior. It's better to explain your side first and support it with the facts.
3. **Attitudes and morale.** Middle and top managers are relatively isolated from direct contact with the work group. This not only frustrates them but deprives them of needed information about how employees feel. So make a point of telling your boss regularly about both the general level of morale and employee reactions to specific issues.
4. **Constructive suggestions.** You can help your boss—and make yourself look good—by offering new ideas, suggestions for changes in policies or procedures, and cost-saving approaches for the organization to consider. This shows that you are going beyond minimum expectations and using your experience, insight, and intellect to improve operations. Most managers will be at least pleasantly surprised, if not delighted, to receive your inputs if they are offered in a positive manner.

Do I need to tailor my communications to fit my employees?

Yes, you should strongly consider doing so. Research indicates that people often fall into one of three preferential categories—visual (relying primarily on what they see), auditory (relying primarily on what they hear), and kinesthetic (relying primarily on what they can touch or actively experience)—with regard to how they learn and how they like to communicate (see Figure 11-2). If you fail to identify their most comfortable pattern, your best communication efforts may still miss the mark. Therefore, for *visual* learners, make sure that you show them charts and diagrams, or give them backup materials in the form of written instructions and memos. For *auditory* learners, give them a chance to not only hear you but to hear themselves and others. Limit the background noise that might interfere with your message, and ask them to summarize what they heard you say. For *kinesthetic* learners, provide them with examples and illustrations; let them work "hands on" with tools and equipment; allow them to move around the workspace. You'll soon find it easy to adapt your communications in this way, and the payoff from doing so will be remarkable!

◆ **FIGURE 11-2**

Characteristics of visual, auditory, and kinesthetic people. **Which description fits your preference?**

Visual People

- Like to "see" an idea
- Love to use figures, models, and maps
- Enjoy concrete examples
- Appreciate visual consistency
- May express understanding in a form such as "I <u>see</u> what you mean."

Auditory People

- Like to "hear" an idea
- Thrive on discussion, argument, and debates
- Find themselves repeating ideas out loud (mostly to themselves)
- May express their understanding in a form such as "I <u>hear</u> what you are saying."

Kinesthetic People

- Like to "learn by doing"
- Are often active individuals, constantly in motion
- See themselves as "hands-on" learners
- Respond well to practice opportunities
- May express understanding in a form such as "I need to get a <u>feel</u> for this."

What can you do to help people understand what you mean?

To begin with, don't be afraid to occasionally repeat what you've stated. You can also ask an employee to repeat to you what you've just said. Another practice is to get the employee to ask questions; this will give you an indication of areas of weak understanding. But the best advice is to be specific and avoid the poor understanding that stems from the unclear meanings of words. Instead of saying, "Speed up the machine a little bit," simply tell the operator, "I want this machine run at 2,100 rpm, not 1,900 rpm." And rather than ordering: "Type this up as soon as possible," say, "I need this letter typed by 2 P.M. today." Similarly, specific expectations can be identified for most quality, quantity, and time standards. But note that sometimes, in your attempt to be precise, you may select a brief but ambiguous word when a slightly *longer* explanation would provide greater clarity! For example, don't say "relocate these boxes" when you really want an employee to examine and sort a pile of boxes before moving only the more recently received ones to a new site. In short, always select your words carefully, and then check to see if they communicated your intent clearly.

7	T or F	It is best to avoid telling your boss about potential problems or controversial issues, for fear of arousing an angry response.
8	T or F	Supervisors should determine whether they are visual, auditory, or kinesthetic persons, and stick to the communication style they use best.

⑤ ORDERS, INSTRUCTIONS, AND REQUESTS

CONCEPT ▶ Supervisors exercise their authority by issuing orders, giving instructions and directions, and making requests.

How are orders and instructions linked to the communication process?

Orders—expectations that supervisors need to have obeyed—are the most direct, authority-based kinds of communications. These can be supplemented with instructions, in which you provide directions and share job knowledge in a systematic way. Orders draw upon a supervisor's authority but may be disliked by employees. *Instructions* are usually

Orders. Commands given forcefully with the expectation of obedience to them.

Instruction. Furnishing knowledge or information in a disciplined, systematic way with the expectation of compliance.

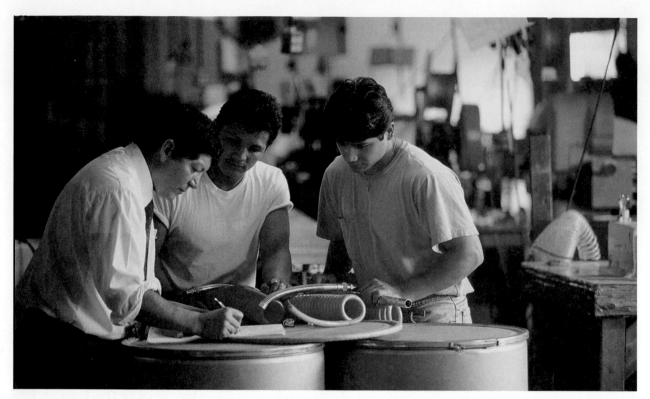

▲ Kinesthetic learners learn best in a "hands on" situation. **Are you a visual, auditory, or kinesthetic learner?**

based on one's expertise and are designed to help workers perform their jobs better. There are appropriate moments for using each approach. Although it is desirable for employees to agree with your rationale for an order, it is absolutely imperative in some circumstances that employees *understand* what must be done and do it. So, as a supervisor, you can draw upon two tools: (a) orders to make sure that employees know *what* to do and (b) instructions to help them *do* it properly and tailor the guidelines to a specific situation. A sound understanding and application of the communication process will help you meet both these responsibilities.

How can you get the best results from the instructions and orders you issue?

By being sure that each instruction or order is the right one for the particular situation at hand and by being specific about what the employee is to do and what kind of results you expect.

Your orders are even more effective when you exercise care in selecting the person most likely to carry them out correctly. And you add power to your orders by expressing confidence as you deliver them. If necessary, repeat or rephrase an order for additional impact. Finally, your orders will be most effective if you regularly check to make sure they are carried out at the time and in the manner you prescribe.

What should you do when an employee willfully refuses to do what you ask?

The first piece of advice, and the toughest to follow, is don't fly off the handle. Review the order's fairness, the selection of the person to carry it out, and the probability that you were understood. If you think you've done your part, find out what the employee objects to and the reasons for the objection. Ask for specifics: "What is it you object to? Why do you think it's unreasonable?" Chances are, a nonthreatening exploration of the situation will let both of you cool down and help you clarify the real problem. Perhaps you can even modify the order so that it will be accepted.

Look under **work** for human resource solutions regarding labor relations, benefits, training, recruiting, leadership, motivation, and legal issues.

But if the employee continues to resist a reasonable request, you're faced with a disciplinary problem. Find a private place where you can talk calmly but firmly. Let it be known that you will take disciplinary steps if the problem isn't resolved. But try to avoid a showdown situation in which one (or both) of you will wind up losing. Resist making threats if you can.

When should you request that an employee do something?

As often as possible. Many of today's employees resent being in positions where they must take orders. They dislike being in subordinate positions (implying that someone else is better than they are); they desire independence and autonomy; or they may have a wealth of experience or education that has prepared them to think for themselves. They want more consideration, they deserve increased respect, and asking for their cooperation helps signal your trust in them. Yet, you may be torn between the need to have something done (now!), and the desire to treat employees in a proper manner.

The solution lies in making ***assertive requests*** for some tasks. A request is a courteous invitation to do something that will fulfill the organization's needs. It also implies that the employees have some discretion in how to respond and is a reflection of an attempt to empower them. Nevertheless, you may feel a strong need to get an employee to cooperate, and adding a bit of assertiveness to the request may stimulate that. Supervisors demonstrate *assertiveness* when they describe a problem, express their feelings about it, request an action, and specify the consequences for either positive or negative responses to the request. All of this is best done, of course, in a direct, open, and confident manner. For example, a supervisor may say, "Please hold your coffee breaks down to 15 minutes," or "I'd greatly appreciate it if you would get your workplace cleaned up before you leave today." Properly phrased and delivered, assertive requests can convey to employees that they have some freedom of action while understanding that the desired behavior is important to the organization.

Assertive request. To ask courteously; to make known your wishes with the implied expectation that they will be fulfilled.

Super SCOPE ▶ Avoiding Trouble When Issuing Orders

How can a supervisor stay out of trouble when directing, ordering, assigning, or instructing an employee? There are no guarantees, but these 10 guidelines should help.

1. **Don't make it a struggle for power.** Avoid the appearance of relying on personal whims. Focus your mutual attention on the demands of the situation and the goals to be met.

2. **Avoid a casual manner.** It's all right to have fun occasionally, but be clear and firm about those matters that are important to you.

3. **Watch your words and tone of voice.** Most employees accept your right to give orders, but they may object to your choice of words and the way in which you convey your thoughts.

4. **Don't assume that the employee understands.** Encourage employees to ask questions. Repeat the highlights of the order. Then watch to see if it is followed.

5. **Seek immediate feedback.** If the employee misunderstands or plans to resist, you might as well discover that right away. Then you'll still have time to iron things out.

6. **Don't give too many orders.** Be selective, or you'll fall prey to communication overload. Be brief, to the point, and don't add new orders until the others are completed.

7. **Provide just enough detail**. Jobs differ on their complexity, and workers vary on their need for detail. Think about, and adapt to, the needs of the person you're addressing.

8. **Avoid conflicting instructions.** Check with other supervisors to make sure you're not telling your employees one thing, and they're sending a different message. Consistency is also key—both from day to day and employee to employee.

9. **Carefully select the recipient.** Don't show favorites, either by picking on complainers or cooperative workers. Employees deserve to have work distributed fairly.

10. **Don't flaunt your authority.** Cracking the whip or letting your ego show won't earn you any respect, and, more than likely, it will backfire on you. Act like one of the team (after all, you are).

Quick Test 5 ▶

9	T or F	The difference between an order and an instruction is that an order tells what to do, and an instruction tells how to do it.
10	T or F	Employees are more likely to respond positively to an assertive request than to an order.

KEY CONCEPTS TO REMEMBER

1. **The Communication Process.** Communication is the process of passing information and understanding from one person to another. Supervisors rely on it daily to give orders and instructions, build team spirit, and receive feedback. Communication relationships must be maintained with employees and bosses, other supervisors, and important groups outside the organization.

2. **Methods of Communication.** Supervisors have a wide array of spoken and written methods—both traditional and electronic—to choose from when communicating with individuals or groups. Successful communication depends on analyzing each major situation and choosing the methods that best match the specific objectives the supervisor wishes to accomplish.

3. **Nonverbal Communication.** Although spoken and written words are generally the most visible element in communication, information exchange is greatly influenced by nonverbal factors. An employee's attitude, personality, tone of voice, and gestures are all important. Accurate receiving of messages is influenced by both observation and listening. Supervisors can reap huge benefits from active, attentive listening.

4. **Communication Guidelines.** There are many errors that supervisors can make when communicating with employees. Many of these can be prevented by staying informed, being sensitive to employee feelings, and anticipating what employees are interested in hearing. Similar guidelines apply to communication relationships with one's superior. It is especially fruitful to analyze the visual, auditory, and kinesthetic preferences of the recipient.

5. **Orders, Instructions, and Requests.** Issuing orders and giving instructions is a fundamental part of most supervisors' jobs. Orders are more likely to be effective if they are clear, delivered confidently, repeated, and followed up to make sure action occurred. But much employee cooperation can be obtained by phrasing most orders as assertive requests and providing explanations for them.

READING COMPREHENSION

1. Why is it important for an organization to have effective communication?
2. Discuss the pros and cons of the grapevine.
3. How can supervisors develop high levels of credibility among their employees?
4. If you are unable to complete a project on schedule, is it preferable to inform your boss about it immediately or to wait until it is done and then provide a detailed explanation?
5. With all this emphasis on communication, isn't there a danger of overcommunicating? Is it ever possible to overcommunicate?
6. Suggest three or more different techniques for helping supervisors listen more effectively.
7. What options does a supervisor have if an employee willfully disobeys an order?
8. Are there any conditions under which a supervisor should refrain from giving orders? If so, what are they?
9. Does listening have any role in the process of giving orders?
10. Discuss the pros and cons of using e-mail for employee communications.

APPLICATION

Self-Assessment

▶ *How good are your communication skills?*

Read the following statements carefully. Circle the number on the response scale that most closely reflects the degree to which each statement accurately describes you. Add up your total points and prepare a brief action plan for self-improvement. Be ready to report your score for tabulation across the entire group.

	Good Description									Poor Description
1. I understand the communication process, and I pay attention to every step within it every time I communicate.	10	9	8	7	6	5	4	3	2	1
2. I recognize the value of 360-degree feedback and actively solicit it from my manager, my peers, and my employees.	10	9	8	7	6	5	4	3	2	1
3. I am alert to the differences in situations and select a communication method to fit each one as best as I can.	10	9	8	7	6	5	4	3	2	1
4. I am aware of the special demands of voice mail and adapt my approach to fit it.	10	9	8	7	6	5	4	3	2	1
5. I find e-mail communications to be beneficial, and I carefully follow the guidelines for its proper use.	10	9	8	7	6	5	4	3	2	1
6. I am careful to point out to my employees the shortcomings of the grapevine.	10	9	8	7	6	5	4	3	2	1
7. I am confident that I demonstrate most of the characteristics of an effective listener.	10	9	8	7	6	5	4	3	2	1
8. I feel very comfortable communicating upward to my boss progress issues, controversial matters, morale problems, and constructive suggestions.	10	9	8	7	6	5	4	3	2	1
9. I recognize the differences in communication preferences among my employees, and adjust my style to their visual, auditory, or kinesthetic preferences.	10	9	8	7	6	5	4	3	2	1

Good Description										**Poor Description**
10	9	8	7	6	5	4	3	2	1	

10. I consciously try to minimize my use of commands, and prefer to seek voluntary cooperation through assertive requests.

Scoring and Interpretation

SCORING

Add up your total points for the 10 questions. Record that number here, and report it when it is requested. _____

INTERPRETATION

81 to 100 points. You seem to have a basic set of communication skills.

61 to 80 points. Take a close look at some of your communication skills (those with lower self-assessments) and discuss them with a manager to see if they need improvement.

Below 60 points. Some of your skills may be substantially inconsistent with effective communication practices and could be detrimental to your success as a supervisor.

Identify your three lowest scores and record the question numbers here: _____, _____, _____.

ACTION

Write a brief paragraph detailing an action plan for how you might sharpen each of these skills. Then pay particularly close attention to the related material in the chapter as you review the relevant sections there.

Skill Development

Listening Skills ◀

Poor listening skills are one of the greatest downfalls of many supervisors. Absence of these skills can imply arrogance, insensitivity, and a lack of concern for employees. You are concerned that your listening skills might need improvement, but you really don't know. Review the list of listening skills below and select the three on which you feel the most confident (mark those with a +). Then identify the three on which you believe you need the greatest development, marking them with a –. Next, engage a close colleague or friend in an extended discussion (e.g., one hour) on a topic of vital interest to you, and then solicit that person's assessment of your listening skills (three strengths and three weaknesses). Compare that assessment to your own evaluation.

Listening Skills	My Assessment		Other's Assessment	
	+ (3)	– (3)	+ (3)	– (3)
1. Positive eye contact	_____	_____	_____	_____
2. Paraphrasing key thoughts	_____	_____	_____	_____
3. Paying attention to feelings	_____	_____	_____	_____
4. Probing nonaggressively	_____	_____	_____	_____
5. Being patient	_____	_____	_____	_____
6. Using pauses	_____	_____	_____	_____
7. Nodding head	_____	_____	_____	_____
8. Making confirming remarks	_____	_____	_____	_____
9. Echoing key words	_____	_____	_____	_____
10. Showing strong interest	_____	_____	_____	_____

ACTION

Prepare a report that suggests how you intend to improve those items on which you both agree need improvement. To prepare your report, review the text's discussion on active listening, scan the Internet for relevant guidelines, and consult with colleagues and staff persons in the human resources department for their advice.

Role Play

▶ *Are You Listening?*

Identify two volunteers from the class. One should take the role of Khrystyne, and the other the role of Elana. After both persons have had an opportunity to read their respective roles, ask them to come to the front of the room to engage in whatever conversation arises. The rest of the class should act as observers.

KHRYSTYNE. You work in Elana's department of 11 employees, where you have been employed for the past seven years. Although you have always enjoyed your job, things seem to have deteriorated badly in recent months, and you are very upset about that. To the best of your knowledge, five new employees have been hired at salaries higher than yours; they have been given their choice of cubicle spaces (nearer the windows, so they have a view and you do not); they have received state-of-the-art computer systems, while yours is almost archaic; and they seem to be receiving much more attention from Elana than you do. You have stewed about these things for two weeks and have finally decided to have a heart-to-heart conversation with Elana to "air out your laundry" with her.

ELANA. You are the supervisor in a department of 11 employees, including Khrystyne. You have always viewed her as a cooperative, productive employee until the past few weeks. Her recent behavior, however, has caused you to seek a heart-to-heart conversation with her to "air out your laundry." She has acted rather coldly to the five new employees hired recently, made several curt comments to you, and started taking the maximum number of personal leave days during each pay period. You realize that times have been tense with the unusual amount of turnover your department has experienced and the necessity of paying higher salaries to attract new employees, but you had hoped that Khrystyne would be a role model for the new hires. Since she has not offered to help them, you have had to spend a large amount of time helping them learn how to operate their new computer systems. You are about to have a conversation with Khrystyne now.

OBSERVERS. Pay attention, in particular, to the listening skills demonstrated by the two parties as they interact with each other. Rate both of them (10 = high; 1 = low) on the degree to which they exhibit each of the following behaviors and characteristics:

	Khrystyne	Elana
Attentive	_____	_____
Concerned	_____	_____
Courteous	_____	_____
Empathetic	_____	_____
Eye contact	_____	_____
Paraphrased	_____	_____
Patient	_____	_____
Probed	_____	_____
Respectful	_____	_____
Summarized	_____	_____

What constructive suggestions can you give to each person?

CASES FOR ANALYSIS

Case 31

The Man Who Wouldn't Move

Rachel Fields was at her wit's end. Office space was in heavy demand at the research laboratory where she was supervisor of the environmental monitoring section. Program funding had grown gradually over the past five years, but no new buildings were constructed to house the newly hired scientists. This had not been a problem until this year, when Rachel reached the absolute limit of her imagination in shuffling people around and even creating offices out of other work spaces. There was literally nothing left but an old work table in the space next to the noisy area where the coffeepot was located. And there was absolutely no construction money forthcoming.

But the problem would have been manageable even this year if it weren't for Dick Lansford. Dick had been with various units of the laboratory for 43 years and loved every minute of it. He never would have retired, except that his family had insisted on it. At first, Rachel thought Dick's announcement of retirement was the answer to her dreams, as she could allocate Dick's office to the newest scientist the laboratory had just hired. Then the bombshell dropped when Dick walked into Rachel's office.

"Rachel, I've been down to the personnel office, and the people there reviewed the policy on retirements for me," Dick said. "They discovered that I'm automatically eligible for status as a scientist emeritus."

"Yes, I believe that's true," Rachel replied cautiously.

"Furthermore," continued Dick, "the policy says that I may be granted office space to support the continuation of my work projects. So I just wanted to tell you how elated I am now that I won't have to move out of my office after all!" With that, Dick turned on his heel and went back to his office, whistling happily all the way.

Rachel called personnel for additional details. She discovered that Dick was right, except he had left out one important detail—the granting of an office to a scientist emeritus was a privilege subject to availability of space. Now Rachel didn't know what to do. On the one hand, Dick had been a loyal and valuable employee for many years and would be heartbroken to be forcibly moved from his office. On the other hand, the laboratory desperately needed to assign Dick's space to the new scientist arriving in one week.

If you were Rachel, which of the following actions would you select to resolve this dilemma? Rank the alternatives on a scale from 1 (most preferable) to 5 (least preferable). You may add another alternative if you wish. Be prepared to justify your ranking.

_____ **a.** Write a memo to Dick, telling him that you're sorry but he simply must be out of the office within one week and that there is no other space available for him.

_____ **b.** Hold your announcement of his eviction from the office until Wednesday, when you can make it at the weekly staff meeting, where it is less likely that an argument will take place (due to the presence of other scientists).

_____ **c.** Place an announcement of the new office assignments on the department's bulletin board, which most employees check daily.

_____ **d.** Don't bother with a formal announcement; simply have the building and grounds staff box up Dick's belongings over the weekend so that they will be all ready for him to pick up on Monday.

_____ **e.** Go to see Dick in his office, explain the problem to him, and ask for his assistance in solving the dilemma you face; then follow up the decision with a short memo of confirmation.

Case 32

Now That I've Got It, What Do I Do With It?

Jay Pierce was a 15-year employee at the Great Lakes marine biology laboratory. About a year ago, he had only reluctantly accepted a promotion to supervisor of the freshwater studies group—he really wanted to continue with his research agenda. This promotion had required that he give up nearly two-thirds of his own research projects and take on the administrative responsibilities for the lab's eight technicians. He warmed to the job slowly, but after several months he began to take it more and more seriously. Of course, he had made a few errors along the way, but he was learning.

After a year, Jay was curious about his success to date. He even volunteered to participate in the laboratory's "360-degree feedback" program—a systematic process of data gathering from key people all around (above, beside, and below) a supervisor regarding his or her performance and needs for improvement. After identifying four other supervisors as his relevant peers, questionnaires were sent to them, his boss, and his eight technicians. Jay also completed the forms himself, rating his performance in six categories on a five-point scale (5 = excellent; 1 = poor).

Analysis ▶

Now the results from all areas of the 360-degree feedback program were back, and he was unsure how to interpret them. What conclusions would you draw from the data?

Category	Jay	Respondents Jay's Boss	Peers	Technicians
Oral communications	3	3	4	3
Written communications	4	4	2	5
Decision making	5	4	5	3
Planning and budgeting	2	2	3	4
Leadership	4	2	4	2
Employee development	3	3	3	1

Case 33 ▶ *Modifying the Medium*

In a classic case of overnight success, Ted's business has grown by leaps and bounds. Starting with a small camera shop, he has recently expanded to a complete line of photographic goods and related developing services in three locations in the city. He used to be able to communicate with his three employees by using a very informal "Hey, you!" approach, simply calling across the aisle to ask about a price, provide advice on the location of a display, or tell a clerk when to take a coffee break. Now, however, he has 26 employees working on two different shifts in the three retail outlet-service center establishments. The "Hey, you!" approach just doesn't work anymore.

Analysis ▶

The following situations arise for Ted during the course of the current week. What communication medium should he use to handle each of them?

a. Mary has been late for work twice this week. She is a new employee, still in her probationary period with the firm, and Ted decides to let her know that she will have only one more chance.

b. One of the developing machines broke down, and a backlog of work to be done on a short schedule has developed. Ted is anxious to discover whether either of the other two shops can handle the overload.

c. Ted is concerned about providing high-quality customer service. Twelve employees come into face-to-face contact with customers, and Ted wants to tell these workers how to greet the customers, take their orders, and handle their problems.

d. Ted's accountant has announced that the firm set dramatic records last year for its level of profits. Ted would like to share his joy with his employees.

e. While attending a camera manufacturer's conference, Ted learned that one of last year's models has a defect in it which, if not corrected, will result in damage to each roll of film used. He feels obligated to tell both prior and future purchasers of that camera model about the defect.

Quick Test 1	Quick Test 2	Quick Test 3	**Answers to Quick Tests**
1. T	3. F	5. T	
2. T	4. F	6. F	

Quick Test 4	Quick Test 5		
7. F	9. T		
8. T	10. T		

Working with Individuals and Teams

CHAPTER 12

Appraisal of Employee Performance

Learning Objectives

After studying this chapter, you should be able to

- Explain the main purposes and benefits of an employee performance appraisal.

- Describe the kinds of factors that are evaluated and some of the formats used, suggest ways of reducing bias, and recognize the influence of the halo effect.

- List the main steps in an appraisal interview and discuss techniques for making it more effective.

- Discuss ways of handling sensitive problems that may arise during, or as a result of, the appraisal interview.

- Explain the legal implications of a performance appraisal, recognize its limited relationship to financial rewards, and identify a number of extenuating circumstances that may cause poor performance.

PURPOSES OF APPRAISAL

CONCEPT ▶ Employees have a right to know, and a desire to know, how well they are performing and how they can improve.

What are the primary purposes of an appraisal?

There are four basic reasons for making an appraisal of employee performance:

1. **To encourage good behavior or to correct and discourage below-standard performance.** Good performers expect positive reinforcement, even if it is only praise. Poor performers should recognize that continued substandard behavior, will at minimum, stand in the way of advancement. At the most drastic, poor performance may lead to termination.

2. **To satisfy employees' curiosity about how they are doing.** People have a fundamental drive to want to know how well they are doing in the eyes of their organization. Employees may dislike being judged by others, but the urge to know is very strong.

3. **To provide an opportunity for developing employee skills.** It is not enough to tell employees of their weaknesses; they must also know how to overcome their shortcomings. A powerful role for the supervisor is to coach employees on ways to improve in the future.

4. **To provide a firm foundation for later judgments that concern an employee's career.** Such matters as pay raises, promotions, or transfers can be handled more smoothly if the employee is aware of the possibilities (and probabilities) beforehand. And in an era of downsizing, appraisals can create a basis for making tough decisions about who must be terminated.

Won't employees resent being evaluated?

The biggest fear in most supervisors' minds is that an employee will dislike being judged. Surprisingly, this fear is almost unfounded—if the appraisal is based on facts (rather than on opinion only), if you have sought input from employees themselves and their peers, if the appraisal is consistent with the pattern of feedback you have previously provided, and if you are flexible enough to change ratings if an employee can show you you're wrong. People want to know where they stand, even if it isn't at the top of the heap. But don't interpret this to mean that appraisal interviews are free from stress for either of you, or that employees will make it easy for you. Some will, but others won't.

Don't treat your employees as you would grade-school children. Mature adults resent that and will resist your suggestions. Instead, use a constructive tone, clarify the purpose, invite their participation, and explore barriers to their performance. And be sure to let them know that you want them to succeed and will help them do so.

Down Side of Appraisal Systems

■ Some of the adverse side effects of appraisal systems—if poorly conducted—include

- Encouraging negative rivalries and hard feelings among workers who feel they are vying for a limited "pot" of merit money.
- Sabotaging company attempts to create high-performing teams.
- Portraying the supervisor as a "superior" who sits in judgment of every employee action.
- Overemphasis on work factors that can be easily observed and quantified, and overlooking other "good citizen" behaviors of employees that are highly valued.

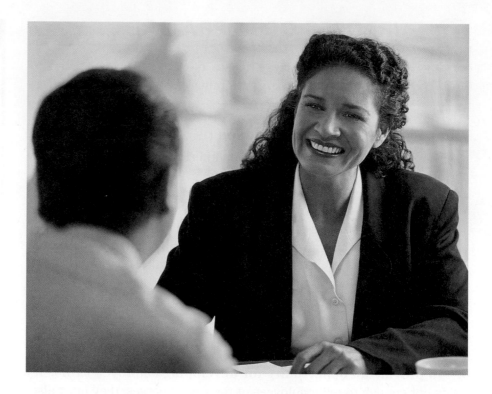

Formal performance appraisals and pay raises should be on different time schedules. Why? ▶

How often should you evaluate an employee?

Twice a year for a formal *performance appraisal* is a happy medium. If you rate too often, you're likely to be too impressed by day-to-day occurrences (as well as being burdened with paperwork). If you wait too long, you're likely to forget many of the incidents that ought to influence your appraisal. Even if your company has a plan that calls for rating only once a year, it's good practice to make appraisals of your own—informally, perhaps—more often. This means that you should observe employee performance routinely and compliment or criticize it on a timely basis. You should do this, of course, regardless of formal appraisal sessions. In other words, *don't wait* for formal appraisals to reinforce good performance or to curb poor performance.

What is the relation of performance appraisals to job evaluation, compensation rates, and merit raises?

This is a sensitive question, often asked by employees. You should approach this issue carefully, since much depends upon your company's policies toward it. *Job evaluation* is a systematic method for appraising the worth of a particular job, *not* the individual who performs it. The compensation set for a particular job is the result of a job-pricing decision based upon the job's evaluation and should have little or nothing to do with the person who actually performs the job. *Merit raises* are salary increases based on merit, or the quality of an individual's performance.

Most organizations strive to separate the performance appraisal session from decisions regarding issuance of merit raises. The purpose is to keep the focus of the appraisal on performance, not salary. This distinction is not always clear to employees.

It is a cardinal mistake, then, for a supervisor to stress the relationship of performance to pay raises during the appraisal interview. It is only human for persons who have been told that their work is good to expect an increase in pay (or other rewards) to follow. If your company's compensation plan doesn't work that way, you may suffer a very red face when an employee tells you later on, "You told me my good work would bring a raise or a promotion—and it didn't." Our best advice is to keep appraisals and pay raises separate by following two different time schedules.

◀ **Quick Test 1**

1	T or F	The primary purpose of appraisals is to provide a basis for merit increases.
2	T or F	Employees should be appraised—at least informally— about twice a year.

 2 FACTORS AND FORMAT

CONCEPT ▶ Appraisals evaluate, in a systematic way, an individual's job-related traits and behavior as they affect performance.

How formal will the performance rating procedure be?

Because of legal implications, most organizations now carefully specify and monitor their performance-appraisal programs. Most appraisal formats incorporate some form of "graphic rating scale." A simple version is shown in Table 12-1. Typically, these formats provide a choice of ratings for each factor, ranging from "superior" or "outstanding" to "expected level" and on down to "unsatisfactory." Numerical weights attached to each factor show its relative importance. Upon completion, a total score for the overall appraisal can be obtained.

A variation of the above is the "forced-choice" format. This provides a series of paired descriptive statements for each factor being rated. One statement is always more positive or less negative than its opposing member. Thus, in making judgments, a supervisor is forced to choose the most accurate phrase very carefully. Regardless of the format, supervisors need to demonstrate objectivity, impartiality, and honesty.

TABLE 12-1

Example of a Weighted Graphic Rating Scale

Factor	Rating* A	B	C	D	E	Score
1. Quality of work	20	16	12	8	4	_____
2. Quantity of work	20	16	12	8	4	_____
3. Dependability	20	16	12	8	4	_____
4. Attitude	10	8	6	4	2	_____
5. Initiative	5	4	3	2	1	_____
6. Housekeeping	10	8	6	4	2	_____
7. Attendance	10	8	6	4	2	_____
8. Potential for advancement	5	4	3	2	1	_____
Total rating score						_____

*A: superior; B: very good; C: at expected level; D: below expected level; E: unsatisfactory

What factors should you consider when appraising an employee?

These can vary from plan to plan. What you are trying to answer about an employee's performance, however, are these questions:

- What has the individual done since last appraised? How well has it been done? How much better could it be?

- In what ways have strengths and weaknesses in the individual's job approach affected this performance? Are these factors ones that could be improved? If so, how?

- What is the individual's potential? How well could the employee do if really given a chance?

Factors that are judged in an appraisal also tend to fall into two categories: objective judgments and subjective judgments. *Objective factors* focus on hard facts and measurable results—quantities, quality, attendance. *Subjective factors* tend to represent opinions, such as those about attitude, personality, and adaptability. Distinguish between the two. Be firmer about appraisal of objective factors than about those involving opinion only. But even subjective factors can be rated with confidence if they are supported by documented incidents. The sample performance rating form shown in Table 12-1 includes both objective (e.g., numbers 1 and 2) and subjective (e.g., numbers 3, 4, and 5) factors. Figure 12-1 presents a rating scale that includes descriptions for each factor.

How can you make sure your standards are consistent from employee to employee?

Before we answer this question, it should be stressed that one employee's rating is almost never measured against another's. Performance is always compared with the stated responsibilities and standards established for a particular job. If there is a variety of skills and experience among your employees, however, you may find it helpful to double check your ratings to make sure that you are not favoring one employee or making an unsupported judgment about another. Accordingly, try this approach:

1. List the name of each employee down one side of a sheet of paper and the factors to be rated across the top.

2. Work down the columns, looking at only one factor at a time. Take quality, for instance. If you have rated Tom only "fair" and Pete and Nicosha "good," ask yourself if you are using the same standards for each. Perhaps upon reconsidering, you'll want to drop Pete's rating to "fair" because Pete and Tom produce the same quality of work, whereas Nicosha's quality is demonstrably better than either Pete's or Tom's.

You may also want to consider whether you are rating *all* employees either too high or too low. In most workforces, there is some sort of variation in performance levels. The performance of some employees will be exceptionally high and of some others exceptionally low, with that of the remainder somewhere in between. Keep in mind, however, that every employee can rate near or at the top if he or she performs well against the stipulated responsibilities and standards.

Doesn't an employee's rating represent only the supervisor's opinion?

A good performance rating includes more than just a supervisor's opinion. It should be based on facts. In considering quality of performance, what is the employee's error record? As to quantity, what do the production records show? As for dependability, what's the absence and lateness record? Can you cite actual incidents in which you have had to discipline the employee, or speak about the quality or quantity of output? Answering such questions makes your rating less opinionated and, consequently, more valid. It also helps you avoid the **halo effect,** which is discussed in SuperScope.

Such documented incidents become examples, called **critical incidents,** of an employee's performance. These incidents should undeniably represent the quality—good or bad—of an employee's work. It is a good practice to make notes of such occurrences and place them in the employee's file. At appraisal time they serve to illustrate what you consider good or subpar performance and to support the ratings you make.

Halo effect. A generalization whereby one aspect of performance, or a single quality of an individual's nature, is allowed to overshadow everything else about that person.

Critical incident. An actual and specific occurrence, either favorable or unfavorable, that serves to illustrate the general nature of an employee's performance.

◆ **FIGURE 12-1**

Example of the behaviorally anchored rating scale. **How will the supervisor use these descriptions?**

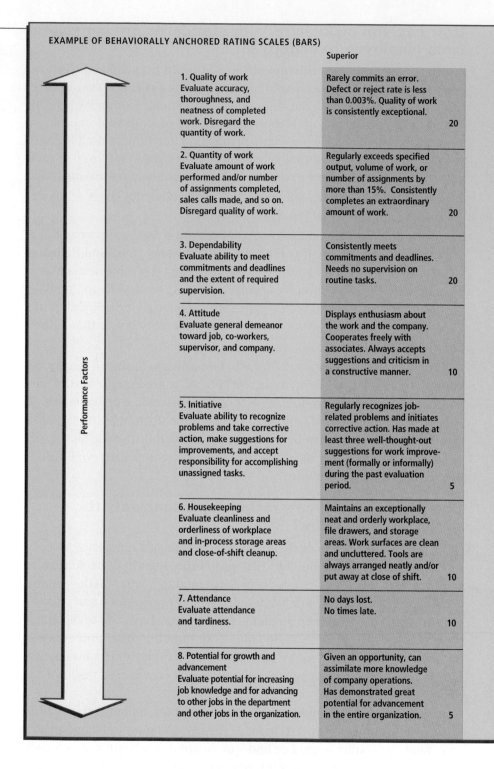

EXAMPLE OF BEHAVIORALLY ANCHORED RATING SCALES (BARS)

Superior

Performance Factors

1. Quality of work
Evaluate accuracy, thoroughness, and neatness of completed work. Disregard the quantity of work.

Rarely commits an error. Defect or reject rate is less than 0.003%. Quality of work is consistently exceptional. **20**

2. Quantity of work
Evaluate amount of work performed and/or number of assignments completed, sales calls made, and so on. Disregard quality of work.

Regularly exceeds specified output, volume of work, or number of assignments by more than 15%. Consistently completes an extraordinary amount of work. **20**

3. Dependability
Evaluate ability to meet commitments and deadlines and the extent of required supervision.

Consistently meets commitments and deadlines. Needs no supervision on routine tasks. **20**

4. Attitude
Evaluate general demeanor toward job, co-workers, supervisor, and company.

Displays enthusiasm about the work and the company. Cooperates freely with associates. Always accepts suggestions and criticism in a constructive manner. **10**

5. Initiative
Evaluate ability to recognize problems and take corrective action, make suggestions for improvements, and accept responsibility for accomplishing unassigned tasks.

Regularly recognizes job-related problems and initiates corrective action. Has made at least three well-thought-out suggestions for work improvement (formally or informally) during the past evaluation period. **5**

6. Housekeeping
Evaluate cleanliness and orderliness of workplace and in-process storage areas and close-of-shift cleanup.

Maintains an exceptionally neat and orderly workplace, file drawers, and storage areas. Work surfaces are clean and uncluttered. Tools are always arranged neatly and/or put away at close of shift. **10**

7. Attendance
Evaluate attendance and tardiness.

No days lost. No times late. **10**

8. Potential for growth and advancement
Evaluate potential for increasing job knowledge and for advancing to other jobs in the department and other jobs in the organization.

Given an opportunity, can assimilate more knowledge of company operations. Has demonstrated great potential for advancement in the entire organization. **5**

Very good		At expected level		Below expected level		Unsatisfactory	
Makes only an occasional error. Defect or reject rate is consistently less than 0.010%. Quality of work is high grade, but not exceptional.	16	Errors are only occasionally troublesome. Defect or reject rate rarely exceeds standard of 0.010%. Quality of work is average.	12	Errors are frequently troublesome. Defect or reject rate often exceeds standard of 0.010%. Quality of work is below average.	8	Errors are frequently troublesome. Defect or reject rate regularly exceeds standard of 0.010%. Quality of work is unsatisfactory.	4
Regularly exceeds specified output, volume of work, or number of assignments. Consistently turns out a good volume of work.	16	Usually meets the specified output, volume of work, or number of assignments. Amount of work completed is about average for this job.	12	Often fails to meet specified output, volume of work, or number of assignments. Amount of work completed is about 10% less than average for this job.	8	Regularly fails to meet specified output, volume of work, or number of assignments. Amount of work is almost always greater than 11% less than average for this job.	4
Meets commitments and deadlines 95% or more of the time. Needs minimum supervision on routine tasks.	16	Meets commitments and deadlines 90% or more of the time. Needs occasional supervision on routine tasks.	12	Meets commitments and deadlines less than 85 to 90% of the time. Needs constant checking, even on routine tasks.	8	Meets commitments and deadlines less than 85% of the time. Work and progress must be checked all the time.	4
Appears to be happy at his or her work. Cooperates freely with associates. Usually accepts suggestions or criticism in a constructive manner.	8	Accepts most assignments without complaint. Cooperates with associates when requested to do so. Follows instructions.	6	Frequently questions suitability of assignments. Complains regularly about the nature of the work. Cooperates with associates when requested to do so. Often rejects suggestions or criticism.	4	Constantly complains about the work and the company. Regularly voices objection to assignments. Does not cooperate with co-workers. Is always negative toward suggestions and criticism.	2
Usually recognizes job-related problems and initiates corrective action. Has made at least one well-thought-out suggestion for work improvement during the past evaluation period.	4	Occasionally recognizes and acts upon job-related problems. Occasionally makes well-thought-out suggestions for work improvement.	3	Fails to recognize job-related problems or to initiate action to correct them. Usually waits to be told what to do.	2	Fails to recognize job-related problems or to initiate action to correct them. Always needs to be told what to do. Never displays any kind of initiative.	1
Maintains a neat and orderly workplace, file drawers, and storage areas. Work surfaces are usually clean and uncluttered. Tools are put away at close of shift.	8	Maintains a reasonably neat and clean workplace. Work surfaces are acceptably free from soil or debris that would interfere with work. Only occasionally does not put tools away.	6	Often fails to maintain a reasonably neat and clean workplace. Work surfaces are often cluttered and not conducive to quality craft. Often fails to put tools away.	4	Consistently fails to maintain a neat and clean workplace or work surface. More often than not, fails to clean up or put tools away at close of shift.	2
1 to 2 days out sick, or 1 day absent of own accord, or 1 time late.	8	2 to 3 days out sick, or 2 days absent of own accord, or 2 times late.	6	3 to 5 days out sick, or 3 days absent of own accord, or 3 times late.	4	More than 5 days out sick, or more than 3 days absent of own accord, or more than 3 times late.	2
Given an opportunity, can assimilate more knowledge of company operations. Has demonstrated good potential for advancement in the department.	4	Has pretty much acquired as much knowledge here as he or she can assimilate. Has demonstrated some potential for advancement in the department.	3	Has difficulty in acquiring knowledge and skills here. Has demonstrated only limited potential for advancement.	2	Has great difficulty in acquiring knowledge and skills here. Has demonstrated no potential for advancement here.	1

Nearly all appraisers have a tendency to let one favorable or unfavorable incident or trait color their judgment of an individual as a whole. This is called the *halo effect*. A range of biases can be introduced this way. Among the most insidious are these eight:

1. **Recency.** Relying too heavily on what happened last week or last month.
2. **Overemphasis.** Placing too much weight on one good or poor factor.
3. **Unforgivingness.** Not allowing an employee's improved performance to outshine a poor record in a prior appraisal period.
4. **Prejudice.** Allowing an individual's contrary personality to affect the appraisal of his or her good work.

5. **Favoritism.** Being positively influenced by a person's likableness, despite a poor performance.
6. **Grouping.** Seeing all employees in a sub-standard work group in the same light, despite individual differences.
7. **Indiscrimination.** Being too critical or too generous; no one gets a good rating, or everyone does.
8. **Stereotyping.** Basing judgments on preconceived notions about such things as race, gender, color, religion, age, or national origin.

The halo effect can be minimized by (a) being aware of the pitfalls, (b) rating all employees on one factor before proceeding to ratings of the next factor, and (c) discussing your ratings with peer supervisors and inviting their questions.

Are all appraisal formats the same?

No. One popular format, which is shown in Figure 12-1, is an example of a ***behaviorally anchored rating scale (BARS)***. Its various items, or standards, are described or illustrated in the form of the behavior expected of an employee. These descriptions are usually based on critical incidents judged to be characteristic of the various levels of performance. This helps to provide greater objectivity in rating, as well as greater consistency across supervisors. The BARS's weakness is that it tends to focus on activity rather than results. Nevertheless, the BARS is generally considered the best and the most effective means of appraisal.

Many of the older formats emphasize an individual's traits, such as "initiative," "dependability," and "cooperation." The weakness with the *trait format*, however, is that the evaluation becomes almost unavoidably subjective. As such, trait evaluations are difficult to defend, especially in the courts.

Management by objectives (MBO) (see Chapter 15, and Table 4-1 in Chapter 4) provides a unique form of *results-oriented appraisal*. This approach is sometimes used for supervisors and other highly motivated employees. It requires that specific objectives, in the form of measurable results, be agreed on beforehand by both superior and subordinate. These objectives become the appraisal factors to be evaluated. The MBO approach is not particularly suitable for employees who rely heavily upon their supervisors to plan and control their work.

Behaviorally anchored rating scale (BARS). A performance-appraisal format that describes, and provides examples of, behavior that can be rated along a scale from outstanding to unsatisfactory behavior.

Management by Objectives (MBO). A planning and control technique in which a supervisor and his or her immediate superior agree on goals to be attained and standards to be maintained.

At the core of all successful appraisal formats, however, are clearly defined and explicitly communicated standards (or expectations) of employee performance on the job. Without these standards, appraisals become vague or contentious, are difficult to support, and lose their value as developmental tools. A good, up-to-date job description can be an invaluable tool as the basis for a performance appraisal.

◀ **Quick Test 2**

3	T or F	Graphic rating scales often provide not only a choice of levels of assessment, but a weighting showing relative importance of each factor.
4	T or F	The halo effect occurs only when you let one positive factor color your appraisal of the individual as a whole.

3 THE APPRAISAL INTERVIEW

CONCEPT ▷ The *appraisal interview* is a developmental exchange between supervisor and employee, aimed at reinforcing appropriate—or correcting unsatisfactory—performance.

What is the best way to handle the appraisal interview itself?

Whereas there are any number of approaches you might use, there are seven steps that form a pretty good path toward understanding and acceptance of the appraisal.

Step 1. Prepare the employee, as well as yourself, to come to the meeting expecting to compare notes. That way, you have your facts at hand, and the employee has the same opportunity to recall performance during the previous period.

Step 2. Compare accomplishments with specific targets—and invite the employee to share a self-assessment with you. Don't be vague or resort to generalizations. Be specific about what was expected and how close the employee has come to meeting these expectations. Then discuss any differences of opinion that arose.

Step 3. Be sure to give adequate credit for what *has* been accomplished. It is a temptation to take for granted those things that have been done well and to concentrate only on the deficiencies.

Step 4. Review those things that have *not* been accomplished. Emphasize where improvement is needed, and explore together with the employee how this can be done and why it is necessary for the employee to improve.

Appraisal interview. A meeting held between a supervisor and an employee to review the performance rating and, using that evaluation as a basis, to discuss the overall quality of the employee's work and methods for improving it, if necessary.

Step 5. Avoid the impression of your sitting in judgment. If there is responsibility to be shared, acknowledge it. Don't talk in terms of mistakes, faults, or weaknesses. Never compare the employee with a third person. Stick to a mutual explanation of the facts and what they imply to both of you.

Step 6. Agree on targets to be met during the period ahead. Be specific about them. Relate them to what has not been accomplished during the current period. This sets the stage for a more objective appraisal discussion next time around.

Step 7. Review what you can do to be of greater help. Then follow through and do it. Improvement is almost always a mutually dependent activity. An employee who knows that you share responsibility for it will approach the task with greater confidence and enthusiasm.

Where should you conduct performance rating or appraisal interviews?

Do it privately, in your own office or in a private room. You'll want to be able to give the interview your undivided attention. And you won't want to be in earshot of other employees, either. Allow yourself enough time—at the very least a half hour. Otherwise, the whole procedure will be too abrupt.

How should you combine feedback on both the favorable and unfavorable aspects of an employee's performance?

Traditionally, supervisors were told to "sandwich" unfavorable comments between favorable comments, as shown in Figure 12-2. For example, say, "I've been pleased with the way you've stepped up your output. You've made real improvement there. I am a little disappointed, however, by the quality of what you produce. The records show that you're always near the bottom of the group on errors. So I hope you'll work as hard to

◆ **FIGURE 12-2**

The "sandwich" technique. **What is the primary advantage of this technique?**

Begin with recognition of work well done

Discuss unsatisfactory areas of performance

End with summary of favorable performance

ASK EMPLOYEE FOR A SUMMARY

■ There are potential problems associated with the sandwich technique. Employees may "hear" the two positive parts (beginning and end) and ignore the critical part (the middle message), or they may do exactly the opposite. To make sure that the employee absorbs the whole sandwich, do this: At the end of the appraisal, ask the employee to summarize *all* that was heard during the session. Then listen carefully to detect if there is a reasonable balance shown. If not, use it as an opportunity to reemphasize your key points (positive or negative).

improve quality as you did quantity. I feel sure you will, since your attitude toward your work has been just fine."

The same technique is a helpful guide to the entire appraisal/review discussion. Use it by starting off the talk with a compliment. Then discuss the work that must be improved. Finish by finding something else good to say about the employee's work.

How are employees likely to respond to an appraisal?

Everyone, when presented with negative feedback, wants to **save face**—to restore their self-image and regain their self-esteem. Some (the really good ones) will do this in the months ahead by simply working harder and performing better. Others, however, will give a variety of explanations for their behavior, which may or may not be valid. Foremost among common excuses for poor performance are "unfair standards," "bad luck," or "inadequate tools, materials, training, and/or equipment."

Most employees will be quick to respond to your appraisal comments. Give them every chance to tell you what obstacles stand in the way of their making good. Don't interrupt them or dismiss their feelings with, "That's just an excuse." Instead, be patient. Let the person talk. Probe for additional explanations. Often the first reason given isn't the real one. Above all, don't get angry, regardless of what remarks the employee makes. Only if you listen carefully will you discover underlying causes for poor performance. Then you can work together to solve the problems. Be sure to negotiate an action plan for future improvements before ending the session.

Should you discuss one employee's rating with another employee?

Never! Always avoid comparisons. And be sure that each employee knows that you treat each rating as confidential. Try to establish the entire procedure on the basis of confidentiality.

Saving face. Employee actions taken to restore their self-image and regain their self-esteem after receiving criticism during an appraisal.

5	T or F	The last typical step in performance appraisal is to set targets for the next rating period.
6	T or F	Providing negative information to employees during an appraisal often creates the need for them to save face.

④ SPECIAL CONSIDERATIONS

CONCEPT ▶ Supervisors must be prepared to handle a variety of sensitive issues that may arise from the appraisal.

How do you handle charges of bias or favoritism?

Unfavorable criticism stings an occasional employee so hard that it's not unusual for the person to react by charging bias or favoritism. Don't try to argue the employee out of it. Your direct denial probably won't be accepted anyway. Instead, point out that you are rating the employee against job *standards*, not other employees. But be prepared to document your reasoning, and explain the entire appraisal process.

Isn't it dangerous to give employees a high rating? Won't they expect to get an immediate raise or a promotion out of it?

Knowledge of where an individual stands with the boss is every bit as important to a top-notch performer as it is to a mediocre employee—maybe even more so. If you fail to show your recognition of a good job, an employee is likely to think, "What's the use of doing a good job? No one appreciates it."

Good workers are hard to come by, and they find it relatively easy to locate other jobs. They should know how you feel, even when you can't show them an immediate reward. Remember, people work for lots more than what they get in their paycheck—for challenge, for accomplishment, for social satisfaction, and for feelings of competency.

How can you tell employees their work is way below par?

First, be especially sure that your previous treatment has encouraged the best kind of performance. Otherwise, they may believe that their poor showing is more your fault than their own.

Your guides should be these: Be candid and direct. Nothing is to be gained by being soft. If the work has been bad, say so. Then stick with the statement.

Be specific. For example: "We've been over this before. During the last six months I've made a point of showing you exactly where you have fallen down on the job. Remember the rejects we had on the X-56 job? And the complaints on the motor shafts? Only last week you put the whole shop in a bad light by the way you mishandled the shaft job again. It looks to me as if you just aren't capable of machine shop work. So I'm recommending that you be transferred out of this department. If there's no other suitable work available, I guess you'll have to look for work elsewhere."

Don't rub it in, though. Leave the employee with some self-respect. End the discussion by summarizing what you have found satisfactory as well as the things that are unsatisfactory.

Ethical PERSPECTIVES

Verbal Abuse

Your boss is verbally abusive and overpowering to subordinates—you included. How do you handle this?

Isn't it true that no matter how well some employees do their job, there's little chance of their getting a better job?

Yes. It's especially hard on a good worker who is bucking a seniority sequence and who knows that until the person ahead gets promoted or drops dead, there is little chance to move up. Suppose a number-two laboratory analyst said to you: "Each time I get reviewed, you tell me I'm doing a good job. But this hasn't done me any good. I'm getting top dollar for the job I'm on, and until the number-one analyst changes jobs, I'm stuck. All the performance review does to me is to rub salt into the wound!"

A good way for you to handle this complaint is to admit the situation exists, but don't oversympathize. Try saying something like this: "Sure, I agree that it's hard waiting for your chance. But some workers make the mistake of depending entirely on seniority for their advancement. I don't want you to fall into that trap. When the next better job opens, I hope both of us can say that you're fully qualified. That's one of the good things about performance ratings. You can find out where your weak spots may be and correct them. For a person who has your ability and does as well on the job as you do, there's no reason why you have to limit your ambitions to the number-one specialist's job here. Maybe you'll be able to jump from a number-two job here to a choice job in another department in the company."

How soon should you appraise a new employee?

Don't wait for the end of the probationary period or the formal appraisal time. Constructively criticize new employees as soon as a problem arises. Identify the cause of poor performance. Ask whether the unsatisfactory performance was due to forgetfulness, carelessness, lack of skill, a gap in their training, or failure to understand the standards expected. Offer whatever assistance is needed. With new employees, you should document the conversation right away by sending them a memo and placing a copy in their personnel file. If the problem occurs a second time, immediately confront the employee and repeat the documentation.

Otherwise, a poor start may deteriorate into an unsatisfactory, but permanent, employee.

Can employees be trusted to appraise themselves?

Self-appraisal. The process of allowing employees to take responsibility for evaluating their own performance.

Some organizations have experimented with *self-appraisal* systems. Employees are asked to evaluate their own performances, just as they are increasingly being allowed to act as their own quality control inspectors. They are told the criteria, given the performance standards, and asked to complete the rating forms. Most employees respond in a highly mature manner, often being even more critical of themselves than their supervisor would have been. Of course, the organization must endorse this procedure first, training must be provided to employees before starting it, and results of such an approach need to be monitored. If this self-appraisal process proves successful, it may help eliminate one of the most frustrating of all supervisory tasks.

Quick Test 4 ▶

7	T or F	To avoid inflating employee egos, it is best to lower the rating of a top performer a little bit.
8	T or F	If employee performance is truly substandard, there is little to be gained by being honest with the individual.

5 LEGAL AND FINANCIAL ASPECTS

CONCEPT ▶ The appraisal represents a critical, legal communication to an employee and should be supported by objective reasoning and documentable evidence.

What are the legal implications of a performance appraisal?

There are several. Most of them are derived from the following legal doctrines:

- Equal pay for equal work.
- Absence of discrimination on the basis of age, gender, religion, race, color, or national origin.
- Accommodation of the physical and mental needs of the disabled and of veterans of the Vietnam era.
- Equal employment opportunity.

To minimize accusations of noncompliance with these legal requirements, try to do the following:

1. Make certain that your appraisals are based on what the job actually requires employees to do, not on a comparison with other employees and not on what you'd like them to be able to do. That's the value of job analysis, a detailed job description, and specific performance standards.

2. Be especially cautious in making subjective judgments. Ask yourself, "Could I back them up if challenged?"

3. Stick to facts that can be documented. When in doubt, keep a record of an occurrence that might be disputed.

4. Never say anything, even in the spirit of "leveling" with an employee, that could possibly be interpreted as meaning that your appraisal was based on a favorable or unfavorable reaction to the individual's race, color, religion, age, gender, national origin, disability, or veteran's status. It is difficult, of course, to be so neutral in your judgments, but you must do everything possible to avoid even the *appearance* of prejudice or discrimination. To do otherwise might bring you and your employer into court.

Should a supervisor keep a written record of what transpires during an appraisal interview?

First ask your employer or human resources department for advice on this one. We believe that you *should* keep a written record. For one thing, your memory may fade over time or you may be transferred to another position. If either of these happens and the employee needs a recommendation from your unit, written documentation of successful performance would be extremely useful.

On the other hand, even if your appraisal has been negative and you expect that improvement may not be forthcoming, it's wise to make a written record that summarizes the interview, especially what you expect from the employee in terms of improved performance in the future. If you do make such a record and place it in the employee's official file, you will be expected by law to give a copy to the employee. That's the problem. You'll have documentation if you need it later on, but you may irritate the employee (or at least make him or her wary).

It is also a good idea to collect in an employee's official file some sort of documentation of critical incidents. These might include regularly kept reports that show the level of and/or quality of output, written complaints or compliments from customers or internal staff members, and examples of very good or very poor work, such as a report filled with arithmetic or factual errors.

How do you convert employee performance ratings to money?

This is strictly a matter of your company's policy. About the only generality that can be drawn is that employees whose ratings are less than satisfactory should not be recommended for pay increases. Where a company has a rate range (maximum and minimum wage rates) for each job, many people believe that only workers who are rated "very good" or "exceptional" should advance to the maximum rate for the job.

Internet CONNECTION

Salaries. Check out one of the salary surveys available on the Internet. It's a great way to compare salaries in various cities.

Some employees try very hard, but their performance remains below par. What is the reason for this? What can be done about it?

If there is a weakness in performance-appraisal programs, it is that management assumes employees have only to try harder in order to measure up to standards. This is often not the case. Many factors can contribute to problems with employee performance. For example:

1. **Individuals may be assigned to work that does not match their capabilities.** It may be too easy or too difficult. One solution is a transfer to a more suitable job. Or the job might be redesigned to give the employee a better fit. An employee may not be able to handle the paperwork required. Perhaps it can be done by someone else. Or the job may require too little judgment for a highly intelligent person. Perhaps it can be rearranged to provide options that use this person's analytic ability.

2. **Employees may not have received proper training.** In any case of continued poor performance, the supervisor should first reexamine the training program and find a way to review the job procedure with the employee from start to finish. A key operating point may have been missed or forgotten.

3. **Individuals may be victims of pressures from the work group.** An employee may be trying to conform to your job standards, but co-workers may be giving him or her a hard time. To correct this situation, you may need to approach it from the group's point of view to change or modify the co-workers' position.

4. **Workers may not be up to the job requirements, physically or emotionally.** A checkup by the company nurse or doctor may be in order. If there are persistent or significant family problems (such as divorce, death, or severe illness), you may try gentle counseling. Your objective should be to show that you are sympathetic but that there is a limit as to how long the related poor performance can be accepted.

5. **Your own supervision may be at fault.** It takes two to tango, and poor performance may be related to a supervisor's failure to provide clear-cut standards, to train employees effectively, or to help with problems and changes as they arise.

6. **Mechanical or procedural problems may exist.** Possibly there is some hitch in the operating process—such as improper tools, materials, or equipment—or a conflict in prescribed paperwork procedures. You may want to review these problems with your own boss or with the appropriate staff departments.

9	T or F	It is generally advisable to create and keep a written record of the highlights of a performance appraisal discussion.
10	T or F	The most likely solution to a performance problem is to get employees to try a little bit harder.

KEY CONCEPTS TO REMEMBER

1. **Purposes of Appraisal.** The objective of performance appraisal is to help an employee improve the caliber of his or her job performance. When made aware of those areas in which he or she is already doing a good job and of those in which there is room for improvement, an employee can be encouraged to develop strengths and to overcome weaknesses. Many employees want to learn what they can do to improve their performance in the future.

2. **Factors and Format.** The careful and fair application of both objective and subjective factors in appraisals will help assure employees that their ratings are based upon facts and not opinions. It is important to minimize the halo effect in making judgments, and it is essential that standards be clearly established for all factors that are evaluated.

3. **The Appraisal Interview.** An appraisal interview should be carefully prepared so that it progresses systematically. The interview should first accentuate the positive by giving credit where credit is due. It may then shift to a discussion of areas where performance is not up to standard. The interview should conclude with an agreement concerning concrete action for improvement or further development. The interview should always be regarded as a two-way street highlighted by a mutual examination of job requirements, a mutual review of how adequately they are being fulfilled, a mutual agreement on new targets, and a mutual responsibility for improvement.

4. **Special Considerations.** Supervisors must be prepared to deal with sensitive issues, such as accusations of bias, negative employee reactions to criticism, and the inability to assure good performers of immediate or tangible rewards. New employees in particular should be appraised often to help them establish successful performance patterns. Some workers can be invited to participate in a self-appraisal process.

5. **Legal and Financial Aspects.** The appraisal of employees is covered by several federal and state guidelines to assure the absence of discrimination. Supervisors need to recognize, too, that carelessness or poor effort is not the only cause of inadequate performance. Mismatches between jobs and workers, physical or emotional stress, poor training or supervision, and unclear procedures may all bring about poor performance in spite of an employee's best efforts.

READING COMPREHENSION

1. What is it that employees expect to gain from a performance appraisal?
2. Distinguish between a job evaluation and a performance rating.
3. Explain the difference between an objective rating factor and a subjective one.
4. Erma complains that her supervisor keeps bringing up a mistake she made months ago, something that rarely occurs anymore. What is the distortion that her supervisor is imposing on the performance appraisal? How might he lessen the tendency to make such distortions?
5. Should an employee accept all the responsibility for his or her future improvement as a result of a performance interview? Why?

6. Should performance ratings be treated confidentially, or is it all right for a supervisor to discuss one employee's rating with another? Why?

7. Why isn't it a good idea to wait until a formal appraisal session to correct the poor performance of an employee?

8. Would it be better for a supervisor to go easy on employees during their appraisal interviews rather than risk hurting their feelings in such a way that they can't save face? Why?

9. What is meant by the fact that the performance appraisal is a legally protected activity? Who protects it?

10. What are at least two possible causes of poor employee performance other than carelessness or lack of effort?

APPLICATION

Self-Assessment

How good are your performance feedback skills?

Read the following statements carefully. Circle the number on the response scale that most closely reflects the degree to which each statement accurately describes you. Add up your total points and prepare a brief action plan for self-improvement. Be ready to report your score for tabulation across the entire group.

	Good Description									Poor Description
1. I am comfortable discussing the reasons for my appraisal with an employee.	10	9	8	7	6	5	4	3	2	1
2. I understand the merits of "doing my homework" before holding an appraisal discussion with an employee.	10	9	8	7	6	5	4	3	2	1
3. I believe that most employees want to know how their supervisor feels they are doing.	10	9	8	7	6	5	4	3	2	1
4. I believe that there are many reasons for poor employee performance, and lack of effort is only one possibility.	10	9	8	7	6	5	4	3	2	1
5. I endorse the practice of creating a written record of the key points discussed during an appraisal discussion.	10	9	8	7	6	5	4	3	2	1
6. I believe that being candid with employees during an appraisal is more likely to give them valid information from which to improve.	10	9	8	7	6	5	4	3	2	1

	Good Description									Poor Description
7. I recognize the value of confidentiality of appraisals, and would not disclose one employee's data to another.	10	9	8	7	6	5	4	3	2	1
8. I think it is important (and fair) to disclose to an employee the purpose(s) of an appraisal discussion.	10	9	8	7	6	5	4	3	2	1
9. I recognize the necessity of including both objective and subjective ratings into most appraisals.	10	9	8	7	6	5	4	3	2	1
10. I am aware of all the types of halo effect biases, and consciously work to eliminate them from my ratings.	10	9	8	7	6	5	4	3	2	1

Scoring and Interpretation

SCORING

Add up your total points for the 10 questions. Record that number here, and report it when it is requested. _____

INTERPRETATION

81 to 100 points. You seem to have a basic set of performance feedback skills.

61 to 80 points. Take a close look at some of your performance feedback skills (those with lower self-assessments) and discuss them with a manager to see if they need improvement.

Below 60 points. Some of your skills may be substantially inconsistent with effective performance feedback practices and could be detrimental to your success as a supervisor.

Identify your three lowest scores and record the question numbers here: _____, _____, _____.

ACTION

Write a brief paragraph detailing an action plan for how you might sharpen each of these skills. Then pay particularly close attention to the related material in the chapter as you review the relevant sections there.

Skill Development

Employee Appraisal Skills ◀

Many supervisors struggle with how to deliver an appraisal to employees and find it to be a difficult task with few rewards. This responsibility can become even more complex when the employee group contains representatives from the Baby Boomer, Generation X, and subsequent eras. Nevertheless, the task cannot be ignored, and (if done well) can produce very positive outcomes for both the appraisee and the organization.

Interview a number of supervisors to obtain a sampling of their experiences with performance appraisal. Record these suggestions of things to do and things not to do in a performance appraisal.

Things to Do	Things Not to Do
1. _____	1. _____
2. _____	2. _____
3. _____	3. _____
4. _____	4. _____
5. _____	5. _____
6. _____	6. _____
7. _____	7. _____
8. _____	8. _____
9. _____	9. _____
10. _____	10. _____

ACTION

Prepare a report that succinctly presents a set of action guidelines that you can follow in the future. This report should contain both lists of what "to do" and what "not to do." To prepare your report, review the text's discussion on employee appraisal, search the Internet for relevant guidelines, and consult with colleagues and staff persons in the human resources department for their advice.

Role Play

Performance Appraisal

Identify two volunteers from the class and assign each of them a role to read. Do *not* allow them to read the other person's role description.

COLLEGIATE DEAN (DR. KIM). You are the dean of a college that employs about 30 full-time faculty. Each year you conduct a performance appraisal interview with each faculty member. This year you are particularly anxious about communicating your assessment of Pat, who is an assistant professor. Pat has been here for three years and from what you have observed has a messy office, dresses too casually for your taste, smokes cigarettes (outside the building, of course), and seems to be trying too hard to relate to the students in matching their language and musical interests. In addition, Pat's grade distributions at the end of the semester are always higher than those of departmental colleagues; you wonder if Pat is just "too easy." You grudgingly admit that Pat has already published several articles and seems to be well-liked by students but wonder if this is the right place for Pat to build an entire career. Pat is about to enter your office now for the appraisal discussion.

ASSISTANT PROFESSOR (PAT). You are an assistant professor in this college and have been on campus for three years already. You have invested an enormous amount of energy in your job here but feel that your accomplishments have gone largely unnoticed until now—presumably because you have been so new on campus. You work long hours, have published several notable articles, and spend enormous energy trying to "connect" with students. For example, you play contemporary music in your office, dress much like students do, try to speak their "language," and talk to them about issues with which they are concerned. You have been especially pleased about the student learning demonstrated in your classes, and this has shown up in the unusually high grades that you have assigned to them. You are looking forward to the annual appraisal discussion with your dean and hope that not only a pay raise but possibly an early promotion might be on the agenda today. You are about to speak with the dean (Dr. Kim) now.

OBSERVERS. Observe the interaction between Dr. Kim and Pat closely, listening especially for not only what is said but how it is received. Watch specifically for opportunities to praise the dean (Dr. Kim) for what is done well and reflects the lessons in this chapter, as well as for possible errors that Pat makes. Be prepared to provide constructive feedback to the dean when the role-play is over.

Case 34

The Downgraded Performance Appraisal

Norma Jean has worked for three years as a buyer in the purchasing department of the Barnwell Company. Her supervisor, Mr. Morgan, consistently rated her performance as "very good," with a point total of 85 out of a possible 100. Typically, Norma Jean got top ratings for her knowledge of the job and the quality and dependability of her work. The only reason that her aggregate score did not move her into the "excellent" range was that her rating for "Quantity of Work Produced" was never better than "fair." Six months ago, Mr. Morgan left the company and was replaced by dynamic young Ms. Conti. When the semi-annual evaluations were filed, Ms. Conti judged Norma Jean's overall performance as only "fair," with a score of 70 points. Yesterday, Ms. Conti called Norma Jean into her office for the appraisal interview.

The news that her present rating was only "fair" upset Norma Jean. "How can that be?" she asked. "I'm working as hard as I always have. My previous supervisor was always more than satisfied with my work."

"I'm sorry, Norma," said Ms. Conti. "That's the way I see it. The amount of work you turn out is deplorably low. If you can't pick up speed, I'm going to have to put you on notice. As it is, I certainly won't be recommending you for a raise when that time comes around."

"That's not fair," said Norma Jean. "I work on purchases that need very precise specifications and quotations. You can look at my record and see that I make hardly any mistakes. No one else in the department is as reliable as I am."

"You're placing emphasis on the wrong thing," said Ms. Conti. "You slow everything down with your nitpicking on every requisition. There is no need for precision on 90 percent of what you do, yet you triple-check every 5-cent item as if it were golden. Either you learn to pick up speed, or you'll be looking for work elsewhere."

◁ *Analysis*

Obviously, there is something wrong with the past and present evaluations of Norma Jean's performance. Of the following five possibilities, which seems most likely to you? Rank them on a scale from 1 (most likely) to 5 (least likely). You may add another alternative, if you wish. Be prepared to justify your ranking.

_____ **a.** Ms. Conti dislikes Norma Jean and is "out to get her."

_____ **b.** Mr. Morgan's standards for Norma's job emphasized quality and dependability rather than output, although even Mr. Morgan had reservations about the quantity of work that Norma Jean produced.

     c. As an entrenched employee, Norma Jean is resisting any change in performance standards applied to her job.

     d. Ms. Conti and Norma Jean will have to have a meeting of the minds about the job's demands before Norma Jean's performance will change and her evaluation improve.

     e. Ms. Conti's threats will shift Norma Jean's concept of her job so that she emphasizes quantity rather than quality in the future.

How might Ms. Conti have improved this interview?

Case 35

Polishing the Halo

David was given an assignment to study and improve the company performance-appraisal system. Specifically, the vice president for human resources gave him a list of different types of halo-effect biases, and asked him to consider the various effects and make recommendations to his colleague supervisors in the company for preventing the occurrence of these problems.

Analysis

Examine David's list of halo-effect biases, shown below. Review the definition, if necessary (see SuperScope on page 300). Then match each halo-effect bias with its most appropriate guideline for prevention.

Halo-Effect Biases

     1. Recency

     2. Overemphasis

     3. Stereotyping

     4. Unforgivingness

     5. Grouping

Guideline for Prevention

a. Use only current performance data as a foundation for employee appraisal.

b. Treat employees as individuals; be alert to their unique strengths and weaknesses.

c. Collect periodic performance information; rely on critical incidents over time.

d. Assign weights to each appraisal factor and use.

e. Examine your biases; share them with peers and ask them to provide feedback if they sense discrimination.

Betty's Carpet-Cleaning Service

Betty Morrison started a small carpet-cleaning service five years ago. (Her motto: "Love your carpet, love your wife; when we shampoo, it'll enrich their life!") The demand for her service has grown so rapidly that she added one employee, then another, until she reached her present staff of four employees. Now she does less and less cleaning herself, spending her time instead on task scheduling, billing and payroll, obtaining and dispensing supplies, and handling advertising and customer relations. She has always used a simple performance-appraisal system, evaluating her cleaners on these criteria: speed, quality, customer satisfaction, equipment repairs, and overall attitude.

This year, after attending a local half-day workshop on performance appraisal, Betty decided to assign weights to the five appraisal factors for the first time. Then she assessed each employee on each of the five factors using her usual scale from 1 to 5 (1 = unsatisfactory; 5 = exceptional), and gave the results to each employee.

Employee Ratings

Factor	Weight	Maria	Trang	Kent	Terry
Speed	.40	4	5	1	3
Quality	.30	4	4	2	3
Customer satisfaction	.20	4	3	3	3
Repairs	.05	4	2	4	3
Attitude	.05	4	1	5	3

When Betty checked the appraisal records from last year, she found that she had rated all four employees precisely the same as she had a year ago. Yet, when she gave the table of ratings to Maria, Trang, Kent, and Terry in individual meetings with them, she got a variety of reactions.

Analysis

a. Calculate the weighted ratings for each employee and the unweighted ratings from a year ago.
b. Predict the reaction of each employee.
c. What should Betty have done differently, if anything?

The Dissatisfied Mechanic

Shawn was very unhappy. He had just discovered that raises had been handed out to several other mechanics in the maintenance shop of the Flyaway Aviation Co., a regional commuter airline. As soon as his shift ended, he stormed into the office of his boss, Myra Maxwell, the shop supervisor.

"What happened to my annual raise?" Shawn demanded.

"Let's get one thing straight," said Myra. "There is no such thing as an annual pay raise at Flyaway."

"That's the first I've heard about it," said Shawn. "I got one last year when everyone got theirs. Now I find that everyone else just got a raise this year, and I didn't. Why was I passed over?"

"Everyone did not get a raise," said Myra. "Raises were given only to those mechanics whom I considered were doing outstanding work in the shop."

"Since when has my work not been outstanding?" asked Shawn.

"For a long time," said Myra. "I did speak to you about it at your last performance-appraisal interview. I suggested then that your work warranted improvement."

"But I didn't think that it had anything to do with my annual merit increase," said Shawn. "I work as hard as anyone else out in the shop."

"I don't think you do," said Myra. "Several times I've noticed you taking a break when the shop was jammed up. And when things are slow, I never see you pitch in with some of the standby, shop-cleanup work I've set aside for off-peak times."

"You never made that clear to me," said Shawn. "I have always thought that shop-cleanup work was voluntary around here. And I don't see anything wrong in taking a break from time to time."

"Then that makes two things you don't seem to know much about," said Myra. "Both affect your performance, and that's enough to keep your work from being considered outstanding."

"That's downright unfair!" said Shawn. "I think that you have discriminated against me in not giving me my annual raise, and these are only excuses you're giving me now."

Analysis ▶

a. Do you agree or disagree with Shawn? Why?
b. What do you think has been wrong with the way Myra has conducted Shawn's appraisal interviews in the past?
c. What would you suggest Myra do in the future to avoid confrontations like these?

Answers to Quick Tests ▶

Quick Test 1	Quick Test 2	Quick Test 3
1. F	3. T	5. F
2. T	4. F	6. T

Quick Test 4	Quick Test 5	
7. F	9. T	
8. F	10. F	

Counseling and Performance Management

Learning Objectives

After studying this chapter, you should be able to

- Describe problem performance and identify the symptoms of a troubled employee.

- Explain the general approach to employee counseling, explain its rules and limitations, and know when a troubled employee should be referred to a professional counselor.

- Identify the various kinds of absenteeism and know the recommended remedial approaches for each.

- Recognize alcoholism and illegal substance abuse among employees, and know the recommended remedial approaches for each.

- Explain the goals of performance management, the most common types of offenses that require disciplinary action, and the range of employee responses to it.

- Differentiate between constructive and progressive discipline, know the four elements of the "hot-stove" rule, and recognize the necessity of due process when firing an employee.

1 PROBLEM PERFORMERS

CONCEPT ▶ Problems with employee performance can often be attributed to troubling personal factors that arise from conditions not related to the job.

How would you define problem performance?

Problem performance encompasses (a) job performance that does not measure up to established standards of output or quality, and (b) behavior that is distracting or disruptive to the normal conduct of operations. The former is routinely dealt with during performance appraisals. The latter problem is far more difficult to identify and to deal with, yet it often leads to the former. It is problem performance of the latter kind that this chapter will focus on.

What kinds of employees become problem performers?

Most people encounter brief periods in their lives when they are troubled by problems away from their employment. At such times, their performance at work may suffer. This is usually a temporary condition (either the problem disappears, or they learn to cope with it), and their performance soon returns to normal.

There are some other people who are especially susceptible to stress, and their resulting performance lapses are more pronounced and more prolonged. They may be troubled by continuing personal problems that make adjustment especially difficult. Examples in today's society include marital discord, personal debts, or addiction to gambling. These people can be described as "troubled." When this state persists, there is a good chance that the troubled person is suffering from a problem with an emotional, rather than a physical, cause. In extreme cases, we speak of a person in this troubled state as emotionally disturbed.

Adjustment is the process by which people modify their feelings and behavior to accommodate the stress of life and work. Individuals adjust to situations with different degrees of difficulty and success.

Supervisors must learn to deal with employees whose difficulty in adjusting to emotional problems is only temporary and with those whose adjustment problems are chronic. More severely disturbed employees should be referred to the organization's *employee assistance program (EAP)*. There, more serious problems can be diagnosed and treated by appropriate professionals.

> **Adjustment.** The process whereby healthy as well as disturbed individuals find a way to fit themselves to difficult situations by yielding to a degree, and by modifying their feelings and their behavior to accommodate the stresses of life and work.

Who are these troubled employees and how do they appear?

Psychologists believe that about one out of five workers is subject to emotional upsets that visibly disturb his or work. Troubled employees may appear as the chronic absentee, the willful rule breaker, the antagonist, or the troublemaker. They may also appear in more sympathetic form as the employee with almost-imaginary ailments, the person who has lost confidence in work-related skills, the alcoholic, or even the work-obsessed individual. Symptoms of emotional upsets may even emerge unexpectedly in the most normal and stable of individuals. Some may demonstrate their emotional distress through **hostility,** the aggressive expression of anger on the job. In extreme cases, this may even be exhibited in various forms of workplace violence. By contrast, other disturbed employees may demonstrate ***withdrawal,*** whereby they retreat from social interaction and confrontation.

Many problem employees fall into these categories: They are perpetually dissatisfied, are given to baseless worries, tire easily, are suspicious, are sure that superiors unfairly withhold promotions, or believe their associates gossip maliciously about them. Some are characterized by drinking sprees, are given to drug abuse, are insubordinate, or have ungovernable tempers.

Among themselves, problem employees differ widely, just as more normal people do. But within the framework of their symptoms, they are surprisingly alike in their reactions.

When do the personal problems of employees become a concern of the supervisor?

The most important rule is this: Intervene when the *performance* of the troubled employee becomes unsatisfactory. (Note the emphasis on performance.) Although some stress can serve to stimulate and challenge individuals, employees under severe stress often function far below their capabilities, or they may disturb the work of others. When either condition occurs, these employees become problems to themselves and to their supervisors. Ultimately, many of these troubled employees, if not helped, become the subject of disciplinary action.

For many workers, the distinction between problems arising from their personal lives and those associated with their work becomes increasingly blurred. Sometimes, an alert supervisor can play a timely role in helping employees sort out their problems. And, difficult as it may be, supervisors have a continuing responsibility to confront employee behavior that affects productivity.

Many supervisors also find that employees will voluntarily look to them for assistance even when their work performance isn't affected. Sensitive supervisors can provide invaluable aid during these times if they project a sincere sense of caring and take the time to practice their listening skills.

Why must so much attention be paid to troubled employees?

Mainly because there are so many of them. Hardly a week goes by in which a supervisor does not deal with problems created by a troubled

Hostility. A feeling of enmity or antagonism; an aggressive expression of anger displayed by problem employees as an unconscious, unwitting relief from fears about their security or other feelings of inadequacy.

Withdrawal. A passive way for emotionally disturbed employees to cope with their anxieties, in which they retreat from confrontations, appear unduly preoccupied, discourage social overtures, and keep very much to themselves.

Did You Know ?

Avoid Burnout

■ Psychologists Christina Maslach and Michael Leiter have found that if you provide the following six factors for employees at work, they are much less likely to experience burnout:

- A manageable workload.
- A sense of control.
- The opportunity for rewards.
- A feeling of community.
- Faith in the fairness of the workplace.
- Shared values.

Source: *Psychology Today,* September/October 1999, pp. 50–53.

employee. Happily, most of these problems are minor. If left unattended, however, they can begin to demand a major portion of a supervisor's time and attention.

There are also many sociological and humanitarian reasons for being concerned about problem workers. One big reason is that a problem employee is probably also a problem husband, son, daughter, or wife. But industry's concern, admittedly, is primarily an economic one. Problem employees are expensive to have on the payroll since their productivity suffers. They are characterized by excessive tardiness and absences. They are difficult to supervise. And they have a tendency to upset the morale of the work group. Consequently, a supervisor should be concerned about (a) hiring problem employees in the first place, (b) handling them on the job so that they reach an acceptable level of productivity with the least disruption of the company's overall performance, and (c) determining whether these employees have become so seriously troubled that they need professional attention.

Super SCOPE ▶ **Behavioral Clues to a Troubled Worker**

Supervisors need to monitor the emergence of, and particularly the pattern of, specific signs of a stressed or troubled worker. In particular, you should note those occasions when an employee who is characteristically acceptable in many ways suddenly exhibits one or more of the following symptoms:

- **Preoccupation.** You begin to observe an employee engaged in frequent daydreaming, and it's hard to catch and hold her or his attention.
- **Irritability.** An employee seems to be really on edge, and even close friends start to steer clear to avoid confrontations.
- **Increased accidents or near-accidents.** An employee with a great safety record starts to accumulate a series of scrapes, bumps, and bruises, while endangering others.
- **Poor treatment of customers or co-workers.** A normally polite individual fails to apologize to a customer when

appropriate and acts brusque with team members.
- **More absences.** An employee calls in "sick" with rather lame excuses and uses up the sick leave allocation early in the year.
- **Increased fatigue.** Although an individual keeps regular hours and claims to be getting a good night's rest, he or she complains of being tired all the time and drags around the workplace.
- **Reduced production.** The level of output is down for an employee, without an apparent reason.
- **Poor quality or excess waste.** Work has to be redone, or several attempts result in wasted effort, time, and materials.
- **Difficulty in absorbing training.** New tasks seem to present an abnormally large challenge for an employee, and you have to repeat instructions several times.

What role does stress play in creating problem employees?

Psychologists suggest that "to be alive is to experience stress; it is inevitable in most jobs as well as home lives." Stress refers to the pressures that people feel in life caused by **stressors**—the physical or human environment (noise, odors, discrimination, boredom), psychological factors (anxiety over job security), or psychosocial factors (interpersonal friction with co-workers). The resulting stress can appear in the form of headaches, upset stomachs, skin disorders, and distractedness (see Superscope for other signs of stress). Some employees have greater **resilience,** or capacity to handle short-term stress. They have learned to handle minor irritations, to find balance between work and home life, and to set realistic goals. They may even find some degree of stress to be a stimulus to their performance (see Figure 13-1). But when major stressors appear, or stress is sustained for long periods of time, some employees with lesser resilience experience **burnout.** This condition is characterized by severe alienation, inability to accept responsibility for errors, sharp declines in work performance, and (sometimes) abrupt resignations. Supervisors need to be aware of the entire range of stress-induced symptoms, and rely on their counseling skills to help employees work through their problems before they become unmanageable.

Stressors. Environmental, psychological, or psychosocial factors that produce stress within employees and often detract from their work performance.

Resilience. The capacity of an employee to handle short-term stress and bounce back from its distractions.

Burnout. The inability of employees to handle major incidents of, or sustained, stress.

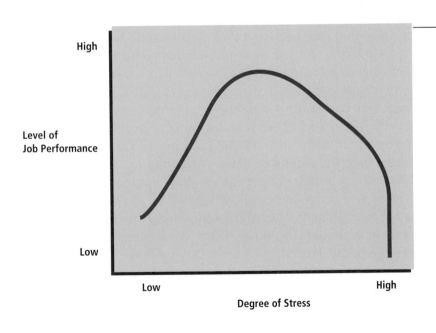

◆ **FIGURE 13-1**

Relationship between stress and performance. **When is burnout likely to occur?**

| 1 | T or F | Supervisors should intervene at the first sign that an employee is experiencing emotional difficulty. |
| 2 | T or F | Ideally, there would be no stress at work to affect employee performance. |

◀ *Quick Test 1*

2 EMPLOYEE COUNSELING

CONCEPT ▶ Counseling—within carefully prescribed limits— offered by a supervisor to a troubled employee may improve performance by providing a degree of relief from anxieties.

What can you do about your troubled workers?

Let's make this clear. We are not talking here about persons with serious personality disorders. *They need professional help.* Nor are we talking about routine performance appraisals, where it can be assumed that criticism will be received and suggestions for improvement will be discussed rationally and objectively. What follows here applies mainly to counseling efforts with mildly troubled employees.

You can help troubled employees toward better adjustment only after establishing an empathic atmosphere. You must first reassure them that you are trying to help them keep their jobs or enjoy their work more. You are *not* looking for ways to punish them or for an excuse to get rid of them. No approach will do more harm to a troubled person than adopting an attitude that says, "Better get yourself straightened out or you'll lose your job." Emotionally upset people are fearful or angry enough without feeling additional pressure from their supervisors. You must genuinely want to help them, and you must project this conviction to them. With such empathy as a foundation, you must then give the troubled employees every opportunity to help themselves.

Employee counseling is essentially a problem-solving technique. It is ultimately task-oriented; that is, it deals with a specific, job-related condition. The supervisor's role is a facilitating one. You do not direct or control the session; the employee does. The counselor listens rather than talks. You do not criticize or argue. Nor do you offer "evaluative" opinions. You do not "judge" an employee's personal problems. Instead, you aim to act as a "sounding board" to help release the pressures that are adversely affecting performance. If the counseling is successful, the employee—not the supervisor—solves the problem.

It cannot be overemphasized, however, that supervisors have great limitations in their counseling roles. *They are not psychologists or social workers*, and they can do more harm than good if they attempt rehabilitation beyond their training and experience. They cannot be "fix-it persons" for employees' personal problems. If they try to do so, they will often spend large amounts of time and energy and their own performance may suffer. Supervisors should be, of course, experts at recognizing these problems and be sympathetic toward them. Beyond that, their counseling roles should be restricted to providing emotional release and support for the employees' efforts to solve their problems.

Employee counseling. A task-oriented, problem-solving technique that features an empathic, interactive discussion—emphasizing listening—aimed at helping an employee cope with some specific aspect of his or her work life.

How, exactly, should you approach employee counseling?

First, take a close look at your attitudes and assumptions. Do you believe that people can be, and must be, responsible for their own actions? Do you agree that employees should solve their own problems (after obstacles are removed)? Do you think it is important for the solution to employees' personal problems to conform to their beliefs and values, not yours? Do you appreciate, and convey, a profound respect for the importance of the other's feelings? Positive answers to all these questions provide a strong foundation for the type of counseling a supervisor must often engage in.

You need to remember that the troubled employee has a very important need to release pent-up feelings, emotions, and stresses. This process, which psychologists call ***catharsis,*** relieves bothersome pressure, just like lifting the lid off a pan of boiling water prevents a scalding accident. As a supervisor, you can best counsel employees if you follow these 10 rules:

Catharsis. The relief that follows release of accumulated feelings, emotions, and frustrations that comes through their expression in a harmless fashion. The supervisor's counseling role and active listening skills contribute to employee catharsis.

1. Let the employee control the direction of the session.

2. Give your undivided attention to the employee who is talking.

3. Listen patiently to what the employee has to say before making any response.

4. Convey, through words, posture, eye contact, and facial expression your attentiveness, receptivity, and empathy.

5. Don't argue, interrupt, criticize, or offer advice about the employee's problem.

6. Look beyond the mere words of what the employee says and attempt to capture his or her feelings. Listen to see if he or she is trying to tell you something deeper than what appears on the surface.

7. Use silence—an extended pause before responding—to encourage the employee to provide an expanded explanation of a brief remark.

8. Don't express surprise or judgment at anything the employee discloses to you.

9. Encourage the employee, through gentle open-ended questions, to take the initiative in deciding what the next appropriate action should be.

10. Polish your skill at *reflecting feelings*—feeding back to an employee the emotional essence of what she or he conveyed to you. This confirms to the employee that you accept feelings as a legitimate topic; it builds trust between the two of you, and it encourages the employee to probe her or his own thoughts at a deeper level.

How do you start a counseling session?

Find a reasonably quiet place where you're sure you won't be interrupted and won't be overheard. Try to put the employee at ease.

You may be helpful simply by letting the employee know how much the current distress is affecting the job—and how much of this the company will tolerate. Above all, a person under stress may add to it materially with fears of what the company might do if and when it discovers the condition. If you can offer some rule of thumb, even if it's not entirely sympathetic, you at least provide something concrete to guide the employee's actions. (For example: "We understand the fact that you have something bothering you. And we're willing to go along with your present performance for a couple of weeks or so. But if it doesn't improve after that, we'll have to find a solution.")

If the employee voluntarily brings the problem to you, you can help most by listening. This is more difficult than it appears. Listening must mean truly *nonevaluative* listening—no interruptions, advice, prescriptions, solutions, pontifications, or preaching.

How many counseling interviews should you have with a problem employee? How long should a counseling interview last?

These are hard questions for clear-cut answers. For a less serious case, one interview might clear the air for a long time. With employees whose emotional problems are more serious, it may take five or ten 15- to 30-minute conversations just to gain confidence. And with still others, the counseling will have to become a regular part of your supervisory chores with them.

You can readily see that counseling can be time-consuming. That's why it's so important to spot worried workers early and take corrective action while you can help them with the minimum use of your time.

As to how long an interview should last—you can't accomplish much in 15 minutes, but if that's all you can spare, it's a lot better than nothing. At the very least, it shows the employee you're interested in the problem. Ideally, an interview should last between three-quarters of an hour and an hour.

What results should you expect from counseling an employee?

Recognize what you are counseling an employee for, and don't look for immediate results. Never mix the counseling interview with some other action you need to take, such as an appraisal or employee discipline.

A counseling interview is aimed at helping employees to unburden themselves—to get worries off their chests. Whether or not the conversation is related to the problem they create for you at work is not

THE DOS AND DON'TS OF EMPLOYEE COUNSELING

■ Nancy Hull, a former chemical-abuse counselor and an authority on the subject, cautions supervisors about the legal aspects of counseling. She suggests a conservative approach to what an employee may otherwise consider a confrontation. Hull's prescriptions for counseling follow.

- **Performance orientation.** Do let the employee know that the company is concerned with work performance.
- **Deterioration.** Do be aware that personal problems generally get worse, not better, without professional help.
- **Confidentiality.** Do emphasize that anything said will not be passed along to others.
- **Exemptions.** Do explain that going for help does not exclude the employee from standard disciplinary procedures and that it does not open the door to special privileges.
- **Improvements needed.** Do explain in very specific terms what the employee needs to do to perform up to the company's expectations.
- **Diagnosis.** Don't analyze what the problem is; you are not an expert.
- **Responsibility.** Don't probe personal problems during counseling unless they occur on the job or are raised by the employee.
- **Moralizing.** Don't superimpose your values on the employee; restrict the confrontation to job performance.
- **Sympathy.** Don't be swayed by emotional pleas or "hard-luck" stories.

Source: Adapted from "The Dos and Don'ts of Confrontation," by Nancy Hull, in *The Troubled Employee*, a film produced by Dartnell Corporation, Chicago. Used with permission of the copyright holder.

initially important. The payoff comes as they get confidence in you—and consequently don't vent their hostility and frustration on the job. This takes patience and time.

Some of the results you can expect include greater employee confidence to handle their future problems, a more relaxed (and rational) individual, and one who is capable of clarified thinking and redirected energy. But don't necessarily expect appreciation in return; for if the counseling is done well, the employees will feel that they have solved their own problems.

How can you recognize when an employee needs professional help?

Dr. Harry Levinson, a nationally recognized authority and founder of the Levinson Institute, advises adhering to the following basic steps (Figure 13-2) in assessing an employee's needs:

1. Recognize the emotional disturbance.
2. Relieve acute distress by listening (counseling).
3. Refer cases beyond your limits to professional help.

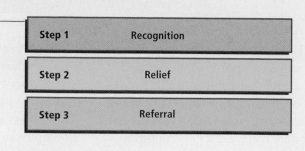

Step 1	Recognition
Step 2	Relief
Step 3	Referral

Dr. Levinson offers this rule of thumb: *If after two listening sessions you seem to be making little headway in establishing confidence, you should report the case (in confidence, of course) to an appropriate professional.* Some possibilities include a physician, a psychologist, a psychiatrist, a social worker, or a financial planner—all depending on the nature and degree of the underlying problem.

Dr. Levinson also advises that your approach in referral should be that of opening another door for additional help.

What do the professionals do for troubled employees that supervisors can't do?

Professionals offer at least two kinds of assistance that may be beyond the scope of the supervisor's capabilities. First, they are likely to have a reservoir of specialized expertise and experiences that they can draw upon to help solve a particular problem (e.g., excessive credit card bills). Such persons can more likely diagnose what an individual's trouble is and prescribe the proper kind of solution or treatment.

Second, the extensive training these professionals have often gives them the ability to listen with great sensitivity to an employee's account of problems and then probe them in depth with their questioning and reflective skills. Further, because these persons don't present a threat of disciplining the employee, they often have a greater chance of winning the employee's confidence and stimulating the emotional release that often precedes constructive problem solving.

Quick Test 2 ▶

| **3** | T or F | In good counseling sessions, the employee determines the focus of the discussion and the topics to be discussed. |
| **4** | T or F | One effective way to help employees relieve their stress is by providing an opportunity for catharsis. |

REDUCING ABSENTEEISM

CONCEPT ▷ Certain forms of absenteeism can be materially reduced by employee counseling.

Absentees are a special kind of problem people. How should you handle them?

It depends on the reasons for absence. Professor P. J. Taylor of London University, who was formerly medical director of Shell (U.K.) Ltd., observes that 60 percent of all absentees have serious or chronic illnesses; 20 percent have acute, short-term illnesses such as the flu; 10 percent complain of minor illnesses such as colds and do or don't report to work according to their attitude about their jobs; and the final 10 percent are completely well but feign illness to enjoy a day off.

It is the group of absentees who make up the bottom 20 percent who are suspect. Industrial psychologists call their virus *voluntary absence.* In many, this is deeply rooted. They may lack an appreciation for the value of hard work. There is an inevitable conflict between the desire for more leisure and more work. This tug is especially evident among some workers who reflect an attitude of "entitlement." They feel that, somehow, the job is owed to them and that they have no responsibility for delivering a fair day's work in return. Regardless of the reason, you can help reduce absenteeism by doing the following:

- Firm up your rules about it.
- Be consistent in applying penalties.
- Try to get at the reasons why an employee is frequently absent.

Absenteeism may have many causes. **Can increased job satisfaction reduce absenteeism?** ▼

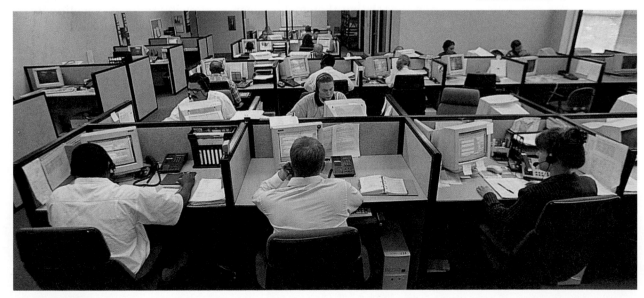

The last method requires the counseling technique. It is important to promptly follow up each individual case. In your discussion of the problem with employees, be sure to permit them to explain their reactions to the job itself, the people they work with, the working conditions, their tools and equipment, and the kind of training they receive. You thus avoid them feeling that you are placing all the blame on them. And if they are specific in their reactions, you then have specific complaints, rather than vague dissatisfactions to deal with.

Don't overlook, however, the power of job satisfaction in luring absence-prone workers back to the job. Surprisingly, however, physical working conditions seem to have little effect. In company after company, attendance figures show little variation between the dirty, unpleasant areas and those that are clean and well lighted. Even most incentive schemes aimed at reducing absences are relatively ineffective. Closeness of the work team, its homogeneity, and the state of its morale seem to have the greatest effect.

How effective is counseling in reducing absenteeism?

Success depends on the root cause of individual absences. See how the patterns and the motivations differ in these groups:

1. **Chronic absentees.** The people who have little capacity for pressure, either on the job or off, may be prime candidates for counseling. But first they must be made fully aware of the consequences of poor attendance. Theirs is a habit, usually of long-standing, and correction requires pressure to attend as well as hand-holding.

2. **Vacationing absentees.** The people who work only so long as they need the cash and who then treat themselves to a day or two off are difficult cases. These employees are often extremely capable on the job, but they feel no deep responsibility for it. Vacationers make a conscious choice to be absent and are rarely helped by counseling.

3. **Directionless absentees.** The younger employees who have as yet found no real purpose in work may simply follow the lead of the vacationer, who appears to lead a footloose, exciting life. A candid, direct talk with the directionless absentee may be more effective than counseling.

4. **Aggressive absentees.** The persons who willfully stay away from work in the hope that their absence will cause an inconvenience for you are probably emotionally troubled. This kind of behavior, however, requires professional counseling to correct it, not the kind of ordinary counseling that a supervisor can provide.

5. **Moonlighters.** The persons who hold more than one job are often either too tired to come to work or faced with conflicting schedules. Straight talk, rather than counseling, is prescribed. When attendance is affected, the moonlighter must be forced to make a choice between jobs.

6. **Occasional absentees.** The persons who seem to have slightly more absences than the rest of your staff are probably prime candidates for counseling. Their absences are legitimate. Their illnesses are real. Their problems are often temporarily insurmountable. These people deserve a mixture of sympathy, understanding, and sometimes outright advice. This might also be the time for you to take a look in the mirror. For example, are you contributing to the absenteeism by lack of support and training?

In summary, you can probably help people who are absent for the following reasons:

1. Getting to work is a problem, real or imagined.
2. Off-job pressures are so strong that they weaken the employee's resolve to get to work.
3. The employee is imitative, easily led or misled.
4. The work appears boring, disagreeable, or unattractive.
5. Working relationships are unpleasant.
6. There are in fact off-job problems—child care, serious illness, court appearances—that need immediate attention.
7. Absence or lateness has become a habit.

You will have difficulty, however, helping people who are absent because of these reasons:

1. The work or the pay associated with it does not hold a strong attraction.
2. Off-job pleasures have a greater appeal than work.
3. The employee is willfully absent in order to disrupt or inconvenience the organization.

5	T or F	Employee counseling works best at reducing absenteeism of those employees who suffer from chronic illnesses.
6	T or F	Firm rules, consistency in applying penalties, and exploration of causes are all useful methods in combating voluntary absences.

◀ *Quick Test 3*

THE PROBLEMS OF SUBSTANCE ABUSE

4

CONCEPT ▶	Increasingly, supervisors must deal with problem performance that stems from substance abuse.

How much distinction should be made between alcohol abuse and drug abuse?

In principle, there may be very little difference between them. In practice, there are significant differences, especially legal ones. Many of the counseling approaches, however, are the same for both problems.

What can you do for alcoholic employees?

Whatever you attempt, proceed slowly and cautiously. Not all heavy drinkers are alcoholics. And the more they drink, the less likely they are to admit to anyone (even themselves) that their ability to handle liquor has gotten out of their control.

An alcoholic employee is really just another kind of problem employee, except that the case is an aggravated one and may need the help of a professional. Nevertheless, many alcoholic workers have rescued themselves with the aid of Alcoholics Anonymous (AA), an association of recovering alcoholics who, because they don't preach and because they emphasize the individual's need to face weaknesses, have perfected the art of listening without being either sympathetic or critical.

Your best bet, however, is to recognize an alcoholic in the early stages. Watch for these characteristic symptoms:

- Sharp rise in absenteeism rate.
- Absenteeism is spread throughout the week (to disguise it).
- Frequent partial-day absenteeism (employee works half a day and then leaves).
- Employee inexplicably leaves work for short periods during the day.
- Employee's actions and behaviors change (deteriorate) as the day progresses.

Then you can apply the same techniques to gain the person's confidence that you would with any other problem employee. Your objective is to provide security at work and to help with talking out problems. If these employees can be helped to recognize that excessive drinking is a problem they aren't handling, then you can refer them to an Employee Assistance program, which, in turn, may be able to persuade them to look into Alcoholics Anonymous or to visit a professional or a special clinic for alcoholics.

How should you approach counseling an employee you believe to be an alcoholic?

Alcoholism requires a special form of counseling, say those who have coped most effectively with it. For example, the U.S. Department of Health, Education, and Welfare (HEW) in its *Supervisors' Guide on Alcohol Abuse* offers these hints to supervisors who are faced with this problem among their employees:

Substance Abuse. Check out the Web site for the **National Clearinghouse for Alcohol and Drug Information**, a service of the Substance Abuse and Mental Health Services Administration.

1. Don't apologize for confronting the troubled employee about the situation. Your responsibility is to maintain acceptable performance for all your employees.

2. Do encourage the employee to explain why work performance, behavior, or attendance is deteriorating. This can provide him or her with an *opportunity* to mention the use of alcohol. Recognize, however, that some alcoholics will deny that they have a problem.

3. Don't discuss a person's right to drink. Don't make a moral issue of it; HEW views alcoholism as a progressive and debilitating illness, which, if untreated, can eventually lead to insanity, custodial care, or death.

4. Don't suggest that the employee use moderation or change his or her drinking habits. A person who is an alcoholic cannot, at the start, voluntarily control drinking habits.

5. Don't be distracted by the individual's excuses for drinking (a difficult spouse, problem children, financial troubles, and so on). The problem as far as you are concerned is that the employee's drinking affects work, behavior, and attendance on the job.

6. Don't be fooled by the employee's assertion that a physician or a psychologist is already being seen. The employee may claim that the physician or the psychologist doesn't consider the drinking a problem or thinks the use of alcohol will subside once the "problems" are worked out. Therapists probably wouldn't say that if they knew an employee's job was in jeopardy because of alcohol abuse; they would attach great significance to the drinking habits.

7. Do remember that the alcoholic, like any other sick person, should be given the opportunity for treatment and rehabilitation.

8. Do emphasize that your major concern as a supervisor is the employee's poor work performance or behavior. You can firmly state that if there is no improvement, administrative action—such as suspension or discharge—will be taken.

9. Do state that the decision to accept rehabilitative assistance is the employee's responsibility.

Ann St. Louis, personnel counselor for Canada's Department of National Revenue, whose program maintains a 90-percent recovery rate among alcoholic government workers, adds this thought: An employer—far better than wife, mother, minister, or social agency—can lead an alcoholic to treatment by "constructive coercion." Give an employee every chance to take treatment, but make it clear that he or she must cooperate or lose the job. This has proven to be more effective than loss of friends or family.

How should an organization respond to drug abuse among employees?

You need only to read the headlines of the daily newspapers to know that drug abuse is pervasive in many areas. Without discounting the terrible impact of drugs on society, the problem is usually less severe in work organizations (but this varies widely by geographical region and even by occupation). Why has drug abuse been slow to achieve notoriety at work? For one thing, many companies attempt to screen out hard-drug users before their employment begins, based in part on conviction records or preemployment drug tests. Second, the trend has been for many organizations to establish much tougher ongoing random drug screenings, security systems, and policies to enable them to dismiss drug abusers. Third, it is difficult for many abusers at work to conceal the symptoms of their habits.

Symptoms of drug use are well known. At work, they manifest themselves objectively in terms of poor or erratic performance, tardiness, absenteeism, requests to leave early, forgetfulness, indifference to deadlines and safety, and in many instances, theft of company property.

Treatment and rehabilitation for drug users are as difficult and complicated as for alcoholics, and the treatments are somewhat similar. Company policies against drug addiction, however, tend to be firmer than those against drinking and alcoholism. For one thing, the addict is different from the alcoholic because many addicts try to involve other people in drugs or endanger their safety. The risk of an alcoholic's inducing another employee to begin alcoholism is slight. Then, too, drug use is illegal; in most instances, use of alcohol is not.

Here again, a supervisor's responsibility should be limited to the detection of drug usage, prevention of the use or sale of drugs on company property, and counseling of drug users, including referral, if indicated, to the appropriate company authority.

Supervisors also need to remember that both alcohol and drug abuse fall under the auspices of the Americans with Disabilities Act (ADA) of 1990. This act protects and addresses the needs of persons with mental and physical disabilities from discrimination at work. Consequently, supervisors who recognize employee abuse problems should immediately consult the human resource department for their advice and counsel in handling a situation so that no discrimination takes place.

What sort of responsibility do supervisors have for counseling employees with major illnesses?

Much has to do with your own sense of compassion, as tempered by your company's policies. Increasingly, supervisors must cope with employees who are suffering from life-threatening illnesses, such as cancer or AIDS. The presence of these employees can affect others on your staff as well. In general, the advice seems to run this way:

- Allow the affected employee to choose whether, when, and how to tell other employees of his or her condition.
- Develop some sort of transitional role for the employee. It should be one that matches the individual's capacity for work and still reflects her or his value to the company.
- Within these limits, avoid special treatment and expect the employee to follow established rules, regulations, and standards of performance. That's what most ill people who choose to keep working prefer. This enhances their sense of worth as adults who are still 100-percent alive and capable of contributing their talent and experience.

7	T or F	Supervisory counseling can be highly appropriate for problems of either alcohol or drug abuse.
8	T or F	If an employee has a life-threatening illness, you should disclose it to other employees as soon as possible to prevent rumors.

◀ *Quick Test 4*

---

5 PERFORMANCE MANAGEMENT

CONCEPT ▶ Properly administered performance management systems serve to guide future behavior in constructive directions, while developing self-control among employees.

What is the real purpose of performance management?

In comparison to the multiple goals in counseling, the real purpose of **performance management** is quite simple. It is to encourage employees to meet or exceed established standards of job performance and to behave sensibly and safely at work. Most employees recognize the legitimate need to keep everyone working toward the same organizational goals and standards. Many employees are capable of self-control—planning their own workday, obtaining necessary resources, coordinating with others, monitoring the results of their effort, and correcting errors.

Performance management. The ongoing process of clarifying and communicating performance expectations to employees, and then providing coaching and feedback to ensure the desired actions.

Employees who observe the rules and meet work standards may be rewarded by praise, financial rewards, job security, and advancement. Those who do not stay in line or measure up to performance standards are possibly subject to discipline. **_Discipline_** is the imposition of a penalty by management on an employee for breaking a rule. A **_penalty_** is a specific punishment or forfeiture, such as suspension, loss of pay, demotion, or in extreme cases, loss of job. It is not designed to be punitive toward employees, but to act as a form of training so they can clearly learn what acceptable performance and behavior are. Because the use of penalties represents an admission by management that it may share in the blame for failure, a supervisor should resort to disciplinary action only after all other attempts at performance management fail. Discipline should never be used as a show of authority or power on the supervisor's part.

What sort of infractions typically trigger the need for disciplinary action?

This varies among companies, and sometimes among departments within a single company. Supervisors, however, are most interested in the specific type, frequency, and degree of the infraction. Some employee behaviors, though frowned upon, may not be prohibited by company policy. And occasional (if rare) infractions of some standard or rule may be tolerated because they are offset by exemplary behavior in some other domain. But when the breach becomes large or persistent, however, the need for discipline becomes obvious and urgent.

In addition to poor performance—either of output or quality—infractions that most commonly result in disciplinary action include excessive absenteeism, insubordination, carelessness, negligence in following procedures, horseplay or fighting, dishonesty or falsification of company records, abusive or obscene language, intoxication, and sexual harassment.

When do employees resent discipline?

Most employees recognize the need for some rules and regulations at work; many welcome the clarity that they provide. They are more likely to object to specific rules that defy logic or tie their hands; they may criticize the organization for adhering too closely to a set of archaic rules; and they may be unable to separate their dislike for discipline received from a supervisor from their general regard for the supervisor who administers it. As a result, effective administration of discipline requires impartiality, good judgment, and courage.

When discipline is not administered fairly, it is likely to threaten employees' pride in who they are and their achievements—their level of **_self-esteem._** And sometimes it doesn't take much to do this. For example, the following actions can lower employees' self-esteem:

- Criticizing an employee in front of peers.
- Talking down to workers.
- Assigning work unevenly.

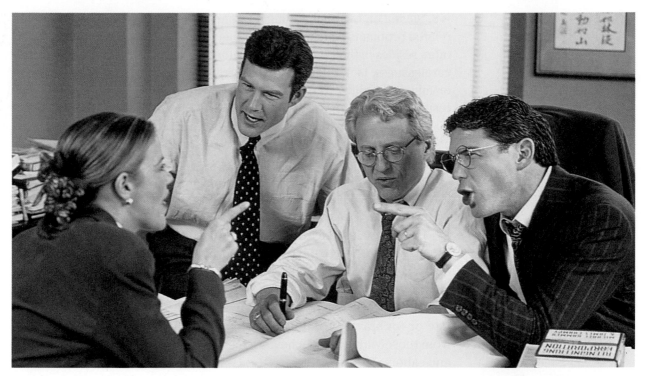

▲ Most employees can accept disciplinary action when it is fair and reasonable. **What happens, though, when it is administered publicly?**

- Not praising adequately.
- Implying that a worker is incompetent.
- Ignoring people or not asking for their input.

When self-esteem is threatened or damaged, the consequences may include distrust, defensiveness, reduced commitment, resentment, and unnecessary conflicts. When these deteriorate further into decreased productivity or excess absenteeism, discipline is called for. But this just continues a negative cycle consisting of problem → discipline → damaged self-esteem → problem → discipline, and so on.

When do employees embrace discipline?

Three major factors affect positive attitudes toward a disciplinary system. First, employees are more likely to support discipline when they participated in its development, which makes a strong case for employee involvement. Second, their support is almost assured when they can see reasonable logic for it (as when worker carelessness threatens their own safety). Third, when groups (such as semiautonomous teams) administer their own justice system, they are more likely to support the process (and, incidentally, take some of the heat off the supervisor).

Why do employees break the rules?

As in most personnel problems, only a small percentage of workers (perhaps less than 10 percent) cause disciplinary problems. People who break rules do so for a number of reasons, including being in the wrong

Did You Know ?

Job Changes

■ According to the Bureau of Labor Statistics, the average worker in the United States holds from six to eight different jobs from ages 18 to 32.

Source: Bureau of Labor Statistics

job, having an overdemanding and unsupportive supervisor, or non-job-related problems causing stress in their lives. But the contributing factor often resides in their personal characteristics—dislike of authority figures, carelessness, lack of desire to cooperate, a poor work ethic, dishonesty, or failure to adjust to the employment world. The supervisor's job, as a result, is to help employees better adjust to their jobs and employers.

What kind of handling do employees expect from a supervisor in the way of discipline?

Justice and equitable treatment. "Let the punishment fit the crime," is the advice in Gilbert and Sullivan's *Mikado*. No one likes to be treated worse than anyone else for the same fault.

People are less inclined to break rules when the supervisor is a good leader, when a sincere interest and real caring is shown toward employees, and when employees get satisfaction from their work. After all, if an employee finds the work uninteresting and the supervisor unpleasant to deal with, is it surprising that the employee will find reasons for being late or for staying away from work altogether? And is it a large step from those withdrawal behaviors to more aggressive forms of resistance and sabotage?

So, when an employee breaks a rule, make discipline your last resort. Search hard to discover the real reason the employee acted that way. Then try to see what you can do to remove the reason.

Quick Test 5 ▶	**9**	T or F	The purpose of performance management is to get employees to meet or exceed job standards and rules.
	10	T or F	At one time or another, nearly 90 percent of employees cause disciplinary problems for supervisors.

6 ADMINISTRATIVE GUIDELINES

CONCEPT ▶ Discipline is most effective when applied constructively, progressively, and in accordance with the "hot-stove" rule.

What is meant by constructive discipline? By progressive discipline?

If a supervisor accepts the goals of getting employees to behave acceptably and perform appropriately, the purpose of discipline becomes primarily positive. From this perspective, you focus on setting performance objectives, coaching for skill development, providing resources,

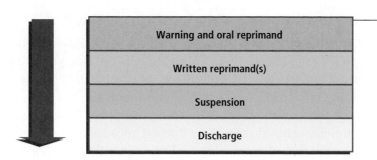

and sharing *constructive criticism.* This requires taking the time to investigate a troublesome situation and compose one's thoughts, carefully selecting the words to use, and stimulating new insights in the employee about how to do the job better. Constructive criticism tries to redirect employee energy and behavior into productive channels by offering feedback and observations, making useful suggestions, and clarifying goals and steps to perform. It requires sensitively protecting their self-esteem and dignity, while simultaneously indicating the urgency for change. A supervisor may say, "Let me show you an easier way to do that," or "I think there'd be less risk of problems if you went through that more slowly the first few times."

   Progressive discipline, however, means that the penalties for substandard performance or broken rules get increasingly harsh as the condition continues or the infraction is repeated (see Figure 13-3). Progressive discipline usually begins with the employee receiving a ***warning***, a formal notification of the consequences of further infractions. Typically, a first offense, unless a dramatic one, may receive an oral warning. A second offense elicits a written warning. A third infraction may bring a temporary layoff or a suspension. The final step occurs when an employee is discharged for the fourth (or a very serious) infraction. This system gives any employee adequate warning of the eventual consequences of repeated violations.

Warning. A reprimand so worded as to give formal notice to an employee that repetition of a particular form of unacceptable behavior, such as infraction of a rule, will draw a penalty.

◆ **FIGURE 13-4**

"Hot-stove" rule for discipline. **Which principle is the most important?**

What is the "hot-stove" rule of discipline?

It is an allegory used to illustrate the four essentials of a good disciplinary policy (see Figure 13-4). If the stove is red-hot, you ought to be able to see it and to know that if you touch it, you will be burned; that is the principle of *advance warning*. If you touch the hot stove, you get burned (penalized) right away; that is the principle of *immediacy*. Everyone who touches a hot stove will get burned because it plays no favorites; that is the principle of *impartiality*. Every time you touch a hot stove, you will get burned; that is the principle of *consistency*.

Does disciplinary action extend to discharge?

That depends on your company's management policy, the autonomy allowed by your own manager and on the labor agreement (if your employees are unionized). Labor unions exist to provide workers with the maximum protection from injustice or unfair treatment. They typically negotiate the basic rules for discipline into the labor agreement but leave its administration to management. However, they reserve the right to *grieve*, or appeal, the results where they feel discipline has been unfairly applied. And supervisors often consult a union representative prior to taking disciplinary action.

How, exactly, do you go about firing someone?

First, bring him or her to a quiet place where privacy is assured. If possible, invite a colleague in to serve as a witness. Bring along whatever documentation you have regarding the compelling problem. Present your rationale, the relevant policy, and your decision. Expect that the person to be discharged may deny the behavior, exhibit extreme anger, or break into tears. Avoid being argumentative, while remaining tactful and assertive. And be sure to provide details of his or her residual rights to employee benefits, if any. Handle any questions, or promise to obtain the answers. And as soon as the meeting is over, make sure you have a plan for communicating the action to the rest of your department, to minimize rumors.

How can you make disciplinary action stick?

By carefully planning it and gathering sound documentation to support it. Actions must be based on genuine evidence, free from bias and discrimination. Avoid impulsive, spiteful actions, for these will surely backfire. Arbitrators, as well as representatives of the EEOC and other investigatory agencies, are quick to spot weak cases and reject them.

Employee discipline is difficult, but penalties and even discharges can be made to stick, provided the supervisor makes none of the following mistakes:

- **Failure to establish a clear-cut breach of rule.** Many areas of enforcement remain "gray" despite efforts to clarify standards of behavior. Although supervisory judgment is always called for, the violation must be clear.

- **Inadequate warnings.** Even the presence of clear rules and guidelines in an employee manual may not be enough; workers need personal warning that their conduct will not be tolerated.

- **Insufficient evidence.** A spot check, a random observation, a little bit of information is not enough. The data gathered must be thorough and complete.

- **Violation of policy or labor contact.** This should be one of the first priorities for supervisory consideration. Discipline imposed following an infraction should accurately reflect an organization's established policies and/or, if a union is present, provisions of the labor contract.

- **Prejudice.** Discrimination or favoritism casts a shadow over disciplinary action. Don't let personal attitudes affect your treatment of a worker.

- **Unequal enforcement of policy.** Because judgment is involved and the supervisor is busy, rules sometimes get applied to one worker but not another. Make sure policies are applied consistently across the board.

- **Inadequate records.** The value of written records documenting an accumulation of offenses over time cannot be overemphasized. Keep a detailed record in the employee's personnel file.

- **Overly severe punishment.** Don't let momentary anger color your judgment. Assess historical records and move only to the next disciplinary step needed.

Supervisory handling of disciplinary actions is always subject to someone else's review—by a manager, the human resource department, the union, an arbitrator or someone in the legal system. Consequently, supervisors must eliminate all of the above mistakes if they expect their disciplinary actions to stand up to external scrutiny.

How can you make sure that your records will support a disciplinary action?

Take care to make the proper records at each step of a progressive disciplinary action. Follow carefully your organization's policies and procedures in this matter. The legal concept of ***due process*** is important in all areas of employment, especially those involving job security. This means that all employees, regardless of union representation, are entitled to a fair and just hearing. Under such circumstances, a supervisor's opinions and vague recollections will not carry much weight. Conclusions will have to be supported by specific documentation. Records that help to provide this documentation include the following:

Due process. An employee's entitlement to a fair hearing before discipline can be meted out. Often, the hearing is conducted by an impartial party, allows appropriate representation, and involves presentation of available evidence.

- Regularly kept records, such as time cards showing absences and lateness, production and quality-control reports, and the like.
- Written complaints from customers, suppliers, or other contacts that can be identified without qualification with the individual who is to be disciplined.
- Examples of unsatisfactory or careless work, including sloppy reports, incorrect tabulations, damaged goods, all tagged or marked in such a way as to identify the culpable individual.
- Written summaries of appraisal and/or disciplinary conferences, which should contain specific rather than general statements, including dates, figures, and clearly described incidents. The hard part here is that the law seems to say that copies of these reports (which are retained in personnel records) must be given to the individual at the time they are written.
- Documentation of information collected from co-workers and others while investigating the events leading to disciplinary action. The important thing to remember here is that these records should be developed on an ongoing basis over time, not reconstructed from memory at the time of a crisis or just prior to a hearing. The stream of incidents thus recorded will then be fresh in your mind and all key details will be easier to support accurately.

Quick Test 6 ▶

11	T or F	Constructive discipline and progressive discipline are basically the same thing.
12	T or F	When firing someone, it is important that supervisors follow the guidelines of due process.

CHAPTER 13 REVIEW

KEY CONCEPTS TO REMEMBER

1. **Problem Performers.** Supervisors have legitimate interest in employee performance that either (a) does not measure up to established standards or (b) is disruptive to the normal conduct of operations. Such problem performance is often a reflection of temporary emotional problems stemming from an inability to adjust to the stress of life or work. This failure to cope sometimes causes employees to behave unproductively or erratically on the job and to interrupt the regular harmony of the workplace.

   Troubled employees can be recognized by such disharmonious conduct as sudden changes in behavior, preoccupation, irritability, increased accidents or absences, unusual fatigue, irrational anger, or hostility. Various sources of stress (stressors) can arise from a wide range of real or perceived factors at work or away from it; the impacts can range from modest to severe, depending on the employee's ability to handle them.

2. **Employee Counseling.** Constructive counseling by a supervisor can help a great many troubled employees improve their performance or control their behavior, provided the degree of their maladjustment is slight and the underlying causes are not intense. The objectives of the counseling process are to (a) recognize the symptoms of a troubled employee, (b) provide relief if the symptoms and causes are minor (to ease the employee's return to satisfactory performance), and (c) *refer the employee to a professional counselor* if the conditions are anything but minor.

3. **Reducing Absenteeism.** Constructive counseling can also reduce absenteeism among chronic and occasional absentees. Other forms of absenteeism respond better to a three-part program involving (a) clear-cut rules, (b) consistent penalties, and (c) counseling to determine—and confront—the reasons for the absences.

4. **The Problems of Substance Abuse.** Alcoholism and drug abuse are found among special kinds of problem employees. Counseling by the supervisor, combined with an insistence that performance standards be met, may be helpful. In anything but minor cases, professional assistance or advice from groups such as Alcoholics Anonymous should be sought.

5. **Performance Management.** When supervisors use performance management correctly, discipline is seldom needed. Most employees are happy to stay out of trouble. Only a few employees find it difficult either to (a) meet work standards or (b) conform to the rules and regulations imposed by an organized activity. Accordingly, effective discipline is aimed not so much at punishing bad performance as at encouraging and rewarding good performance. The objective of discipline is to train erring employees to develop their own self-control so that they are not drawn over the line that separates acceptable from unacceptable behavior.

6. **Administrative Guidelines.** Effective discipline should be an essentially positive effort. Its three hallmarks are (a) punishment that is suitable to the importance of the offense, (b) penalties that

become progressively severe (e.g., warning, suspension, discharge) as offenses are repeated, and (c) discipline that is consistent with the "hot-stove" rule (that is, discipline should be given only if there has been adequate warning, and it should be immediate, impartial, and consistent). Severe violations may result in suspension or firing, but only if the supervisor has carefully thought through the process in advance. Employees are entitled to, and expect, due process; without it, labor unions, the EEOC, and other federal, state, and local agencies might intervene on behalf of the employee.

READING COMPREHENSION

1. Why is it so important for supervisors to identify and attempt to help troubled employees in their workforce?
2. When a supervisor is thinking of counseling an employee, should the emphasis be placed on behavior, performance, or attitude? Why?
3. List at least five symptoms of an employee with a possible emotional problem.
4. Describe the characteristics of the counseling approach.
5. List five specific counseling skills that you could use in counseling a troubled employee.
6. Discuss the difference between valid absences that result from bona fide illness and absences that psychologists describe as *voluntary* absences. What is a supervisor's role in minimizing the latter?
7. Why might a company have policies for confronting drug abuse that are different from those for dealing with alcohol abuse?
8. Summarize these four arguments: why a well-behaved employee, and another prone to bending the rules, would like and dislike the presence of disciplinary regulations in the workplace.
9. Progressive discipline suggests a sequence of four steps. What reasons can you suggest for *not* using all four, such as starting at step 1 and jumping to step 3, or starting directly at step 2?
10. The "hot-stove" rule is meant to help supervisors remember four important points about discipline. Briefly describe each.

APPLICATION

Self-Assessment

▶ *How good are your counseling and performance management skills?*

Read the following statements carefully. Circle the number on the response scale that most closely reflects the degree to which each statement accurately describes you. Add up your total points and prepare a brief action plan for self-improvement. Be ready to report your score for tabulation across the entire group.

	Good Description									Poor Description
1. I recognize that any employee can develop emotional problems occasionally that might negatively affect performance.	10	9	8	7	6	5	4	3	2	1
2. I am generally alert to sudden changes in a person's normal behavior at work.	10	9	8	7	6	5	4	3	2	1
3. I have the patience to recognize that most employee problems won't be solved in a single counseling session.	10	9	8	7	6	5	4	3	2	1
4. I recognize that employees who lack resilience may become candidates for burnout if their stressors continue to accumulate.	10	9	8	7	6	5	4	3	2	1
5. I am skillful at allowing catharsis by using silence and listening skills, nonverbal responses, and reflecting feelings.	10	9	8	7	6	5	4	3	2	1
6. I feel comfortable confronting chronic absentees and occasional absentees about their disruptive behaviors.	10	9	8	7	6	5	4	3	2	1
7. I am aware of the common symptoms of alcoholic employees.	10	9	8	7	6	5	4	3	2	1
8. I actively use the practice of performance management to help employees become more productive.	10	9	8	7	6	5	4	3	2	1
9. I am acutely aware of the ways in which my behavior can affect employee self-esteem.	10	9	8	7	6	5	4	3	2	1
10. I am conscious of the important steps in progressive discipline, and I practice the four essentials of the "hot-stove" rule.	10	9	8	7	6	5	4	3	2	1

Scoring and Interpretation

SCORING

Add up your total points for the 10 questions. Record that number here, and report it when it is requested. _____

INTERPRETATION

81 to 100 points. You seem to have a basic set of counseling and performance management skills.

61 to 80 points. Take a close look at some of your counseling and performance management skills (those with lower self-assessments) and discuss them with a manager to see if they need improvement.

Below 60 points. Some of your skills may be substantially inconsistent with effective counseling and performance management practices and could be detrimental to your success as a supervisor.

Identify your three lowest scores, and write the question numbers here: _____, _____, _____.

ACTION

Write a brief paragraph detailing an action plan for how you might sharpen each of these skills. Then pay particularly close attention to the related material in the chapter as you review the relevant sections there.

Skill Development

▶ *Counseling*

Many employees go through periods of substantial stress in their lives, caused either by work-related or nonwork problems (or both). When they find it desirable to "let off steam" at work, supervisors need to take the time—and demonstrate the skills—to allow for their catharsis in a psychologically safe setting. This requires the acquisition and development of some basic counseling skills, as outlined in this chapter. When done well, this type of counseling can produce very positive outcomes for both the stressed employee and the organization.

Pair up with another person. Assume that this person has asked to speak with you on an urgent basis. The problem that he or she presents to you may be of any kind (e.g., family crisis, alcohol abuse, financial difficulties, temporary depression around the holidays, or frustration with another employee at work). Spend several minutes counseling this person until it appears that she or he is more relaxed and in control emotionally. (To prepare yourself, you will likely wish to review the text's discussion on employee counseling, scan the Internet for relevant guidelines, and consult with colleagues and staff persons in the human resources department for their advice.) When you are finished, ask the other person to provide constructive feedback to you on the following dimensions:

1. Degree to which you let the person control the direction of the conversation.
2. Degree to which you gave your undivided attention.
3. Degree to which you listened patiently.
4. Degree to which you were attentive, receptive, and empathic.
5. Degree to which you refrained from arguing, interrupting, or offering advice.
6. Degree to which you were alert to underlying feelings.
7. Degree to which you used silence to draw out the other person.

8. Degree to which you refrained from expressing surprise or judgment at anything that was said.
9. Degree to which you used gentle, open-ended questions.
10. Degree to which you appropriately reflected the other person's feelings.

ACTION

Based on the feedback from your partner, make a list of the ways in which you can improve your counseling skills.

Group Exercise

Performance Management ◄

STEP 1: Form groups of three to five persons. Viewing the classroom as an organization, your task is to develop a performance management system for it.

STEP 2: Decide what your goals are in several areas—safety, room cleanliness, attendance, participation, learning, etc. Be as specific as possible. Then anticipate what types of (student) problems might arise in each of these areas.

STEP 3: Create a model set of policies for addressing potential problems, incorporating the text's guidelines for progressive discipline. Prepare to present your report to the class, anticipating members' reactions and criticisms.

STEP 4: After class presentations are completed, compare and contrast the various approaches, followed by discussion of these issues:
1. How difficult was this task?
2. What additional information would be desirable? Where might you get it?
3. What is the likely response if you implement such a performance management program in this classroom?
4. How did your model program differ from the others? What have you learned by listening to the class presentations?

CASES FOR ANALYSIS

Case 38

The Irrational Documents Clerk ◄

Benny was not exactly a knockout as a documents clerk for the Northern Empire Power and Light Company, but he was reasonably dependable. He got most of his work done on time, and his error rate on document coding was no worse than the average clerk's rate. His manner was generally pleasant, although he was considered somewhat of a loner by his associates.

That has all changed during the past three months. Benny's output has deteriorated markedly. He no longer meets his deadlines. And his boss, Aretha Ford, keeps discovering costly miscodings in the documents Benny prepares. Benny appears to be working hard, but his results are no longer satisfactory. When approached by other clerks to make corrections in the documents he sends them, Benny flares up. On some occasions, he has been downright insulting.

Yesterday, Aretha asked Benny to come to her office to talk about this problem. She opened the discussion by saying: "Your error rate on document preparation has become entirely unacceptable lately. So has your output. This can't keep on. What can you do to bring your work back into line?"

Benny was silent for a few minutes, so Aretha repeated her question. Then, without warning, Benny slammed his fist down on the desk. He shouted obscenities and heaped abuse upon Aretha: she was unfair, played favorites, expected too much of him, didn't understand his situation; if she wanted him to quit, why didn't she say so; and so on.

Analysis ▶

If you were Aretha, what would you do now? Of the following five alternatives, which do you think would be most appropriate? Rank the alternatives on a scale from 1 (most preferable) to 5 (least preferable). You may add another alternative if you wish. Be prepared to justify your ranking.

_____ **a.** Don't say anything for the time being; allow Benny to keep on talking.

_____ **b.** Advise Benny that he isn't making sense; tell him that when he is ready to talk rationally, you'll resume the discussion.

_____ **c.** Carefully show Benny why his accusations are not justified by the records.

_____ **d.** Wait a while; then tell Benny that you want to help him if he's suffering from some sort of emotional problem.

_____ **e.** Tell Benny that you understand how he feels, but say that it would be better if he faces up to his problem now.

Case 39 ▶ *A Difference of Opinion*

Twenty-two supervisors, all from different local companies, met for an all-day workshop on "Effective Supervision for the 21st Century." They heard presentations about, and engaged in discussions on, a range of topics including communication, motivation, leadership, and counseling. During the afternoon refreshment break, Josie, a supervisor who had been rather quiet all day, directed a question toward the instructor and another workshop participant who was standing close by.

"I have a problem with an employee," said Josie. "One or two days a week one of my drivers comes to work with liquor on his breath. Although he's not had an accident yet, I'm afraid that if he gets stopped by the police for any reason, they'll ticket him for DWI (driving while intoxicated). That could be bad for the company's reputation in the community and for our insurance rates. What should I do?"

Before the instructor could reply, the other supervisor said, "Your role as a supervisor is to identify and solve problems, isn't it?" Josie nodded.

"Well, then, tell the employee you think he's an alcoholic. Say he'd better control himself right now. Threaten him with immediate discharge if he doesn't shape up. You've got to take prompt action on these matters, or you lose all control."

Josie turned to the instructor. "I guess he's got a good point there," she said. "What do you think?"

◀ *Analysis*

Respond to Josie, commenting both on the other supervisor's perspective and any ideas you have for a different approach.

She's a Charmer, But . . .

◀ **Case 40**

Julie Garvo is 23 years old and serves as a paralegal clerk in a large law firm. She's been employed there for six months. Julie is charming and energetic, and is very popular with the office staff and with the lawyers.

Julie, however, is frequently late for work. She takes long lunch hours and has been absent from work an average of two days a month for the past three months. She apologizes when she saunters in late but seems unconcerned about this or her absences. To her co-workers, Julie readily admits that she doesn't have a great deal of interest in her work. The best thing about the job, she says, is that it pays well enough for her to do some of the things she enjoys in her off-hours.

◀ *Analysis*

Julie's supervisor, the office manager, notes, "She's a charmer, but she's become a problem." If you were her supervisor, what would you do?
a. Encourage Julie to improve. Sympathize with her lack of interest and try to make the job less boring for her.
b. Have a shoulder-to-shoulder talk with Julie, pointing out the importance of her creating a good work record.
c. Have Julie seek professional help to "get her head on straight."
d. Tell Julie to either stop the lateness and absences, or she will be fired.

Can you make any other suggestions to Julie's boss?

Case 41

"That Was the Week That Was"

It was finally Friday afternoon, and Martina breathed a big sigh of relief. It had not been, in anyone's eyes, a very good week. As the supervisor of a large crew working on clearing a mountain trail for hikers, she had a challenging job. She was responsible for the efforts of 24 workers, organized into four teams of six people each. The teams were spread out over nearly one-half mile, with team A cutting large trees, team B removing stumps, team C clearing smaller brush, and team D building footbridges across small streams and swampy areas.

Unfortunately, Martina was having trouble controlling several of her crew members. This was probably due, she reasoned, to the fact that she had split her time across the four crews, and she couldn't be everywhere at once. Just this week, she had to discipline several individuals for a variety of infractions:

- She gave an oral reprimand to Andrea, because when Martina walked up to one crew, she thought she saw Andrea quickly jump up and grab her tools to start working.
- Jackie had been coming to work late almost every other day for the past two weeks. "This can only set a bad example for the entire crew," reasoned Martina one night. Finally, on Thursday, Martina had put up with enough of Jackie's tardiness and fired her when she arrived at work.
- Mickey was one of those workers who moved so slowly that Martina sometimes wondered if she should check his pulse to see if he was even alive. "He's just lazy," concluded Martina. "Maybe a written reprimand will stimulate him to work a little faster!"

Analysis

Will Martina's disciplinary actions hold up if they are challenged? Should her manager support her? What errors in discipline did she make?

Answers to Quick Tests

Quick Test 1	Quick Test 2	Quick Test 3
1. F	3. T	5. F
2. F	4. T	6. T

Quick Test 4	Quick Test 5	Quick Test 6
7. T	9. T	11. F
8. F	10. F	12. T

Building Cooperative Teams and Resolving Conflicts

Learning Objectives

After studying this chapter, you should be able to

- Explain the formation, roles, and influence of formal and informal groups in an organization.

- Discuss the use of participatory management with groups of employees, and know how to conduct a group meeting.

- Identify the clues to good and bad teams, and explain how teams develop over time.

- Identify the most common sources of conflict in an organization and describe some effective ways to resolve conflict.

- Discuss ways in which cooperation can be obtained from associates, staff people, individuals, and groups.

Group dynamics. The interaction among members of a work group and concurrent changes in their attitudes, behavior, and relationships.

| CONCEPT ▶ | Supervisors need to understand *group dynamics*— the complex behavior of groups of employees and of employees within groups. |

Why are group relations more important today than they were in years past?

Business, industrial, service, and government enterprises are larger and more complex. As a result, they depend more on the effectiveness of group effort. At the beginning of the twentieth century, employees worked more by themselves, and their productivity often depended on their efforts alone. Then, too, many of the jobs were unskilled. People were hired to do routine work or to perform a specific task that a machine performs today. Automation, computers, and modern technology made those jobs scarce. Instead, modern jobs involve great interdependence among individuals and among departments, and demand close cooperation among all parties.

As Casey Stengel, the eccentric but immensely successful manager of baseball's Dodgers, Yankees, and Mets, observed: "It's easy to get the players. Gettin' 'em to play together, that's the hard part."

Which groups take priority: the formal or the informal ones?

Formal work group. A group or team of employees who are assigned by management to similar activities or locations with the intent that they work together in a prescribed way toward goals established by management.

Formal groups do, such as your own department or assigned work teams within your department. *Formal work groups* have been set up by management to routinely carry out the work in the best fashion. But informal groups require your attention and consideration, too. A supervisor must be realistic about the emergence of informal groups within the department because:

1. **Informal groups are inevitable.** They'll form at the water fountain and in the locker room. They will be made up of carpoolers and those with common interests in sports or politics. You will find them everywhere. There is no way to blot them out.

2. **Informal groups can be very powerful.** They strongly influence your employees. To enforce compliance among group members, such groups often establish sanctions that run counter to a supervisor's formal authority. Most informal groups, however, will work with you, depending on your relationships with them.

3. **Informal leaders tend to emerge within these groups and to guide opinion within them.** Supervisors should be aware of such leaders and be prepared to contend with their influence. Strive to win their support and cooperation.

What causes employees to create their own informal groups?

There are a number of causes. Most powerful is a common specialty or skill. For example, the customer service representatives in a telemarketing office are naturally going to find things in common to talk about. Other common experiences, backgrounds, or interests will also serve to pull parts of a formal grouping of employees into "cliques." Proximity plays a role, too. Workers who are physically close together tend to form close relationships to the exclusion of others in the department who are in more remote locations.

Membership in *informal work groups* is developed gradually. Over a period of time, an individual begins to feel accepted (or rejected) by the others. In return for acceptance, the individual begins to accept—and carry out—the interests and behavior of the group. The bonds are tighter when the attraction is fostered by a desire for protection or support (often with regard to the company or management). Groups are less cohesive when the common bond is more casual, as with hobbies and sports.

A supervisor must be careful in his or her relationships with informal groups. They can't be ignored; more often they can be helpful. On the other hand, giving these groups too much attention, especially to the exclusion of those outside the groups, will surely bring about dissension, feelings of favoritism, and lack of cooperation.

Informal work group. A group that forms spontaneously among employees who work near one another, who have common personal interests, or who work toward common job goals.

How does a group of employees differ from a single employee in the group?

Take a group of 10 employees who work in a small can-filling line in a food-packing plant. This group is respected by its supervisor as one of the most productive groups in the plant. It also has a collective reputation for advocating work stoppages over many issues. Yet in the group are three people who, polled separately, are strongly against a walkout. And there are another three who, when working with other groups, are low producers. This is typical. Each person in a group may be a fairly strong individualist when working alone. But when people work in a group, the personality of the group becomes stronger than that of any single individual in the group. The group's personality will reflect the outlook and work habits of the various individuals, but it will bring out the best (or worst) in some and will submerge many individual tendencies of which the group does not approve.

Furthermore, each group sets the standards of conduct—or *group norms*—for its members. Norms are accepted ways of doing things, an accepted way of life within the group. The group's ways may not be the best ways. Often, group norms stand in the way of doing things the way the company and the supervisor want them done. But the group will support the group standards. Individuals who don't conform will be cut off

Group norms. Beliefs held by a group about what is right and what is wrong as far as performance at work is concerned.

What Factors Contribute to and Detract from Cohesion?

Supervisors can predict, with some accuracy, whether a group will become cohesive. According to a review of research on cohesiveness, these are the two sets of factors that allow a supervisor to estimate how cohesive a group will be.

Contributors:

- Opportunity for frequent interaction.
- Prior group attractiveness (e.g., past successes; enjoyable experiences by early members).
- Similar attitudes, values, and backgrounds of members.
- Presence of a superordinate goal (one that can be reached only through cooperative efforts of the members).
- Existence of a common "enemy" or threat (such as an authoritarian supervisor, risk of job loss, or even physical danger).

- Competition with other groups.

Detractors:

- Favoritism shown by supervisors toward some group members.
- Domination of the group by one or more members.
- Absence of interpersonal attractiveness (liking) among members.
- Actions by members that prevent or destroy trust within the group.
- Disagreement over goals or standards of performance.
- Large groups (often those with more than 10 members).
- Scarce resources, leading to competition within the group.

Source: Allan R. Cohen et al., *Effective Behavior in Organizations* (5th ed.), Homewood, IL: Irwin, 1992, pp. 105–120.

---

from the group's gossip sessions, informal rewards, and social activities. It's not uncommon for the group to ridicule those who don't "play ball" or to purposely make it difficult for outsiders to get their own work done.

What makes some groups stronger than others?

It all revolves around **cohesiveness**—the members' desire to join, remain a part of, and participate in the group and its activities. In a cohesive group, members are attracted to it, willing to make personal sacrifices for the good of the group, and are enthusiastic about what the group is doing. They enjoy a common sense of identity and feel close to each other. And a cohesive work group tends to have greater similarity of output among its members and higher productivity *if* the group's norms support the organization's goals. However, high cohesiveness also has its limitations. It could lead to restricted risk-taking by individuals, withholding of unpopular views, failure to confront areas of conflict, and suppression of unique perspectives from individual members. The key to determining whether a cohesive group will be for or against the organization's goals lies in its level of **morale**. Often defined as a group's

Cohesiveness. The degree to which team members are attracted to the group, feel a part of it, and wish to remain in it.

Morale. A measure of the extent (either high or low) of voluntary cooperation demonstrated by an individual or a work group and of the intensity of the desire to meet common work goals.

collective job-satisfaction level, morale is a measure of the team's voluntary cooperation and desire to meet common work goals. If a group's morale level is high, its members are more likely to cooperate with management and contribute to its goals. But if it is low, watch out!

A fascinating by-product of group activity can sometimes be the experience of *synergy*. This is the supplemental energy, creativity, and productivity that emerges when a group of individuals "click" together to produce a better product than the sum of their individual efforts would have predicted. It doesn't occur in all groups, and it doesn't emerge automatically, but when it happens it is nearly magical to observe. It is almost the collective parallel to the term athletes use to describe their feelings when everything goes perfectly for them—they are in a *zone*.

In what ways are groups most likely to cause problems?

By ganging up to present mass resistance (spoken or silent) and by pressuring individual members to conform to the group's standards. Strong work groups stick together. They will protect one of their loyal members, and they will force a nonconformist to go along with the majority. The pressure can be so strong that even an eager beaver or a loner can be made to fall in line—or to quit. Groups are powerful. Their support is to be cherished. Their enmity can be awesome. For these reasons, prudent supervisors seek a group's help in establishing attainable work goals.

What are work groups likely to do best?

Solve work problems. Groups, formal or informal, seem to have an uncanny knack for unsnarling complex work situations. In a few minutes, they can straighten out crossover procedures between employees. They often know causes of difficulty hidden from the supervisor. Typically, they are acutely aware of personality conflicts between their members. Thus, a group's ability to put together jointly held know-how in a constructive manner is one that experienced supervisors like to tap. The technique of securing group aid this way in solving departmental problems is called ***participation.***

Participation. The technique in which a supervisor or manager shares work-related information, responsibilities, decisions, or all three, with the work group.

1	T or F	Informal groups are inevitable, usually weak, and have informal leaders.
2	T or F	Cohesive groups with organizationally supportive norms are usually more productive.

◄ *Quick Test 1*

2 GROUP PARTICIPATION

CONCEPT ▶ A participative approach tends to enhance a supervisor's effectiveness with employee groups.

How can a supervisor set goals with the work group without sacrificing authority?

Unless the people you supervise believe that what you want them to do is to their advantage as well as to yours, you'll have little success as a supervisor. The solution lies in permitting the members of the work group to set their goals along with you and in showing them that these goals are attained through group action: teamwork.

It may be only natural for you to feel that to permit the group to get into the decision-making act will be hazardous to your authority. It needn't be. First of all, make it clear that you'll always retain a veto power over a group decision (but don't exercise it unless absolutely necessary). Second, establish ground rules for the group's participation beforehand. Explain what's negotiable and what's not. Make these areas of freedom, as well as the limitations, clear. Finally, provide enough information for the group so that its members can see situations as clearly as you do. It's when people don't have enough facts that they rebel against authority.

Internet CONNECTION

The Web site for **Guide to Personnel Management and Policies** provides guidance in establishing policies and procedures.

In dealing with work groups, try to make your role that of a coach. Help employees to see why cost cutting, for instance, is desirable and necessary to prevent layoffs. Encourage them to discuss ways to cut costs. Welcome their suggestions. Try to find ways of putting even relatively insignificant ideas to work—at least on a trial basis. And report the team's achievements frequently. Emphasize that good records are the result of the team's united effort, not your own bright ideas.

Of course, it goes without saying that certain decisions, such as those concerning work standards or quality specifications, may be beyond the group's control or even yours (see Figure 14-1). Consequently, you should make it clear at the start what work conditions are off limits as far as group participation is concerned.

What makes group participation so effective?

You've probably heard about many forms of participation, ranging from simple and time-honored methods such as suggestion systems to dramatic experiments with self-managing work teams. Both Japanese and European organizations have successfully introduced systems of consensus management, quality circles, and industrial democracy. Each of these programs has its advocates, and the results have often been widely acclaimed. They all tap into two important phenomena—(a) widespread desire on the part of many employees to be more actively involved in their

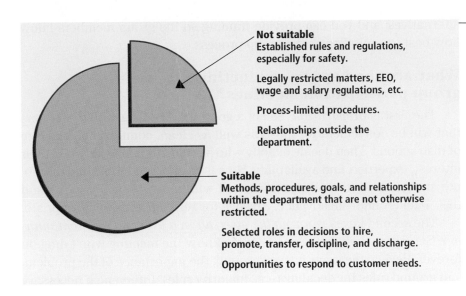

Not suitable
Established rules and regulations, especially for safety.

Legally restricted matters, EEO, wage and salary regulations, etc.

Process-limited procedures.

Relationships outside the department.

Suitable
Methods, procedures, goals, and relationships within the department that are not otherwise restricted.

Selected roles in decisions to hire, promote, transfer, discipline, and discharge.

Opportunities to respond to customer needs.

◆ FIGURE 14-1

Areas suitable for and areas usually not suitable for participatory management methods. **What is the supervisor's role in those areas where participatory management methods are suitable?**

work organizations, and (b) the predictable joint products of such participation, which are a better quality of decisions and employees committed to carrying them out successfully. As a result, participative techniques have been very useful in developing harmony and attaining common goals in the organizations that have made a sincere effort to infuse these methods from top to bottom.

Participation is an amazingly simple way to inspire people. And its simplicity lies in its definition: "to share in common with others."

Sharing, then, is the secret. You must share knowledge and information with others to gain their cooperation. You must share your own experience so that employees will benefit from it. You must share the decision-making process itself so that employees can do some things the way they'd like to. And you must share credit for achievement.

How often can group participation be expected to work in your behalf?

Only as often as the group's perception of a situation leads the members logically or emotionally, or both, to the conclusion that what you wish is good for them. Keep in mind that merely permitting participation will not necessarily produce decisions similar to those you would have made—nor should it! And the larger the group, the more forces are at work in it that complicate the process.

There are two rules of thumb to guide you: (a) Without group support your chance of achievement is slim, and (b) your best chance for winning group support is to let the forces within the group itself work toward a decision with minimum interference from you. This isn't to say you must stand by helplessly while the group strikes off in the wrong direction or struggles to solve a problem while lacking appropriate skills. You can still apply sound direction by providing facts that might otherwise be overlooked; you can ask the group to weigh pros and cons of various alternatives; and you can provide training so the group members know how best to capitalize on the group process.

What are the keys to conducting successful group participation meetings?

The first is *preparation*. Select a good time and place to meet—one that will be convenient for most, as well as clean, comfortable, and free of distractions. Then decide exactly who should attend, based upon their interest, expertise, and availability. Now is the time to create and distribute an agenda so that everyone invited will know the key issues—and their background—in advance. Arrange for refreshments, if appropriate.

The second key is *running the meeting in a fair and efficient manner*. Set a time limit so the participants know the meeting won't drag on forever. Review the issue, its background, the importance of the problem, and ground rules for deciding (e.g., majority rule). Intervene if necessary to prevent tensions from escalating. And make sure that everyone has the opportunity to be heard, while firmly limiting anyone who tries to dominate the process. Avoid reaching premature closure by consciously soliciting from the group the possible pitfalls and weaknesses of a proposal. Then check for the level of commitment to the solution.

The final key lies in *ending the meeting and preparing for future actions*. Stick to the time limit as closely as possible. Give credit to key individuals and the group as a whole for the roles they played. Summarize the major conclusions, and make specific assignments for further action. Try to end the meeting on a positive note. If possible, send out a brief summary of the agreed-upon decision to all who attended plus others who need to be informed. Finally, be sure to follow up to assure yourself that all actions are fulfilled.

What is the major difference between a group and a team?

In one sense, a **group** is simply a collection of individuals. They may be located in the same area, they may hold similar job titles, they may have the same supervisor, they may even aim for the same goals, they may interact occasionally to achieve them, and they may even refer to themselves as a team. But none of this guarantees they *will* be a team.

Teams generally have a compelling common objective that pulls them together intensively to achieve it. They are so committed to success that they are willing to devote extra energy—not only to the overarching goal, but also to the interpersonal processes—necessary to attain it. In short, they *work* on becoming more effective, and this often results in more open communication, occasional conflict, and higher levels of cohesiveness.

Group. Two or more people who are aware of one another and interact with one another.

Teams. Groups of people who must work together to achieve common goals.

3	T or F	Group participation generally produces both higher quality decisions, and higher commitment among employees to their success.	
4	T or F	The key to running a successful meeting is to clearly let the group know what solution you want them to select.	

◄ Quick Test 2

③ DEVELOPING COOPERATIVE TEAMS

CONCEPT ► Supervisors can apply the methods and skills of organizational development to improve the operation of their work teams.

What are the signs that a group of workers is not acting as a team?

They're usually pretty obvious, if you're paying attention. A simple sign may be just the absence of laughter and friendly banter among workers. You may overhear one employee bad-mouthing another one frequently, or you may notice increasing friction among factions. Incidents of littering, graffiti, complaints, and insubordination may increase. When you ask an employee to step in and help out another one, you may hear a variety of excuses for not doing so. At the extreme, employees may request transfers out of your unit, while asserting that it is nothing you did that caused them to leave. All of these are clues to low morale and the absence of teamwork, and they demand your attention.

What are the indicators you'll see when teamwork is present?

The differences will be as clear as the contrast between the darkest night versus the sunniest day. Workers will show up on time with a fresh attitude most days. They'll volunteer for tasks, willingly tackle assignments, exhibit pride in their performance, and pitch in when others need help. The whole atmosphere will be different, with employees having fun and engaging in good-natured teasing. And perhaps most important, a sense of community will emerge, with co-workers genuinely caring about each other. As a result, the teamwork will pay off in terms of increased quality and efficiency.

What can supervisors do to create more effective work units?

Organizational Development (OD). A set of values and assumptions about individuals, groups, organizations, and their environments that suggests they must embrace change and find ways to deal more effectively with each other.

Interventions. A variety of activities designed to make individuals, groups, or the entire organization more effective.

They can apply some of the techniques of *organizational development (OD)*. OD is a set of approaches to creating and sustaining high-involvement, high-performance organizations and their subunits. It assumes that employees have much to offer, want to do so, and will grow and mature through various activities. It assumes that highly effective teams are essential to organizational success, while recognizing that teamwork does not develop overnight. Also, OD assumes that most organizations have been controlled, filled with detrimental conflict, and too rigid to respond to their dynamic environments.

OD typically consists of a series of steps, as shown in Figure 14-2. A manager, often working with an OD consultant, makes an initial diagnosis that a problem exists. For example, employees may be confused about their roles, or priorities may conflict, or groups may be competing with each other. Then some data are usually collected to serve as a basis for understanding and discussion. The data are fed back to the interested parties so that they are forced to confront the issues. Action plans are developed and implemented, and after they have been given a chance to work, the results are evaluated.

A key feature of OD is its use of one or more forms of *interventions,* which are a variety of activities designed to make individuals, groups, or the entire organization more effective. Typical interventions include the following:

- **Process consultation**—helping others see themselves and their behavior more clearly by observing, asking probing questions, and confronting them with new information about their impact on others.
- **Feedback mechanisms**—collection of data and perceptions from others that are then provided to an individual or group, allowing them to see themselves as others see them and take action on that data.

◆ **FIGURE 14-2**

Typical steps in the OD process. **What assumption about employees underlies OD?**

Preliminary problem diagnosis

↓

Data-gathering

↓

Feedback and confrontation of issues

↓

Action plan development

↓

Implementation of an intervention

↓

Evaluation of results

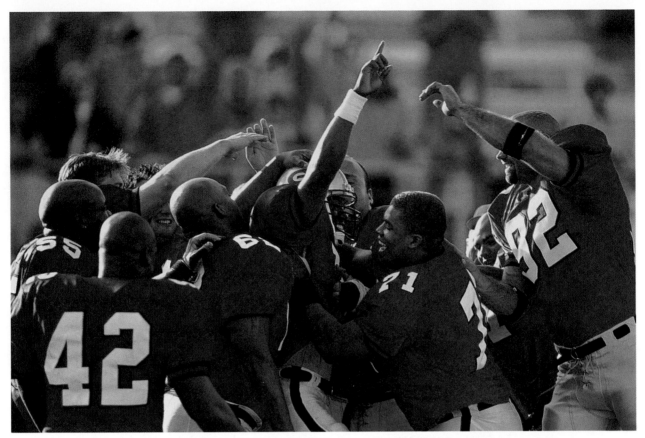

▲ Just as in athletics, teamwork in the workplace is crucial. **What can a supervisor do to encourage teamwork?**

- **Encounter groups**—unstructured small-group interactions, often with some degree of stress, designed to get participants to understand themselves and others more clearly.
- **Job design and strategic approaches**—a range of methods that may focus on job enrichment, management by objectives, career planning systems, or organizational transformations.

What can be done to help a collection of individuals work as a team?

A popular OD intervention is known as **team building**. In situations where employees must work closely with each other, share resources, and act to achieve overall goals, it is imperative that they become a team. Team-building interventions take many forms but generally involve an activity that encourages members to explore how they work together, identify the nature and intensity of their problems, and develop more effective ways of interacting with each other. Trust is often a key ingredient in effective teams, and members are encouraged to take risks, share significant information with each other, and provide support and encouragement to other members.

Team building. Activities designed to help group members develop more effective ways of problem solving and interacting with each other.

Can teams develop to the point where they don't need active supervisory leadership?

Yes. When they do this, they become ***self-managing*** (self-directed, or self-reliant) ***teams***. And the best ones produce productivity gains and cost savings ranging from 30 to 70 percent when compared to traditional systems.

How are these self-managing teams different from others? They keep their own time records, analyze quality problems, assign jobs to each other, train team members, redesign production processes, set team goals, and analyze internal performance and quality results. Some teams maintain their own inventory control, adjust production schedules, prepare annual budgets, and resolve internal conflicts. They elect their internal team leaders, administer competency tests to each other, and make selection decisions regarding the hiring or transfer of new members. They truly assume many "management" roles!

The results may include leaner staff units, fewer job classifications, lower absence and turnover rates, higher commitment and job satisfaction, and improved efficiency and customer service. These gains are possible only if employees are willing to learn multiple skills, substitute pay-for-knowledge for seniority-based compensation, and be perpetually in a learning mode. But supervisors must also give up their traditional roles based on authority, giving directions, disciplining, appraising, and controlling resources. The new roles for a supervisor may include being a mentor, buffer, champion, counselor, and coach.

Are there any predictable patterns in the evolution of a team?

Bruce Tuckman, a noted researcher, has found that most teams go through five key stages as they develop (see Figure 14-3). In the *forming stage*, members are concerned about their own "fit" with the group. Will they be accepted? Do they have adequate competence to make a contribution? And who are all these other people? In the *storming stage*, predictable conflicts arise as the group struggles to create an identity and develop a mode of operation. As they move toward the *norming stage*, members examine their goals and resources, and develop fairly explicit statements about their beliefs and values (e.g., what is and is not acceptable to the group). In the *performing stage*, members start to take risks, step into predictable roles, empower each other to change, and become action-oriented. Finally, most teams eventually disband (after achieving the goals, of course!) in the *adjourning stage*. Here, they engage in retrospective reviews to document and celebrate their accomplishments, record what they have learned, and relive what they have struggled through, as well as look to the future to see what lies ahead of them. Often, the process begins anew as members are assigned to other teams.

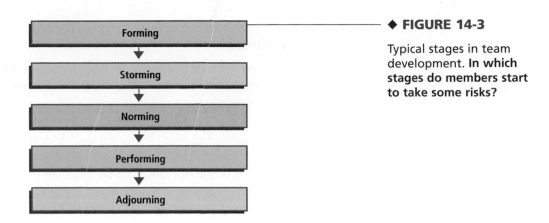

The supervisor of a self-managing team faces many new challenges. While the team is developing its new skills, the supervisor must learn to embrace a broad set of new values. These include a recognition of the need for continual change, collaboration with others, open communications, shared power, and constructive confrontation. And one of the new values lies in looking at conflict as both predictable in its emergence and potentially useful in bringing issues into the open.

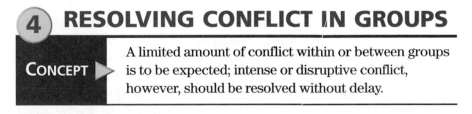

5	T or F	It is generally difficult to detect the differences between a team and just a group of workers.
6	T or F	Teams usually cannot be effective unless a strong element of trust is present among the members.

◀ *Quick Test 3*

④ RESOLVING CONFLICT IN GROUPS

CONCEPT ▶ A limited amount of conflict within or between groups is to be expected; intense or disruptive conflict, however, should be resolved without delay.

Is the presence of bickering and disputes a sign of poor supervision?

Not necessarily. It is human to quarrel and complain. When many people must work together, conflict is inevitable. Accordingly, a small amount of conflict can be a good thing. It is when there is no end of quarreling and confrontation that supervisors should begin to worry about how good a job they are doing.

Where are the main sources of conflict in an organization?

There are many. People with different ideas about what should be done and how to do it are a common source. Departments that are sometimes at cross-purposes—such as production and maintenance, production control and sales, sales and credit, accounting and retailing, purchasing and engineering—cause intergroup difficulties. But most of the causes of conflict in a supervisor's department are closely related to the work itself: how it is laid out and the way in which the supervisor manages the employees. In particular, a supervisor should be on guard against the following:

1. **An appearance of an unfair allocation of tools, materials, supplies, and other resources.** There is seldom enough of everything to go around equally. The supervisor must often make the hard decisions about who will have what, how much, and when. When these decisions are made openly and fairly, employees are more likely to accept them without quarreling with one another. If allocations are made slyly or on the basis of favoritism, trouble will brew.

2. **Expressed disagreements about what is and is not important.** If these are the result of lack of information or misinformation, they should be cleared up right away. If the disagreements arise because individuals see things differently, the supervisor must try to get to the root of the problem. For example, a press operator may constantly push his benchmate for work to be processed, whereas the benchmate may insist that her work can't be released because its quality isn't good enough. The first individual sets priority on output, the other on quality. The supervisor must find an answer to this question: Are these priorities (or goals) merely a reflection of each individual's values—or are they related to the department's established goals and standards?

3. **Changes in work flow or conditions that imply a change in status.** If in the past Anita handled incoming orders first before passing them on to Jack for posting, Anita may regard her work as more valued than Jack's. A change in the order of flow so that Jack handles the orders first may disturb Anita's sense of status. And she may begin finding fault with everything that Jack does. Experienced workers tend to develop "territorial rights." Hence, they feel that they should resist outside forces such as a new supervisor, new employees, or any changes in which they have not participated.

4. **A growing sense of mistrust among employees.** This is liable to occur when things in the department are generally going wrong. If business is bad, or if the department has been criticized for mistakes or low productivity, employees may look around for others on whom to place the blame. The production department, for example, will blame off-grade products on the maintenance people, suggesting

that the equipment was faulty. The floor salesperson may blame the cashier for a lost sale. The nurse may blame the nurse's aide for upset patients.

5. **Lack of stability in departmental operations.** Change is so threatening to many people that they will naturally take out their fears and anxieties in quibbling and complaints. Many times, change is something beyond the supervisor's control. But, as a supervisor, you can calm troubled waters simply by maintaining open channels of communication. You can, for example, talk with employees about the reasons for the change, how long it will last, and how it will affect—or not affect—normal operating conditions.

How does competition differ from conflict?

The former is usually productive; the latter is often counterproductive. The right kind of *competition* can stimulate a healthy, controlled discussion between two individuals. Informal contests allow employees to try to excel at meeting departmental goals that are mutually beneficial. Carried too far, however, the contestants may lose sight of the common good and become antagonistic. *Conflict* tends to pit individuals and groups against one another in trying to control the department's resources in pursuit of their own goals. A lathe operator, for example, may insist on taking the only available tool in order to finish her own quota on time. She may not worry about whether this slows up another operator or the department in meeting its goals. Or a salesperson may demand the major portion of the section's travel expenses because his own customers are most important.

Competition. A relatively healthy struggle among individuals or groups within an organization to excel in striving to meet mutually beneficial, rather than individual, goals.

Conflict. A disruptive clash of interests, objectives, or personalities between individuals, between individuals and groups, or between groups within an organization.

What's a good way to handle conflict in your department?

First, be alert to its presence. Next, seek out its causes. Then meet it head-on. A basic approach involves five steps:

1. **Decide what it is that you want to have accomplished.** Do you want peace and quiet at any price? Or do you want better quality? Greater productivity? A project finished on time? Fewer mistakes in transcribing? An end to delays caused by quarrels between the maintenance person and your production operator? Nothing will be resolved unless you first make up your mind what the desired outcome should be.

2. **Call together the people who can best settle the issue.** If the conflict is strictly between you and an individual, limit the confrontation to the two of you. If others are involved, invite them into the discussion. If a disinterested party, such as the quality-control department, can shed light on the subject, ask for that person's participation. If a referee or someone who can speak authoritatively about the company's viewpoint is needed, then get your boss into the act.

3. **Be ready to bargain; don't hand out edicts.** Conflicts are truly settled by negotiation. A short answer tends only to put off the problem, and it will keep recurring. If you keep your eye on the objective you have set, there are usually many ways to attain it. Remember that each individual has an objective, too. If the maintenance department, for example, can provide the necessary repairs while still keeping its costs in line, and dependable repairs are your objective, then let the maintenance people do it their way.

4. **Don't be distracted by personalities.** Whereas many people do rub one another the wrong way, most conflicts have a much more tangible basis. That's the value of keeping the eyes of all concerned on the main objective. It tends to push personality conflicts into the background. Finally, try not to get emotionally involved yourself. Most importantly, don't choose sides.

5. **Focus attention on mutually beneficial outcomes.** Above all, don't make performance comparisons between individuals. This will only heighten competition and stress. Instead, hold up total organizational results as the criterion for success. If Kevin insists that Sharon takes up more than her share of the keyboard time, for example, try to reach a solution that makes the most effective use of the keyboard. That way, both Sharon and Kevin can contribute to departmental effectiveness, even though both may have to give in a little while doing so.

Quick Test 4 ▶	**7**	T or F	When employees bicker and quarrel, it is a sure sign of poor supervision.
	8	T or F	Competition inevitably leads to disruptive conflict.

(5) SECURING COOPERATION

CONCEPT ▶ Cooperation from employees and associates can be encouraged by showing how cooperation protects or advances their interests.

Why don't some people cooperate?

For a very natural reason: They see no personal advantage in doing so. A terrible attitude? Not at all.

Not one of us does anything for nothing. We do some things for money, others for lots of other reasons. Joe works well because he likes the feeling of being with a group of people. Jane works hard because she gets a sense of accomplishment from what she is doing. Louise puts in top effort because her job makes her feel important.

Hardly anyone works for money alone. We all expect different satisfactions in different proportions from our work. So don't be annoyed when a worker's attitude when asked to cooperate seems to say, "What's in it for me?" That's your signal to get busy and to find some way of providing satisfaction for that person on the job.

How can "I'm okay, you're okay" help to build cooperation?

This kind of analysis, often called ***transactional analysis (TA),*** helps to provide insights because it simplifies some of the apparently complex interactions that take place between people. This analysis maintains that there are four possible views of a relationship that can be held by the employee, the supervisor, or both:

1. **I'm not okay. You're not okay.** This is a negative view that implies an employee's dissatisfaction with her or his own behavior but also, in effect, says that the supervisor's actions are just as bad. It is somewhat like the attitude of a rebellious child quarreling with a parent. At work, it might arise when an employee accused of pilfering materials says that the boss does the same thing.

2. **I'm not okay. You're okay.** This is often the mark of the person who has lost self-respect or of a person who places all the responsibility on the boss's shoulders. This person often feels unable to do the job without continual assistance from the supervisor. Supervisors should strive to get out from under this kind of dependence.

3. **I'm okay. You're not okay.** This is the parental kind of role that many supervisors traditionally displayed. Essentially it means treating the employee like a child. Such an attitude invites rebellion or loss of any hope the employee may have that the job can be done to the supervisor's satisfaction.

4. **I'm okay. You're okay.** This is the mature, or adult, way to handle conflicts. It assumes that each individual respects the other. Starting from a point of mutual respect, each person tries to understand— without necessarily agreeing with—the other's point of view. The supervisor says to the employee: "I understand why you may think I'm taking advantage of your good nature, but listen to me long enough so that you understand my point of view. Once we're sure we understand one another, maybe we can come to some sort of agreement that gives you some satisfaction while making sure that the job gets done."

Any of the first three approaches tends to drive people apart. The fourth approach, which encourages positive stroking, can be very effective if carried out honestly. It helps provide a solid basis for cooperation and compromise.

Transactional analysis (TA). A way of improving relationships between people that is based on an understanding of each individual's (mature) attitudes and behavior toward one another.

Ethical PERSPECTIVES

A Less Stressful Work Environment

Ergonomic rules have been put in place to require employers to minimize the physical daily stress of certain jobs. Would this be good for the employer? The employee? What's the ethical responsibility of the employer to employees to provide a physically comfortable working environment?

▲ Cooperation from employees should not be assumed. **What question will employees ask themselves before giving their cooperation?**

How do you go about getting cooperation from your associates?

The secret of getting along well with other supervisors is much the same as that of winning cooperation from your employees: *Find out what they want most from their work; then satisfy these desires.* With your associates, though, it's not so much a problem of providing satisfaction as it is of not blocking their goals and ambitions.

Face up to the fact that, to a degree, you and your associates are competing—for raises, promotions, praise, popularity, and a host of other things. If you compete too hard or compete unfairly, you won't win much cooperation from the other supervisors. And your chances of getting ahead depend on your ability to run your department in harmony with those departments that interface with yours.

Winning friends among other supervisors means intelligent sacrifice. Occasionally you'll have to put aside your wish to make your department look good so that you don't put the supervisor of the next department behind the eight ball. Willingness to lend a hand when another supervisor falls behind, and avoiding hairsplitting when allocating interdepartmental charges and responsibilities will also help.

Above all, let other supervisors run their own shows. Don't try to give orders in their departments or encourage disputes between your workers and theirs.

As in the case of an individual employee who doesn't play ball with the others, if you don't conform to a reasonable degree, you'll have the

MEETINGS, TEAMS, AND CONFLICTS

■ There are many useful skills that supervisors can use to facilitate effective group meetings, help teams increase their cohesiveness, and resolve interpersonal conflicts. These skills include the following:

- Observing groups unobtrusively to gather information and gain insights.
- Negotiating so that all parties feel like they "won" something.
- Stimulating deeper explorations of issues through effective questions.
- Facilitating new insights by providing feedback on team behaviors.
- Demonstrating your own self-esteem, and fostering high self-esteem in others.
- Encouraging others to accept uncertainty in their lives.
- Showing concern and empathy for people.
- Soliciting commitment to objectives.
- Coaching individuals and groups to become more sensitive and skillful.

supervisory group down on you—and cooperation will be slow in coming. To turn this group solidarity to your advantage, aim at giving your supervisory colleagues the advantage of your own positive leadership. Help other supervisors set worthwhile goals, and the chances of all of you working together will be improved.

How can you get along best with staff people?

Generally speaking, staff people in your organization are almost entirely dependent on the cooperation of you and other supervisors. And in this case, cooperation will breed cooperation. When you cooperate with staff people, their jobs are made infinitely easier. Their superiors judge them by their success in giving you assistance and by the degree to which you accept and act on their advice. So when you cooperate with staff people, you're actually helping them get more satisfaction from their work. And you can be pretty sure that they'll go a long way toward helping you make a good showing on *your* job.

Wouldn't you like to have a staff specialist report to your boss: "It's a pleasure to work with a supervisor like Jill. She never seems to hide things or get offended when I offer suggestions. She is quick to see how what we're doing will improve operations in the long run. Not that Jill buys everything I say. She doesn't. She has her ideas, too. But together, I think Jill and I are really accomplishing things out there."

Individual or group of individuals. What's the best way to avoid misunderstanding and to gain willing cooperation?

The starting place is respect for others' points of view, no matter how much they vary from your own. For the manager, this implies an appreciation of subordinates for what they really are. It's wishful thinking—and downright harmful—to measure someone against a mythical ideal such as the perfect person for the job.

Try to remind yourself that by definition you, as a supervisor, deal in other people's lives. An order to take any action in the company is interpreted all down the line in terms of personal effects on people. And the effectiveness of the implementation of any order is a matter of approval or disapproval on the part of your subordinates and your associates.

Many managers never learn that their subordinates are constantly evaluating the manager's actions and varying their efforts accordingly. It's certainly the rare subordinate who will risk telling the boss when he or she is making mistakes, particularly if the boss isn't one who takes criticism willingly. Thus, many supervisors never get any critical feedback about themselves. Fortunately, if you can make the first step, you'll find yourself a new and better kind of supervisor. You'll gain a new awareness that there are more consequences to any action involving people than those on the surface. And the consequences often interfere with productivity because people who are working on their own frustrations have less energy to devote to the job.

Of course, it isn't always possible to solve the human problems that can result from a necessary and unpleasant management action. But sensitive supervisors enjoy two distinct advantages over their less sensitive counterparts:

1. An awareness of others' needs aids in avoiding unnecessary human problems that ordinarily seem to be cropping up each day.
2. A pattern of awareness of others' needs in itself tends to blunt the edge of problems and conflicts that cannot be avoided because subordinates and associates know that the supervisor has tried.

| **Quick Test 5** ▶ | **9** | T or F | Gaining cooperation from others is usually a function of satisfying their desires. |
| | **10** | T or F | Many supervisors are virtually starved for constructive feedback on their performance. |

CHAPTER 14 REVIEW

KEY CONCEPTS TO REMEMBER

1. **Group Dynamics.** Since supervision is involved with organized human effort, group dynamics—group relationships—are present in every situation. Work groups may be either formal, established by management, or informal, spontaneously created by their members because of mutual interest.

   Because groups can exert such tremendous influence in work situations, supervisors must weigh the characteristics of a group's norms and behavior just as carefully as those of an individual.

2. **Group Participation.** With groups especially, the principle of participation presents an effective approach. By recognizing a group's ability to attain (or block) goals, a supervisor who invites participation encourages the group to direct its influence in a productive manner. While respecting the power and legitimate interests of work groups, supervisors should not abandon the management's responsibility to the group or relinquish their essential authority.

3. **Developing Cooperative Teams.** A new model of supervision is emerging, stressing collaboration, sharing of power, and open communication. These values can be demonstrated and instilled through the use of various organizational development (OD) intervention methods. Team building is one method that most supervisors can use to build trust and a cooperative spirit within their departments. Teams develop through a series of five stages, and some teams may achieve "self-managing" status.

4. **Resolving Conflict in Groups.** Conflicts are natural in any organization. The supervisor's responsibilities are to try to understand the causes of these conflicts and to resolve them in a way that will contribute to meeting the objectives of the work group and the organization. Conflict is best resolved by focusing on mutually beneficial goals, by seeking areas of compromise, by examining facts, and by keeping personality differences out of the discussion.

5. **Securing Cooperation.** Listening to an employee's point of view and the reasons for it can be one of the most effective ways for a supervisor to obtain cooperation. Transactional analysis (TA) can be a useful tool for understanding different points of view.

READING COMPREHENSION

1. Describe a situation in which you might be a part of both a formal group and an informal group at the same time.
2. Give an example of how a group's norms might differ from the standards of performance set by the company.
3. Why would an experienced supervisor encourage group participation in solving a work problem?
4. What are the primary benefits of allowing employees to be involved in decision making?
5. What areas of supervision are not usually appropriate for participatory management? Is it possible that more of those could be candidates for involvement?
6. What accounts for the current interest in OD?
7. Examine the new skills and values for a supervisor under conditions of self-managing teams and team building. How do they compare?
8. Distinguish between competition and conflict in an organization.

9. John and Mary are quarreling over who should have the use of a lift truck first while loading cartons into a truck for shipment. What steps would you take to settle this dispute?

10. Can cooperation be forced on others? Why or why not?

APPLICATION

Self-Assessment

▶ *How good are your team and conflict management skills?*

Read the following statements carefully. Circle the number on the response scale that most closely reflects the degree to which each statement accurately describes you. Add up your total points and prepare a brief action plan for self-improvement. Be ready to report your score for tabulation across the entire group.

	Good Description									Poor Description
1. I am aware of the presence and power of informal groups in my organization.	10	9	8	7	6	5	4	3	2	1
2. I avoid doing the things that detract from work group cohesiveness, and practice the actions that contribute to it.	10	9	8	7	6	5	4	3	2	1
3. I can see multiple opportunities for work groups to be involved in participative decision making.	10	9	8	7	6	5	4	3	2	1
4. I consciously practice at least 10 of the text's ideas for running effective meetings.	10	9	8	7	6	5	4	3	2	1
5. I could identify at least three clues that a group is not functioning effectively as a team.	10	9	8	7	6	5	4	3	2	1
6. I could identify at least three indicators that a group is functioning effectively as a team.	10	9	8	7	6	5	4	3	2	1
7. I could feel comfortable with the new roles required of a supervisor of a self-managing team.	10	9	8	7	6	5	4	3	2	1

		Good Description									Poor Description
8.	I can envision specific things I could do to help a team at each stage of its development process.	10	9	8	7	6	5	4	3	2	1
9.	I am comfortable helping others resolve their interpersonal conflicts.	10	9	8	7	6	5	4	3	2	1
10.	I actively seek to identify and then satisfy what other people want from their work.	10	9	8	7	6	5	4	3	2	1

Scoring and Interpretation

SCORING

Add up your total points for the 10 questions. Record that number here, and report it when it is requested. _____

INTERPRETATION

81 to 100 points. You seem to have a basic set of team and conflict management skills.

61 to 80 points. Take a close look at some of your team and conflict management skills (those with lower self-assessments) and discuss them with a manager to see if they need improvement.

Below 60 points. Some of your skills may be substantially inconsistent with effective team and conflict management practices and could be detrimental to your success as a supervisor.

Identify your three lowest scores, and write the question numbers here: _____, _____, _____.

ACTION

Write a brief paragraph detailing an action plan for how you might sharpen each of these skills. Then pay particularly close attention to the related material in the chapter as you review the relevant sections there.

Skill Development

Group Meeting Skills ◄

Most organizations hold meetings, and sometimes it seems as though supervisors spend their whole day in meetings! But supervisors also must conduct frequent meetings, and these represent opportunities to demonstrate one's effectiveness at getting results while also leaving participants satisfied with their contributions. This requires the acquisition and development of some basic group meeting skills, as outlined in the chapter.

When done well, these group leadership skills can produce very positive outcomes for both the participants and the organization.

Pair up with another person, who will be your observer. Identify a small group of individuals who are willing to attend a short meeting to discuss and decide on some key problem or issue (such as how to lower college tuition rates by 30 percent!). (To prepare yourself, you will likely wish to review the text's discussion on conducting group meetings, search the Internet for relevant guidelines, and consult with colleagues and staff persons in the human resources department for their advice.) When you are finished, ask the other person to rate you on a 10-point scale (1 = poor, 10 = great) and provide constructive feedback to you on each of the following dimensions:

1. Degree to which you created and shared an agenda in advance.
2. Degree to which you set a reasonable time limit for the meeting.
3. Degree to which you reviewed the background and importance of the problem.
4. Degree to which you clearly established how decisions were to be made.
5. Degree to which you gave everyone the opportunity to be heard.
6. Degree to which you avoided reaching premature closure.
7. Degree to which you checked for the group's level of commitment to the decision.
8. Degree to which you stuck to the original time limit for the meeting.
9. Degree to which you gave appropriate credit to individuals who contributed input.
10. Degree to which you summarized conclusions and ended on a positive note.

ACTION

Based on the feedback from your partner, make a list of the ways in which you can improve your meeting skills.

Role Play

Resolving Conflict

Form groups of three individuals, and assign one of the following roles to each person. Do *not* read each other's roles. When everyone is ready, hold a conversation among the three, with Amber playing the role of a mediator who is trying to help Bobbi and Carl reconcile their differences.

AMBER. You are a mutual friend of Bobbi and Carl, who are two co-workers in your office. They have been squabbling for several days, and you have asked them to meet with you to iron things out. Before the session begins, you review the five suggestions for handling conflict as presented in the text. You vow to yourself to give these principles an honest effort today, as your goal is to eliminate the conflict between Bobbi and Carl.

BOBBI. Sometimes, it seems, your co-workers just rub you the wrong way, and Carl is one of those persons. He's actually a pretty decent person, but he has some peculiar habits, too. Whenever he comes to your work area to chat about something, he always picks up your personal objects (such as family photos), examines them, and then sets them back down in a different position. And he's always rubbing your nose in the fact that he has more seniority than you do, even if it is by just a few weeks. You've also noticed that he spends a lot of time in the supervisor's office, and you assume that he is just "polishing the apple" to get on the good side of your boss. You really want to get along with him, but Carl can be pretty irritating sometimes. Amber—a mutual friend and co-worker—has asked you to meet together with her and Carl today. You hope that Amber can get Carl to see things your way. You are about to meet with both of them now.

CARL. You have worked here for several years, and see yourself as one of the senior people in the department. As a matter of fact, you were hired several weeks before Bobbi came on board, and you like to tease her about it once in a while. Your supervisor also consults with you quite a bit to obtain your opinions and tap into your experience, and that gives a big boost to your ego to spend time in the "corner office." You hope, however, that others haven't noticed this, as it might be interpreted differently. Lately, you've noticed that Bobbi has acted irritably and even snapped at you as you chatted with her at her desk. You suspect that something is causing her to be stressed out, and speculate that it must be some kind of problem at home. Another co-worker, Amber, has commented on the shaky relationship between you and Bobbi and asked the two of you to meet today to iron things out. You agreed that a meeting was needed and are about to meet with both of them now.

Discussion Questions

1. What issues arose during the conversation?
2. What did each party learn about the other that they were not aware of before?
3. Why did the conflict come about? How could it have been prevented?
4. What actions taken today by Amber were helpful in resolving the relationship? What else could Amber have done?
5. Will Bobbi and Carl get along better in the future, based on this conversation? Discuss.

CASES FOR ANALYSIS

Case 42

> ### *Problems, Problems, Everywhere!*

Addie's emotional state had gone from low to high in less than a week. Before she left for the workshop on "Organizational Development for Supervisors," she felt overwhelmed by the problems that her employees seemed to cause for her. Everyday it was something new, and there were issues including bickering, jealousy, scarce resources, and misunderstandings. At times, it seemed like a lost cause, and Addie wished she'd never accepted supervisory responsibility for her group.

Then, in just three days, Addie's hopes were lifted. She was introduced in the seminar to a wide range of OD interventions, and each of them seemed to have some merit. "Now," she thought as she flew home from the workshop, "if I could just figure out which one to use with each of my employees, I might make some progress."

Addie has identified the following five key problems and placed them in priority order. (She believes that Ahmad's problem requires immediate solution; the "retreat" issue can be confronted last.)

1. Ahmad's morale has been steadily sagging for months, and several symptoms of boredom and monotony have appeared. For example, she was absent three times in the last month alone. When asked for the cause, Ahmad blurted out "I hate to keep doing the same reports over and over again each month!"

2. Addie's department consists of three sections, A, B, and C, each with about seven employees. The B section never gets into trouble, but people from the A and C sections always seem to be fighting with each other and nobody really seems to know why.

3. Frans has been a technical star—a real whiz at his job—but when it comes to interacting with others, he is a total bomb. Frans just seems totally unaware of his impact on other employees, and it is beginning to affect their cooperation with him. As Marissa said, "Frans just doesn't get it, does he?"

4. The members of B section get most of their work done on schedule, but problems seem to arise whenever the members have to communicate with each other. No one tells anyone else what they are doing or when they need something until the last minute, and then tempers flare up.

5. Once a year, Addie calls all members of sections A, B, and C together for a one-day "retreat," in which she attempts to share vital

information, obtain ideas for improvements, and encourage empathy for problems in each other's sections. However, in each of the past two years, the meeting has deteriorated rapidly after the first hour. People go off on tangents, break into small cliques, ignore the speaker, and interrupt each other.

◀ *Analysis*

Each of Addie's problems may lend itself to the application of at least one OD intervention. Of the following five possibilities, which one should she use first (e.g., with Ahmad)? Second? Rank them on a scale from 1 (immediate use) to 5 (delayed use for the "retreat" issue).

_____ **a.** Team building

_____ **b.** Process consultation

_____ **c.** Job enrichment

_____ **d.** Encounter group

_____ **e.** Feedback mechanisms

◀ Case 43

Tell Them to Lay Off Me!

Deep in the Ozarks is a knitting mill that moved there from New England during the Great Depression of the mid-1930s. The mill has grown during the last decade, however. From what had been essentially a subcontracting facility, manufacturing its goods for large eastern apparel firms, the mill now operates independently. It produces its own line of sportswear under its own, well-known brand name. Its sales representatives call directly on major department stores and retail chains throughout the country. The mill, now known nationally as Linda Kay Fashions, could be considered a major success story.

Inside the home office at Linda Kay Fashions, however, a small drama is unfolding, with many of the aspects of a soap opera. Nevertheless, it is a very real situation to its participants.

Here is what is happening. In a group of seven Linda Kay employees who work as a team to receive, record, and process sales orders, Stella is the least productive. Typically, she takes the most time at coffee breaks and spends more time in the lounge than any of the other employees. Yesterday, she complained to the group's supervisor that others in the group were "petty and impossible."

"What makes you say that?" asked the supervisor.

"Because they continually harass me and pressure me for more production."

"Perhaps they are right about your production," said the supervisor.

"Right or wrong," said Stella, "tell them to lay off me. Who is running this department, anyway? You or them?"

Analysis ▶

    a. What do you think of Stella's complaint?

    b. What is the problem here?

    c. How should the supervisor handle it?

Case 44 ▶ *Inviting Participation*

    Oprah is the newly appointed supervisor of the clients' records department of a large commercial service firm in California. She is to supervise 17 workers; nearly all of these employees have been with the company for some time and have established lasting friendships and informal groups. Oprah wants to invite the employees to participate in decision making at regular meetings she plans to hold. She wants to be sure to use good practices in conducting these meetings.

Analysis ▶

    Your assignment is to prepare a checklist of important ideas for Oprah to review before each meeting. These should help Oprah achieve her goals of productive participation. Use the guidelines given in concepts 2, 3, and 5 of this chapter.

Factors That Encourage Participation

    a. Extent of authority: _____

    b. Information available: _____

    c. Topic areas to cover: _____

    d. Suggestions to make: _____

    e. Teamwork to stress: _____

    f. Credit to be given: _____

    g. Other factors: _____

    h. Other factors: _____

    i. Other factors: _____

Answers to Quick Tests ▶

Quick Test 1	Quick Test 2	Quick Test 3
1. F	3. T	5. F
2. T	4. F	6. T

Quick Test 4	Quick Test 5	
7. F	9. T	
8. F	10. T	

PART Six

Controlling

CHAPTER 15

Keeping People, Plans, and Programs on Track

> ## Learning Objectives

After studying this chapter, you should be able to

- Understand the dual nature—judgmental as well as problem solving and decision making—of the supervisor's role in carrying out the control function.

- Define and recognize a control standard, and explain and evaluate the sources of these standards.

- Discuss the four steps of the control process, be alert to the dangers of overcontrol and undercontrol, and explain the three major types of controls.

- Identify the seven major areas of organizational control that guide supervisory actions and explain the technique of management by exception.

- Discuss employee resistance to controls, explain some of the ways to reduce it, and explain the relationship of management by objectives to the control process.

1 A DUAL ROLE

CONCEPT ▶ Supervisors act both as judges and problem solvers in an organization's control process.

What is the basic purpose of a supervisor's control function?

To keep things in line and to make sure your actions hit their planned targets. In the restrictive sense, you use ***controls*** to make sure that employees are at work on time, that materials aren't wasted or stolen, and that some persons don't exceed their authority. These controls tend to be the don'ts of an organization, the rules and regulations that set limits of acceptable behavior. In the more constructive sense, controls help to guide you and your department to achieve production goals and quality standards.

Controls. Those rules, regulations, standards, and specifications that enable a supervisor to measure performance against a department's goals and to determine causes and to take corrective action when necessary.

How much will control rely on the information system and how much on the supervisor?

That depends. In a large, well-managed organization with surveillance information constantly available, the supervisor may play only a small part in the control system. That's the exception, however. Most supervisors will be an integral part of the control system, and it won't function without their participation, informally as well as formally.

Day-to-day control means that most of the time supervisors should be on their feet—walking around—observing, listening, counting, taking nothing much for granted. In other words, the supervisor's desk is only a part-time workstation. Especially regarding clerical work, much that goes on is not detailed by a master control system. There are daily and seasonal fluctuations in employee workloads, for example. Only an alert and observant supervisor can provide standards and enforce controls for these conditions.

What is control, and what are the supervisor's roles in the control process?

Control always begins with establishment of some *standards*, which are advance expectations for something (e.g., quality of raw materials received). Next, actual conditions, activities, or results are *measured* to determine their real characteristics. In the critical third step, the measurements are *compared* to the standards to see if there is a significant difference between them that warrants some action. In the fourth step, *corrective action* is taken (if necessary). These steps will be explained further, in section 3. Now let's see how two supervisory roles relate to the major steps in the control process (see Table 15-1).

TABLE 15-1

Roles* of the Supervisor in the Control Process

Control Steps	Stages of a Process		
	Inputs	Conversion	Outputs
1. Standards set	P	P	P
2. Measurement	J	J	J
3. Comparison	J	J	J
4. Corrective action	P-S	P-S	P-S

*P = planning; J = judgmental; P-S = problem solving/decision making

Supervisors fulfill two principal functions. In the first role, a supervisor acts somewhat like a *judge*, watching what happens in the department to see whether activities, conditions, and results are occurring as they are supposed to. In the second role, supervisors act as *problem solvers* and *decision makers*. They do so to find out why something is going (or has gone) wrong and then to decide what to do about it.

In their *judgmental role*, supervisors observe what is happening (or has happened) throughout the conversion process and then compare these observations (or measurements) with the standards of what was supposed to happen. These standards are derived from, or may be exactly the same as, the goals that were set during the planning process. Here are two examples of how the judgmental role is handled: In the first, a supervisor in a check-processing unit of a bank expects that all 10 operators will be at their stations within five minutes after the lunch break (a standard she has set for the operators). Now she observes that only eight operators are regularly at their stations when they should be. The supervisor knows that a standard condition is not being met; it is temporarily out of control. In the second example, an assembly supervisor in a video game factory has set a goal of completing 300 assemblies a day. At the end of one day, the production report tells her that only 255 games were assembled. The supervisor knows that her department is 45 assemblies below standard; production is temporarily out of control.

In their *problem-solving* and *decision-making role*, supervisors not only must find out why conditions or results are below standard but also must correct conditions and bring results up to expectations. Here's how the supervisors might handle the two control problems in the last paragraph: In the first case, the supervisor makes certain that the word processing equipment is in good operating order and that there is plenty of work available for all 10 operators. Then she speaks to the latecomers to find out if any extenuating circumstances prevent them from being at their stations immediately following the lunch break. She then outlines the need for promptness to ensure full usage of the equipment and the penalties for being late. Finally, she continues to watch for late arrivals to keep this condition in line with her standard. In the second case, the assembly-line supervisor conducts a similar problem-solving search to find the cause of the missed standard. She might find a number of conditions: faulty assembly tools, shortages of parts, changed specifications, employee absences, lack of training, or failure of one or more employees to apply themselves to their work. Once the true cause has been identified, the supervisor decides what to do and takes the steps needed to correct the problem and bring the conditions and/or results back under control.

Controlling or coaching? Which comes first?

Increasingly today, the two are inseparable. Many employees view control as a negative thing, akin to criticism or scolding, regardless of how necessary it may be. They respond more positively to coaching, wherein the control is offered in the form of constructive advice and suggestions for improvement. At AT&T, for instance, a spokesperson recently said, "While we haven't yet attained our goal of having managers and supervisors less control minded, we are working toward a redefinition of a leader from a controller to a coach." The trend seems clear: To be an effective controller, a supervisor should, as often as is possible, approach control problems as a coach rather than a critic. Why? Because criticism looks backward, whereas coaching looks forward.

In what way are controls linked to plans?

Controls are directly related to the goals that are set during the planning process. In many instances, controls (or control standards) are actually goals that have been sharpened to make them more detailed and specific. Suppose, for example, that you are the supervisor of the commercial office of a telephone company and your office has been given a goal of handling 2,000 service calls for the next month. For a month with 20 working days, that goal can be converted into a control standard of 100 service calls a day. If your office handles 100 calls a day, it has met the target and you need no corrective controls. If, however, your office handles fewer than 100 calls a day, it is performing below the control standard. If this persists, your office may not meet the goal planned for that month. You must take some sort of action to improve this performance, to "bring it into control."

1	T or F	The control process cannot be complete unless the supervisor performs the problem-solving function.	◀ **Quick Test 1**
2	T or F	The first step in control lies in setting appropriate standards.	

2 CONTROL STANDARDS

CONCEPT ▶ Effective controls are based on sound standards.

Exactly what is a control standard?

A control standard, usually called simply a ***standard***, is a specific performance goal that a product, a service, a machine, an individual, or an organization is expected to meet. It is usually expressed numerically: a weight (14.00 ounces), a rate (200 units an hour), or a flat target (4 rejects). The numbers may be expressed in any units, such as inches, gallons, dollars, or percentages.

Many companies also allow a little leeway from standard, called a ***tolerance.*** This implies that the performance will be considered to be in control if it falls within specified boundaries. A product, for instance, may be said to meet its 14.00-ounce standard weight if it weighs no less than 13.75 ounces or no more than 14.25 ounces. The control standard would be stated as 14 ounces, ±0.25 ounce. The tolerance is the ±0.25 ounce.

Where do the control standards come from? Who sets them?

A great many standards are set by the organization itself. They may be set by the accounting department for costs or by the industrial engineering or methods department for wage-incentive (or time) standards. They may be issued by the production-control department for schedule quantities or by the quality-control people for inspection specifications. It is typical for control standards in large organizations to be set by staff specialists. In smaller companies, supervisors may set standards themselves. But even in large companies, the supervisor may have to take an overall, or department, standard and translate it into standards for each employee or operation.

On what information are control standards based?

Standards are based on one, two, or all three of the following sources:

Past performance. Historical records often provide the basis for controls. If your department has been able to process 150 orders with three clerks in the past, this may be accepted as the standard. The weakness of this historical method is that it presumes that processing 150 orders represents good performance. Perhaps 200 would be a better target. This might be especially true if improvements have recently been made in the processing equipment and workplace layouts.

High hopes. In the absence of any other basis, some supervisors ask for the moon. They set unreasonably high standards for their

Standard. The measure, criterion, or basis—usually expressed in numbers and/or other concrete terms—for judging performance of a product or service, machine, individual, or organizational unit.

Tolerance. The permissible deviation, or variance, from standard.

employees to shoot at. Whereas it is a sound practice to set *challenging* goals, standards should always be *attainable* by employees who put forth a reasonable effort. Otherwise, workers will become discouraged, or will rebel, and won't try to meet them.

Systematic analysis. The best standards are set by systematically analyzing what a job entails. This way, the standard is based on careful observation and measurement, as with time studies. At the very least, standards should be based on a consideration of all the factors that affect attainment of the standard, such as tooling, equipment, training of the operator, absence of distractions, and clear-cut instructions and specifications.

Internet CONNECTION

Check out **control standards** on the Internet for more information on cost controls, setting performance standards, and maintaining standards.

3	T or F	Once a standard is set, there should be no deviation from it.	◀ *Quick Test 2*
4	T or F	Past performance is the best basis for setting control standards.	

3 THE CONTROL PROCESS

CONCEPT ▶ The control process involves standard-setting, measurement, comparison, and corrective action.

How is the control process carried out?

The control process follows four sequential steps. The first step, setting performance standards, often takes place "off camera." That is, the standards may have been set before the supervisor arrives on the scene. Other times, it is up to the supervisor to set the necessary performance standards for his or her department. Steps 1, 2, 3, and 4 of the control process were outlined in Table 15-1. Following are the four process steps in order:

1. **Set performance standards.** Standards of quantity, quality, and time spell out (a) what is expected and (b) how much of a deviation can be tolerated if the person or process fails to come up to the mark. For example, the standard for an airline ticket counter might be that no customer should have to wait in line more than five minutes. The standard could then be modified to say that if only 1 out of 10 customers had to wait more than five minutes, no corrective action needs to be taken. The standard would be stated as "waiting time of less than five minutes per customer with a tolerance of 1

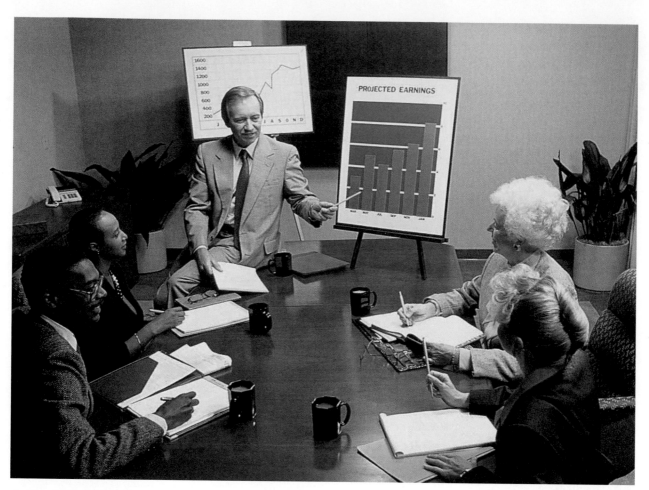

▲ Most companies and employees like to know how they are doing. **How do they know if they are successful or not?**

out of 10 who might have to wait longer." The guideline is that the more specific the standard, the better, especially when it can be stated with numbers as opposed to vague terms such as "good performance" and "minimum waiting time."

2. **Collect data to measure performance.** Accumulation of control data is so routine in most organizations that it is taken for granted. Every time a supervisor or an employee fills out a time card, prepares a production tally, or files a receiving or inspection report, he or she is collecting control data. Whenever a sales ticket is filled out, a sale rung up on a cash register, or a shipping ticket prepared, control data is being recorded—often with a computer-related terminal. Of course, not all information is collected in written form. Much of what a good supervisor uses for control purposes is gathered by observation, by simply watching how well employees carry out their work.

3. **Compare results with standards.** From top manager to first-line supervisor, the control system flashes a warning if there is a gap between what was expected (the standard) and what is taking place or has taken place (the result). If the results are within the

MEASURE PERFORMANCE

■ Many motivational experts have long argued, "The things that get rewarded are the things that get done"—and we agree. But we can also modify this statement to fit this chapter with equal validity: "The things that get *controlled* (measured and analyzed) are the things that get done."

So try to get better results by informing your employees of what you will be monitoring, and then follow through and actually measure their performance in those domains. You'll be surprised how a little bit of emphasis will pay off!

tolerance limits, the supervisor's attention can be turned elsewhere. But if the process exceeds the tolerance limits—if the gap is too big—then action is called for.

4. **Take corrective action.** You must first find the *cause* of the gap (called ***variance***, or deviation from standard). Then you must take action to remove or minimize this cause. If travelers are waiting too long in the airline's ticket line, for example, the supervisor may see that there is an unusually high degree of travel because of a holiday. One possible corrective action is to add another ticket agent. If, however, the supervisor observes that the agents are taking extra-long coffee breaks, this practice will have to be stopped as soon as possible.

Variance. The gap, or deviation, between the actual performance and the standard, or expected performance.

How much control should be applied to a process, and where?

There are two major dangers in designing and applying control systems. *Overcontrol* suggests that standards are too tight, that monitoring takes place too frequently, and that even trivial deviations receive major attention. It is equivalent to oversteering an automobile to avoid an obstacle in the road (and possibly causing a tragic accident as a result). *Undercontrol* is just the opposite; it implies that measurement and adjustment does not take place frequently enough (or in time) to prevent a serious situation from arising. Accordingly, supervisors should look for key places—make-or-break points—in their operations where control makes the most sense. These are often called ***strategic control points*** because a measurement, comparison, and correction takes place early enough in a process before the impact of an error reaches significant proportions.

Strategic control points. Key places where it makes the most sense to measure performance and take corrective action.

The selective locale of observation points can also provide three distinct types of control opportunities. Refer to Table 15-1 as you read their explanations.

Preventive controls. These take place at the input stage before the conversion process begins. Materials are inspected. Machinery undergoes inspection and preventive maintenance. The proper kinds of employees are selected for each assignment and trained

Preventive controls. Controls applied, primarily to an examination of resources, before the conversion process begins.

beforehand. By catching problems before they can affect later operations, preventive controls have the greatest potential for savings.

Concurrent controls. These are controls that take place during the conversion phase of a supervisor's operations. In manufacturing and processing plants, pressures and temperatures are checked and online inspections are made as partially converted products flow through the process. In offices and retail shops, supervisors monitor output and quality of employee performance during the workday. Concurrent controls make their biggest contribution by catching and correcting problems before they get out of hand.

Corrective controls. These controls take place at the output stage after an operation is completed, a product is finished, or a service is delivered. Such "final inspections" occur too late to do much good for what has already happened. Their value is in alerting supervisors to ongoing performance problems to be avoided in the future.

To what extent is control automatic?

Increasingly, operating processes depend upon automatic, or computer-driven, control systems. These try to minimize the human element. We expect *feedback* from a thermostat, for example, to tell the furnace to keep the room warm. In many automobiles, we expect a buzzer to let us know whether a seat belt is not fastened. Many processes in industry are controlled according to the same principle. A worker feeds a sheet of metal into a press, and the machine takes over. A clerk slips a sheet of paper into a copying machine, and the machine automatically reproduces the number of copies the clerk has dialed onto the control mechanism. There will be much more of this in the future.

Computer monitoring of employee performance is the latest in this trend. The computer, by sensing a terminal at which a clerk works—or any mechanism related to an employee's output—automatically counts, times, and records an employee's performance. Such impersonal computer measurement, while viewed as a boon to management, arouses resentment in the minds of many employees. It also raises social issues that are under continuing debate and attack from labor unions and others that believe the practice is an invasion of privacy.

Quick Test 3 ▶			
5	T or F	It is better to undercontrol a process than to overcontrol it.
6	T or F	Concurrent controls focus on the conversion stage of an operation.

4 CONTROL TARGETS

CONCEPT ▶ The primary targets of supervisory control are output, quality, time, materials, equipment, costs, and employee performance.

What specific kinds of organizational controls are most likely to apply to supervisory actions?

These depend largely on the nature of the organization in which the supervisor works. The following controls, however, are most common:

Output controls. These relate to the demand of almost every organization for some standard of output or production. The quantity of production required is often the basis for all other aspects of control. In other words, a supervisor must first make sure that output quantities measure up. Then the supervisor's attention can turn to controls that specify a certain quality or time, for example.

Quality controls. If, in meeting the production standard, a department sacrifices the quality of its work, there will likely be trouble. Quantity and quality go hand in hand. The inspection function is intended to make sure the final product or service lives up to its *specifications*, its quality standards. As a supplement to routine inspections, many companies practice *statistical quality control*, a way of predicting quality deviations in advance so that a supervisor can take corrective action before a product is spoiled. (See Chapter 17 for more on quality controls.)

Time controls. Almost every organization must also meet certain deadlines or live within time constraints. A product must be shipped on a certain date. A service must be performed on an agreed-on day. A project must be completed as scheduled. Such time standards point up the fact that it is not enough just to get the job done if it isn't finished on time.

Material controls. These are related to both quality and quantity standards. A company may wish to limit the amount of raw or finished materials it keeps on hand; thus, it may exercise *inventory controls*. Or an apparel firm, for instance, may wish to make sure that the maximum number of skirts is cut out of a bolt of cloth so that a minimum amount of cloth is wasted—*a material-yield standard*.

Equipment controls. These include those that the manufacturer builds into the machinery and also those that are imposed upon the operator to protect the equipment or the process. The most common controls are for speed, pressure, temperature, and loads.

Did You Know ?

Using Analytical Tools

■ Many organizations—including paper mills, mining companies, and utilities—are training their supervisors to become proficient at using a wide array of analytical tools for control purposes. These tools include fishbone diagrams (for assessing cause-effect relationships), flow charts (for examining a desired or actual sequence of events), scatter diagrams (for visually seeing the correlation between two variables), and control charts (for determining whether a process is operating within an acceptable range). Are you familiar with these?

Specification. A collection of standardized dimensions and characteristics pertaining to a product, process, or service.

Cost controls. Another crunch in exercising controls involves costs. A supervisor may meet the quantity and quality standards, but if in so doing the department has been overstaffed or has been working overtime, it probably won't meet its cost standard.

Employee performance controls. These cover a wide spectrum and are often inseparable from all the above controls. The difference is that employee performance controls focus on individuals or groups of employees, rather than on a department, a machine, or a process. Such controls may be concerned with employee absences, tardiness, and accidents as well as with performance directly related to the quantity or quality of the employees' work.

Where do budgets fit into this picture?

You'll have an opportunity to learn about these in greater detail in Chapter 16. For the moment, it is enough to say that many controls and control standards are often incorporated in a single control document—a budget. A *budget* is typically cost- or expense-related, since it is usually prepared by an accounting or finance department. The budget is not limited to cost items, however. It may also include allowable items for quantities of materials to be used and units of product or service to be produced, as well as any other quantifiable activity or condition an organization may wish to control.

Must supervisors spend all their time controlling?

It would appear that way. But by using a simple principle called management by exception, time taken by a supervisor for control activities can be held to a reasonable level. *Management by exception* is a form of delegation in which the supervisor lets things run as they are as long as they fall within prescribed (control) limits of performance. When they get out of line, the supervisor steps in and takes corrective action.

Figure 15-1 shows how a supervisor can use the management by exception principle as a guideline for delegating much of the control work to subordinates.

Let's look at the example in Figure 15-1, a broiler chef in a fast-food restaurant. The supervisor says that the chef should expect to broil between 180 and 200 hamburgers an hour. This is control zone 1. As long as results fall within the prescribed limits, the chef is completely in charge.

If the requests for hamburgers, however, fall below 180 but above 150, the chef keeps the grill hot but puts fewer hamburgers into the ready position; or, if requests build up to 225, the chef moves more hamburgers to the completed stage. This is zone 2. The chef takes this action without first checking with the supervisor but tells the supervisor what has been done.

If business falls below 150 but is more than 100 hamburgers an hour, the chef may ask the supervisor whether the grill can be turned off for a

---

Budget. A planning, reporting, and control document that combines standards for various departmental operating conditions with allocations for operating expenses.

Management by exception. A principle of control that enables a supervisor to delegate corrective action to a subordinate as long as the variances in performance are within specified ranges.

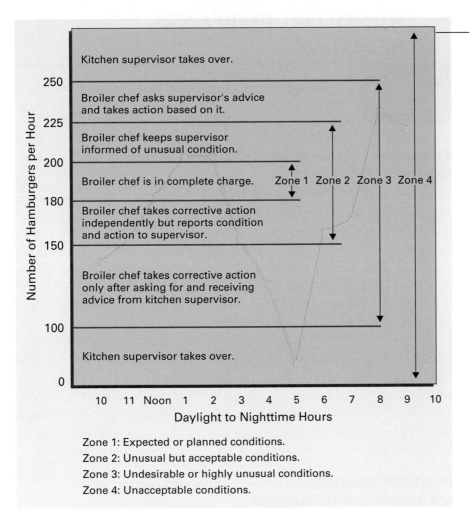

♦ **FIGURE 15-1**

Use of management by exception chart for controlling the operation of a hamburger grill. **When do the exception conditions occur?**

Zone 1: Expected or planned conditions.
Zone 2: Unusual but acceptable conditions.
Zone 3: Undesirable or highly unusual conditions.
Zone 4: Unacceptable conditions.

while; or, if the requests build up to 250 an hour, the chef may ask if one of the counter clerks can help. This is zone 3.

If conditions now move to either extreme—hamburger requests drop below 100 or exceed 250, the chef calls this to the supervisor's attention. This is zone 4. The supervisor may in the first instance (below 100) decide to shut down the grill, or in the second instance (above 250) decide to start up an auxiliary grill.

◀ *Quick Test 4*

7	T or F	The first kind of control a supervisor should use relates to outputs.
8	T or F	In a management by exception system, supervisors only monitor and react to the very best levels of performance—those that are truly exceptional.

HANDLING EMPLOYEE RESISTANCE

5

The human element in the control process: How important is it?

It is probably the most critical element. Regardless of management's efforts to automate the control system, human activities remain the vital factors. Supervisors provide the eyes and ears for the system. They must continually find ways to make sure that employees meet (or exceed) job standards. Especially sensitive is performance relating to (a) attendance, (b) speed and care in feeding or servicing of automatic operations, and (c) relationships with other departments and with customers or client organizations.

As noted earlier, organizations are moving toward greater employee participation in decision making. As this occurs, it becomes essential that a supervisor—through observation—determine which employees can work with little supervision (or control) and which ones cannot. This should determine the degree of personal control a supervisor should exert in each particular case. It is a fact of life that many employees will resist control from their supervisors, yet willingly provide self-control of their own.

What key characteristics of the control process are important to include?

We've already talked about a couple of these: acceptance by the people being controlled and identification of strategic control points. But there are several others that ideally should be considered, too. They include:

- **Timeliness.** Since controls are designed to identify problems in time for them to be fixed before too much damage is done, the best control systems provide key information to supervisors as soon as possible.
- **Accuracy.** In many processes there is little room for error, and therefore the data reported must be trustworthy or the resulting actions could even make matters worse.
- **Conciseness.** Too much information can overwhelm a supervisor. Usually, the best data are brief and easily understood, with additional information readily available if more analysis is necessary.
- **Beneficial in comparison to cost.** All controls cost money, directly or indirectly. Therefore, don't measure more often than necessary or you'll spend all your time controlling and not enough on the other important tasks you have facing you.

Did You Know ?

Workforce Statistics

■ In 2001, the first of 76 million members of the Baby Boom generation reached early retirement at age of 55.

By 2005, median age of U.S. workforce will be 40.6 years.

By 2006, the number of workers ages 45 to 54 will increase more than 50 percent . . . ages 25 to 34 will decline by 9 percent.

Source: "Boomers put new wrinkle in retirement," *Dallas Morning News,* December 29, 1999.

Many supervisors, understandably, dislike those aspects of the control process that require a confrontation with an employee. "It may remind you uncomfortably," says W. Steven Brown, chairman of the Fortune Group, an Atlanta-based consulting group, "of being called on the carpet by your father, the principal, or your own raging boss." Brown advises that you forget these memories. "Constructive confrontation is not a matter of angry accusations or character assassination," he says. "Your object here is not to punish or to humiliate offenders, but to get them back on the track. Don't be wishy-washy or vague, however. The criticism must be clear and direct."

To exert control effectively, Brown suggests using this confrontational, but empathetic, approach:

1. State the specific behavior you have observed or the performance that is not acceptable.
2. Express how you feel about it.
3. Explain the problems that this nonconformance to standards has created—for the individual, the supervisor, and the department.
4. Listen to the employee's explanation.
5. Together, evaluate the situation and explore ways to correct the behavior.
6. Agree on a plan for bringing the employee's performance back within the standard.

Brown concludes, "If you're clear and considerate in confronting problem behavior, you don't risk damaging your relationships with your employees."

Source: Adapted from "Looking the Other Way," by W. Steven Brown, *Manage*, April 1993, p. 10.

How can you soften employee resistance to controls?

Many people do not like to be "controlled." They don't like to be told what to do, and they feel boxed in when faced with specific standards. Few persons like to be criticized or corrected. Yet criticism or correction is what control often comes down to. When correction means discipline or termination (see Chapter 13), controls can seem very harsh indeed. For this reason, a supervisor should be realistic about controls. Controls can have a very negative effect on employees, to say nothing of what they may do to the supervisor.

The negative aspects of controls, however, can be minimized. Supervisors should consider the following more positive approaches.

Emphasize the value of controls to employees. Standards make it possible to provide employees with feedback that tells them whether they are doing well or not. Standards actually minimize the need for the supervisor to interfere and often allow the employee to choose a way of doing the job as long as standards are met. It's like telling the employee, "You do the job, and I will stay out of your hair."

Avoid arbitrary or punitive standards. Employees respond better to standards that can be justified by past records that support the standards. "Our records show that 150 a day is a standard that other operators have consistently met." Standards based on analysis, especially time studies, are even more acceptable. "Let's time this job for an hour or two so that we can be sure the standard is

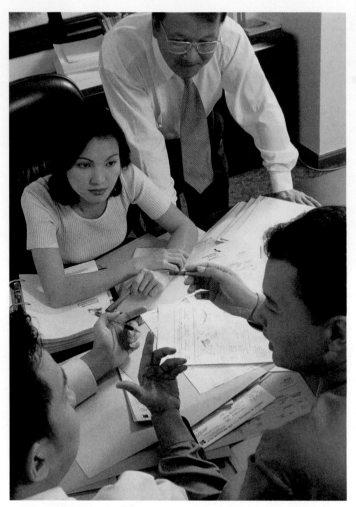

▲ Management by Objectives requires that managers and subordinates develop goals together. **What is the advantage in doing so?**

reasonable." Compare this with, "We'll have to step up our production rate to 175 units each day."

Be specific: Use numbers if possible. Avoid such expressions as "improve quality" and "show us better attendance." Instead, use numbers that set specific targets, such as "fewer than two days' absence in the next six months" or "decrease your error percentage from 7 out of 100 to 3 out of 100."

Aim for improvement rather than punishment. Capitalize on instances of missed standards to try to help employees learn how to improve their work. "Your output was below standard again last month. Perhaps you and I ought to start over to see what is preventing you from meeting standards. There may be something I haven't shown you about this particular operation."

Make the penalty for nonconformance absolutely clear. A supervisor must balance rewards with punishment. Most employees respond to positive motivation. Some do not. All employees, however, good and poor alike, want to know what the "or else" is about their jobs. The guiding rule is to hold off punishment if you can, but to make it clear to everyone that standards must be met. Specify in advance what the penalty will be for those who don't meet them.

Avoid threats that you can't or won't back up. If you must discipline an employee for failing to meet a quota or a standard of workmanship, be specific about the nature and timing of the discipline. "If you don't get your production up to 150 a day by the first of April, I will recommend that you be laid off for good." Don't say, "If you don't shape up soon, your head will be in a noose." If you do make the specific threat, it is good to make certain in advance that the company will help you make it stick.

Be consistent in the application of controls. If you have set standards that apply to the work of several employees, it should go without saying that you will be expected to make everyone measure up to them. If you do feel that exceptions can be made, be prepared to defend that position. In the main, however, standards should be the same for everyone doing the same work. Similarly, rewards and punishment should be the same for all those who meet or fail to meet these standards.

What about encouraging self-control?

Self-control is beautiful for those who can exert it. Douglas McGregor, a notable pioneer in human relations research, insisted that many people need only to be given the targets for their work—the standards. After that, he said, they wish to be left alone and to be judged on the basis of their results in meeting or not meeting these targets. Many employees will, McGregor said, provide their own control and do not need a supervisor to threaten them or cajole them into meeting standards.

Our advice is to give an employee the benefit of the doubt. Give a free hand to those who take charge of themselves. Keep the rein on those who soon show that they need, or expect, the control to come from the supervisor.

When do management goals become control standards?

Very often, as shown when we discussed the link between planning and controlling. More specifically, however, many companies convert their organizational goals into control programs by using a system of management by objectives. ***Management by Objectives (MBO)*** is a planning and control process that provides managers at each organizational control point with a set of goals, or standards, to be attained. The process is usually repeated every 6 to 12 months. These MBO goals are similar to the supervisory performance goals listed in Table 4-1. It is presumed that if all supervisors reach their goals, the organization will also reach its goals. In companies where MBO is practiced to its full extent, the supervisors' goals literally become the standards of performance that must be met. The assumption is that the supervisors are capable of, and will exert, their own controls in striving to meet these objectives. The MBO system also presumes that the supervisors have been given enough freedom of action to meet these goals with the allocated resources. In essence, MBO is simply a formalization at managerial levels of the principle of self-control. Typically, the goals in MBO are jointly set by the boss and the subordinate, with the subordinate taking the leading role.

Management by Objectives (MBO). A planning and control technique in which a supervisor and his or her immediate superior agree on goals to be attained and standards to be maintained.

◀ *Quick Test 5*

9	T or F	There is little a supervisor can do to counteract employee resistance to controls .
10	T or F	Self-control is not always appropriate for all employees to engage in.

KEY CONCEPTS TO REMEMBER

1. **A Dual Role.** The control function is inseparably linked to planning, in that planning goals are converted to control standards. Good control requires that a supervisor keep continual track of progress toward departmental goals so that corrective action can be taken as soon as possible. In exercising control, supervisors (a) apply judgment in determining whether deviations from standard are significant and (b) engage in problem solving and decision making when taking corrective action.

2. **Control Standards.** Good controls are based upon reliable, attainable standards of performance. The best standards are those that are based on systematic analysis.

3. **The Control Process.** The control process entails four steps, usually taken in sequence: (a) setting standards, (b) measuring performance, (c) comparing performance with standards, and (d) taking corrective action. To avoid over-controlling, supervisors should place controls selectively at key, make-or-break points in the process. Preventive controls are those exerted before the conversion process begins; concurrent controls take place while operations are under way; and corrective controls occur after the conversion process is completed.

4. **Control Targets.** The most frequently used organizational controls are targeted at output, quality, time, materials, costs or budgets, and employee performance. Supervisors must take advantage of the management by exception principle to delegate some of the decisions regarding corrective controls to qualified employees.

5. **Handling Employee Resistance.** The human factor in the controlling process is a vital one. Key characteristics of good control systems include acceptance, strategic control points, timeliness, accuracy, conciseness, and cost-benefit. While employee resistance to controls is a very natural human reaction, too much of it will disrupt the control system. For this reason, if for no other, controls should (a) be fair, (b) be specific and numerical, (c) motivate rather than coerce, (d) be consistently applied, and (e) encourage the greatest degree of self-control possible. Management by objectives (MBO) is a method of control that higher management sometimes extends to supervisors to give *them* an opportunity for exercising the greatest degree of self-discipline in controlling their own work.

READING COMPREHENSION

1. What is the ultimate purpose of the control process?
2. Explain the difference between a supervisor's judgmental role in organizational control, and his or her problem-solving and decision-making role.
3. Which do you think is better: to over-control or undercontrol a process?
4. Of the three chief ways of setting standards, which is the best? Why? What's likely to be wrong with the other two?
5. If a supervisor has been given the standards for her or his department, what three other steps in the control process will she or he still have to deal with?

6. Tammy relies mainly upon checking merchandise just before it is shipped from her department. What kind of control is she relying on? What are the dangers in waiting until then to exercise control?

7. Briefly describe the seven areas of organizational control that warrant the most supervisory attention.

8. How are management by exception and control-standard tolerances related?

9. How should supervisors approach the issue of self-control for their employees?

10. What technique, involving self-control or self-discipline, is sometimes made available to supervisors for controlling their own performances?

APPLICATION

Self-Assessment

How good are your controlling skills?

Read the following statements carefully. Circle the number on the response scale that most closely reflects the degree to which each statement accurately describes you. Add up your total points and prepare a brief action plan for self-improvement. Be ready to report your score for tabulation across the entire group.

		Good Description									Poor Description
1.	I feel equally comfortable playing either the judgmental or problem-solving roles in the control process.	10	9	8	7	6	5	4	3	2	1
2.	I consciously and systematically follow the four-step model of control.	10	9	8	7	6	5	4	3	2	1
3.	I strive to balance my controlling actions between criticism and coaching.	10	9	8	7	6	5	4	3	2	1
4.	I tell each employee what the desired standard is for each major task, and I make this as specific as possible.	10	9	8	7	6	5	4	3	2	1
5.	I make sure that employees know how much tolerance is allowed around the standards I set.	10	9	8	7	6	5	4	3	2	1
6.	I regularly check with my employees to make sure that I am neither undercontrolling nor overcontrolling them.	10	9	8	7	6	5	4	3	2	1
7.	I do *not* place all my emphasis on corrective controls; I pay considerable attention to using preventive and concurrent controls also.	10	9	8	7	6	5	4	3	2	1

	Good Description									Poor Description
8. I make sure that my employees are involved in the control process by practicing management by exception with them.	10	9	8	7	6	5	4	3	2	1
9. I carefully monitor my employees' resistance to controls and follow several of the guidelines to minimize their negative effects.	10	9	8	7	6	5	4	3	2	1
10. I seek to make the control feedback I give timely, accurate, and concise.	10	9	8	7	6	5	4	3	2	1

Scoring and Interpretation

SCORING

Add up your total points for the 10 questions. Record that number here, and report it when it is requested. _____

INTERPRETATION

81 to 100 points. You seem to have a basic set of controlling skills.

61 to 80 points. Take a close look at some of your controlling skills (those with lower self-assessments) and discuss them with a manager to see if they need improvement.

Below 60 points. Some of your skills may be substantially inconsistent with effective controlling practices and could be detrimental to your success as a supervisor.

Identify your three lowest scores, and write the question numbers here: _____, _____, _____.

ACTION

Write a brief paragraph detailing an action plan for how you might sharpen each of these skills. Then pay particularly close attention to the related material in the chapter as you review the relevant sections there.

Skill Development

▶ *Self-Control Skills*

The opportunity—and the need—to engage in control is everywhere, both at work and in our personal lives. And since many of us tend to resist being controlled by others, we need to practice and demonstrate our self-control skills. When we can provide strong evidence of our capacity for self-control, others around us will see that they can practice management by exception with greater confidence. As a result, both parties will feel more comfortable.

Select some area of your life in which you would like to make a change. (This might include weight reduction, smoking cessation, cursing less, exercising more, etc.) Follow the control model's four steps, and lay out a plan for engaging in self-control that incorporates many of the guidelines for effective control. (To prepare yourself, you will likely wish to review the text's discussion on control, scan the Internet for relevant guidelines, and consult with colleagues and staff persons in the human resources department for their advice.)

ACTION

Invite another person to monitor your attempt at self-control across the next several weeks or months, and rate you on a 10-point scale (1 = poor, 10 = great) on each of the following dimensions:

1. Degree to which you set a specific standard (goal) for yourself.
2. Degree to which you allowed exceptions for variation within control limits.
3. Degree to which you regularly measured your own behavior and progress.
4. Degree to which you reacted only to major deviations from the standard.
5. Degree to which you gave constructive feedback to yourself.
6. Degree to which you demonstrated both judging and problem-solving roles.
7. Degree to which you took responsibility for your success and failure.
8. Degree to which you stuck to the original standard despite possible setbacks.
9. Degree to which you gave yourself rewards for short-term progress.
10. Degree to which you demonstrated independent thought and action.

Role Play

Implementing Controls ◀

Assume that you are part of a management team that is in charge of designing and implementing a control system. Your organization is just about to begin hiring employees who will apply their skills to the assembly of key components for a computer manufacturer. These components must conform to the customer's specifications for quality and performance. Anne-Marie, the company's CEO, has asked two of the team members to take different sides of a "mini-debate" so as to raise all relevant issues prior to setting up a control system.

TOMAS. You have been asked to argue for *more* and *tighter* controls. Pull together all the major arguments you can as to why this is appropriate and useful, and prepare to present them in front of your boss.

VANG. You have been asked to argue for *less* and *looser* controls. Pull together all the major arguments you can as to why this is appropriate and useful, and prepare to present them in front of your boss.

ANNE-MARIE. You will soon listen to two sets of arguments (one each from Tomas and Vang), designed to bring up key issues regarding the control system you will implement in the near future. Listen to both sides and be prepared to provide feedback to both presenters regarding the effectiveness of their arguments. Then lead a brief discussion in which the three of you reach a resolution regarding the degree of control to implement in your new assembly operations.

For Discussion

1. What arguments were raised on each side?
2. Which ones were the most important in deciding the outcome?
3. What makes this a difficult decision to resolve?
4. How might the final decision be different in a different company or industry?

CASES FOR ANALYSIS

Case 45

The Overworked Copying Machine

Bill Blake was the first to admit it. Use of the copying machine at the Regional Water Board, where he was office manager, had gotten out of control. Employees were indiscriminately making copies of everything, not only of official documents but also of personal items. This put Bill's office way over its paper budget. Not unexpectedly, word came down from state headquarters to "get things under control."

Bill's first effort was to post a notice over the copying machine, reminding employees that the machine could be used only for official business. At the end of the month, however, the number of copies run was still as high as ever.

Bill fumed over this development. He called his employees together and read the riot act to them. "The next person I find using that machine to copy personal items will be suspended on the spot," he threatened. Only a day later, Bill saw two employees laughing as they came away from the copier. When he asked to see what they had been copying, they held out a dozen or so sheets of paper. They had been copying a slightly off-color limerick that someone in the office had typed. "Aw, Bill," one said, "we were just having a little fun. After all, what's a few sheets of paper to the government? Why, only last week, we ran off dozens of copies of a report that the State Board later canceled."

"That's not the point," said Bill. "In the future, nothing personal goes on that copying machine. Do you hear me?"

"We hear you," said the employees.

At the end of the month, however, the situation had not improved. So Bill decided to take firmer action. He posted a log sheet next to the copier. It instructed employees to record their names and the date, time, number of copies, and purpose each time the machine was used. "Anyone I find cheating on this new system *goes!*" Bill announced.

Two weeks later, Bill checked paper usage and found that the rate of consumption had dropped only a fraction. This month, the regional office would again exceed its budget.

That did it! Bill got the key to the copying machine and locked it. Next, he posted a sign over the machine that read: "From this time forward, anyone who wishes to use the copying machine must fill out a request form and present it to me. The individual will also show me exactly what has been run off when the key is returned."

With this measure, Bill thought he had gained control of the situation. However, Bill now found that he was interrupted several times a day to hand out the key and to check paper usage when the key was returned.

◀ *Analysis*

If you were Bill, which of the following actions would you select to attain a more effective form of control? Rank the alternatives on a scale from 1 (most preferable) to 5 (least preferable). You may add another alternative, if you wish. Be prepared to justify your ranking.

_____ **a.** Explain to State Headquarters that it costs more to exert control over copier usage than the extra paper is worth.

_____ **b.** Post the monthly paper usage next to the machine. Ask one employee to check each day's usage and post the cumulative totals daily. Explain that when the budget total is reached, the machine will be inoperative until the beginning of the next month.

_____ **c.** Meet with employees to explain the budget and the resulting control problem. Ask for their ideas about control procedures that might work. Try to follow their suggestions.

_____ **d.** Call your employees together and tell them that the copy machine problem has gotten ridiculous. You have been too soft so far. You are going to unlock the machine and use the original log-sheet method. From now on, however, you will act on your threat to suspend anyone using the machine for personal items.

_____ **e.** By means of a log sheet, analyze usage during the next month. On the basis of what you find, set up an allotment system for the various legitimate usages needed for official work. If there is too little paper in the budget, then ask State Headquarters to increase the paper allowance.

Case 46

Seven Situations Under Control

Supervisors are especially concerned with the seven areas, or types, of organizational control presented in the alphabetic list that follows the numbered list. The numbered list contains examples of control situations related to these areas.

Analysis ▶

Your assignment is to match the correct organizational control (a–g) with each of the numbered situations (1–7). Next to each number on the list below, write the letter of the appropriate organizational control. (You may decide that some examples illustrate more than one type of organizational control. If so, enter more than one letter for that numbered item, but be prepared to justify your choices.)

The Situations

_____ **1.** At Metro City, the city purchasing director instructs the city's department supervisors that they should not order new supplies of computer paper until the supply level in their department drops below five boxes.

_____ **2.** At Crystal Soft Drinks Co., the bottling supervisor sets a production quota of 5,000 bottles each day for the capping machine operator.

_____ **3.** At the Seaside Warehouse, employees must "keyboard" into a data recorder the starting and ending times for each order pulled.

_____ **4.** At JR's Chicken-in-the-Rough fast-food restaurant, the counter help has been told that the fried potato servings should weigh between eight and nine ounces each and should be discarded if the fries have been on the holding rack for more than a half hour.

_____ **5.** At Handy Home Builders, construction workers who do not intend, for any reason, to report to work on a given day must notify the building-site office by 8:00 A.M.

_____ **6.** At WMQQ, a local radio station, the station manager states as policy that travel expenses cannot exceed $500 per month for each news person.

_____ **7.** At Western Utilities, power plant operators are advised to hold steam-turbine temperatures between 220 and 235 degrees F.

The Kinds of Organizational Control Exercised

a. Output, or quantity, controls
b. Quality controls
c. Time controls
d. Cost, or expense, controls
e. Material controls
f. Equipment controls
g. Employee performance controls

Case 47

The Wayward Bus Line

Things had gotten out of hand lately for Manuela M., the bus dispatching supervisor at the Hometown Transit Authority. Drivers were arriving late for their shifts. Buses were not running on time. There was an inordinate number of breakdowns on the road, which required that the maintenance department send out special buses to continue the route and to tow the disabled bus back to the dispatching shed. There were also frequent reports of buses not following their specified routes and of short-cutting scheduled stops on their return trips. On the other hand, many drivers who started their trips on time returned to the garage late from their runs, with unsubstantiated excuses. Nevertheless, they still had to be paid the extra monies that their union contract guaranteed them. In a disturbing number of cases, too, a driver's cash receipts did not conform to the normal expectation of fare collections for a scheduled run.

Manuela had been puzzling for some time over what to do about this deteriorating performance, when the situation was brought to a head by a call from the transit commissioner. "The mayor and I have been receiving far too many complaints from bus riders this year. The complaints include just about everything, including the rudeness of our drivers, being deliberately passed by at a bus stop, and unreliable timetables. For my part, I've reviewed the expense reports for the last few months, and your department is way over budget, especially for overtime. Fare collections are down, too.

"I know that you can't be responsible for everything that's happened, but I do want you to come up with a plan that can put a stop to these irregularities."

"I'll do my best," said Manuela.

Analysis

1. What can you suggest in the way of control measures that would help Manuela to correct these conditions? On a separate sheet of paper, write the following headings: (a) preventive controls, (b) concurrent controls, and (c) corrective controls. Under each heading, enter the problems or conditions in the case that might be solved best by the particular type of control. Then, for each problem or condition, write the ideas you have for correcting it.

2. Discuss the problems Manuela may encounter when instituting these controls and what she might do to overcome these problems.

Answers to Quick Tests

Quick Test 1	Quick Test 2	Quick Test 3
1. T	3. F	5. F
2. T	4. F	6. T

Quick Test 4	Quick Test 5	
7. T	9. F	
8. F	10. T	

Controlling Costs and Budgets

Learning Objectives

After studying this chapter, you should be able to

- Discuss the importance of record keeping and differentiate among unit costs, standard costs, and budgeted costs.

- Explain the purpose of budgets in cost control, describe the cost-variance report, calculate unit costs, and explain the way in which flexible budgets are designed.

- Understand how to select cost targets, assign priorities to them, and recognize a belt-tightening program.

- Identify and evaluate the principal sources of cost improvement ideas, list some positive approaches, and explain why some cost improvement suggestions might be rejected.

- Discuss the reasons for employee resistance to cost reduction programs and describe several ways for securing workers' support and cooperation.

1 ACCOUNTING RECORDS

CONCEPT ▶ Effective cost control begins with accurate records of costs as they occur and an understanding of the accounting reports that document them.

Which comes first: cost control or cost reduction?

Pressure to hold costs within prescribed limits, cost control, often comes first in the life of a supervisor. This is closely followed by calls to reduce (or "improve") existing costs. Note that the term *cost improvement* is often used to soften the implication of the real objective: *cost reduction*.

How important is record keeping to cost control?

Unless you have furnished to you—or you keep—accurate and up-to-date records, controlling costs is next to impossible. When you say "control," it's the same as saying "keep within acceptable limits." If you don't know what the limits are and how well you're holding costs within those limits, you can't very well take any meaningful action.

What must you know about accounting?

You don't have to know double-entry bookkeeping to understand cost figures. But you should make a point of understanding the accounting terms your company uses. Don't be afraid of appearing dense: You're a supervisor, not an auditor. Ask questions, if need be, until meanings are clear.

There are three basic measures of cost, however, that accountants use for their own cost control. You are very likely to encounter all three:

1. ***Unit costs.*** These are the costs, partial or total, which a department (or the company as a whole) accumulates per unit of product or service processed or produced. Unit costs can be expressed in dollars and cents per unit, per pound, per gallon, per ton, per sales call, per order, per dollar of billing, per insurance policy issued, and so on.

2. ***Standard costs.*** These are unit costs that have been set down as "allowable" costs—for materials, for direct and indirect labor, for manufacturing, for marketing, for administration, and the like. As such, these costs become the standards toward which a supervisor is expected to strive and against which cost performance is judged as either good or bad.

3. ***Budgeted costs.*** These are the cost guidelines (or targets) agreed to by supervisors and managers at the beginning of an accounting period. The ***budget*** is a plan, or forecast, of foreseen and allowable expenses for a company's operation over a specified period

---

Unit cost. The cost of producing a single product or unit; measure of output of a product or service.

Standard costs. The normal, or expected, costs of an operation, product, or service (usually including labor, materials, and overhead charges) computed on the basis of past performance, estimates, or work measurement.

Budgeted costs. Costs that are stipulated as acceptable in a particular budget for a specific accounting period.

Budget. A plan, or forecast, especially of expenses that are allowable in the operation of a department.

of time. It provides a supervisor with a figure for each item of expense that can be charged to the operation during that period. A supervisor may be able to control some of these figures, while others may be apportioned to her or him. The budgeted figures may cover only a few items, or they may be presented in considerable detail. In either case, the expectation is that the supervisor will live within, or not exceed, the budget. The budget may be called either an expense budget or an operating budget.

Costs are often further categorized by accountants: (a) **direct costs** are those that can be identified as materials entering the product or directly associated with manufacturing a product or with producing a service; (b) **indirect costs** are those expenses that are necessary in producing a product but do not contribute directly to its value, such as heat, rent, insurance, and so forth; (c) **variable costs** are those that tend to vary (directly or indirectly) according to the volume of goods produced, services rendered, and/or sales generated.

Direct costs. Variable costs that can be clearly identified as adding value directly to the goods produced or services rendered.

Indirect costs. Variable costs that are essential to the production of goods or rendering of services but which do not clearly add value to them, or do not do so in an easily measurable way.

Variable costs. Costs that tend to vary (directly or indirectly) according to the volume of goods produced, services rendered, and/or sales generated.

*Super*SCOPE ▷ Where Do Cost Data Come From?

Sometimes it seems that the records of costs and expenses arise from some mysterious source. Actually, data are gathered from a number of sources, the most common of which follow:

Work-order forms are used to request and authorize some sort of internal work such as that performed by a maintenance or other service department. The actual charges against the work order, however, come from employee time sheets, material requisitioned from internal stock rooms, and purchase orders.

Material requisitions are used to withdraw materials and supplies from internal stock or store rooms. When the order is filled, a copy is sent to accounting, which translates the number of units withdrawn into dollars and charges the appropriate cost center (such as the supervisor's department) or job at that center.

Purchase orders contain cost data related to materials purchased from an outside supplier for use at a particular cost center, either as "consumable" supplies or to be included in the finished product.

Time cards and time sheets gather the time employees spend at work, often with a breakdown of the time spent on a particular job. For many salaried employees—especially supervisors, upper-level managers, and some kinds of professionals—100 percent of their time may be automatically charged to a cost center by the accounting department without additional paperwork.

Travel expense sheets gather data to verify travel, lodging, meal, and related expenses while company employees are at work away from their regular duty station. These expenses will be charged back to a particular cost center or job.

Prorated costs, which may include charges for a variety of utilities, supplies, and services, are collected for the entire enterprise and then apportioned to a cost center based upon some preconceived formula.

The accounting department consolidates (often through a data processing system) all the expenses to be charged to a particular job or cost center, compares these on an item-by-item (line-item) basis, and prepares the kind of summary report shown in Table 16-1.

TABLE 16-1

Cost-Variance Report

Department: *Forms Control*		Location: *Arlington*		Month: *July*
No. of units scheduled to be processed		15,000		
No. of units actually processed		13,000		
Output variance		–2,000		

Line-Item Account Titles	Budgeted	Actual	Variance*
Salaries	$16,750	$15,050	$–1,700
Fringe benefits	3,400	3,010	– 390
Supplies	1,750	1,450	– 300
Telephone	1,650	1,400	– 250
Equipment leases	2,090	2,090	0
Purchased services			
Postal, UPS, FedEx	1,070	850	– 220
Cleaning services	450	450	0
Temporary help	240	1,450	+1,210
Recruiting ads	0	350	+ 350
Occupancy charges	2,500	2,500	0
Other	100	0	– 100
Total Controllable Budget	$30,000	$28,600	$–1,400

* + means over budget; – means under budget

② BUDGETED COSTS

CONCEPT ▶ Budgets establish departmental cost standards and targets and are used to monitor cost performance.

How do budgets fit into the cost control picture?

Budgetary controls are very similar to cost controls and standards. Typically, the accounting or financial department provides a supervisor with a list of allowable expenses for the month. These are based on the expectation of a certain output, or "throughput," say, 4,000 units of production. These allowable expenses become the department's cost standards to be met for the month. At the end of the month, the accounting department may issue the supervisor a ***cost-variance report*** (Table 16-1). This tells whether the department has met its standards, exceeded them, or fallen below them. Note that in Table 16-1 the department was under budget by $1,400. Closer examination of the figures, however, shows that Temporary help was over budget by $1,210 and Recruiting ads by $350. Furthermore, there is an output variance, shown on the third line of the table, of 2,000 units. The supervisor will be expected to explain all the significant variances, either over or under, and decide what will be done to bring these back into line next month. If a certain account (or line item) were to persist for long under budget, however, the accounting department might develop a new standard for those expenses and allow the supervisor less money for them in the future.

Some account items shown in Table 16-1 are, of course, largely beyond the supervisor's control, such as Equipment leases, Cleaning services, and Occupancy charges.

Supervisors and others in management use the cost variance to guide cost control actions. In effect, the report says to a supervisor: "When your costs are under or equal to budget, they are in control. When your costs are over budget, you must exert control to bring them back into line."

Will unit costs vary in relation to how much work a department is doing?

Yes. Total costs, studied alone, may be misleading. Look again at Table 16-1. Total costs are $1,400 under budget. Is that really good? Probably not. Since department output dropped from a scheduled 15,000 units to 13,000 units, only a comparison of unit costs will tell the whole story. Here's how that's done:

Budgeted:
$30,000 ÷ 15,000 units = $2.00 per unit processed

Actual:
$28,600 ÷ 13,000 units = $2.20 per unit processed

This means that unit costs were $0.20 (or 10 percent) over budget. The supervisor must explain this variance. Here's what happened:

A veteran employee quit just before the first of the month. This lowered salary expenses by $1,700 and fringe benefits by $390. The supervisor advertised for a replacement, which sent recruiting expenses up by $350, but to no avail. By the middle of the month, a temporary was hired, causing this account to go $1,210 over budget. The combination of the loss of a skilled employee and the inexperience of the temporary inevitably led to the 2,000-unit drop in output. On the other hand, as output fell, associated expenses also fell: $300 in supplies, $250 for telephone, and $220 in postal charges.

Cost-variance report.
A listing of allowable expenses compared with the actual expenses incurred.

Did You Know ?

Replacement Costs Are High

■ According to independent consulting firms (Hewitt Associates and Saratoga Institute) the cost of replacing an employee is 1 to 2.5 times the salary of their position. The more sophisticated the job, the higher the costs.

Source: "Sanity, Inc.," in *Fast Company*, January 1999, No. 21, p. 84.

Given these circumstances, the supervisor's control efforts will be on (a) finding and training a full-time replacement so as to bring (b) output up to budget and (c) unit costs back to normal. And, as that happens, supplies, telephone, and postal charges are expected to return to normal.

Is that where flexible budgets come in?

Flexible budget. A budget that presents several options based on possible variations in output levels.

More or less. Many expense budgets are presented as a set of budgets in order to anticipate the impact of possible changes in output levels. Such a *flexible budget* may offer several budget options to make allowances for variations in justifiable expenses for varying levels of output. If, for example, a department is scheduled to produce 2,000 tons of materials during the budget period, the allowance for direct labor may be pegged at $10,000. If the production schedule is to be raised to 2,500 tons, the budget may allow $12,500 for direct labor.

TABLE 16-2

Flexible Budget

Account Title	Monthly Allowances*			
	3,500 tons	**4,000 tons**	**4,500 tons**	**5,000 tons**
Direct labor	$ 7,000	$ 8,000	$ 9,000	$ 10,000
Indirect labor				
Material handling	600	600	900	1,200
Shop clerical	500	500	500	500
Supervision	1,200	1,200	1,200	1,200
Overtime premium	0	0	450	450
Shift premiums (2nd and 3rd)	0	0	0	100
Operating supplies	350	400	450	500
Maintenance and repairs	1,200	1,400	2,000	2,800
Gas, water, steam, compressed air	1,500	1,800	2,100	2,400
Electrical power	700	800	900	1,000
Total controllable costs	$ 13,050	$ 14,700	$ 17,500	$ 20,150
Insurance	$ 120	$ 120	$ 120	$ 120
Taxes	80	80	80	80
Depreciation of equipment	400	400	400	400
Building occupancy	800	850	900	950
Total allocated costs	$ 1,400	$ 1,450	$ 1,500	$ 1,550
Total allowable costs	$ 14,450	$ 16,150	$ 19,000	$ 21,700

*Based on four operating levels in terms of tons produced.

This flexibility is not necessarily absolutely proportional to the changes in output level. The concept, however, is that when output rises, expense allowances will also rise, and when output falls, expenses will also drop.

Furthermore, many expenses (for example, rent, heat, light, and indirect labor) tend to remain the same regardless of output levels. Even on a flexible budget, these so-called *fixed costs* may be the same for each output level.

An example of a flexible budget is shown in Table 16-2.

Fixed costs. Costs that tend to be constant, at least on an annual basis, and that are not related to the rate of production, services rendered, or amount of sales.

Quick Test 2

3	T or F	A cost variance may be either above or below the standard.
4	T or F	Under a flexible budget, fixed costs vary according to the expected level of output.

3 COST IMPROVEMENT STRATEGIES

CONCEPT ▷ Cost reduction strategies can be either broadly focused or specific in nature, but their success depends on carefully planned priorities.

How sweeping are cost reduction programs likely to be?

It depends. A strategy for cost reduction can be either applied to the entire organization or confined to the operations of a single department. If it is organization-wide, the program is likely to be sweeping in nature and administered from the top down. If it is a departmental effort, the chances are that the strategy will be a piecemeal one. It will nibble away at costs under a plan conceived and implemented by the department's supervisor.

Supervisors will be expected to accept the disruptions and to clear the path for changes dictated by large-scale, long-term cost improvement programs. Usually, however, supervisors are concerned with modest, ongoing plans for cost reduction, which they often initiate themselves. The success of these plans, especially when initiated by supervisors themselves, depends on how well they have been conceived and how creatively and persistently supervisors pursue them. As the hare and tortoise fable points out, "Slow and steady wins the race"—even the cost race.

Where are the most promising cost targets to be found?

These usually emerge from a systematic search of the most obvious sources of expense, which include the following:

Product or service costs. Both the total and unit costs.

Process, or operations, costs. All, or any part, of the department's operating procedures.

People costs. Both direct and indirect. The latter refers to labor costs that support the central operations of a line department—such functions as maintenance, material handling, inspection, housekeeping, and other service functions.

Equipment and tools costs. Either in general or for a particular machine or device.

Materials costs. The materials that go into a product and, often just as important, the operating supplies consumed during the process or while providing the service.

Utilities costs. Power, fuels, water, steam, compressed air, and other utilities used by the department.

Communications costs. Telephone, facsimile, copying, mail, and so forth.

Information costs. Data collection, processing, retrieval, reporting, and analysis.

How should you set your cost-target priorities?

Approaches vary here. Short-term priorities are usually assigned to obvious "action-now" projects. Those projects that take time to carry out, however, are usually held back for an assessment of what they might entail as compared with their returns. On the basis of such an evaluation, targets can be picked and their priorities assigned according to ratings such as the following:

1. **Most obvious.** Sometimes the cost element that is most out of line is so obvious that you need search no further. Occasionally, this choice can be misleading; the true cause of the high cost may lie elsewhere, and the obvious element is only a result.

2. **Easiest.** The course of least resistance also is often the best path to follow to achieve cost savings. A small savings that is quickly reaped with little effort cannot be ignored. Starting with a sure thing can be a good way to build momentum in a cost reduction campaign.

3. **Worst first.** Sometimes a cost situation is so critical that it begs for immediate attention. If such is the case, it is probably wise to attack that cost target first. Otherwise, it may interfere with a more orderly progression toward long-term goals.

4. **Fastest payback.** Sometimes a company's financial policy dictates that those projects that pay back their investment fastest be given highest priority. Certainly, for those cost reduction projects that do require significant investment, this is a sensible choice.

What is meant by a "belt-tightening" program?

This usually refers to a short-term plan, often dictated from above, to cut costs as rapidly as possible. Such an approach is negative in nature, in that it allows little room for creative cost "improvements." Instead, belt-tightening will emphasize any of the following approaches:

Stop spending. Costs are cut through the simple expedient of restricting spending to necessities only. Spending for frills, conveniences, and luxuries is stopped. Sometimes the halt can become a permanent way of life. In that case, a supervisor and staff must learn to operate frugally, always.

Do without. This is much like stopping, except that the implication here is that the belt-tightening will be of short duration. The expenses not incurred during this period, however, represent a real contribution to savings. Money not spent for wiping rags today, for example, may never have to be spent later on.

Postpone what you can. With this approach, spending is postponed, or deferred, until a later time when the pressure to cut costs is not so severe. Unlike stopping or doing without, postponing implies that the money will be spent, but at a later date. Deferred maintenance work is the most common of these postponed costs. This approach has a potentially serious flaw: Many times the money that must be spent to do the job later is greater than what might be needed now. A machine not lubricated today may need a new bearing tomorrow. A building that needs only one coat of paint this year may need total replacement of its siding in the future.

◀ Quick Test 3

| 5 | T or F | Attacking the "worst first" cost reduction areas is likely to produce the fastest payback, by definition. |
| 6 | T or F | Most belt-tightening programs are somewhat negative in nature. |

4 COST IMPROVEMENT SOURCES

CONCEPT ▶ Cost improvement ideas may be gathered from a variety of sources, using a number of proven techniques.

Who can provide the necessary cost-cutting ideas?

Three good sources follow, all close to home:

1. **Yourself.** Build up a backlog of ideas the year round. Whenever you see, hear, or read about something that might work in your department, jot it down in a notebook or place it in a folder. Call these files your "idea banks." Later, when your attention is drawn to costs for any reason, check over your files to see what might be useful. (See especially Chapters 17 and 18 for ideas on improving productivity- and quality-related costs.)

2. **Your employees.** Employees probably know more about the ins and outs of the job than you do. If you encourage employees properly, they are likely to have ideas for cutting production corners or for reducing waste. (See Concept 5 of this chapter for ways to stimulate the flow of employee ideas.)

3. **Staff departments.** Once you have pinpointed a cost target, staff specialists, such as industrial engineers and methods and systems people, can provide expert help. They can call on vast reservoirs of examples of how costs were reduced in similar target areas in other departments or other companies.

How helpful are cost-reduction committees?

Cost-reduction committees were the forerunners of quality circles. Quality circles changed the emphasis from relying mainly upon the

Continuous improvement. The ongoing process of searching for cost reductions (and process improvements) by taking a critical view toward the present situation.

Super SCOPE ▶ **Continuous Improvement**

Many organizations today engage in cost control through the process of ***continuous improvement.*** This approach sets aside the "crisis" orientation of many cost-reduction efforts, and encourages employees to search for a better way to do things (such as find less expensive methods or materials) on an ongoing basis. Employees and their supervisors are asked to break out of old habits and routines, take a positive approach to reducing costs (*expecting* to find room for improvement), correct errors and implement new ideas immediately, and take a critical view toward existing practices. Many corporations, such as GE, Motorola, Pacific Bell, and Chase Manhattan Bank, have aggressively cut costs and saved expenses by implementing continuous improvement practices.

contributions of experts and specialists to that of broadening participation to small groups of well-trained and concerned employees. Members of quality circles are volunteers, and they contribute their ideas to work improvement as well as to cost reduction. Today, cost reduction committees are often inseparable from quality circles, and these groups may go by many names. Regardless of designation, they rely on broad and informed participation that taps a large reservoir of people in the organization for ideas.

What about positive ways to improve costs?

As compared with belt-tightening, the following six approaches to cost improvement tend to accentuate the positive. Each technique provides a different tool for cutting at the roots of cost problems. If one technique doesn't work, try another, or a combination of two or three.

Reduce waste. Where can you find waste in raw materials and operating supplies? How about people? Are you wasting their efforts? Are you getting the most from utilities, or are you wasting water, steam, or electricity?

Save time. Can you speed up or upgrade your equipment? Will time studies show you where time itself can be saved? Are you doing everything you can to get full use of your employees' time?

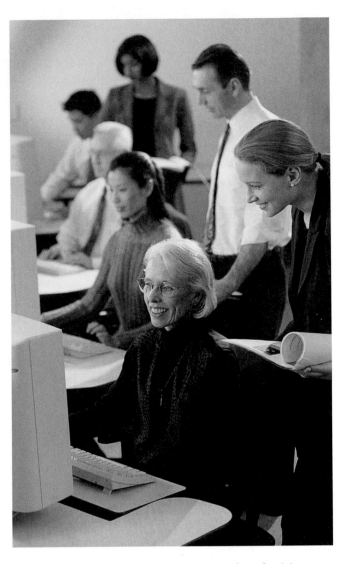

▲ Increased productivity through improved technology. **How does improved technology help to lower costs?**

Increase output. You can cut cost rates—and improve productivity—by stepping up the amount of work put through your department. Sometimes there's a rhythm that goes with high production that's lost with lower production. Sometimes when you cut back, you need the part-time services of several different people, whereas if you increased output, these same people would be working 100 percent of the time. With the higher output base, unit cost rates would actually be lower.

Spend wisely. Cutting costs doesn't always mean that you stop spending. In fact, it's a popular and true expression that you have to spend money to make money. Often top management is more attentive to the need for wise spending during a cost-cutting campaign than at other times. So look for ways to spend money that will ultimately save money, such as on mechanization or on replacement of slow machines with newer, faster ones.

Use space more intelligently. Space—for storage, manufacturing, and shipping—costs money. This cost goes on whether output is high or low. If you can figure out how to get more use out of the same space, you cut costs. Double or triple stacking of pallet loads, for instance, may cut charges for storage space by one-half to two-thirds.

Watch your inventories. It may make supervisors feel comfortable to know they have a big backlog of materials and supplies to use or to be shipped, but this is a very costly practice. Generally, it's best to stock as little as you can safely get away with, especially if supplies can be purchased and delivered quickly and reliably. When using up materials in storage, use the oldest stock first (where possible), before it gets soiled or damaged or becomes obsolete.

Why might an apparent money-saving idea sometimes be turned down by top management?

Mainly because the idea doesn't pay off quickly enough. It is exasperating, of course, for a supervisor to come up with an idea for saving $500, for example, only to have it rejected. Here's the way upper management may have evaluated the idea: Your plan will clearly save $500 a year, but its implementation (hooking up a new keyboard network, for example) will cost the company $3,000. This means that it will take six years for your idea to pay off. The cost of financing investments is so great that many companies have adopted the policy that a new machine or piece of equipment must pay for itself in five years or less. In fact, some companies insist on a payoff period of only one year!

Another factor is that your idea is often in competition for investment money with ideas suggested by other supervisors. Obviously, higher management will choose the ideas with the best and fastest payoffs.

Quick Test 4 ▶	**7**	T or F	The best cost-cutting ideas will invariably come from specialized staff.
	8	T or F	Ironically, some cost-cutting programs require that you spend money.

⑤ EMPLOYEE REACTIONS

CONCEPT ▶ Employee resistance to cost-cutting changes is likely to be high, so employees require special motivational efforts on the part of their supervisors.

Why do employees fear cost reduction?

Unless you can sell cost reduction to employees, they are likely to be indifferent at best, rebellious at worst. After all, to employees, cost cutting may mean loss of work, overtime, or their jobs. They feel that cost cutting threatens their security—or at least disrupts their work habits.

What are some chief criticisms employees have toward cost-cutting or productivity-improvement campaigns?

Employees often think that management itself throws away money through poor planning and downright misjudgment as to what's really important—and that applies to supervisors, too.

Following are some typical worker comments:

- "One employee saved the company about $2,000 one day and the next day I almost got laid off for turning in 20 minutes overtime."
- "We put in a new machine, then ripped it apart and sent it away. It probably cost the company $500 to do it. They waste lots of money by not planning the big things."
- "They changed construction of this particular item four or five times, got just short of production, and then the whole thing was called off. What that cost I couldn't even guess!"

Sitting as you do on the management side of the fence, you can understand the reason behind many moves that look wasteful to employees. But the tipoff for you is this: Employees frequently don't see the situation the way you do because *no one has taken time to make it clear*.

Your cue to selling cost reduction is to give employees the facts and help them see that cost cutting (or productivity improvement) helps them; it does not work to their disadvantage.

Internet CONNECTION

What does your salary equal in another city or state? Check **cities/salaries** on the Internet.

What is the union's attitude likely to be?

Not much different from that of a rank-and-file employee, except that the union's official opinion may be more contentious. Here are five reactions often heard from labor union leaders when asked to cooperate in cost-reduction activities:

- "Talk of downsizing and reengineering is a strategy the company uses to pressure us into accepting unfair cost-reduction programs."

- "Layoffs blamed on the need for cost reduction are aimed at weakening the union."
- "This industry is trying to speed up operations in order to produce the same amount of goods and services with more profit and fewer jobs."
- "Management isn't doing a good job of managing. Why should it tell our workers to do a better job before it mends its own fences?"
- "Management keeps 'crying wolf' about international competition, and then it tries to switch our jobs overseas."

Make no mistake about it; much of what the labor leaders say may be true in particular instances. Consequently, if you have a union that actively supports your cost-cutting efforts, you—and your company—have made a convincing case for the need for cost improvement.

Over the long haul, what is the best way to cut through employee resistance and build support for cost improvement?

It will take a long-range effort on your part and must be reinforced by sound planning and a genuine concern for employee welfare. The seven suggestions that follow will provide a firm foundation for your efforts:

1. **Talk to employees about cost reduction in terms of their interests.** You must see their point of view, or they'll never be able to see yours. In face-to-face conversations, show them how the company's interest in profits relates directly to a worker's interest in higher wages and job security. Show that one can't be achieved without the other.

2. **Bring the cost picture down to earth.** Don't talk in global terms of standard costs, of productivity ratios, or even about hard times. If company sales have fallen off, talk in terms of its impact upon the services produced in your department: "We processed 10,000 forms the first quarter, but our schedule calls for only half as many to be handled this quarter." If rising materials charges are a factor, pick up a product your employees make and tell them: "Last year, fabric for this item cost 50 cents; now it costs 60 cents—a rise of 20 percent."

3. **Set specific goals.** Don't say, "We've got to cut costs to the bone." Instead, suggest a specific program: "Our records show that keyboarding costs must be lowered by 10 percent. We'll have to figure a way to improve our methods to do this." Or, "Defective production that had to be scrapped cost us $1,200 last month. This month, let's get it down below $1,000."

4. **Invite participation.** Let employees know that you need their help in solving cost problems—and that help means more than cooperation. Tell them you need their ideas, too, and will welcome any suggestions.

5. **Explain why and how.** Spell out the reasons for each specific change. And remember that employees need your help, too, in deciding how to attain the cost-cutting goals you set.

6. **Train for cost improvement.** One of the key elements in quality circle programs is the training provided to employees in the techniques of problem solving and methods improvement. Try to incorporate these self-development elements into your cost-improvement training activities.

7. **Report cost progress.** Scorekeeping appeals to the achievement needs in many employees. Reports of progress toward cost goals (posted on bulletin boards, for example) stimulate competitiveness and self-motivation.

JOB tip!

TUNE IN TO THE RUMOR MILL

■ In today's electronic society, news—and rumor—travels very rapidly. Astute supervisors keep their ears tuned to the rumor mill and respond quickly to lay false rumors to rest. Employees may have heard exaggerated tales of impending cost cutbacks, retrenchments, or downsizings. Gather information, validate it, and share what you can with employees as soon as possible to diminish their fears. Above all, speak the truth to them, for they will judge your integrity through every word you speak.

◄ Quick Test 5

| 9 | T or F | Most employees are likely to welcome the opportunity to cut costs. |
| 10 | T or F | Good supervisory practices (e.g., goal setting, participation, training, explanations, and progress reporting) can help reduce potential resistance to cost cutting. |

CHAPTER 16 REVIEW

KEY CONCEPTS TO REMEMBER

1. **Accounting Records.** Effective cost control and cost improvement both depend on the availability of accurate records. Costs may be measured and reported as total costs, unit costs, or standard costs, or in the form of budgeted costs (or expenses). Costs may also be categorized as direct, indirect, or variable.

2. **Budgeted Costs.** Budgets establish departmental cost standards, or targets. They are essentially tables of allowable expenses for a given period, like a month or a year. Unit costs are especially useful, since they translate total costs into comparable measures. Flexible budgets are used to provide a number of optional tables of expenses in order to anticipate variations in output levels during the period.

3. **Cost Improvement Strategies.** Cost improvement efforts can be large scale and long term, or piecemeal and short range. Supervisors usually initiate the latter. The most promising cost targets are close at hand, including the costs of products or services, processing, people, equipment and tools, materials and supplies, utilities, communications, and information. Many cost-reduction programs are negative in nature, featuring several belt-tightening approaches, including stopping or postponing spending and doing without.

4. **Cost Improvement Sources.** Ideas for cost improvement come from supervisors, their employees, staff departments, and cost-reduction committees, including quality circles. Positive programs for cost improvement include reducing waste, saving time, increasing output,

spending wisely, conserving space, and controlling inventories. Cost-improvement ideas that require expenditures for their implementation often compete with other ideas that require financing.

5. **Employee Reactions.** Employees often are fearful that cost-reduction programs will bring about unpleasant changes and/or threaten their job security. Labor unions tend to have similar reactions, and they support the resistance that these attitudes induce. Supervisors must struggle to modify these fears to obtain employee cooperation and support for cost and productivity improvements. This is accomplished by (among other things) honest, candid, factual communication and by inviting employee participation in solving cost-related problems.

READING COMPREHENSION

1. Jane has been told that cost control in her department is all right but that she must now make some cost improvements. What is the distinction?
2. Distinguish between total costs and unit costs.
3. "You are over budget this month," the plant manager told the department supervisor. What report would have given the manager that information?
4. Bud's total cost for computer paper was $1,000 in January and $750 in February. His department serviced 80 accounts in January and 50 in February. Did his unit cost for paper go up or down in February? Show your calculations.
5. Marty supervises a manufacturing department. His payroll for assembly workers has varied with his department's output, but the payroll for clerical help has stayed constant. How can this be?

6. Compare a belt-tightening cost program with a cost-improvement program.

7. How are cost-reduction committees and quality circles alike? How are they different?

8. Why can better use of space be considered a cost-improvement method? Who actually benefits?

9. How might a labor union's attitude differ from an employee's attitude toward cost-reduction programs?

10. Which approach is more likely to stimulate employee cooperation in cost reduction? Why? (a) "Your jobs are threatened now by price-cutting competitors." (b) "You can help protect your jobs from price-cutting competitors if we can find a way to reduce our department's scrap percentage from 5 to 2 percent per month."

APPLICATION

Self-Assessment

How good are your cost-control skills? ◄

Read the following statements carefully. Circle the number on the response scale that most closely reflects the degree to which each statement accurately describes you. Add up your total points and prepare a brief action plan for self-improvement. Be ready to report your score for tabulation across the entire group.

	Good Description									Poor Description
1. I recognize the importance of, and carefully study, relevant cost records.	10	9	8	7	6	5	4	3	2	1
2. I place more emphasis on controlling unit costs than I do on total costs.	10	9	8	7	6	5	4	3	2	1
3. I closely examine cost variances that are either above or below budget.	10	9	8	7	6	5	4	3	2	1
4. Although flexible budgets are more challenging to understand and use, I recognize their value in dealing with varying levels of output.	10	9	8	7	6	5	4	3	2	1
5. I try to balance the need for both short-term and long-term cost-reduction efforts.	10	9	8	7	6	5	4	3	2	1
6. I encourage my employees to understand the need for continuous improvement in departmental costs.	10	9	8	7	6	5	4	3	2	1
7. I actively involve my employees in the search for ways to lower costs.	10	9	8	7	6	5	4	3	2	1

	Good Description									Poor Description

8. I recognize that employees may resist my cost-cutting efforts, and I search for ways to reduce their resistance.

10 9 8 7 6 5 4 3 2 1

9. I actively seek to reduce costs through both direct (e.g., wise spending) and indirect (e.g., space-saving) methods.

10 9 8 7 6 5 4 3 2 1

10. I view cost-control as resting on a "three-legged stool," with inputs from myself, my employees, and staff departments.

10 9 8 7 6 5 4 3 2 1

Scoring and Interpretation

SCORING

Add up your total points for the 10 questions. Record that number here, and report it when it is requested. _____

INTERPRETATION

81 to 100 points. You seem to have a basic set of cost-control skills.

61 to 80 points. Take a close look at some of your cost-control skills (those with lower self-assessments) and discuss them with a manager to see if they need improvement.

Below 60 points. Some of your skills may be substantially inconsistent with effective cost-control practices and could be detrimental to your success as a supervisor.

Identify your three lowest scores, and write the question numbers here:

_____, _____, _____.

ACTION

Write a brief paragraph detailing an action plan for how you might sharpen each of these skills. Then pay particularly close attention to the related material in the chapter as you review the relevant sections there.

Skill Development

▶ *Cost Control*

Costs—and waste—are everywhere, it seems. We can see them in airports, in hospitals, in educational institutions, and in restaurants. It is often more difficult, however, to see them in our own domains. For this reason, it is often helpful to invite someone else into an operation and ask them to view it with a critical eye toward cost reduction. In this assignment, you will play the role of a cost consultant who is searching for ways to save costs.

Select an organization (or unit thereof) as the focus of your investigation. Obtain access to it (if necessary), and spend a little time observing what people do, where materials are stored, the quantity of inventory on hand, how time and space are used, and more.

Cost-improvement suggestions

1. _____

2. _____

3. _____

4. _____

5. _____

6. _____

7. _____

8. _____

9. _____

10. _____

ACTION

Prepare a brief report that summarizes your 10 best suggestions for cost improvement from your limited analysis. (To prepare yourself, you will likely wish to review the text's discussion on cost control, search the Internet for relevant guidelines, and consult with colleagues and staff persons in the human resources department for their advice.) If possible, share the results of your study with a responsible person in the host organization and obtain his/her reactions.

Role Play

Responding to a Rumor ◀

Triple-A Window Cleaning Service has been in operation for 20 years. It has gradually grown in size, as more and more organizations became aware of the need for its service and its reputation for doing a good job at a reasonable price. Recently, however, a competitor sprung up—College Students Cleaning Windows—and the price for their services is about 15 percent less than that of Triple-A. A rumor has spread among Triple-A employees of cutbacks in its workforce unless drastic cost reductions are achieved. A meeting has been called by the owner of Triple-A to discuss the current situation. Divide into groups of five, and each person should take one of the five roles shown below. All participants should read only their own roles before the meeting.

JUSTIN (TRIPLE-A'S OWNER). You are very concerned about the potential impact of the new competitor and fear that a significant loss of revenue will occur through loss of contracts unless you are able to initiate cost reductions of about 15 percent, or make other operating improvements that justify your higher prices. You have called a meeting of your employees and are about to present the topic to them now. Prepare a mental plan for how you will conduct this meeting.

ABBY. You are the newest and youngest employee of Triple-A, and therefore worried about your future with the company. However, you are also attending college on a part-time basis, and have been thinking about applying for a job with a new company—College Students Cleaning Windows. If things really get bad here, you could always "jump ship" and switch companies.

BENITO. You have the most seniority at Triple-A and therefore are not too concerned about the rumor of a cost-reduction program. As far as you are concerned, Justin (the owner) can just go ahead and lay off a few of the newer employees; all they ever do is loaf and talk about the parties they have every night anyway!

CANDY. You have recently read some material on the idea of "continuous improvement," and are intrigued by the possibility of finding ways to put it to work at Triple-A. You hope that all the other employees will go along with your suggestions; this could be a fun experiment to liven up the workplace and make it more efficient, too!

DARREN. You have read about cost-reduction programs at other organizations and are convinced that they always result in work speed-ups, job loss, insecurity for employees, and a negative work atmosphere. You are inclined to resist any cost-reduction program with all your energies.

CASES FOR ANALYSIS

Case 48

▶ *The High-Flying Sales Staff*

Trina's boss had a real head of steam. "Your department is too much. I've put up with a lot from them, but now they have reached the top of my list."

"That sounds great," said Trina, who supervised over a dozen of the division's best salespeople.

"Don't get funny with me," said her boss. "You know what I'm talking about. The list I had in mind was the company's big spenders. Of all the staffs in my division, yours is absolutely the worst when it comes to expense control. They have become too used to high living, and it's got to stop."

"Wait a minute," said Trina, "you're talking about a dozen of the best outside-sales people a distributor ever had. They bring in top dollar for the company."

"They may be good, but they're not that good," said Trina's boss. "Let me make it perfectly clear. Your department's expenses are way too high. I expect you to get them down to a reasonable level. And soon!"

"Okay," said Trina, "I'll get on it."

To herself, however, she said, "I'm sick and tired of taking the heat for those high-flyers on my staff. None of them give a hoot about what they spend or waste so long as they get the job done. I'll have to sit down with the whole gang of these artful dodgers now and straighten them out."

When Trina did sit down with her staff, here's what she told them:

"The division is throwing one of its cost-cutting tantrums right now, and I'm taking a lot of heat on your behalf. From now on, I want you to get your expenses back in line."

"Back in line with what?" asked one salesperson.

"Don't you worry about where the line is. I'll tell you if you step over it. Here's what I mean:

"First of all, your auto expenses are way too high. I'm going to stop paying for your side trips to the seashore.

"Second, you have been wasting our costly brochures by dumping them all over the territory as if there were no tomorrow. That's got to stop.

"Third, you don't have to take every distributor's counter clerk out to lunch to make a sale. You know that's not necessary.

"Fourth—" but she was interrupted.

"What do you want us to do," said another salesperson, "stop selling and sit around the office instead?"

"Kidding aside," said still another salesperson, "how are we to cut down on our expenses and still bring in the sales you expect?"

"That's your problem, not mine," said Trina. "You know what you've got to do. Do it!"

Time passed, and a couple of months later, Trina was called into the boss's office. "I thought I told you to get your department's expenses in line," the boss said. "If anything, they are worse than ever."

Analysis ▶

Why do you think that expenses in Trina's department did not fall back into line? Of the five alternatives provided below, which do you think is the most likely cause? Rank the alternatives on a scale from 1 (most likely) to 5 (least likely). You may add another alternative, if you wish. Be prepared to justify your ranking.

_____ **a.** The staff believed that it was really sales that counted to the company, not expense control.

_____ **b.** Trina had not laid out specific standards or budget targets for the staff to measure up to.

_____ **c.** The staff was not interested in saving Trina's neck.

_____ **d.** Trina hadn't given the staff a chance to suggest how they might go about cutting down on their expenses.

_____ **e.** The sales staff knew they were good and were not about to cut back on a lifestyle they enjoyed.

Case 49 ▶ *Kindly Make Every Effort . . .*

Leopold G., the supervisor of the weaving department, received this note from the controller of the textile plant: "Kindly make every effort to reduce your operating costs this month by 5 percent. Our schedules call for a throughput the same as last month." The supervisor looked at last month's total charges, which came to $20,000. Of that total, $10,000 was a direct labor charge; he decided that since these men and women were on piece rates, this figure could not be cut. However, he felt that the $2,500 he had incurred in indirect labor might be reduced drastically, since he had "borrowed" much of it from the labor pool to do a cleanup job. Operating supplies had come to $1,500, and that surprised him. But, on thinking about it, he recalled that $500 had come from a requisition for wiping rags, and he would not have to reorder them this month. Maintenance was still running heavy, he felt, and the charges of $3,000 were sure to be repeated this month. His prorated share of electricity came to $1,200, and he felt that there was nothing he could do about that. Water, too, at $1,800 a month, was a steady charge that he could not avoid.

Analysis ▶

a. How many dollars must Leopold save this month to meet the 5 percent reduction "requested" of him?

b. From which two of his budget items will he be able to make these savings?

c. How much will he save from each?

The "Up-Up-and-Away" Computer Supplies

Over the last few years, the Ajax Computer Center had grown and grown. Last year, its accounting section alone had obtained 50 contracts, but now this figure was forecast to remain constant for the next couple of years. Beth, who supervised the accounting contracts, thought about this forecast as she set up her budget for next year. She felt that most of her expenses would remain rather constant, too, except for supplies, such as computer paper and printer ribbons. She had noticed that the amount of such supplies consumed while fulfilling a contract had been increasing alarmingly. Two years ago, the total cost of these supplies had been about $9,500. Last year, the total was $10,000. Based upon her best estimate, Beth thinks that next year the total consumption would increase by about 5 percent every three months.

◀ *Analysis*

a. What was the unit cost of supplies per contract last year?
b. If the increase in consumption of supplies continues as Beth thinks it will, what will be the total cost of supplies next year?
c. What will that make the unit cost of supplies per contract next year?
d. What might Beth do to reduce these costs next year?

Quick Test 1	Quick Test 2	Quick Test 3	◀ *Answers to*
1. F	**3.** T	**5.** T	*Quick Tests*
2. F	**4.** F	**6.** T	
Quick Test 4	**Quick Test 5**		
7. F	**9.** F		
8. T	**10.** T		

PART Seven

Improving Productivity and Quality

CHAPTER 17

Stimulating Productivity, Quality, and Innovation

Learning Objectives

After studying this chapter, you should be able to

- Calculate productivity ratios and percentages, and understand what contributes to rising or falling productivity rates.

- Understand and describe the various approaches to work measurement and improvement, including reengineering and value analysis.

- Explain the meaning of quality, and discuss a number of ways for carrying out a supervisor's responsibility for quality improvement.

- Understand the concepts of statistical quality control, make use of frequency-distribution and quality-control charts, and explain a reliability measure.

- Describe the main features of zero defects, quality circle, and total quality management programs and explain the value of participative approaches for solving quality problems.

- Explain various approaches to creative thinking and innovation for solving productivity and quality problems, including free association of ideas and brainstorming.

UNDERSTANDING PRODUCTIVITY

> **CONCEPT** ▶ Productivity measures how much output is being created by a given set of inputs.

What is productivity?

There are many definitions and most of them are complex. Yet ***productivity*** is a very simple and vital concept. Dr. C. Jackson Grayson of the American Productivity Center says it most clearly: "Productivity is the process of getting more out of what you put in. It's doing better with what you have."

> **Productivity.** The measure of efficiency that compares the value of outputs from an operation with the cost of the resources used.

How is it measured?

Technically, *productivity* is a measure of how efficient a person or work activity is; it is determined by comparing (a) the value of the output result with (b) the cost of the input resource. It is usually expressed as a ratio (or rate):

$$\text{Productivity} = \frac{\text{output}}{\text{input}}$$

Take a simple example. The productivity of a telephone salesperson might be stated as 10 sales completed per salesperson hour. That would yield a productivity rate of 10:1. A productivity rate can also be established by comparing the dollar costs of output and input. Suppose the dollar value of each sale averaged $25, for a total of $250. If the telephone salesperson is paid $10 per hour, then the productivity rate would be $250 divided by $10, or 25:1.

Once a productivity ratio has been established as a standard for a work activity, it is very helpful to compare current productivity with this standard. This comparison is usually expressed as a percentage increase or decrease. Take the preceding example of the 10:1 ratio. Suppose the salesperson increased this productivity ratio next year to 12 completed calls per hour, or 12:1. It would then be correct to state that productivity had improved by 20 percent. Here's how it is calculated:

New rate minus Old rate, divided by Old rate = Percent change

$(12 - 10) \div 10 = 2 \div 10 = 0.20 = 20 \text{ percent}$

Note that when using the dollar-based productivity rate, the productivity improvement comes to the same 20 percent. Here's how this is arrived at:

The value of the new output is 12 calls × $25, or $300, while the cost of the input remains the same $10 per hour. Hence, the new ratio is $300:$10 = 30:1. The comparison is calculated as before:

$(30 - 25) \div 25 = 5 \div 25 = 0.20 = 20 \text{ percent}$

What you'll hear most about productivity is not the standard or basic rate, but whether the rate is increasing or decreasing.

How can supervisors tell how good their departmental productivity is?

Only by comparing it with the standard rate or an industry rate for the particular work activity, if either one is available, to see if yours is better or worse. Otherwise, you must make a judgment based on a comparison of your current rate with a previous one. In most ongoing organizations, your productivity performance will be judged by whether it is rising or falling.

A simple concept should guide you here. Productivity will increase if the number or value of the outputs increases *relative* to the number or value of the inputs. When the reverse occurs, productivity will decrease. Said another way, if the size of your output goes up while the size of the input remains the same, productivity will increase. Conversely, if the size of your output goes down while the size of the input remains the same, productivity will decrease. This concept is illustrated in Figure 17-1.

◆ **FIGURE 17-1**

Showing how productivity ratios are computed and compared. **How might supervisors use productivity measures when making decisions for their units or departments?**

Graphic Display	Units	PRODUCTIVITY		
		Ratio	Movement	Percent Change
				$\dfrac{\text{latest} - \text{original}}{\text{original}}$
	$\dfrac{10}{10}$	= 1.00 : 1	Original	
	$\dfrac{12}{10}$	= 1.20 : 1	Increase	$\dfrac{1.20 - 1.00}{1.00} = +0.20 = +20\%$
	$\dfrac{10}{8}$	= 1.25 : 1	Increase	$\dfrac{1.25 - 1.00}{1.00} = +0.25 = +25\%$
	$\dfrac{8}{10}$	= 0.80 : 1	Decrease	$\dfrac{0.80 - 1.00}{1.00} = -0.20 = -20\%$

Can productivity measurements be made anywhere?

Just about anywhere. It used to be thought that productivity was only a concern of the goods-producing industries, like manufacturing. Today, productivity measures are applied to government work, educational and charitable institutions, and to almost every kind of clerical or service operation. A word processor's productivity, for example, would be measured by the number of lines or pages of copy keyboarded, or forms completed per hour worked. A supermarket checkout counter clerk's output would be the number of items checked (or dollars taken in) a day. A bank teller's productivity would be the number of transactions handled an hour, day, week, or month.

The main limit to the application of productivity is the need to obtain a reliable measurement of output. It is difficult, for example, to measure the value of a nurse's output, although many hospitals talk about the number of patients tended by one nurse per shift as a measure of productivity.

Another factor to watch is the impact that quality demands have on productivity. If quality requirements are raised, output may drop accordingly. Or, if product specifications are loosened, output may rise solely because of this change and not represent a real improvement in productivity.

Is that all there is to productivity measurement?

Not quite. There is another important aspect to grasp if you are to understand it fully. Up until this point we have understated what makes up the true cost of the input portion of the productivity measurement. The examples have focused only on labor costs. We have done so because these costs are what have traditionally been measured. Nevertheless, when you think about it, something besides human energy goes into the creation of an output. At the very least, there is the cost of the power, equipment, and facilities involved in most work activities. A comprehensive measure of productivity would include the costs of all these inputs. But because of the complexity involved in the calculations, very few organizations add these factors into their measurements. On the other hand, it is readily acknowledged that the creative manipulation of these factors can contribute greatly to productivity improvement. Accordingly, you'll want to keep this in mind when you set about to improve the productivity of your unit.

On what factors should supervisors focus for obtaining productivity improvements?

Supervisors can work on two basic ingredients to improve productivity—technology factors and human factors. The technological factors usually include product or service design, facilities and equipment, automation, computer controls, robots, process layout and methods, better materials, more efficient power usage, and rapid access to job-related information. The relatively obvious human factors include ability, knowledge, motivation, education, experience, levels of aspiration, work schedules, training, organizational groupings, personnel policies, and pay practices. In addition, an easily overlooked factor is supervisory leadership and its role in contributing to employee job satisfaction.

What role does employee job satisfaction play in improving productivity?

It is the most important factor not yet fully exploited. In high-technology industries—such as petroleum refining—job satisfaction may be a smaller, though still vital, factor than technology. In most work, however, there is an increasing need to place major emphasis on the role of job satisfaction. In the long run, people control the work pace. They can be devilishly clever in thwarting machines.

Supervisors must try to match jobs with each person's own kind of job satisfaction. Productivity gets its strongest boost from the human side when supervisors support employees in their individual search for job satisfaction. The trick, of course, is to balance employees' needs for satisfaction with the organization's need for productivity and cost control.

JOB tip!

WARNING SIGNS

■ You can obtain many clues regarding negative employee attitudes (and your own!) that will affect productivity and quality by listening to some of the phrases and clichés commonly used at work. In particular, watch for these warning signs that there may be a "quality-hostile" work environment:

- "We are smarter than our customers."
- "Continuous improvement is unrealistic to expect."
- "Workers are paid to do, not to think."
- "If it ain't broke, don't fix it."
- "To err is human; we all make mistakes.

Source: Adapted from Robert E. Cole, "Learning from the Quality Movement," *California Management Review,* Fall 1998, p. 50.

Quick Test 1

1	T or F	Productivity is usually measured as the ratio of inputs over outputs.
2	T or F	Job satisfaction represents a largely untapped area for productivity improvement.

◀ Knowledgeable employees, at any level in the organization, can positively impact productivity. **How can organizations educate their personnel?**

② METHODS IMPROVEMENT

CONCEPT ▶ The systematic way for increasing productivity is to measure, and then improve, the methods used for performing work.

What has work measurement got to do with productivity improvement?

It is the foundation stone of productivity improvement. Work—human effort especially—is the basic input in a great many processes. Unless you have a good idea of how much work is entailed, it is almost impossible to know where to look for productivity improvements or to tell whether or not you've accomplished anything when you're through. ***Work measurement*** is the term generally applied to any method of determining how long it would take an individual (or group of individuals) to perform a specific task.

Work measurement. The determination, by systematic and (ideally) precise methods, of the time dimension of a particular task.

What are the main ways in which work is measured?

Making *time studies* of the actual job as it is performed (using some sort of stopwatch) is by far the most common way. Other methods range from rough-and-ready measures to ultrasophisticated techniques.

The crudest measures involve simply looking at historical records that show how much an employee has produced in a day, week, or month.

The most elaborate approach uses tiny building blocks of time units based on *motion studies*. Experts add the time for every motion required on a job (lifting, pulling, straightening, and so forth) to find the total time needed. The measuring units are called *predetermined elemental time standards*.

Work sampling is a rough-and-ready approach to work measurement. It is relatively easy to do. It has some shortcomings, but it is especially suitable for supervisors who wish to get a quick idea of the productivity of their departments.

Work sampling is accomplished by making random observations of various activities in the work area (see Table 17-1). It enables a supervisor to find the proportion of delays and interruptions that occur as related to the total time required to do a job.

Whatever the work-measurement technique—precise or rough-and-ready—the times that are found become time standards, or simply **standards**. These standards for various jobs are accumulated in a company's record files, and are often available (for jobs commonly performed in commerce and industry) for purchase from consulting firms.

What is implied by the term methods improvement?

Any change in the way a task is performed so that it lowers the cost, shortens the time, or improves the quality of the product or service provided by the task is called a ***methods improvement.*** The *process* of methods improvement is simply the organized use of common sense to find better ways of doing work.

Methods improvement has many names, and it takes many forms. It may be known as work simplification, work study, time-and-motion study, operations analysis, methods engineering, systems engineering, methods and systems analysis (especially for clerical and service work), waste reduction, motion economy, or even quality circles.

Methods improvement has been applied by expert and novice alike to such diverse fields as construction, supermarkets, and endless paper-work systems in offices. For example, Lillian Gilbreth, a noted pioneer in work simplification, made great improvements in hospital care by re-arranging nurses' stations and by simplifying food service, housekeeping, and patient-care activities.

While the methods-improvement process has many variations, it usually involves observing each minute segment of a job and then examining these segments for ways to do the job better as a whole. That's the kind of "up-close, small-scale" methods improvement we'll talk about here. There are, of course, many other approaches (involving large-scale application of automation and computers) that are used effectively by methods engineers and other analysts. For your part, however, you'll need no stopwatch, video camera, or computer—only pencil and paper, some guidelines we'll provide you with, good judgment, patience, and ingenuity.

TABLE 17-1

Example of Work-Sampling Study of Clerical Employees

Observation Sheet
Random Observation Times

	9:09	9:57	11:18	1:15	2:43	3:11	3:52	4:21	4:39
Chavez	7	8	1	1	3	5	6	3	1
Yost	2	1	6	4	1	3	7	6	2
Albers	7	4	5	1	8	1	1	3	8
Dowdy	7	8	7	4	1	1	2	1	8
Rozetti	4	1	2	5	7	5	1	4	1

Activity Category Code Numbers

1. Keyboarding
2. Copy machine
3. Operating calculator
4. Clerical activity at desk

5. Away from desk, but in office
6. Telephoning
7. Personal
8. Not in office

Date: 7/21

Supervisor (Observer): F. Diehl

Summary of 990 Observations

Category	Number of Observations	Percentage of Observations
1. Keyboarding	487	49.2
2. Copy machine	23	2.3
3. Operating calculator	86	8.7
4. Clerical activity at desk	71	7.2
5. Away from desk, but in office	36	3.6
6. Telephoning	68	6.9
7. Personal	113	11.4
8. Not in office	106	10.7

Which elements of a work activity are highly valued and which are thought to be wasteful?

During a work activity, five distinct things can happen to a product or service. Only one of them adds directly to the value of the product or service. The other four elements may be necessary, and are often costly, but they do not add value. See Figure 17-2(a). Here's how experts separate the "valued" element of a work activity from the "wasteful" ones.

The Valued Element. An *operation* occurs when the subject (object, person, or service) is changed in any of its physical characteristics, is assembled or disassembled, or is arranged in a special way. An operation also occurs when a person is served or when information is given, received, or processed. What really makes an operation unique is that it *does* something to improve and/or add value to the object. All other elements of a work activity are considered wasteful, no matter how necessary they may at first appear.

The Wasteful Elements. These are the four troublesome auxiliary elements of a work activity:

1. **Inspection.** This occurs when an item is checked, verified, reviewed, or examined for quality—and nothing is done at that time to change it.

2. **Delay.** Also called *idle time*, this occurs to an object while waiting to be worked on, equipment that is available for work but is not operating for any reason, or a person who waits for materials, instructions, or available equipment.

3. **Transportation.** Also called *movement* or *transfer*, this occurs when an object is moved from one place to another, or a person moves from one place to another—not as the key operation, as with bus or plane travel—but solely to support another element in the work activity.

4. **Storage.** This is a special kind of delay, mostly purposeful, in which something remains in one place for a measurable amount of time. Typically, such storage is not a part of a regular process and occurs while an item is awaiting further action at a later date, often in a storage area, file cabinet, data bank, stockroom, or warehouse.

Where should you begin your attempt to improve methods?

Experts in this field usually take the position that the wasteful elements should get your attention first. Once each of these has been broken out of the pack as a separate element, examined and improved, you can then concentrate on the value-adding operation.

How do you go about improving the value-adding operations?

Think of an operation as consisting of three distinct segments, as illustrated in Figure 17-2(b).

Makeready. This includes the effort and time that go into setting up the particular job, such as arranging equipment and materials beforehand. A painter, for instance, makes ready to paint a house by mixing paint, raising the ladder, spreading the drop cloths, and so forth. A word processing

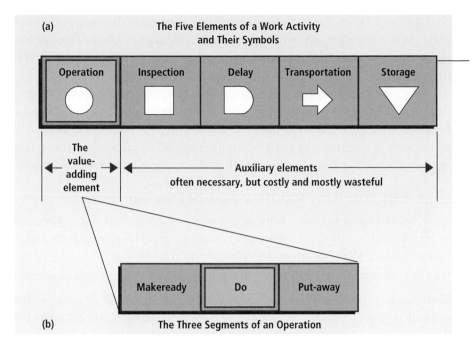

◆ **FIGURE 17-2**

How to break down a work activity for analysis and improvement. **What is the primary difference between the valued element and the auxiliary element?**

employee turns on the computer, obtains and stacks the batch of reports to be keyboarded, and adjusts the copy holder.

Makeready, as necessary as it often is, adds no value to the product or service that is being performed by the job. It is a prime target for combining or elimination.

Do. This is the segment of the operation that actually adds the value. The painter adds value to the house by applying the paint. The word processing employee adds value to the service by placing the data into the computer where it will be automatically processed into a more useful format. A bank teller adds value to the checking operation by verifying the endorsement, stamping it with a new endorsement and either exchanging it for cash or preparing a deposit slip. A machinist adds value to a piece of iron rod by cutting it into two-inch lengths for bolts.

Since the "do" operations are the essential ones, they are hard to eliminate. They do, however, lend themselves to speeding up and simplifying or to combining with another operation. Furthermore, the great advantage of eliminating a "do" segment is that it simultaneously eliminates both the "makeready" and the "put-away" associated with it.

Put-away. This segment covers anything that's done after the "do" is finished. It includes unloading, disposing, storage, transfer, and cleanup. The painter takes down the ladder, removes the drop cloth, cleans up spots on the floor, washes brushes, and stores material and equipment. In like manner, the word processor closes down the computer, puts a protective cover on it, and files away the completed and uncompleted source forms.

And the bank teller, for each "do" operation, sets aside the canceled check and makes a notation of the transaction on a calculator ribbon. The machinist, also after each "do" operation, sets aside the bolt for the next "do" operation.

The makeready and put-away segments are often the choicest targets for improvement. They are prime candidates for (a) elimination, (b) combination either with the "do" segment itself or with the "make-ready" of the next "do" segment, or (c) for handling automatically, since these segments normally require the least skill and attention from human hands.

How can you develop new and better methods?

Uncovering delays and finding out what's wrong with a work activity or job operation are valuable accomplishments, and their worth shouldn't be minimized. But this effort doesn't pay off until you've devised a better way to perform the job. There are many approaches from which to choose:

Eliminate. First look for the chance of dropping out a part of or the entire operation. There's no point in wasting time improving methods if the job doesn't have to be done at all.

Combine. Doing two or more things at once saves time. Often it saves additional time by eliminating the transportation, storage, and inspection that previously took place between operations.

Change sequence. Frequently you can do things more easily or cheaply by changing the order in which they are done. For example, it is best to finish a part only after the shaping operations have been completed.

Simplify. After you've searched the first three approaches in this list, look for ways of doing the job in a simpler manner. Here's where you try to cut down on wasted motions, replace hand operations with mechanical ones, and provide fixtures for positioning and chutes for feeding. But remember, don't try to simplify until you've first tried to eliminate, combine, or change sequence.

In what ways does motion economy help improve productivity?

Motion economy is the use of the human body to produce results with the least physical and mental effort. It's been given long study by methods engineers and physiologists. Here are principles of motion economy that are generally agreed on as aids to getting a job done with the least labor:

- **Motions should be productive.** Every motion a person makes should be concentrated on "do" operations that bring the job closer to a finish. Hands, for instance, should not be wasted in holding the work; they should be released for more value-added operations.

- **Motions should be simple.** The fewer parts of the body used, the better. Use a finger and a thumb rather than the whole hand. Grasp an object by reaching with the forearm rather than with the whole arm. Motions should be along curved paths rather than straight lines because most of the body members swing from joints in a circular motion.

- **Motions should be rhythmic.** Arrange the work so that it's easy to work with smooth motions. It's easier, too, for hands to move in opposite directions and in similar motion paths.

- **Make workers comfortable.** The workbench, the keyboard, and the chair should all be arranged so that the operator feels comfortable, whether the work requires sitting or standing or walking.

- **Combine two or more tools.** Picking up and laying down tools takes time. It's quicker to reverse a tool with a working edge on either end than to pick up and lay down two separate tools.

- **Pre-position tools and materials.** Having things arranged so that they are already aligned before the operator picks them up speeds up the job. If a form needs to be turned over or around, the job needs positioning.

- **Limit stretching.** A person works comfortably within the swing of the arms forward and up and down. If the person has to reach or stretch beyond that normal work area, turn around, bend, or stoop, it takes time and is fatiguing. *Ergonomics* is the name given to the study of how workers react to their physical environment. Its goal is to create more comfortable, and therefore more productive, workstations. In current terminology, workplaces should be ergonomically sound.

Who takes care of high-tech improvements?

The highly engineered and/or large-scale approaches to improving productivity are usually the responsibility of engineering specialists and computer systems people. *Automation*, once thought of as simply a form of stepped-up mechanization with a degree of self-control in the process, has exploded in some industries. In fact, hundreds of thousands of fully automatic devices, called *robots*, are already in place in hundreds of manufacturing plants. But it is the computer that has made the big difference. It has enabled engineers to look at an entire process—department-sized or even plant-sized—and to tie the scheduling and operation of dozens of separate machines and subprocesses into a whole.

Similarly, *office automation* links together by means of computers any number of previously independent clerical and administrative activities. "Workflow automation" goes even further in that many such activities are programmed to be performed within the computer network itself. One unanticipated result is the shrinking, not only of office staffs in some circumstances, but also of the work space allotted to the employees themselves.

Reengineering. A top-down, broad-based approach to improvement that can lead to sweeping changes in goals and methods throughout an organization.

On an even broader scale, *reengineering* is seen by some authorities as a major source of company-wide methods improvement. The reengineering approach asks the same questions of the entire organization that improvement-oriented supervisors ask about work activities within a department:

Why are we doing this?

How can we do it better?

How can we achieve more with less?

The net effect is that the organization may redefine its purpose, its customers, and the very way your department functions.

Whatever the approach, whenever high-tech improvement takes place, supervisors should be alert to changes such as these:

- **Accelerated time frames.** That is, there will be shorter leadtimes for making changes, much faster-paced operations, and the need to provide quicker answers.

- **Less forgiving monitoring of output.** Control of a process won't be considered satisfactory unless the results are acceptable, too.

- **Closer coupling with outside forces.** The activities of an internal department are likely to be linked up with customers and clients, suppliers, and distributors.

Overall, supervisors may or may not have an opportunity to participate in these high-tech decisions. One thing is certain, however, supervisors are the ones who will be charged with making these improvements work. As a consequence, supervisors will be expected to ease the problems associated with shop-floor changes, to counsel employees about relocations and displacements, and to train them to handle the new systems.

Where does value analysis fit into this picture?

Internet CONNECTION

Check out the **Centre for Applied Ethics** website for samples of corporate codes of ethics and other business ethics resources.

To our way of thinking, *value analysis* (also called *value engineering*) is simply a productivity improvement that focuses on a product rather than on a process. It has another unique aspect in that it studies the value of the functions that a product or service performs *from a customer's or client's point of view.* Functions for analysis are classified two ways, *use* and *esteem:*

- The *use* function provides the action that customers want from the product. An automobile's use function is to provide transportation. A hotel's use function is to provide lodging.

- The *esteem* function pleases a customer and stimulates the purchase. An auto's esteem function might be its styling and optional features such as a multidisc CD player. A hotel's esteem function might be its attractive lobby and the decor of its rooms.

The objective of value analysis is not only to retain those use and esteem functions that customers want, but also to provide them at a lower cost. As a consequence, value analysis focuses on (a) simplifying a product's design features and (b) minimizing the amount and cost of materials used in it.

◀ **Quick Test 2**

3	T or F	Work measurement methods typically result in time standards.
4	T or F	Productivity improvements are best sought through a focus on the valued elements of a job.

③ QUALITY AND THE SUPERVISOR

CONCEPT ▶ Supervisors have a major responsibility for making an organization's quality assurance effort successful.

To begin with, what exactly is meant by quality?

Quality is a measure of the degree to which a process, product, or service conforms to the requirements that have been established for it. This means that quality is not merely a descriptive term; to have meaning, quality must be defined in highly specific terms. For example:

- "This process (operating an air-driven nut runner) must conform to the requirement that the machine's pressure be held to 90 pounds per square inch (psi), plus or minus 5 psi."
- "This product (a box of cereal) must conform to the requirement that it weigh no more than 16¼ ounces and no less than 16 ounces."
- "This service (recording of telephone sales orders) must conform to the requirement that *all* prices be exactly as they appear in the published catalog."

Quality. The measure of the degree to which a process, product, or service conforms to the requirements that have been established for it.

How do you differentiate among the many other terms that are associated with quality?

Unfortunately, many quality-related terms have evolved without precise definition. It helps, however, to classify them as either conceptual terms or operational terms. The paragraphs that follow will clarify generally accepted usage of some of the more important terms.

Conceptual terms include:

Quality control (QC) is the basic term. Unfortunately, its emphasis on control projects a narrow, negative, or corrective connotation. Its usage is often supplemented by the broader, more positive and preventive concepts of quality assurance and total quality performance.

Quality Assurance encompasses *all* the efforts taken by an organization to ensure that its processes, products, and services conform to the requirements set for them. This concept has gained general acceptance, and companies around the world are likely to insist that their suppliers maintain active quality-assurance programs. See Table 17-2 for an international standard for such programs.

Total Quality Management (TQM) is an even broader concept than quality assurance. TQM implies that all constituents of an enterprise (suppliers and distributors as well as the internal members of the organization) must (a) accept responsibility for the quality of the goods and services that are linked to providing customer and client satisfaction, and (b) must become involved in the process that produces them.

Return on Quality (ROQ) is a modification of TQM in that it foregoes quality for quality's sake alone and focuses on providing only that degree of quality that a customer or client values highly and is willing to pay the price to obtain.

TABLE 17-2

International Standards for Quality Management

The most widely accepted international standards for judging systems that organizations use to manage quality are the ISO 9000 series. These were set by the International Standards Organization of Geneva, Switzerland, in 1987 and have been identified in the United States as the ANSI/ASQC Q90 series. ANSI is the American National Standards Institute, and ASQC is the American Society for Quality Control. The ISO 9000 standards serve to identify and certify a supplier's ability to meet a customer's product and service requirements. This is increasingly important for companies that participate in global markets.

To become certified, a company must pass an audit against the appropriate quality-management standard. The series consists of four parts:

ISO 9000 is a guide to the selection and use of total quality-management and quality-assurance standards.

ISO 9001 is a standard for quality assurance in design and development, production, installation, and servicing of products. This is the most important standard.

ISO 9002 provides additional details on the standard for quality assurance in production and installation.

ISO 9003 elaborates on the assurance standards for final inspection and test activities.

The Malcolm Baldrige National Quality Awards, while having no direct connection with ISO 9000, recognizes U.S. companies that excel in quality management and quality achievement. These awards are sponsored by the National Institute of Standards and Technology of the United States Chamber of Commerce and are administered by the American Society for Quality Control.

◀ In the 1990s, many American companies responded to the perceived superior quality of many foreign-made products. **Is that perception still present?**

Operational terms include:

Acceptable Quality Level (AQL) is an expression of the limits of deviation from a specified quality characteristic of a product or service that is accepted as having met the quality requirement. A required dimension or characteristic of quality is called a ***specification.*** The allowable limits of a deviation from a specification are called the ***tolerance.*** Despite the practicality and wide usage of AQL, many purists do not like the concept that underlies the term because it implies an acceptance of less-than-perfect performance. In fact, many Japanese firms have adopted the *Taguchi Method,* which sets specifications with no tolerance. They believe that the presence of an AQL inevitably leads to faulty products and services. Worldwide, however, most organizations find the AQL approach to be effective.

Any deviation in a product (or service) from its specified quality characteristics (or AQL) constitutes a ***defect*** or an error. The consequences of a defect or an error are that the product or service may either (a) require *rework* such as repair, adjustment, or repetition of all or part of the process that produced it, or (b) be classified as a ***reject*** to be discarded or destroyed.

Inspection is the process of examining a process, product, or service to determine whether it conforms to the established requirements and, if not, the extent of the deviation. Inspections can be made before, during, or after a process cycle is completed, or after a product is finished or a service delivered.

Nondestructive testing is an inspection that does not break, distort, or otherwise damage the product being made. A farmer who candles

Acceptable Quality Level (AQL). A general form of specification that tells a supervisor the kind of tolerance limiting that will be judged as acceptable performance.

Specification. The definitions of expected performance of a product (or quality of a service).

Tolerance. A statement of precision that establishes limits within which the product or the service must meet the specification.

Defect. Any variation (in the product or service) from specifications that falls outside the prescribed tolerances.

Reject. A product that needs to be discarded or destroyed.

an egg is applying nondestructive testing. Industry techniques include X-rays, sound waves, temperature flow patterns, magnetic fields, and ultraviolet rays. Some of these techniques—such as ultrasound and CT Scans—are widely used in the medical field to determine the internal conditions of the body without damaging the tissues.

How great is a supervisor's responsibility for quality assurance?

It is a very large, but shared, responsibility. First of all, it should be made clear that the attainment of quality does not reside in a single person or even a single department. Every activity of an organization contributes to, or detracts from, the quality of its products or services. These include, especially, such functional departments as product design, methods engineering, purchasing, and maintenance and repair. The functions that receive the greatest amount of heat, however, are (a) the inspection and quality-control departments and (b) the supervisor's own operations. Inspection and QC are expected to catch errors and defective work before they leave the department. Supervisors are expected to make certain that the errors and defects do not occur in the first place.

There is a long-standing guideline that should govern any supervisor's approach to a responsibility for quality: *Quality must be built into the product. No one can inspect it in.*

In what ways does poor quality add to costs?

Off-grade quality costs industry billions of dollars each year. It is most obvious in the form of product liability suits (a million claims for a total of $50 billion in damages in a year is not unusual) and manufacturers' recalls to repair defective goods. Billions of dollars are lost to poor quality, however, in two other ways:

Corrective Costs. These costs include money down the drain for any of the following: (a) damaged parts and materials that must be scrapped or, at best, reworked; (b) the time and effort of redoing poor work; (c) the cost of warranties that presume errors will be made that must be corrected later; and (d) the cost of handling customer complaints. Corrective quality is by far the most costly approach to quality problems, accounting for 2 to 10 percent of sales revenue.

Preventive Costs. These are the costs of trying to prevent poor workmanship or defective goods in the first place. They include routine (a) inspection, (b) testing, and (c) quality-control procedures, including education and motivation programs. It is a rare organization where the costs of preventive quality, however, exceed 3 percent of total sales revenue.

Obviously, prevention is less costly than cure.

How can you make your own checks of quality?

Keep in mind these 10 points:

1. Set up some specific quality standards, such as dimensions and appearance. Keeping examples of acceptable and nonacceptable work on exhibit helps.
2. Put quality specifications or standards in writing. See that your employees get a copy to guide them.
3. Allocate some of your own time for inspection. The total amount isn't so important as doing a certain amount each day.
4. Pick the spots where quality can best be made or lost. There is no point in spending your time checking operations where nothing much can go wrong.
5. Make inspection rounds from time to time. Change the order of your trips frequently.
6. Select at random 5 or 10 percent of the pieces produced (for example, letters typed) at a particular station. Inspect each one carefully.
7. Correct operating conditions immediately where your inspection shows material to be off grade or equipment to be faulty.
8. Consult with employees to determine the reason for poor workmanship or unacceptable products. Seek their cooperation in correcting conditions and improving quality.
9. Check the first piece on a new setup or a new assignment. Don't permit production until you are satisfied with the quality.
10. Post quality records, scrap percentages, and so forth, to keep employees informed of the department's performance.

5	T or F	Quality control and quality assurance mean basically the same thing.	◀ *Quick Test 3*
6	T or F	The responsibility for quality basically resides in a single department assigned those duties.	

④ STATISTICAL QUALITY CONTROL

CONCEPT ▶ Statistical quality control makes valuable use of mathematical techniques for monitoring and controlling the quality of processes, products, and services.

What is meant by statistical quality control?

Statistical Quality Control (SQC) simply means that numbers—statistics—are used as a part of the overall approach to controlling quality.

> **Statistical Quality Control (SQC).** Numbers are used as a part of the overall approach to controlling quality.

Statistics are tools and in no way relieve supervisors or employees from a concern with quality. Used properly, however, statistics can be of considerable aid.

In many industries, it is only the techniques of SQC that make rigid specifications economically attainable. For example, JC Penney Co., Inc., orders millions of knitted garments each year. It uses various inspection and statistical methods to screen the thousands of samples submitted to the company for purchase. As a consequence, the company often rejects 30 percent of the submissions, thus preventing subsequent disasters at the sales counters.

In Japan, the practice of SQC is so widespread that a great many employees, including truck drivers and workers of all kinds, prepare and maintain their own quality-control charts.

What are some of the tools of statistical quality control, and how do they affect the supervisor's job?

Greatly increased demands for precision parts have stepped up the need for better methods to measure and record the accuracy with which manufacturing people meet product specifications. Statistical methods speed up this measuring process, and more and more companies in all kinds of industries use them in some form or other. Don't let any fear you may have of mathematics prevent your using statistical methods.

Three statistical quality-control tools are most commonly encountered:

1. **Frequency-distribution chart.** Hold on. It isn't as bad as it sounds. Probably you'll recognize it by its more popular name—a tally card. If you were asked to place an X in the appropriate space for every shaft diameter you gauged in a given lot, chances are that you'd come up with a tally that looks something like Figure 17-3.

   In this case, the nominal shaft diameter was 0.730 inch with a tolerance of ± 0.002. This tally gives you a picture of just what and where the shaft variations are instead of merely recording whether a

◆ **FIGURE 17-3**

Simple frequency-distribution chart (histogram) used in statistical quality control. **What is its purpose?**

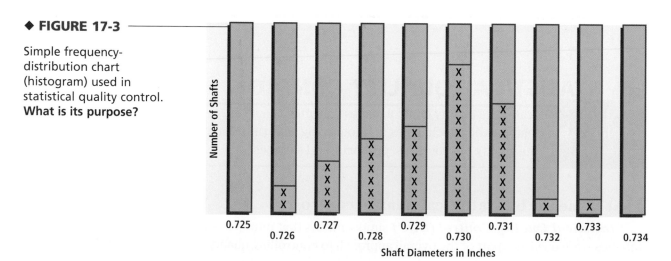

shaft is good or bad. This frequency-distribution chart (or histogram) helps tell you the causes of the variation. The wide distribution in this case indicates tool wobble. A picture that showed parts bunched around a point below or above the nominal 0.730 inch (say, at 0.728) might mean that the setup must be adjusted.

2. **Quality-control chart.** This is an hour-by-hour, day-by-day graphic comparison of actual product quality characteristics. On the chart are limits that reflect the person's or the machine's ability to produce, as shown by past experience. Statisticians make use of their knowledge of shop tolerances and analysis of previous frequency distribution tallies to establish these limits. Whenever the inspections plotted on the control chart show that the product is getting outside the predicted control limits, that's a signal for the supervisor or the operator to correct what is being done so that the product comes back into specification.

In Figure 17-4 the part being made is supposed to measure 0.730 inch. The tolerance is ± 0.002, or from 0.728 to 0.732 inch. The quality-control statistician has predicted in advance from a frequency-distribution diagram that most production will vary within these control limits—the 0.7285 and 0.7315 lines. When quality stays within these limits, it is said to be "on the highway." It is to be expected that a few products will fall outside the limits, into the "shoulder." But when the trend of measurements indicates that

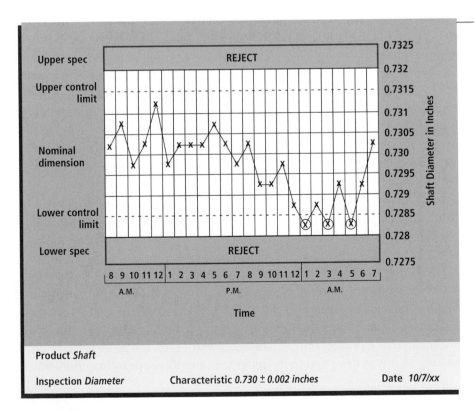

◆ **FIGURE 17-4**

Quality-control chart. **What does it mean to be "on the highway"?**

product quality is drifting progressively into the shoulder area, it's time to check the process. Any product that goes beyond the upper or lower specification limits (goes "into the ditch") is rejected.

The value of the chart lies in its ability to tell the supervisor and the operator whether they are within bounds or whether they are losing control of the process, before the process goes completely haywire.

3. **Sampling tables.** The trend today has been away from 100 percent inspection, which is costly and often misleading. (In a 100 percent check of a load of oranges, does this mean that each orange has been inspected for color, ripeness, thickness of skin, and appearance? Or does it mean that each orange was inspected for appearance only?) The first solution to less than 100 percent checking was spot checking, but this proved unreliable. Today, most sampling is done according to the size of the lot of goods produced and according to tables designed by statisticians for this purpose. These sampling tables guide the quality-control manager in the determination of how large a sample to take and how often to take it.

Is there a connection between reliability and statistical quality control?

Yes, indirectly, and it often has a direct relationship to product liability claims. *Reliability* is defined as the probability of a product's performing a specific function, under given conditions, for a specified time without failure. It must measure up specifically, therefore, to (a) what it's supposed to do (such as, for a bolt, hold 500 pounds of direct pull); (b) the circumstances under which it will be used (such as temperatures up to 185°C in an acid atmosphere); and (c) the length of time it should perform before it breaks or stops working (such as 25,000 fastenings or 39 months). Reliability can be determined either by direct test (using the product until it fails) or by statistical computation (based on assumptions about the design and work characteristics of the product). Reliability is usually expressed as the (mean) time expected between failures, for example, 500 hours.

Because the assumptions made vary in the degree of confidence the estimator has in them, reliability figures are often qualified as having, say, 85 percent confidence (being 85 percent sure to last as long as predicted, with a 15 percent risk of not lasting that long).

Reliability enters statistical quality-control considerations when you are deciding on the tolerance limits of variation, on how far from standard the product can be without being rejected. Obviously, the tighter the variable limits, the greater the reliability of the product. However, this does not mean that a perfect part will be reliable forever. It will be reliable only as long as it was designed to be under the specified operating conditions.

Reliability. A measure (usually a statistical estimate) of the probability of a product's performing specific functions, under given conditions, for a specified time without failure.

| **7** | T or F | Statistical quality control is too complex for all but the most sophisticated experts to use. |
| **8** | T or F | Quality-control charts rely on previously set tolerances to indicate when a system is in or out of control. |

(5) TOWARD TOTAL QUALITY MANAGEMENT

CONCEPT ▶ The ultimate in quality achievement depends upon complete commitment and maximum participation by the entire organization.

Commitment to quality? How inclusive must it be?

When it comes to succeeding with quality, commitment must involve every member of an organization, as well as constituents outside the enterprise. Organizations have been slow to come to this conclusion. Originally, it was thought that a good inspection team was all that was needed to ensure acceptable quality. Then, with the introduction of the zero-defects approach, commitment from top to bottom became the guideline. Broad commitment led to participation at all levels, together with deep involvement by the workforce. Gradually there emerged the belief that customer satisfaction must be drawn into the quality planning, as well as a commitment from suppliers and distributors. This principle formed the basis for total quality management (TQM). And TQM is now being fine tuned by the idea of benchmarking and return on quality, as explained later in this section. Figure 17-5 illustrates this evolution.

What is the zero defects program, and why did it work so well?

Philip Crosby, a quality-control expert intimately involved with the NASA space program and later corporate vice-president for quality for ITT Corporation, removed the emphasis on statistical quality control and expert inspectors and placed the responsibility for quality in the hands of the employees. *Zero defects (ZD)* stressed personal motivation. It attempted to instill in each individual a pride in his or her work. It was the first quality program to put quality on a personal basis. ZD techniques were aimed at stimulating everyone involved to care about accuracy and completeness, to pay attention to detail, and to improve work habits. In this manner, everyone worked toward reducing his or her own errors to zero.

Ethical PERSPECTIVES

Taking Credit

Indira Gandhi said, "There are two kinds of people, those who do the work and those who take credit. Try to be in the first group; there is less competition there." What do you think of employees who reach their goals at the expense of others?

The evolution of quality management techniques. **What is the primary target of quality management?**

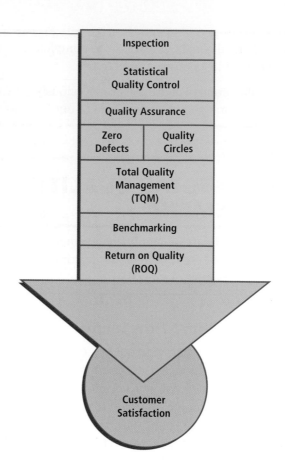

Zero defects techniques got great results for three good reasons:

1. **The quality standard was very explicit: Do it the right way from the start.** As Philip Crosby said, "What standard would you set on how many babies a nurse should be allowed to drop?"

2. **There was complete commitment by everyone.** From sweeper to top executive, from production worker to clerical employee, everyone was encouraged to spot problems, detect errors, and prescribe ways and means for their removal.

3. **Action was taken immediately to change behavior and to remove conditions that cause errors.** Crosby maintained that 90 percent of all error causes could be acted upon and fully removed by first-line supervisors. In other words, top management had to do its part to improve conditions, but supervisors and employees could handle most problems right at the operating level.

If ZD was so good, what caused all the excitement about quality circles?

If you agree with the participative aspect of ZD, then you'll probably agree that the quality circle movement is the next logical step forward. Both programs are based on the belief that quality cannot be produced or controlled by a single individual or department. Both programs conceive of quality as the result of dozens, perhaps hundreds, of interactions. These take place between the designer and the manufacturing department, between manufacturing and purchasing, between sales and production, between the data-entry operator and the computer programmer, and so on. Quality is the end result of a complex system. The quality circle concept accepts quality as a starting point (as with ZD) and *then* concludes that only by bringing together the people who are directly involved in the system will the obstacles that block good quality and error-free performance be removed.

Quality circles were conceived of by an American statistician, W. Edwards Deming (abetted by Joseph M. Juran, a noted quality consultant) and introduced in Japan in the 1950s. Gradually, firms in the United States, such as General Motors and Westinghouse Electric Corp., got wind of the idea. These companies formed small groups of 10 to 15 employees to meet regularly to examine and suggest solutions to common problems of quality. Now, the number of U.S. firms using these circles has grown into the thousands. Circles are found just about anywhere, in small companies as well as large, in hospitals as well as banks, in government agencies, and in offices as well as factories.

How does a quality circle operate?

Since the quality circle concept is based on maximum—and voluntary—involvement of employees from top to bottom of an organization, quality circle programs are almost always initiated at the executive level. If the program doesn't get all-out support at that level, it probably won't work at any level. Next, the quality circle idea is fanned out into the total organization. It is typically spearheaded by a "facilitator" or "coordinator." That person helps to organize the departmental and interdepartmental circles. He or she also provides the necessary training in problem and opportunity identification and in methods improvement and problem solving.

Each circle is made up exclusively of volunteers, who meet on company time. They place personnel and labor relations problems off limits. Also prohibited are discussions about the performance or lack of performance of specific individuals. Typically, a new quality circle will focus on simple workplace problems. Early achievements build confidence and experience. Later on, the circle will tackle more ambitious problems, ones that extend beyond its own control and involve other departments and other circles. As its expertise grows, the circle will shift gears from problem solving to problem preventing.

Supervisors should be cautioned that under current labor law in the United States, an employee team such as a quality circle must function in such a way that it does not encroach upon labor union prerogatives or employees' rights to union representation and collective bargaining. *Generally speaking, a quality circle must stick to its charter: investigating problems involving quality and productivity and the like, and suggesting ways to improve them.* This means that team leaders and members should avoid appearing to represent or negotiate for employees in matters such as wages, hours of work, working conditions, or grievances.

Is quality the only focus of a quality circle?

It started that way, but most circles have found that quality is inevitably tangled up with every imaginable kind of operating problem. As a consequence, most circles will turn their attention to any troublesome problem. And most organizations with a quality circle program cite example after example of productivity improvement.

You may have observed by now that all quality-improvement approaches have much in common with productivity- and cost-improvement programs. There is a great deal of desirable overlap. Many of the techniques of quality improvement have been borrowed from work simplification, for example. The reason for these similarities is that at the heart of all improvement programs are the problem-solving and decision-making techniques described in Chapter 6. The effective quality circle program makes special use of all the approaches associated with problem solving and methods improvement (see Figure 17-5).

Where does Total Quality Management (TQM) fit in?

A simple answer is that TQM is bigger than either zero defects or quality circles. To begin with, TQM focuses on ultimate customer or client satisfaction. Satisfaction in this context applies not only to the primary goods or services contracted for, but also to the way in which they are delivered and serviced. And it doesn't stop there. Under TQM, the customer must be satisfied with the manner in which all contacts with the provider are conducted. This means no "brush-offs," "round-robins," or buck-passing when a customer or client seeks information or registers a complaint. Obviously, this is a tall order and a difficult one for an enterprise to fill. Nevertheless, that is the main idea of TQM.

The implementation of TQM typically involves some aspects of both ZD and quality circles. For instance, TQM adheres to the belief that attitudes, education, and motivation can play a large part within an organization as its various functional departments strive for quality. That's the ZD way. The quality circles approach is reflected in the emphasis that TQM places on teamwork and on specifications-oriented, systematic, problem-solving programs.

Benchmarking? What's that?

In a way, **benchmarking** is much like TQM, but with an added twist. It, too, is vitally concerned with customer satisfaction. Benchmarking often begins with finding out exactly what customers and clients really want in the product or service. This establishes the "customer benchmark." That way, productive efforts can be devoted to giving customers what will satisfy them, rather than wasting time producing something that

Benchmarking. A quality management technique based on finding the best product, service, process, or procedure and adopting it as the standard of quality performance.

isn't valued much. Once the customer benchmark has been set, its impact may be felt (in the form of changed specifications and procedures) all the way back to the supervisor's department.

A related phase of benchmarking focuses on the quality of competitors' products and services—and the way they provide these services. The guideline is "Identify the best there is in your field . . . and do it that way yourself." This phase of benchmarking may also look, not only to competitors, but also to any company that has a reputation for doing something in particular very well. It may be order processing, inventory control, or any phase of manufacturing. Here again, the objective is to identify the best way of doing something and to copy it. These "competitor" or "external" benchmarks, too, may change the way things are done in a supervisor's department.

Finally (although many companies begin with this phase), there is a search for "internal" benchmarks, which are usually cost and/or quality related. In this phase, the idea is to locate the place in the organization where a particular work activity is best performed. The procedures used there then become the benchmark (or model) for all departments that perform similar work.

Ultimately, the goal of a benchmarking program is to establish a set of benchmarks in the form of goals, standards, or specifications (a) for products and services that will provide the optimum in customer satisfaction and (b) for internal methods and procedures that will be most cost- and quality-effective.

Is the concept of Return on Quality (ROQ) a step forward or backward in quality assurance?

It is not so much a step in either direction as it is a reaffirmation of the TQM policy of focusing all quality efforts on customer or client values. ROQ rejects quality for quality's sake alone. Instead, it takes a hard look at the cost of providing the specified characteristics of a product or service. It then weighs these costs against what a customer or client is willing to pay for these characteristics.

In effect, ROQ advises against "gilding the lily" unless the customer wants it gilded and is willing to pay the price to have it that way. ROQ is also somewhat like value analysis, as discussed earlier, wherein the product or service is designed to meet only the use and esteem functions that are valued by the customer.

◀ Quick Test 5

9	T or F	Zero defects and quality circles are both based on requiring all employees to search actively for ways to improve quality.
10	T or F	An important thrust in the search for quality is to identify what the customer wants and is willing to pay for.

6 INNOVATION AND CREATIVITY

CONCEPT ▶ Creative supervisors and employees are valuable sources of innovative ideas for improving work methods and quality.

How can you get employees more interested in productivity and quality?

It has been popular to complain about the "I don't care" attitude of some employees. Your viewpoint should be that if employees don't care about quality, it's because you have failed to convince them of its importance.

To get a worker to become performance conscious, start right from the first day by stressing quality as well as output. Emphasize that the two must go hand-in-hand in your department. Whenever you show an employee how to do a job—especially a new employee or a new job—be specific as to what kind of work is acceptable and what kind will not meet specifications. Explain the reason behind product- or service-quality limitations, and try to give your employees the little tricks of the trade that help to make productivity and quality standards easy to attain.

Why do employees make errors?

Generally speaking, employees make mistakes for six reasons—and most begin with management inadequacies rather than with employee shortcomings. The experience of companies that have improved their productivity and quality shows these potential causes of errors:

- Lack of training
- Poor communication
- Inadequate tools and equipment
- Insufficient planning
- Incomplete specifications and procedures
- Lack of attention or concern

Poor communication, for example, can be overcome by taking the extra time to make sure each person fully understands the instructions. In written orders, don't leave loopholes that can lead to misinterpretation. One small company with a large staff of Spanish-speaking people had the workers repeat the orders that were given to them. It took a few minutes, but it actually saved time. Rejects and rework tumbled to a fraction of 1 percent.

Lack of concern, however, is completely different from the other potential causes of error and is perhaps the most serious. This is very personal and stems from employees' attitudes. You must reaffirm that management is interested in employees and will help them do their jobs to perfection. You, as a supervisor, must re-create the old-fashioned pride in one's craft. You must motivate employees so that they have a personal attachment to their jobs and will be proud of the quality of the work they do. And you must use a variety of ways to stimulate the application of creative thinking toward productivity and quality improvement.

Exactly what is creative thinking?

It is simply the ability to put your mind to a problem that hasn't been solved by a routine method and to come up with a brand-new solution or batch of solutions. Many experts think that the secret of creativity lies in *free association of ideas,* that is, the mind's ability to make a connection between two vastly different objects or ideas. Take this example: A factory was spraypainting bedsprings automatically. Drips and "teardrops" were a big problem. The engineer tried all the obvious ideas. He speeded up the spraying and then slowed it down; he changed paint consistency, surface preparation, drying heat, and airflow. No luck. Then the supervisor of the operation came up with the bright idea of whacking the painted springs automatically with a rubber hose. It worked! Paint flew off like the dust from a rug she had seen her grandmother beat with a rug beater. Not only was the drip problem solved, but also enough paint was collected in gutters beneath the springs to paint twice as many springs as before.

The free association of ideas was linking the painting problem with getting dust out of a rug.

Free association of ideas. The ability of the mind to unconsciously visualize relationships between seemingly different objects and ideas.

What isn't creative thinking?

Critical, negative thinking tends to discourage the flow of ideas. Alex Osborn, the advocate and popularizer of brainstorming, always advised innovators to think the "green-light" way. When the green light is on, you don't stop to judge the merit of the ideas that emerge. The time to apply "red-light" thinking is after you've created a batch of ideas and want to evaluate their potential for improving the methods under review.

What is the best way to generate innovative ideas on your own?

There is no one best way, but successful innovators follow a systematic approach something like this:
1. **Narrow down the problem or the target.** It's easier to think of ideas for changing the way day-old reports are filed, for example, than to redesign the entire filing system.
2. **Learn to concentrate.** Try writing the problem on a sheet of paper and keeping it in front of you to focus your attention.
3. **Persevere.** Good ideas don't always come quickly. So if you can't produce a workable solution today, try again tomorrow.
4. **Preserve.** When you come across good ideas, write them down before they're forgotten. Put these in a special file (an "idea bank"), and search it occasionally for possible applications.
5. **Build your confidence.** Look for early breakthroughs on small matters; then raise your sights to more difficult challenges.

6. **Use your unconscious mind.** Remove blockages by sleeping on a problem, letting your mind wander, taking a break.
7. **Keep ideas flowing.** When you're hot, don't stop generating ideas just because it's quitting time.
8. **Take action.** Ideas may strike you in a sudden burst of inspiration. Nothing much will come of them, however, unless you convert them to practical usage.

What's the difference between brainstorming and creative thinking?

Brainstorming is the group approach to idea generation. The term was coined by Alex Osborn, an advertising executive, and he set four rules for a successful brainstorming session:

1. **Don't criticize ideas.** There's a time for judicial thinking, but not while brainstorming.
2. **Welcome ideas freely.** That is, the wilder the idea, the better. A "can you top this?" attitude is encouraged. Participants use others' ideas as jumping-off places for their own.
3. **Strive for quantity.** Experience shows that the more ideas there are the better they are likely to be. A seemingly remote idea from one person may trigger a more valuable idea from another.
4. **Combine and improve.** Ideas are like building blocks. Brainstorming participants are encouraged to suggest how an idea can be expanded upon or how two ideas can be combined into a single idea that is better than either idea alone. (Note the use here of work-simplification techniques.)

> **Brainstorming.** A group approach to idea generation that encourages free association of ideas among participants, while forbidding negative judgments, in order to generate a maximum number of ideas in a short period of time.

Quick Test 6 ▶	11	T or F	When employees make errors, the dominant cause lies within them, not in management.
	12	T or F	A key principle in brainstorming is to strive for quality ideas.

KEY CONCEPTS TO REMEMBER

1. **Understanding Productivity.** Productivity is akin to efficiency. It compares (a) the output value of the product or service produced with (b) the costs of the input resources (labor, materials, equipment) that are used to make the product or provide the service. Productivity is the "bottom line" for supervisory performance evaluation. Productivity increases whenever the output rises faster or falls slower than the input; it decreases when the opposite occurs. Productivity improvement is affected by the contributions of two factors: technological and human.

2. **Methods Improvement.** The time needed to perform a task is directly proportional to the way in which the job is performed. The time needed can almost always be reduced through the application of various techniques for methods improvement and motion economy that simplify work procedures and utilize work-assisting devices, tools, and machinery. Large-scale productivity gains are mostly achieved through the introduction of automation, robots, and computers using such techniques as workflow automation and reengineering. Value analysis is a form of productivity improvement that focuses on the product, rather than on the process by which it is made.

3. **Quality and the Supervisor.** Quality is a measure of the degree to which a process, product, or service conforms to the requirements that have been established for it. The cost of correcting defects and errors is high compared with the cost of preventing poor quality in the first place. Concerns for quality extend far beyond the manufacture of products into every kind of service that is provided internally, as well as externally, to customers. The first-line supervisor is in a key position to see that quality is built into the product or service as it is produced.

4. **Statistical Quality Control.** Statistical quality control (SQC) provides a valuable method for monitoring and controlling quality performance. The three principal tools of SQC are frequency-distribution charts, quality-control charts, and sampling tables. Reliability is a special concept that establishes the probability of a product's performing a specific function, under given conditions, for a specified number of times (or period of time) without failure.

5. **Toward Total Quality Management.** The concepts of zero defects and quality circles have been especially effective in quality-assurance programs. They both illustrate that most errors of workmanship can be eliminated if each individual is properly motivated and supported throughout the entire organization. The success of quality circles is highly dependent on group participation techniques applied to solving problems of quality and productivity. Both approaches usually are incorporated now in total quality management (TQM), which enlarges the scope of quality management to focus on customer satisfaction and to include suppliers and distributors. Benchmarking is a related technique for finding the best there is in a product, service, process, or procedure and adopting that as the standard of quality performance. Return on quality (ROQ) modifies TQM so as to focus on providing only that degree of quality that is

valued highly by customers and for which they are willing to pay.

6. **Innovation and Creativity.** Supervisors and their employees, because of their nearness to the work, can be especially creative in suggesting new ways for improving productivity. Such innovation is related to an individual's ability to obtain a free association of seemingly unrelated ideas. When this process is carried out in group sessions, it is called *brainstorming*.

READING COMPREHENSION

1. What two factors determine the productivity measurements of an operation? Why is higher productivity so greatly valued by an organization?

2. A collection agency estimated that each transaction a clerical worker recorded contributed 25 cents to the total value of the agency's services. The average clerk receives $8.00 per hour, and can record 800 transactions during an 8-hour day. What is the productivity rate stated in units per hour for an average clerk? Express this rate as a ratio. What is the productivity rate stated in dollars per hour for an average clerk? Using dollars for calculating both outputs and inputs, what is the productivity ratio for an average clerk? Why are the two ratios different? Which is the correct one? Why? For what purpose might each be used?

3. Name the five elements used in analyzing a work activity for methods improvement and explain why one of these is considered value-adding and the others wasteful.

4. Compare, for the sake of value analysis, the use function and the esteem function.

5. What are some of the things supervisors should do for themselves in seeking to ensure quality performance in their departments?

6. Besides poor workmanship, what are some of the things that can contribute to defects and errors?

7. How does statistical quality control differ from inspection?

8. In what way are zero defects programs and quality circle programs alike?

9. In what way is ROQ like TQM? Value analysis?

10. Why do brainstorming sessions strive for large quantities of ideas? Wouldn't it be better to stress the quality of the ideas?

APPLICATION

Self-Assessment

▶ *How good are your productivity/ quality improvement skills?*

Read the following statements carefully. Circle the number on the response scale that most closely reflects the degree to which each statement accurately describes you. Add up your total points and prepare a brief action plan for self-improvement. Be ready to report your score for tabulation across the entire group.

		Good Description									Poor Description
1.	I understand how the basic productivity ratios are determined.	10	9	8	7	6	5	4	3	2	1
2.	I am open to exploring both technological and human avenues for productivity improvements.	10	9	8	7	6	5	4	3	2	1
3.	I am continuously on the alert for potential productivity improvements in the areas of inspection, transportation, delays, and storage.	10	9	8	7	6	5	4	3	2	1
4.	I can, in my mind, see the useful distinction between the use function and esteem function in the product or service my unit is responsible for.	10	9	8	7	6	5	4	3	2	1
5.	I can explain the difference between quality control and quality assurance to employees.	10	9	8	7	6	5	4	3	2	1
6.	I fully understand the value of exercising preventive control versus corrective control when it comes to achieving quality.	10	9	8	7	6	5	4	3	2	1
7.	I feel comfortable with my ability to use a variety of statistical quality-control tools such as histograms and quality-control charts.	10	9	8	7	6	5	4	3	2	1
8.	I fully endorse the three underlying principles of zero defects: explicit standards, complete commitment, and immediate action to improve conditions affecting quality.	10	9	8	7	6	5	4	3	2	1
9.	I would strongly support the use of employee participation for identifying and solving both productivity and quality problems.	10	9	8	7	6	5	4	3	2	1
10.	I would feel very comfortable conducting a group brainstorming session on ways to improve quality.	10	9	8	7	6	5	4	3	2	1

Scoring and Interpretation

SCORING

Add up your total points for the 10 questions. Record that number here, and report it when it is requested. _____

INTERPRETATION

81 to 100 points. You seem to have a basic set of productivity/quality improvement skills.

61 to 80 points. Take a close look at some of your productivity/quality improvement skills (those with lower self-assessments) and discuss them with a manager to see if they need improvement.

Below 60 points. Some of your skills may be substantially inconsistent with effective productivity/quality improvement practices and could be detrimental to your success as a supervisor.

Identify your three lowest scores and record the question numbers here: _____, _____, _____.

ACTION

Write a brief paragraph detailing an action plan for how you might sharpen each of these skills. Then pay particularly close attention to the related material in the chapter as you review the relevant sections there.

Skill Development

▶ ### *Productivity/Quality Improvement*

Opportunities for productivity and quality improvement are almost everywhere, if we are alert to them, creative enough to address them, and receptive to the inputs of others to assist us in this process. But supervisors must also be humble enough to recognize that not all good ideas need to come from within themselves; many employees can generate amazingly useful suggestions for change, too. The trick lies in soliciting their ideas in a fashion that convinces them that you are serious about using the best of the suggestions.

Identify a problem that lends itself to a fresh look from a variety of perspectives. Recruit a handful (three to six) of people to participate in attacking the problem. Conduct a brainstorming session to generate a large number of possible improvements. Be sure to brief the group first on the guidelines for brainstorming, and designate someone to record all the ideas the group produces. (To prepare yourself, you will likely wish to review the text's discussion on brainstorming, search the Internet for relevant guidelines, and consult with colleagues and staff persons in the human resources department for their advice.)

Productivity/quality improvement suggestions from the brainstorming session

1. _____
2. _____
3. _____
4. _____
5. _____
6. _____
7. _____
8. _____
9. _____
10. _____

ACTION

After assessing all the ideas produced, prepare a brief report that summarizes the group's 10 best suggestions for productivity or quality improvement from the brainstorming session. If possible, share the results of your study with a responsible person in the host organization and obtain his or her reactions.

Group Exercise

Role Reversal ◄

Assume that your instructor for this course has asked you, the students, for help in improving the instructor's productivity, quality, and innovativeness. In short, *you* are the expert consultants, and your instructor is the client for your services (a role reversal from the usual relationship). Your task is to help your instructor examine the roles she or he performs, identify barriers to high quality, and begin to shape a strategy for productivity improvements in the service that she or he provides to students.

STEP 1: Divide into groups of four to five persons. Prepare a set of interview questions designed to explore with your instructor the following topics:
   a. *Nature of his or her job* (major duties and responsibilities; key outcome measures for assessing productivity and quality).
   b. *External reasons* (obstacles and barriers) that work to prevent a higher level of performance.
   c. *Internal factors* (within the instructor) that work to prevent a higher level of performance.

STEP 2: Ask the questions, and gather the results.

STEP 3: Scan Chapter 17 to identify relevant concepts and tools that could potentially be applied to your instructor's situation to attain productivity improvements.

STEP 4: Present a brief report to your instructor, and assess the reaction to your suggestions. How relevant are the concepts and tools to a professional occupation? How likely is it that your instructor will implement some of your suggestions? Why or why not?

CASES FOR ANALYSIS

Case 51

As the Wheels Turn

This actually happened in a British lawnmower factory.

Regina, a methods engineer, was timing the work of an employee who was attaching wheels to a lawnmower body. The job instruction card read: "Mount 5-inch black wheels with red inserts, half-inch nuts, two spring washers and two flat washers, torque to 28 pounds." First, however, the workman rolled a dolly of 10 bodies from the painting room to his workbench. Then he went to the tool room for a torque wrench. Next, he went to the stockroom to pick up wheels and parts. He then set up a jig, or holding fixture, to simplify the handling of the lawnmower body. To do the actual work that Regina was timing, the workman placed each body in the jig, inserted the wheels onto the body's axles, placed the washers and nuts and tightened them to a torque of 28 pounds. When he had fitted the wheels to 10 bodies, he inspected his work, rejecting one of the bodies because of paint drips, and placed the remaining bodies on a dolly to be moved to the next operation.

Regina checked her watch: It had taken the workman only 75 minutes from start to finish. But the workman had clocked in at 8:00 and it was now 9:45, so that made a total of 105 minutes for 9 bodies, and he was about to go on tea break. That meant 105 minutes for 36 wheels.

As Regina was thinking about this, she noticed an inspector in a white coat measuring the gap between the wheels and the body on the nine finished assemblies. The inspector then put a pink tag on two of these bodies, and they were set aside to be reworked. Another inspector also came along, and he was checking the torque settings on the wrench that the workman had used. He saw that the torque measured only 22 pounds, and he adjusted it up to the prescribed 28 pounds.

When Regina went back to her office, she spoke to the assembly supervisor. "I watched a fellow spend 105 minutes working this morning, but he spent only 75 minutes of that time actually screwing 40 wheels on to 10 lawnmower bodies. Worse still, three of these bodies were rejected and will have to be reworked. That's really only 28 wheels in 105 minutes."

"Wait a minute," said the supervisor. "The standard for the wheel mounting job is 1.88 minutes, or about 2 minutes per wheel. If all 10 bodies had been okay, that would have been 40 wheels in 75 minutes actual time taken, or about two minutes per wheel. That's right on target!"

◀ *Analysis*

a. What's wrong with the supervisor's argument?

b. How do you explain the difference between the 75 minutes the employee spent actually mounting the wheels and the 105 minutes he was on the job?

c. What other problems that affect productivity do you see in this case?

Adapted from "A Changing View of Factory Labor," by J. Roger Morrison, *The McKinsey Quarterly*, Spring 1988, p. 79.

The Hard-to-Meet Quality Standards

◀ **Case 52**

Rhonda is the housekeeping supervisor for a 200-room motel located near the airport in a major southwestern city. Ten full-time and 15 part-time room-cleaners report to her. Hours are staggered to allow for housekeeping services throughout the day, although most room-cleaners report at 9 A.M. and finish by 5:30 P.M. Some night coverage is provided, and of course, service must be provided on the weekends, too. Because of the nature of the work and the hours, turnover among housekeeping employees has traditionally been high.

The motel, which is a franchise of a national chain, has been furnished with standards that specify not only the amount of work to be done by a room-cleaner during a shift, but also a long list of quality conditions that a serviced room should meet. Typically, a room-cleaner should service 3 rooms per hour, or 24 on an 8-hour shift. Exceptions to this standard can be made when the cleaner encounters unusual conditions in the room. Generally speaking, the room-cleaners meet this standard.

Where Rhonda has trouble is with the room-cleaner's ability to meet the quality standards. These standards specify such details as the way in which a finished bed must look, arrangement of furniture, replacement of stationery in the desk, and placement of soaps and towels in the bathroom.

There are over 20 of these details per room. Each is demonstrated in a training video shown to new employees and is also reproduced on an illustrated poster mounted in the housekeeper's office. Nevertheless, a day never goes by that Rhonda doesn't have to send a cleaner up to one or more rooms that haven't been properly serviced.

There is an even bigger quality problem, too. This has to do with the less definable conditions of quality, such as how completely the wall-to-wall carpet has been vacuumed, whether or not the drapes and curtains have been dusted, and the degree of cleanliness of the tub and shower, tile flooring, and mirrors in the bathroom. Verifying the quality of these conditions is difficult and subject to debate, at which Rhonda has learned her employees are expert.

Here are some of the arguments Rhonda has heard from the room-cleaners:

"The last cleaning person didn't do the job right, and it would have taken me another 10 minutes to get it in shape."

"The mops we're using need replacement. It's a wonder I can get the tile floors clean as it is."

"You're scheduling too many rooms early in the day. Many times, I've got to slip in and out while a lodger is still shaving."

"They must have had some party in that room last night. You should be happy I got it ready in time for the couple who were checking in."

"The vacuum cleaner on my floor is faulty and has needed maintenance for two weeks now."

"I did a super job of cleaning that room. You just show me where I didn't do it right."

"The supply man was late with the linens and towels, so I had to rush through several rooms in order to catch up."

"I can't clean three rooms an hour if you expect me to cover every one of the 20 details and still do a first-rate job of vacuuming and mopping."

Analysis ▶

What do you think Rhonda should do to improve the level of cleanliness and conformance to detail specs in the rooms her staff services? Of the five alternatives provided below, which do you think would be most appropriate? Rank them on a scale from 1 (most appropriate) to 5 (least appropriate). You may add another alternative, if you wish. Be prepared to justify your rankings.

_____ **a.** Agree that the room-cleaning job is difficult, but urge the cleaning persons to "do the best you can."

_____ **b.** Ask the maintenance department to examine all vacuum cleaners, mops, and other equipment to make sure that these are in good operating order.

_____ **c.** Take her employee's complaints seriously, investigate them one by one, and take action on those that have merit.

_____ **d.** Post this notice on the employees' bulletin board: "From now on, all rooms will be spot-checked for cleanliness. Employees with more than one room a week that doesn't meet cleanliness standards will be subject to dismissal."

_____ **e.** Notify the national chain headquarters that the room-cleaning standards are unreasonable and should be adjusted.

◀ **Case 53**

The Dried-Out Burger

"I can't eat this hamburger," declared the irate customer. "It's completely dried out!"

"I'm sorry," said the assistant manager of the fast-food restaurant, "we'll make you a fresh one."

"I don't have time to wait," said the customer. "This will be the last time I eat here."

When Gilda, the assistant manager, spoke to the counter person, he said that he had served the customer a wrapped hamburger that the fry cook had placed on the serving rack. "I assumed that it was okay," he said. "That customer seemed like an old crab. Nothing would have satisfied her. The hamburger wasn't that bad. She must have just gotten tired of waiting 'til we could get around to her."

The fry cook, when asked for her explanation of the dry hamburger, said, "We had been very busy earlier, and I made up an extra large batch so that I could stay ahead."

"You know," said Gilda, "that our standard says that you should never put more than 10 hamburgers up at a time. From the look of things, you must have had a couple of dozen in the serving rack. When they dry out, we can't serve them; they must be thrown away."

"Maybe I did," said the fry cook, "but I can't see what difference an occasional dry hamburger is going to make."

◁ *Analysis*

a. What do you think of the counter person's view of the situation?

b. How valid was the fry cook's explanation?

c. If you were Gilda, what would you do to prevent the serving of dried-out hamburgers in the future?

◀ **Case 54**

The Best and the Worst of It

On the quality-control chart for the production of a high-priced facial lotion, the pH specification is 7.0, with tolerance limits of ± 0.02. The control of pH is very important, because it measures acidity, with 7.0 being neutral. The manufacturer wishes to maintain this reading to avoid potential skin irritation, which could mean possible product liability suits from customers. Operators make check readings of the pH meter on the lotion flow line once each hour and record them on a chart, like the one provided in Figure 17-6.

Here are the readings made by operators on the first, second, and third shifts:

8 A.M. to 4 P.M.: 7.00, 6.99, 6.98, 7.00, 7.01, 7.02, 7.01, 7.00
4 P.M. to 12 A.M.: 6.98, 7.00, 7.02, 6.99, 7.02, 7.03, 6.99, 6.98
12 A.M. to 8 A.M.: 6.99, 7.00, 6.98, 6.97, 6.98, 6.96, 6.97, 6.95

Analysis

a. Using the information supplied, complete the quality-control chart in Figure 17-6. (Refer to Figure 17-4 for guidance.)
b. Which shift operator has the best control of the operation?
c. Which shift operator appears to have lost control of the operation?
d. Which operator appears to have more consistent control, the one on the first shift or the one on the second?

◆ **FIGURE 17-6**

pH specification quality-control chart.

pH Quality-Control Chart		
First Shift	Second Shift	Third Shift

Desired Specification

8 9 10 11 12 1 2 3 4 5 6 7 8 9 10 11 12 1 2 3 4 5 6 7

Hourly Readings

Answers to Quick Tests

Quick Test 1	Quick Test 2	Quick Test 3
1. F	3. T	5. F
2. T	4. F	6. F
Quick Test 4	**Quick Test 5**	**Quick Test 6**
7. F	9. F	11. F
8. T	10. T	12. F

PART Eight

Contemporary Concerns of Supervision

CHAPTER 18

Managing a Diverse Workforce

Learning Objectives

After studying this chapter, you should be able to

- Discuss the nature and workplace implications of a culturally diverse society.

- Identify and interpret the major equal employment opportunity legislation, explain the intent of affirmative action plans, and describe the role of the Equal Employment Opportunity Commission.

- Discuss the special problems of disadvantaged workers and suggest ways for integrating these employees successfully into the workplace.

- Discuss the importance of women in the workplace and their difficulties in advancing from their traditional roles, including related subjects such as job evaluation, comparable worth, and sexual harassment.

- Discuss the unique assets and drawbacks of older workers.

- Explain the legal and social aspects of an employee's right to privacy and the impact this has on a supervisor's right to manage.

A DIVERSE WORKFORCE

CONCEPT ▶ Society and our resultant workforce is becoming more culturally diverse every year.

What is the general makeup of the workforce today?

It has changed dramatically in the past few decades. Just 25 years ago, half of the members of the labor force were native-born white men. Today, although they still comprise a major segment of the existing workforce, only 15 percent of the new workers are native-born white men. In contrast, about 40 percent of the new entrants are white women. Other significant groups entering the labor force include immigrant men, native-born nonwhite women, and native-born nonwhite men. In addition, the number of young workers (ages 16 to 24) has dropped slightly. Today, about 60 percent of all women of working age are employed. Clearly, the labor pool is richly heterogeneous from many perspectives—gender, race, and age.

Good supervisors will seek a workforce reflective of these changes in the labor pool. They will also recognize that they must understand and accept *cultural diversity,* the cultural differences between ethnic and racial groups, in order to be a completely effective supervisor. For example, members of many Native American cultures do not make eye contact when speaking to a superior. They do this as a gesture of respect but it is often misunderstood as failure to pay attention, or as disrespect. Participation in cultural awareness and cultural diversity workshops can give supervisors a better understanding of the range of people they will encounter as supervisors and provide helpful suggestions to assist them in managing that diversity.

Is workforce diversity limited to ethnic and gender differences?

Definitely not. In addition to differences by race and gender, supervisors should also be aware of differences resulting from marital status, disability, age, sexual orientation, veteran's status, and religious belief. It is not the supervisor's responsibility to have a professional opinion on the correctness of the differences that they will note in their workforce. Pay attention to work performance, knowing that part of successfully managing people is understanding their needs and focusing their attention on work goals and objectives. The better you understand people and what motivates them, the more effective you will be in your supervisory responsibilities.

Cultural diversity. The recognition that society and the workforce are composed of a variety of groups, each of whom has, in addition to similarities with other groups, unique differences in beliefs and experiences that can be assets at work.

Quips & Quotes

Success is to be measured not so much by the position that one has reached in life as by the obstacles which he has overcome while trying to succeed.

—Booker T. Washington

② THE LEGAL BASIS

CONCEPT ▶ A strong body of law establishes the rights and privileges of all job applicants and employees, regardless of race, color, national origin, gender, disability, or age.

Protected groups. Certain minority and/or disadvantaged groups in the population, which warrant special protection in employment matters.

Discrimination. Any managerial action or decision based on favoring or disfavoring one person or member of a group over another on the basis of race, color, ethnic or national origin, gender, age, disability, Vietnam-era war service, or union membership.

Stereotype. The characterization of an individual on the basis of a standardized, oversimplified view of the characteristics believed (often wrongly) to be held in common by the group to which the individual is assumed to belong.

In the eyes of the law, who is a minority employee?

Just about everyone who is not under 40 years of age and a white male of European heritage. The generally more useful term applied to minorities today is *protected groups*. A **protected group** consists of people who, historically, have encountered discrimination in the American workplace. **Discrimination** is defined as any managerial action or decision that either favors or penalizes individuals based on characteristics that are not related to their work performance or professional qualifications. Most of the relevant laws specifically identify these people as ethnic and racial minorities (African Americans, Hispanics, Asians, and Native Americans, in particular), women, disadvantaged young persons, disabled workers, veterans of the Vietnam war era, and persons over 40 years of age.

The basic equal employment opportunity laws say that an employer cannot discriminate because of race, color, religion, gender, sexual orientation, national origin, or age. In trying to make these laws work, various agencies of the U.S. government have interpreted them to apply to all victims of prejudice and discrimination.

What has caused this intensified concern for minorities?

Great social forces at work in the past 40 years have altered the values of many people. What were once widespread **stereotypes** (oversimplified and often unfounded group characteristics applied indiscriminately to individual members of that group) of blacks and women, for example, are no longer tolerated, either by law or by society in general. Family lifestyles and marriage patterns have radically changed. And with them, our notions of what are appropriate occupations and behavior for women—and men—have changed, too. A great many people enjoy relatively affluent

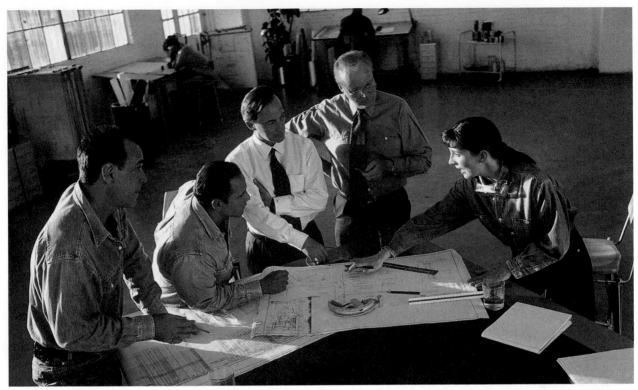

▲ Discrimination against job applicants and employees is generally forbidden by law. **Can you identify specific protected groups?**

and privileged livings. This makes for harsh comparisons with those who do not have jobs or who are relegated to less-skilled work and often poverty-level pay. The power of television and instant communication intensifies the awareness of these differences. People—especially those who believe that their lesser status is the result of discrimination (as it often is)—are impatient for improvement. The newer laws are a direct expression of the public's general dissatisfaction with these conditions and its wish to provide equal employment opportunities for all.

What is the legal basis for equal employment opportunity programs?

There is a great body of federal, state, and local laws. These have been reinforced by a number of significant rulings in the courts. The laws are further supported by guidelines laid down by the Equal Employment Opportunity Commission (EEOC), the federal agency charged with enforcing the law.

A discussion of the legal basis for nondiscriminatory legislation is beyond the scope of this text. A synopsis of the major federal laws, popularly referred to as the *equal employment opportunity (EEO)* laws, is provided for your review in Table 18-1. Most importantly, these laws specify that the great majority of business firms and public institutions cannot do any of the following:

Equal Employment Opportunity (EEO). A system of organizational justice, stipulated by law, that applies to all aspects of employment and is intended to provide equal opportunity for all members of the labor force.

TABLE 18-1

Synopsis of Major Federal Laws Enacted Since 1960 That Affect Equal Employment Opportunity

LAW

Equal Pay Act (1963)

PROVISION

Prohibits job discrimination in all employment practices on the basis of race, color, sex, religion, or national origin. This includes recruiting, selecting, compensating, classifying, assigning, promoting, disciplining, and terminating, as well as eligibility for union membership. The EEOC administers these laws and monitors related affirmative action programs.

LAW

Executive Order 11246 of 1965 as amended by Executive Order 11375 of 1967

PROVISION

Prohibits discrimination in employment in organizations having contracts of $10,000 or more with the federal government. The orders require that these organizations institute affirmative action programs and recruit and promote women and minorities where necessary.

LAW

Age Discrimination in Employment Act (1967) as amended in 1975

PROVISION

Prohibits discrimination in hiring and employment of workers over 40 years of age unless BFOQ can be established.

LAW

Rehabilitation Act of 1973 and Executive Order 11914 of 1974

PROVISION

Prohibits discrimination by federal contractors of applicants and employees with physical and mental disabilities.

LAW

Vietnam Era Veteran's Readjustment Assistance Act of 1974

PROVISION

Prohibits discrimination—by federal contractors—in employment of disabled veterans and veterans of the Vietnam war; also specifies certain affirmative actions in the employment of veterans.

LAW

Americans with Disabilities Act of 1990

PROVISION

Prohibits discrimination by all governmental units and private employers with 15 or more employees in the employment of qualified applicants or employees with a disability if reasonable accommodation to a job or a work environment is possible.

LAW

Family and Medical Leave Act of 1993

PROVISION

Requires public and private employers with 50 or more employees to provide eligible employees with the opportunity to take up to 12 weeks of unpaid leave per 12-month period for specifically defined family and medical situations.

- Make any distinctions based on race, gender, or national origin in any condition of employment, including hiring, setting wages ("equal pay for equal work"), classifying, assigning or promoting, and allocating the use of facilities, and in training, retraining, and apprenticeship programs.
- Distinguish between married and single people of one sex and not of the other.
- Deny employment to women with young children unless the same policies apply to men with young children.
- Penalize women because they require time away from work for childbearing.
- Maintain seniority lists based solely on gender or race.
- Establish jobs as either men's or women's. The only exceptions allowed are jobs for which the employer can prove that there is a bona fide occupational qualification (BFOQ).
- Discriminate against workers 40 years of age or over in hiring, firing, promoting, classifying, paying, assigning, advertising, or determining eligibility for union membership.
- Similarly discriminate against qualified disabled persons. The law defines persons with disabilities as individuals who (a) have a physical or mental impairment (many prefer the terms *challenged* or *differently abled*) that substantially limits one or more major life activities, (b) have a record of such impairments, or (c) are regarded as having such impairment.

Obviously, EEO legislation was designed to protect minority groups of all definition from discrimination. Its principal intent, however, was to encourage utilization of all the potential and talent of all minority groups in the workforce. Note that the law is not a labor-management law: It is directed at employers, and they must comply without obstruction from labor unions.

Internet CONNECTION

Check the website for the **Equal Employment Opportunity Commission** for diversity-related issues.

Where does affirmative action apply?

In enforcing the provisions of the equal employment opportunity laws, the EEOC and its state and local equivalents have encouraged firms to engage in affirmative action programs. An ***affirmative action*** program consists of action taken to ensure nondiscriminatory treatment of all groups that are protected by legislation that forbids discrimination in employment because of race, religion, gender, age, disability, Vietnam-era war service, or national origin. The EEOC emphasizes that results count, not good intentions. If company statistics on pay and promotion, for example, show that the current status of protected groups is inferior to that of most other employees in that company or geographic area, the company may be directed to set up an affirmative action program. Companies with federal contracts over $50,000 and with more than 50 employees have no choice. They must have a written program in place and follow it.

Affirmative action. An in-company program designed to remedy current and future inequities in employment of minorities.

In investigating EEO discrimination charges, what areas are most sensitive?

The EEOC will look for three possibilities:

1. **Differential treatment.** This occurs when a member of a protected group is treated differently from a nonmember in the same situation.
2. **Disparate effect.** When a job requirement acts to exclude a protected group, it creates a disparate effect. The employer must demonstrate that the requirement is a "business necessity" and thus a BFOQ.
3. **Evil intent.** This is present, for instance, when an employer or supervisor is "out to get" a member of a protected group.

These infractions are most likely to occur in recruiting, interviewing, selecting, assigning, appraising, training, promoting, and disciplining employees. Supervisors are intimately involved in all these areas. Accordingly, they bear a great deal of the responsibility for carrying out the spirit, as well as the requirements, of the law.

What is meant by *reverse discrimination*?

Reverse discrimination is what many believe happens to men, or to Caucasians in general, when preference in employment is shown to women, minorities, or both. In *Bakke v. University of California Board of Regents* (1978), the U.S. Supreme Court said in effect that it was wrong to use quotas designed to accommodate women and minorities in such a manner as to withhold employment from eligible men and whites. At the same time, however, the Court upheld the principle of affirmative action programs.

As you can infer, supervisors must tread a very unbiased line in this matter. They must be sure to support the principle of equal employment opportunity and affirmative action; yet they must also be careful not to use these guidelines unfairly to discriminate against nonminorities.

What is the ADA and how does it affect my job?

The Americans with Disability Act of 1990 (ADA) applies to private employers with 15 or more employees. State and local governments of any size are also included. ADA prohibits discrimination in all employment practices including job application procedures, hiring, firing, advancement, compensation, training; and other terms, conditions, and privileges of employment. It applies to recruitment, advertising, tenure, layoff, leave, fringe benefits, and all other employment-related activities.

ADA defines an *individual with a disability* as a person who has a physical or mental impairment that substantially limits one or more major life activities, has a record of such impairment, or is regarded as having such an impairment. Individuals with minor nonchronic conditions of short duration, such as sprains, infections, or broken limbs, generally would not be covered.

Differential treatment. The act of treating a member of a minority, or protected group, differently from other applicants or employees in a similar situation.

Disparate effect. The existence of job requirements that have the effect of unfairly excluding a member of a protected group.

Reverse discrimination. The notion that implementing affirmative action programs deprives qualified members of nonprotected groups from their rightful opportunities.

If persons with a disability meet the legitimate requirements of a job and can perform the essential functions of that job, they should be accepted as candidates for employment without considering their disability. In fact, it is expected that an employer will make *reasonable* accommodations to a job or a work environment to enable a qualified applicant or employee with a disability to perform the essential job functions. An employer is not required to make accommodation if it would impose an undue hardship on the employer's business. In most cases, accommodations for employees covered by this act are possible within the economic resources of most employers. The act also requires that physical barriers to facilities be removed when readily achievable.

Examples of barrier removal measures could include installing ramps, making curb cuts, modifying sidewalks and entrances, rearranging tables, chairs and other furniture, widening doorways, installing grab bars in toilet stalls, and adding raised letters or Braille to elevator control buttons. Before a supervisor makes any specific change, the ADA accessibility guidelines should be consulted to be sure that the alterations meet those requirements.

Who is covered by the Family and Medical Leave Act (FMLA) of 1993?

All public and private employers with 50 or more employees are covered by the FMLA. Part-time employees are counted as long as they are on the payroll for each day of the work week. To be eligible for a leave, an employee must work at a worksite with 50 employees or for an employer who has 50 or more employees within 75 miles of that worksite; have worked for the employer at least 12 months; and have worked at least 1,250 hours (about 24 hours per week over the previous 12-month period). Eligible employees may take up to 12 weeks of unpaid leave per 12-month period for the birth of a child and in order to care for a child; for the placement of a child with the employee for adoption or foster care; in order to care for an immediate family member, spouse, child, or parent, if such immediate family member has a serious health condition; or in response to a serious health condition that makes the employee unable to perform the functions of his or her position.

After completing the leave, employees must be restored to their former position or an equivalent position. If the need for a leave is foreseeable, an employee must give 30 days notice to the employer before taking it. FMLA does not supersede state laws or collective bargaining agreements that require more generous leave policies, including provisions that may provide for paid leave for all or a portion of the 12-week leave period.

Quick Test 2 ▶	**3**	T or F	A 46-year-old white male employee would be considered a minority.
	4	T or F	Reverse discrimination occurs, for example, when a minority supervisor discriminates against a minority employee.

③ DISADVANTAGED MINORITIES

CONCEPT ▶ A significant part of the population has traditionally been "disadvantaged" and requires especially supportive treatment from their supervisors.

You hear of unemployed persons and of the hard-core unemployed. What's the difference?

The majority of unemployed persons are people who move in and out of the workforce temporarily as they lose or quit one job and seek another. There are millions of other unemployed persons, however, who are out of work more of the time than they are employed. These are the especially disadvantaged, or hard-core unemployed. Typically, they have the following characteristics that make them a challenge to their supervisors when they finally find what they hope will be good jobs:

- They are school dropouts, usually with only a sixth- or seventh-grade education. Many are functionally illiterate, and do not speak or write English. As many as 30 percent have less than fifth-grade reading and arithmetic skills.
- They are single heads of households, men and women with large family responsibilities that tend to overwhelm them with problems.
- They have poor work histories. Few have worked at anything but day labor or in casual service as dishwashers or porters, for example. They have not been prepared for work by their families, their communities, or their schools.

- They are plagued by personal problems, such as undependable transportation to work. They have little experience in managing a regular income and may need help in handling credit, balancing a budget, or even learning how to cash a paycheck.

Recently employed hard-core or disadvantaged persons are troubled by job and business conditions that others accept as routine. They may have difficulty in getting along with the boss or with their co-workers. For example, one 24-year-old ghetto youth said that he reacted at first to orders from his supervisor the way he'd react to being pushed around by a street-gang leader: "I had to learn not to take orders personally. When someone told me to get this or do that, I'd get mad. Finally, I learned that the boss was reacting to the pressure of his job and had nothing against me." In like fashion, many of the disadvantaged view work rules and regulations as something devised to harass them, not as reasonable guidelines for organized behavior that everyone has to follow.

Is it true that many disadvantaged people get "tested" out of jobs?

It was true to a great extent until 1971, when the U.S. Supreme Court *(Griggs v. Duke Power)* handed down a decision barring "discriminatory" job testing. Few tests, however, are intentionally discriminatory; it is just that most tests have been built around cultural models of white, middle-class people. As you can see by definition, such people are not typical of the hard-core unemployed, and tests, when used indiscriminately, screened out the latter. Nevertheless, as a result of the Supreme Court decision, testing for selection, placement, or training in industry has been modified to identify aptitudes and skills of disadvantaged persons rather than unwittingly separating out from the labor force people with untapped potential.

Federal guidelines for employment testing require that tests be validated (if adverse impact is present) so that a test really measures what it says it measures and does not discriminate against protected groups. Tests must be *validated* on two counts:

1. **Content validity.** This means that the test content appropriately represents all key elements of the job. It would be unfair to use only the results of a keyboarding speed test for selection of an individual when keyboarding represents only 20 percent of that job. Clearly, the other job requirements also need to be assessed.

2. **Construct validity.** This means that the test is put together in such a way that it does not screen out applicants who could pass the content part if only they could understand the test questions themselves. For example, applicants might be able to demonstrate mechanical aptitude if they could read the questions. Perhaps the test should be administered orally rather than in writing.

5	T or F	Jeff has recently been the victim of job loss through a massive downsizing in his organization. He is a good example of the hard-core unemployed segment of society.
6	T or F	In order to demonstrate that they are nondiscriminatory, tests should have both content and construct validity.

④ WOMEN IN THE WORKPLACE

CONCEPT ▶ Women have traditionally been denied equal opportunities in the workplace, and their rights must now be protected and enhanced.

How important are women to national productivity?

They are absolutely essential. Out of every five persons working in the United States, two or more are women, and this number is growing rapidly. Women now occupy more than 40 percent of all managerial and professional positions; nearly two-thirds of all technical, sales, and administrative support jobs are filled by women.

The increase in the proportion of women working has been nothing less than spectacular, as illustrated in Figure 18-1.

But what about compensation for women?

Unfortunately, that's another story, and it is one that makes many women justifiably unhappy. Estimates vary, but it would appear that, on average, women receive only about three-quarters of the pay that men do in the labor market. How can that happen? Mainly because women have traditionally been shunted toward lower-paying, lower-status jobs and then blocked from advancement into higher ones, a condition referred to as the *glass ceiling*.

Why doesn't job evaluation put an end to this discrimination in pay?

It does, but only for work that is performed and compensated for under a job-evaluation plan. Even then, it does not close all the possible loopholes. And, of course, it can do nothing to remedy the lack of opportunities, which is the role of the EEO legislation.

The relevant law of the land (the Fair Labor Standards Act as amended by the Equal Pay Act of 1963 and again by Public Law 92-318 in 1972) stipulates that all employees, regardless of gender or other discriminatory identification, should receive the same pay for the same kind and amount

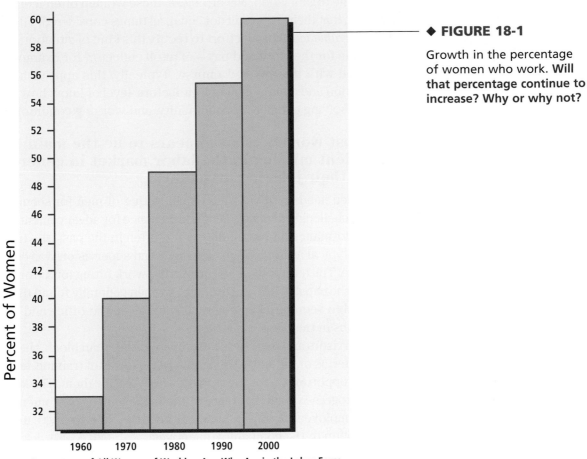

◆ FIGURE 18-1

Growth in the percentage of women who work. **Will that percentage continue to increase? Why or why not?**

Percentage of All Women of Working Age Who Are in the Labor Force

Source: U.S. Department of Labor

of work. *Job evaluation* is the basic means for making sure that this occurs. The "equal pay for equal work" standard, like job evaluation, requires scrutiny of the job as a whole. Its intention is that job titles be ignored and attention focused on actual job requirements and performance. The law examines four factors in particular: equal skill, equal effort, equal responsibility, and similarity of working conditions. Whereas the law does acknowledge some exceptions, it will not permit the concepts of "women's jobs," "men's jobs," "job lists for nonwhites," and the like. On the other hand, the law does permit the use of merit pay plans that recognize a difference, within a job pay range, of different levels of performance among individuals or as reflected by seniority.

What is meant by *comparable worth*?

This is a concept used for evaluating widely dissimilar jobs. The Equal Pay Act of 1963 charges discrimination if women aren't given pay equal to men's pay for equal work. In a great many instances, however, women perform work that is radically different from the work performed by men in the same organization. Nevertheless, these women often feel, with justification, that their pay is still not equal, all things considered. The concept of *comparable worth* is an effort to rectify this kind of situation. It makes it possible for the work and pay—of a toll collector, for example—to be compared with that of, say, a nurse. Typically, this approach involves examination and comparison of four factors: level of know-how required, problem solving entailed, accountability, and working conditions.

For most women, what appears to be the main ingredient missing in the labor market in general and in their jobs in particular?

Women need an opportunity equal to that of men for securing intellectually challenging employment and a chance for advancement based on their performance and capabilities. Too often in the past, the traditional or stereotypical attitude of management and supervision was essentially protective. The question asked was, "Is the work fitting for a woman?" not "What is she capable of?" Accordingly, women generally found themselves restricted to secretarial and clerical routines in the office and to lesser-skilled jobs in the plant.

Supervisors and managers must open, rather than block, the way outward (in terms of job scope) and upward (in terms of training, status, and financial opportunity) for the women who work for them. The supervisor who is progressive and liberated in the management of women will find that *all* employees are more highly motivated and have a greater loyalty and devotion to the company's objectives.

How differently from men should you treat women at work?

There should be no basic difference in how you supervise women and men. The principles of sound, equitable, and considerate management should apply just as fully to the supervision of women as to the supervision of men. Simply stated, a person is a person is a person, regardless of gender—and color and national origin and religious preference. A good supervisor will recognize and adapt to each person's unique individuality, with the conviction that he or she will respond most favorably when treated with respect and thoughtfulness.

What is sexual harassment?

Sexual harassment. Repeated or unwarranted verbal or physical advances or sexually explicit remarks that are offensive or objectionable to the recipient.

The Equal Employment Opportunity Commission has defined *sexual harassment* as "unwelcome sexual advances." Requests for sexual favors and other verbal or physical conduct of a sexual nature constitutes sexual harassment when (a) submission to such conduct is made, either explicitly or implicitly, a term or condition of an individual's employment, (b) submission to or rejection of such conduct by an individual is used as the basis for employment decisions affecting such individual, or (c) conduct has the purpose or effect of unreasonably interfering with an individual's work performance or creating an intimidating, hostile, or offensive working environment.

The supervisor's role in preventing sexual harassment is a crucial one. In fact, according to EEOC guidelines, if you as a supervisor know or should have known about an act of sexual harassment and respond in an inappropriate way, including failure to act, you may be placing yourself and your employer at significant risk of personal and corporate liability.

How should I respond to a complaint of harassment?

The precise answer to this question depends to a large extent on your company's policy with regard to handling an accusation of sexual harassment. In any case, you must know who will conduct the investigation. Often cases of sexual harassment are initially investigated by the human resource department or an affirmative action officer of the Equal Opportunity Employment Office. It's also possible that you will be the first source of intervention. In those cases, be sure to document all actions you take, including any contacts you have with the alleged victim, perpetrator, and often company officials. After a full investigation of the facts related to a case, it is important to consider appropriate discipline, up to and including termination. Remember, sexual harassment is not primarily about sex; it is about power. Victims often endure the pain of harassment for long periods of time until they have the courage to come forward and express their anger, frustration, and outrage. It is also much more prevalent than most males believe. Several reputable national studies have suggested that more than 50 percent of all women in the workforce, at some point in their work lives, have been the victims of sexual harassment. Encourage the victim to participate in whatever employee assistance programs are available.

The message sent to employees must be clear. Men, and women, who want to play games or seek favors with sexual implications must not do so at work. Supervisors have the responsibility for maintaining the proper levels of sexual decorum, including the treatment of employees by suppliers and customers.

How can I prevent the harassment of my employees?

1. One important way is by stating clearly that you will not tolerate sexual harassment and that any case reported to you will be investigated completely and, if proven, dealt with severely. Make sure your employees know your organization's sexual harassment policy by offering periodic training sessions on the topic.
2. Review your physical environment. Suggestive photos, offensive humor, and physical sexual intimidation cannot be tolerated.

Ethical PERSPECTIVES

Sexual Harassment

How would you respond to the following statement? "The problem with sexual harassment is all these women the company has hired. If the company would fire all of them, there would be no more problems."

Begin your response with the definition of sexual harassment, and keep in mind that business ethics is coming to know what is right or wrong in the workplace and doing what's right.

AFFIRMATIVE DEFENSE

■ Organizations that wish to achieve two objectives—prevent sexual harassment and protect themselves in court if a lawsuit is filed against them—are well advised to establish an "affirmative defense," according to the Society for Human Resource Management. Here are some of the key ingredients of an affirmative defense:

• Develop a zero-tolerance policy on harassment.

• Disseminate the policy widely and frequently.

• Provide multiple avenues for reporting of alleged violations.

• Conduct relevant training for all employees and managers regarding what the likely judgment of a "reasonable person" might be with regard to various actions.

• Investigate allegations promptly and thoroughly; take swift disciplinary action where it is appropriate.

Sources: "Finally, a Corporate Tip Sheet on Sexual Harassment," *Business Week*, July 13, 1998, and *Workforce* magazine's Web site at *www.workforceonline.com*.

3. Encourage employees to report acts of sexual harassment they experience or overhear. The victims of sexual harassment need to know that they will be supported by their employer. If they have that confidence, they are more likely to use the internal investigation process for the resolution of sexual harassment complaints. If not, they may, and will be encouraged to, take advantage of the state or federal agencies that will investigate these complaints on their behalves. A sensitive, caring supervisor can make all the difference in resolving harassment complaints and creating a climate where it is clear that harassing behavior is unacceptable. Perhaps one major employer gave the best advice to its employees when advising them to evaluate their behavior with co-workers and determine whether they would act in that manner with that individual in front of their spouse, parents, or children. If not, a reevaluation of that behavior is probably in order.

Quick Test 4 ▶	**7**	T or F	Comparable worth suggests that women must be paid the same as men, regardless of differences in their job responsibilities.
	8	T or F	Supervisors have the responsibility for preventing, as well as investigating and resolving, sexual harassment at work.

YOUNGER AND OLDER WORKERS

CONCEPT ▶ Younger, as well as older, workers require a special kind of nurturing from their supervisors.

What characterizes the younger workforce?

First of all, it is within this group that the highest levels of unemployment occur, especially among African-American teenagers. As a consequence, many younger workers under 25 enter the labor force with a jaundiced eye toward business. The disadvantaged younger worker, especially, enters the labor market keenly distrustful of business's intent.

Younger workers may come from backgrounds that are rich or poor. Their education may be complete, or they may be dropouts from school. They may have ambition in the traditional sense—to achieve—or they may wish only to collect enough paychecks to underwrite their next adventures. Their distinguishing characteristics are (a) a deep preoccupation with themselves as individuals with unique prerogatives and (b) an almost universal suspicion of everything traditional.

The disadvantaged younger workers begin the battle for survival, let alone work, with several handicaps, most of which are neither of their own choosing nor of their own making. They suffer from all the usual wounds of the poor—nontraditional family structure at home, poor education, poor diet, poor health, poor legal protection. The probability is that they have never worked at a decent job with fair pay or in an enlightened environment. They may never have enjoyed many of the "social comforts" that the middle class and others experience. Their politics may be militant but are more likely to be nonexistent. Their distinguishing characteristics are (a) an outlook that recognizes few values beyond those of today, (b) a disbelief in the possibility that business will ever provide an honest opportunity to succeed, and (c) a hopeless feeling that the cards are stacked against them.

Deep down, the typical younger worker asks, "What's in it for me now?"

Deep down, the disadvantaged younger worker asks, "What's the use of trying?"

How serious does this make the generation gap in business?

It is at its most critical in the realm of what any older person will accept without complaint and what a younger person will refuse to do, regardless of pay. Whereas an old-timer may brag about the scars from

▲ Younger and older workers must often work together. **How are their views of work likely to differ?**

welding sparks, a 22-year-old might pack up and quit. A veteran grimly clenches his nostrils as he seals up a coke-oven door in a steel mill; the recent high school graduate balks at that and asks his union steward to get him off that job. A woman who has worked for years as a clerk in a stockbroker's office swallows her boredom; a young woman says that life is too short for that.

What is the root of this difference? The answers vary. Some say it is the permissiveness and the relative affluence in which many young people have grown up. Others say it is simply the difference between a compelling reason to earn a full-scale livelihood (as most older, married persons must) and the wish only to make enough cash for walking around. Then, too, younger people today are better educated, have higher levels of expectation, are more mobile, and are more aware of attractive conditions elsewhere. For whatever reason, younger persons are not docile. They often demand that their job be acceptable—and rewarding—for them, or they will walk away from it. However, this can make supervisors feel like they are coddling such workers.

What can a supervisor do to better motivate and manage young workers?

Supervisors should take their cues from younger workers' complaints. Specifically, a supervisor must be mindful of the following:

1. **Exert authority only from reason.** Dependence on power invites rebellion. A supervisor's authority ought to make sense in terms of its conservation of effort and resources, its recognition of the humanness of employees, and its understanding of the value in change as well as in conformity.

2. **Learn to move faster in making changes.** The twenty-first century will move ever faster in its development of knowledge and technology. Tradition has lost much of its value and meaning. It should be tested constantly against current needs. Learn to let go of the old. Neither progress nor capable young workers will wait very long for you to embrace the new.

3. **Convey the meaning of each assignment.** There is nothing unique about the younger worker's cry for relevance. Men and women have wished to gain this from their work since time began. To apply oneself, one needs to know why a job must be done a certain way, why it must be done at all, and how it relates to what is going on around one.

4. **Make sure the younger workers know what results are expected of them.** Vague and critical admonitions ("use your head") rather than specific goals and targets will sound too much like a parent speaking—and probably induce a comparable response. Make certain, too, that the wage system is clearly understood— exactly how pay will be related to accomplishment.

5. **Provide support and assistance.** Especially in job training, a supervisor's desire to help employees become proficient is welcomed as an expression of respect and confidence.

6. **Praise freely when it is deserved.** Younger people are less confident of their performance and need frequent feedback as to its quality. Conversely, when you criticize, it is important to be tactful. Similarly, discipline must be reasonable rather than arbitrary.

7. **Enrich the nature of the work.** Monotony stems from repetition that allows no room for improvisation and ingenuity. Give employees the freedom, should they choose it, to provide their own variety while they are still committed to a specific, demanding goal.

When does a worker become considered as older?

The Age Discrimination in Employment Act categorizes people over 40 years of age as older. They are mature, settled, experienced, and usually

Quips & Quotes

Age is something that doesn't matter unless you are cheese.

—Billie Burke

well-trained. But they already have family responsibilities, often heavy ones; and signs of both physical aging and emotional wear will soon become evident.

What is important to keep in mind is that age affects each person differently. Its effect depends on a large number of factors: heredity, durability, physical condition, exposure to weather, extreme living or working conditions, climate, indulgence in food or drink, drug abuse, and emotional and psychological strains. Consequently, it is a good rule of thumb for a supervisor to monitor signs of change due to age in any employee over 50 years old. Changes may be physical or mental, slight or marked. Changes may affect the older worker's performance for better or for worse. Or not at all. Just keep your eyes open for changes.

What are the chief assets of older workers?

Older workers have many assets. According to Dr. William A. Sawyer, formerly medical director of the Eastman Kodak Company and later medical consultant to the International Association of Machinists, AFL, older workers take these and other assets to work:

Safety. They have far fewer accidents.

Attendance. They have a better absence record. They are sick less often, although their illnesses tend to last longer than those of younger people.

Judgment. The variety of their work and social experiences tends to improve older workers' judgment and to familiarize them with a variety of work situations.

Loyalty. Broad experience has helped older workers to recognize good supervision when they get it—and to reward that supervision with the loyalty it deserves.

Skill. Once acquired, job skills rarely start to fade before a person reaches 60, often not until much later.

What are the potential drawbacks of older workers?

Older workers have one or more liabilities. But their experience and skills often permit them to compensate for their limitations. On the whole, older workers tend to have the following limitations:

Slower. Age slows athletes and workers. But whereas older people work more slowly, they may make fewer mistakes.

Weaker. Their strength fades, too, although by now they may have learned to work more intelligently, not harder.

Less resilient. Older workers often don't have the endurance they once had. Fatigue—mental and physical—sets in faster. And illnesses and accidents keep them off the job longer than they would a younger person. But remember, older workers are less likely to have either happen.

Suffer from poor eyesight. Near vision may suffer; older workers may need bifocals to correct it. But if vision also includes the ability to understand what we see, then older workers are at least as well off as their sharper-eyed children.

Is it true that older workers learn less readily than younger ones?

This is a tricky question because the learning process is so complicated. It's best answered by saying that older persons, with their greater experience, could learn just as quickly as younger persons—if the older persons were as well motivated. Younger people sometimes learn faster because they want to learn, because they see learning as a key to their futures. Older persons may see no benefit from learning. They have done their bit, they may think, so why try to learn something new?

Older workers are likely to learn best when they are kept apprised of how well they are doing. Experience has made them especially sensitive to this form of motivation. It satisfies both their achievement need and their need for respect. The value that older workers place on their pride is so high in a learning situation that an error is often less acceptable to them than to younger persons.

Under what conditions do older workers have the most difficulty in learning a new job?

Older adults have the most trouble learning a new skill when that skill conflicts with one they have already learned. Experience grows strong roots. When learning a new skill means cutting off those roots, the older workers may not be psychologically ready to learn something new.

To make a difficult learning task easier, it's wise to demonstrate to older workers the similarities between what they have been doing and what you're asking them to do now. For instance, the supervisor could show that the procedures for performing a new task are basically the same as for the previous one and that the differences are mainly a matter of degree. It's always easier for anybody to learn if the move is gradual from the familiar to the unfamiliar.

How can you best motivate older workers?

By understanding them and helping them to understand themselves. As all of us grow older, the gap widens between what we are and what we'd like to be. It's only natural for us to adopt an "I am what I am" attitude—especially when someone asks us to improve or to change our ways. In fact, the very stability that makes older workers an asset also makes it harder for them to change, since this stability is based on their having found contentment with their present lot. So the problem of getting them to want to change, or to do better, resolves itself in your ability to get them to try.

To get older persons to try, you must help them to be less critical and less self-conscious. Show them what other older workers are doing—in your company, if possible. Urge them to talk to others who have changed.

A word of caution: Keep performance standards high for both output and quality for older workers. There should be no rewards for age in terms of relaxed requirements.

Quick Test 5 ▶	**9**	T or F	There are few meaningful differences between younger and older workers today.
	10	T or F	From a legal standpoint, any worker over 40 years of age is considered to be older.

6 SPECIAL PROBLEMS IN A CHANGING ENVIRONMENT

CONCEPT ▶ Changes in both the social and legal environments create special problems of supervision in handling sensitive issues of privacy and other employee rights.

What are the ways in which an employee's rights for privacy may be threatened?

The explosion in applications of technology has unleashed a wide array of devices allowing employers to monitor some aspects of employee behaviors. These include

- Viewing interpersonal e-mail messages.
- Monitoring voice mail messages.
- Observing images on computer monitors.
- Overhearing conversations in a variety of work and nonwork areas.
- Counting the number of keystrokes at a computer terminal.
- Electronically monitoring employee movement around the work facility.

The frequency of such practices has risen sharply in recent years, such that nearly half of all firms now report some forms of such "snooping" being used.

Employers defend themselves, arguing that they have the right to check employee backgrounds as well as monitor productivity. Employers routinely engage in drug testing, criminal record examinations, and credit checks. But employees are becoming more vocal about their rights to privacy, too. Unfortunately, the law regarding privacy at work is not as clear as it might be. It varies from state to state, too. In general, however, three things stand out: (1) employees are entitled to know what information is on file about them, (2) employees should be informed in advance about what activities will be monitored, and (3) supervisors are restricted in their efforts to find out confidential information about their employees or to pass on to others outside the company information that has been gathered about an employee.

When can lie detectors and drug tests be used?

The use of lie detectors is severely restricted to specified occupations (such as security guard) or for particular situations. They can no longer be randomly used. In general, such tests (including testing for drug usage) are acceptable only if it can be clearly demonstrated that they are needed (a) to protect the business itself or its customers from damage or theft, or (b) to protect employees from interference or harm. Most organizations adopt and publish a policy on these matters. It is the supervisor's responsibility to assist in the dissemination and enforcement of this policy.

Does privacy extend to sensitive issues such as AIDS?

To a large extent, the answer is yes. In most instances, supervisors must rely upon policies adopted by their employers and comply with them. This must be done regardless of how employees may view the matter. It is important to support the letter of whatever law applies and your company's policy for implementing it. With regard to the specific issue of AIDS, it is now clear that those suffering from this disease can have long, productive work lives. As a supervisor, you should be prepared to offer reasonable accommodations should changes in the illness require them. If other employees express concerns about working with the person who has AIDS, get the facts about the illness and share them with your employees.

To what extent does the concern for protected employees and for employee rights affect a supervisor's right to manage?

It complicates a supervisor's life, for sure. But it can be handled if you follow these priorities:

1. First things should come first. It's a supervisor's job to deal promptly and firmly with subordinates whose performance is unsatisfactory, who act in an unsafe manner, or who are uncooperative or abusive. This is consistent with laws about management and labor relations. Furthermore, it matches what most employees expect of their supervisor.

2. Thereafter, full respect and attention should be given to equal employment opportunity laws and other legislation intended to protect the rights and welfare of people while at work. This should include an attitude of accommodation toward social concerns that are increasingly reflected in workplace practices, such as family leaves and child care or parental-assistance programs.

| **Quick Test 6** ▶ | **11** | T or F | Supervisors need to be sensitive to, and protect, employee rights to privacy. |
| | **12** | T or F | A supervisor's primary responsibility is to ensure a safe, fair, and productive workplace. |

KEY CONCEPTS TO REMEMBER

1. **A Diverse Workforce.** The composition of the workforce is changing, and it is doing so at a dramatic pace. The number of white males as a percentage of the total workforce is getting smaller. The vast majority of new job holders are now women, minority men, and immigrants. With these changes come increased responsibility for the supervisor to understand effective and productive ways of managing that diversity.

2. **The Legal Basis.** A large body of equal employment opportunity (EEO) legislation has been enacted to protect and enhance the rights of protected groups, including women, African Americans, Native Americans, Hispanics, Asians, disabled workers, older workers, and Vietnam-era veterans. This places great responsibility upon supervisors to make sure that these laws are effective in the workplace.

   The federal agency charged with enforcing EEO laws is the Equal Employment Opportunity Commission (EEOC). The EEOC encourages, and often requires, the formation of affirmative action programs to ensure a more equal representation of minorities in a company's workforce. The EEOC looks, especially, for evidence of differential treatment, disparate effect, or evil intent.

3. **Disadvantaged Minorities.** Disadvantaged workers represent a special kind of supervisory problem in that they often enter the workforce poorly prepared in terms of education and job skills. For this reason, it is essential that employment and advancement tests demonstrate their content and construct validity.

4. **Women in the Workplace.** Women are a major and valued portion of the workforce. Nevertheless, the quality of their participation continues to need protection and enhancement. This is evident in the difference between women's compensation and that of men, despite the efforts of job-evaluation programs to equalize pay. Most women ask only that their worth be judged on their merits and that they be given opportunities equal to those given to men for higher paying and higher status jobs. Sexual harassment in the workplace also continues as a threat to a woman's dignity, welfare, and opportunities. Supervisors share a direct responsibility with higher management to prevent such harassment.

5. **Younger and Older Workers.** Younger workers represent a special kind of supervision problem in that they bring to work very high expectations but very little self-discipline. On the other hand, older workers may begin to suffer limitations caused by deterioration in pace, strength, eyesight, and resilience. These are more than counterbalanced, however, by older workers' experience, skills retention, superior attendance, steadiness, safe working habits, and loyalties to their company and supervisors.

6. **Special Problems in a Changing Environment.** Increasingly, both the law and society in general believe an employee's right to privacy should be protected. This view has many ramifications in the areas of drug testing, lie detectors, and workplace monitoring, and in policies toward employees with life-threatening illnesses, such as AIDS. Nothing in any of the laws designed to protect the rights, or enhance the opportunities, of

employees deprives supervisors of their fundamental right—and responsibility—to manage.

READING COMPREHENSION

1. What changes are occurring in our workforce today and are likely to continue into the future?

2. What is meant by affirmative action, and how does it tie in with EEO legislation?

3. In seeking to ensure conformance to EEO laws, what evidence of discrimination does the EEOC look for? In which areas of management are these most likely to occur?

4. Lupe's mother has just been involved in a serious car accident. Lupe has asked her supervisor for an extended period of time away from the job to care for her mother. How should the supervisor respond? If a leave is approved, can Lupe be transferred to a different, lower-paying job when she returns? Why?

5. Distinguish between the content validity and construct validity of employment tests.

6. Which approach do you think would motivate the company's "hard-core" van driver more: offering the driver membership in the company's recreational club or allowing the driver to take the keys of the van home at night? Why?

7. The men in Jane's work group repeatedly—but jokingly and admiringly—address her as "Marilyn," an obvious reference to her physical resemblance to Marilyn Monroe. Jane doesn't particularly like this and complains to her supervisor. What should the supervisor do?

8. If 19-year-old Pete is dissatisfied with his job and blames his unrest on the meaninglessness of his work, what is the possibility of this charge being justified? What might Pete's supervisor do about this situation?

9. Why might an employee who works at a computer keyboard object to the number of her keystrokes being counted electronically as a measure of her performance? Do you believe that her employer has a right to make these measurements?

10. If, as a supervisor, you suspected an employee of drug dealing, would it be all right to inspect that employee's locker? Why?

APPLICATION

Self-Assessment

▶ *How good are your diversity management skills?*

Read the following statements carefully. Circle the number on the response scale that most closely reflects the degree to which each statement accurately describes you. Add up your total points and prepare a brief action plan for self-improvement. Be ready to report your score for tabulation across the entire group.

	Good Description									Poor Description
1. I am aware of, and sensitive to the need for, cultural diversity.	10	9	8	7	6	5	4	3	2	1
2. I take special care not to discriminate against the member of any minority group.	10	9	8	7	6	5	4	3	2	1
3. I make a conscious effort to eliminate the use of stereotypes by me and my co-workers.	10	9	8	7	6	5	4	3	2	1
4. I have a clear understanding of the various laws affecting equal employment opportunity.	10	9	8	7	6	5	4	3	2	1
5. I understand and support the nature and purpose of affirmative action.	10	9	8	7	6	5	4	3	2	1
6. I would feel comfortable making reasonable accommodations for a person with a disability.	10	9	8	7	6	5	4	3	2	1
7. I understand and support the intentions of the Family and Medical Leave Act.	10	9	8	7	6	5	4	3	2	1
8. I fully support equal pay for women and men who are performing similar or comparable jobs.	10	9	8	7	6	5	4	3	2	1
9. I understand what constitutes unwelcome sexual advances, and would feel comfortable intervening immediately to stop them if I were aware of them happening.	10	9	8	7	6	5	4	3	2	1
10. I understand the ways in which I need to relate differently to younger and older workers.	10	9	8	7	6	5	4	3	2	1

Scoring and Interpretation

SCORING

Add up your total points for the 10 questions. Record that number here, and report it when it is requested. _____

INTERPRETATION

81 to 100 points. You seem to have a basic set of diversity management skills.

61 to 80 points. Take a close look at some of your diversity management skills (those with lower self-assessments) and discuss them with a manager to see if they need improvement.

Below 60 points. Some of your skills may be substantially inconsistent with effective diversity management practices and could be detrimental to your success as a supervisor.

Identify your three lowest scores, and write the question numbers here: _____, _____, _____.

ACTION

Write a brief paragraph detailing an action plan for how you might sharpen each of these skills. Then pay particularly close attention to the related material in the chapter as you review the relevant sections there.

Skill Development

▶ *Diversity Management Improvement*

Some organizations and some communities are rich melting pots of various racial and ethnic groups, but others are not. However, despite a possible absence of cultural diversity, almost all work organizations contain a reasonable mixture of male and female employees. Although many major organizations (e.g., Avon Products, Colgate-Palmolive, Coopers & Lybrand, Dow Chemical, and Motorola) have made major strides in creating a healthy environment for the advancement of females, others have lagged behind and still have a glass ceiling.

Select an organization and gain access to it to chat with some of its employees. Solicit their reactions regarding the problems they have encountered or observed, and the specific actions that their employer could take to break down the glass ceiling. (To prepare yourself, you will likely wish to review the text's discussion of the glass ceiling, search the Internet for relevant guidelines, and consult with colleagues and staff persons in the human resources department for their advice.)

Problem Areas

1. _____

2. _____

3. _____

4. _____

5. _____

Suggestions for Improving Opportunities for Women

1. _____
2. _____
3. _____
4. _____
5. _____
6. _____
7. _____
8. _____
9. _____
10. _____

ACTION

After talking to several different people and assessing all the ideas produced, prepare a brief report that summarizes the problems and your 10 best suggestions for improvement in the opportunities for women. If possible, share the results of your study with a responsible person in the host organization and obtain his or her reactions.

Role Play

Dealing with Diversity ◀

Five persons are asked to volunteer to play the role of one of five supervisors who are about to hold a meeting with their employees. Each volunteer is assigned one of the supervisory roles shown below and asked to prepare a brief statement to be delivered orally to a group of their employees. Then each supervisor will have the opportunity to receive feedback from your employees.

FIRST SUPERVISOR. You have recently attended a supervisory development workshop on various aspects of diversity. At the end of the workshop, you decided that it would be appropriate to share some of your feelings with your employees as a way to ensure that everyone acts in a consistent manner and doesn't cause either intentional or inadvertent difficulties. You have chosen to make a brief statement on the topic of older workers—their unique characteristics, the challenges they present to co-workers, their rights to be different, and the importance of tapping into their strengths and attributes.

SECOND SUPERVISOR. You have recently attended a supervisory development workshop on various aspects of diversity. At the end of the workshop, you decided that it would be appropriate to share some of your feelings with your employees as a way to ensure that everyone acts in a consistent manner and doesn't cause either intentional or inadvertent difficulties. You have chosen to make a brief statement on the topic of younger generation—their unique characteristics, the challenges they present to co-workers, their rights to be different, and the importance of tapping into their strengths and attributes.

THIRD SUPERVISOR. You have recently attended a supervisory development workshop on various aspects of diversity. At the end of the workshop, you decided that it would be appropriate to share some of your feelings with your employees as a way to ensure that everyone acts in a consistent manner and doesn't cause either intentional or inadvertent difficulties. You have chosen to make a brief statement on the topic of ethnic minorities—their unique characteristics, the challenges they present to co-workers, their rights to be different, and the importance of tapping into their strengths and attributes.

FOURTH SUPERVISOR. You have recently attended a supervisory development workshop on various aspects of diversity. At the end of the workshop, you decided that it would be appropriate to share some of your feelings with your employees as a way to ensure that everyone acts in a consistent manner and doesn't cause either intentional or inadvertent difficulties. You have chosen to make a brief statement on the topic of the female gender—their unique characteristics, the challenges they present to co-workers, their rights to be different, and the importance of tapping into their strengths and attributes.

FIFTH SUPERVISOR. You have recently attended a supervisory development workshop on various aspects of diversity. At the end of the workshop, you decided that it would be appropriate to share some of your feelings with your employees as a way to ensure that everyone acts in a consistent manner and doesn't cause either intentional or inadvertent difficulties. You have chosen to make a brief statement on the topic of monitoring employee behaviors—the fact that your organization feels it is necessary and appropriate to keep tabs on employee behavior, and the various ways in which it does so.

ALL OTHERS (THE EMPLOYEES). Listen attentively to each of the supervisory talks. When each one of the talks is finished, you should react to what you heard and respond with questions, expressions of support, statements of concern, and so forth (expressing your honest reactions to the supervisor). Respond as you think typical employees might respond upon hearing such a talk.

Questions (*Answer after all five talks have been delivered.*)

1. What did the supervisors say or do that was highly effective?
2. What did the supervisors say or do that might be viewed as inappropriate or offensive?
3. How could the presentation of information such as that heard today be presented in such a way that it is well-received and adhered to by the employees?
4. Based on the feedback received, the five supervisors should indicate how they might have improved upon their presentations.

CASES FOR ANALYSIS

◄ **Case 55**

Jackrabbit Jokers

Dave's Jackrabbit Delivery Service is a small local package delivery service in the Midwest. Three of the 15 truck drivers are women. At the start of every day, it was common for all the drivers to get together in the lunchroom for a morning cup of coffee and a chance to discuss the day's events before going out on the run. After work, they would gather at the Cueball Bar for a couple of drinks before going home. The crew had no turnover in the past five years. It was a close-knit group that enjoyed one another's company. It wouldn't be uncommon when they got together to tease one another about an unusual or distinctive habit—their weight, their bodies, or even their love lives. Everyone seemed to enjoy themselves.

Eight months ago, one of the women, Theresa, got married to someone not well-known to the rest of the group. The before- and after-work routine continued, much as before Theresa's wedding. One day, as Theresa came into the lunchroom, Hector said, "Hey, Theresa, you look like you had a real workout last night." Marty commented that if his wife had a body like that, he'd be "coming to work with bags under his eyes."

Everyone laughed, and why not? It was typical of the type of interplay that they had with each other over the years. You can imagine their surprise when Dave came into the lunchroom the next day and announced that Theresa had filed a charge of sexual harassment against Hector and Marty. Someone responded to Dave, "I don't get it. We've always been able to kid each other like this."

◄ *Analysis*

Based on the information that you have above, prepare a brief response to each of the following statements:

a. Sexual harassment did not occur because no requests for sexual contact or physical touching occurred in this case.

b. No sexual harassment occurred because, whether we like it or not, this kind of behavior had gone on for years and Theresa had never complained about it before.

c. Theresa has a good case for sexual harassment because the environment in which she worked was clearly hostile, intimidating, and offensive.

d. Hector and Marty should receive no discipline for their action because Theresa never told them she found their behavior offensive.

e. This entire work group was looking for trouble and some action needs to be taken to ensure this behavior doesn't continue in the future.

Case 56

Upward on Cannery Row

In a West Coast cannery, Luis Valdes, a 45-year-old ex-migratory worker, was hired into the steam-pack operation. For his first few weeks on the job, Luis performed general labor, helping the operator to load the vats and to mop up spills. He was eager and attentive; and, although his English was not particularly good, he seemed to get the idea of what was wanted from him. Accordingly, the steam-pack supervisor suggested that Luis might swing over to the second shift as a number 2 operator.

Analysis ▶

In preparation for this move, the supervisor should do which of the following?

a. Assemble a series of operating manuals for Luis to study.

b. Ask the day-shift operator to tell Luis exactly what will be expected of him.

c. Show, by demonstration, how each step of the steam-pack operation is performed, and have Luis repeat each step while the supervisor watches him.

d. Tell Luis that he should clear up any questions he has about the steam-pack operation now before he swings over to the second shift.

Case 57

Banking Jobs for All Ages

If you were the branch manager of a bank in a booming industrial area where it was very difficult to attract and hold younger people, how might you suggest to your various supervisors that they adjust their job openings and work assignments to accommodate and make the most valuable use of the larger supply of older people in the local labor market? You know that business at the tellers' windows has a great deal of variety: some is routine, such as accepting deposits and cashing checks; other transactions are more complex, such as making out certified checks, selling traveler's checks, and opening up new accounts. Then, too, at some hours of the day, business is hectic and fast-paced; at other times, it is relatively slow. In the cashier's department, keypunching is generally a "high-production" job, whereas resolving and verifying balances is a more painstaking one.

◀ *Analysis*

What are your suggestions for making the most of the younger and older workers in the local labor market?

Think first about the characteristics of younger workers, their attitudes toward their work, what they expect and enjoy most and what they like least. Then think about what the text says about older workers, their strengths and their weaknesses. With this knowledge in mind, what might be done to modify and restructure work at the bank to make it more appealing and more effective for both younger and older workers? Consider, especially, changes that affect the following:

- Work schedules
- Division of work
- Employee training
- Job progression

Quick Test 1	Quick Test 2	Quick Test 3
1. F	3. T	5. F
2. F	4. F	6. T

Quick Test 4	Quick Test 5	Quick Test 6
7. F	9. F	11. T
8. T	10. T	12. T

◀ **Answers to Quick Tests**

CHAPTER 19

The Supervisor's Role in Employee Safety and Health, and Labor Relations

▶ Learning Objectives

After studying this chapter, you should be able to

- Discuss the extensive list of factors in addition to human error that contribute to occupational injuries and illnesses.

- Explain various facets of the Occupational Safety and Health Act, compute occupational accident incident and severity rates, and understand the procedures for investigating and analyzing an accident.

- Evaluate several common approaches to accident prevention—including the three Es of *engineering*, *education*, and *enforcement*—and discuss the effectiveness of safety committees, safety inspections, and wellness programs.

- Discuss a supervisor's responsibilities in labor-management relations, as affected by significant provisions of the main labor-management relations laws.

- Explain the collective-bargaining process and the supervisor's role in implementing a labor agreement.

- Describe a typical grievance procedure, and discuss how a supervisor can contribute to its effectiveness.

① SAFETY AT WORK

CONCEPT ▶ Accidents and hazards to health represents costly factors in the work environment and must be guarded against constantly.

What causes accidents?

People do, mostly. In fact, study after study shows that approximately 91 percent of accidents can be attributed to unsafe acts, compared to about 9 percent caused by environmental factors or faulty equipment. Of course, people don't have accidents on purpose. An ***accident,*** by definition, is an unplanned or uncontrolled event, usually one that results in personal injury or property damage. Accidents happen for a variety of reasons. Sometimes, it's just plain carelessness. Sometimes, people haven't received proper instructions or have not been alerted to a ***hazard,*** a known, potentially dangerous object or condition, associated with their work. Sometimes, the person's attitude is to blame. Sometimes, equipment fails. Sometimes, machines are not properly guarded. But, almost always, there is a person, usually the person who gets injured, who could have prevented the accident by taking proper protective or control action.

This is not to remove the responsibility from the company, institution, or agency involved. Ownership and management must be committed to the principle of accident and health protection. This often means a sizeable investment as well as costly and time-consuming safety and health measures.

How costly are work-related accidents?

Very costly, indeed. The annual bill to industry is over $50 billion, and it is rising. The human costs, however, are even greater. At least one worker in the United States is killed every hour of every day on the job. That's more than 10,000 deaths each year. And it doesn't stop there. Every five seconds, another worker is injured on the job, or some 6 million a year. Consider the physical pain and suffering, the loss of self-esteem that can accompany becoming dependent upon others, or the disruption to a family when the breadwinner loses his or her normal source of income.

How much of the blame can be placed on accident-prone employees?

Some blame belongs there, but it would be wrong to overemphasize their presence. Examination of safety records often shows that just a few employees account for the bulk of the accidents—that the great majority of employees rarely have accidents. Those people who get injured frequently are spoken of as *accident prone.* This means that for one reason or another, they have a tendency to have accidents and hence are prone to injury. Psychologists have shown, however, that only a small percentage

Accident. An unplanned or uncontrolled event in which action or reaction of an object, material, or person results in either personal injury or property damage, or both.

Hazard. A potentially dangerous object, material, condition, or practice that is present in the workplace, to which employees must be alert and from which they must be protected.

■ Gangs have begun to infiltrate many industries and organizations in corporate America. According to some estimates, as many as 400,000 gang members live and work in corporations, and they regularly engage in a wide variety of activities, including theft, extortion, drug sales, and hijackings. Some even stage workplace accidents to cover up gang-related injuries so they can collect huge reimbursements from health insurance companies. What can organizations do? Supervisory actions include the following:

- Don't assume that any workplace is immune from gang activity.
- Carefully screen prospective employees.
- Watch for clues that gang members may be present in your workforce.
- Install—and use— a variety of security measures (e.g., video cameras).
- Strictly enforce existing policies for security and behavioral violations.

of so-called accident-prone employees are truly accident prone. Most of these habitual sufferers can actually be made accident free by proper job placement, training, and encouragement. If one or more of your workers appear accident prone, don't assume it is not your responsibility. Instead, encourage the development of work habits that will protect these employees from themselves.

Where else, then, does the blame lie?

Finger-pointing isn't the most effective way to prevent accidents. There are many commonly recognized causes of accidents besides those immediately attributable to employee carelessness or inattention. Among them are the following:

- Absence of, or faulty, protective devices.
- Ineffective specifications for safety clothing.
- Inadequate ventilation or the presence of fumes.
- Presence of hazardous or unauthorized materials.
- Wrong tools, materials, or supplies issued for the job.
- Absence of a safety standard for the operation.
- Lack of safety training for a specific task.
- Inadequate or improper instructions.
- Safety rules or procedures not enforced.
- The wrong person placed on an unsuitable task.
- Poor housekeeping or sanitation at the workplace.
- Pressure from supervision to disregard safe procedures in the interest of faster movement or greater output.

Do not disregard the fact, of course, that each of these causes is directly or indirectly related to the faulty performance of an individual or group of individuals somewhere along the line.

Where do most industrial accidents occur?

They have their greatest frequency and severity in the manufacturing, mining, food processing, construction, transportation, and hotel industries. They occur less frequently in banks and insurance companies.

It bears repeating here that accidents *can* be prevented. Du Pont Co. and its 100,000 employees, for instance, have an exemplary safety record despite the fact that the company manufactures explosives and heavy chemicals, which can be extremely hazardous processes. In one recent year, Du Pont had a lost-time incident rate of 0.04 when the national average for their industry was over 70.0. The company is justified in asserting that its employees are safer at work than at home.

The Occupational Hazard of Chicken Plucking and Computer Keyboarding

The latest occupational illness, repetitive strain injuries (RSI), has found very strange bedfellows. It has been known to strike just about anyone who spends the day tapping away at a computer keyboard or who wields a knife on a chicken processing line. The common denominator? The use of the hands and arms to repeat the same motions over and over again throughout the workday. The incidence of this affliction can be minimized in three important ways:

1. By stretching, changing position, alternating tasks, moving about, or otherwise interrupting the muscular routines.
2. By redesigning the workplace so that it can be adapted to the needs and size of the workers (an ergonomic workplace).

Examples: a desktop that can be raised or lowered at will, a fully adjustable chair, positioning devices to hold the work, glare-free illumination.

3. By the use of special tooling, machinery, and accessories intended to help the body accommodate to the routines imposed by the work assignment.

Not all of these devices are proven antidotes to RSI, but nowhere are they so commonly employed as at the computer keyboard. An ergonomically correct computer workplace often includes wrist-, arm-, and footrests, a glare filter on the screen, a copyholder, a telephone headset, and a fully adjustable chair.

Where are ergonomic hazards most likely to occur?

Increasingly, organizations are paying close attention to risk factors arising from **ergonomic hazards.** These are workplace conditions that have the potential for inducing injury from an occupational activity that involves repetitive motion and stress. The technical term for such an injury is a *repetitive strain injury (RSI)*. See the Superscope above. Employers are most concerned with ergonomic hazards associated with

Ergonomic hazard. A workplace condition that requires the job holder to repeat or sustain a fixed motion or stress pattern over an extended period of time, and that may include a repetitive strain injury (RSI).

- Performance of the same motion pattern for a prolonged period of time, such as at a computer keyboard.
- Use of vibrating or impact (jarring, jolting) tools.
- Using forceful hand, leg, or foot exertions repeatedly.
- Maintaining a fixed or awkward posture for an extended period.

			◀ **Quick Test 1**
1	T or F	Basically, a hazard and an accident are the same thing.	
2	T or F	Accident-prone employees have usually just been in the wrong place at the wrong time.	

OSHA'S MANDATED SAFETY STANDARDS

2

CONCEPT ▶ The federal government establishes and monitors (through OSHA) strict standards for protection of safety and health at work.

What role does the federal government play in the prevention of accidents?

Occupational Safety and Health Act. Comprehensive legislation that establishes standards and calls for the inspection of safety and health conditions and the investigation of all serious accidents and alleged safety or health hazards. Created Occupational Safety and Health Administration.

A major one. In earlier times, the safety of an employee at work was largely the result of efforts on behalf of state governments, insurance companies, independent safety organizations such as the National Safety Council, and the employer. Passage of the Williams-Steiger *Occupational Safety and Health Act* of 1970 (effective April 1971) and the creation of the *Occupational Safety and Health Administration (OSHA)* put the federal government and the Department of Health, Education, and Welfare (HEW) squarely into the safety act in every significant plant and office in the United States. The purpose of OSHA is to establish safety and health standards with which every employer and every employee must comply. And to make sure that there is compliance, OSHA makes thousands of inspections annually.

How much leeway for variances does OSHA permit?

Very little. The act minces no words. For example, the General Duty clause states that each employer

1. Shall furnish to each employee, employment and a place of employment that is free from recognized hazards causing, or likely to cause, death or serious harm to employees.
2. Shall comply with occupational safety and health standards promulgated by the act.

The poster that OSHA requires each employer to display in the area adds, "The act further requires that employers comply with specific safety and health standards issued by the Department of Labor."

The standards (called National Consensus Standards) are set down in a tightly packed, 250-page volume called "Occupational Safety and Health Standards; National Consensus Standards and Established Federal Standards," and specify just about everything imaginable. They include specifications for guarding walks and walking surfaces, means of egress, powered platforms, environmental controls, noise, radiation, hazardous materials, sanitation, first-aid services, fire protection, compressed gases, material handling, machine guards, portable tools, welding, and electrical installations and pay particular attention to paper, textile, laundry, sawmill, and bakery operations.

The OSHA standards are regularly revised and updated and published in the *Federal Register*.

To what extent does OSHA specify accident record keeping?

It insists that every company or separate establishment maintain a log of illnesses and accidents as they occur. Beyond that, the forms already used by your organization to monitor these matters and to investigate accidents are probably satisfactory.

The OSHA log (Form 200) is used to record each occupational injury or illness and identify whether it has caused a fatality, a lost workday, a permanent transfer to another job, or a termination of employment. Whereas your company will probably specify what records must be kept and who will maintain them, the supervisor—as in so many other areas—is a pivotal person in collecting the data.

There are numerous governmental agency websites. Check out **OSHA's** site for workplace regulations.

How are accident rates classified and measured?

OSHA and the U.S. Bureau of Labor Statistics have worked together to establish (a) what constitutes an incident (or accident case) and (b) how to measure the incident rate (frequency rate) and severity rate.

A *recordable incident* (or *accident case*) is one that involves occupational injury or illness, including death. Not recordable are (a) first-time ailments that involve one-time treatment or (b) minor cuts, scratches, or burns that do not ordinarily require medical care, even if such treatment is provided by a physician or registered nurse.

Accident rates are measured by two very similar formulas. The first formula measures an *incident rate* (also called *frequency rate)* by comparing the number of accident cases that have occurred with the total number of hours worked by all employees during the same period. The second formula measures a *severity* rate by comparing the number of lost workdays that have occurred with the total number of hours worked by all employees during the period. For consistency's sake, all rates are computed using a standard based upon the expectations of 100 employees working 2,000 hours per year, or 200,000 hours.

To illustrate the use of these formulas, suppose that plant XYZ has 200 employees each averaging 40 hours a week for 50 weeks (or 2,000 hours per year each). During the year, 12 accident cases are recorded, and a total of 88 workdays are lost as a result.

$$\text{Incident rate (Frequency rate)} = \frac{\text{number of recordable cases} \times 200{,}000 \text{ hours}}{\text{total hours worked by all employees during the year}}$$

$$= \frac{12 \text{ cases} \times 200{,}000 \text{ hours}}{200 \text{ workers} \times 40 \text{ hours/week} \times 50 \text{ weeks/year}}$$

$$= \frac{2{,}400{,}000}{400{,}000}$$

$$= 6 \text{ incidents per 100 full-time employees}$$

▲ It may not be possible to eliminate accidents entirely, but their numbers can be reduced. What is the supervisor's role in workplace safety?

Using the data provided, the severity of these accidents, as gauged by the total lost workdays they caused, is measured in the following way.

$$\text{Severity rate} = \frac{\text{number of workdays lost} \times 200{,}000 \text{ hours}}{\text{total hours worked by all employees during the year}}$$

$$= \frac{88 \text{ workdays lost} \times 200{,}000 \text{ hours}}{200 \text{ workers} \times 40 \text{ hours/week} \times 50 \text{ weeks/year}}$$

$$= \frac{17{,}600{,}000}{400{,}000}$$

$$= 44 \text{ workdays lost per 100 full-time employees}$$

Similar incident and severity rates can be calculated for disabling injuries only or for illnesses only.

It should be noted that some organizations compute these rates according to 1,000,000 hours worked per year rather than the 200,000 hours used by the Bureau of Labor Statistics. Such rates would be five times greater.

How do you investigate an accident?

If an accident should happen in your department or to an employee under your supervision, one of the best ways to prevent its happening again is to investigate the accident to find out exactly why it happened.

Once you have determined this, you can establish safeguards to protect individuals from any unnecessary dangers. When you are checking on accidents, your primary goal is to find causes, not to fix blame. Look for answers to such questions as these:

- **What happened?** Who got hurt? How badly? What material was spoiled? Was any equipment damaged? Does it need repair before being put into operation again? Who, besides the injured individual, was involved?
- **Why did it happen?** Was it solely human error? If so, was it due to a lack of skill? Of knowledge about key points? Was it mainly carelessness? What part did the process play? Was it functioning properly or erratically at the time? How about the equipment involved? Was it in good working order? Did the individuals involved know how to operate it properly?
- **What needs to be done to prevent this from happening again?** Does it require special training? A specific new rule or regulation? A change in process or procedure? Different kinds of equipment? Additional safeguards on the equipment?
- **What steps have you taken to prevent recurrence?** How much of the above have you put into practice with improved training and instruction? Have you worked out a prevention plan with process engineers, systems designers, or housekeeping and maintenance staffs?
- **What still needs to be done?** Do you need further assistance from your boss or from the appropriate staff departments? Should you enlist the help of the safety committee? Have you set up a follow-up procedure that won't be dropped until the entire prevention plan is implemented?

What happens to a company when it doesn't meet the OSHA standards?

It receives a citation. A severe penalty and fine will follow if the problem is not corrected. More specifically, the citation is issued to the manager in charge of the facility. It may even be issued, for example, to a supervisor who refused to make certain that a prescribed machine guard was in place. A company and an individual may seek a temporary variance from the standard, but in most instances the only recourse is to take corrective action as soon as possible. In many cases, heavy fines and even jail sentences have been imposed on companies and managers who failed to comply promptly with the citation.

How has OSHA affected safety training?

It has made it mandatory. Supervisors are expected to make certain that safe procedures are taught not only to new employees but also as an ongoing program.

Ethical PERSPECTIVES

Ergonomic Hazards!

According to the Bureau of Labor Statistics, work-related musculoskeletal disorders (MSDs) constitute the largest job-related injury and illness problem in the United States. MSDs account for $1 out of every $3 spent on workers' compensation.

OSHA's proposed new ergonomic standard would provide workers with ergonomic protection. Will this standard benefit employees? Employers? Or both?

General safety training applies to the proper observance of safety regulations, routing for emergency egress in case of fire or other common danger, accident and injury treatment and reporting, and fire and explosion emergency activities.

Specific employee training required by OSHA applies to occupational health and environmental controls, hazardous materials, personal protective equipment, medical and first aid, fire protection, material handling and storage, machine guarding, and—for welding—cutting and brazing.

Where do employees fit into the OSHA picture?

The law insists that they, too, act safely within established standards—provided that employers live up to their responsibilities. In other words, an employee who refused to wear the safety glasses provided by the employer in prescribed areas could be cited. A bearded employee might be required to shave to make his respirator fit. Specifically, OSHA states, "The Williams-Steiger Act also requires that each employee comply with safety and health standards, rules, and orders issued under the Act and applicable to his conduct."

Employees have several important rights under OSHA, however. For example, they may do the following:

1. Request an inspection if they believe an imminent danger exists or a violation of a standard exists that threatens physical harm.
2. Have a representative (such as a union steward) accompany an OSHA compliance officer during the inspection of a workplace.
3. Advise an OSHA compliance officer of any violation of the act that they believe exists in the workplace, and question, and be questioned privately by, the compliance officer.
4. Have regulations posted to inform them of protection afforded by the act.
5. Have locations monitored to measure exposure to toxic or radioactive materials, have access to the records of such monitoring or measuring, and have a record of their own personal exposure.
6. Have medical examinations or other tests to determine whether their health is being affected by an exposure, and have the results of such tests furnished to their physicians.
7. Have posted on the premises any citations made to the employer by OSHA.

Should a supervisor give an injured employee first aid?

That depends on the practice in your company and on your own qualifications. There should be no question, however, about your responsibility to see that an injured employee gets first aid—quickly and properly. Permit only trained people (such as graduates of the Red Cross first-aid course) to attend the patient. Know who these people are ahead of time and how to summon them without delay.

If your plant has a nurse or a physician who has been called, stay until you are sure that the injured employee is under medical care.

3	T or F	OSHA requires organizations to record any injury to or illness of its employees.
4	T or F	The accident incident rate focuses on the frequency of accident cases, whereas the severity rate focuses on the number of lost hours as a result of accidents.

ACCIDENT PREVENTION: (3) THE BASICS

CONCEPT ▶ Supervisors play the key role in accident prevention by emphasizing safety awareness, education, and enforcement.

With whom does accident prevention begin?

Good supervision is the starting place for an effective accident-prevention program. No amount of machine guards or safety rules will stop accidents from happening if supervisors aren't absolutely sold on the fact that it can be done—and that it's their responsibility.

Shouldn't employees have a responsibility for safety?

By all means! People failure is at the heart of most accidents. Supervisors cannot be everywhere at once, and they shouldn't want or need to be. So in the long run, it will be your employees who cause—or prevent—accidents in your department. But you've got to take the lead in showing them how prevention is achieved.

1. **Instill in employees the belief that they are the most influential source of accident prevention.** Do this with the aid of your safety engineer, if you have one. Discuss the particulars of the accidents that have occurred in your organization. Seize every opportunity to let employees see cause and effect for themselves.

2. **Show employees how to develop safe working habits.** People have to be trained to work safely just as they must be trained to work accurately. Few persons are naturally cautious, or know instinctively where danger lies. After training, remind them frequently to help them maintain safe habits and to integrate these habits into their work routines.

3. **Pay special attention to new employees.** Statistics show that a majority of accidents involve first-year employees. The first day on

the job isn't too early to start this indoctrination. The first day on the job in a foundry, for example, a worker may be worried about burns from hot metal and hardly realize that eye injuries, dermatitis, and crushed toes are just as likely to happen.

4. **Be specific about prevention techniques.** For example, don't say, "Use caution when operating this machine." Instead, say, "Wear a face shield when operating this machine." Often a demonstration is needed to supplement the instructions. For example, you might begin by saying, "Stack boxes carefully on this shelf and not too high; otherwise, they may fall and hurt someone." Then *show* the employee how to stack cartons safely, and also make a mark on the wall above which they must not be stacked.

5. **Enlist safety suggestions from employees.** When an accident happens close to home, for instance, talk it over with one or many of your employees. Get their ideas of how it could have been prevented. Ask them if similar situations could arise in their areas. Continually bring the conversation around to the role of the human element.

6. **Set a good example.** Supervisors should go out of their way to observe the letter of every safety rule themselves. Never—*never*—yield on safety in favor of your own convenience.

7. **Firmly enforce job safety standards.** Don't be surprised that many employees think of safety as a matter of "Don't do this or that," or as just so many rules and regulations. Let employees know immediately the danger to themselves—and your dissatisfaction—when they don't follow the safety guidelines you've outlined for them. Reason and encourage first, but penalize if you don't get the necessary conformance.

What is the basis for accident prevention?

Accident prevention requires a balanced, three-pronged attack. For years, the National Safety Council has stressed the three Es: engineering, education, and enforcement. (See Figure 19-1.)

◆ **FIGURE 19-1**

The three E's of safety and accident prevention.
Who is responsible for worker safety?

You can observe the three elements of accident protection in the workplace, too. For instance:

- To *engineer* a job for safety is to design the equipment, lay out the work, plan the job, and protect the individual—all with accident prevention as a first ingredient. Placing safety guards on machines is one example of engineering.
- To *educate* for safety is to show employees where, why, and how accidents can happen and to develop in them safe work habits and the desire to avoid injury. Helping workers to analyze the danger spots in their jobs and training them to build a defense against each is an example of education for safety.
- To *enforce* safety is to make an actuality of the slogan, "Safety first." Employees need guidance in the form of regulations and discipline to protect safe workers from those who would cause accidents through unsafe acts.

But isn't accident prevention really the safety specialist's job?

Safety engineers do an excellent job of carrying out the three Es of safety. But they would be the first to admit that without the supervisor's help, safety programs would flop. The supervisor is the key safety person, especially in education and enforcement.

What can be done to make safety committees more useful?

If you or your company have organized departmental safety committees, see that the committee has a real job to do. Don't let meetings turn into nonproductive rap sessions. And don't use them solely as a sounding board for your inspirational appeals for safety. Treat the safety committee as a business organization:

Assign specific problems. If your medical department or first-aid room tells you there's been a rash of small cuts on hands and arms, get the committee to investigate this condition to find out what the facts are, where the cuts occur, and to whom. Then ask for a specific recommendation on how to correct the situation.

Expect results. Make it clear that being on a safety committee entails more than sitting in on a meeting. Assign area safety responsibilities to the members. Let them assist with inspections. Ask for a report on the minor accidents in each area. Have the members tell what improvements have been made and what more can be done.

Have members participate in investigations. Talking about safety isn't as effective as getting out on the floor to see what's being done about it. Use this opportunity to demonstrate the company's efforts and expenditures for safe working conditions. Emphasize that unsafe practices are just as important to watch out for.

REWARD SAFETY

■ Reward employees for safe work practices and accident-free results. Why? Because, in general, every dollar spent on safety-recognition programs saves about $10 in injury costs (lost time, medical expenses, and workers' compensation). But the real art lies in *how* to reward employees, especially if the rewards are combined with safety-awareness programs and safety training. In general, follow these rules:

- Don't provide cash awards to employees for good accident records (the amount is too low to be meaningful).
- Set targets for employees to achieve (e.g., six-month or yearly goals).
- Provide a variety of company-related items as rewards (e.g., inexpensive coolers, hats, or flashlights) with the company's safety slogan imprinted on them.
- Provide team rewards for a team's safety achievements.

Delegate duties. If the committee plans a safety competition, let it handle the publicity, the method of making awards, and the establishment of rules. Committee members know their co-workers better than anyone else does and can guess what will work best.

Safety inspections: Are they useful, or are they another example of window dressing?

Safety and sanitation inspections are an essential part of a successful accident prevention and control program. It is important, however, that they (a) be conducted regularly, (b) be based on verifying compliance with the company's and OSHA's rules and standards, (c) seek also to detect new areas of necessary coverage, and (d) be followed up quickly by rigorous action to correct unsatisfactory conditions.

How prevalent are wellness programs?

Increasingly, prevention programs extend beyond safety to health and wellness. For example, the U.S. Department of Health and Human Services reported that the following wellness programs were most common in industry: smoking control, health-risk appraisals, back care, stress management, exercise and physical fitness, off-the-job accident prevention, nutrition education, blood-pressure control, and weight control. They indicate how broad an employer's concern for safety and health enhancement can grow.

Quick Test 3 ▶			
	5	T or F	Supervisors represent the first line of defense in preventing accidents.
	6	T or F	The three Es of accident prevention focus on engineering, education, and elimination.

4 LABOR UNIONS AND LABOR LAW

CONCEPT ▶ Supervisors are considered legal representatives of management in matters affecting labor union recognition and contracts: therefore they need to be aware of relevant labor laws.

What role does the first-line supervisor play in labor matters?

In the eyes of the law, supervisors are responsible agents of their organizations. Your employers are held responsible for any action you take in dealing with employees or with labor unions, just as if they had taken the action themselves. For this reason, if for no other, it is essential that a supervisor be familiar with the legal aspects and terminology of labor relations. This is especially true on two particular points: (a) your actions may be considered violations of laws, and may affect a union's attempts to gain or retain bargaining rights for employees; and (b) the *labor agreement* that your organization has signed with a union (a mutually binding contract stipulating wages and benefits, hours, and various working conditions) can exert a powerful impact on policies, practices, and procedures that make for effective operation of the organization as well as constructive employee-employer relations.

Labor agreement. The written agreement that binds a company's management and its employees' organization (labor union) for a stipulated period of time to certain conditions of pay, hours, work, and any other matters the parties deem appropriate. (Also called *union agreement* or *labor contract.*)

Why do employees join labor unions?

Employees join labor unions for at least three reasons:

1. **The union offers bargaining power and takes risks through collective activity that many individuals cannot, or do not wish to, provide by acting alone.** That's the underlying purpose of labor (or trade) unions; to promote, protect, and improve—through joint action—the job-related economic interests of their members.

2. **Membership is often compulsory.** In three-quarters of the labor agreements (but not in all states), an individual must join or at least pay dues if she or he wants to keep a job. The idea behind compulsory membership is that everyone should pay their fair share of the cost of benefits derived from unionism and that no one should get a free ride.

3. **Membership provides both a real and perceived countervailing power from management's power to hire, promote, or fire at will.** No matter how fair-minded an organization's management may try to be, many individuals feel "pushed about" or helpless in today's increasingly large and complex organizations. Others may believe they have received unfair or arbitrary treatment. For these individuals, union membership provides a feeling of strength and security that is otherwise lacking.

What should your attitude be toward an existing union?

Adopt the attitude that once your company has made an agreement with a union, your best bet is to work as hard as you can to get along with that union. Don't waste your energy trying to undermine the union. Instead, put your efforts into making your department a better place in which to work. It's more important than ever, when your company has a union, to show employees that you still consider them your department's greatest asset. If you abandon their interests, you're likely to find employees looking to their union representatives rather than to you for leadership.

How should you react when your employees display strong loyalties to their union?

Don't feel hurt. An extensive study of employees' loyalties showed rather conclusively that it's natural for workers to have dual loyalty—to their supervisors and to their union leaders. Employees look to their boss for sound business judgments and for the satisfactions that come from doing a purposeful job under good working conditions. But employees look to their union for the social prestige of belonging to an influential group and as a protector of their economic interests and job security. An employee who works for a good company and a considerate boss and who also is represented by an honest, active union enjoys both relationships.

What is the impact of the Wagner Act?

The Wagner Act (formally called the National Labor Relations Act) describes the conditions under which workers can organize and bargain collectively through their authorized representatives. It does not set out any specific working conditions that employers must give to their employees. Nor does it concern itself with the terms of the union agreement. All it does is guarantee that employees may act in a group together—rather than as individuals—if they so desire, in bargaining for three key items: wages, hours, and working conditions. There is also considerable evidence that, perhaps as the result of greater attention, supervision has actually become much better trained and more effective since the right of employees to organize has been protected by law.

For example, supervisors have learned that they need to be especially careful to avoid *interference* during a union's organizing drive or representation election. They must avoid (a) any actions that affect an employee's job or pay, (b) arguments that lead to a dispute over a union question, (c) threats to a union member through a third party, or (d) interactions without advice from top management with any of the organizing union's officers. These could all be deemed ***unfair labor practices*** under the Wagner Act.

Unfair labor practices. Those practices engaged in by either management or labor unions that are judged by the federal labor law (National Labor Relations Act) to be improper, especially in that they (a) interfere with the rights of employees to organize or (b) discriminate against employees for labor union activities.

How did the Taft-Hartley Act change the Wagner Act?

The National Labor Relations Act (the Wagner Act) was amended by the Taft-Hartley Act (Labor-Management Relations Act) in 1947. The Taft-Hartley Act clarified and added to the list of unfair practices that could be charged against management. But more significantly, the act provided better balance between the parties by imposing on unions certain restrictions over their organizing activities and ability to make use of certain types of boycotts.

Under the amended law, unions and their agents are forbidden to engage in the following unfair labor practices:

- Attempt to force an employer to discharge or discriminate against former members of the union who have been expelled for reasons other than nonpayment of regular union dues or initiation fees.
- Attempt to force an employer to pay or deliver any money or other things of value for services that are not performed. This outlaws featherbedding and other make-work practices.
- Restrain or coerce other employees into joining or not joining a union.
- Require excessive or discriminatory fees of employees who wish to become union members.

In addition, the act made clear that employees are protected in their desire to bargain or not to bargain collectively. For example, they may take up a complaint directly with management—but only where the issue and the settlement do not involve issues covered by a union contract. However, a union representative must be given an opportunity to be present.

Closed shop, union shop—what are they?

In a *closed shop*, a prospective employee had to belong to the union before being hired. The closed shop was outlawed by the Taft-Hartley Act. The *union shop* is still a form of compulsory unionism, but with a big difference: the person need not be a union member at the time of hiring. But a new employee (usually after a 30- or 60-day trial period) must *become* a member of the union to stay on the payroll. Of course, the union shop is not automatic in all collective bargaining cases—it must be negotiated and agreed on contractually by the union and management.

Under the Taft-Hartley Act, the only reason for which a union may force a company to fire a worker is that she or he does not pay union dues. This protects the individual from being discriminated against by the union. In the union shop agreement, it's common for a company also to sign a *checkoff agreement* with the union. This means that the company will collect employees' union initiation fees and dues through payroll withholding and turn them over to the union. The employee must first sign an authorization card that gives the company permission to do so.

▲ Labor and management must work together to assure a harmonious relationship. **What issues are likely candidates for discord?**

Right-to-work laws.
Legislation passed in nearly two dozen states that makes it illegal to negotiate for a union shop after a union gains recognition.

What is a right-to-work law?

When the Taft-Hartley Act outlawed the closed shop, it also permitted the individual states to pass laws making the union shop illegal. Such laws, enacted in 21 states, are called *right-to-work laws.* In these states, compulsory membership in a labor union is illegal. Then, where unions do gain recognition in an organization, it is illegal to negotiate for a union shop. Thus, it is possible for 51 percent of a company's bargaining-unit employees to be union members and 49 percent to be nonmembers because they have the right to choose their own status and still work.

What other labor-related laws should a supervisor know about?

Two important laws are the Walsh-Healey Public Contracts Act and the Fair Labor Standards Act. Generally, your company will watch for compliance, but since the laws influence decisions that affect you, here's a fast rundown.

Walsh-Healey Public Contracts Act. Walsh-Healey sets the rules for any company that works on a government contract in excess of $10,000. The act sets minimum ages for the hiring of teenagers, and limits the basic hours of work to 8 per day and 40 per week. The employer must pay time and a half for overtime hours on a daily basis. The act also sets up strict standards for safety, health, and working conditions. A very important feature is the right to establish a minimum wage for a particular industry.

Fair Labor Standards Act. Also known as the Wages and Hours Law, this act regulates methods of wage payment and hours of work for any industry engaged in commerce between two or more states. The law restricts the employment of children over 14 and under 16 to nonmanufacturing and nonmining positions and prohibits the employment of children between 16 and 18 in hazardous jobs, including driving or helping a driver of a motor vehicle. The law sets the minimum wage (periodically adjusted by Congress) and prescribes that time and a half must be paid for all hours worked over 40 in a week. It also establishes what is "work" and what is not—such as waiting in line to receive paychecks, changing clothes, washing up, and checking in or out. (All of these may be considered work in a union agreement if the parties agree.)

The Fair Labor Standards Act also sets guidelines for determining which supervisors and other employees must be paid overtime and which should not. To be classed as an exempt employee (and thus not subject to the provisions of the act), a supervisor must meet the following requirements:

The **Department of Labor's** website provides a summary of all major statutes and regulations administered by the Department.

- Have as a primary duty the management of a recognized department or subdivision.
- Customarily and regularly direct the work of two or more other employees, exercise discretionary powers, and have the power to hire or fire or make suggestions and recommendations that will be given particular weight in the hiring, firing, and promotion of subordinates.
- Not perform nonexempt (clerical, nonadministrative) work more than 20 percent of the time (40 percent in retail trade).
- Receive a minimum level of weekly salary specified by federal law.

Nonexempt employees (those who are directly covered by the act) include almost all wage-based and clerical people; overtime provisions of the law apply to them. Professional employees who require advanced knowledge, customarily acquired through prolonged instruction and study of a specialized field, are usually considered exempt. However, apprenticeship, a college degree, and routine training will not necessarily qualify an employee as a professional.

What is the purpose of the Landrum-Griffith Act?

Officially designated as the Labor Management Reporting and Disclosure Act of 1959 (also known as the Landrum-Griffith Act, for its primary sponsors), it compels employers to report the following types of financial items:

- Payments to labor union officials, agents, or stewards (for purposes other than pay for work).

- Payments to employees (other than regular wage payments) or to groups or committees of employees for purposes of persuading other employees regarding choice of a union or other union matters.
- Payments to a consultant on labor union matters.

Payments that must be reported also include reimbursed expenses. More important, the law also compels a labor union to make a more complete disclosure regarding the sources and disbursement of its funds. The law also strictly regulates the internal affairs of unions and clearly defines the rights of individual union members.

The law is aimed primarily at (a) preventing unethical collusion between a company and a union or other interference with the due process of collective bargaining, (b) preventing the misuse of a union's funds by its leaders, and (c) otherwise minimizing the possibility of labor "racketeering."

Quick Test 4 ▶			
7	T or F	Not all employees have the freedom of choice as to whether or not they will join the union.	
8	T or F	Unions commonly—and legally—coerce employees into joining a union.	

⑤ COLLECTIVE BARGAINING AND CONTRACT REPRESENTATION

CONCEPT ▶ Collective bargaining sets the organizational context for labor relations, but supervisors are the primary implementors of labor contracts.

Collective bargaining.
The process of give-and-take engaged in by the management of an organization and authorized representatives of its collective employees (a labor union) to reach a formal, written agreement about wages, hours, and working conditions.

What does collective bargaining include?

Collective bargaining takes place only after a labor union has won a representation election. When authorized representatives of the employer and authorized representatives of the employees bargain together to establish wages, hours, and working conditions, this process is called *collective bargaining.* Various labor laws have determined what are fit matters for collective bargaining and what are not. Generally speaking, however, the term *working conditions* is so broad that almost anything that affects employees at work or the manner in which they carry out their jobs can be included.

The mere fact that a matter, such as wage rates or pensions, is a fit subject for collective bargaining doesn't necessarily mean that the union can control the way it is handled. The union can bargain for its position, and both sides must bargain in good faith over the issue. But the company does not have to accept the union's position. Several considerations will determine the issue's final disposition: the reasonableness of the union demand; the desirability of the demand to employees, management, and stockholders; the ability of the company to pay for its cost; the judgment of management as to its worth; and, finally, the relative bargaining strength of the union and the company.

Does collective bargaining end with the signing of the contract?

Collective bargaining usually starts with the negotiation of the labor agreement. But it doesn't end there. Supervisors, managers, employees, and union stewards must live with the agreement for the duration (or term) of the contract—usually 1, 2, or 3 years. Applying the contract and interpreting its meanings from day to day are what make collective bargaining effective—and exciting. The labor agreement, like any other contract, is rarely changed during its life. But there are dozens, sometimes hundreds, of occurrences between supervisor and employees that require astute judgment on how the situation should be handled to best carry out the meaning of the contract. It is such interpretation and differences of opinion between management and unions that make labor relations a key supervisory headache and responsibility. And it is also the source of many grievances, as we shall discuss later in this chapter.

What is a supervisor's authority in labor relations?

Your primary responsibility to your organization in labor matters is to protect the interests and the rights of management. How far supervisors can exercise authority in carrying out this responsibility will depend on the extent to which upper management feels that supervisors can act without first checking to see if their decisions are in line with company policy.

The first-line supervisor is usually the first contact between employees and management and between union representatives and management. Since what you do and say in labor matters has such vital consequences to your company's overall relationship with employees and their representatives, you must be knowledgeable of the major provisions of the contact and your company's labor practices. Your actions are not confined only to yourself and a single employee; they could very well have companywide impact. Under certain circumstances, your actions could cause your employer to be charged by the union with violating the contract or even with breaking the law.

Supervisors in the past have been charged with unfair labor practices of discrimination. What is that all about?

One supervisory unfair labor practice—interference—was discussed earlier. Another one—discrimination—is also governed by the Wagner Act. *Discrimination* applies to any action (such as discharge of an employee, layoff, demotion, or assignment to more difficult or disagreeable work) taken by any member of management because of the employee's union membership or activity.

There is an easy way to avoid charges of discrimination. Simply disregard completely an employee's union membership, activism in union affairs, or general attitudes toward the union when you make decisions regarding job assignments, discipline, and promotions. Before you act, make sure in your own mind that you have separated ability, performance, and attitude toward the job from the employee's stand on unionism or zeal in supporting it.

How far does a union shop steward's authority go?

A *steward* is to the union what you are to the employer. It's a union steward's job to protect the rights of union members just as it's yours to protect the rights of management. But in protecting these rights, a union shop steward has no authority to run your department or to tell you or any employee what to do about work.

You may get the impression that a steward is telling you what to do. A new steward may even feel that it is his or her job to do so. All the steward has authority to do, however, is to advise you or employees of his or her understanding of how the contract limits your actions and decisions. It goes without saying that you are the department supervisor, and you are not obligated to share your responsibility with anyone.

It is good practice, however, to keep stewards informed of your actions—so that they can make their position known. Better yet, if you wish to build a strong working relationship with the steward under an overall atmosphere of company-union cooperation, you may occasionally even wish to ask the steward's input in advance of making a decision. Their job experience—and worker perspective—could prove invaluable.

How friendly should a supervisor be with a steward?

Be as cooperative, understanding, and patient as you can without giving up your right to run your department. You may personally resent an aggressive steward who is a continual thorn in your side. But remember, the steward is an elected representative of the group. Stewards speak not only as individuals but also for the employees they represent. They, too, want to do the best job possible.

You can gain confidence, if not cooperation, from union stewards if you let them know what's going on. They have status to protect, just as you do, and they don't want to be blindsided with surprise information. If you try to keep them in the dark or treat them as if they are insignificant, they may react by showing you just how important they are. So don't keep a steward at arm's length. Get to know her or him as you would any other employee—or better. You will have many mutual problems. There's nothing wrong with enlisting a steward's help in solving some of them with you.

Suppose you are planning to start up a second shift on one of the machines in your department. You intend to post a bidding sheet for a new operator. You lose nothing by telling the steward of the new job opportunity in advance. And it gives you a chance to enlist the steward's help when you say, "We're going to be needing a good operator to run the number 6 machine on the second shift. We agree with the union that the job should go to the worker with the most seniority who is really qualified to do a good job. But how about helping to see that we get some good people bidding on it?"

What do you do if a steward just won't cooperate?

You can help aggressive stewards channel their energies constructively if you remain under control and show them you understand their problems. After all, their jobs can be thankless ones. Check yourself, too, to be sure that it's not your own aggressive actions that make a steward hard to get along with. Try to approach each problem, not as a battle between the two of you, but as a problem that you are both trying to solve in accordance with the labor agreement. Don't say only, "Let's see what the contract says." Show that you, too, are interested in justice for your employees: "Let's see how we can do the most we can for this employee without making a decision that is out of line with the contract."

9	T or F	The three primary and legitimate areas for contract negotiations include working conditions, working hours, and wages.
10	T or F	A duly-elected union steward has the same authority as a supervisor in running the department.

◄ *Quick Test 5*

6 GRIEVANCE PROCEDURES

CONCEPT ▶ The grievance procedure provides a systematic, objective way of dealing with employee grievances.

Why is there a grievance procedure? Wouldn't it be better to settle gripes informally without all the red tape?

Most union contracts establish a step-by-step *grievance procedure.* Experience has shown both management and labor that it's best to have a systematic method of handling complaints. Without a formalized procedure, management (in dealing with unionized employees) would find it difficult to coordinate labor and personnel practices from department to department.

The formal procedure provides an easy and open channel of communication for employees to bring complaints to the attention of management, and guarantees that these complaints won't be sidetracked or allowed to ferment without corrective action being taken. Good supervisors and wise higher managers know that an unsettled grievance, real or imaginary, expressed or hidden, is always a potential source of trouble. The grievance machinery helps uncover the causes and get the grievance out into the open.

Does the law dictate a standard grievance procedure?

No. The actual grievance procedure will vary from organization to organization. It will depend on what the employer and the union have agreed on and have written into the labor contract.

A typical grievance procedure has from three to five steps, as shown in Figure 19-2, and usually originates after an employee is dissatisfied with a supervisor's actions or initial response to a complaint.

Step 1. Supervisor discusses the complaint with employee and union steward.

Step 2. Superintendent and labor relations manager discuss complaint with union grievance committee.

Step 3. Site manager and labor relations manager discuss complaint with union grievance committee.

Step 4. General company management discusses complaint with national union representative and union grievance committee.

Step 5. Dispute, if unresolved, is referred to an impartial arbitrator for decision.

It should be emphasized that a serious and prolonged effort should be made by both parties to settle the grievance at each step—including the first. As a matter of fact, many companies appraise their supervisors on

Grievance procedure. A formalized, systematic channel for employees to follow in bringing their complaints to the attention of management. Typically, it prescribes a progression of appeals from lowest to highest authority within the company and the employees' organization. It often has arbitration as a final step.

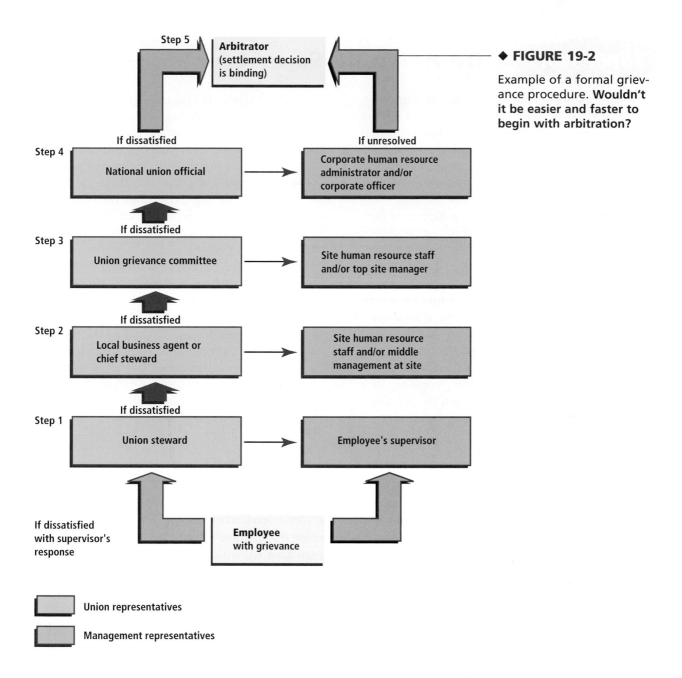

◆ **FIGURE 19-2**

Example of a formal grievance procedure. **Wouldn't it be easier and faster to begin with arbitration?**

a number of relevant criteria, such as the number of grievances filed per employee per year, or the proportion of grievances resolved at the first step. Prompt action by supervisors has been shown to be effective in solving as many as 75 percent of all grievances at the first step.

Why don't grievances go right to the arbitrator in the first place?

Arbitration, the settling of labor-management disputes by a mutually acceptable, impartial third party, is not popular among members of either unions or management. They seem to agree on this point: they'd

Arbitration. The settlement of a labor dispute or employee grievance by an impartial umpire selected by mutual agreement of the organization and the union.

Most supervisors make a strong effort on a regular basis to be sure their decisions and actions are in line with their employer's interpretation of the union contract. Nevertheless, they are sometimes overruled at subsequent steps of the grievance process. Why? Experience shows it may be due to any of five major reasons:

1. **Bad information.** The supervisor may have acted on insufficient or incorrect information. Unfortunately, this is the most common reason, despite its ease of prevention in many cases.

2. **Reinterpretation.** The supervisor may occasionally be made the sacrificial lamb when the company realizes at the third or fourth step of the procedure that its interpretation of the contract won't stand up to the union's position. Worse yet, the employer may have changed its own mind during the intermediate steps and reversed its own earlier position.

3. **Arbitration decision.** The supervisor and the company may be overruled by the arbitrator at the last step. Here, the company isn't at fault for not supporting the supervisor, but an independent party saw greater merit in the union's case.

4. **Rigidity.** The supervisor may be too concerned about saving face (sticking with an earlier decision so as to maintain an image of never making a mistake) to back down. And that same supervisor may have difficulty seeing the situation objectively when he or she is too close to the problem.

5. **Overindependence.** The supervisor may have failed to consult with other colleagues or the human resource department on issues of contract interpretation. Sometimes a bit of insight, a word of caution, or a shared lesson from another's experience can be invaluable.

both rather settle their household quarrels between themselves than invite a stranger in to settle disputes. Both parties reason, and rightly, that they know more than anyone else about their affairs. In the long run, union and management must learn how to settle their differences themselves without continually depending on a third party. It has been said by both union and management that nobody wins an arbitration. But when it's needed, peaceful arbitration is far better than strikes or lockouts.

Quick Test 6 ▶

11	T or F	A formal grievance procedure is usually advantageous for both labor and management.
12	T or F	Historically, about 75 percent of all grievances advance to the level of an impartial arbitrator before they are resolved.

KEY CONCEPTS TO REMEMBER

1. **Safety at Work.** An accident is evidence of something wrong in the workplace—with an employee, a machine, methods, materials, or a supervisor. Although there is evidence that some people are accident prone, the great majority of accidents are attributable to human error by ordinary people somewhere along the line. Only aware and responsible people can recognize these wrongs—and correct, guard against, and avoid them.

2. **OSHA's Mandated Safety Standards.** The Occupational Safety and Health Act of 1970 created a large body of standards for safe working conditions, sanitation, and the handling of hazardous materials. The law is enforced by the Occupational Safety and Health Administration (OSHA), which places a great deal of responsibility for its implementation upon supervisors. Employees, too, are expected to participate actively and are given certain rights in that regard. OSHA specifies that a great many accident records be maintained in a prescribed fashion. Calculation of accident incident (frequency) and severity rates is a helpful way to measure the effectiveness of safety programs. Supervisors are directly involved in the investigation and analysis of accidents and their causes.

3. **Accident Prevention: The Basics.** Accident prevention is a major supervisory responsibility that is shared with employees, often under the guidance of a company safety specialist. Most accidents can be prevented by a unified program that encompasses (a) engineering—proper job and equipment design; (b) education—effective employee communication and training; and (c) enforcement—consistent adherence to, and enforcement of, the prescribed safe practices.

4. **Labor Unions and Labor Law.** In dealing with employees and labor unions, courts view supervisors as responsible agents of the organizations for which they work. Regardless of a supervisor's attitude toward organized labor, she or he is bound to behave in accordance with labor laws and to abide by the agreements that may be derived from collective bargaining.

    The basic labor-management law in the private sector is the National Labor Relations Act, or Wagner Act (which protects the rights of employees to bargain collectively for wages, hours, and working conditions), as amended by the Taft-Hartley Act. Other related legislation includes the Labor Management Reporting and Disclosure Act, Walsh-Healey Public Contracts Act, and the Fair Labor Standards Act. Most of these are under the supervision or administration of the National Labor Relations Board (NLRB).

5. **Collective Bargaining and Contract Representation.** Collective bargaining between management and a labor union takes place only where a union legally represents the employees. The end result of a collective-bargaining negotiation is a labor contract. Supervisors play vital roles in administering the labor contract. Accordingly, it is important that supervisors (a) maintain their own interest in, and responsibility toward, the well-being of their employees and (b) protect their own authority and rights as managers to direct, motivate, and control their staffs—modified only by contractual

limitations. Supervisors need to refrain from discrimination at all times, but especially during contract administration.

6. **Grievance Procedures.** Supervisors have a special interest in employees' grievances. It is in the supervisor's interest to listen to, understand, and resolve them at the first level of management rather than to have them move beyond his or her control into the formal channels of referral specified by the grievance procedure.

READING COMPREHENSION

1. Many accidents are caused by the ever-present human factor. Name at least six other possible causes of accidents.

2. Vivian, housekeeping supervisor in a state mental institution, devotes time each day to safety training for her employees. This activity fits into which phase of the three E's of accident prevention? What are the other two phases?

3. Distinguish between an accident incident (or frequency) rate and an accident severity rate.

4. What can a supervisor do to instill safety consciousness in employees?

5. Why should a supervisor want to investigate an accident?

6. Suggest two good reasons why a supervisor should know about the basic principles of labor-management relations.

7. Compare the objectives of the Wagner Act with those of the Taft-Hartley Act.

8. How do the closed shop and union shop differ? Which is most closely associated with right-to-work laws?

9. Contrast a union steward's responsibility with that of an employee's supervisor.

10. Describe a typical grievance procedure. What role does a supervisor play in the process?

APPLICATION

Self-Assessment

▶ *How good are your safety and labor-relations management skills?*

Read the following statements carefully. Circle the number on the response scale that most closely reflects the degree to which each statement accurately describes you. Add up your total points and prepare a brief action plan for self-improvement. Be ready to report your score for tabulation across the entire group.

Good Description									Poor Description
10	9	8	7	6	5	4	3	2	1

1. I believe that I can improve the safety record of "accident-prone" employees by working closely with them.

	Good Description									Poor Description

2. I understand and appreciate the positive role that OSHA plays in encouraging safe working conditions.
    10 9 8 7 6 5 4 3 2 1

3. I understand the difference between accident incident rate and severity rate.
    10 9 8 7 6 5 4 3 2 1

4. I feel comfortable approaching a safety problem from the perspectives of the three Es: engineering, education, and evaluation.
    10 9 8 7 6 5 4 3 2 1

5. I know several actions I could take to help make employees feel responsible for their own safety.
    10 9 8 7 6 5 4 3 2 1

6. I can explain several reasons why employees might join a labor union.
    10 9 8 7 6 5 4 3 2 1

7. I can explain the difference between a closed shop and a union shop.
    10 9 8 7 6 5 4 3 2 1

8. I understand the four prerequisite conditions that define an exempt employee.
    10 9 8 7 6 5 4 3 2 1

9. I understand the role of a union steward as it relates to that of a supervisor.
    10 9 8 7 6 5 4 3 2 1

10. I can explain a number of reasons why my decision on a grievance might be overturned at a higher level of the process.
    10 9 8 7 6 5 4 3 2 1

Scoring and Interpretation

SCORING

Add up your total points for the 10 questions. Record that number here, and report it when it is requested. _____

INTERPRETATION

81 to 100 points. You seem to have a basic set of safety and labor-relations management skills.

61 to 80 points. Take a close look at some of your safety and labor-relations management skills (those with lower self-assessments) and discuss them with a manager to see if they need improvement.

Below 60 points. Some of your skills may be substantially inconsistent with effective safety and labor-relations management practices and could be detrimental to your success as a supervisor.

Identify your three lowest scores, and write the question numbers here: _____, _____, _____.

ACTION

Write a brief paragraph detailing an action plan for how you might sharpen each of these skills. Then pay particularly close attention to the related material in the chapter as you review the relevant sections there.

Skill Development

▶ *Safety and Labor-Relations Management Improvement*

No matter how hard an organization tries, there are often still some overlooked or temporary safety hazards present in its operations. As a result of either negligence during internal safety inspections, careless actions by employees, or lack of familiarity with relevant laws, even the best of organizations can sometimes receive citations when an OSHA inspector makes a surprise visit. Nevertheless, a prepared organization can do much to minimize such problems.

Select an organization, and gain access to it. Conduct a personal walk-around inspection, identifying the unsafe conditions (problem areas) that you encounter or observe, and the specific actions (unsafe practices) that employees are demonstrating that could lead to an accident. (To prepare yourself, you will likely wish to review the text's discussion on the safety investigations, search the Internet for relevant guidelines, and consult with colleagues and staff persons in the human resources department for their advice.)

Problem Areas

1. _____
2. _____
3. _____
4. _____
5. _____

Unsafe Practices

1. _____
2. _____
3. _____
4. _____
5. _____

Suggestions for Creating a Safer Work Environment

1. _____
2. _____
3. _____
4. _____
5. _____
6. _____
7. _____
8. _____
9. _____
10. _____

ACTION

After studying your findings, prepare a brief report that summarizes your 10 best suggestions for making the work environment safer. If possible, share the results of your study with a responsible person in the host organization and obtain his or her reactions.

Role Play

Making Task Assignments ◄————————————————

BACKGROUND. Many supervisors make task assignments to employees on a daily, or even hourly, basis. On the positive side, this provides great flexibility to shift resources where needed and to respond to fluctuations in demand for human resources. On the negative side, this practice might result in undertrained employees being assigned to tasks, uncertainty in the minds of employees as to where they will work next, and a limited ability to enjoy sustained social relations with co-workers. This role-playing incident deals with such an incident of task assignments and the employee's reaction to it. Class members should break into groups of three persons, with one each assigned to the role of Olga, Daryl, or Mickey. After they have read (only) their own roles, they should hold a three-way meeting among themselves.

OLGA. You are a word-processing operator in a state agency whose employees are represented by a union of government workers. You work in a word-processing pool made up of employees with low seniority. You have no regularly assigned job but report each morning to the pool's supervisor, Daryl Dowd, to find out where you will work that day. Sometimes you work in the same area you did the day before, but other times Daryl pulls you out of a job to place you on a particularly demanding or short deadline job. When the workload is relatively light, Daryl lets you and the other operators pick the job each wants to work on. When the calls for operators from various departments are frequent, however, Daryl makes all the assignments and is not receptive to counterarguments.

Lately, you have begun to feel that Daryl is taking advantage of your good work and your good nature. You rarely get to stay on the same assignment (which is desirable because it means a chance to get the feel of the work and the people in a particular department) more than one day at a time. Besides, many of the jobs that Daryl gives you are unattractive ones. The work is especially painstaking; for example, it has to be done under pressure, or the people in the department are largely unfriendly.

This morning, Daryl wants to send you up to the tenth floor to work in the budget-review department. Suddenly, you boiled over. "Send someone else up there to do their kind of picky work today," you tell him. "I won't take another assignment like that until every other operator in the pool has been rotated to as many rotten jobs as I've had." Then Daryl replies, "You've got to work any assignment that is legitimate, so get going!" With that, you storm off to talk to Mickey, the union steward. After briefing the steward on the interaction with Daryl and your frustrations, the three of you agree to meet. You hope that with Mickey on your side, the two of you can convince Daryl to be more fair about task assignments.

DARYL. You are the supervisor of a group of word-processing operators in a state agency whose employees are represented by a union of government workers. You head up a word-processing pool made up of employees with low seniority. They have no regularly assigned job but report to you each morning to find out where to work that day. Sometimes they work in the same area they did the day before, but other times you have to pull them off a job to place them on a particularly demanding or short deadline job. When the workload is relatively light, you let the operators pick the job they want to work on. When the calls for operators from various departments are frequent, however, you must make all of the assignments and you don't feel any reason to be receptive to counterarguments.

Lately, the pressure to provide operators to various departments has been particularly intense. You rarely get to keep an operator on the same assignment (which is desirable because it means a chance for him or her to get the feel of the work and the people in a particular department) more than one day at a time. Besides, many of the jobs the operators do are unattractive ones. The work in some departments is especially painstaking; for example, it has to be done under pressure, or the people in the department are largely unfriendly.

This morning, you assign Olga, one of your operators, to the tenth floor to work in the budget-review department. Suddenly, she boils over. "Send someone else up there to do their kind of picky work today," she tells you. I won't take another assignment like that until every other operator in the pool has been rotated to as many rotten jobs as I've had." Then you reply, "Olga, you've got to work any assignment that is legitimate, so get going!" With that, she storms off to talk to Mickey, the union steward. The steward calls and says that Olga has reported on the interaction with you and her frustrations, and asks that the three of you meet now to resolve the situation. You are about to talk to them and hope to convince Mickey and Olga that what you said and did was clearly within your rights as a supervisor.

MICKEY. You are the union steward, representing several dozen word-processing operators in a state agency. Your job is to make sure that employees are treated fairly and the union contract is followed by supervisors. A little while ago, Olga came storming in to see you and related her story in the following fashion.

"I have begun to feel that Daryl is taking advantage of my good work and my good nature. I rarely get to stay on the same assignment (which is desirable because it means a chance to get the feel of the work and the people in a particular department) more than one day at a time. Besides, many of the jobs that Daryl gives me are unattractive ones. The work is especially painstaking; for example, it has to be done under pressure, or the people in the department are largely unfriendly.

This morning, Daryl wants to send me up to the tenth floor to work in the budget-review department. Suddenly, I just boil over. I tell him to send someone else up there to do their kind of picky work today. I won't take another assignment like that until every other operator in the pool has been rotated to as many rotten jobs as I've had."

"What did Daryl say?" you ask Olga. "He told me in no uncertain terms that I had to work any assignment that is legitimate, so I'd better get going! That's when I came up to see you; I just don't think it's fair!" said Olga.

You think it over for a few minutes and then call Daryl to arrange a three-way meeting. Somehow you have to get this problem resolved before Olga decides to quit her job, or Daryl starts to treat all employees this way.

Questions for discussion:

1. What is the outcome in each group (what is decided)?
2. Will Olga take the assignment that Daryl gave to her? Why or why not?
3. What basic issues are presented in this incident?

4. What is the appropriate way to resolve the disagreement before it deteriorates further?
5. How can further incidents such as this be prevented?

CASES FOR ANALYSIS

Case 58

▶ *Their Aching Backs*

"Not another one!" moaned Jerry, supervisor of the shelf-stocking unit at the SuperDuper Mart, a 60,000-square-foot discount hardware and lumber supply store. He had just received a call from the company doctor, reporting that one of his crew had suffered a severe strain in the lumbar region of his back. Not only would this employee be off duty for a week or two, the injury would also be recorded as a lost-time accident. Jerry would hear lots about that from his boss, especially since the company's insurer had been threatening to raise its premium due to the high incidence of back-related injuries at SuperDuper Mart.

To forestall further incidents, Jerry immediately toured the facility, stopping to admonish each of his crew. His message was essentially the same for everyone:

"Too many of you are going to the company doctor complaining about your aching backs. When you were hired, you knew you had to lift 50- to 70-pound cartons on a regular basis.

"There's no excuse for all these back injuries if you will only be more careful when you're lifting heavy cartons.

"Furthermore, I'm ordering a batch of those new back-support belts so everyone will have one. Don't let me catch you not wearing it.

"Remember, from now on around here, it's going to be Safety First."

Analysis ▶

Despite these admonishments, employees in Jerry's department continued to have frequent back injuries. What might Jerry have done to be more effective in reducing back injuries in his department? Of the five alternatives listed below, which do you think might be most effective? Rank them on a scale from 1 (most effective) to 5 (least effective). You may add another alternative, if you wish. Be prepared to justify your rankings.

_____ **a.** Post a summary of his message on the bulletin board and hang "Safety first" signs throughout the shop.

_____ **b.** Be sure to wear the new back-support belt himself.

_____ **c.** Hold regular safety meetings with his crew so that he can keep emphasizing his safety message.

_____ **d.** Train or retrain all employees in proper lifting techniques.

_____ **e.** Appoint an employee safety committee to study the lifting problems in the store and to recommend appropriate safety equipment and protective clothing.

Case 59

Mary's Pinched Ring Finger

While filing computer reports in a steel filing cabinet, Mary McDonald pinched the knuckle of her ring finger. It happened when the sleeve of her jacket caught in the steel drawer as she slammed it shut. Her supervisor examined the operation of the drawer and declared that the accident should not have happened. Other file clerks, however, observed that the opening and closing of the file drawers was a constant hazard. In fact, many of the clerks declared that they had torn a blouse or had a finger pinched.

◀ *Analysis*

a. To what extent do you think that these accidents were caused by the file clerks rather than by the design and operation of the drawers in the file cabinets?

b. Using the three E's of accident prevention, what sort of a safety program would you recommend for this particular hazard?

Case 60

Nine Who Did Wrong

Each of the following nine labor actions is a violation of one of the principal labor and employment laws. On a separate sheet of paper, write the name of the law that is violated by each action.

◀ *Analysis*

a. The Jasper Company refuses to talk about its wage scale to a union agent duly selected by employees.

b. A labor union insists that the Axe Construction Company discharge Tony, one of its employees, because he was expelled from the union for disagreeing with its policies.

c. The supervisor of the receiving department insists that a worker uncap a tank car of chemicals even though a needed safety respirator is not available.

d. A company refuses to hire Audrey Hill solely because she is married and her future supervisor thinks that she will quit soon to have a baby.

e. Torger Branson, who works for National Distributors, did not receive time-and-a-half pay for the hours over 40 that he worked last week.

f. Astro Metals Manufacturers hires 17-year-old George Cone to work on a job connected with a large government contract it has recently acquired.

g. A union prohibits one of its employees from speaking up on a complaint she has against the company's management.

h. Stan's supervisor assigns Stan to a very unpleasant task to discourage him from asking other employees to sign union membership cards.

i. The Texto Company fails to report to the government its arrangement for reimbursing shop stewards for their expenses while attending union conventions.

Answers to Quick Tests ▶

Quick Test 1	Quick Test 2	Quick Test 3
1. F	3. F	5. T
2. F	4. T	6. F

Quick Test 4	Quick Test 5	Quick Test 6
7. T	9. T	11. T
8. F	10. F	12. F

PART Nine

Personal Development Portfolio: Toward Mastery of Your Job

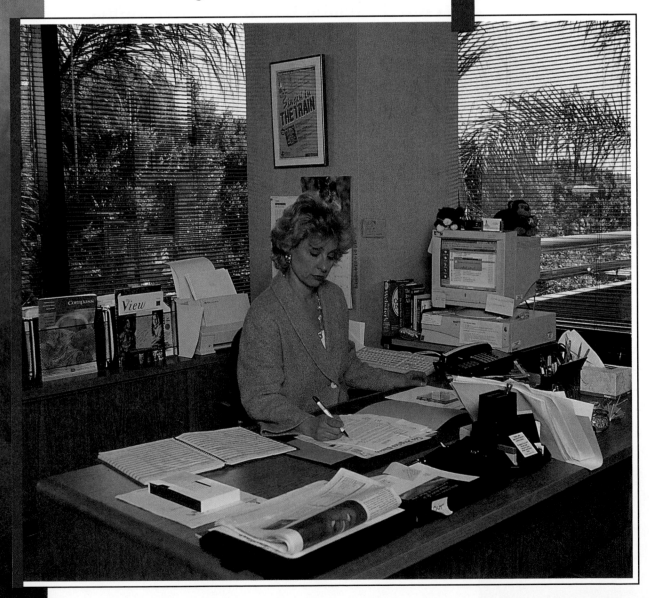

What Skills Will You Need to Succeed and Survive as a Supervisor?

FILE ① Taking Charge of Your Career

- A candid self-assessment, p. 540
- Establishing a career path, p. 541
- Preparing a timetable, p. 542
- Networking and mentors, p. 543
- Improvement and development, p. 545

FILE ② Managing Job-Related Time

- Surveying your time-usage habits, p. 547
- Controllable and uncontrollable time, p. 548
- Seven ways to manage your time better, p. 548
- ABCs of time control, p. 550

FILE ③ Coping With Stress

- Rating your stress potential, p. 553
- Stress management, p. 553
- Recognizing basic sources of stress, p. 554
- Controlling job-related stress, p. 554
- Guidelines for coping, p. 556

FILE ④ Moving Up in Your Organization

- Finding out how well you are accepted, p. 557
- Putting your best foot forward, p. 557
- Avoiding negative attitudes, p. 559
- Inviting favorable attention, p. 560
- How to ask for a raise, p. 561

How Can You Get the Most From This Portfolio?

Apply Yourself to Each of the Four Portfolio Files This Way

Complete the self-assessment exercise that appears on the second page of each file. It will help show you where you stand before you review the material that follows.

Study the advice presented in each file. It is arranged in the question-and-answer format that was used in the previous chapters of the text.

Where indicated, prepare your own career paths, objectives, time-tables, and developmental programs as illustrated in the file.

Make notations of the material that seems especially appropriate to you. Use these notations as a guide to searching for, and collecting, information elsewhere that will enhance and personalize your own file.

- *Study the Key Concepts to Remember*, which appears on page 563. They provide a summary of the high points in the Personal Development Portfolio.

- *Complete the final four Case Studies*, which appear on pages 564 to 566. These will provide you with experience in analyzing and solving problems that can occur while you are following a self-development program.

FILE ① TAKING CHARGE OF YOUR CAREER

Career planning begins with a candid self-assessment. Before doing anything else, complete the Personal Effectiveness Inventory (Table PDP-1) on the facing page. This is for your guidance in planning a self-improvement program, so do be realistic. Get a second opinion, too. Ask a friend—or even your boss—to make a similar assessment of your effectiveness for comparison purposes. The inventory consists of criteria that many authorities believe are needed for success in supervisory and management positions. Accordingly, the purpose of the assessment is not only to affirm your strong points but, especially, to identify areas that need further development.

To complete the table, place a check mark in the column to the right of each numbered skill that best matches your assessment of your proficiency. If you believe that you are *less than strong* in a skill that stands in the way of your career advancement, place a check mark in the "Needs Improvement" column, too.

On what is a career development program based?

It has four vital components:

- **A candid self-assessment.** You have already begun your self-development if you have completed the Personal Effectiveness Inventory in Table PDP-1.
- **Firm and realistic job goals.** These should be based on what you want to accomplish in your career specifically and in your life generally. They will be limited, of course, by the unimproved weaknesses that stand out in your Personal Effectiveness Inventory.
- **A concrete program for development.** Every weakness points toward a corrective course of action. These actions should be spelled out in detail—a course to take, a book to read, a seminar to attend, an on-job practice to engage in. Action plans should also pin down the time to begin and complete each phase. A modest but concrete development program is better than an ambitious but vague one.
- **Motivation and commitment.** Career growth has its pluses and minuses. Upward movement usually means greater status and a more affluent lifestyle. It also means very hard work, sacrifice of leisure time, removal from the easy friendship with people in the department, and an occasional unpleasant decision to make. That is the tradeoff. To go ahead, supervisors have to value the benefits above the new obligations. Without personal drive and commitment to the goals you have chosen, a self-development program becomes an exercise in self-deception.

TABLE PDP-1

Personal Effectiveness Inventory

Skills	Proficiency			
	Weak	Adequate	Needs Improvement	Strong
1. *Oral communication:* Ability to express ideas effectively in individual or group situations.	_____	_____	_____	_____
2. *Written communication:* Ability to write clearly, concisely, and correctly.	_____	_____	_____	_____
3. *Leadership:* Ability to get ideas accepted and acted upon by an individual or a group.	_____	_____	_____	_____
4. *Interpersonal sensitivity:* Ability to be perceptive about the concerns and needs of others and the impact of your own behavior on others.	_____	_____	_____	_____
5. *Planning and organizing:* Ability to plan a course of action for self and others and to get results.	_____	_____	_____	_____
6. *Problem solving:* Ability to identify causes, analyze problems, and propose workable solutions.	_____	_____	_____	_____
7. *Decisiveness:* Ability to make sound decisions and a willingness to take action.	_____	_____	_____	_____
8. *Time management:* Ability to make effective use of job-related time to meet schedules, deadlines, and other commitments.	_____	_____	_____	_____
9. *Stress tolerance:* Ability to perform under pressure.	_____	_____	_____	_____
10. *Creativity and innovation:* Ability to conceive, recognize, and accept or implement new and/or imaginative ideas.	_____	_____	_____	_____
11. *Flexibility:* Ability to recognize changing conditions and to implement necessary changes.	_____	_____	_____	_____

What is a career path? How is it found?

A **career path** maps out the most logical and practical roadway to a position, or series of positions, that an individual believes holds the most attractive occupational and personal rewards. As stated earlier, you may decide that your career lies in your present job. If so, you'll be mainly concerned with the improved performance, broader scope of responsibilities, larger salary, and heightened personal satisfaction.

If, however, your sights are on a career beyond your present position, you'll need to develop a more complex plan. Your target can be the next higher position in your organization, or it can be one at the same level but with a different range of responsibilities, or it can be a job much further up the management hierarchy. An example of a career path is illustrated in Figure PDP-1. This individual—let's call her Patty—has picked a long-range target of becoming the general manager of a profit center. To get there, Patty has plotted a path that will move her from a staff-supervisory position in quality control (1) to being a production-line supervisor (2), then upward to production manager in a different division (3), across to an entirely different functional area as a marketing manager (4), and, it is hoped, after a number of years, to general manager of her original division (5).

To make her career path workable, Patty should include target dates for each move, say "in two or three years" or "in five years." And, most important, Patty's plan must identify (a) any personal weaknesses in her present performance and (b) the knowledge, skills, or experience needed to move her from one step to another along her career path. For example, Patty's performance on her present job may be marred by a poor employee safety record. She'll have to plan to do something to get that straightened out before she can realistically expect to get a crack at the line production

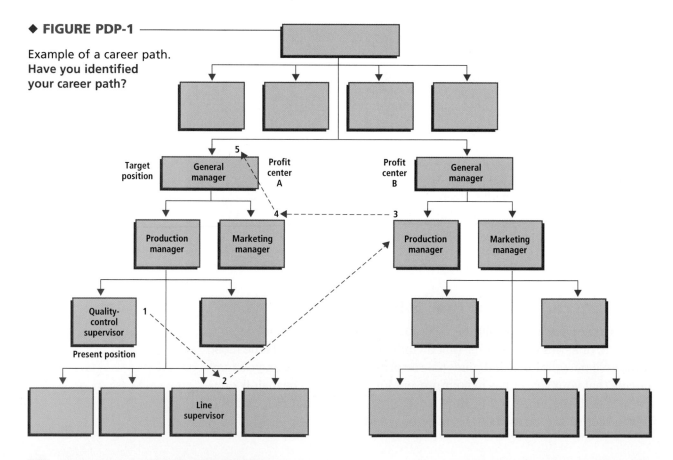

◆ FIGURE PDP-1

Example of a career path. Have you identified your career path?

job. Looking ahead to what it will take for her to move from the line job (2) to the divisional production manager's job (3), Patty may decide that she has to acquire a broader technical knowledge of the process. To do so, she may enroll in the appropriate course at a local technical institute. The point is that each new job will have its own particular set of requirements. Patty will need to anticipate them and acquire the necessary credentials before she can seriously think about moving ahead to the next position in her career plan.

How can you make sure that your plan for self-improvement or for career advancement becomes reality?

Self-delusion is paved with good intentions. To avoid shortfalls in your improvement plans, don't try to do too much too soon. Plan ahead for one step at a time. Do this planning in detail and do it realistically. Set targets that can be reached and place some kind of deadline for them, as shown in Figure PDP-2. Put both your goals and your plans into writing. Tack them up in a place where they will constantly remind you of your commitment to them. Check your progress regularly.

What about networking and mentors?

You'll help your career along with either or both. **Networking** is what used to be called "connections." Today's differences are that networks are built by, or tapped by, an individual along lines of knowing what's going on and what's opening up in an organization rather than on formal lines of authority and status. Networks are very informal, and the individuals in them often have little or no direct influence. But, by working the network, you can do a better job of planning your career moves and selecting the best preparation for them.

A **mentor**, on the other hand, is someone in a position of influence or authority who is interested in you and your career. A mentor is best utilized as an adviser. He or she will have a good idea of the best path to travel and the kind of training and skills you'll need to pursue it. It is not a good idea to expect a mentor to do much more than point the way. It is unfair to ask him or her to risk personal security and reputation on your behalf. If, however, a mentor goes out on a limb for you, don't let him or her down.

How can you attain the formal education needed for your career?

Face it, the person with the better education has an advantage over the person without it. But this doesn't mean you can't do anything about it. There's plenty you can do to improve your knowledge.

First, examine your own attitude toward further education. Is it strictly negative? If so, you'd better change in a hurry. Convince yourself that you, too, can learn new techniques and accept new ideas. If you want to learn, learning is made easier.

Supervisor: _____ Joane Carleo _____

Self-development schedule. **How many areas of self-development are on your schedule?**

Weak Spots	Plan for Corrective Action	When to Do It	Action Complete
Telling employees where they stand	Prepare calendar with a different worker to be talked to each week	At once	✔
Poor department safety record	Hold monthly meetings with work group	Begin June	✔
Keeping up with job technology	Subscribe to *Personal Computing*	At once	✔
No activities outside of work	Join Data Processing Association	Next year	
Speaking in front of groups	Enroll in Dale Carnegie course in public speaking	Next winter	
Cost estimating	Take correspondence course in accounting	Not scheduled	

☐ This year's plan   ☐ Next year's plan   ☐ Future

Next, pick out the soft spots in your educational armor. Is it reading and writing? Is it a weakness with figures? These can be improved quickly through correspondence and home-study courses or in an evening course at a local community college or university. Adult education courses at your local high school also offer help in these areas.

If your weakness is in a technical line—say, your company is processing chemicals or constructing complicated electronic equipment or your job involves simple metallurgy—you can find courses at technical institutes and universities that will help you understand such processes better even if you don't become an expert.

Caution: You may not be able to take a course in computer programming, for instance, if you haven't had a previous course in basic computer operations. So your plan for improvement may often have to be a long-range one. Here's a suggestion: You may be able to enroll in an advanced course just as a listener. You can thus get a feel for the subject and its terminology, with only a little prior preparation.

In your programming, don't scatter your efforts indiscriminately. Pinpoint your educational efforts to strengthen your weak spots. Later on, if you like, you can add frills.

How can you take best advantage of your company's training and development program?

Show that you're interested. In most progressive companies today, the human resource development manager or the training director is eager to help supervisors who want to help themselves. Don't be ashamed to ask for help, and don't think you'll be revealing a secret weakness. One of the necessary qualities of an executive is the ability for self-analysis and the determination to improve.

Stay alert, too, to **management development** opportunities. Management development (it may also be called executive or supervisory development) is the term applied to the systematic inventory, appraisal, and training of management people. Programs vary according to an individual company's policies. Sometimes they include only top management people and often are not extended to the first-line supervisory level.

If there's a program in your company that applies to you, you'll probably hear about it from your boss. But don't expect your company to take care of your self-development program. It's really up to you.

Where can you go for outside help and guidance?

For educational guidance outside your company, try your local center for adult education or vocational guidance, a nearby community college or technical institute, or a university extension service. Another source to try is any nearby chapter of the American Society for Training and Development or the International Personnel Management Association.

Additionally, you should be aware of three nationwide management associations of particular importance to supervisors:

International Management Council
430 S. 20 Street
Omaha, NE 68102

National Management Association
2210 Arbor Boulevard
Dayton, OH 45439

Institute of Certified Professional Managers
James Madison University
Harrisonburg, VA 22801

For information about specific correspondence or technical courses, write to

American Society for Training and Development
1640 King Street
Alexandria, VA 22313

American Society for Engineering Education
1 DuPont Circle, N.W.
Washington, DC 20036

International Personnel Management Association
1617 Duke Street
Alexandria, VA 22314

National Home Study Council
1601 18th Street, N.W.
Washington, DC 20009

American Personnel and Guidance Association
5999 Stevenson Avenue
Alexandria, VA 22313

What will outside reading do for you?

Some people can learn a lot just by reading. Others find it difficult to get much from the printed page. But if you're one of the former, try to set up a planned reading program. Include in it at least one good newspaper (such as *USA Today* or *The Wall Street Journal*), one good news magazine (such as *Time* or *Newsweek*), one good management magazine (such as *Business Week* or *Industry Week*), and one good technical magazine or journal that serves your field (such as *Modern Office Technology* or *Popular Computing*). Don't just subscribe to them or have your name put on the routing list. Read them—and try to apply what you find in them. In addition, you ought to set up a library of business and professional reference books for yourself.

To what extent will career goals conflict with other aspirations in life?

They can be compatible, but the higher you move in a career, the more likely it is that other life values will suffer. This need not be, if you also build into your career plans a place for the other things you hold dear—family, friends, leisure, health, service, faith. You will be able to make such plans only if you have developed maturity, however. Maturity requires the ability to stand outside yourself and make an honest judgment of your thoughts and behavior. It usually means—among other things—exercising a great deal of self-control, being able to hold your temper when others are losing theirs, accepting an occasional failure as well as success, and evaluating the talents and the intent of others fairly, regardless of your personal views.

FILE ② MANAGING JOB-RELATED TIME

How *purposefully* busy are you? The Time Management Survey (Table PDP-2) is designed to help you answer that question. Your responses should lead you to the major challenge of **time management.** It involves dividing your time into two compartments: (1) the time that you *can* control and (2) the time that you *can't* control. When your boss wants you at a meeting, for example, that's time you can't control. So is the time you have to spend on an unexpected breakdown or an emergency. In your

TABLE PDP-2			
Time Management Survey			
Time Management Practices and Styles	**Least Like Me**	**Neither Least nor Most Like Me**	**Most Like Me**
1. It is difficult for me to meet delivery or project deadlines without working overtime or letting other work slip.	3	2	1
2. I usually can be depended upon to meet my time commitments.	1	2	3
3. My estimates about how quickly something can be done are usually correct; they rarely take longer than I expected.	1	2	3
4. I carefully examine schedules that I am given beforehand, rather than waiting until the work is behind schedule to complain.	1	2	3
5. When making promises about getting a new job done, I take into account how long it takes to get started on something new.	1	2	3
6. I base my time decisions on concrete knowledge of how long it has taken me to do a similar job in the past.	1	2	3
7. I regularly use some sort of systematic plan for the use of my time.	1	2	3
8. I often find myself caught up in disruptive, time-consuming telephone calls.	3	2	1
9. I rarely find the opportunity to let someone else do a job that I can do better.	3	2	1
10. I like to get a head start on work that I know will be time consuming.	1	2	3

Scoring: 24 to 30, *outstanding!*
17 to 23, *satisfactory*, but there is room for improvement in some areas, notably those you circled as "1."
10 to 16, *poor.* Time gets away from you. Go to work on the items you circled as "1."

own situation, there are probably a number of other demands placed on your time, not at your convenience but at that of someone else. It's a good idea to make a list of these potentially uncontrollable occurrences right now. This is important because you'll want to think about them differently from the way you think about time demands that you can control. As a consequence, your approach to time management can be guided by two general rules:

1. Systematize and prioritize the management of your controllable time.
2. Minimize the amount of your uncontrollable time. This has to be done in bits and pieces, and probably over a long period of time. And, since this time is often controlled by others, you'll have to work out ways to gain some concessions from them in the interests of your own flexibility while still accommodating their needs.

What can you do to manage your time better?

Here are seven good guidelines to follow:

1. **Make up your mind fast.** This is not to advocate snap judgments, but it's a fact that 85 percent of the problems that face you aren't worth more than a few minutes of your time. So learn to say "yes" or "no," "we will" or "we won't." Employees and associates like working with decisive people—even when they aren't right all the time. And few things save time like a decisive answer—time saved for you and your employees.

2. **Be specific about dates.** You promise to get out an order "sometime next week." What happens? You're likely to find several deadlines coming due at the same time. If you're specific—Wednesday for Triangle and Thursday for Superior—you've started to systematize your thinking.

   Or let's say Pete calls you. Can he drop by to see you? Any time, you say. So Pete drops by just when you're up to your ears in a line changeover. Pete doesn't get much attention, your changeover gets the "good enough" treatment, and your time budget suffers.

3. **Control the telephone.** It's a monster to supervisors in some shops. But it needn't be (if your boss will cooperate). If you can get someone else to answer it for you, do. Then call back when you have the time. Avoid using the telephone for routine messages that can be forwarded through the interoffice mails or by E-mail. And watch yourself so that you don't develop telephonitis and bother others with it unnecessarily.

4. **Write down reminders.** Don't trust yourself to remember things to do. Use a surefire reminder system, such as jotting down important jobs to be done on your desk calendar or in a personal digital assistant. One supervisor we know jots down anything she feels she should remember or act upon on a little sheet of paper. Then she tosses it into a desk drawer. Each morning she reviews the

notes to see what she must do out of the ordinary for that day. When it's done, she simply tears up the slip.

5. **Limit chitchat.** Conversation, with employees and other supervisors, is vitally important to your role as supervisor. But you've got to keep it under control or it will eat up all your spare time. So limit casual conversation to a few pleasantries when you can. Nothing ruins your day quite so well as a couple of 20-minute conversations with your associates about the fish they didn't catch or the status of a do-it-yourself project.

6. **Set up a time budget.** Try preparing a time budget beforehand like the one charted in Figure PDP-3, by which you plan to distribute your daily time usage into four scheduled categories:

   a. *Routine work*, such as checking time sheets, answering mail, and handling normal paperwork.

   b. *Regular job duties*, such as the important ones of supervising, training, controlling, and appraising.

   c. *Special work*, such as serving on committees or assisting on special projects.

   d. *Creative work*, such as developing new methods to improve your department's quality or productivity.

◆ **FIGURE PDP-3**

Example of a time budget. **Are there other categories you would add?**

	MONDAY	TUESDAY	WEDNESDAY	THURSDAY	FRIDAY
8					
	ROUTINE	ROUTINE	ROUTINE	ROUTINE	ROUTINE
9	Inspection and supervision of operations REGULAR	Individual work with staff REGULAR	Inspection and supervision of operations REGULAR	Individual work with staff REGULAR	SPECIAL WORK
10		Inspection and supervision of operations REGULAR		Control studies and reports REGULAR	Inspection and supervision of operations REGULAR
11					
12			Division staff meeting REGULAR		Our staff meeting REGULAR
1	L	U	N	C	H
	Interviews and contacts REGULAR	Interviews and contacts REGULAR	Interviews and contacts REGULAR	Interviews and contacts REGULAR	CREATIVE WORK
2					
3	Planning and organizing REGULAR	Inspection and supervision of operations REGULAR	SPECIAL WORK	Inspection and supervision of operations REGULAR	
4					
5	ROUTINE	ROUTINE	ROUTINE	ROUTINE	ROUTINE

7. **Begin each workday with a plan.** Each day will present a new set of problems, so take five minutes to tailor your plans before the workday begins. Use your desk calendar to list the things you want to do that day.

How can you use ABC analysis to control time?

ABC analysis is a concept that predicts that 80 percent of your time will be spent on only 20 percent of your problems. (See pages 109 to 110 and Figure 5-4.) To make this idea pay off for you, the 20 percent of the problems that you work on should be rated as class A—the **vital few.** The president of a major appliance firm, for example, begins his day by labeling each task ahead as A, B, or C. Class B items aren't quite so important as A items. And class C problems are very small fish, even though there are lots of them. The president goes after A items first and then tries to get to the Bs. Invariably, says the president, a surprising thing happens. When he gets to the Cs, he can "wipe out a lot of them in one sweep." These are the tasks, of course, that can be disposed of quickly with a telephone call, a jotted note, or a brief instruction to employees as you walk through the shop.

In planning to concentrate your time on the "vital few" problems and let the "trivial many" await their turn, how do you recognize the vital few?

Experience will provide a good basis. You may waste a couple of hours the first time around on what turns out to be an inconsequential problem. The next time it comes up, however, either you will know how to dispose of it quickly or you will know that you should put it far down on your priority list.

There are other ways, too, of judging a problem's importance. For example, ask yourself any of these questions:

Where did it come from? If the problem arose as a directive from your boss or a request from the sales department, it may need top priority. If it came from a lesser source, perhaps you can delay it. In organizational matters, you must be realistic and hard-headed politically.

What is its potential for trouble? Some unsolved problems can cause other problems to pile up elsewhere. Suppose there is a machine that needs a minor repair. You put it off. But that machine is in the main line of flow in your operation. It is in a position to cause quality problems, and if it breaks down altogether, it will hold up production. The repair problem is minor, but its potential for trouble is great. Get to it sooner rather than later.

Is it aimed at results rather than activity? Dr. George Odiorne, who popularized MBO, warned that supervisors and managers devote too much time going through motions that are essentially trivial. On paper, their efforts may look good; they write reports, keep their files up to date, and attend all the meetings. But they don't get results in terms of greater output, better quality, or lower costs. Odiorne said that these managers have wasted their time by falling into the "activity trap."

How quickly can it be disposed of? Watch your answer on this one. It is what R. Alec Mackenzie calls the "time trap." Many problems look as if they can be handled quickly. It is a temptation to jump into them without thinking. But what was supposed to be done with a three-minute phone call turns into several phone calls. What should have taken only a minute or two of discussion grows into a major hassle. Tasks that can truly be handled quickly should be grouped together and finished in one block of time. Problems that need a major effort should be budgeted for your undivided attention, with enough time allotted for their solution.

If you delegate a big share of your work to your subordinates to save time, won't you be charged with passing the buck?

Not necessarily. Subordinates expect that they'll have to carry the ball along with you. After all, that's the name of the game. Furthermore, most people want to feel important enough to the operation to be asked to do some of the boss's work. But even if this weren't so, it's imperative for other urgent reasons that you learn to delegate a good portion of your personal workload.

Delegation is an essential ingredient of good management. And, to be painfully frank, it's often the only way you'll be able to keep your head above water. The average managerial job is so fraught with responsibilities that you could worry yourself into an 80-hour, jam-packed week just checking up on every detail yourself. If you allow yourself to fall into that trap, you're on your way out as a supervisor.

Delegation means, of course, that you've got to trust and train others on your staff to do the job nearly as effectively as you'd do it yourself. And if you can steel yourself to leave them alone, they usually will. With a big difference, however. Others won't do the job exactly the way you'd do it yourself. They'll also regard some factors as more important than you think they are. Worse still, they'll overlook or ignore other factors that you think demand top priority. That's the way of delegation. So learn to accept the fact of less-than-perfect results and to delegate just the same. Without delegation, you won't be able to make the grade as a supervisor and still maintain your peace of mind.

In delegating to make better use of your time, there are two good rules of thumb to follow:

1. Try not to spend time working on tasks that are below your capabilities. These are the things that you can do, of course, but that others should be doing for you.

2. Don't give your priorities to a series of trivial jobs while putting the big job on "hold." It's important that you take on the big job first. If the trivial jobs are urgent, then you should delegate them right away to the most qualified subordinates.

TABLE PDP-3			
Stress Indicator Barometer			
		Frequency	
Conditions	**Never**	**Sometimes, or Mild**	**Frequently, or Severe**
1. General irritability.	1	2	5
2. Difficulty in getting along with others.	1	2	5
3. Feelings of guilt.	1	2	5
4. Worry about seemingly small matters.	1	2	5
5. Depression, or lack of enthusiasm.	1	2	5
6. Concern that nothing gets done on time.	1	2	5
7. Overeating.	1	2	5
8. Insomnia.	1	3	10
9. Substance abuse, excessive use of alcohol, or use of illegal drugs.	1	5	10
10. Use of prescribed sleeping pills, pain killers, or pep pills.	1	3	10
11. Increased use of tobacco.	1	3	10
12. Feelings of weakness or dizziness.	1	5	10
13. Difficulty in concentrating.	1	2	5
14. Loss of appetite.	1	2	5
15. Increased occurrence of cuts, bruises, falls, or minor accidents.	1	3	10
16. Stomach cramps, upsets, diarrhea.	1	3	10
17. Temper tantrums.	1	5	10
18. Impatience with delays.	1	2	5
19. Changes in bodily functions, missed menstrual period, unusual premenstrual tensions.	1	3	10
20. Unusual spate of lost personal objects like keys, glasses, and notebooks.	1	3	10

Scoring: 20 to 50, *normal.* Indicates good tolerance of, or management of, stress.
51 to 99, *marginal.* Indicates greater-than-average difficulty in coping with stress.
100 or above, *watch out!* Indicates very low tolerance and/or severe difficulty in managing stress.

FILE 3
COPING WITH STRESS

Poor time management often leads to stress. The supervisory job is the kind of position in which, by its nature, you are asked—or expected—to do more than most people can in a normal workday. When you find that you are not accomplishing what you believe you should be, you may become frustrated. Frustrations exert pressure on your mind and eventually on your nerves and body. Such pressure is popularly known as **stress**. In its exaggerated state, it is often called "burnout." As a matter of practical fact, almost everybody suffers from stress. It is when stress places a load on the body or mind beyond a point that can be tolerated that stress becomes a medical problem.

To get some indication of whether or not you are buckling under stress at this time, complete the Stress Indicator Barometer in Table PDP-3.

Twenty stress indicators are listed in the table. For each condition, circle the number of the answer at the right that best describes the frequency with which that condition occurs in you. Add the numbers you have circled. Then use the scoring key at the end of the table to assess your ability to manage stress.

Why do some individuals thrive on pressure, whereas others seem to be crumpled by it?

Probably because those who don't show signs of wear and tear (a) have learned their stress limits and (b) have kept their stress load within them. Your mind and body flexes freely under tolerable stress, somewhat like a steel beam flexes under a heavy load. If the load is within its stress limits, the beam will snap back into line when the load is removed. If, however, the beam is overloaded, it will be bent out of shape. Loads that are too heavy for *you* to carry will bend your mind or body out of shape, too. There is always a limit beyond which the mind or body will flex no longer. At that point, you show some of the signs indicated in Table PDP-3. Accordingly, you "manage" this stress by finding ways of relieving it, by redistributing it, or by removing it.

For example, you shift some stress to others by delegating. You remove some of it by obtaining additional resources (people, tools, information, and the like) to help out in your department. You can also make sure that stress doesn't all come at once by planning and controlling your personal time more effectively. The steel beam, for example, can carry a load of 100 tons in 24 hours, *provided* that no more than 5 tons are placed on it at a time. That's why so many bridges bear signs that read "Maximum load is 10 tons." You can't go around wearing such a sign; employees and associates often have little sympathy for one's limits, anyway.

Instead, you must learn exactly how much stress you can bear before you suffer a strain, and then you must develop a plan for managing stress so that it never exceeds that limit.

Where is stress likely to come from?

Career counselors tell us that stress at work originates from three sources:

1. **The work environment.** This includes just about everything, from malfunctioning machinery, faulty materials, tight schedules, pinching budgets, and pressure-cooker deadlines to your hardheaded boss, your uncooperative associates, and your disinterested employees.

2. **Your inner self.** This is pretty deep stuff, but it includes such things as a loss of self-confidence, sensitivity to criticism about your performance, fear of failure, and doubts about your ability to cope with stress, wherever it originates.

3. **Interpersonal relationships.** This combines the worst elements of the first two. Most work situations involve some sort of interpersonal transaction. For example, you may want a machine repaired in a hurry so that a critical order can be shipped. You've got to persuade the maintenance supervisor that this job should get her top priority. The degree of stress generated by this situation may depend entirely on your interpersonal skills. If you handle this transaction well, the machine will be back on line without delay. On the other hand, if you end up quarreling with the other supervisor, the stress of the machine breakdown will be compounded by the stress of the quarrel.

In regard to the stress coming from the supervisory job itself, which conditions are likely to need a fundamental improvement?

Former U.S. President Harry Truman was partly right when he said, "If you can't stand the heat, stay out of the kitchen." The supervisory job is, by its nature, stressful. That's what makes it so invigorating and challenging. As another wise person once said, "If there were no stress, you might as well be dead." But there is a great difference between an invigorating amount of stress and too much stress. A basic goal in stress management, therefore, is to try to eliminate persistent but unnecessary stress. There's enough of the other kind already to make many of your days hectic. Among the basic sources of stress that should be corrected are the following:

- **Ambiguity about the results for which you are held responsible.** If your organization provides a job description for your position, make sure that it is specific about vital results such as output expected per shift, the acceptable percentage of rejects or errors, allowable expenses, and tolerance for employee absences, tardiness, and accidents. Be wary about performance expectations in these and any other areas that are described with such loose terms as *good, better, soon,* and *improved.* Ask, politely but firmly: "How good?" "How much better?" "How soon?" "How big an improvement?" These are reasonable questions, and they will do much to take the vagueness—and stress—out of the measurements by which you will be judged.

- **Inadequate resources for the job at hand.** Few things are more frustrating than being pressed to get results without having been given the resources to get the job done properly. You'll want to try to make certain that the performance demands that are made of you are matched from the start with adequate labor, equipment, materials, and supplies. Supervisors often make their biggest mistake by saying "yes" to a request before carefully sizing up the situation. This doesn't mean that you should say "no" all the time, either. It may mean that you'll need to say: "Yes, it can be done, *but only* by postponing the Smith job 2"—or by allowing the staff to work overtime, or by subcontracting a part of the project, or by purchasing partially finished components, or by making any other necessary increase or adjustment in your resources, methods, and deadlines.

- **Conflicting demands and instructions.** These often stem from having two bosses. This situation shouldn't happen, of course, but it does. And, as matrix organizations increase in number, it will happen more often. When faced with the stress of conflict in orders or instructions, don't let it pass by simply blowing off steam. Instead, make the results of such a conflict clear to both parties as soon as you can. Show them how it affects productivity, costs, or customer relations. Here, again, situations are most likely to be corrected for reasons that bring benefits to those who cause the situation.

There are sources of stress outside work, aren't there?

Of course. Not only that, but the sources of stress outside business are probably more powerful and less manageable. So far, we've talked about how to avoid or minimize stress at work, especially stress arising from time pressures. You should not overlook the very important matter of stress sources outside work. These are often just as hard to avoid or reduce. The same principles prevail, however. You must

1. Alter or change the conditions of your personal environment to reduce stress, if you can.
2. Be realistic about your personal ambitions and capabilities, but don't undersell yourself to yourself.
3. Identify those necessary interpersonal transactions where your performance is unsatisfactory, and do something to improve your skills in those areas. Admittedly, none of this is easy to do. Accordingly, if the strain you feel—from stress at work or elsewhere—is great, you'll need professional counseling. This might be obtained from a

variety of professionals, including doctors, lawyers, and accountants; marriage counselors, psychologists, and clinical social workers; and religious or spiritual advisers.

Besides trying to control stress at the source, what else can you do personally to lessen its impact?

The three fundamental approaches to management of stress, no matter what its origin, were outlined in the last section. In a more specific context, however, there are several other constructive things you can do to lessen the impact of stress on your system:

1. **Understand your limitations and live within them.** Acknowledge such truisms as "Everybody can't be president" and "Rome wasn't built in a day." This calls for you to (a) be realistic about your true capabilities, (b) exploit them only as far as they'll carry you, (c) try not to move too far too fast, and (d) accept the fact that it's usually more satisfying to do well at a lesser job than to feel relentlessly pressured at one slightly above your capacity.

2. **Break away, if necessary, before you break yourself.** Don't run away from every crisis, but if you find yourself crumbling, do make time to remove yourself physically from the stressful situation. Take fifteen minutes or more to think, meditate, pray, relax—so you can get a fresh perspective.

3. **Get more genuine exercise.** It's a fact that tensions are reduced when the blood circulation rises. Even if you're not athletically inclined, find a half hour each day to loosen up your body in some relaxing form of exercise. Such activity need not be too vigorous—walking, bike riding, bowling, or lawn mowing may do you as much good for relaxation purposes as jogging, tennis, or swimming.

4. **Select and pursue at least one diversion.** Most important, this should be something you truly enjoy doing, not something that you feel is a matter of obligation. Let it be stamp collecting, woodworking, or machine-shop work, local politics, gardening, gourmet cooking, card playing, or needlepoint. If it's a true diversion, you will find that you are totally absorbed in it, that time flies and cares are forgotten during your involvement. The purpose of the diversion is to give your mind a rest from stress so that it can recharge its psychological energy cells.

5. **Take time to look at the world around you.** Most people who are troubled by stress tend to turn their vision inward. This is like trying to climb out of a pit by digging downward. The escape from pressure usually lies in the other direction, outside oneself. The world is a very big place, and simply taking five minutes to look at the morning or evening sky helps to place personal matters in perspective. Similarly, the act of getting concerned about other people's problems has a tension-relaxing effect. To test the degree to which you are inwardly turned, observe how well you can listen to others

without interruption. Ask yourself how often you try to top another person's miseries with a story about one of your own. Does only the work that you do seem important? Many of us who would never think of ourselves as egotists are concerned only with ourselves. It's a malady brought on by stress. And one of the best proven cures for it is to immerse yourself in trying to come to the aid of others.

FILE MOVING UP IN YOUR ORGANIZATION

You will succeed as a supervisor not only because of the extent of your basic competencies but also to the degree that you learn to fit into and master the organization you serve. Call it politics, organizational sensitivity, or just plain practicality, you must learn to go with the flow most of the time rather than swimming upstream. Your relationship with your boss is probably the best barometer of your organizational fit. By completing the Organizational Acceptance Rating Sheet in Table PDP-4, you can get an indication of how you stand with your current organization and with your boss, in particular.

To complete the table, circle the number to the right of each item that most nearly describes the condition in your organization. Add the numbers you have circled. Then use the scoring key at the end of the table to assess your standing in the organization.

How can you put your best foot forward in an organization?

There are many ways to gain personal acceptance in an organization, but here are some that have been particularly effective.

1. **Demonstrate your job competence.** Few things gain as much respect as an individual's ability to do a job well. Your job is supervision. So show that you can run your operation like a clock, that company-wide problems never have their origin in your department, and that you've got your employees well motivated and under control.

2. **Become an integral part of the information network.** Almost all organizations, public and private, derive a great deal of their power from the information they assemble and control. By becoming a part of the information network of an organization, you become an integral part of the organization. Accordingly, make an early effort to know (a) the extent of unique information the organization possesses, (b) how to gain access to it, (c) how to contribute to it, and (d) how to use it in your operation. This does not imply that you should try to tap secret documents. It does mean, however, that you should know how to obtain and exchange the data you

TABLE PDP-4

Organizational Acceptance Rating Sheet

Conditions	Not True	Partly True	Mostly True
1. You receive raises as frequently as your associates.	1	2	3
2. Your boss gives you a free hand with your employees.	1	2	3
3. Your boss knows very little about your life away from work.	3	2	1
4. Others in your organization are always encroaching on your turf.	3	2	1
5. When you've made a mistake, your boss will stand up for you.	1	2	3
6. You are among the last to learn about impending changes in the organization.	3	2	1
7. You don't like the way your company does a lot of things.	3	2	1
8. You have found a number of supportive associates within your organization.	1	2	3
9. The other people in your organization seem to carry grudges forever.	3	2	1
10. Your boss gives weight to your opinions before making decisions that affect you.	1	2	3

Scoring: 24 to 30, *insider*. You're part of the team! However, review the items you circled as "1" or "2" to see how you can strengthen your position even more.

17 to 23, *"fringesider."* You are not fully accepted yet. Check the items you circled as "1" to see why you haven't yet been welcomed onto the team.

10 to 16, *outsider*. You are definitely not one of the team. Examine the items you circled as "1" to plan a comprehensive program for gaining the support of your boss and your colleagues.

---

need to improve productivity and smooth out operations in your department.

3. **Go with the flow of the organization.** That is, try to find a way to go along with the organization's standards and its general style of management. A maverick has a hard time proving his or her worth. It's better to give up a little of your independence in return for the support you'll eventually need if you are to be fully effective in any organization. After all, that's what an organization is—a cooperative effort. Loyalty, too, plays a part here. If you disagree with some of the things that are going on, don't stand aside and criticize; try constructively to improve them.

4. **Build a personal support system.** It can be awfully lonely in an organization without friends, especially without influential friends. Accordingly, it is wise to be somewhat selective about the people

in the organization with whom you develop special rapport. Be cordial and courteous to everyone, of course. These qualities provide the lubrication that enables interpersonal contacts to thrive. But it is important that you go beyond that by making friends (business friends, not necessarily personal friends) with those people who are—or whose positions make them—influential in the organization. A first step is to develop a good relationship with the key person in the department that precedes or follows yours in the product or service flow. If you make things reasonably comfortable for that person, he or she may be expected to come to your aid when you need help. A next step is to establish contacts in key staff departments (if you're a line supervisor, or in line departments if you're a staff supervisor). You'll want to be able to get confidential advice, and perhaps a little extra cooperation, from those in a position to do you good in payroll, accounting, sales order, field service, inventory, production control, and information systems, for example. In a great many instances, you will be able to develop this network only by first demonstrating that you will discharge your own responsibilities in a way that, at the very least, does not create problems for these key people. *People for whom you do favors do you favors.* People about whom you say good things speak well of you. That's politics, of course, but it's also the fact of organizational survival and success. Make no mistake: your personal support network depends on such tradeoffs.

What sort of attitudes and actions should you avoid?

Always keep in mind that an organization is a group of people working together toward common goals. Large organizations are made of many smaller, overlapping organizations. These are groups within groups. As a consequence, at any one time at work you'll be a member of many organizations. What you say and do to make you a hero in one organization may make you an outcast in another. If you're strong enough and right enough often enough, you can say and do just about anything you please and few people will take sides openly against you. Most of us, however, are not like the eight-foot bear who can "sleep anywhere he pleases." We've got to be more politically astute. This means that it's not too wise to take extreme positions. You needn't always be in the middle of the road, but you don't want to get so far away from the consensus that you can't make a compromise when good judgment dictates one. Here are some additional points to remember:

- It's important that you show others that you are willing to pull your weight in the total organization. There are always a number of unpleasant assignments; make sure that you take your share.
- You can't go far—or for long, either—with a win-lose attitude toward your peers. Resource allocations can spark battles between departments. Each wants the new clerk, the extra lift truck, first access

to the computer upgrade, and the like. If you insist on getting the most or the best every time, you'll inevitably make enemies. Organizations create mutual dependencies. You'll need to learn when to fight for a particular resource and when you will contribute more to the organization's goals if you let another department have the resource without a quarrel.

- It's also wise to avoid being characterized as a "negative," a person who resists every change. Try to check yourself before you think or say: "We've tried that before and it didn't work." "It isn't practical in the shop." "We're too busy with more important matters to be bothered right now."

- Finally, don't hog all the credit. Most of your accomplishments depend on the contributions of others. When reporting progress, give others the credit they deserve, and then some. Go out of the way to tip your hat (in your reports to your superiors) to anyone who can reasonably be said to have been a party to a success. It costs very little to be generous, and it goes a long way toward defusing any potential undercutting of your organizational ambitions.

How can you draw favorable attention to your capabilities without appearing offensive or objectionable?

The larger the organization, the more difficult it is for you to gain broad visibility. Doing a superb job in your own niche usually isn't enough. Your good works will go unrecognized elsewhere, unless you make a conscious effort to display them. This does not mean that you should make a nuisance of yourself in this regard. However, to help you in both your present job and your career, you should practice the two techniques described below.

- **Find ways to exhibit your leadership and initiative.** It may be more comfortable for you to sit back and let others start a project rolling. After all, the old army saying "Never volunteer!" has its merits; it keeps your extra burdens light. But if you really want to show your talents, this is one way of separating yourself from the pack. You'll want to pick your spots, of course. You don't want to become the company dray horse who can be counted on to carry *all* the heavy loads. Instead, try to be a part of the leading edge of those committees, projects, and operational changes that are being watched over or spurred on from above. Sometimes all that is needed is for you to speak up in favor of a project that is stalled on dead center.

    There are always opportunities, too, to institute a new method or procedure in your own department without waiting for a company-wide program. When you do so, be sure to go on record with a memorandum to your boss and to any of the staff departments to which it may have special interest. Suppose, for example, you institute a daily error-watch reporting system for your employees, and it makes an observable inroad into reducing errors. Send a copy of the form you use and the results obtained to your boss and to other interested persons.

- **Look for, or accept, challenging responsibilities.** This idea is an extension of gaining visibility for your leadership and initiative qualities. It will require an extra effort on your part, since these opportunities often will not come to you; you'll have to seek them out. They may be found, however, wherever a problem exists—within your own operations or anywhere in the total organization. You may many times encounter a condition that you know to be unsatisfactory. You may assume that either nothing can be done about it or it is the affair of someone else, usually one of the adjacent line or staff departments. Don't let the problem die there. Instead, try tackling a material shortages problem, a duplication-of-effort problem, or a communication problem, for example. These often occur at the interface between departments. They give you a chance to work with others in positions of responsibility outside your department. It will usually be up to you to be the spearhead, but if you can bring about a solution or an improvement, you'll have something to show, not only upstairs but next door.

How do you go about asking for a raise?

Assuming your timing is correct, you'll want to approach the raise problem in much the same manner you would if you were trying to sell your boss a new idea. Here are a few tactics to consider.

- **Come right out and ask for it.** The direct approach will force a "yes" or "no" answer, so be certain your performance warrants more money before you try it. To be on firm ground, have some facts on hand that can show how your job has grown bigger or how your efforts have become more effective: "I know the company expects to get a return on all the money it spends—including my salary. So I've made a list of new duties I've picked up since last year. And the shop records show that absences in my department are down 3 percent over last year, scrap is down 4 percent, and direct labor cost per unit has been reduced 7 cents."

- **Pick a salary goal.** Instead of vaguely asking for "more money," it puts you in a better negotiating position if you can name the dollar figure you have in mind. Be certain that it is reasonable in light of (a) your performance and (b) the salaries of others in your organization. Don't set it too low, however. The chances are great that your boss will interpret your salary target as a top figure to consider and will work downward from there. The point of naming a salary goal is to establish the range of your request, with the thought that you may be willing to compromise between your goal and your current salary.

- **Stress the value of your contribution.** People who get ahead are those who can—and do—point to their efforts to help the organization attain its goals. Specifically, find ways to document your productivity, dependability, management-mindedness, and initiative. Show that you do more than the minimum required without having to be pushed. Guard against making the plea that you need the money, however. It's a poor business argument. Your personal finances are your own affair. You weaken yourself in the boss's eyes by asking for a raise because you can't manage at home.
- **Wait and see.** In many companies, this is the only tack you can follow. But, generally speaking, it's wise for you to remind the organization of your values from time to time. For instance, you might say, "I'm not asking for a raise at this particular moment, Ms. Jones, but I'd like to review my past six months' performance with you so that when raises are possible again, I'll be sure that my performance will warrant one."

KEY CONCEPTS TO REMEMBER

1. **Taking charge of your career.** Personal growth and improvement are the direct result of self-development. Other people may offer valuable advice and guidance, but each individual must furnish his or her own initiative, application, and persistence.

   Plans for career development should be based on an objective assessment of present performance as compared with job demands and future opportunities for growth and advancement.

   Self-development is essentially a form of adult education directed at improving personal knowledge, skills, and attitudes. This education can be accomplished through formal instruction, guided experience, and relevant reading.

   It is essential that plans for self-improvement be (a) practical, (b) specific in nature, and (c) firm in setting goals and timetables for attainment.

2. **Managing job-related time.** An awareness of time, its incredible value, and its fleeting elusiveness, together with an ability to utilize and conserve it, is what distinguishes an outstanding supervisor from an ordinary one.

   It takes self-discipline and conscious control to prevent personal time from being frittered away on nonessential, nonproductive activities. Inevitably, wasted time leads to job stress.

   Capable supervisors are tempted to consume too much of their own time by doing too much themselves, retaining too many responsibilities instead of delegating time-absorbing routines to their subordinates.

3. **Coping with stress.** An overload of stress can come from (a) the work environment, (b) your inner self, and (c) poorly handled interpersonal relationships. Job stress is often magnified by (a) ambiguity concerning responsibilities and results, (b) resources that do not match responsibilities, and (c) conflicting demands and instructions. Individuals manage stress by (a) understanding their limitations and living with them, (b) breaking away to regroup when pressures become extreme, (c) getting the proper exercise, and (d) developing outside interests that distract and relax.

4. **Moving up in your organization.** Few people rise far in management without having found a way to harmonize their personal goals and actions with those of their superiors and the organization as a whole. To do so requires tact and a degree of compromise, but it does not necessarily mean that you must sacrifice your independence or integrity.

   Your acceptance and support by the organization will depend in large measure upon (a) how well you demonstrate competence in your work, (b) the readiness with which you accommodate group goals and consensus, (c) your contribution to, and use of, the information network, and (d) the power and influence of the personal support system that you build.

   Raises and promotions are not the inevitable reward for good work. Your petitions for either should follow a well-conceived program that demonstrates the value of your contributions to the organization.

CASES FOR ANALYSIS

Case 61

▶ **Passed Over Again**

"I work hard," complained Connie to a fellow supervisor over coffee, "but I don't get much for it. Oh sure, I get an occasional merit increase or pat on the back. But that's not enough. I feel like I'm just marking time here. I'm really down now. Last week, when my boss retired, I thought for sure that I'd get his job. But I was passed over again. And that's the third good job that's passed me by."

"What reason did they give this time?" asked the other supervisor. "Was it the old 'glass ceiling' treatment?"

"No, I can't say that," said Connie, "As you must know, Mary from Dept. C got the job. But I did hear some of the old excuses."

"Like what?" asked the other supervisor.

"Like they didn't think I was really interested, that I was satisfied where I am. That Mary was better qualified. That the new information-control system needed someone who had advanced training. Mainly, but without being specific, they thought I hadn't demonstrated that I have the skills the new job would require."

"What really bothers me," continued Connie, "is that I *am* interested in moving ahead. I'd have liked advanced training if someone had offered it to me. And I do have a lot of skills that I haven't been asked to use on my present job. The system is so unfair. Why can't they see that?"

Analysis ▶

a. How unfair has the system been to Connie? Whose fault is it?
b. What might Connie do to improve her chances for advancement in the future?

Case 62

▶ **"Get Your Priorities Straight!"**

Tomas was deep into his review of the week's time sheets when the phone rang. It was a call from the plant manager's office advising him that there was a productivity committee meeting for all supervisors at 11:00 that morning. Tomas looked at his desk calendar. He was supposed to deliver his time sheets to the payroll office by noon, and it was 10 A.M. already. Just then, the chief inspector walked into Tomas's office. "There's a small problem developing out there on the assembly line right now. If you don't get it straightened out soon, it may end up with having to shut down the line." Tomas dropped everything and went out into the shop. The quality problem was a sticky one, and it was 11 A.M. before it was corrected.

When Tomas got back into his office, the phone was ringing. "Where are those time sheets?" queried the payroll supervisor.

"I'll get them up to you in a few minutes," Tomas said. And he set to work on them again.

At noon, the phone rang again. This call was from a very angry plant manager, who wanted to know why Tomas had not attended the productivity meeting. Tomas explained the quality-control problem and the need to get the time sheets into payroll. The plant manager was not sympathetic. He said, "You better get your priorities straight in the future."

◀ *Analysis*

a. Should Tomas have gone to the meeting? Why?
b. How would you have advised Tomas to arrange his priorities for handling the problems he faced that morning?

◀ **Case 63**

The Unfaceable Day

"I can't face this day," said Vito to his wife as he drank his third cup of breakfast coffee.

"What's wrong?" asked his wife.

"Just about everything," said Vito. "We just got through laying off a third of the office staff to cut costs. That was bad enough. Telling people they'd be going on unemployment, with no hope of their being called back. Now, we've got a big surge of orders to process. And my boss says that we've got to make do with the help we have. No temporaries. No callbacks. How am I ever going to press the remaining help to do more than normal? As it is, they've all slowed down the pace to stretch out the work."

"You'll manage, somehow," soothed Vito's wife.

"Maybe," said Vito as he chewed on a couple of antacid tablets before he lit up his first cigarette of the day. "I guess I'll have to put more pressure on to get everyone back into line!"

◀ *Analysis*

a. What's wrong with Vito's approach to his staff?
b. How would you suggest he handle this situation?
c. What kind of advice can you give Vito, generally, to enable him to cope better with his stress?

Case 64

Who Should Get the Pay Raise?

The area manager of a large insurance company was puzzling over the budget for allotting pay increases for her supervisory staff. The budget was especially slim this period. As best she could figure, the budget would allow only one pay increase. Looking down the list of supervisors, two stood out. Both did good jobs. On the one hand, there was Jerome, who headed the claims section. He was as solid as a rock. Last year, at performance-appraisal time, he had expressed a desire to progress steadily ahead, salarywise. Nevertheless, he was patient and understanding, and he would not be expected to make much of a fuss if he were passed over from time to time.

On the other hand, there was Julia, customer service supervisor. She, too, was a solid performer, but certainly no better than Jerome. At her last appraisal, however, Julia had made several points citing her contributions to the area's success. She had been forceful, too, about saying that she expected to receive a pay increase at the very next possible time.

"I can only approve a pay increase for one supervisor this time," the area manager mused. "Who should it be, Jerome or Julia?"

Analysis ▷ _____

a. How would you evaluate the case for Jerome and for Julia?

b. To whom would you give the pay increase? Why?

Appendixes

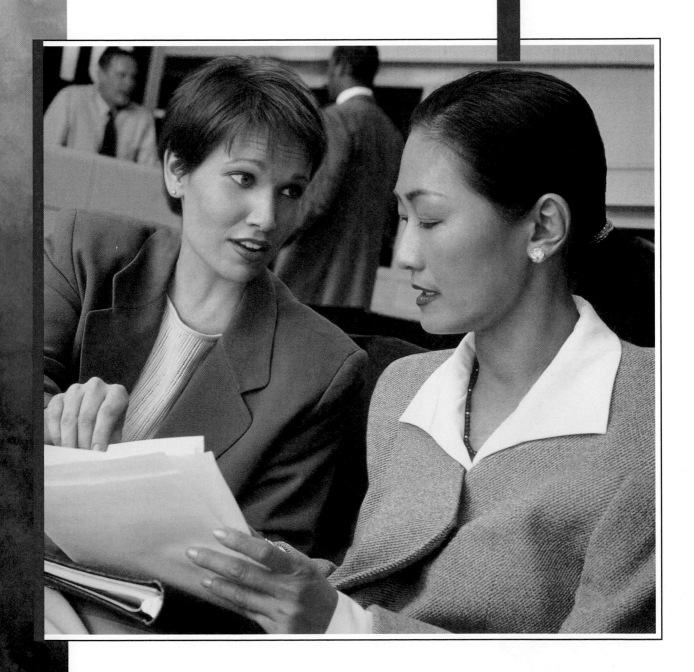

Planning the Day's Work

1. Do before the shift begins (15–30 minutes)
   a. Check production schedule and/or work orders for the day.
   b. Check equipment to be used—its availability and condition.
   c. Check supply of materials for the day.
   d. Check tools needed for the day.
   e. Arrange equipment, materials, and tools for the day.
   f. Prepare a firm work schedule for the day.

2. Do at the beginning of the shift (15–30 minutes)
   a. Check attendance and assign employees to workstations.
   b. If necessary because of absences, balance the workforce against the workload by rearranging assignments or by securing additional help from other departments.
   c. Assign production and/or work orders to employees.
   d. Stress critical quality areas to watch for.
   e. Specify when work should be completed.

3. Do during each work day (6–7 hours)
   a. Check quality of work with each employee. Approve, correct, instruct, or train as needed.
   b. Check work progress with each employee. Add help, allow more time, or assign additional work as appropriate.
   c. Check on housekeeping. See that it is satisfactory at all times. Good work cannot be done in an untidy place.
   d. Stay on the floor most of the time supervising and/or being available for questions, assistance, and instructions.
   e. Be on the floor immediately before and after all breaks and for a full 15 minutes before quitting time.
   f. Inspect critical quality points as work progresses. Correct problems as soon as they are detected.
   g. Provide a final inspection of parts, subassemblies, reports, and paperwork before they move on to other departments or to customers.

    h. Check periodically to see that tools and equipment are in proper operating condition.

    i. Check periodically to see that materials and supplies are on hand.

    j. Report and/or request maintenance, repair, or replacement of defective tools and equipment.

    k. Check accident hazards. Be sure that employees are following safe practices and OSHA safety and health specifications, and that they are wearing proper protective clothing and equipment.

    l. Prepare time cards, work-distribution sheets, work orders, material distributions, and other routine reports.

4. Do once a day (15–30 minutes)

    a. Observe one employee or workstation continuously for 15 minutes. Look for time wasted, dull or improper tools, need for work-positioning jigs and fixtures, interferences, delays and bottlenecks, and excess time getting materials, orders, or parts. Try to find ways to cut costs or to make improvements in any of these.

    b. Alternatively, select one employee or small group of employees with whom to interact. Ask about problems they are presently encountering and for suggestions they have for overcoming them.

5. Do before going home (15 minutes)

    a. Make a list of unsolved problems that came up during the day. Think about ways to handle them.

    b. Complete all paperwork. Avoid holding any paperwork for the following day.

    c. Make a notation of any critical problems or exceptional accomplishments of each employee for that day—for later use in personnel appraisals and actions, or making immediate commendations or corrections.

    d. Make a list of jobs that must be done the following day. Take it home with you and review it before coming to work.

Supervisory Responsibility Survey

SUPERVISORY RESPONSIBILITY SURVEY

Do you feel it is your responsibility to...

	Yes	No	Don't Know

...select and train your employees?

1. Request that additional employees be hired as needed? ____ ____ ____
2. Approve new employees assigned to you? ____ ____ ____
3. Explain benefit plans to employees? ____ ____ ____
4. Tell employees about upgrading and pay ranges? ____ ____ ____
5. Make sure employees know rules of conduct and safety regulations? ____ ____ ____
6. Train an understudy? ____ ____ ____
7. Hold regular safety meetings? ____ ____ ____

...make work assignments and maintain discipline?

8. Prepare employee work schedules? ____ ____ ____
9. Assign specific duties to workers? ____ ____ ____
10. Assign responsibilities to assistants or group leaders? ____ ____ ____

SUPERVISORY RESPONSIBILITY SURVEY

Do you feel it is your responsibility to...   Yes   No   Don't Know

...make work assignments and maintain discipline?

		Yes	No	Don't Know
11.	Delegate authority?	____	____	____
12.	Discipline employees?	____	____	____
13.	Discharge employees?	____	____	____
14.	Specify the kind and number of employees to do a job?	____	____	____
15.	Determine the amount of work to be done by each employee in your group?	____	____	____
16.	Authorize overtime?	____	____	____
17.	Enforce safety rules?	____	____	____
18.	Transfer employees within your department?	____	____	____

...handle employee problems with the union?

		Yes	No	Don't Know
19.	Interpret the union contract?	____	____	____
20.	Process grievances with shop stewards?	____	____	____
21.	Prepare vacation schedules?	____	____	____
22.	Recommend changes in the contract?	____	____	____
23.	Lay off employees for lack of work?	____	____	____
24.	Grant leaves of absence?	____	____	____

...know how pay and incentive systems work?

		Yes	No	Don't Know
25.	Explain to employees how their pay is calculated?	____	____	____
26.	Determine allowances for faulty material or interruptions?	____	____	____
27.	Approve piece rates or standards before they become effective?	____	____	____
28.	Answer employees' questions regarding time studies or allowances?	____	____	____

...make these operating decisions?

		Yes	No	Don't Know
29.	Start jobs in process?	____	____	____
30.	Stop jobs in process?	____	____	____
31.	Authorize setup changes?	____	____	____
32.	Approve material substitutions?	____	____	____
33.	Requisition supplies to keep your department running?	____	____	____
34.	Determine whether material should be scrapped or reworked?	____	____	____
35.	Replan schedules upset by breakdowns?	____	____	____
36.	Take unsafe tools out of service?	____	____	____
37.	Correct unsafe working conditions?	____	____	____

SUPERVISORY RESPONSIBILITY SURVEY

Do you feel it is your responsibility to...	Yes	No	Don't Know

...tie in with other departments?

38. Know how an order flows through the company from start to finish? ____ ____ ____

39. Understand what the staff departments do? Your relationship to them? ____ ____ ____

40. Authorize maintenance and repair jobs? ____ ____ ____

41. Requisition tools? ____ ____ ____

42. Investigate accidents? ____ ____ ____

...be concerned with the way the job gets done?

43. Make suggestions for improvements in operating procedures in your department? ____ ____ ____

44. Recommend changes in department layout? ____ ____ ____

45. Suggest material handling methods to be used in your department? ____ ____ ____

46. Discuss with staff members the operating problems caused by proposed design changes? ____ ____ ____

...think about how much things cost?

47. Cut down on waste of materials and supplies? ____ ____ ____

48. Keep adequate production records for checking output per machine and per worker-hour? ____ ____ ____

49. Participate in setting up your department budget? ____ ____ ____

50. Investigate charges against your budget? ____ ____ ____

Checklist for Accepting the Assignment of a New Department

1. Operational information
   a. What is the basic function of this department?
   b. Is there a current set of departmental objectives?
   c. Is there a current departmental expense budget?
   d. Where are the current operating schedules? Is the department ahead, behind, or on schedule?
   e. What are, and where are, the various performance standards for output, quality, units costs, etc.?
   f. What historical, statistical data is available?
   g. When do the seasonal peaks or troughs occur?
   h. When do busy periods of the day, week, or month occur?
   i. What are the basic safety precautions, rules and regulations, and problem areas that pertain to this department?

2. Organizational relationships
   a. How is the department organized? Is there an organization chart?
   b. What are the main working relationships with (i) other line departments, (ii) other staff departments, (iii) the central office or headquarters, (iv) vendors and suppliers, (v) customers or clients, and (vi) regulatory agencies or bodies? Who are the contacts? Telephone numbers?
   c. What support services are available? Purchasing? Maintenance? Custodial? Personnel? Payroll? Reproduction? Transportation? Who are the contacts? Telephone numbers? E-mail addresses?
   d. What, if any, labor union is recognized in the department? Who is the local representative, or shop steward?

3. Departmental staff
   a. Is there an assistant supervisor or administrative assistant? Who is it? What are the normal duties of this person?
   b. Who could substitute for the supervisor in an emergency?
   c. Which employees have the longest service? How long have they been on their present assignments?

  d. What sort of turnover has the department experienced, generally and by position?

  e. Are the performance-appraisal records for all the staff available? Do they include absence, sickness, and accident histories?

  f. Are any employees due soon for transfer or retirement?

  g. For each employee, how much leave or vacation time has been taken this year? How much remains?

  h. Which positions are most strongly staffed? Which need strengthening?

  i. What training programs are currently in progress?

4. Facilities and security

  a. What equipment, tools, machinery, utilities, and the like are assigned to this department? What are their capacities and/or operating rates? What is their downtime and repair history? Who are their qualified operators?

  b. Who, or what department, is responsible for repairs, window washing, floor polishing, and so forth?

  c. Where are raw materials and operating supplies stored? How and when are they obtained? Who has authority to withdraw them?

  d. What keys to equipment, files, safes, stockrooms, warehouses, or premises are there? How many duplicates exist? Who holds them?

  e. Is there a schedule for opening and closing the premises? Who opens up and locks up?

  f. Where are the appropriate, nearby (i) fire station, (ii) first-aid facility, (iii) doctor, and (iv) police station? What are their telephone numbers?

Your Career in Supervision and Management With Action Planning Checklists

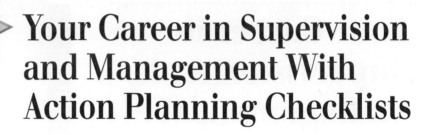

Your Career in Supervision and Management With Action Planning Checklists

The success—or shortcomings—of your career will depend largely on the skills you acquire and develop by yourself and the programs you devise to capitalize on them. Other people may offer advice and guidance—and even an occasional assist—but, in the main, advancement in supervisory and management careers is a bootstrapping operation.

Starting from scratch

If you are just now beginning to seek a career in supervision and management, it is important to find a starting point that best suits your aptitudes and potential. Your first place of employment will probably not be your last, but some places provide a better springboard than others. These are some of the more important aspects of employment to consider:

Blue collar or white collar? Do you prefer activities associated with production or construction, working close to tools and machinery? Or is your preference for clerical, desk-related, and clean-hands operations?

Inside or outside? Do you like to be close to your support system, along with the comfort of daily routines that are clearly set? Or does the independence and challenge of sales and other field-related activities exert a greater appeal?

People relationships versus technical expertise? Do you favor activities in which interpersonal relationships play a large part? Most supervisory and management positions place greater emphasis on interpersonal skills than on technical expertise.

Line versus staff? Line jobs often carry with them the authority and visibility that lead to advancement. Work in line activities also tends to provide more action and a sense of being at the heart of an operation. Staff activities, on the other hand, may be less stressful and more rewarding from a creative and intellectual point of view.

Manufacturing or services? The downtrodden manufacturing industries are now experiencing a rebirth, with opportunities for advancement growing again. The major economic growth, however, continues to be in service-related industries such as banking and finance, food service, hotel and restaurant management, and in wholesaling and retailing.

Large or small company? Relative job security, good working conditions, and opportunities for advancement make work in many large organizations attractive. There are drawbacks, of course, with the pressure to conform, reels of red tape to put up with, and responsibilities that are narrowly specialized. Work for smaller organizations, on the other hand, presents an opposing set of advantages and disadvantages. Pay and benefits are often less attractive, as are job security and chances for advancement. Responsibilities in small companies, however, are usually more varied and challenging, with a minimum of red tape and a great deal of informality.

Private or public employment? Risks of employment in private industry are generally considered to be greater, but with the possibilities of greater financial rewards. Public employment, while usually less remunerative, is more secure and may provide a greater sense of social contribution.

An awareness of the flames. The better positions in supervision and management are always challenging and demanding. Some jobs, however, are characterized by too much heat. These are the ones that cause "burnout"—since they often demand the impossible. This kind of pressure isn't always apparent at the start, so it pays to explore advancement opportunities carefully before pursuing them. You should expect a good job to demand much of you, but not so much that you can't do it well every day without feeling exhausted.

Planning a career search inside or outside your present organization

The competition for good jobs in supervision and management is now more intense than ever. This is especially true of the higher-paying, more interesting positions. Curiously, neither the available positions nor the better ones necessarily go to the most qualified candidates. In a great many instances, these jobs are won by those people who plan and carry out the most appropriate search. So, whether you are exploring opportunities for advancement with your present employer or somewhere else, your career search should combine at least five essential elements: (a) a seek-and-search timetable, (b) a realistic list of job factors that you consider necessary to make a job attractive and appropriate for you, (c) a résumé that clearly and concisely demonstrates your most valuable qualifications, (d) preinterview research and preparation, and (e) a strategy for handling interview questions so as to favorably differentiate you from other candidates.

Elements (d) and (e) will be discussed in detail later. Suffice it to say about elements (a), (b), and (c) that diligence is required in making out applications and seeking interviews. Résumés should be carefully prepared. Persistence is a strong tool for prying open the best positions in supervision and management. On the other hand, you should also be ready to accept something less than the perfect assignment in order to get a foothold in the area or field that is attractive to you. Most people have to perform work that has its menial, tedious, and unattractive facets so that they can show their potential. Good supervisory and management positions are obtained by building on a record of sound performance in lesser assignments.

Preparing for a career-advancement interview

Many a good position is lost before the candidate walks in the door for an interview. A successful advancement interview requires planning, research, and rehearsal—even for jobs within your own company. Days before your interview, you should:

1. **Find out more about your potential employer, department, or boss.** Consult the company's annual report, published reports about it found in a library, or someone who is working there now. You'll want to know something about the background of the company or department, its financial condition, its products, services, and personnel along with any problems it is seeking to solve. After all, your application will have told the interviewers something about you; it will give you an equal edge to know something about the company or department that is interviewing you.

2. **Review your strengths and weaknesses.** Plan to put your strongest qualities forward, as they relate to the job in question. Be prepared also to defend your weaknesses. You must be ready to acknowledge, for example, that you may have little experience in a particular line of work. If you are prepared, however, you can counter with a reply that this has not been a serious problem in the past since you are an attentive and diligent learner.

3. **Anticipate the kinds of questions that you might be asked.** Generally speaking, interview questions fall into two categories:

   - **Substance questions.** These seek out concrete information about you, your education, and your work history. Reply to them in short, specific sentences. Be concise: you'll want to guard against rambling. Typical questions are: "Tell me about your background." "What are your major accomplishments?" "How does your education or experience qualify you for this position?" "Why should we hire you for (or promote you to) this position?"

   - **Poise questions.** These are asked by interviewers to judge your personality, your ability to reply under stress, and the extent to which you would fit in with the people at that company (or department) and its philosophy. There are usually no "right" or "wrong" answers to these questions, so try to answer directly and honestly. Often, the interviewer doesn't care so much about what you say as about how you answer. Obviously, don't get angry. Don't allow yourself to become too negative. Your objective is to project a pleasant, positive outlook. Typical questions here are: "What kind of people do you enjoy working with?" "What kinds of situations have you found most unsatisfactory?" "How would you handle a disagreement between you and one of your employees?" "Tell me about your worst boss."

4. **Rehearse your interview beforehand.** Like an actor before a play or a golfer practicing her swing, it helps to rehearse beforehand what your answers and behavior will be during the interview. Have a friend ask you the questions outlined above. Try out your answers by speaking aloud. Record them on tape to see how they sound and whether the tone of your voice reflects confidence. Think through what you want to say and revise your answers so that you can make the most concise and effective replies.

Your interview strategy

Some authorities describe the job interview as "the 60 most critical minutes of your life." That may be an exaggeration, but it points up the wisdom of having a preplanned strategy for making the most of a brief period of time. You won't be able to control the interview; the interviewer will. Nevertheless, you can contribute greatly to its success by following a strategy that places you and your capabilities in the best possible light. For example, a winning strategy can be based on the following nine points:

1. **Make a good appearance.** Neatness in dress and care in grooming are absolutely necessary. Generally speaking, your clothing choice ought to be conservative so as neither to distract from your person nor from what you are saying.

2. **Be on time.** It is even better if you arrive a few minutes early. This gives you a chance to catch your breath and to become comfortable in strange surroundings. If kept waiting for the interview, don't be impatient or demonstrate nervousness. It's not unusual for someone to observe, and to report on, your behavior while you're waiting.

3. **Take advantage of the "warm-up" period.** Most interviewers use the first few minutes to get a "feel" of your personality before they proceed to the substance questions. During this period, try to relax yourself and to tune your ear to the voice and manner of the interviewer.

4. **Be pleasant and cordial.** As in most human exchanges, a smile goes a long way in gaining acceptance. As a job candidate, you are a guest, even when applying for advancement in your own company. Your behavior should readily indicate appreciation for the opportunity to present yourself for consideration. Don't approach the interview as an imposition placed upon you or as an opportunity to debate.

5. **Project a positive image.** This is especially true when applying for a supervisory or managerial position, which implies that you would be representing the employer, both to employees and to the community. A positive image can be projected in a number of ways. Shake hands firmly. Look the viewer in the eye in a friendly fashion. Listen attentively. If you miss a question or don't understand it, ask that it be repeated: this demonstrates your interest. Don't be afraid to display enthusiasm. Take your time, if needed, to think through what you want to say before answering difficult questions. Try to keep your replies short. Don't smoke, even if a cigarette is offered you.

6. **Ask the interviewer questions.** If you have done your homework, you can ask questions that demonstrate the validity of your interest in the position. Don't dwell on pay or benefits. Do ask about the company's or department's product or service line, its plans for growth, and what the normal promotion paths might be for a person of your qualifications.

7. **Differentiate yourself from other candidates.** Your career-search preparation should help here. Try to focus on the two or three things that you do best, such as: "I have a strong sense of commitment." "I meet my objectives." "I work well with people." "I can handle, and am ready to perform, a variety of assignments." Show how these can contribute to a solid performance as a supervisor. In replying to questions, don't be afraid to repeat these qualifications.

8. **Close the interview firmly.** Most employment interviewers will control the close of the interview. Nevertheless, it is appropriate and it makes a good impression if you also sum up clearly and confidently your understanding of what has transpired and your concluding view of the job opening. Say something like this: "I understand that you will be interviewing several other candidates, but I do wish to emphasize how interested I am in filling this position. I believe that my qualifications, by reason of education, experience, and motivation, would enable me to perform this job very well. You would find me an excellent employee and supervisor." When the interview is concluded, thank the interviewer. Shake hands if possible. Leave in a businesslike fashion.

9. **Follow up.** Regardless of the outcome of the interview, it makes a good business impression for you to write a brief note, thanking the company or department head for the interview and expressing your continued interest in the position. (If the job no longer appeals to you, write anyway, asking that your name be removed from the list of active candidates.) It is also appropriate to telephone the interviewer periodically to determine the status of the job opening and to ask that your application be kept active. Don't, however, persist to the point of becoming a nuisance, especially if you are told that the job has been filled. As an applicant, you will "lose" many interviews before you "win" one. Approach each as an opportunity

for improving your job-advancement skills, and be appreciative of the company or department that gave you the chance. Persistence in your career search and maintaining a positive outlook will eventually pay off.

A strategy for survival and advancement

Once you have secured the particular position in supervision and management that you want, you'll have to work just as hard to succeed in it. Don't let this phase be accidental. It requires a plan and policies, too, for your personal guidance.

1. **Be a team player.** The big difference between academic pursuits and those of business or other real-life occupations is that you will be able to accomplish very little at work without the support of your co-workers, whether they are supervisors, managers, or other professionals. Almost everything productive that happens in organizations takes the combined and coordinated efforts of many people with many different skills. Trouble lies ahead if you try to go it alone. It is far better to acknowledge your interdependency with others.

2. **Establish credibility.** Your previous achievements won't be mounted on a plaque and hung on a wall in your office. Your new boss will judge you, not by what you say or may have done before, but by what you accomplish now—and every day thereafter. *It is performance that counts.* Performance means discharging your responsibilities productively and with a minimum of complaints or callbacks. It also means being dependable, showing that you can meet your obligations by the designated times. Your reputation for performance will be established, or discredited, within your first few months on a new assignment. If it is good, you are on your way upward. If it isn't so good, you may be heading toward a dead end—or even on your way out.

3. **Do right by your boss.** Will Rogers, the cowboy philosopher, once said, "I never met a man I didn't like." The reason for these almost unbelievably happy circumstances is that Rogers found a way of finding something in everybody to like. It may seem too much to ask for you to like every boss that you have. It is almost certain, however, that your bosses will always like you a little better if you try to perform your job so that it helps them to meet their performance goals, too. Few bosses will exploit you. Most will want to do right by you. Many bosses may seem unreasonably demanding at times, but this is usually in response to the pressures imposed by the organization on them. It will be counterproductive to set yourself against your boss. Instead, try to cultivate a productive, friendly relationship. Put yourself on the boss's side, for example, by asking about the direction the company is moving in and what your department can do to help cope with upcoming changes.

4. **Dress appropriately.** Advising women or men about what to wear at work is a sensitive issue, but there do appear to be certain agreed-upon guidelines for business wear.

   For women, for most supervisory and management positions, one experienced counselor advises, "Tailored clothing only. No frills, ruffles, straps, or plunging necklines. Don't affect a 'feminine' style of dress. Try suits and blazers in plain, neutral colors, or understated plaids. Choose dresses in dark colors, worn with or without blazers. Use scarves for accents. Wear dark pumps with medium or low heels. Stud earrings and modest necklaces are all right, but avoid dangling bracelets."

   For men, for most office, sales, or clerical supervisory and management positions, the same counselor suggests, "Dark or gray suits, solid, pinstripe or shallow plaids. Navy blazers and gray trousers are popular. Wear dress shirts in solid colors, mostly white, pale blue, or yellow. Choose from a variety of ties in muted colors in contrast to the suit. Solids, stripes, or small patterns are preferred. Wear calf-length hose in dark colors to match the suit, and black or brown, 1-inch belts. Tassel loafers, wingtips, or lace-up shoes are fine. Avoid flashy cuff links, rings, or neck chains."

   More companies today are permitting employees to wear casual business attire. In such cases, the company must define for employees what clothing is acceptable.

5. **Build a network.** Networking is now an accepted dynamic of business and organizational life. At its simplest, networking is just another name for making friends. Among these friends, however, should be people who are supportive to you careerwise as well as personally. Your work associates will provide an important part of this network. Most importantly, you should try to make business friends of people at higher levels of management in your own organization.

   The main purpose of such a network, however, is not to use these friends in seeking advancement, but as a means of exchanging information, contacts, and resources. A good way to expand your network is to join a professional association related to your field and to volunteer your time to it. That way, you can establish credibility based on your service and can exchange useful information as a result.

6. **Observe these guidelines.** Management development experts generally agree on these ten fundamental guidelines to help keep your supervisory and management career on an upward path:

   - Know where your job fits into the organization.
   - Put your efforts into tasks that your boss values.
   - Don't be afraid to ask questions, and learn where to go for answers.

- Learn to communicate—and with the right people.
- Always share credit; never spread blame.
- Let others know when you've done a good job. It's not enough to be good; influential people have to know about it.
- Be sensitive to office politics.
- Cultivate a career-support network.
- Don't let emotions control your actions; try to stay cool and reasonable.
- Learn how to manage stress before you need to.

Review and Upgrade Your Career-Advancement Potential with These 19 Action Planning Checklists

Advancement in supervision and management depends far more on action than on words. The 19 checklists that follow are designed to help you plan to put effective action behind your supervisory performance. Each checklist contains 15 action points. Taken together, they summarize the key points presented in the text's 19 chapters. In that way they provide a quick and comprehensive review of the book's highlights. They will also help you to assess the current state of your effectiveness and to prepare a program for bootstrapping your career in supervision and management.

By comparing each checkpoint with conditions on your present job, or with your present qualifications, you can decide whether or not corrective action is needed now. If your review assures you that a particular item is in good shape or has already been taken care of, then check "No" under the Action Needed heading. On the other hand, if you feel that conditions need improvement, check "Yes" for Action Needed. This means that you are not satisfied with conditions or with your present qualifications—and that you intend to take positive steps to improve them. Don't stop with the check mark. Also write down a date for when you intend to have the particular condition under control or your qualifications upgraded. When you have completed the corrective action, you can then mark that item off your Action Needed list.

The Supervisor's Role in Management

	Action Needed		Date Completed
	Yes	No	

1. Made a commitment to no longer work with your "hands on" the job and to embrace the management viewpoint. ___ ___ _____

2. Resolved to maintain good health, work hard, set a good example for your employees, and continue to learn. ___ ___ _____

3. Identified those individuals and groups to whom you now owe a responsibility: higher management (especially your boss), staff departments, fellow supervisors, and your employee work group. ___ ___ _____

4. Checked out the resources that enable you to carry out your job responsibilities: facilities, equipment, tools, power, utilities, materials, supplies, and information (dollar value of all this). ___ ___ _____

5. Gotten the "basic personnel" particulars about your workforce: personal data on each employee—age, length of service, work history, present job title and description, and pay rate. ___ ___ _____

6. Found out about current and upcoming production schedules and other output requirements and project deadlines. ___ ___ _____

7. Found out exactly what the quality requirements or specifications of your product or service are. ___ ___ _____

8. Pinned down the cost and expense limitations under which you will be expected to operate. ___ ___ _____

9. Accepted the fact that pressures on you will be many and varied, with changing worker attitudes the most pressing of all. ___ ___ _____

10. Given thought to how well your present abilities measure up to the demands for technical, administrative, and human relations skills—and what you might do to improve them. ___ ___ _____

11. Prepared to balance your supervisor efforts between task-centered concerns and employee-centered ones. ___ ___ _____

12. Reviewed the managerial process so that you can anticipate problems and decisions requiring planning, organizing, staffing, energizing, and controlling. ___ ___ _____

13. Accepted the fact that your supervisory role will often be ambiguous and will occasionally put you in the middle between higher management and your employees. ___ ___ _____

14. Guarded against pitfalls for new supervisors: poor relationships with others in the organization, failure to plan ahead, confusion about your managerial role, lack of initiative, discouragement, and the inability to successfully meet changing conditions. ___ ___ _____

15. Adopted an attitude of doing the best you can today with a plan for developing your knowledge and skills so that you can do even better tomorrow. ___ ___ _____

Creating a Positive Workplace Within a Dynamic Environment

	Action Needed		Date Completed
	Yes	No	

1. An awareness of the seven environmental factors with which supervisors must cope: technology, legal restrictions, pressures from above, organizational policies and procedures, competition for scarce resources, a burgeoning information load, and the rising expectations of employees.

2. Allowances made for the impact of the time factor on departmental operations.

3. A weather eye out for changes that will affect operations.

4. An understanding of what work really is and how it applies to departmental operations.

5. An understanding of why people work.

6. An ability to differentiate work from other human activities.

7. Consideration of the effect that job satisfaction may have on employee effort.

8. Recognition of the extent to which job challenges can influence employee performance.

9. An awareness of "entitlement expectations" and the possible impact of "downsizing" on your workforce.

10. An awareness of the differences with which individuals perceive their work and the reasons why.

11. A plan for anticipating negative perceptions of work in your department and for presenting it in a more favorable light.

12. A sensitivity to, and allowances made for, a good employee's occasional bad day.

13. A determination to make accurate and sufficient information available to employees regarding their work.

14. Recognition of the possible relationship between the lack of job satisfaction on an employee's part and poor management on the supervisor's part.

15. Ways and means devised for improving the quality of work life in your department by (a) soliciting employee feedback, (b) facilitating rather than directing, (c) providing flexibility in assignments, and (d) conveying a sense of meaning to employees' work.

ACTION PLANNING CHECKLIST ③

Supervision and the Management Process

	Action Needed Yes	No	Date Completed

1. Determination to think—and act—like a manager, in a truly professional manner.   ___ ___ _____

2. Recognition that there is an established body of management principles and practices to draw upon for guidance.   ___ ___ _____

3. Identification of the five management process functions: planning, organizing, staffing, activating, and controlling.   ___ ___ _____

4. An ability to relate the five managerial functions to operations at the supervisory level.   ___ ___ _____

5. An understanding of the conversion process that transforms input resources into output results as it applies to your operations.   ___ ___ _____

6. Identification of the resources available to you for the conversion operations in your department.   ___ ___ _____

7. Identification of the results expected from the conversion process in your department, in terms of products or services created and their related quality and cost specifications.   ___ ___ _____

8. An ability to relate management principles to the management process.   ___ ___ _____

9. Adherence to Fayol's main principles of management:
   a. Division of work   ___ ___ _____
   b. Responsibility matched by authority   ___ ___ _____
   c. Discipline matched by loyalty   ___ ___ _____
   d. Unity of command   ___ ___ _____
   e. Unity of direction   ___ ___ _____
   f. Personal interest second to the organization   ___ ___ _____
   g. Fair pay for employee contributions   ___ ___ _____
   h. Chain of command   ___ ___ _____
   i. Persistence of order   ___ ___ _____
   j. Equity   ___ ___ _____
   k. Initiative   ___ ___ _____

10. An understanding of, and proficiency in using, the systematic (or "scientific") management approach.   ___ ___ _____

11. An understanding of, and proficiency in using, the human relations (or behavioral) management approach.   ___ ___ _____

12. An understanding of, and proficiency in using, the quantitative management approach.   ___ ___ _____

13. An understanding of, and an awareness of the prevalence of, systems in organizational relationships.   ___ ___ _____

14. An understanding of the relationship of Japanese "consensus" management to the participation concept advocated under human relations management.   ___ ___ _____

15. An awareness of the significance of, and application of, the contingency (or situational) management approach.   ___ ___ _____

ACTION PLANNING CHECKLIST ④

Setting Goals, Making Plans, and Carrying Out Policy

	Action Needed		Date Completed
	Yes	No	

1. Time set aside for planning: 5 to 10 minutes daily, 15 to 30 minutes weekly, 1 to 2 hours monthly. ____ ____ _____

2. Knowledge of organizational policies and procedures that affect departmental goals, plans, and operating practices. ____ ____ _____

3. Goals based on a realistic appraisal of departmental strengths and weaknesses and company-imposed limitations. ____ ____ _____

4. Departmental goals arranged in a hierarchy (in order of their priorities). ____ ____ _____

5. Goals clearly stated (a) as measurable output expected, (b) in explicit and quantified terms, and (c) in relation to a specific period of time. ____ ____ _____

6. Consideration of What, Where, When, How, and Who in making plans. ____ ____ _____

7. Plans, procedures, and regulations that fit into chosen goals. ____ ____ _____

8. Plans flexible enough to permit change if needed. ____ ____ _____

9. Control limits and procedures set for plans so that you can monitor progress toward attainment of goals. ____ ____ _____

10. Schedules set that neither underutilize nor overload departmental staff and equipment. ____ ____ _____

11. Care not to overcommit your staff or equipment or to make delivery promises that can't be met. ____ ____ _____

12. Ability to prepare and use, where appropriate, a Gantt-type production planning and/or progress-control chart. ____ ____ _____

13. An understanding of how PERT or CPM works so that you can make valid contributions in the form of task sequences and time estimates to the specialists who prepare such plans. ____ ____ _____

14. Ability, for clerical work, to prepare and use a work-distribution chart as a basis for making job assignments. ____ ____ _____

15. Prudence in checking company policy implications before taking trend-setting action at the departmental level. ____ ____ _____

Problem Solving and Managing Information

	Action Needed		Date Completed
	Yes	No	

1. Skills developed for detecting and describing existing and potential problems in your department.   ____ ____ _____

2. An ability to distinguish between what actually is occurring and what should have occurred, in order to precisely define the problem gap.   ____ ____ _____

3. An ability to pursue a systematic procedure in analyzing and solving problems.   ____ ____ _____

4. Persistence in tracking down real causes of problems so as not to be misled into treating symptoms.   ____ ____ _____

5. Not being satisfied with the first, seemingly easy, solution; searching always for alternatives to remove root causes.   ____ ____ _____

6. A recognition of the point where problem solving ends and decision making begins.   ____ ____ _____

7. An ability to assist a specialist in preparing a decision-tree analysis for problems affecting your areas of responsibility.   ____ ____ _____

8. An understanding of cost-benefit judgments in evaluating proposed solutions to operational problems.   ____ ____ _____

9. Balance maintained between intuitive judgments and those based on systematic and logical analysis of a situation.   ____ ____ _____

10. A willingness to seek opinions and advice from employees in problems that affect them, especially those problems that will require employee support for their solutions.   ____ ____ _____

11. A knowledge of the nature and extent of your company's management information system (MIS) and how it serves your operational area.   ____ ____ _____

12. Specific knowledge of how your department feeds data into the company's MIS and the exact form in which this information should be provided.   ____ ____ _____

13. Preparation of a diagram illustrating the information system within your own department (using Figure 5-5 in Chapter 5 as a model).   ____ ____ _____

14. An awareness of how information and computer systems in your organization have changed, are changing, and will change the content of employees and jobs.   ____ ____ _____

15. A sensitivity toward employees' fears of the impact of computerization and other technological changes on their jobs and their job security; a continuing effort to counteract these fears by your personal interest and intervention.   ____ ____ _____

ACTION PLANNING CHECKLIST 6

Organizing an Effective Department

	Action Needed		Date Completed
	Yes	No	

1. An understanding of the steps in the organizing process. ____ ____ _____
2. The work of your department organized in such a way as to focus on its objectives and responsibilities. ____ ____ _____
3. An awareness of, but not conflict with, the informal organization in your operational areas. ____ ____ _____
4. Identification of both line and staff responsibilities, in your department and with other company departments. ____ ____ _____
5. Identification of your company's organizational structure—divisional or product, geographic, customer, or matrix. ____ ____ _____
6. An estimate of the degree of centralization and decentralization in your company and in your department; satisfaction with the extent of your own span of control, neither too narrow nor too broad. ____ ____ _____
7. Construction of an organization chart for your areas of responsibility. ____ ____ _____
8. A clear understanding of your responsibilities and related authorities according to class 1—complete, class 2—limited, and class 3—none. ____ ____ _____
9. Full development and utilization of your personal sources of authority. ____ ____ _____
10. Cooperation with, and utilization of, company staff departments. ____ ____ _____
11. Identification of operational areas in your department where a staff department may exert functional authority. ____ ____ _____
12. Regular use of delegation within your department to relieve yourself of unnecessary work and to develop the skills and confidence of subordinates. ____ ____ _____
13. Knowledge of the chain of command in your organization and a general conformity to it. ____ ____ _____
14. Regular review of your department's organization structure to minimize communications problems, avoid having an employee answer to two people, ensure clear designation of work duties, and retain flexibility for contingencies. ____ ____ _____
15. Recognition of the nature of the culture of your organization as well as its relationship to the formal structure. ____ ____ _____

Staffing with Human Resources

	Action Needed		Date Completed
	Yes	No	

1. An understanding of the six-step staffing process and the supervisor's role in it. ____ ____ _____

2. An awareness of the supervisor's responsibility in having the right workers on the right jobs in sufficient numbers at the right time. ____ ____ _____

3. Alertness to symptoms of poor human resource staffing: high labor costs; excessive absenteeism, latenesses, and turnover; poor quality of work; lowered productivity. ____ ____ _____

4. Periodic review to make certain that employees are placed in jobs that best suit their capabilities. ____ ____ _____

5. Periodic forecasts of your department's workforce needs. ____ ____ _____

6. Care taken to neither understaff nor overstaff. ____ ____ _____

7. As an aid in carrying out your forecast, preparation of a workforce trial balance sheet that anticipates (a) payroll separations and (b) changes in departmental workloads. ____ ____ _____

8. An ability to interview job candidates objectively, using open-ended questions, especially to probe the suitability of education and experience for the open position. ____ ____ _____

9. Knowledge of legal (especially EEOC) guidelines that must be observed in conducting employment interviews and in selecting and placing employees. ____ ____ _____

10. Improvement of your interviewing skills such as question asking, listening, and evaluation. ____ ____ _____

11. An ability to describe a job accurately and to specify the qualifications of the person who might fill it. ____ ____ _____

12. Periodic review to assess the applicability of performance tests as aids in selection of applicants for jobs in your department. ____ ____ _____

13. Knowledge of, and an ability to calculate, your department's turnover rate. ____ ____ _____

14. Knowledge of, and an ability to calculate, your department's absenteeism rate. ____ ____ _____

15. A plan for keeping turnover and absenteeism rates within standards acceptable to the parent organization. ____ ____ _____

ACTION PLANNING CHECKLIST (8)

Training and Developing Employees

	Action Needed		Date Completed
	Yes	No	

1. A continuing alertness for symptoms of training needs, such as lowered output, off-standard quality, higher costs, accidents, or poor morale. ____ ____ _____

2. Use of a systematic, rather than hit-or-miss, approach to each and all training problems in your department. ____ ____ _____

3. Training in your department based on (a) an analysis of skills needed and (b) a planned timetable for completion (modeled after Figure 8-1 in Chapter 8). ____ ____ _____

4. Formation of a working partnership with the professional training staff so that you may benefit from their advice and assistance. ____ ____ _____

5. Care in orienting each new employee to your department, using the list of items in the text as a guide; seizing upon the teachable moment. ____ ____ _____

6. Preparation of a simple job breakdown sheet, with key points identified, before beginning employee training on a particular job (see Figure 8-2 and Table 8-1 in Chapter 8). ____ ____ _____

7. Knowledge and use of the four-step, job-instruction-training method (JIT). ____ ____ _____

8. Proper employee preparation and motivation provided before training begins. ____ ____ _____

9. Use of training demonstrations that combine telling and showing. ____ ____ _____

10. Training coverage broken into easily learned segments; not attempting too much during a single session (as illustrated in Figure 8-3 in Chapter 8). ____ ____ _____

11. The training sequence arranged so that the learner begins with the least difficult segments and progresses to the most difficult. ____ ____ _____

12. Encouragement of questions from the trainee throughout the entire training process. ____ ____ _____

13. Provision of feedback and followup to the trainee throughout, offering either encouragement or correction as the training progresses. ____ ____ _____

14. Use of programmed learning and computer-assisted training materials, as well as a variety of audiovisual aids, to supplement, stimulate, and reinforce the learning process. ____ ____ _____

15. Training efforts tailored to fit the needs and learning capabilities of each individual, rather than simply provided across the board without thought to need and relevance. ____ ____ _____

Motivating People at Work

	Action Needed		Date Completed
	Yes	No	

1. An acknowledgment that people act as they must, that their behavior is essentially rational in terms of their needs.

2. Identification of the inevitable differences among your employees as to motivation, goals, and personality, and the influence of these favors on their performance.

3. Recognition of the impact of heredity, environment, and experience on an individual's personality.

4. Restraint in jumping to conclusions about the consequences of an individual's personality; an attitude of "live and let live" with respect to personal preferences.

5. An assessment of each employee's current level of need according to Maslow's hierarchy: survival, security, social, respect, and self-fulfillment.

6. In trying to provide motivation, always searching for conditions that can fill an unsatisfied need.

7. An attempt to create conditions at work that Herzberg characterizes as "satisfiers": recognition for achievement, interesting and meaningful work, opportunities for utilization of one's capabilities, responsibility for one's own work.

8. Feedback to higher management of the absence of "hygiene" factors that may become "dissatisfiers" to your employees.

9. Open praise for an employee's good work and opportunities for employees to provide their own self-discipline.

10. An understanding of the concept of "expectancy" that influences the degree to which an employee will undertake unpleasant or difficult work.

11. Wariness of your own inclination to overachieve to the extent that you become so task oriented that you minimize human relationships.

12. Maintenance of equity and fair treatment of all employees despite personal differences.

13. A readiness to modify (or redesign) existing jobs in your department so as to accommodate physical and psychological needs among your employees: ergonomic compatibility, provision of a whole job, contact with users and clients, variety of skills, freedom for self-direction, feedback from the work itself, and a chance for self-development.

14. Consideration given to enlarging or enhancing the narrower, more monotonous, and less demanding jobs in your department.

15. Emphasis placed on ways to empower employees so they can attain organizational goals without sacrificing the quality of their own work life.

Leadership Skills, Styles, and Qualities

	Action Needed		Date Completed
	Yes	No	

1. An awareness of the importance of leadership skills (persuasion, influence, rapport) as contrasted with so-called "inborn" leadership traits.

2. An acknowledgment that effective leadership depends on providing motivation rather than on manipulation.

3. A determination, through self-analysis, of whether your assumptions about employees represent a Theory X or Theory Y viewpoint.

4. An attempt to help employees to discover personal goals consistent with those of the organization.

5. Development of skills in applying all three kinds of traditional leadership approaches: autocratic, democratic, and participative.

6. Differentiation between results-centered and situational leadership approaches.

7. Balanced application of leadership styles contingent on the particulars of each situation.

8. A concern for people (people-centered leadership) equal to your concern for results (task-centered leadership).

9. An awareness of the multiple reasons why participative management practices might fail.

10. Recognition of the choices that can be made by a supervisor along the continuum of leadership styles.

11. Consideration of the maturity (not age!) of an individual when selecting an appropriate style of leadership.

12. An attempt to match your leadership style to the followership inclinations of each employee as well as to that of your boss.

13. Consistency in the nature of your relationships with others—superiors, subordinates, and peers alike.

14. Maintenance of good examples of personal commitment and a willingness to make sacrifices to help your employees meet department objectives.

15. A conscious effort to treat employees equitably in similar situations, to neither play favorites nor pick on those you don't particularly like.

ACTION PLANNING CHECKLIST (11)

Effective Employee Communication

	Action Needed		Date Completed
	Yes	**No**	

1. Communications whose purpose is to link plans to action. ___ ___ _____
2. Repetition, feedback (especially 360-degree feedback), and questioning regularly used as techniques to avoid misunderstandings and to reinforce understanding. ___ ___ _____
3. A minimum of "noise" in your communication system: employees ready to listen, absence of conflicting instructions, employees and supervisors talking about the same thing. ___ ___ _____
4. Expertise in, and reliance on, many methods rather than a single method of communication. ___ ___ _____
5. Emphasis on the free flow of information up, down, and across your department. ___ ___ _____
6. Development of your person-to-person communication skills: spoken—informal talks, planned appointments, telephone calls, etc.; written—interoffice memos, letters, e-mail, reports. ___ ___ _____
7. Development of your group communications skills: spoken—informal staff meetings, planned conferences, mass meetings; written—bulletin board notices, posters, displays, audio and visual aids. ___ ___ _____
8. An awareness of body language; a realization that your actions often speak more convincingly than your words. ___ ___ _____
9. Knowledge of the grapevine, but its use avoided for supervisory communications; rumors spiked as soon as possible. ___ ___ _____
10. Development of your active listening skills, using your responses to establish empathy and rapport; a willingness to listen without interrupting or taking offense, with your emphasis on face-to-face communications. ___ ___ _____
11. A willingness to track down and retrieve job-related information for employees who need it or request it. ___ ___ _____
12. Guarding against overcommunicating and talking on sensitive subjects. ___ ___ _____
13. Your boss kept regularly informed of accountable, controversial matters and employees' attitudes toward organization policy, but without betraying confidences. ___ ___ _____
14. Care in issuing orders and instructions so that they are clear in terms of quantity, quality, and time factors: an awareness that words mean different things to different people and that hard facts are better than vague generalities. ___ ___ _____
15. Avoidance of any semblance of a power struggle when issuing orders, using requests as often as possible and commands only in emergencies or when a high degree of coordination is needed. ___ ___ _____

Appraisal of Employee Performance

	Action Needed		Date Completed
	Yes	**No**	

1. An attitude toward appraisals that focuses on the major goal of improvement of the individual's performance so as to match the job's requirements. ____ ____ _____

2. Care in separating the discussion of an employee's appraisal rating from any talk, or consideration, of money. ____ ____ _____

3. Knowledge of the distinctions between a graphic rating scale and a forced-choice appraisal format. ____ ____ _____

4. A conscious effort to apply the same standards to all, so that your expectations are consistent from employee to employee. ____ ____ _____

5. Maintenance of a file of critical incidents, or specific and representative examples, of each employee's behavior so as to support the appraisal you make. ____ ____ _____

6. Your guard up against the halo effect, which discriminates for or against a person, based on a single incident or trait. ____ ____ _____

7. Proper preparation for and conduct of the appraisal interview: privacy, enough time, emphasis on job standards, credit where it is due, mutual examination of the facts supported by critical incidents, focus on the future, and sharing by you of responsibility for the individual's performance. ____ ____ _____

8. Establishment of a positive, constructive atmosphere during the appraisal interview so that employees do not feel that they sit in the judgment of a person who believes himself or herself to be infallible. ____ ____ _____

9. Willingness to listen to an employee's rebuttal of your ratings and to change those ratings if the argument is sound. ____ ____ _____

10. Treatment of an individual's appraisal as confidential, with respect to his or her associates or peers. ____ ____ _____

11. Strict observance of legal (especially EEOC) regulations as they affect the performance appraisal and the interview. ____ ____ _____

12. Maintenance of the proper records of the appraisal interview and discussions that take place during it. ____ ____ _____

13. A continuing interest in, and appraisal of, the individual's performance, so that your judgment isn't a one-time thing. ____ ____ _____

14. Your active assistance to the employee in helping to overcome specified weaknesses or to develop desirable skills. ____ ____ _____

15. Thoughtful reexamination of conditions beyond an employee's control that may be contributing to substandard performance: a poor skills–job match, inadequate training, work group pressure, physical or emotional problems, insensitive supervision, and technical problems in the process or procedures. ____ ____ _____

ACTION PLANNING CHECKLIST ⑬
Counseling and Performance Management

	Action Needed		Date Completed
	Yes	**No**	

1. An awareness and sensitivity to employees who display emotional problems, without overreacting to them. ___ ___ _____

2. Recognition that all people have soft spots in their emotional armor, and that this does not mean they are crazy. ___ ___ _____

3. A focus on performance and job-related behavior that indicates a troubled reaction to stressors, especially those in the workplace. ___ ___ _____

4. An ability to distinguish between evidence of neurotic behavior (which may be tolerated) and psychotic behavior (which is bizarre and may become threatening to the individual or to others in the workplace). ___ ___ _____

5. Recognition of the signs of poor emotional adjustment—sudden changes in behavior, preoccupation, irritability, increased absences, fatigue, accidents, waste, too much drinking, and substance abuse. ___ ___ _____

6. A desire to help employees to adjust to their emotional problems, rather than to ridicule them for these problems or to minimize their importance to the individual. ___ ___ _____

7. Time set aside in your schedule to counsel employees who need attention. ___ ___ _____

8. Conduct of your counseling sessions in a nonthreatening manner, with emphasis on nondirective interviewing, so as to provide catharsis. ___ ___ _____

9. Development of your listening skills so as to become a nonevaluative listener—a person who does not comment or pass judgment on what is said. ___ ___ _____

10. Readiness to refer an emotionally troubled person to your company nurse, doctor, or psychologist for professional advice and treatment whenever your own efforts are not fruitful. ___ ___ _____

11. A combination of firmness and empathy when counseling employees with problems of absenteeism, alcoholism, or substance abuse. ___ ___ _____

12. Selective use of different counseling approaches for the willful absentee (vacationers, the directionless, moonlighters, and the aggressive) and the chronic and the occasional absentee. ___ ___ _____

13. An alertness for early warning signs of alcoholism and substance abuse in an employee. ___ ___ _____

14. A willingness to confront an alcoholic employee—or a substance abuser—with the choice of acceptable performance or losing her or his job. ___ ___ _____

15. A sensitivity, along with an expectancy of useful performance, in dealing with employees who have terminal illnesses. ___ ___ _____

Building Cooperative Teams and Resolving Conflicts

	Action Needed		Date Completed
	Yes	**No**	

1. A sensitivity to the dynamics of group relationships in your department. ___ ___ _____

2. An awareness of, without prying into, the attitudes of informal work groups in your department. ___ ___ _____

3. Respect for, and utilization of, the power of cohesiveness that an employee group can develop. ___ ___ _____

4. Recognition that many individuals will look to you for protection from unreasonable group pressures so as to ensure personal freedom of performance. ___ ___ _____

5. A determination to integrate individual and group goals with those of the organization. ___ ___ _____

6. An opportunity offered for employees—collectively—to participate in solving work-related problems. ___ ___ _____

7. A firm stand to uphold goals, policies, procedures, and rules that are judged to be inflexible if work is to be coordinated in a safe and productive way, regardless of a group's attitudes toward them. ___ ___ _____

8. Determination to build a cooperative departmental team. ___ ___ _____

9. An understanding of the purpose—and potential effectiveness—of an intervention in the Organizational Development (OD) process. ___ ___ _____

10. An acceptance of a limited amount of conflict or competition as normal so long as it is not intense or disruptive. ___ ___ _____

11. An awareness of common sources of conflict and competition: unequal distribution of resources, disagreements about what are important changes in work flow, infringement on territorial rights, mutual mistrust, and constant change. ___ ___ _____

12. Prompt settlement of disputes in an objective and professional manner. ___ ___ _____

13. Maintenance of an "I'm okay, you're okay" attitude when dealing with stress situations, by stroking and by placing emphasis on performance rather than on attitudes. ___ ___ _____

14. Cooperating with, rather than resisting, advice and suggestions from staff personnel. ___ ___ _____

15. Encouraging cooperation from employees and peers by focusing on common objectives. ___ ___ _____

ACTION PLANNING CHECKLIST 15

Keeping People, Plans, and Programs on Track

	Action Needed		Date Completed
	Yes	No	

1. Knowledge of your company's information system and how it affects controls in your area of responsibility. ____ ____ _____

2. Understanding of a supervisor's judgmental, problem-solving, and decision-making roles in implementing controls. ____ ____ _____

3. Knowledge of how control standards and procedures are linked to plans and goals. ____ ____ _____

4. Ability to define and identify control standards and tolerances as they affect your operations. ____ ____ _____

5. Ability to use historical records and systematic analysis to establish standards for your department. ____ ____ _____

6. An understanding of the control process and a supervisor's role in it. ____ ____ _____

7. An ability to distinguish among preventive, concurrent, and corrective controls and to identify the application of these in your area of responsibility. ____ ____ _____

8. Departmental standards and controls established to cover employee performance, machine operations, product or service quality, costs and expense, time-related factors, and materials usage. ____ ____ _____

9. Control standards that are clearly written, numerically expressed where possible, and based on historical records or systematic analysis. ____ ____ _____

10. A periodic review to make sure that existing control standards are correct and relevant to the person or process being monitored. ____ ____ _____

11. An understanding of the intent and use of budgetary controls received and the extent to which you must conform to them. ____ ____ _____

12. Application of the management by exception principle to the control process as much as is possible. ____ ____ _____

13. Sensitivity to the people problem when exercising control. Emphasis on motivation rather than punishment. ____ ____ _____

14. Encouragement of employee self-control whenever feasible and appropriate. ____ ____ _____

15. An understanding of, and receptivity to, management by objectives (MBO) if applied to your area of responsibility. ____ ____ _____

Controlling Costs and Budgets

	Action Needed		Date Completed
	Yes	No	

1. Knowledge of costs and expenses for your department and maintenance of appropriate records for your guidance and action. ___ ___ _____
2. An understanding of basic cost and accounting terms, such as unit costs, standard costs, and budgeted costs. ___ ___ _____
3. An ability to interpret a budget and take action based on a cost-variance report, as illustrated in Table 16-1 of Chapter 16. ___ ___ _____
4. An ability to compute and compare unit costs. ___ ___ _____
5. An understanding of a flexible budget and how it is prepared, as illustrated in Table 16-2 of Chapter 16. ___ ___ _____
6. Acceptance of your responsibility in routine, recurring, organization-wide cost reduction programs. ___ ___ _____
7. An ongoing search for cost reduction targets: in processes, procedures, personnel, equipment, materials and supplies, utilities, communications, paperwork, and information. ___ ___ _____
8. An ability to plan and implement an intense, but temporary, "belt-tightening" program. ___ ___ _____
9. Use of participative approaches to seek cost-cutting ideas from employees and staff departments. ___ ___ _____
10. Development of a program for ongoing cost curtailment, such as: reducing waste, saving time, increasing output, spending wisely, using space more intelligently, and trimming your inventories. ___ ___ _____
11. An understanding of why some cost-saving ideas may be rejected (for good reason) by higher management. ___ ___ _____
12. A sensitivity to employee—and labor union—resistance to cost reduction efforts, with a plan to minimize or overcome such resistance. ___ ___ _____
13. Establishment of specific, attainable cost reduction goals with and for employees—for factors and conditions that they can affect or control themselves. ___ ___ _____
14. Encouragement of, and receptivity toward, employee ideas and suggestions for cost reduction. ___ ___ _____
15. A continuing communications program to inform employees of the genuine need for cost control, using concrete examples and specific figures; enhanced by training for cost improvement, and reports of progress toward cost goals. ___ ___ _____

Stimulating Productivity, Quality, and Innovation

	Action Needed		Date Completed
	Yes	No	

1. Knowledge of which input resources and output values can be used to measure productivity in your department. ____ ____ _____

2. A record kept of the basic productivity trend in your department. ____ ____ _____

3. Identification of the specific technological factors that can affect productivity for better or worse in your department. ____ ____ _____

4. A knowledge of how much time it does, and should, take to perform the various tasks and work under your supervision, given the quality of workmanship expected. ____ ____ _____

5. Periodic work-sampling check of your workforce to observe the degree of travel, delay, or idleness that prevails. ____ ____ _____

6. Periodic review of tasks under your supervision to identify those that most need a methods-improvement analysis, especially those with many "wasteful" elements. ____ ____ _____

7. Routine thought given to improvement of each of the three task elements—"makeready," "do," and "put-away"—of jobs in your department. ____ ____ _____

8. A challenging attitude toward existing procedures in terms of what is being done, where, when, why, and how. ____ ____ _____

9. Systematic application of (a) the methods-improvement checklist—eliminate, combine, change sequence, and simplify—and (b) the motion-economy checklist—productive, simple, and rhythmic motions; comfortable workplaces; combining of tools; prepositioning of tools and materials; etc. ____ ____ _____

10. Acceptance of high-technology innovations from automation, computer-assisted systems, and office automation and reengineering. ____ ____ _____

11. An appreciation of people-oriented participative approaches, such as quality circles, to improve productivity. ____ ____ _____

12. An alertness to value-analysis applications, especially by substituting less expensive, easier-to-work-with materials and parts in the product being made. ____ ____ _____

13. Seeking, stimulating, and accepting creative ideas and suggestions from employees—through either formal suggestions systems, quality circles, or brainstorming sessions. ____ ____ _____

14. When stimulating innovative thinking on the part of your employees, brainstorming principles are observed: no criticism, anything welcomed, quantity stressed, combining and improving on what already has been suggested; evaluating later on. ____ ____ _____

15. Development of your own ability to create new ideas, using the list of suggestions in the text. ____ ____ _____

Managing a Diverse Workforce

	Action Needed		Date Completed
	Yes	No	

1. Accommodation of the needs and expectations of an increasingly diverse workforce and full utilization of its diverse talents. ____ ____ _____

2. An acceptance of a very broad definition of "minorities" as "protected groups" under the law: including African Americans, women, ethnic minorities (such as Hispanic, Asian, and Native Americans), disadvantaged, disabled, Vietnam War veterans, and workers over 40 years of age. ____ ____ _____

3. Knowledge of, and respect for, the basic legal protections against discrimination in all aspects of employment because of race, religion, national origin, age, or gender. ____ ____ _____

4. Understanding of the legal and practical implications of an affirmative action program. ____ ____ _____

5. An understanding of EEOC's three culpable variations of discrimination: differential treatment, disparate effect, and evil intent. ____ ____ _____

6. A determination to give all employees a fair chance to learn a job and to prove their ability to perform satisfactorily, and a recognition of the need to document a bona fide occupational qualification (BFOQ) exception to the EEO laws. ____ ____ _____

7. An expectation of satisfactory performance from all minorities once they have become an integral part of your workforce. ____ ____ _____

8. Assurance that workplace conditions and procedures conform to the requirements of the Americans With Disabilities Act. ____ ____ _____

9. Proper implementation of the rights and privileges afforded employees by the Family and Medical Leave Act. ____ ____ _____

10. Avoidance of stereotyped thinking about why women work—as well as about their interest in, and capability to perform, various types of work. ____ ____ _____

11. Absolutely equal pay and treatment for women who perform the same work as men (and vice versa) with equal opportunities for training, development, and advancement. ____ ____ _____

12. A strict avoidance of any form or implication of sexual harassment, either by you or by any member of your staff. ____ ____ _____

13. A determination to bridge the generation gap between you and younger employees, by being supportive of their efforts, trying to make work more meaningful, and providing feedback. ____ ____ _____

14. An alertness to obsolescence among workers over 50, with job assignments that make the most of their skills and good work habits. ____ ____ _____

15. Strict observance of an employee's right to privacy (including AIDS-related matters) and restrictions affecting drug and lie detector tests. ____ ____ _____

The Supervisor's Role in Employee Safety and Health and Labor Relations

	Action Needed		Date Completed
	Yes	No	

1. A recognition of the potential for immense financial costs and human damage due to work-related accidents and health hazards. ____ ____ _____

2. Knowledge of the prime causes of work-related accidents, as listed in the text. ____ ____ _____

3. Knowledge of OSHA standards as they apply to safety and health conditions in your areas of responsibility. ____ ____ _____

4. Careful safety training for new employees and an ongoing program for all employees. ____ ____ _____

5. Knowledge of and protection of employees' rights under OSHA. ____ ____ _____

6. A continuing search for better accident prevention and safety procedures—the engineering of safety. ____ ____ _____

7. An ongoing program to educate and motivate employees to work safely, with emphasis on accident awareness and prevention. ____ ____ _____

8. Enforcement of safety and health rules and regulations—no matter how small—without exception. ____ ____ _____

9. Insistence that employees wear the designated protective clothing and in the prescribed way. ____ ____ _____

10. Knowledge of accident potential and prescribed safe working conditions associated with lifting and material handling, machinery, hand tools, falls, low-voltage electricity, computer keyboarding, and other office and clerical activities. ____ ____ _____

11. Relentless surveillance of potential fire conditions in your department, making sure that employees have foreknowledge of what to do if a fire occurs. ____ ____ _____

12. Prompt reporting of occupational injuries and illnesses that occur in your department so that they may be entered in the company's OSHA log. ____ ____ _____

13. An ability to make calculations of accident incident and severity rates. ____ ____ _____

14. Prompt investigation of accidents and occupational illnesses large and small—to identify and remove causes, not to fix blame. ____ ____ _____

15. Maintenance of approved conditions and procedures affecting environment and sanitation in your department: ventilation, waste disposal, food handling, washrooms, lighting, and handling and storage of hazardous materials. ____ ____ _____

GLOSSARY OF TERMS

A

Absenteeism rate The average number of days absent per employee, or the percentage of scheduled worker-days lost.

Acceptable Quality Levels (AQL) A general form of specification that tells a supervisor the kind of tolerance limiting that will be judged as acceptable performance.

Accident An unplanned or uncontrolled event in which action or reaction of an object, material, or person results in either personal injury or property damage, or both.

Accountability A nonassignable liability for the way in which an organizational obligation held by a supervisor is discharged, either personally or by subordinates.

Active listening The conscious process of securing information of all kinds (including feelings and emotions) through attention and observation.

Adjustment The process whereby healthy as well as disturbed individuals find a way to fit themselves to difficult situations by yielding to a degree, and by modifying their feelings and their behavior to accommodate the stresses of life and work.

Affirmative action An in-company program designed to remedy current and future inequities in employment of minorities.

Application blank A form used by an organization to legally and systematically gather and record information from a job applicant about his or her qualifications, education, and work experience.

Appraisal interview A meeting held between a supervisor and an employee to review the performance rating and, using that evaluation as a basis, to discuss the overall quality of the employee's work and methods for improving it, if necessary.

Arbitration The settlement of a labor dispute or employee grievance by an impartial umpire selected by mutual agreement of the organization and the union.

Assertive request To ask courteously; to make known your wishes with the implied expectation that they will be fulfilled.

Attrition The gradual reduction of a workforce by means of natural events and causes, such as retirements, deaths, and resignations, as opposed to reductions planned by management, such as discharges, layoffs, and early retirement programs.

Authority The legitimate power to issue orders to other people in an organization and to obtain resources from it.

B

Behavioral management A management approach that seeks to stimulate cooperation on the basis of an understanding of, and genuine concern for, employees as individuals and as members of a work group.

Behaviorally Anchored Rating Scale (BARS) A performance-appraisal format that describes and provides examples of, behavior that can be rated along a scale from outstanding to unsatisfactory behavior.

Benchmarking A quality management technique based on finding the best product, service, process, or procedure and adopting it as the standard of quality performance.

Body language Nonverbal body movements, facial expressions, or gestures that may project and reveal underlying attitudes and sentiments.

Brainstorming A group approach to idea generation that encourages free association of ideas among participants, while forbidding negative judgments, in order to generate a

maximum number of ideas in a short
period of time.

Budget A planning, reporting, and control document that combines standards for various
departmental operating conditions with
allocations for operating expenses. Also a
plan, or forecast, especially of expenses
that are allowable in the operation of a
department.

Budgeted costs Costs that are stipulated as
acceptable in a particular budget for a
specific accounting period.

Bureaucracy An organized system of work
characterized by policies and rules, a chain
of command, an emphasis on organizational
goals, and many written records.

Burnout The inability of employees to handle
major incidents of, or sustained, stress.

 _____

Catharsis The relief that follows release of
accumulated feelings, emotions, and frustrations that comes through their expression
in a harmless fashion. The supervisor's
counseling role and active listening skills
contribute to employee catharsis.

Chain of command The formal channels in an
organization that distribute authority from
top to bottom.

Coaching Helping employees learn through
supervisory observation, demonstration,
questioning, and timely feedback.

Cohesiveness The degree to which team
members are attracted to the group, feel
a part of it, and wish to remain in it.

Collective bargaining The process of give-and-
take engaged in by the management of an
organization and authorized representatives
of its collective employees (a labor union)
to reach a formal, written agreement about
wages, hours, and working conditions.

Communication The process of passing information and understanding from one person
to another.

Competition A relatively healthy struggle among
individuals or groups within an organization
to excel in striving to meet mutually beneficial,
rather than individual, goals.

Concurrent controls Controls applied to
conditions to be maintained and results to
be obtained during the conversion process.

Conflict A disruptive clash of interests, objectives, or personalities between individuals,
between individuals and groups, or between
groups within an organization.

Contingency management The selection and
use of a management practice that is most
appropriate for a particular problem or situation, based on prior research.

Contingency model of leadership The belief
that the leadership style that will be most
effective in a given situation can be predicted by examining the intensity of three
interacting factors.

Continuous improvement The ongoing
process of searching for cost reductions
(and process improvements) by taking a
critical view toward the present situation.

Continuum of leadership A range of leadership approaches that progresses from the
extremes of autocratic control by the supervisor to complete freedom for subordinates.

Controls Those rules, regulations, standards,
and specifications that enable a supervisor
to measure performance against a department's goals and to determine causes and
to take corrective action when necessary.

Corrective controls Controls applied, mainly
to results related to products or services
produced, after the conversion process has
been completed.

Cost-benefit analysis A technique for weighing the pros and cons of alternative courses of action.

Cost-variance report A listing of allowable expenses compared with the actual expenses incurred.

Critical incident An actual and specific occurrence, either favorable or unfavorable, that serves to illustrate the general nature of an employee's performance.

Cultural diversity The recognition that society and the workforce are composed of a variety of groups, each of whom has, in addition to similarities with other groups, unique differences in beliefs and experiences that can be assets at work.

D

Decision making The part of the problem-solving process in which alternatives are evaluated and a choice is made.

Decision tree A graphic portrait of the possible outcomes of alternative solutions.

Defect Any variation (in the product or service) from specifications that falls outside the prescribed tolerances.

Delegation The assignment, or entrustment, to subordinates of organizational responsibilities or obligations along with appropriate organizational authority, power, and rights.

Differential treatment The act of treating a member of a minority, or protected group, differently from other applicants or employees in a similar situation.

Direct costs Variable costs that can be clearly identified as adding value directly to the goods produced or services rendered.

Discipline The imposition of a penalty by management on an employee for the infraction of a company rule, regulation, or standard in such a manner as to encourage more constructive behavior and to discourage a similar infraction in the future.

Discrimination Any managerial action or decision based on favoring or disfavoring one person or member of a group over another on the basis of race, color, ethnic or national origin, gender, age, disability, Vietnam-era war service, or union membership.

Disparate effect The existence of job requirements that have the effect of unfairly excluding a member of a protected group.

Dissatisfaction The state that exists when "maintenance" or "hygiene" factors such as good pay, job security, fringe benefits, and desirable working conditions are lacking.

Division of work The principle that performance is more efficient when a large job is broken down into smaller, specialized jobs.

Downsizing A reduction in the number of people employed by an organization, usually in order to respond to unfavorable economic conditions or in an attempt to improve efficiency.

Due process An employee's entitlement to a fair hearing before discipline can be meted out. Often the hearing is conducted by an impartial party, allows appropriate representation, and involves presentation of available evidence.

E

E-mail Use of the Internet or Intranet (local area network) to send and receive messages electronically.

Employee-centered supervision Places an emphasis on a genuine concern and respect for employees, and on the maintenance of effective relationships within a work group.

Employee counseling A task-oriented, problem-solving technique that features an empathic, interactive discussion—emphasizing listening—aimed at helping an employee cope with some specific aspect of his or her work life.

Employee turnover A measure of how many people come to work for an organization and do not remain employed there, for whatever reason.

Employment interview A face-to-face exchange of information between a job applicant and an employer's representative designed to develop qualitative information about the applicant's suitability for employment.

Empowerment Providing lower-level employees with the authority to examine problem situations and resolve them as they arise.

Entitlement The perception by employees that they ought to receive certain benefits, protections, and privileges from their employer.

Equal Employment Opportunity (EEO) A system of organizational justice, stipulated by law, that applies to all aspects of employment and is intended to provide equal opportunity for all members of the labor force.

Equity An employee's perception of the fairness in the application of rewards to oneself and others for their efforts.

Ergonomic hazard A workplace condition that requires the job holder to repeat or sustain a fixed motion or stress pattern over an extended period of time, and that may include a repetitive strain injury (RSI).

Executive A top-level manager in charge of a group of subordinate managers; this person establishes broad plans, objectives, and strategies.

Expectancy An individual's judgment about the attractiveness and probability of an assignment.

F

Facilitating An approach to management in which a supervisor assists and guides employees in their efforts to perform their jobs rather than emphasizing orders, instructions, and control.

Feedback Information provided by those engaged in the communication process that serves to clarify and/or verify understanding and to indicate either agreement or dissent. Also the process of relaying the measurement of actual performance back to the individual or unit causing the performance so that action can be taken to correct, or narrow, the variance.

Fixed costs Costs that tend to be constant, at least on an annual basis, and that are not related to the rate of production, services rendered, or amount of sales.

Flexible budget A budget that presents several options based on possible variations in output levels.

Flexible work schedule A system by which employees can choose—and periodically change—the blocks of time in which they will work.

Formal work group A group or team of employees who are assigned by management to similar activities or locations with the intent that they work together in a prescribed way toward goals established by management.

Free association of ideas The ability of the mind to unconsciously visualize relationships between seemingly different objects and ideas.

Functional authority The legitimate authority granted to a staff department to make overriding organizational decisions involving its particular functional specialty.

Functional organization An organizational structure in which tasks are grouped according to a particular operating function, such as production, sales, information handling, and so on.

G

Gantt chart A visual device for scheduling jobs in the most productive sequence and then controlling work progress.

Goals Short-term and long-range targets (objectives) toward which an organization strives.

Grapevine The informal communication network that employees use to convey information of interest to them.

Grievance procedure A formalized, systematic channel for employees to follow in bringing their complaints to the attention of management. Typically, it prescribes a progression of appeals from lowest to highest authority within the company and the employees' organization. It often has arbitration as a final step.

Group Two or more people who are aware of one another and interact with one another.

Group dynamics The interaction among members of a work group and concurrent changes in their attitudes, behavior, and relationships.

Group norms Beliefs held by a group about what is right and what is wrong as far as performance at work is concerned.

H

Halo effect A generalization whereby one aspect of performance, or a single quality of an individual's nature, is allowed to overshadow everything else about that person.

Hazard A potentially dangerous object, material, condition, or practice that is present in the workplace, to which employees must be alert and from which they must be protected.

Hostility A feeling of enmity or antagonism; an aggressive expression of anger displayed by problem employees as an unconscious, unwitting relief from fears about their security or other feelings of inadequacy.

I

Indirect costs Variable costs that are essential to the production of goods or rendering of services but which do not clearly add value to them, or do not do so in an easily measurable way.

Informal work group A group that forms spontaneously among employees who work near one another, who have common personal interests, or who work toward common job goals.

Information Data that has been selected, arranged, and analyzed to make it useful for supervisory decisions. Also the knowledge, skills, and feelings that are exchanged in the communication process.

Instruction Furnishing knowledge or information in a disciplined, systematic way with the expectation of compliance.

Interventions A variety of activities designed to make individuals, groups, or the entire organization more effective.

J

Japanese management The participative practice of seeking consensus of agreement from employees and other managers before choosing or implementing a course of action.

Job aids Materials placed on or near the work area that help employees to remember key points and to perform effectively.

Job breakdown analysis The segmentation of a particular job into important steps that advance the work toward its completion.

Job enlargement Extends the boundaries of a job by adding differing tasks at the same level of expertise.

Job enrichment Expanding a job vertically by adding higher skill activities and delegating greater authority.

Job evaluation A systematic technique for determining the worth of a job, compared with other jobs in an organization.

Job Instruction Training (JIT) A systematic four-step approach to training employees in a basic job skill.

Job redesign The process of carefully restructuring a job to foster productivity and to appeal to the interests of the employees who carry it out.

Job sharing The process of taking one job and splitting its duties into two such that the combined time and efforts of two persons will satisfy all the work demands.

K

Key points The essential elements that make or break the job.

Knowledge Job-relevant information.

Knowledge management The process of creating and using human and technological networks to capitalize on a company's expertise, experience, and learning.

L

Labor agreement The written agreement that binds a company's management and its employees' organization (labor union) for a stipulated period of time to certain conditions of pay, hours, work, and any other matter the parties deem appropriate. (Also called *union agreement* or *labor contract*.)

Leadership The process of influencing and supporting others to follow you and to do willingly the things that need to be done.

Learning organization A company in which new ways of thinking are nurtured, people are continually learning how to learn, and the results are widely shared and used at all levels.

Line-and-staff organization The most common form of organizational structure, in which line managers hold accountability for results that most directly affect profits or institutional goals, and staff managers hold accountability for results that most directly affect the processes by which line managers accomplish their goals.

M

Management The process of obtaining, deploying, and utilizing a variety of essential resources in support of an organization's objectives.

Management by exception A principle of control that enables a supervisor to delegate corrective action to a subordinate as long as the variances in performance are within specified ranges.

Management by Objectives (MBO) A planning and control technique in which a supervisor and his or her immediate superior agree on goals to be attained and standards to be maintained.

Management Information System (MIS) A system (usually computerized) which collects, analyzes, exchanges, and delivers information in a way that helps managers make timely and valid decisions.

Management principles A set of guidelines established by Henri Fayol and others for carrying out the management process.

Management process Covers the five key functions of planning, organizing, staffing, energizing, and controlling organizational resources for the attainment of results.

Manager An individual who plans, organizes, directs, and controls the work of others in an organization.

Merit raises Increases in an employee's salary based on the supervisor's assessment of an individual's job performance.

Methods improvement Any of many systematic methods of work analysis aimed at finding simpler, faster, less physically demanding ways of accomplishing a given task while at the same time increasing productivity and reducing costs.

Middle manager A person who reports to an executive and who directs supervisory personnel toward the attainment of goals and the implementation of plans of an organization.

Mission statement A statement that clarifies the nature and purpose of a business.

Modeling The process in which a skilled co-worker or supervisor explains and demonstrates the performance of a key job skill.

Morale A measure of the extent (either high or low) of voluntary cooperation demonstrated by an individual or a work group and of the intensity of the desire to meet common work goals.

Motivation The process that impels a person to behave in a certain manner in order to satisfy highly individual needs.

Multi-skilling The development of capacities to perform two or more key tasks by a single employee.

Noise Any kind of distraction, physical or emotional, within an individual or the environment that distorts or obstructs the transmission of a message.

Nonmanagerial employees (often referred to as "employees" or "associates"). Workers who receive direction from managers and then perform specific, designated tasks.

Occupational Safety and Health Act Comprehensive legislation that establishes standards and calls for the inspection of safety and health conditions and the investigation of all serious accidents and alleged safety or health hazards. Created Occupational Safety and Health Administration.

Open-book management The practice of sharing extensive information with employees, training and empowering them to use it, and rewarding them for the results.

Orders Commands given forcefully with the expectation of obedience to them.

Organization The structure derived from systematically grouping the tasks to be performed and from prescribing formal relationships that strengthen the ability of people to work more effectively together in pursuing common objectives.

Organizational culture The underlying (often implicit) set of assumptions, beliefs, attitudes, and expectations shared by members of an organization.

Organizational Development (OD) A set of values and assumptions about individuals, groups, organizations, and their environments that suggests they must embrace change and find ways to deal more effectively with each other.

Orientation The process in which new employees are introduced to their jobs, co-workers, and work environment through tours, personal introductions, and explanations.

Participation The technique in which a supervisor or manager shares work-related information, responsibilities, decisions, or all three, with the work group.

Participative leadership The act of fully involving employees in decision-making processes such that their ideas are used and they are fully committed to the solution's success.

Penalty A punishment or forfeiture imposed by management on an employee as a form of discipline. Typically, such penalties include suspensions, loss of time and/or pay, demotion, or loss of job—that is, firing.

Performance appraisal A formal and systematic evaluation of how well a person performs his or her work and fills the appropriate role in the organization.

Performance management The ongoing process of clarifying and communicating performance expectations to employees, and then providing coaching and feedback to ensure the desired actions.

Performance test An employment test that enables job applicants to demonstrate that they can actually perform the kind of work required by the job in question.

Personality An individual's unique way of behaving and of seeing and interpreting the actions of other people and events.

PERT chart A graphic project-planning device that shows relationships among many tasks and the critical bottlenecks that could delay progress toward completion.

Policies Broad guidelines that must be followed in pursuit of goals.

Preventive controls Controls applied, primarily to an examination of resources, before the conversion process begins.

Problem solving A process of systematically analyzing gaps between expected and actual conditions to find and remedy their causes.

Productivity The measure of efficiency that compares the value of outputs from an operation with the cost of the resources used.

Programmed decision A solution to a recurring problem that can be established for continual use every time the problem reappears.

Protected groups Certain minority and/or disadvantaged groups in the population, which warrant special protection in employment matters.

Q

Quality The measure of the degree to which a process, product, or service conforms to the requirements that have been established for it.

Quality assurance An approach to quality control that encompasses all the efforts taken by an organization to ensure that its processes, products, and services conform to the requirements set for them.

Quality of Work Life (QWL) The extent to which the work itself provides motivation, satisfaction, and the chance for personal growth.

Quantitative management A management sciences approach to management that emphasizes the use of advanced mathematics and statistics and the application of information theory.

R

Realistic job preview A balanced presentation of positive and negative features about a job that allows a candidate to reach an informed judgment.

Reengineering A top-down, broad-based approach to improvement that can lead to sweeping changes in goals and methods throughout an organization.

References People who give information on those seeking employment.

Reject A product that needs to be discarded or destroyed.

Reliability The demonstrated ability of a test to yield similar scores for a candidate if the test were repeated (after a sufficient period of time to allow forgetting). Also a measure (usually a statistical estimate) of the probability of a product's performing specific functions, under given conditions, for a specified time without failure.

Resilience The capacity of an employee to handle short-term stress and bounce back from its distractions.

Responsibility The duty or obligation to perform a prescribed task or service or to attain a specified objective.

Return on Quality (ROQ) A modification of TQM in that it focuses on providing only that degree of quality that a customer or client values highly and is willing to pay the price to obtain.

Reverse discrimination The notion that implementing affirmative action programs deprives qualified members of nonprotected groups from their rightful opportunities.

Right-to-work laws Legislation passed in nearly two dozen states that makes it illegal to negotiate for a union shop after a union gains recognition.

S

Satisfaction The positive state that exists when truly motivating factors (satisfiers)—such as interesting and challenging work, full use of one's capabilities, and recognition for achievement—are provided.

Saving face Employee actions taken to restore their self-image and regain their self-esteem after receiving criticism during an appraisal.

Schedules Detailed date-and-time indications of how facilities, equipment, and employees are to be used to accomplish organizational goals.

Self-appraisal The process of allowing employees to take responsibility for evaluating their own performance.

Self-directed learning The process by which trainees learn at their own pace by consulting resources and asking for guidance when they feel it is needed.

Self-esteem The degree of self-confidence that employees have, often based largely on their personal expectations and prior levels of performance.

Self-managing team A group of employees who perform most managerial activities themselves, thus dramatically changing the roles of a traditional supervisor.

Sexual harassment Repeated or unwarranted verbal or physical advances or sexually explicit remarks that are offensive or objectionable to the recipient.

Skill The ability to perform a job-related action.

Span of control The number of activities or people that a single manager can supervise.

Specification A collection of standardized dimensions and characteristics pertaining to a product, process, or service. Also the definitions of expected performance of a product (or quality of a service).

Standard The measure, criterion, or basis—usually expressed in numbers and/or other concrete terms—for judging performance of a product or service, machine, individual, or organizational unit. Also the normal or expected time required to perform an operation or process or make a product, computed on the basis of past performance, estimates, or work measurement.

Standard costs The normal, or expected, costs of an operation, product, or service (usually including labor, materials, and overhead charges) computed on the basis of past performance, estimates, or work measurement.

Statistical Quality Control (SQC) Numbers are used as a part of the overall approach to controlling quality.

Stereotype The characterization of an individual on the basis of a standardized, oversimplified view of the characteristics believed (often wrongly) to be held in common by the group to which the individual is assumed to belong.

Stewardship The view that supervisors are stewards of resources and must play the role of servant-leader to help others achieve their goals.

Strategic control points Key places where it makes the most sense to measure performance and take corrective action.

Strategies The major methods for achieving an organization's vision and mission.

Stressors Environmental, psychological, or psychosocial factors that produce stress within employees and often detract from their work performance.

Substitutes for leadership Factors in the task, organization, or employees that diminish the need for various kinds of supervisory leadership behaviors.

Superleader A supervisor who places a high priority on developing the skills of employees to manage themselves and engage in self-leadership.

Supervisor A manager who is in charge of, and coordinates the activities of, a group of employees engaged in related activities within a unit of an organization.

System An interrelated set of elements functioning as a whole.

Systematic management The traditional approach to management that emphasizes the functions performed in the management process as well as systematic measurement and analysis of the various tasks and activities of the workplace.

T

Task-centered supervision Places an emphasis on the job or task that employees are expected to perform so as to produce results.

Teachable moments The specific times when employees are most likely to learn.

Team building Activities designed to help group members develop more effective ways of problem solving and interacting with each other.

Teams Groups of people who must work together to achieve common goals.

Telecommuting Working at one's home, while being connected electronically to the employer's office.

Theory X A set of assumptions in which a supervisor acts as if she or he believes that most people don't like to work and that they wish to avoid responsibility and prefer job security above all.

Theory Y A set of assumptions in which a supervisor acts as if she or he believes that most people can set challenging goals and provide their own initiative and exert self-control to attain their goals.

Tolerance The permissible deviation, or variance, from standard. Also a statement of precision that establishes limits within which the product or the service must meet the specification.

Total Quality Management (TQM) An approach to quality control that focuses on customer satisfaction and embraces not only all the internal functions of an enterprise, but also external contributors.

Training need A demonstrated gap between expected and actual performance.

Transactional Analysis (TA) A way of improving relationships between people that is based on an understanding of each individual's mature attitudes and behavior toward one another.

Transfer of training The process in which trainees effectively apply to their jobs knowledge and skills gained in off-the-job training.

U

Unfair labor practices Those practices engaged in by either management or labor unions that are judged by the federal labor law (National Labor Relations Act) to be improper, especially in that they (a) interfere with the rights of employees to organize or (b) discriminate against employees for labor union activities.

Unit cost The cost of producing a single product or unit; measure of output of a product or service.

Unity of command The principle that each individual should report to only one boss.

Unity of direction The principle that there should be a single set of goals and objectives that unifies the activities of everyone in an organization.

V

Validity The proven ability of a test to measure what it purports to measure.

Values What an organization believes in and guides its practices by.

Variable costs Costs that tend to vary (directly or indirectly) according to the volume of goods produced, services rendered, and/or sales generated.

Virtual classroom The use of Web-based electronic programs to provide just-in-time training to employees.

Vision A statement of an organization's ideal future.

Voice mail The use of electronic recording to capture, save, and transmit telephone messages.

Warning A reprimand so worded as to give formal notice to an employee that repetition of a particular form of unacceptable behavior, such as infraction of a rule, will draw a penalty.

Withdrawal A passive way for emotionally disturbed employees to cope with their anxieties, in which they retreat from confrontations, appear unduly preoccupied, discourage social overtures, and keep very much to themselves.

Work An activity involving physical or mental effort to perform tasks and overcome difficulties so as to attain valued organizational results and a means of personal livelihood.

Work distribution chart A visual device for allocating tasks equitably among the members of a department, according to time required and skill levels available.

Work measurement The determination, by systematic and (ideally) precise methods, of the time dimension of a particular task.

Work sampling A technique for finding out what proportion of employees' time is used productively on job assignments, compared with the proportion that is not.

INDEX

A

ABC analysis, 109–110, 550

Absenteeism, 329–331

    counseling for, 330–331

    negative effects of, 172–173

    reducing, 173, 329–330

    staffing process and, 170–171

    types of absentees, 330–331

Absenteeism rate, 172–173

Acceptable Quality Level (AQL), 445

Acceptance theory of authority, 139

Accident prevention, 506–514

    basis for, 512–514

    employee responsibility for, 511–512

    federal government role in, 506–507, 509–510

    safety committees and, 513–514

    safety inspections for, 514

    safety specialist and, 513

    wellness programs and, 514

Accidents

    accident-prone employees, 503–504

    causes of, 503–504

    costs of, 503

    defined, 503

    first aid for, 510–511

    frequency and severity of, 504

    investigating, 508–509

    rates of, 507–508

    record-keeping process for, 507

Accountability, 139–140

    authority and responsibility versus, 139–140

    defined, 139

Accounting records, 406–408

    basic concepts, 406–407

    information sources for, 407

Achievement motivation, 221

Actions, 61

Active listening, 273–274

Adjustment, 320

Advance warning, 340

Affiliation motivation, 221

Affirmative action, 475

Age

    older workers, 487–490

    younger workers, 485–487

Age Discrimination in Employment Act of 1967, 474, 487–488

Alcohol abuse, 332–334

Alcoholics Anonymous (AA), 332

American Association of Career Education, 510

American Management Association, 37, 72

American National Standards Institute (ANSI), 444

American Productivity Center, 431

American Society for Quality Control (ASQC), 444

Americans with Disabilities Act (ADA) of 1990, 162, 334, 474, 476–477

Application blank, 160, 161

Appraisal interviews, 301–303

Aptitude tests, 161

Arbitration, 525–526

Assertive requests, 279

AT&T, 226, 383

Attitudes, 275, 559–560

Attrition, 171

Auditory learners, 275–276

Authority, 55

    chain of, in bureaucracy, 34

    defined, 138

    delegation of, 138, 141–144

    functional, 140–141

    responsibility and accountability and, 139–140

    responsibility versus, 138

    sources of, 138–139

    of supervisor, 140

Autocratic leadership, 245

Automation, 441–442

Baby boomers, 81, 392, 489

Bakke v. University of California Board of Regents, 476

Barner, Robert, 33

Bay, Tom, 31

Behavioral management, 57, 58–59

Behaviorally Anchored Rating Scales (BARS), 298–299, 300

Belt-tightening program, 413, 415

Benchmarking, 454–455

Bias, 102, 304

Black, James Menzies, 165

Blanchard, Ken, 250–251

Blau, Gary, 172

Blindsiding, 56

Block, Peter, 253–254

Body language, 264, 273

Bona Fide Occupational Qualification (BFOQ), 475

Boundary managers, 61

Brainstorming, 458

Broedling, Laurie, 18

Brown, W. Steven, 393

Buddy system, 201

Budget

    budgeted costs, 15, 406–407, 408–411

    in control function, 390

    defined, 390, 406

    flexible, 410–411

Bureau of Labor Statistics, U.S., 58, 61, 81, 337, 507, 508, 509

Bureaucracy

    components of, 33–34

    defined, 34

Burke, Billie, 487

Burnout, 321, 323

Capacity, in scheduling process, 81

Career

    advancement in organization, 557–562

    development, 540

    education in, 543–545

    help and guidance, 545–546

    mentor in, 50, 543

    networking and, 543, 557–558

    path, 541–543

    planning, 540–546

    raises, 304, 308, 561–562

Carr, Clay, 219

Case, John, 115, 121

Catharsis, 325

Centralized organization, 135, 136

Chadderdom, Lisa, 242

Chain of command, 56, 144, 146

Challenged employees, accommodating, 166

Chamber of Commerce, U.S., 444

Channels, 144–145

Charisma, 239

Chase Manhattan Bank, 414

Checkoff agreement, 517

Cheney, Lynn V., 20

Chitchat, 549

Cleaver, Eldridge, 101

Closed shop, 517

Coaching, 187–188, 383

Cohen, Allan R., 354

Cohesiveness, 354–355

Cole, Robert E., 434

Collective bargaining, 520–521

Communication
    defined, 264
    (*See also* Employee communication)
Company policy, 87
Company training department, 190
Comparable worth, 481–482
Competition
    conflict versus, 365
    defined, 365
Compressed work week, 39
Computer-assisted instruction, 197
Concurrent controls, 388
Confidence, delegation and, 143
Confidentiality, 303
Conflict resolution, 363–366
    bickering and disputes, 363
    competition versus conflict, 365
    conflict, defined, 365
    main sources of conflict, 364–365
    methods of, 365–366
Confrontation as control, 393
Construct validity, 479
Constructive criticism, 338–339
Consultative leadership, 246, 250
Content validity, 479
Contingency management, 57–58, 62
Contingency model of leadership, 248–249
Continuous improvement, 414, 434
Continuum of leadership styles, 250
Control function
    analytical tools for, 389
    budgets in, 390
    dual role of, 381–383
    employee resistance and, 355, 392–395
    in management process, 16, 53
    in planning process, 80
    process of, 385–388, 392

standards in, 381, 384–385
    supervisor role in, 382–383
    targets for, 389–391
Control standards, 381, 384–385
    information for, 384–385
    nature of, 384
    source of, 384
Controls
    defined, 381
    planning, 80, 383
Cooperation, 366–370
    from associates, 368–369
    individual versus group of individuals, 369–370
    lack of, 366–367
    with staff people, 369
    Transactional Analysis (TA) and, 367
Corrective action, 381
Corrective controls, 388
Cost-benefit analysis, 108
Cost control
    accounting records in, 406–408
    budgets in, 15, 406–407, 408–411
    cost improvement sources, 414–416
    cost improvement strategies, 411–413
    employee reactions to, 417–419
    labor union and, 417–418
Cost targets, 412–413
Cost-variance report, 408, 409
Counseling (*See* Employee counseling)
Covey, Stephen, 272
Creative thinking
    brainstorming versus, 458
    generating ideas, 457–458
    nature of, 457
Critical incidents, 297
Critical-path method, 84–86
Crosby, Philip, 451–452

CSX Railroad, 77

Cultural diversity, 471

Current problems, 99

Customer organization, 134

D

Daimler/Chrysler, 200

Data, 112

Data bank, 112

Davis, Keith, 10

Deadlines, 82–83

Decentralized organization, 135–136

Decision making

    in control function, 382–383

    cost-benefit analysis in, 108

    decision trees in, 106–108

    defined, 102

    effective, 109–110

    group, 108–109

    in hiring process, 160–163

    intuition in, 106

    mathematical, 106

    problem solving and, 102

    programmed decisions, 108

    rational, 106

    recognizing need for, 105

    seeking help in, 104

    seeking information for, 111–112

    systematic, 106

Decision trees, 106–108

Defects, 445

Delegation, 138, 141–144

    employee acceptance of, 143

    improving, 141–142

    of jobs to employees, 142–143

    problems in, 144

    reasons for, 141

    tasks appropriate for, 142

    in time management, 551–552

Deming, W. Edwards, 453

Democratic leadership, 246, 250

Demonstrations, 200

Department of Health, Education, and Welfare, U.S., 333

Department of Health and Human Services, U.S., 514

Department of Labor, U.S., 171, 506

Depersonalization, 116

Differential treatment, 476

Direct costs, 407

Directive leadership, 245

Disadvantaged minorities, 478–479

Discharge, 340

Discipline, 55, 336–342

    common pitfalls of, 341

    defined, 336

    effectiveness of, 340

    hot-stove rule of, 340

    infractions that trigger, 336–338

    progressive, 339

    recordkeeping for, 341–342

Discrimination

    defined, 472, 522

    reverse, 476

Disparate effect, 476

Dissatisfaction, 219

Distance learning, 189

Diversions, 556

Diversity (*See* Workforce diversity)

Division of labor, 130

Division of work, 55

Divisional organization, 133–134

Downsizing, 37

Drexel University Center for Employment Futures, 488

Drexler, Mickey, 20

Drucker, Peter, 52

Drug abuse, 334–335

Drug tests, 491

Du Pont Co., 504

Due process, 341–342

E

E-mail, 270

Eastman Kodak Company, 488

Edison, Thomas, 302

Education
formal, 543–545
importance of, 184
(*See also* Training)

Educational Development Center, 184

80/20 principle, 109–110

Emotional intelligence (EQ), 247, 296

Employee
delegation to, 138, 141–144
development as leader, 252–253
doing work of supervisor, 7
expectations of, 35–36
health problems, 335, 491, 514
interest in productivity and quality, 456–457
leadership and maturity level of, 250–251
and management information system, 115, 116–117
nonmanagerial, 4
perceptions of, 36–39
performance of (*See* Performance appraisal)
quality of work life, 32, 40–41
reactions to cost control, 417–419
resistance to controls, 355, 392–395, 417–419
responsibility for safety, 511–512
supervisor doing work of, 6
and supervisor responsibility for policy, 89
supervisor responsibility to, 12
as term, 36
transition to supervisor, 8, 9–11
troubled (*See* Troubled employee)
workforce diversity and (*See* Workforce diversity)

Employee Assistance Program (EAP), 320, 332, 483

Employee-centered supervision, 19

Employee communication
communication process, 264–266
with group of employees, 268–270
guidelines for, 275–277
of instructions, 277–278
methods of, 266–271
nonverbal, 272–274
of orders, 277, 278, 280
of requests, 279
spoken, 267–268, 269
written, 268, 269–270

Employee counseling, 324–328
beginning session, 326
length of sessions, 326
number of sessions, 326
professional referral, 327–328
to reduce absenteeism, 330–331
results from, 326–327
rules of, 325

Employee loyalty, 37

Employee ownership plans, 247

Employee turnover, 170–173
causes of, 172
defined, 171
measuring, 171
reducing, 173
staffing process and, 170–171

Employment interviews, 163–166

building rapport in, 164

objectives of, 163

open-ended questions in, 164–165

questions to avoid in, 166

realistic job preview in, 163–164

Employment references, 160, 162–163

Empowerment

defined, 226–227

job redesign and, 227

End user, 113

Energizing, in management process, 16, 53

Entitlements, 37

Equal Employment Opportunity (EEO), 473–478

Equal Employment Opportunity Commission (EEOC), 166, 340, 473, 477, 482–483

Equal Pay Act of 1963, 474, 480–481

Equitable Life Assurance Society, 200

Equity, 56, 222–223

Equity theory of motivation, 172

Ergonomic hazards, 367, 505, 509

Ergonomics, 441

Errors, 456–457

Esteem needs, 218

Executive, 3–4, 31

Exercise, 556

Expectancy, 222

Expectations, of employees for work, 35–36

Facial expression, 165

Facilitating, defined, 40

Facilitators, 112

Fair Labor Standards Act (FLSA) of 1938, 5, 6, 518, 519

Family and Medical Leave Act of 1993, 474, 477–478

Favoritism, 304

Fayol, Henri, 54–56

Feedback

in control process, 388, 393

defined, 265, 388

on employee performance (*See* Performance appraisal)

360-degree, 266

Fiedler, Fred, 248–249, 250

Filipczak, Bob, 489

Firing, 340

First aid, 510–511

Fishman, Charles, 136

Fixed costs, 411

Flexible budget, 410–411

Flexible work schedules, 39

Forecasting, workforce requirements, 157–159

Formal organization, 130

Formal work group, 352

Free association of ideas, 457

Frequency-distribution chart, 448–449

Freud, Sigmund, 19

Functional authority, 140–141

Functional organization, 131

Gandhi, Indira, 451

Gangs, 504

Gantt, Henry Laurence, 57, 82

Gantt chart, 82, 83–84

Gap, The, 20

Gen-Xers, 81

Gender (*See* Women in the workplace)

General Electric, 77, 414

General Motors, 453

Generalizations, 200

Generation Xers, 253, 489

Geographic organization, 134

Gestures, 165

Gilbreth, Frank B., 58

Gilbreth, Lillian, 436

Glass ceiling, 382, 480–481

Goal setting, 74–77

    career, 546

    group participation in, 356

    planning versus, 74–76

    supervisors and, 76–77

    work group, 356

Goals

    controls and, 383

    defined, 73

    performance, 275

    in planning process, 78–79

Goleman, Daniel, 247, 296

Grapevine, 271

Grayson, Dr. C. Jackson, 431

Greenberg, Eric Rolfe, 186, 334

Grievance procedures, 524–526

Griggs v. Duke Power, 479

Group

    communication with, 268–270

    defined, 358

    (*See also* Work group)

Group decision making, 108–109

Group dynamics, 352–355

    cohesiveness, 354–355

    defined, 352

    formal work group, 352

    group versus single employee in group, 353–354

    importance of, 352

    informal work group, 352, 353

    mass resistance, 355

    problem solving, 355

Group norms, 353–354

Group participation, 356–363

    effectiveness of, 356–358

    group versus team, 358

    participation, defined, 355

    in setting goals, 356

H

Halo effect, 297, 300

Hawthorne Works of the Western Electric Company, 58–59

Hazards, defined, 503

Health problems, 335, 491, 514

Hersey, Paul, 250–251

Herzberg, Frederick, 219, 220, 223

Hierarchy of needs, 215–217, 220

Hill, Kenneth D., 18

HireSystem, Inc., 242

Hiring process, 160–163

Hobbies, 556

Hochwarter, W. A., 77

Honesty tests, 161

Hostility, 321

Hot-stove rule of discipline, 340

Hull, Nancy, 327

Human resource planning, 157–158

I

Iacocca, Lee, 217

Imperato, Gina, 6

Indirect costs, 407

Individuality, 213–215

Informal organization, 130

Informal work group, 352, 353

Information, 38, 112

    defined, 264–265

Information management, 111–117

    cutoff point in seeking information, 111–112

data versus information and, 112

employees and, 115, 116–117

Management Information Systems (MIS) in, 112, 113–114

supervisors and, 113–114

systematic, 115–116

Inputs, 61

input-output analysis, 108

in productivity measurement, 431–433

Inspection, 445

Institutional theory of authority, 139

Instructions, 277–279

Intelligence tests, 161

Interest tests, 161

International Standards Organization (ISO), 444

Interventions, 360–361

Interviews

appraisal, 301–303

employee counseling, 324–328

employment, 163–166

Intuitive decision making, 106

Inventories, 416

IQ (mental capacity), 247, 296

 J

Japanese management, 59–60

JC Penney Co., Inc., 448

Job aids, 197

Job breakdown analysis, 191–192

Job-centered supervision, 19

Job enlargement, 227

Job enrichment, 227

Job evaluation, 294–295, 480–481

Job Instruction Training (JIT), 194–195

Job redesign

defined, 225

dimensions of, 226

empowerment and, 227

impact of, 227

payoff from, 227–228

Job satisfaction, 37, 116, 143, 217–220

absenteeism and, 330

employee perceptions of work, 36–39

expectations for work, 35

extent of, 35

productivity improvement and, 434

Job security, 116–117

Job sharing, 39

Jobs, Steve, 434

Juran, Joseph M., 453

 K

Kanter, Rosabeth Moss, 106

Kerr, Steven, 18

Key point, 191, 192–193

Kinesthetic learners, 275–276

Kipling, Rudyard, 80

Kirkpatrick, Shelley, 238

Knowledge, defined, 190

Knowledge management, 117

 L

Labor agreement, 515

Labor-Management Relations Act of 1947, 5, 517–518

Labor Management Reporting and Disclosure Act of 1959, 519–520

Labor union

collective bargaining, 520–521

cost controls and, 417–418

employee membership in, 515, 516

Fair Labor Standards Act, 5, 6, 518, 519

grievance procedures, 524–526

Landrum-Griffith Act, 519–520

rules of discipline, 340

supervisor and, 12, 515, 516, 521–523

Taft-Hartley Act and, 5, 517–518

union steward and, 522–523

Wagner Act and, 516, 522

Walsh-Healy Public Contracts Act, 518

Landrum-Griffith Act of 1959, 519–520

Lawlor, Edward E., III, 362

Leadership

charisma in, 239

defined, 238

exhibiting initiative and, 560–561

followers and, 253–254

and motivation, 241–244

personality and, 239

popularity of, 254

situational, 248, 250, 251

skills required for, 240

supervisors and, 252–254

traits of, 238

Leadership styles, 245–251

autocratic, directive leadership, 245

defined, 245

democratic, consultative leadership, 246, 250

participative leadership, 246–248, 250

selecting appropriate, 248–251

Learning multiplier effect, 184

Learning organization, 117

Legal issues

equal employment opportunity, 472–478

in performance appraisal, 306–307

supervisor status, 5

union grievance procedures, 524–526

Leigh, Pamela, 52

Leiter, Michael, 321

Levinson, Harry, 327–328

Lie detectors, 491

Line-and-staff organization, 132–133

Line organization, 132–133

Listening, 273–274, 325, 326

Literacy, 510

Locke, Edwin, 77, 238

Lockheed Martin, 200

Long-range plans, 72, 79

Louis Harris and Associates, 172

Mackenzie, R. Alec, 551

Mahadeva, Kabir, 436

Malcolm Baldridge National Quality Awards, 444

Management

defined, 3

supervisor responsibility to, 11

Management approaches (schools), 56–62

behavioral, 57, 58–59

contingency, 57–58, 62

quantitative, 57, 60

systematic, 57, 58, 60–62

Management by exception, 390–391

Management by Objectives (MBO), 300, 395, 550–551

Management development, 545

Management Information System (MIS), 112, 113–117

employees and, 115

human approach to, 115–117

importance of, 112

supervisors and, 113–115

Management principles, 54–56

list of, 55–56

in management process, 54–55

Management process, 16, 51–54

defined, 16, 51

functions of, 16, 52–53

importance of, 51

management principles in, 54–55

objective of, 54

supervisor knowledge of, 51

supervisor role in, 16

Manager

defined, 3

levels of, 3–4

supervisor transition to, 50

Manz, Charles, 252

Maslach, Christina, 321

Maslow, A. H., 215–217, 220, 241

Mass resistance, 355

Mathematical decision making, 106

Mathys, N. J., 77

Matrix organization, 134

Mayo, Elton, 58, 59

Mays, Benjamin E., 73

McClelland, David, 221, 241

McGregor, Douglas, 242, 244, 395

McLaughlin, Ellen E., 477

McLean, Lachlan, 324

Medical evaluation, 162

Meetings, 369

Mentor, 50, 543

Merit raises, 294–295

Methods improvement, 435–443

Middle manager, 4, 31

Mintzberg, Henry, 137

Mission statement, defined, 71

Modeling performance, 200

Morale, 275, 354–355, 359

Motion economy, 440–441

Motivation, 38

career, 540

defined, 215

drives in, 221

expectancy and, 222

importance of individuality in, 213–215

leadership and, 241–244

needs in, 215–218, 222

of older workers, 217, 489, 490

pattern of, 215–217

rewards and, 223–225

satisfaction and dissatisfaction and, 217–220

in work itself, 225–228

of younger workers, 487

Motorola, 77, 184, 414

Multi-skilled employees, 194

N

National Consensus Standards, 506

National Endowment for the Humanities, 20

National Highway and Traffic Safety Administration, 511

National Institute of Standards and Technology, 444

National Labor Relations Act, 516

National Safety Council, 512–513

National Sleep Foundation, 86, 511

Networking, 543, 557–558

Nexters, 489

Noise, 264–265

Nondestructive testing, 445–446

Nonexempt employees, 519

Nonmanagerial employee, 4

Nonverbal communication, 272–274

Normal distribution, 110

Norms, group, 353–354

O

Objectives, 73
    of employment interviews, 163
    in goal setting, 75
    management by, 395, 550–551
Occupational Safety and Health Act of 1970, 506
Occupational Safety and Health Administration
    (OSHA), 169, 412, 506, 507, 509, 510, 514
Odiorne, George, 550–551
Off-the-job training methods, 197–198
Office automation, 441–442
Older workers, 487–490
    assets and drawbacks of, 488–489
    learning process of, 489–490
    motivating, 217, 489, 490
    training, 196, 489–490
Open-book management, 115
Open-ended questions, 164–165
Orders, 277–279, 280
Organigraphs, 137
Organization
    defined, 129
    formal, 130
    informal, 130
    organizing versus, 129
    responsibility for job satisfaction, 219–220
    work to be done versus, 131
Organization charts, 136
Organizational Acceptance Rating Sheet, 557, 558
Organizational culture
    defined, 146
    learning about, 146–147
    organizational structure and, 146
Organizational Development (OD), 360–361

Organizational structure, 129, 131–137
    centralized, 135, 136
    charts of, 136–137
    customer, 134
    decentralized, 135–136
    divisional or product, 133
    functional organization, 131
    geographic, 134
    line-and-staff organization, 132–133
    matrix organization, 134
    organizational culture and, 146
    span of control and, 136
Organizing
    guidelines for, 144–147
    importance of, 129–130
    in management process, 16, 52
    organization versus, 129
    process of, 130
Orientation training, 168–170
    contents of, 168–170
    importance of, 168
    increased chances of success and, 170
    orientation, defined, 168
Osborn, Alex, 457, 458
Outputs, 61
    in productivity measurement, 431–433
Overstaffing, 158–159
Overtime, 6, 82

P

Pacific Bell, 414
Participation, 355 (*See also* Group participation)
Participative leadership, 246–248, 250
    formal programs to encourage, 247
    potential problems of, 248
    prerequisites for, 247

Penalty, 336

Perception of fairness, 222–223

Performance appraisal

    appraisal interview, 301–303

    defined, 294

    factors in, 296

    financial aspects of, 294–295, 304, 308

    formats of, 295–301

    frequency of, 294

    halo effect and, 297, 300

    legal aspects of, 306–307

    problems of, 293, 308–309

    purposes of, 293–295

    record-keeping for, 307

    rewarded activities and, 387

    special considerations, 304–306

    standards for, 297

    timing of, 305–306

Performance goals and standards, 275

Performance management, 18, 335–338

    defined, 18, 335

    disciplinary action, 336–338

    problem performance, 320

Performance measures, for supervisor, 14–15

Performance motivators, 219

Performance standards, 385–387

Performance tests, 161–162

Personal Effectiveness Inventory, 540–541

Personal references, 160, 162–163

Personal support system, 558–559

Personality, 213–214

    conflict based on, 366

    of supervisor, 239

Personality tests, 161

PERT chart, 84–86

Physical examination, 162

Planning

    controls and, 383

    goals versus, 74–76

    in management process, 16, 52

    by supervisor, 71–74

Planning process, 78–80

    career, 540–546

    classification of plans in, 79

    controls in, 80, 383

    double-checking in, 80

    goals in, 78–79

Policies, 87–89

    applying, 88

    company policy, 87

    defined, 73

    deviating from, 89

    responsibility for, 89

    unwritten, 88–89

Potential problems, 99, 100

Power motivation, 221

Prejudice, 102

Preventive controls, 387–388

Primary data, 113

Prime source, 113

Privacy, 490–491

    drug tests, 491

    lie detectors, 491

    protected employees and, 492

    and sensitive issues, 491

    threats to, 490–491

Problem solving, 101–105

    in control function, 382–383

    decision making and, 102

    defined, 100

    employee counseling, 324–328

    group dynamics, 355

    methods of, 101

roles in, 110

seeking help in, 104

seeking information for, 111–112

systematic, 102–105

Problems

causes of, 100, 103

current, 99

defined, 99

potential, 99, 100

recognizing, 100

Procedures, 73

Product, 54

Product organization, 133–134

Productivity

defined, 431

encouraging employee interest in, 456

high-tech improvements in, 441–442

improving, 433–434

job satisfaction and, 434

measuring, 431–433

motion economy and, 440–441

overtime work and, 82

value-adding operations, 438–440

value analysis, 442–443

wasteful elements and, 437–438

Productivity Benchmark Index (PBI), 455

Programmed decisions, 108

Programmed learning, 198

Progressive discipline, 339

Promotion, delegation and, 143

Protected groups

defined, 472

disadvantaged minorities, 478–479

older workers, 487–490

privacy of, 492

women, 471, 480–484

Public Agenda Foundation, 35

Q

Quality

attainment of, 15

defined, 443

encouraging employee interest in, 456

standards of, 13, 444

statistical quality control, 447–450

terms related to, 443–446

Total Quality Management (TQM), 247, 444, 451–455

Quality assurance, 444

Quality circles, 247, 415, 452–454

focus of, 454

operation of, 453–454

Quality Control (QC), 443

Quality-control chart, 449–450

Quality of work life, 32, 40–41, 228

Quantitative management, 57, 60

Questions, employment interview, 164–166

R

Raines, Claire, 489

Raises, 304, 308, 561–562

Rapport, building, 164

Rate of turnover, 171

Rational decision making, 106

Realistic job preview, 163–164

Reasonable accommodation, 477

Recognition, personal, 224–225

Record-keeping process

cost control and, 406–408

for disciplinary action, 341–342

for performance appraisal, 307

for training, 186, 187

for work-related accidents, 507

Reengineering, 225, 442

References, 160, 162–163

Regulations, 73

Rehabilitation Act of 1973, 474

Rejects, 445

Reliability, 162

    defined, 162, 450

    and statistical quality control, 450

Reminders, 548–549

Repetitive Strain Injuries (RSI), 505

Replacement costs, 409

Requests, 279

Resilience, 323

Respect, 216

Responsibility, 55

    authority and accountability versus, 139–140

    authority versus, 138

    for policies, 89

Return on Quality (ROQ), 444, 455

Reverse discrimination, 476

Rewards, 33

    money as, 223

    personal recognition, 224–225

    safety, 514

Right-sizing, 158

Right-to-work laws, 518

Robots, 441

Roethlisberger, Fritz, 59

Role

    defined, 17

    of supervisor in management process, 16

    of supervisor versus other managers, 17, 30–32

Rules, breaking, 337–338

Rumors, 419

Rush deliveries, 82–83

Ryun, Jim, 223

S

Safety

    accident prevention, 506–514

    accidents at work, 503–504

    ergonomic hazards, 367, 505, 509

    OSHA standards, 506–511

    rewarding, 514

Safety committee, 513–514

Safety needs, 215

Safety specialists, 513

St. Louis, Ann, 333–334

Salary, 561–562

    overtime versus, 6

    raises, 304, 308, 561–562

Sampling tables, 450

Sandwich technique, 302, 303

Satisfaction, 219

Saving face, 303

Sawyer, Diane, 250

Sawyer, William A., 488

Schedules, defined, 73

Scheduling, 81–87

    capacity and, 81

    Gantt chart, 82, 83–84

    overtime and, 82

    PERT chart, 84–86

    rush projects, 82–83

    work distribution chart, 86, 87

Schmidt, Warren H., 251

Schwarzkopf, H. Norman, 139

Secondary data, 113

Selection decision, 167

Self-actualization, 216

Self-appraisal, 306

Self-control, 395

Self-directed learning, 189

Self-esteem, 336–337

Self-fulfilling prophesy, 170

Self-improvement, 239

Self-managing teams, 7, 362

Self-respect, 216

Senge, Peter, 194

Service, 54

Sexual harassment, 482–484

    affirmative defense, 484

    defined, 482

    preventing, 483–484

    responding to complaints, 483

Shell (U.K.) Ltd., 329

Shop steward, 522–523

Short-range plans, 72, 79

Silberstein, Nina, 106

Silence, 274, 325

Sims, Henry, Jr., 252

Single-use plans, 79

Situational leadership, 248, 250, 251

Skill, defined, 190

Skill-based pay, 194

Sleeping, 86, 511

Social needs, 215, 218

Society for Human Resource Management, 484

Southwest Airlines, 106

Span of control, 136

Specification, 389, 445

Spoken communication, 267–268, 269

Staff organization, 132–133

    functional authority and, 140–141

Staff specialists, supervisor responsibility to, 12

Staffing process

    absences and, 170–171

    employment interviews in, 163–166

    human resources planning in, 157–158

    importance of, 157

    improving hiring decisions in, 160–163

    in management process, 16, 52

    orientation training in, 168–170

    overstaffing and understaffing, 158–159

    selection decision in, 167

    six-step procedure for, 159–160

    turnover and, 170–171

Stamps, David, 184

Standard costs, 406

Standards, 73

    control, 381, 384–385

    defined, 384, 436

    performance, 275, 385–387

    for performance appraisal, 297

    for quality, 13, 444

Standing plans, 79

Statistical Quality Control (SQC), 447–450

    defined, 447–448

    reliability and, 450

    tools of, 448–450

Stengel, Casey, 352

Stereotypes, 472–473

Stewards, 253–254

Strategic control points, 387–388

Strategy, defined, 71

Stress

    defined, 553

    lessening impact of, 556–557

    personal style and, 553–554

    sources of, 554–556

    Stress Indicator Barometer, 552, 553

Stressors, 323

Substance abuse, 332–335

    alcohol, 332–334

    drugs, 334–335

Substitutes for leadership, 253

Suggestion systems, 247

Superleader, 252

Supervisor

    attainment of results, 15

    becoming, 7–8

    behaviors associated with results, 18

    benefits from training, 198–200

    controlling function, 380–395

    defined, 4

    delegation by, 141–144

    discipline and, 338

    employee communication and, 264

    employee counseling, 324–328, 335

    employees doing work of, 7

    frontline, 6

    goals of, 76–77

    helping employees become leaders, 252–253

    job pressures of, 30–32

    job responsibilities of, 11–12

    key tasks of, 13

    and labor union, 12, 515, 516, 521–523

    leadership roles of, 252–253

    leeway in taking authoritative action, 140

    legal status of, 5

    and management information system, 113–114

    management of resources, 14–15

    in management process, 16, 52–53

    in new workplace, 33

    normal day in life of, 19

    other management levels versus, 17, 30–32

    overruling, 526

    performance measures for, 14–15

    personal characteristics of, 9

    planning by, 71–74

    problem performers and, 320–328

    productivity and, 432–443

    quality and, 443–455

    quality of work life, 40–41

    reading by, 9

    responsibility for job satisfaction, 219–220

    responsibility for policies, 89

    responsibility for training employees, 187–190

    roles in control function, 382–383

    span of control, 136

    staffing process and, 157–158

    supervisory balance, 19

    as term, 4–5

    transition to supervision, 8, 9–11, 50

    work of employees and, 6

Synergy, 355

Systematic approach

    to decision making, 106

    to information management, 115–116

    to problem solving, 102–105

    to training, 184–185

Systematic management, 57, 58

    contingency management and, 62

    systems in, 60–61

Systems

    defined, 60

    in systematic management, 60–62

T

Taft-Hartley Act of 1947, 5, 517–518

Taguchi Method, 445

Tannenbaum, Robert, 251

Tardiness, 173

Task-centered supervision, 19

Taylor, Sir Edward Burnett, 146

Taylor, Frederick W., 57

Taylor, P. J., 329

Teachable moment, 188

Team building, 361, 369

Team leader, 7

Teams, defined, 358

Teamwork, 359–363

    indicators of, 359

    lack of, signs of, 359

    Organizational Development (OD), 360–361

    patterns in evolution of team, 362–363

    self-managing teams, 7, 362

    team building, 361, 369

    teams, defined, 358

    (*See also* Work group)

Telecommuting, 38, 39, 336

Telephone calls, 267–268

Telephone use, 548

Tests, employment, 161–162

Theory X, 242–243, 253

Theory Y, 243–244, 246

Thompson, K. R., 77

360-degree feedback, 266

3M, 77

Time and motion studies, 435–436

Time budget, 549–550

Time horizons, 31–32

Time management, 547–552

    ABC analysis, 550–551

    delegation in, 551–552

    guidelines for, 548–550

    vital few problems, 550–551

Time orientation, 77

Time trap, 551

Tolerance, 384, 445

Tone of voice, 165

Total Quality Management (TQM), 247, 451–455

    benchmarking in, 454–455

    defined, 444

    implementation of, 454

    quality circles and, 452–454

    Return on Quality (ROQ), 444, 455

    zero-defects approach and, 451–453

Towers Perrin, 37

Train-the-trainer courses, 188–189

Training

    costs of, 198

    employee learning without, 184

    factors in learning, 190–196

    importance of, 184

    obtaining results from, 198–201

    of older workers, 196, 489–490

    orientation, 168–170

    purpose of, 185–186

    record-keeping process for, 186, 187

    safety, 509–510

    supervisor responsibility for, 187–190

    systematic, 184–185

    training methods and aids, 196–198

    (*See also* Education)

Training needs, 186–187

Transactional Analysis (TA), 367

Transfer of training, 200

Troubled employee, 320–323

    administrative guidelines, 338–342

    behavioral clues to, 322

    employee counseling, 324–328, 330–331

    performance management, 18, 320, 335–338

    problem performer, 320–323

    reducing absenteeism, 329–331

    substance abuse, 332–335

Truman, Harry, 554

Trust, 239, 361, 364–365

Tuckman, Bruce, 362

Turnover (*See* Employee turnover)

U

Understaffing, 158–159
Unfair labor practices, 516
Union (*See* Labor union)
Union Pacific, 77
Union shop, 517
Unit costs, 406, 409–410
United Airlines Inc., 218
Unity of command, 55
Unity of direction, 55

V

Validity, 162
Value-adding operations, 438–440
Value analysis, 442–443
Values, defined, 71
Van der Heyden, Ludo, 137
Variable costs, 407
Variance, 387
Veterans, 489
Vietnam Era Veteran's Readjustment Assistance Act
    of 1974, 474
Virtual classroom, 189
Vision, defined, 71
Visual aids, in training, 196–197
Visual learners, 275–276
Vital few, 550–551
Voice mail, 268

W

Wagner Act, 516, 522
Wal-Mart, 36, 166
Walsh-Healey Public Contracts Act, 518
Warnings, 339
Washington, Booker T., 471

Weber, Max, 34
Wellness programs, 514
Western Electric, 200
Westinghouse Electric Corp., 453
Withdrawal, 321
Williams-Steiger Act, 510
Women in the workplace, 471, 480–484
    comparable worth for, 481–482
    glass ceiling, 382, 480–481
    importance of, 480
    job evaluation and, 480–481
    sexual harassment and, 482–484
Work
    in bureaucracy, 33–34
    defined, 32
    employee expectations for, 35
    employee perceptions of, 36–39
    motivation in, 225–228
    quality of work life, 32, 40–41, 228
    reasons for, 33
    rewards for, 33, 223, 224–225
Work distribution chart, 86, 87
Work group
    formal, 352
    goal setting by, 356
    group dynamics, 352–355
    group participation, 356–363
    informal, 352, 353
    (*See also* Teamwork)
Work measurement
    defined, 435
    time and motion studies in, 435–436
Work sampling, 436, 437
Workforce diversity
    age, 471, 485–490
    cultural, 471
    disadvantaged minorities, 478–479

equal employment opportunity and, 472–478

gender, 471, 480–484

privacy concerns, 490–492

Workforce requirements, forecasting, 157–159

Written communication, 268, 269–270

Yankelovich, Daniel, 35

Younger workers, 485–487

characteristics, 485

generation gap, 485–486

motivating and managing, 487

Zemke, Ron, 489

Zero-defects approach, 451–453

Ziglar, Zig, 227